comedy
plays, theory, and criticism

Marvin Felheim   *University of Michigan*

Under the General Editorship of
DAVID LEVIN
Stanford University

Harcourt, Brace & World, Inc. *New York · Burlingame*

A NOTE ON THE COVER: from the Michael Benthal production of *Twelfth Night* for The Old Vic Company. Photograph by Angus McBean.

ACKNOWLEDGMENTS   *The editor wishes to thank the following for their permission to reproduce materials in this book:*

EDWARD ARNOLD (PUBLISHERS) LTD.: For selections from *The Origin of Attic Comedy* by Francis M. Cornford, 1914. By permission of W. K. C. Guthrie.

BASIL BLACKWELL: For selections from *The People of Aristophanes* by Victor Ehrenberg, 1951.

THE CLARENDON PRESS: For selections from *Poetics* from *The Student's Oxford Aristotle* translated by Ingram Bywater, 1942, and selections from *Restoration Comedy* by Bonamy Dobrée, 1924.

COLUMBIA UNIVERSITY PRESS: For "The Argument of Comedy" by Northrop Frye from *English-Institute Essays, 1948*, edited by D. A. Robertson, Jr., 1949.

DOUBLEDAY & COMPANY, INC.: For "Laughter" from the book *Comedy*, copyright © 1956 by Wylie Sypher, which contains "Laughter" by Henri Bergson. Reprinted by permission of Doubleday & Company, Inc.

GROVE PRESS, INC.: For *A Wedding* from *The Brute and Other Farces* by Anton Chekhov, Edited by Eric Bentley, in new versions by Eric Bentley and Theodore Hoffman. Published by Grove Press, Inc. 1958, Copyright © 1958 by Eric Bentley.

HARCOURT, BRACE & WORLD, INC.: For *The Misanthrope* by Molière, translated by Richard Wilbur, copyright 1954, © 1955 by Richard Wilbur. For Notes to *Twelfth Night* from *Shakespeare: The Complete Works* edited by G. B. Harrison, copyright 1948, 1952, by Harcourt, Brace & World, Inc. Aristophanes: *The Birds*. An English Version by Dudley Fitts. © 1957 by Harcourt, Brace & World, Inc. Selection from *World Drama* by Allardyce Nicoll, 1950, by permission of Harcourt, Brace & World, Inc.

GEORGE G. HARRAP & COMPANY LIMITED: For selection from *World Drama* by Allardyce Nicoll, 1950.

HILLARY HOUSE PUBLISHERS LTD.: For "Twelfth Night" from *Shakespeare's Sources*, Vol. I, by Kenneth Muir, 1957.

ALFRED A. KNOPF, INC.: For "Some Prefatory Words on Comedy" from *The Thread of Laughter* by Louis Kronenberger, by permission of Alfred A. Knopf. Inc. Copyright 1952 by Louis Kronenberger.

METHUEN & CO. LTD.: For "Twelfth Night" from *Shakespeare's Sources*, Vol. I, by Kenneth Muir, 1957.

THE NATIONAL COUNCIL OF TEACHERS OF ENGLISH: For "Satiric Strategy in *The Importance of Being Earnest*" by Otto Reinert in *College English*, Volume 18, No. 1, October, 1956. By permission of the author.

THE NEW AMERICAN LIBRARY: For selections from *The Satyricon of Petronius*, translated by William Arrowsmith, copyright © 1959 by William Arrowsmith, published by arrangement with The New American Library of World Literature, Inc., New York.

NEW DIRECTIONS: For "Le Misanthrope" from *The Classical Moment* by Martin Turnell, 1948. All rights reserved. Reprinted by permission of New Directions.

OXFORD UNIVERSITY PRESS, INC.: For *A Phoenix Too Frequent* by Christopher Fry. Copyright 1946 by Christopher Fry. Reprinted by permission of Oxford University Press, Inc.

RANDOM HOUSE: For selections from *Wit and Its Relation to the Unconscious* in *The Basic Writings of Sigmund Freud*, trans. and ed. by Dr. A. A. Brill, Copyright 1938 by Random House, Inc. Reprinted by permission of the Brill Trust.

CHARLES SCRIBNER'S SONS: For "The Great Dramatic Forms: The Comic Rhythm" reprinted with the permission of Charles Scribner's Sons from *Feeling and Form* by Susanne Langer, copyright 1953 Charles Scribner's Sons.

THE SOCIETY OF AUTHORS: For *The Man of Destiny* from *Plays: Pleasant and Unpleasant* by Bernard Shaw, 1898, Herbert S. Stone & Co. Reprinted by permission of the Public Trustee and The Society of Authors.

JOSEPH H. SUMMERS: "The Masks of *Twelfth Night*" from *The University of Kansas City Review*, XXII, Autumn, 1955. By permission of the author.

Introduction

> . . . there remained only Socrates, Aristophanes, and Agathon, who
> were drinking out of a large goblet which they passed round, and
> Socrates was discoursing to them. Aristodemus was only half awake,
> and he did not hear the beginning of the discourse; the chief thing
> which he remembered was Socrates compelling the other two to
> acknowledge that the genius of comedy was the same with that of
> tragedy, and that the true artist in tragedy was an artist in comedy
> also. To this they were constrained to assent, being drowsy, and not
> quite following the argument.
>
> Plato in the *Symposium*

Comedy, as the materials in this Harbrace Sourcebook show, has been one of mankind's persistent modes of thought, of action, of self-awareness. Men have always written comedies; they have, as well, tried to explain why. No single satisfactory answer has emerged. Rather, we have the rich variety of comedy, from its obscure and scurrilous Greek origins through its delicate but razor-sharp observations, as made by a Molière or a Jane Austen, to its current provocative brilliance in the existential absurd, in the grotesque worlds of Faulkner, Beckett, and Ionesco.

No longer do we see comedy simply as a delightful escape from life or merely as a form of social corrective, although it still performs both those functions; on the contrary, we perceive it, at its greatest moments, approaching the realm of the tragic. Just as Plato in the *Symposium* brings together the comedian, Aristophanes, and the tragedian, Agathon, so Shakespeare links Lear and his Fool; and the modern artist, a Camus or a Chaplin, is still concerned to mix the genres. Freud explains the origin of wit in the unconscious, where at a level below what the mind articulates the emotions have their true comic and tragic existence. Even in *Ecclesiastes*, where laughter is treated as vanity, it is nevertheless granted that

To everything there is a season, and a time to every
   purpose under heaven:
A time to weep, and a time to laugh: a time to mourn,
   and a time to dance.

The intent behind the selection of the plays in Part I has been to provide as wide a range as possible for the protean genius of comedy. The time between the first performance of *The Birds* and that of *A Phoenix Too Frequent* is two thousand three hundred and sixty years. The eight comedies of Part I indicate clearly that the comic spirit has ever indulged itself in joy, in farce, in blunt and smooth criticism. Both long and short plays have been chosen to provide examples from the various historic periods of comedy and from different dramatic approaches. Dramas in both poetry and prose have been reprinted. Where translations have been used, those which best capture the essential thrust of the playwright—rather than mere literal transcriptions—have been selected.

The section *Sources*, Part II, has been devised for two major purposes: to provide necessary and interesting background on a few of the plays—and thus to enrich the student's experience—and, in the case of Allardyce Nicoll's discussion of *commedia dell'arte*, to supply information about a significant but shadowy period in the history of comedy. Further, each of these four essays is organized on a different principle, so that the section as a whole offers a varied approach to the study of sources.

The essays in Part III—*Theory*—were chosen on the same basis as the plays in Part I: to obtain range, in the historical sense, and variety, in the points of view represented. Most of the selections

are complete sections taken from longer works. A
few of the selections are excerpts because some
commentators, such as Aristotle and other philosophers, have discussed comedy as one aspect of a
larger problem, or because other writers, Freud
for example, have developed theories of comedy
which are too long to reprint in their entirety.

In Part IV—*Criticism*—the aim has again been
to provide the student with a helpful range of
critical materials. Four plays—*The Birds, Twelfth
Night, The Misanthrope*, and *The Importance of Being
Earnest*—have been selected for discussion. Again,
as in Part II, these critical essays not only present
imaginative insights but also illustrate differing
approaches to the practice of criticism. Critical
works on the other plays are pointed out in the
Suggestions for Further Reading and are readily
accessible in college libraries.

The Suggestions for Written Assignments are
arranged in an approximate sequence of increasing
length and complexity; those suggestions which
are not used for written assignments might serve
as study questions and subjects for class discussion.

In documenting his paper, the student may
simply refer to the pages of this edition. However,
the source of each selection is fully identified to
make it possible for him to cite the sources themselves. References to a nondramatic work can cite
the original paginations which have been inserted
into the texts. References to plays can be made by
means of act and scene numbers and, in the case
of verse drama, line numbers.

The editor is indebted to two earlier Harbrace
Sourcebooks, *Julius Caesar in Shakespeare, Shaw, and
the Ancients*, edited by G. B. Harrison, and *Tragedy:
Plays, Theory, and Criticism*, prepared by Richard
Levin, for having set the standard and shown the
way. The suggestions of Professor Alvin B. Kernan
of Yale University were most helpful. Dr. Harold
Swayze of the University of Michigan has provided encouragement.

MARVIN FELHEIM

University of Michigan
January, 1962

Contents

IV   Criticism

I
Eight Comedies

Aristophanes The Birds

in a Translation by Dudley Fitts

The Birds was first produced by Callistratus at the City Dionysia, a religious festival, in 414 B.C. The procedure was a long established one: each year, the magistrate in charge of festivals chose from among many applicants the three poets whose works were to be presented. A chorus and five actors were provided and paid for by the State; other expenses were met by wealthy citizens, one of whom, a "choragos," chosen by lot, was assigned to each production. *The Birds* won second prize for Aristophanes, the first award going to Ameipsias for his *Revelers*. At this time Aristophanes was about thirty years old. *The Birds* is one of only eleven of his plays which have survived; in all, he wrote about forty theatrical pieces.

The characteristic feature of Aristophanic comedy is the intermingling of elements: serious political satire which occasionally involves bitter personal attacks, uproarious low-comic farce, and lovely lyric poetry. Although some mocking of persons (especially of Euripides and Socrates) and some rather pointed political comments (aimed particularly at Athenian litigiousness and sycophancy) are present here, *The Birds* is chiefly distinguished for its lyricism (such as the famous invocation by Epops in ll. 211 ff., p. 5).

Athens was enduring desperate times in the period just after the sailing of the Sicilian Enterprise, when this play was written; and although the war may have seemed endless in prospect to Aristophanes' audience, this is not essentially a war play. It attacks civic evils and corruption and may be said to suggest a utopia of which even the gods might be jealous. More significant than these contemporary effects is the larger comic vision, the creation of a perfect world. Cloudcuckooland the Beautiful is a place of joy, not an escapist paradise. Aristophanes' first object was entertainment, and it is in this sense that we must learn to read his play.

The designations of the parts of the play (Párodos, Agon, Parábasis, etc.) are explained in the critical essay by Cornford in Part IV (pp. 254–56); much valuable background and explanatory material is also included in the excerpt from *The People of Aristophanes* in Part II (pp. 256–58). The version used here is by Dudley Fitts (N. Y.: Harcourt, Brace, 1957), whose notes and index of proper names have been retained.

PERSONS REPRESENTED

* Asterisk refers the reader to the Index of Proper Names, p. 30.

EUELPIDES	A TRAVELLING PROPHET	A PARRICIDE
PISTHETAIROS[1]	METON*	KINESIAS*
A BIRD SERVANT	AN INSPECTOR	AN INFORMER
EPOPS*	A DECREE-VENDOR	PROMETHEUS*
CHORUS OF BIRDS	THREE MESSENGERS	POSEIDON*
A PRIEST	IRIS*	A TRIBALLIAN* GOD
A POET	A HERALD	HERAKLES*

The supernumeraries include various servants and liturgical attendants, PROKNE the Nightingale wife of EPOPS, MANES* a slave, and BASILEIA* the bride of PISTHETAIROS.

---

[1] The Protagonist's name is in doubt. "Peisthetairos," attested by most of the mss., is unsatisfactory; of various other forms, "Pisthetairos"—"trusty friend"—seems to be the best.

PROLOGUE

[*A waste region.*[2] *Rocks, low bushes, a few thin trees. In the background, a steep rock face surmounted by a single tree. Enter two old men,* PISTHETAIROS *and* EUELPIDES, *followed by slaves carrying baggage.* PISTHETAIROS *has a raven perched upon his wrist;* EUELPIDES *has a jackdaw. Weariness and frustration.*]

EUELPIDES. [*to the jackdaw*] Straight ahead?
    Over by that tree?

PISTHETAIROS. [*to the raven*]
                            Oh, damn your feathers!
—Euelpidês, this fool fowl keeps cawing
a retreat.

EUEL. I know. What's the use?
All this humping up and down hills,
we'll be wrecks before we find the right road.

PISTH. Miles and miles, walking around in
    circles,
all because of a brainless bird.

EUEL.   Yes,
tramping my toenails off for a damned jackdaw.

PISTH. I wonder where we are.

EUEL.   Do you think we
    could find our way back?   10

PISTH. Exekestidês[*] himself couldn't find his
    way back.

EUEL. Hell!

PISTH.   That's a road you'll have to go on
    your own.

EUEL. No, damn it, but I was thinking of that
    birdseller.
Nice service that was,
swearing that these two specimens would lead us
    straight
to Tereus,[*°] the king who turned into a Hoopoe;
selling us a jackdaw for a penny, the damned
    jackass,
and three pennies for that raven. What a pair!

[2] The scene is deliberately vague. Although Pisthetairos and Euelpidês have come on foot from Athens, the site of the future Cloudcuckooland seems neither terrestrial nor aerial: a dream region, suitable for a dream city. If the transformed King Tereus[*] has chosen to remain in the country that he ruled as a man, the location is Thrace[*]—northward, at any rate, in the direction of witchcraft and delusion.

16. Tereus was a king of Thrace who violated Philomelê, the sister of his wife Proknê, and tore out her tongue so that she should not tell. The sisters avenged themselves by cooking Itys, Tereus' infant son, and serving him up to his father at dinner. The gods' criticism of this Faulknerian episode took the form of changing all three agonists into birds: Tereus became a Hoopoe, Proknê a Swallow, and Philomelê a Nightingale. It is worth noting that Aristophanes follows the variant that transforms Proknê, not Philomelê, into the Nightingale. Moreover, she seems to have forgiven Tereus for his affair with her sister, and Tereus has forgotten the dreadful business about Itys. The Nightingale and the Hoopoe are on exemplary domestic terms with each other.

All they can do is peck. [*to the jackdaw*]
                    —What's the matter now?
Forgotten how to shut your beak? Or a brilliant
    thought   20
like leading us bang up against that rock?
I don't see any road.

PISTH.   Not so much as a path.

EUEL. Do you think that raven of yours is still
    conscious?

PISTH. I don't know. He sort of grunts, every once
    in a while.

EUEL. I mean, do you think he knows what he's
    up to?

PISTH. He seems to know enough to chew on my
    finger.

EUEL. Silly, isn't it?
Here we are, two of us for the birds,
and we can't even find the road. [*addresses the
    audience*]   —Gentlemen:
Our trouble's just the reverse of Sakas's.[*]   30
He isn't a citizen, and he's dying to become one;
but we,
native born, pure strain, citizens all our lives,
we can't get away from Athens[*°] fast enough.
Not that we don't like Athens:
it's a fine city, progressive, full of opportunities
to appear in court, citizens
happy as locusts droning in the shade—
only I must say they seem to do most of their
    droning
before a judge.
                    To come right down to it,   40
that's why the two of us are taking this walk,
fitted out with baskets and braziers and myrtle
    boughs.
We're looking for a less strenuous residence,
a City where we can pass our lives in peace;
and we thought of Tereus:
what with all the flying he's done, maybe
he'll know a nice restricted—

PISTH.   Look! Look!

EUEL. What's the matter?

PISTH.   The rock! Look at
    my raven!

EUEL. Yes, and my jackdaw sees something: his
    beak's

34. A losing war is hard on the national nerves, but Aristophanes' grievance against Athens is that of any intelligent citizen whose government has yielded to fanaticism and public hysteria. Certainly there were traitors and dangerous malcontents in Athens, working for Sparta[*] or for their own interests, but it is also true that the inevitable Informer was providing harmless citizens and defenceless aliens with all too many "opportunities / to appear in court" on "loyalty" charges. After the scandals that attended the sailing of the Sicilian Expedition (415 B.C.) professional patriotism had become a golden racket.

open again. I'll give you odds 50
there's birds around that rock. Let's do something.

PISTH. Why don't you go bang your foot against
that rock?

EUEL. You go bang your head. It'll make twice
the noise.

PISTH. Pick up a stone and knock.

EUEL. Anything you
say.

—Porter! Porter!

PISTH. Idiot, that's no way
to call a Hoopoe. You should say "Hoop! Hoop!"

EUEL. Hoop! Hoop!
Have I got to knock again?
Hoop! Hoop! Hoop!

[*A door in the rock face opens; enter* SERVANT, *wearing
an enormous bird mask.*]

SERVANT. Whoop are youp? What do
you want?

PISTH. Holy Apollo,* what a beak! It's a canyon!

SERV. That's all we needed: a couple of bird-
watchers! 61

EUEL. Not so bad as all that.
—Come, let's think
this thing through.

SERV. You'd better make it good.

EUEL. Well, first of all,
we're not really men, you see.

SERV. Then what are you?

EUEL. I am a Yellowyammer, a Libyan* bird.

SERV. Never heard of you.

EUEL. Just look at the mess
on my feet.

SERV. I see.—And your friend: what kind of
bird is he?

PISTH. A Crapulet, from Phartia.

EUEL. For that matter,
what animal are *you*, for all the gods' sake?

SERV. A slave bird.

EUEL. You mean you were beaten
by some cock? 70

SERV. Not that, no. But when the Chief became
a Hoopoe,
he made me turn into a bird, too, to keep him
company
and do little jobs for him.
Say he wants a mess
of sardines from Phaleron:* off I run with my jug
to buy some. Or maybe it's pea soup,
and we need a tureen and a ladle: well, off I go
and arrange everything. See?

EUEL. I'd call this bird a
Kitchen.
Well, Kitch, you can do a little job for us.

Bring out Tereus.

SERV. I wouldn't think of it!
He's just had a lunch of ant and myrtle salad, 80
and now it's time for his nap.

EUEL. Bother his nap!

SERV. He won't like this a bit. But if you say so,
I'll do it. It's no skin off my beak.

PISTH. Get going!
[*Exit* SERVANT.]
To hell with him and that chasm he calls a beak!

EUEL. He scared away my jackdaw.

PISTH. You got scared,
you mean, and let it loose.

EUEL. How about you?
When you were falling flat on your face over there,
didn't you let your raven fly away?

PISTH. I certainly did not.

EUEL. Then where is it?

PISTH. Absent.

EUEL. You can wash your hands of it now, old
lion-heart. 90

EPOPS. [*within*] Open the door. I'm going out to
to meet them.

[*Enter* EPOPS, *the Hoopoe. He is inadequately covered
by thin drooping feathers, and wears a mask with a very
long pointed beak and a tall radiant crest.*]

EUEL. What in the name of High Heraklês is
that?
Those feathers! That tiara!

EPOPS. Gentlemen,
your names, if you please? The purpose of your
visit?

EUEL. The Twelve Gods° seem to have visited
something, friend,
on you.

EPOPS. You find my feathers laughable?
Remember: once I was a man.

EUEL. We are not laugh-
ing at you.

EPOPS. At what, then?

EUEL. That damned funny beak
of yours.

EPOPS. I can't help it. It's Sophoklês'* fault,°
the way he misrepresented me in his plays. 100

EUEL. You are really Tereus? A bird, or a
parody?

EPOPS. Every inch a bird.

EUEL. What's the matter
with your wings?

EPOPS: Feathers missing.

---

95. The Twelve Gods: Zeus,* Hêra,* Poseidôn,* Deméter,*
Hephaistos, Arês,* Athenê,* Artemis,* Aphroditê, Hestia,*
Apollo,* Hermês.* **99. It's Sophoklês' fault:** The reference
is to the *Tereus* of Sophoklês, a play no longer extant.

EUEL.   Some bird disease, or what?
EPOPS. Every bird moults in the wintertime.
We get new feathers in the spring.
                              —But tell me:
who are you two?
EUEL.   Mortal men.
EPOPS.   Nationality?
EUEL. Land of the Free. Home of the Brave.
EPOPS.   I suppose
you're jurymen?
EUEL.   No; you might call us *de
jure* men.
    EPOPS. Isn't that a new crop down there?
    EUEL. If you work hard enough you can grow it
        in some fields.   110
    EPOPS. Well, well.—But what brings you to this
        place?
    EUEL. We want to integrate ourselves with you.
    EPOPS. Why?
    EUEL.   Because you were a man once, like us;
because you owed money, like us, and because,
like us, you hated to pay it. Now you are a bird,
with a bird's-eye view of things and a man's
        knowledge
of all lands under the sun, of every sea.
So we have come to you
as to an authority, meaning no disrespect,
to ask if you can tell us where to find   120
a soft snug woolly city
where a man can loaf and stretch and lie down in
        peace.
    EPOPS. A nobler city than Kranaos'* town?
    EUEL. Not nobler, no; but something more to
        our taste.
    EPOPS. More aristocratic?
    EUEL.   The Social Register
pains me in a spot I needn't describe.
    EPOPS. What sort of city?
    EUEL.   What I have in mind
is a place where the worst of your troubles would be
friends crowding in early in the morning
with invitations: "Look, Euelpidês,   130
I'm giving a dinner today. For God's sake,
get a bath somewhere, pick up your wife and kids,
come early and stay late. If you forget,
I'll never turn to you when I need a friend."
    EPOPS: I can see that you're fond of troubles.
                              —How about you?
    PISTH. I feel the same way he does.
    EPOPS.   For example?
    PISTH. I'd like to live in a town
where a friend of mine, father of a goodlooking
        boy,
would meet me and, "You old bastard," he'd say,

"what's this I hear about you from that son of
        mine?   140
He tells me he ran into you outside the gymnasium,
and though he was fresh from his bath
you didn't say anything nice to him, or kiss him,
or feel his balls or his biceps—
Why, I thought you were a friend of the family!"
    EPOPS. It's clear that both of you want to live the
        hard life.
Well, this city of yours
does exist, after all. You'll find it on the Red Sea.°
    EUEL. And have the *Salaminia** turn up some
        morning
with a constable on board? Thanks, no sea for
        us!   150
Haven't you a Greek city you can recommend?
    EPOPS. How about Lepreon?*
    EUEL.   No. I've never
        been there,
but the name reminds me of Melanthios.*
    EPOPS. Then there's Opoûs,* over in Lokris.*
    EUEL.   No.
You couldn't pay me enough to be Opountios.*
But tell me,
what is life like up here among you Birds?
    EPOPS. Not bad, take it by and large. No money,
        of course.
    EUEL. There go most of your problems right
        away.
    EPOPS. As for food, we have poppy seed and
        myrtle,   160
white sesame, mint—
    EUEL.   It's a non-stop honeymoon!°
    PISTH. I have it! I have it!
I've just dreamed the most powerful dream in the
        world
for you Birds, if you only do what I tell you to.
    EPOPS. What's that?
    PISTH.   Well, first of all
I advise you to stop flying around aimlessly
with your beaks open. It isn't dignified.
Back in Athens when we see a man running around,
somebody asks "Who's that?", and Teleas*
or someone else says, "Him? He's a hot bird,
        he is!   170
Jittery, ants up his tail, all over the place, un-
dependable type."

148. the Red Sea: "He means Arabia Felix," says Σ. [Σ =
Scholiast, an anonymous commentator, generally from the
medieval period.] Actually he means Cockaigne or Arcady,
Bali or Boston, or whatever your personal Eldorado may be.
161. It's a non-stop honeymoon: Bridal wreaths were made
of mint leaves and myrtle-berries. Poppy seeds dipped in honey
were esteemed as an aphrodisiac and eaten at weddings. The
sesame plant was associated with Aphroditê.*

EPOPS.   You're right, by Dionysos!*
What else do you advise?
    PISTH.   I advise you to found a city.
    EPOPS. We birds? Found a city?
    PISTH.   O ye of little faith!
Look down there.
    EPOPS.   I'm looking.
    PISTH.   Now up there.
    EPOPS.   I'm
        looking.
    PISTH.   Look all around you.
    EPOPS.   Whatever
        you say.
I hope you're not trying to make me sprain my
        neck.
    PISTH. Do you see anything?
    EPOPS.   Clouds, and a lot of sky.
    PISTH. That's the birds' sphere.
    EPOPS.   Sphere? What
        do you mean?
    PISTH. It's a space, really; but it revolves,   180
and everything passes through it, so we scientists
call it a sphere.
                    Very well. You settle this sphere,
build walls around it, and you'll have a city.
And what's more,
you can lord it over the human race as though
they were so many grasshoppers. And the gods—
why, you can starve them out like the Mêlians.*
    EPOPS. How?
    PISTH.   Just as we manage these things on
        earth.
Suppose a man wants to consult the Oracle
at Delphoi:* well, he has to get a pass   190
from the Boiotians, because Boiotia's* on the
        way
to the Shrine. And so it will be with the gods:
there's all that air between earth and the top of
        Olympos,*
so if they won't pay tribute to the Birds
you can make it illegal
for the smoke of offering to pass up to them.
    EPOPS. Oh by Earth, by Nets, by Traps, by
        Springes,
I never heard a cleverer idea in my life!
With you to help me, I will build that city—
that is, if we can get the other Birds to agree.   200
    PISTH. Who will explain it to them?
    EPOPS.   You.
I've lived with them so long that they have learned
to speak Man now instead of twittering.
    PISTH. Can you call an Assembly?
    EPOPS.   Nothing easier.
I'll just step back into the coppice here

and wake my darling wife, my Nightingale.
We'll summon them, she and I,
and they'll come racing when they hear our voices.
    PISTH. Oh do, do! Dear Tereus, be quick!
Into the woods, wake the Nightingale!   210
[*Exit* EPOPS; *presently his voice is heard singing within.*]
    EPOPS. Awake, Love, lazy sleeper,
            Awake, and pour
The lilting glory of your golden throat
For Itys, ours no more.
        Ah, the liquid trill
            Of the holy monody rising
To God's house from the stillness of the woods!
        Phoibos* himself, that high
Singer, struck by your music, would sweep
The lutestrings with his delicate fingers   220
        Antiphonal, and all the air along
            Lead the quiring
Of the tireless gods responsive to your song.
    EUEL. Heavenly God, what a voice that little
        bird has!
He is drowning the forest with honey.
    PISTH. You!
    EUEL.   What?
    PISTH.   Be quiet, can't you?
    EUEL.   Why?
    PISTH. The Hoopoe is going to sing for us again.
[*During the following monody, birdcalls are heard from
various points behind the scene, distant and uncertain at
first, but increasing in volume and in urgency until the
CHORUS OF BIRDS enters for the* Párodos.]
    EPOPS. [*within*] *Epopoí*
                    popoì epopopoí
    popoì
        iô
    iô
        iô
            To me,   230
            to
    me here, here, here, O
        friends, O feathery
    myriads!
            Leave your
    fields now, furrows
            deep
        in seed, beak-
    wielders,
            swift
        spiralers,
                melodists
    of delight   240
    tíotíotíotí
        All you
    divers for stingvoiced gnats

in dusky wet ravines,
          you
curlew, curlew crying,
          you,
     spume-guests of the halcyon
on the enchanted water:
          Come to me, come,   250
hear this remarkable old man
     whose brain
brims for our common gain:
          Hear him,
          come
     here, here, here,
          hear him!

CHORUS. [*within*] *Tórotorotórotíx*
                    totoĭx
               whit tuwhít tuwhít   260
          Tórotorotórotorolílilíx

PISTH. Do you see any birds?

EUEL.   Not a single bird.
There's not so much as a feather in the sky.

PISTH. It seems to have done no good for the
Hoopoe to go gargling in the glade.°

PÁRODOS³

[*The* CHORUS *is composed of twenty-six persons dressed
in stylized representation of various birds, each with a
large beak-mask. These enter separately from every direction, gathering about their leader, the* Flamingo, *in the
orchestra. The entrance should be complete by the end
of the* Hoopoe's *catalogue.*]

A BIRD. Torotìx torotíx.

PISTH.   Look, there's one coming now!

EUEL. What do you suppose it is? A peacock,
     maybe?

PISTH. The Hoopoe can tell us.

                              —What kind of
     bird is that?

EPOPS. That, Sir, is a water bird; you don't see
that sort every day.

EUEL.   Nice colour; flame-y.

EPOPS. Naturally. He's a Flamingo.

EUEL.   Oh look!

PISTH. Now what?

EUEL.   Another bird.

PISTH.   I should say so!

---

265. gargling in the glade: The word (ἐπῷζε) is unexpectedly harsh. Pisthetairos is disappointed by the Hoopoe's appar-
rent failure to attract an audience.

³ The *Párodos* is the formal entrance of the Chorus into the
orchestra, and in *Aves* it is almost entirely spectacle. There is
relatively little singing for the Chorus, and the chief interest
lies in the costumes of the individual Birds and in the com-
menting dialogue. Here, as throughout the play, the Choragos
is spokesman for the Chorus as a whole.

He's a weird sister, all right, as the poet puts it.
See how he struts! I wonder what he is.

EPOPS. We call him the Bird of Araby.°

PISTH.   Araby?   10
Did he come on a flying camel?

EUEL.   There's another one!
By Poseidôn, he looks as if he had been dyed!

PISTH. This is astonishing. Do you mean to say
there's more than one Hoopoe in the world?

EPOPS. He's the son of Philoklês* and a lady
     Hoopoe,
and I am his grandfather. It's like the formula
"Kallias* : Hipponikos* : : Hipponikos : Kallias II."°

EUEL. So that's Kallias II. I see he's losing his
     feathers.

EPOPS. A man about town, you know, always
     getting plucked
by parasites and party girls feathering their own
     nests.   20

PISTH. Here comes one with a crest. What's he
     called?

EPOPS. That one? Gobbler.

EUEL.   I thought Kleony-
     mos* was the Gobbler.

PISTH. This can't be Kleonymos: he hasn't
     thrown away
his crest.

EUEL. Speaking of that, why do birds
wear crests? To compete in the Armed Men's Race?

EPOPS. It's like the Karians:* crests make
     fighting safer.

PISTH. I never saw so many birds! They make
     me nervous.

EUEL. You said it.
When they lift their wings you can't see where
     you're going.

EPOPS. That's the Partridge; and that's—let's
     see—that one's   30
the Francolin; the Egyptian Mallard; and that
     female's
a Hen Kingfisher.

---

10. Bird of Araby: This is the Cock, the Persian Bird, here
called *Mêdos*, "the Median." (The phallic pun is the same in
Greek as in English.) My "Araby" is a licence, intended to
make the "camel" more assimilable. **17. "Kallias...Kallias
II":** The names are *ad hoc*, for illustrative purposes. In ordinary
circumstances the grandson takes his grandfather's name. The
Hoopoe is explaining the presence on stage of a younger
Hoopoe, whom we may call Hoopoe II. Philoklês was a tragic
poet of unsavoury reputation (Σ) who plagiarized the *Tereus* of
Sophoklês: that is to say, the monstrous cohabitation of Philoklês with Sophoklês' "Lady" Hoopoe produced Hoopoe II.
Kallias, grandson of Kallias I, was a real enough person: dissolute and wasteful ("always getting plucked"), he is best remembered for Plato's making his house the scene of the *Protá-
goras*.

PISTH.   What's that in back of her?
EPOPS. A Shavetail, of course.
PISTH.   Do birds shave tails?
EPOPS. Doesn't Sporgilos?*
                    —And that's a female
Owl.
EUEL. That's an idea! Bringing Owls to Athens.
EPOPS. Magpie. Turtledove. Lark. Warbler.
    Spryneck.
Pigeon. Snirt. Falcon. Ringdove. Cuckoo.
Redleg. Firepate. Purple Hatch. Kestrel.
Grebe. Bunting. Lämmergeier. Woodpecker.° 40
    PISTH. Birds and more birds!
    EUEL.   Even white Blackbirds!
    PISTH. The way they chatter and screech at each
    other!
    EUEL. Do you think they're dangerous?
    PISTH.   Their
    beaks are wide open,
and they're certainly looking hard at both of us.
    EUEL. I think so, too.
    CHORAGOS.   Who-oo-oo called this Assembly?
Where is he?
    EPOPS.   Here I am, your tried
and trusted old friend.
    CHORAG.   Spea-pea pea-peak:
What clever new message have you to give us?
    EPOPS. A profitable one, safe, correct, ingenious.
These two gentlemen, both of them keen
    thinkers,   50
came here looking for me.
    CHORAG.   Looking for you? Why?
    EPOPS. I am telling you.
                    —These elegant old men
have detached themselves temporarily from
the human race and brought us what I am sure
is a plan of promising proportions.
    CHORAG.   I think
you have made the greatest blunder in history.
What are you talking about?
    EPOPS.   Be not afraid.
    CHORAG.   Why not?
What have you done to us?
    EPOPS.   I have lent an ear
to two respectable bird-struck Senators.
    CHORAG. You have?
    EPOPS.   I have. And I am proud
    of it.   60
    CHORAG. What, in our house?
    EPOPS.   As sure as I'm
    standing here.

CHORUS.   Oh misery!   [Strophe.]
        Duplicity!
            Oh horror without end!
        Who lays the snare
        And leaves us there?
            Our old familiar friend!
    Is this the Hoopoe of our heart,
        Copartner of our fields and skies,
    Who bids our ancient laws depart   70
        And sells us to our enemies?
    CHORAG. We can take care of him later. Just now
it's a matter of these two old fools. Look at them!
The usual penalty is clearly in order:
death by dissection.
    PISTH.   Done for, by God Almighty!
    EUEL. Your fault, your fault entirely. Why did
    you ever
lead me here?
    PISTH.   So that you could follow me.
    EUEL. It's blood and tears for us!
    PISTH.   Hardly tears for you,
once the Birds have pecked out both your eyes.

CHORUS.   The cock-trump sings. [Antistrophe.]
        Advance both wings,   81
            O army of the air!
        The hour has struck
        That ends the luck
            Of this repulsive pair.
    No clouds that cluster in the sky,
        No raindark mountain peaks,
    Shall save them from the battery
        Of our insulted beaks.
    CHORAG. Forward! Peck them apart! Flay them!
                    —Where's   90
that Wing Commander? Tell him to get moving
on the right!
[Immense confusion of movement among the Birds in the
orchestra. EUELPIDES and PISTHETAIROS confer apart.]
    EUEL.   That settles that.
How do we get out of this mess?
    PISTH.   Why not
stick around?
    EUEL.   Of course. And get pulled apart?
    PISTH. I suppose you have figured out some way
    of escape?
    EUEL. You know I haven't.
    PISTH.   Then listen to me.
Let them come on. We'll stand here and fight them
with these kitchen pots.
    EUEL.   Pots? What good are pots?
    PISTH. They'll keep the Owl from attacking us.°

---

40. Magpie, etc.: Some of Aristophanes' birds, in this list and
later, are no longer identifiable—"a bird of some sort," says
Σ—; and the translation reflects this uncertainty.

99. They'll . . . us: Athenê invented pottery; hence the Owl,
sacred to her, will not attack pots.

EUEL. How about those fellows with the
    horrible claws?   100
PISTH. Stick that spit up in front of you like a spear.
EUEL. But our eyes?
PISTH.   Use a couple of saucers.
EUEL.   What a mind!
You remind me of Nikias.* You ought to be
on the General Staff, in charge of secret weapons.
    CHORAG. *Eleleú!*
Ready, beaks at the charge! Let 'em have it!
Grab! Claw! Tear! Gouge! Break the pots first!
[*Much noise on both sides, but no other activity; the
                Hoopoe intervenes.*]
    EPOPS. Permit me. Just a minute, please.
                                            —With
    the best intentions,
you are behaving like besotted beasts.
What is the good of killing two harmless men,   110
both of them perfect strangers and, what's more,
related to my wife?°
    CHORAG.   Are you promoting
a Be Kind to Wolves week?
    EPOPS.   Oh, come. I'll admit,
men are our natural enemies; but these men
are different, they really mean us well.
More than that,
they have a practical plan for the good of us all.
    CHORAG. A practical plan? Nonsense. Our
            enemies,
our fathers' enemies—what can they teach us?
    EPOPS. Why, people before this have learned
    , from their enemies.   120
An open mind's a weapon in itself.
It's not our friends teach us resourcefulness,
but our wise enemies. Cities and princes
have learned the use of warships and fortresses
from necessity, not friends. Enmity saves
our homes, our children, everything that we love.
    CHORAG. You may be right.
                            At least it can do no harm
to hear what they have to say.
                            It may be
we shall take some profit even from what we hate.
[*The Birds cluster in doubtful conference about the
                CHORAGOS.*]
    PISTH. [*apart to* EUELPIDES] They're coming to
        their senses. Easy, now!   130
    EPOPS. [*to the Birds*] Think over what I've said.
        You'll thank me for it.
    CHORAG. We have always admired the Hoopoe's
        intellect.

PISTH. Now we can breathe again.
Leave your pot there on the ground. Pick up your
    spear—
your spit, I mean—and let's walk around
and see what the place is like.
                                Keep this side
of the pots, and keep your eye on those Birds.
    Above all,
don't act as though you were nervous.
    EUEL.   I'd like to know:
if they kill us, where'll we get buried?
    PISTH.   I should hope,
in the National Cemetery.° For a first-rate funeral
at the public expense, we'd say we fell gloriously
in combat with the common enemy   142
at Gettysbird.°
        [*The Birds decide upon a truce.*]
    CHORAG.   At ease! Stack arms!
Now we must find out who these strangers are
and what they want.
                        Listen, Epops!
    EPOPS.   I am listening.
    CHORAG. Who are these men? Do you know
        where they are from?
    EPOPS. Travelers from Greece, where education
        is general.
    CHORAG. What brings them to the Birds?
    EPOPS.   Ornithophily.
They have heard of your laws and customs and
        they long
to live with you for ever.
    CHORAG.   Is it possible?   150
What else do they say?
    EPOPS.   Incredible things, transcending
utterance.
    CHORAG. What do they ask from us?
Does "living with us" mean living as honest friends,
or serving their own interests at our cost?
    EPOPS. This savant speaks of benefits to you
that fairly rob me of words to describe them.
It's all for you. He will tell you so himself.
    CHORAG. Is the man crazy?
    EPOPS.   His sanity defies
definition.
    CHORAG. Really?
    EPOPS.   Pure fox, subtle, deep.
    CHORAG. Then let him speak, let him speak!   160
These hints of yours have got me all a-twitter.

---

112. **related to my wife:** Proknê was the daughter of King
Pandiôn of Athens, hence of the same "tribe" as Pisthetairos
and Euelpidês.

140. **National Cemetery:** Here were buried those Athenians
who died in battle for their country. The reservation was called
Kerameikos, which is "Pottersville" rather than "Potter's
Field."   143. **Gettysbird:** The bloodless one-day siege of
Orneai (416 B.C.); hence, no one died in that battle. The Greek
name makes the pun inevitable.

AGON

[*Order is now restored. As* EPOPS *takes command of the situation, the* CHORUS *forms itself at opposite sides of the orchestra to listen to the ensuing debate.*]

EPOPS. You there, and you,
carry these weapons in and hang them up
in the kitchen again, next to the tripod.
Fair fortune befall them!
[*Exeunt two Bird Servants with the pots, spits, and other utensils.*]
                    —And you, friend,
inform the Birds why I have summoned them
to this Assembly. Expound.
          PISTH.   No, by Apollo!
Not unless they promise me first
what Monk the Knifeman° made that wife of his
promise *him*: no biting, no tickling, no unseemly
prodding in the—
          EUEL.   The arse, you would say?
          PISTH.   No;   10
I mean my eyes.
          CHORAG.   Sir, you have our promise.
          PISTH. Swear it.
          CHORAG.   I swear it; but on condition that
this Comedy of ours wins First Prize
by unanimous vote of the judges and audience.
          EPOPS. NOW HEAR THIS:
Break ranks! Every private will pick up his arms
and go back to barracks. See your bulletin boards
for further announcements.

          CHORUS.   [*Strophe.*]
Men were deceivers ever; and it may be,
Friend, that the quality of our guilelessness   20
          Tempts you to gull us. Nevertheless,
          Nothing risked may be gain rejected when

Truth as a Stranger comes. If you have discerned
New forces in us, talents earthed over, dis-
          used instruments of old artifice:
          Speak out. Let age edify unfledged youth.

          CHORAG. You are at liberty to say whatever you
          like.
You have our promise:
We shall not be the first to break the truce.
          PISTH. I thank you.
                    —Gentlemen, you will find
much to chew on in the following message.   31
But first, with your permission—[*to a* SERVANT]

Boy, bring me
a garland and a bowl of water to wash my hands.
          EUEL. [*apart*] Do you see dinner coming?°
          PISTH. [*apart*]   No;
          I am trying to think
of something to tell them, some enormous concept
that will knock them silly.
                    —Gentlemen: My heart
bleeds—bleeds, I say—when I reflect that you
who once were kings—
          CHORAG.   Kings? Kings of what?
          PISTH. Why, kings of everything! Kings of
          myself, of this
poor friend of mine, yes, kings of Zeus the King!
Before Time was, you were: you antedate   41
Kronos,* the Titans,* Earth—
          CHORAG.   Earth?
          PISTH.   Yes, by Heaven!
          CHORAG. That's something that I never knew
          before.
          PISTH. Ignorance, accdia. There are authorities
for what I say: Αἰσῶπος,* to go no farther.
He tells us—don't you remember?—that the Lark
was the first Bird born in those chaotic times
before even Earth was thought of; and the Lark's
father died—have you forgotten?—, and because
there was no earth on Earth to bury him in,   50
the Lark finally laid him away in her head.
          EUEL. Exactly. That's how Hyde Lark° got its
          name.
          PISTH. You see my point, I hope? If birds existed
before the Creation, before the gods themselves,
then you Birds must be heirs apparent: the royal
          power
belongs to you.
          EUEL.   Of course. At the same time,
they'd better keep their beaks in fighting trim:
Zeus won't give in to the first woodpecker.
          PISTH. In those glorious days it was not the gods
          who ruled
over men, but the Birds. Let me cite you a few
          proofs.   60
Consider the Cock.
Long before any Dareioses* or Megabazoses*
the Cock was King of the Persians, and such a king
that ever since he's been called the Persian Bird.
          EUEL. That's why, even now,

---

8. **Monk the Knifeman:** From the disorderly gossip of Σ we gather that this was one Panaitios, a grumpy ugly cutler who had an actively amorous wife. The general purport seems to be: "You lay off me, and I'll lay off you." Panaitios' nickname was Pithêkos, "Monkey."

34. **Do you . . . coming?:** Pisthetairos, in accordance with correct procedure at the beginning of an address, has asked for the ceremonial wreath and the lustral water. Euelpidês affects to mistake this for preparation for a formal dinner.   52. **Hyde Lark:** The Greek says that when the Lark's father died he was encephalated, or hidden in the Lark's head—an absurd allusion to the gestation of Athenê. Euelpidês sees a chance for a joke about the place-name Kephalai, which means "heads."

Cocks strut like the Shah; and of all birds living
only they have a right to the tiara.

PISTH. What power he had! Why, to this very day
when the Cock sings at dawn
everyone jumps out of bed and goes to work: 70
blacksmiths, potters, tanners, shoemakers,
grocers, masseurs, lyre-&-shield-manufacturers—
Some of them are hard at it before it's light.

EUEL. Some of them certainly are! That's how
    I lost
a perfectly good new Phrygian* all-wool coat.
I'd been asked to a party to celebrate
naming somebody's baby. Well, when I got there
I had a couple of short ones, so I felt sleepy
and lay down for a minute; and—would you
    believe it?—   79
some damned cock began to crow, and I woke up
and thought it was morning, before the other guests
had even sat down to dinner! Well, I started out
on the Halimos* road, but I'd hardly poked my
    nose
past the drive when, baff! somebody boffed me
with something blunt, and I went down for the
    count.
When I came to, my coat was somewhere else.

PISTH. At that same time the Kite reigned over
    the Greeks.

CHORAG. The Greeks?

PISTH.   The Greeks. That's when
    they learned
to prostrate themselves° when the kites come back
    in the spring.

EUEL. I remember I prostrated myself one day
when I saw a Kite, or I tried to, but somehow   91
I fell on my back by mistake and my market money
went down my throat. That day I ate no more.

PISTH. Then there's the Cuckoo.
Once upon a time
in Egypt and in Phoinikia* the Cuckoo
was king. As a matter of fact, when the Cuckoo
said "Cuckoo!",
all the Phoinikians went out and mowed their
    fields.

EUEL. "Cuckoo! Back to the furrows, you
    foreskinless!"°   100
as the proverb has it.

PISTH.   Another thing: You will find
that whenever a man managed to become a king,

an Agamemnon,* say, or a Menelaos,*
he would always carry a bird on the end of his
    sceptre
to share the royal gifts.

EUEL.   That explains something.
I used to go to the theatre; and whenever Priam*
came on in the tragedies, he'd have a bird
on his sceptre, just as you say. I used to think
the bird was there to keep an eye on our friend
Lysikratês* when the bribes were passed around.

PISTH. But the best proof is that Zeus, the current
    King,   111
wears an Eagle on his head as a sign of power.
His Daughter has an Owl; his son Apollo,
as a medical man, has a Hawk.

EUEL.   That's perfectly true.
Why do you suppose those gods have those birds?

PISTH. Why? So that when the sacrificial roasts
are offered to the gods, the birds may taste them
    first.
And here's something else:
In the old days men never swore by the gods,
but always by birds.

EUEL.   Lampôn* still does today.   120
He always says "Holy Kites!"° when he makes a
    mistake.

PISTH. You understand, then, that years and
    years ago
you were great, even holy, in the minds of men.
    But now? Now you are rejects, fools,
    worse than slaves, stoned
    in the streets by arrogant men, hunted
    down even in your sanctuaries
    by trappers with nets, springes, limed
    twigs, cages, decoy-
    boxes;
        caught, sold   130
    wholesale, goosed, prodded
    by fat fingers, denied
    even the grace of wholesome frying,
    but served up sleazily, choked
    with cheese, smeared with oil,
    sprayed with vinegar, doused
    as though you were dead meat, too gamy,
    in rivers of sweet slab sauce.

CHORUS.   [Antistrophe.]
Tears, and no idle tears, Stranger, distress us
Hearing your plain account of calamity.   140
    Clearly our primeval dignity

---

89. to prostrate themselves: Probably a genuflection (Σ). At
any rate it is to be taken literally: the Kite was so greeted as
the harbinger of spring. Euelpidês, carrying his market money
in his mouth, seems to have genuflected too vigorously.
100. "Cuckoo! Back to the furrows . . .": The meaning of
the proverb is obscure; *sed latet*, as the Commentators happily
remark, *spurci aliquid*.

121. "Holy Kites!": Lampôn, possibly because he didn't
want to be bound by his oracles, used to confirm them with
this diluted oath; or maybe he was one of those mistaken persons
who think that "My Cow!" or something of the sort avoids the
profanity of "My God!"

Has lapsed in the long sliding of the years.

You, by a happy chance or some divine influence sent to guide us, have indicated
    Future recovery, joy ahead.
            Ourselves, our wives, our chicks depend on
            you.

    CHORAG. What can we do? Instruct us, since
            you say
you have a plan. Life's no life for us
till we win back the power that we have lost.
    PISTH. My plan is a great City for All Birds,   150
a single City, with the surrounding air
and all the space between encircled by
massive brick walls like those at Babylon.*
    EUEL. Bring on your Giants! What a mighty
            fortress!
    PISTH. Once the wall's built, you must send an
            embassy
to Zeus and lay your grievances before him.
If he denies them, if he temporizes,
then you should declare a Holy War
against the whole of Olympos: no more free pas-
            sage
for divinities in an obvious state of erection   160
on their way through your land to flirt with their
            Alopês,*
their Sémelês,* their Alkmenês!* No; once across
            the border,
each strutting member must be stamped and
            sealed.
That should give them something to think about!
                            As for Mankind,
you must send another bird to them, a herald
to announce that from now on, since the Birds are
            kings,
the first sacrifices must be made to them,
and then (if convenient) to the Olympian* gods.
But even in sacrifices to the gods
an appropriate Bird° must be adored as well: 170
thus, Aphroditê and a Phalarope; Poseidôn
and a Duck; Heraklês and a Cormorant;
or, if the victim is offered up to King Zeus,
let the Wren, the Wren, the king of all birds,
            receive
the flesh of the Balled Gnat.
    EUEL.   What price gnat-flesh?
Let the Good Gosh° bounce thunderballs in the
            sky!

170. The attendant or surrogate birds are appropriate.
Aphroditê's phalarope is suggested by *phallos;* as a sea god,
Poseidôn should have a water bird; cormorants, like Heraklês,
are greedy; and it has always been the wren, not the eagle, who
is King of the Birds.   **176. the Good Gosh:** Not a softening,
like Lampôn's oath noted above, but a whimsical variation:
Zan for *Zeus.*

    CHORAG. What if men refuse to treat us as gods?
What if they say, "Them? Jackdaws, that's all,
flying around up there with their silly wings"?
    PISTH. I can't believe you are serious. Why, good
            Lord!   180
Hermês has wings, and he flies; yes, and Nikê,
she has wings; and Erôs*—all sorts of gods
fly, don't they? Why, even Iris,
the one that Homer* refers to as "Trembling
            Dove"–
Iris has wings, Iris flies.
    EUEL.   Speaking of wings,
what if Zeus drops one of his wingèd bolts on us?
    CHORAG. But what if Mankind is so unregenerate
that only the regulars of the Olympos clique
are recognized?
    PISTH.   We'll draft a regiment
of Sparrows and march them off to steal the seeds
in the new-planted fields. Deméter can set up   191
a Farm Program to fend off starvation.
    EUEL. Deméter will also find a thousand ways
to get around any program that she sets up.
    PISTH. If the Sparrows fail, we'll send some
            Elite Crows
to the grazing lands and have them bite out the
            eyes
of herdsmen and herds. Let Apollo cure them.
he's a doctor, he gets paid.
    EUEL.   Let me know in advance:
I'll want to sell my yoke of oxen first.
    PISTH. But if they sense the indwelling divinity
of the Birds, as they should, knowing that you are
            God,   201
and Life, and Earth, and Kronos, and Poseidôn—
then everything will end as they would have it.
    CHORAG. Everything? What do you mean?
    PISTH.   For
            example,
locusts will not touch their budding vines:
the Hawks and Owls will see to that. Then, too,
a single platoon of indoctrinated Redwings
will be assigned to keep the gall-flies and emmets
from chewing up fig-shoots.
    CHORAG.   But how shall we manage
money? Men seem to set great store by money.   210
    PISTH. The Auspice birds will show them where
            rich mines
lie in the earth. The Augurs, too, will learn
the secret of quick returns. Shipwrecks will end—
    CHORAG. How so?
    PISTH.   They'll consult the Birds be-
            fore each voyage:
"Is it safe to sail?" "Not today; a storm's blowing
            up."

EUEL. I'll invest in a boat. Yo-ho for the briny
   deep!

PISTH. Then, of course, there are those buried
   pots

of treasure. The Birds know. Haven't you heard
"A little bird told me where to look for it"?   219

EUEL. I'll sell my boat. Me for the buried pots!

CHORAG. But what about health? That's the gift
   of the gods.

PISTH. When business is good, health takes care
   of itself.

EUEL. I never heard of a bankrupt whose
   health was good.

CHORAG. How will they ever live to reach old
   age?

Surely that's an Olympian dispensation.
Or must they die in the cradle?

PISTH.   Not at all.
The Birds will add three centuries to their lives.

CHORAG. Where will they get three centuries?

PISTH.   From
   themselves.
The poet says: 229
"One crow caws down five generations of man".°

EUEL. Almost thou persuadest me to be a bird.

PISTH. Why not be birds? They demand no
   marble temples

intricate with golden doors; their shrines
are the ilex, the sparkling shrubs. Their highest
   gods
live in the sanctuary of olive trees.
We need no Delphoi or Ammon* for this worship,
but at home, on our own ground,
in peace among our own familiar flowers,
we can raise hands full of grain to them in prayer,
invoking their dear aid: 240
and when our words fly up, they will be answered
in blessings that fall upon the scattered grain.

CHORAG. Dearest of old men, you have won me
   utterly

to your cause. From this hour your words are my
   words.

CHORUS.   My mind applauds.
           Swear faith to me,
           And I will swear
           Death to the gods.
           The fight is fair:
           Sing Victory.   250

CHORAG. We are ready to do whatever must be
   done.
The plans and stratagems we leave to you.

EPOPS. Action, quick action. By God, this is no
   time
for taking naps or dawdling like Nikias!
But first, gentlemen,
this is my nest, a poor thing of twigs and straw,°
but my own. Will you permit me to entertain you
inside? And will you tell me who you are?

PISTH. Of course. Pisthetairos is the name. That
   one's
Euelpidês; comes from Kriôa.*

EPOPS.   Very happy   260
to meet you both.

PISTH.   Not at all.

EPOPS.   Will you please step in?

PISTH. After you.

EPOPS.   Right this way.

PISTH.   There, I almost
   forgot!
Tell me, how can a couple of men like us
live with birds? You can fly. We don't know how.

EPOPS. I see.

PISTH.   And speaking of Aisôpos again,
he has a fable about a fox and an eagle.
The fox lost.

EPOPS.   Really, it's no problem at all.
There's a useful little herb. You nibble it
and, presto!—you sprout wings.

PISTH.   That's fair enough.
—Here, Xanthias,* Manodôros:* pick up the
   baggage.   270

CHORAG. Hi! Epops! Before you go—

EPOPS.   What's the
   matter?

CHORAG. You'll invite our venerable guests to
   dine, of course;
but the Nightingale,
the Muses'* love, sweet cataract of song—
will you send her out and let us play with her?

PISTH. A sound idea, by God, and I second it.
Ask the delightful bird to step this way.

EUEL. Yes, just for a minute. You can't imagine
   how long
we've longed, my friend and I, for a nightingale.

EPOPS. You are too kind.

                          —Proknê, Proknê,   280
come here and show yourself to our noble guests.
[Enter the Nightingale: a flute-girl, nude except for her
                          mask and wings.]

PISTH. God of our fathers, what a heavenly
   little bird!
So soft, so white—

---

230. "One crow . . . man": A parody of a line of Hesiod (Frag.
50): "Nine generations lives the cawing crow." [Σ]

256. a poor thing of twigs and straw: The Hoopoe's nest is
proverbially filthy, Proknê being a career musician rather than
a housewife.

How I should like to get between those thighs!

EUEL. The gold, all the gold, like a bride on her
wedding day!

I can't help it; I am obliged to kiss this young
woman.

PISTH. Stupid, don't you see the little spikes on
her beak?

You'll get hurt.

EUEL.   No, I shan't. It's like opening an egg.

Tap her on the head, the shell falls away,
and there's my kiss.

EPOPS. [indicating the door] Gentlemen.

PISTH.   Let's go
in.   290
                                                [Exeunt.]

PARÁBASIS[4] I

[In the orchestra the CHORUS turns to face the audience;
the Nightingale accompanies the lyric passages on her
flute.]

CHORUS [a solo voice]   [Kommation.]
        Tawnythroat, Partner
        In song, dark
        Muse, dearest of Birds:
        Come, let the curving long
        Line of our fluting
        Fall, sparkling
        Undersong to our words.

CHORAG.   [Parábasis.]
Come now, let us consider the generations of Man,
Compound of dust and clay, strengthless,
Tentative, passing away as leaves in autumn   10
Pass, shadows wingless, forlorn
Phantoms deathbound, a dream. Let Men turn
To the Birds, aerial philosophers of
Forever, safe from age, from change, from death.
Let them be humble and learn from us
The truth of Being, the essential germ,
The Bird, first Cause of Gods and Rivers,
Of Erebos,* and of the great Void of Chaos.*

Here is the absolute Theogony:
Professor Pródikos* can lecture somewhere else.

CHAOS and NIGHT: that was the start of it,   21
And black Erebos, and the long nothing of
        Tártaros;*

No Earth as yet, no Air, no Heaven. There,
In the untried lap of Erebos, sombre Night
Laid a wind-egg,° whence, with the circling year,
Erôs was hatched, golden Erôs, wind-swift
Love, the world's longing. His was the sleight
Joined Night and wingèd Chaos in that first
Tartarean marriage and brought the race of Birds
To the shores of light. It was Erôs   30
Created the line of Gods also, mixing
The urgent elements in adorable ways
To make the Sky and Sea and Earth and all
The Blessèd Ones.
              So it appears that we
Are móre ancient than these same Blessèd Ones,
Older in the line of Love. What I say is clear
In a thousand proofs:
                    We are wing'd, and so is Love.
Love is our art: how many a handsome boy
Has armed his heart with scorn, only to yield
His proud thighs to the persuasion of the Birds, 40
Won by a gift of quail, or geese, or cocks!

And birds are good to men in numberless ways.
We lead in the seasons. The clanging Crane
Flies towards Libya, and the sowing begins;
She it is who tells the mariner
When it is time to take his winter sleep,
The unshipped rudder hanging against the wall.
This same Crane
Inspires our friend Orestês* of the Alleys°
To knit himself a shirt against the cold,   50
Thus winning the gratitude of citizens waylaid
Who otherwise would shiver in nudity.
Later, the Kite brings back the brilliant Spring
And you barber your sheep; and then the summer
        Swallow
Suggests bargains of thin dress at the shops.

We are Ammon, Delphoi, Dodôna,* Phoibos
        Apollo.
Are you not always taking the advice of birds
In matters of business, of marriage, of daily life?
You see Bird in everything:° your rumours are
        what
A small Bird told you; your sneeze is a Bird, your
        chance   60
Hello in the street's a Bird; a stranger encountered;

---

[4] At this point the action of the play is suspended while the
author, speaking through the Choragos, addresses the audience.
The Parábasis proper begins as a parody of the Theogonies, the
philosophical accounts of the origin of the gods and the creation
of the world; but this tone, which is precariously balanced
between the solemn and the bantering, passes into mild topical
satire.

25. laid a wing-egg: This is an unfertilized egg, appropriate
for the genesis of Love. Σ obscurely alludes to the Ledaian egg
from which the Heavenly Twins, Kastor and Polydeukês, were
hatched.   **49. Orestês of the Alleys:** This hoodlum with the
glorious nickname, who is mentioned again by the Chorus,
seems to have impressed Aristophanes rather deeply. He must
also have had a sense of humour, for there is something comic, to
the non-participant, in his habit of stripping his victims of all
their clothes after robbing them.   **59. you see Bird in everything:** Birds as omens, a fashionable fad.

An ass on the road: all Birds, all signs of Birds.
Are we not right to call ourselves your Apollos?

Therefore confess us gods, for so   [*Makron.*]
We are, to you; and you shall have
Feathery Muses to foretell
The winter wind, the summer breeze.
We will not perch like Zeus, at ease
In some remote cloud-citadel,
But live with you and with your sons,   70
Your sons' sons, and their sons as well,
Bringing you gifts of youth and peace,
Love, laughter, wealth, new dances, brave
Festivals, more than the human tongue
Can tell, more than the heart can know.
This is our pledge, this is our song.

CHORUS. Woodland Muse   [*Ode.*]
                 tíotiotínx tíotínx
                         Lucency
         Darting voice   80
                 Valley
         Wanderer, circling flight
                 tíotinx tíotiotínx
                         on the bright hills:
                 My singing
         Spills
                 duskiness into the light
         For Pan*
                         and thou hearest
                                 For
         The Great Mother, Mountaindweller,
                 tótototótótototínx
                         and thou   90
                         hearest
         In air
                 on the heights
                                 fields
                 where Phrynichos*
         Tastes the ambrosial finality
                 tíotínx
                                 of song.

CHORAG.   [*Epirrhema.*]
If any gentleman in the audience is interested
In a pleasant life, he should get in touch with us.
We practise what your laws forbid: You would
    like to beat
Your father? Good. According to your code
It's an off-colour pastime and, moreover, illegal.
All right; but if you were one of us Birds,   101
You'd just walk up to the old man, tap him
On the snout, and say: "Put 'em up, if you want
    to fight!"
Or say you're on the lam, branded and all that:
    here,

We'd refer to you as a Mottled Francolin, and
    forget you.
You're a sub-Asiatic type like Spíntharos?*
Here you'd be a Migrant Finch, Philémon* species.
Even a creeping calamity like Exekestidês
Can hatch ancestors up here and become
    respectable.
Why, if Peisias'* son himself   110
Should take after the old man and cohabit
With subversives by the dozens, we'd only say
"What a clever bird he is, always drumming up
    trade!"

CHORUS. So the wild Swans   [*Antode.*]
                 tíotiotínx tíotínx
                         calling
         Above the roar
         Of their great wings,
                                 cry
                 tíotínx tíotiotínx
                         "Apollo!"   120
                         on the Hebros*
         Shore:
                 The company
         Of spotted wood-beasts fly
                         for dread,
         The sea
                 hearing
                 tótotototótototototínx
                         falls
                 hearing
                 and is still:
         Olympos
                 is hushed
                                 The Graces*   130
                 shriek back against
         The liquid instancy
                 tíotínx
                         of song.

CHORAG.   [*Antepirrhema.*]
There is nothing more practical or more enjoyable
Than a pair of wings. Suppose you go to the theatre
And find it's some Tragedy or other: well, of course
You're bored, and hungry, so off you fly home,
Take care of your belly, and get back for the last act.
Or say you develop a sudden case of the runs.
Do you sit there and spoil your suit? No. You
    simply   140
Zoom up into air, do your job, fart twice,
Catch your breath, and coast back to your seat
    again.
Or maybe you're an Adulterer, of all things, and
    there's

Your girl's husband in the front row gawking at
   the Chorus.
A flap of the wings, and you're off you know where;
   and when
You've laid the lady—a flap of the wings, and
   you're back.
Wings? There's nothing like them!
Look at Dieitrephês,* if you want a good example:
Those wicker wing baskets he manufactures got
   him
A captaincy, then a colonelcy, and now, rags to
   riches,   150
He's a full-fledged Horsecock° in a yellow uniform!

SCENE

[*Re-enter* PISTHETAIROS *and* EUELPIDES. *Both are now
absurdly feathered, winged, and beaked.*]

PISTH. So far, so good.
EUEL.   By God, it's the funniest thing
I ever saw in my life!
   PISTH.   What is?
   EUEL.   You,
with those pinfeathers. Know what you look like?
   PISTH. *You* look like a cut-rate reproduction
of an unsuccessful sketch of a goose.
   EUEL. Do I?
You look like a blackbird tonsured in the dark.
   PISTH. These similes are futile. Remember the
   poem.
"I shot an arrow into the air . . ."°
   CHORAG.   Next business?
   PISTH. First we must find   10
a name for our City, a glorious name;
and then we must sacrifice to the gods.
   EUEL.   You said it.
   CHORAG. Let's get busy. What shall we call this
   City of ours?
   PISTH. Shall we go in for a touch of Lakonian*
   je ne sais quoi
and name it New Sparta?
   EUEL.   I want no part of Sparta.
Gosh, I wouldn't tie a name like that
to a flop-house bunk!
   PISTH.   Well, have you any ideas?
   EUEL. Somewhere, what with all these clouds
   and all this air,
there must be a rare name, somewhere . . .

PISTH.   How
   do you like
"Cloudcuckooland"?
   CHORAG.   That's it! That's it!   20
What a name, what a jewel of a name you've
   thought of!
   EUEL. Cloudcuckooland. Isn't that the place
where Aischenês* and Theogenês* rent castles?
   PISTH. Yes; and it's where the Giants met the
   Gods
and got themselves bluffed off the battlefield.
   CHORAG. Cloudcuckooland's a city with a future!
What god or goddess shall we choose for Patron?
   EUEL. Why not Athenê?
   PISTH.   In a City with a Future,
"what boots a mailèd warrior goddess° in arms,"
since Kleisthenês* tends to the weaving?
   CHORAG.   But the
   Akropolis?*   30
Who will guard the Pelargic Wall?*°
   PISTH.   A bird.
   CHORAG. One of us? What kind?
   PISTH.   Something Per-
   sian, I should say,
something with a reputation for ferocity.
An Arês-chicken, maybe?
   EUEL.   Hail, Arês, Master Cluck!
He's used to uncomfortable roosts, at any rate.
   PISTH. [*to* EUELPIDES] But now,
off you go into the air! See what the builders
are up to. Make sure they have enough stones.
Get plenty of tubs. Make the mortar yourself.
   (Better
strip first.) Carry the hods up—
   EUEL.   And fall off the
   ladder.°   40
   PISTH. Bank the fires. Post sentries in the right
   places.
Make the round of the guards at night—
   EUEL.   And take a snooze.
   PISTH. Send out two heralds, one to the gods
   above,
one to mankind below.
When you have done this, report back here to me.
   EUEL. And here you'll be on your back! I wish
   to God
you'd do some of the work.

29. "what boots a mailèd warrior goddess": The whole
speech parodies a passage from the lost *Meleagros* of Euripidês.*
31. the Pelargic Wall: This was a part of the fortifications of the
Akropolis. The more common name was "Pelasgic"; "Pelargic,"
however, has the advantage of meaning "Stork [Wall]."
40. and fall off the ladder: There is no authority for assigning
this interpolation and the next one to Euelpidês, but surely the
conjecture is allowable. Incorporated in Pisthetairos' speech
they have no comic force at all.

151. a full-fledged Horsecock: An unhappy Aischylean
compound, which Aristophanes ridicules again in *Ranae*.
Aischylos intended it as a kind of heraldic beast, half fowl, half
horse, a figurehead for a ship.
   9. "I shot an arrow...": Pisthetairos quotes a verse from the
lost *Myrmidones* of Aischylos, where a wounded eagle recognizes
his own feathers on the shaft of the arrow that struck him.

PISTH.   Friend, that's not like you.
We all depend on you to get things done.
I shall be busy too: [*Exit* EUELPIDES.]
I must arrange for the dedication service   50
and collar a priest to recite the liturgy.
Boy!—You, boy!—Bring me the basket and the
    lavabo.

CHORUS.   [*Strophe.*]
        Inevitably right! My mind
            Melts in your mind's embrace.
        High rituals of any kind
            Are proper in this place.
        Here let our piety devote
        To the blest gods one skinny goat.

        So may they look down from above
            Upon our sacred feast,   60
        Accept our sparsely offered love,
            And overlook the rest.
        Sing one, sing all! Sing deaf, sing mute!
        Chairis,* assist us with your flute.

PISTH. [*to the* FLUTEPLAYER] You, there, stop that
    futile tooting!
What a man! I swear by my God, I've seen
strange sights in my life, but this is the first
crow I ever saw with a leather beak-rest.°
                    [*Enter a* PRIEST.]
Holiness, get busy. Sacrifice to the gods.
    PRIEST. I would fain do so.
                    —Where is my acolyte?   70
LET US PRAY:
TO HESTIA NESTIARCH,* TO THE HIGH
    HAWK OF THE HALL, TO ALL OLYM-
    PIAN BIRDS AND BIRDETTES—
    PISTH. Hail Storkissimo! Hail, Super of
        Sounion!*
    PRIEST.—TO THE PYTHODELIAN* SWAN,
    TO LETO CORNCRAKE, TO ARTEMIS
    SISKIN°—
    PISTH. That's a pretty association of ideas!
    PRIEST.—TO SABAZIOS* THE PHRYGIL-
    LATOR, TO THE GREAT OSTRICH
    MOTHER OF GODS AND MEN—   83
    PISTH. Lady Kybelê,* Ostrichess, Mother of
        Kleokritos!*
    PRIEST. THAT THEY MAY VOUCHSAFE
    HEALTH AND LENGTH OF DAYS TO
    ALL CLOUDCUCKOOLANDERS, and also
    to the Chians*—

---

68. a leather beak-rest: The Crow, as *auletês*, or flute accom-
panist for the singing, would be wearing a leather lip-guard.
79. Artemis Siskin: One of the mystical names of Artemis was
Kolainis (Σ). The *Akalanthis* is a bird, the siskin. This is straining
for a pun; but a pun of sorts emerges.

PISTH. My heart leaps up when someone men-
    tions the Chians!
PRIEST. AND TO ALL HERO BIRDS AND
BIRDSONS OF HEROES: MORE ESPE-
CIALLY TO THE PORPHYRION,* THE
WRY PECKER, THE PELICAN, THE
PYROPHLEX, THE RUDDY GUINEA,
THE PEACOCK, THE MAJOR OUSEL,
THE TEAL, THE BANDED BITTERN,   96
THE HERON, THE DISTELFINK, THE
BALMY PETREL, THE PIPIT, THE GOAT-
GREEN TITMOUSE, THE—
    PISTH. Birds, birds, birds! Enough! Why, what
        a man
you are, to summon all those vultures and sea-eagles
to our Eucharist! Can't you see that a single hawk
could take our entire victim at one gulp?
Go away, and take your portable altar with you.
                    [*Exit* PRIEST.]
I'll finish the service myself.   105

CHORUS.   [*Antistrophe.*]
        If that is so, it seems that I
            Must tune my voice again
        In sacramental hymnody
            Of even deeper strain:
        O Gods, and thou our Patron's God,
        Exact no more from us than laud.

        Behold our sacrificial beast,
            Sick bones and stringy hair:
        If you partake of the thin feast,
            How shall we laymen fare?
        Reject our poor oblation, then,
        And feed your worshipers. Amen.

PISTH. Let us propitiate the Feathery Gods.
            [*Enter a* POET, *singing.*]
    POET. Cloudcuckooland, my happy home,
Sung by the Muses Nine—   120
    PISTH. How did this one get in?
                    —Who are you?
    POET. Who am I? A honeythroated bard,
a "willing slave of the Muse," as Homer puts it.
    PISTH. A slave? With that haircut?
    POET.   You misunderstand.
I am a poet. All we poets are
"willing slaves of the Muse," as Homer puts it.
    PISTH. That cloak of yours has seen service,
        willing or not.
Speak, O Bard: What catastrophe brings you here?
    POET. In honour of Cloudcuckooland, that great
        City,
I have composed the following lyric items: 130

a] a batch of cyclic verses
b] a few simple virginations
c] some odes in the manner of Simonidês.*

PISTH. God forbid. When did you start writing
them?

POET. Long have I meditated on this City, long.

PISTH. Impossible. Why, only a minute ago
I was dedicating the place, giving it a name!

POET. Ah, swift is the speech of the Muses,
Yea, swifter than swivelling steeds!
Mark me, man: 140
 Thou Author of Aitna,*° Father,
 At whose dire doom do foregather
  All the high hierarchs—
 Och! wad
 Thy nod
  Some giftie gi'e me:
I don't care what, just a token of your regard.

PISTH. He'll be around all day if we don't pay
him off.
Here, you in the new overcoat:
take it off and give it to this lyric has-been.   150

—Put it on. You look as though you were catching
cold.

POET. Thy, Sir, high gratuity
 Compels gratitudinity.
Brace yourself. I will now address you
in the vein of Pindar.*

PISTH.   It's a vein I can do without.

POET. Ill fares the man amid the Skythian spears,
Beset by Nomads, who no 'pparel wears.
Nil is his number, nameless is his name,
 Who hath no garment to refúge his shame.
Do you get me?   160

PISTH. I get the idea that you want some
underwear.
—Take that off too, man, and let him have it.
He's a poet, after all.
                          —There you are. Get out!

POET. Out, out, poor poet!
Sing, O Muse in gold enthroned,
 This chilly City!
Naked in many a snowbank have I moaned,
 Which seems a pity.
  But still I'll chant, where'er I roam,
  Cloudcuckooland my happy home.   170
Alalaí!   [Exit POET.]

PISTH. God, what a nuisance! I hope I never meet
another one like that. How did he hear so soon

---

141. **Author of Aitna:** The Poet's lyrics are a farrago of im-
perfectly remembered fragments from the standard poets. Here
he is mutilating a Pindaric* ode on Hiero, Tyrant of Syracuse
and founder of the town of Aitna.

---

about our City? Well . . .
                          —You, there:
Go around again with the holy water.
                  [Enter a TRAVELLING PROPHET.]

DEARLY BELOVED: WE GATHER TO-
GETHER IN—

PROPHET.   Silence!
Begin not the sacrifice of the goat!

PISTH. Who says so?

PROPH.   I; an Expounder of Oracles.

PISTH. Expounders be damned!

PROPH.   Tut. We mustn't blaspheme.
I come to reveal an oracle of Bakis*   180
that bears directly on Cloudcuckooland.

PISTH. In God's name, why did you wait to
reveal it
until I'd gone and founded Cloudcuckooland?

PROPH. God moves in a mysterious way.

PISTH.   He does.
Well, since you're here, let's have your revelation.

PROPH. WHAT TIME WOLVES AND
WHITE CROWS
CONFECT BUNGALOWS
'TWIXT SIKYON AND KORINTH*—

PISTH. It's a lie! I never had any dealings with
Korinth.

PROPH. That is Bakis' way of referring to the Air.
Now listen: 191
 TO PANDORA* THIS DAY
 A WHITE RAM THOU MUST SLAY,
 AND TO WHOSO DIVINES ME THOU
  SHALT NOT REFUSE
 A WARM WINTER SUIT AND A PAIR OF
  NEW SHOES.

PISTH. Does it say shoes?

PROPH.   Look in the book.
 PLUS A GENEROUS CUP,
 PLUS A SLICE OFF THE TOP—

PISTH. A slice off the top, hey?

PROPH.   Look in the book.
AND IF, GODLY INFANT, THOU DOST
AS I SAY,   200
A HEAV'N-KISSING EAGLE SHALT
 THOU BE TODAY,
NOT SO MUCH AS A TITTYMOUSE IF
 THOU SAY'ST NAY.

PISTH. Is that there too?

PROPH.   Look in the book.

PISTH. Strange. It's so unlike the oracle
I took down from Apollo's dictation.

PROPH.   What was
that one?

PISTH. BUT IF BY ILL HAP A CHEAP
ORACLE-MONGER

DISTURBETH THE SERVICE WITH LIES
  BORN OF HUNGER,
THOU SHALT BASH IN HIS RIBS—
PROPH.   I don't
  believe it says that.
PISTH. Look in the book.
AS FOR HEAV'N-KISSING EAGLES AND
  ARSE-KISSING SEERS,   210
TO HELL WITH THEM ALL. END OF
  MESSAGE. [LOUD CHEERS]
PROPH. Is that there too?
PISTH.   Look in the book.
          [*Suddenly losing patience.*]
Damn you, get out of here!
          [*Strikes him with his staff.*]
PROPH.   Ouch! I'll go! Ouch!
                    [*Exit* PROPHET.]
PISTH. [*calling after him*] Peddle your damned
  oracles somewhere else!
[*Enter* METON, *wearing a saffron gown embroidered with
          geometrical figures.*]
METON. My aim in coming here—
PISTH.   Another headache!
What's your project? And, above all,
why that absurd costume?
MET.   I have come
to subdivide the air into square acres.
PISTH. May I ask who you are?
MET.   You may. My
  name is Metôn.
The word's a commonplace in Greece and
  Kolonos.*   220
PISTH. What's that you've got with you?
MET.   An aerial
  straight-edge.
Observe:
The conformation of the air, considered as
a total entity, is that of a conical damper.
Very well. At the apex of this cone we apply
the ruler, bracketing in the dividers to allow
for the congruent curve. Q.E.D.
PISTH.   Q.E.D.?
MET. We calculate the declination by ca-
  thexis
according to the sine. Thus we square the circle.
In the centre we postulate a forum, the focus 230
of convergent streets that, stelliform,
subtend the radii extended from this point.
Q.E.D.
PISTH. Q.E.D.! The man's a Thalês!*
Metôn.
MET. Yes?
PISTH.   I admire you. I really do.
Take my advice and subdivide somewhere else.

MET. Why? Is it dangerous here?
PISTH.   Yes, here and
  in Sparta.
You know how they're treating aliens these days:
nasty demonstrations in the streets.
MET. You apprehend
seditious manifestations in Cloudcuckooland? 240
PISTH. God forbid.
MET.   Then what?
PISTH.   Well, we've passed
  a law
that charlatans shall be whipped in the public
  square.
MET. Oh. Then I'd better be going.
PISTH.   You're almost
  too late.
Here's a sample, God help you!
          [*Knocks him down.*]
MET.   My head! My head!
PISTH. I warned you. On your way, and be
  quick about it!
[*Exit* METON; *enter an* INSPECTOR, *elegant in full uni-
    form, carrying two urns for balloting.*]
INSPECTOR. Summon the Consuls.
PISTH.   Who's this
  Sardanápalos?*
INSP. My good man, I am a legally designated
Inspector, empowered to investigate
the civic status of Cloudcuckooland.
PISTH. Your warrant?
INSP.   This illegible document
endorsed by Teleas.
PISTH.   My dear Inspector,   251
it seems a pity to waste your valuable time.
Suppose you collect your pay and go right
  home?
INSP. A first-rate idea! As a matter of fact,
I ought not to have left Athens at all.
There are certain sensitive foreign affairs—you
  know?—
that Pharnakês* leaves to me.
PISTH.   Is that so?
Here's your pay.
          [*Slaps his face.*]
INSP.   Sir, I demand the meaning of this.
PISTH. It's a sensitive foreign affair.
INSP.   I make formal
  protest
that you have assaulted and battered an Inspector.
PISTH. Take your voting-jugs and get out of my
  sight!   261
It's an outrage:
Inspectors before there's a City to inspect!
[*The* INSPECTOR *withdraws, but hides behind one of the*

Acolytes; enter a DECREE-VENDOR, *who begins to read from a scroll.*]

DECREE-VENDOR: "AND IF ANY CLOUD-CUCKOOLANDER WHATSOEVER SHALL CAUSE INJURY OR DISTRESS TO ANY ATHENIAN CITIZEN WHATSOEVER—"

PISTH. Another one! A walking law-book this time.

DECR. Your Honour, I am a dealer in the latest decrees.   270
Satisfaction guaranteed.

PISTH.   As for example?

DECR. "VOTED: THAT FROM THE DATE HEREINUNDER SUBSCRIBED ALL WEIGHTS MEASURES AND STATUTES WHATSOEVER OF CLOUDCUCKOO-LAND SHALL BE IDENTICAL WITH THE SAME OBTAINING IN OLO-PHYXOS.*"

PISTH. That ought to fix us.
                          —Look here, you!

DECR. What's the matter with you? Something you ate?   280

PISTH. Go back where you came from with your silly laws,
or you'll get some rough and ready legislation.

[*Strikes him; exit* DECREE-VENDOR *hurriedly; the* INSPECTOR *reappears.*]

INSP. I charge Pisthetairos with felonious assault, returnable April Session.

PISTH.   How did *you* get back?

[*The* DECREE-VENDOR *re-enters.*]

DECR. "AND IF ANY MAN SHALL SCUTTLE A MAGISTRATE AFTER THE NAME OF SAME HAS BEEN POSTED ON THE PILLAR IN ACCORD-ANCE WITH THE LAW—"

PISTH. Holy God! You too?   290

[*Drives him away with blows.*]

INSP. I'll have your license! This will cost you a cool thousand!

PISTH. I'll smash those jugs of yours in a thousand pieces!

INSP. Do you remember the evening you polluted the pillar?

PISTH. Go pollute yourself!
                      —Grab him! That's it!

[INSPECTOR *escapes.*]

Let's hope that's the end of him.
                              —Gentlemen:
If we're going to sacrifice our goat at all,
I'm afraid we'll have to do the job inside.

[*Exeunt; manet* CHORUS.]

PARÁBASIS II

[*The* CHORUS *again addresses itself to the audience.*]

CHORUS.   [*Ode.*]
We are Lords of Earth and of all upon it,
Marking all, all-knowing, in tireless session
Guiding, weighing, judging the varied drama.
  Come and adore us!

Guardians of young fruit in the open orchards,
Our swift beaks transfix the insect marauder,
And he falls, struck down by the feath'ry ictus
  Whirring from heaven.

CHORAG.   [*Epirrhema.*]
You see CRIMINAL WANTED notices every-where:
"Whoever kills Diágoras* the Mêlian,"   10
So much reward; "Whoever kills
A dead tyrant or so," still more
Reward. Well, then, I proclaim:
"Whoever kills Philókratês* the Birdseller,
One talent, cash; whoever brings him in
Alive, four talents"—twice as much
As for poor old Diágoras. This Philókratês
Hangs bullfinches on hooks in his shop
And sells them at cut rates; he inflates thrushes
With air pumps and exposes their abused puffy 20
Bodies for sale; he mutilates blackbirds; he
Stuffs live pigeons into nets and makes them
Act as decoys. That's Philókratês for you!
                                          —And
If any members of this audience
Maintain a bird in a gilded cage at home,
We beg you let it go. Refuse, and you'll see
How quickly the Birds will make decoys of you!

CHORUS.   [*Antode.*]
  Joy of birds! In summer the long thick sunlight
  When the locust drones in the trance of noon-
    time:
  Mad with sun we shout, and the forest
    dances   30
    Heavy with music.

  Wintertime is sun on the tropic headlands
  Where the Nymphs play counterpoint to our
    singing;
  Spring is myrtle, pang of the pink sweet
    prickling
    Buds of the Graces.

CHORAG.   [*Antepirrhema.*]
Now for a word or two, Judges, about
This Competition. If you give us the Prize,
We'll pay you better for it than Prince Paris*
Was paid by the Goddess. First of all,

The Owls of Laureion*° will never desert you: 40
They'll be everywhere in your houses, nesting
In your purses, maniacally producing
Miniature Owls. Judges are fond of Owls.
More than that, we'll add new wings
To your houses: you'll dream that you dwell
In marble halls, and you'll be right.
                                    If your jobs
Are slow pay, if your fingers begin to itch,
We'll send you a little confidential Hawk
To perch on your wrist. For state dinners you can
     have
The loan of a bird-crop to solve capacity prob-
     lems.   50
But if we lose the Prize,
Take portable canopies with you on your strolls,
Or your new white robes will suffer
Avine criticism dropping from the skies.

SCENE

[*Re-enter* PISTHETAIROS *with his attendants.*]
PISTH. The omens are favourable, I'm glad to
     say.
Strange that we've had no news
about the wall.
               —But here comes a messenger now,
puffing like an Olympic* sprinter.
     [*Enter* FIRST MESSENGER, *wildly.*]
MESSENGER. Where is he? Where is he? Where
     is he?
PISTH   Where is who?
MESS. The Chief. Pisthetairos.
PISTH.   Here.
MESS.   Great news! Great news!
Your Wall is finished!
     PISTH.   That *is* great news.
     MESS.   Oh how
shall I describe the splendour of that Wall,
The apocalyptic hugeness? Take two chariots,
hitch four fat Wooden Horses to each one,   10
let Theogenês and old Proxenidês
of Belchertown meet head-on—, they'd pass each
     other
without a scratch. It's that big.
     PISTH.   Holy Heraklês!
MESS. And tall? Look, I measured it myself:
it stands six hundred feet!
     PISTH.   Merciful Poseidôn!
What workmen could build a wall as high as that?
     MESS. Birds, only birds. Not a single Egyptian

hodcarrier° or stonemason or carpenter
in the gang; birds did it all, and my eyes
are popping yet.
               Imagine thirty thousand Cranes
from Libya,° each one with a belly full of stones 21
for the Rails to shape up with their beaks; ten
thousand Storks, at least,
all of them making bricks with clay and water
flown up by Curlews from the earth below.
     PISTH. Mortar?
     MESS.   Herons with hods.
     PISTH.   How did they
        manage it?
     MESS. *That* was a triumph of technology!
The Geese shovelled it up with their big feet.
     PISTH. Ah feet, to what use can ye not be put!°
     MESS. Why, good Lord! There were Ducks to set
        the bricks,   30
and flights of little apprentice Swallows
with trowel tails for the mortar in their bills.
     PISTH. Who wants hired labour after this?
—But the joists and beams?
     MESS.   All handled by birds.
When the Woodpeckers went to work on those
        portals
it sounded like a shipyard!
                           —So there's your Wall,
complete with gates and locks, watchfires burning,
patrols circling, the guard changed every hour.

But I must wash off this long trek of mine.
You'll know what to do next.   40
                        [*Exit* FIRST MESSENGER.]
     CHORAG. Surprises you, hey? That quick job on
        your Wall?
     PISTH. Surprises me? Why, it's a lie come true!
But there's another non-stop messenger,
and this one looks like trouble.
     [*Enter* SECOND MESSENGER: *tragic manner.*]
     MESS. Alas! Alas! Alas!
     PISTH.   What's the matter with *you?*
     MESS. Confusion now hath made his master-
        piece!
One of the gods, I do not know his name,
has invaded our air and slipped through the gate
right under the beaks of the Jackdaws on day duty.
     PISTH. Murther and treason!
                           —What god did
        you say?   50
     MESS. Identity not established. But he has wings,
we know that.

40. Owls of Laureion: Coins begetting smaller coins.
   17-18. Egyptian hodcarrier: Aristophanes is thinking of
the accounts—Herodotos, for example —of the building of the
Pyramids by the slave workmen of Cheops.

20-21. Cranes from Libya: Because of their improbable
shape, cranes were supposed to need a ballast of stones in order
to fly.   **29. Ah feet...:** A proverb; but Pisthetairos substitutes
"feet" for the "hands" of the original.

PISTH.   Alert the Air Cadets!

MESS. Cadets! We've alerted everything we have.
Ten thousand mounted Arrowhawks,
to say nothing of claw-to-claw raiders
of every calibre: Kestrels, Buzzards,
Kites, Vultures, Nighthawks, Eagles—
every mortal inch of air
they've ploughed up with their wings, looking for
    that god.
He won't get away,   60
he's somewhere around here; I feel it in my
    feathers.

PISTH. Slings and arrows, slings and arrows! All
    of you,
here: get shooting, quick! Give me my bow!

CHORUS.   War to the end,   [Strophe.]
              Inexpressible war,
              God against Bird!
              Arm to defend
              Our fathers' Air!
              Olympos' host
              Must not get past   70
              Our border guard!

CHORAG. Each one of you keep watch on every
    side.
I hear, or seem to hear, an ominous clack
of wings, as though some Deity were descending.
[The goddess IRIS appears from above, suspended in the
machina; she has broad static wings and wears a large
    rainbow around her head and shoulders.]

PISTH. Heave to! Let go halyards! Lower the
    flaps! Easy all!
        [The machina stops with a violent jerk.]
Who are you? Where are you bound? What's your
    home port?

IRIS. [tragic tone] I come to you from the Olymp-
    ian gods.

PISTH. Your name? Are you sea-going, or a
    flying
hat-rack?

IRIS.   Fleet Iris am I.

PISTH.   Deep sea or
inland waters?

IRIS.   What are you talking about!   80

PISTH. Some of you birds had better get on the
    balls
and board this crate.

IRIS.   Board me? I never
heard such a thing!

PISTH.   Well, you heard it now.
We'll give you something to squawk about.

IRIS.   Well, really!

PISTH. All right, all right. What gate did you
    come through?

IRIS. How should I know? Gates mean nothing to
    me.

PISTH. Oh. So that's the way it is.
                            —Well, then,
did you report to the Chief Jackdaw? Say some-
    thing!
Did you get your passport countersigned by the
    Storks?
You did not?

IRIS.   Are you in your right mind?

PISTH.   Not a single
bird there punched your card for you?

IRIS.   No, or punched
anything else for me, you poor idiot.

PISTH.   So   92
you're flying over foreign territory
without any papers.

IRIS.   How else should gods fly?

PISTH. Good God, how should I know?
                            But they
    can't do it here!
I don't care if you're a whole fleet of Irises;
you've committed a violation, and the penalty
for that is death.

IRIS.   Mortal, I am immortal.

PISTH. Death just the same!
                    Things have come
    to a pretty pass
if we set up a system of border controls, only to
    have   100
you gods flying back and forth whenever you feel
    like it.
But tell me:
What was the destination you had in mind?

IRIS. Destination? I am about my Father's
    business.
He has commanded me to remind mankind
that they must sacrifice to the eternal gods,
smiting the hornèd beasts upon their altars
and filling their streets with the smoke of im-
    molation.

PISTH. What do you mean? Sacrifice to what
    gods?

IRIS. Why, to us gods in Heaven.

PISTH.   So you are gods too?

IRIS. Can you think of others?

PISTH.   I am thinking of the Birds.
So far as mankind is concerned, Birds are now
    gods.   112
It's they must have sacrifices—not God, by God!

IRIS. Alas, deluded worm, think not to stir
the guts of wrath eterne: else heavenly Justice,
with Zeus's pitchfork arm'd, drops from on high
to man's undoing and leaves not a rack
behind. Fried and consumèd shalt thou be,

as i' th' Euripidean Tragedy!°

PISTH. Madam, wipe the foam from your mouth,
and do stop quivering so. Am I a slave,　121
some Lydian or Phrygian slave,° that you imagine
you scare me with talk of this kind?

As for Zeus:
you can inform your Zeus
that if he gets in my way I'll burn him out,
yea, I will blast him in Amphíon's* hall
with eagles lightningbeak'd that heed my call.
Notify him furthermore
that I command a squadron of six hundred
sky-scaling porphyrion birds in panther skin.　130
That will hold him, I think: a single Porphyrion
　　once
kept him busy enough.

　　　—And if *you* get in my way,
Iris or no Iris, messenger or whatever you are,
I'll just hoist up your legs and get in between:
then, by God, you can tell your wondering friends
how you met an old battleship with a triple prow!

IRIS. No gentleman would address a lady so.

PISTH. On your way! Scat!

IRIS.　　　　　　　　　I shall certainly tell
　my Father.

PISTH. Next time, consume someone your own
　age!

[*Exit* IRIS *in the* machina.]

CHORUS.　　My word is sure:　[*Antistrophe.*]
　　　　　Children of Zeus,　141
　　　　　No entrance here!
　　　　　And it shall stand.
　　　　　Let no man dare
　　　　　Cajole the skies
　　　　　With ritual brand
　　　　　Or sacrifice.

PISTH. Speaking of mankind, I am worried about
　our herald.
It's strange that his commission should keep him
　so long.

[*Enter a* HERALD, *in haste.*]

HER. O Pisthetairos! O Blessedest! O Saga-
　ciousest!

O Superlativest! O Sagaciousest! O Perspicacious-
　est!

O Thrice Blessedest! O And-so-forth!

PISTH.　　　　　　　　　Did you speak?

HER. I crown you with this golden crown, the
　gift

of your admiring public.

PISTH.　　　　　　　I thank you.
Tell me: Why does mankind admire me?

HER. O Pisthetairos, mighty father of
Cloudcuckooland the Beautiful, how slight
your skill in understanding human thought
if you must ask that question!

　　　　　　What is man?
Or, rather, what was man before your triumph?
An abject Spartomaniac°—long hair,　161
infrequent baths, bad honest food, knobbly
accessories, the Sokratês* pose.°

　　　　　　What is man now?
Mad about birds! Birds, birds, from the moment
they get out of nest in the morning: eggs and bird-
　seed
for breakfast, and then bird business,
reeding and piping till clucking-off time.
They even affect bird names:
"Partridge" is any man gone in one leg;
Menippos is "Swallow"; Opountios,　170
"Monocle de Mon Oncle"; Philoklês
is "Lark"; Theogenês, "Gypsy Goose"; Lykour-
　gos,*
"Ibis"; Chairephôn, "Bats"; Syrakosios,* "Jay-
　bird";
and Meidias,* of course, is called "Goon Quail"—
one look at that bashed-in face of his
will tell you why.

　　　　　As for song-writing,
you can't so much as buy a hearing unless
you stuff your lyrics with assorted wild ducks
and swallows, or doves, or geese, or maybe
a few last feathers from a cast-off wing.　180

That's what it's like down there. And mark my
　words:
you'll soon be getting visitors by the thousands,
all sorts of men begging to be fitted out
with wings and beaks and claws. Take my advice
and lay in a pile of pinions.

PISTH.　　　　　　　　Heavens, yes!
I can see we'll be busy.

　　　—Quick, you: [*to a* SERVANT]
fill every last basket you can find with wings
and tell Manês to bring them out to me here.
I want to be prepared for these gentlemen.

---

119. **Euripidean Tragedy:** "In the [lost] *Likymnios* of Euripidês, somebody or something gets struck by lightning." [Σ] 122.
some Lydian or Phrygian slave: A parady of Euripidês:
Alkestis 675, Pherês to Admêtos.

161. **an abject Spartomaniac:** It is curious that in a long war
it should become fashionable among certain people to ape the
manners of the enemy.　163. **the Sokratês pose:** Here, as in
the *chorikon* on p. 26, Aristophanes reveals his inability to admire
the Great Martyr. The full-dress attack takes place in *Nubes*, but
even in these minor skirmishes the animus is apparent, and only
by shutting our minds to the plain sense of words can we conclude
that this is a friendly raillery.

CHORUS. My City is Cloudcuckooland, [*Strophe.*]
　　　And men of every nation　　　191
　　　Confer on us, I understand,
　　　Ecstatic approbation.

PISTH.　　　And surplus population.

CHORUS. What wonder though it should be so?
　　　Here Love and Wisdom dwell,
　　　And through the streets the Graces go,
　　　And Peace contrives her spell.

PISTH.　　　The servant problem's hell!

CHORUS.　　　　　　[*Antistrophe.*]
　　　Manês, awake! New wings, new beaks!
　　　Surely there never was　　　201
　　　A slower slave. Your master speaks!
　　　The precious moments pass!
　　　[*Enter* MANES *emptyhanded.*]

PISTH.　　　This Manês is an ass.
　　　　　　　　[*Exit* MANES.]

CHORUS. Wings make the man; let each man
　　　wear
　　　The crest that suits his bent:
　　　Musician, merchant, privateer,
　　　Cleric, or laic gent,
　　　[*Re-enter* MANES *as before.*]

PISTH.　　　Or slave of snail descent.

Manês, I swear by All Hawks, I'll haul you　210
hairless if you don't get busy! Come on; service!
[*General confusion.* MANES *and other servants appear and
reappear carrying wings of all shapes and sizes. These are
arranged on a bench.*]
　PARRICIDE. [*within, singing*] "Ah that the eagle's
　eager wings were mine,°
To gyre above the waste of bloomless brine!"
　PISTH. That messenger seems to have been right.
Here comes somebody singing about eagles.
　　　　[*Enter a young* PARRICIDE.]
　PARR. Here we are!
I vow, there's nothing like flying.
　　　　　　　—Sir,
I'm mad about birds, I'm
always up in the air. More than that,
I apply for citizenship under your laws.　　220
　PISTH. What laws? We Birds have many laws.
　PARR. All of them; especially that glorious
　statute
that gives Birds the right to strangle their own
fathers.

PISTH. We *do* consider it a sign of manliness
when a chick stands up to his father and faces him
　down.
　PARR. Exactly my own motive in emigrating:
I propose to throttle the old man for his property.
　PISTH. At the same time we have an ancient
　decree
(you'll find it in the Book of Storks) that says:
STORKLINGS　CARED　FOR　BY　THE
　STORK　THEIR　SIRE　　　230
AND　BY　HIM　TAUGHT　TO　FLY　SHALL
　IN　THEIR　TURN
CARE　FOR　THE　STORK　THEIR　SIRE　IN
　HIS　OLD　AGE.
　PARR. What was the use of my coming all this
　distance
if I've got to support my father after all?
　PISTH. Come, it's not so bad.
You obviously mean well, and we'll make
a decent orphan bird° of you yet, young man.
But first
permit me to recite a useful thought
　　"that was given me　　　240
　　at my mother's knee":
Sons, don't beat your fathers. It's unkind.
[*During the following speech* PISTHETAIROS *arms the
　　PARRICIDE with a toy sword, shield, and helmet.*]
Stick out your hand: receive this bright cock-spur.
Your other hand: receive this shining wing.
Stick out your neck: receive this crested helm.
Now you're in the Army, cock.
Keep awake on guard duty, live on your pay, and
　let
your father alone. If you feel like fighting,
take a trip to Thrace: there's always a war on there.
　PARR. You're right. I'll do it, by God!
　　　　　　　　[*Exit.*]
　PISTH.　　　　By God,
　you'd better!　　　250
　　　[*Enter the dithyrambic poet* KINESIAS.]
　KINESIAS. [*singing*] "Lifted aloft on wings of song,°
　　Towards high Olympos winging—"
　PISTH. This man needs wings if ever a poet did!
　KIN. [*singing*] "Pure in mind, in body strong,
　　Ever of thee, love, singing—"
　PISTH. Kinêsias, as I live. Old limpety-lop,
why did your limping feet bring you up here?
　KIN. [*singing*] "I aim, nor shall my purpose
　fail,
　　To be a Neo-Nightingale."

---

212. **"Ah that the eagle's . . .":** Σ notes that these verses are
quoted [in parody?] from the lost *Oinomaos* of Sophoklês.

237. **a decent orphan bird:** A male war-orphan would be
educated by the State. There are vestiges of a dim ornithological
pun.　251. **"Lifted aloft . . .":** Kinêsias enters singing a love-
poem by Anakreôn.

PROM. What's the weather like?

PISTH.   Hey?

PROM.   I said, "What's
the weather like?"

PISTH.   Go to hell!

PROM.   Splendid. I'll just
take off these cerements.

[*Throws off the cloak and stands revealed in scarlet
tights.*]

PISTH.   Well, I'll be
damned! Prometheus!   10

PROM. Sh, sh, keep your voice down!

PISTH.   What's the
matter?

PROM. Just don't mention my name. If Zeus finds
me here
he'll scalp me. You don't know the half of it.
I'll tell you; only,
please hold this umbrella over my head
so the gods can't look down and see me from up
there.

PISTH. The same old Prometheus! All right; get
under,
and begin to talk.

PROM. Listen.

PISTH.   I am.

PROM.   Zeus is through.

PISTH.   Since when?

PROM. Since you organized Cloudcuckooland. 20
There's not been so much as a sniff of sacred smoke
coming up to us from a single human altar.
I swear, we're hungrier
than a Thesmophoria* fast-day; and, what's
worse,
the damnedest lot of starving yowling gods
from the back country are talking about revolt
if Zeus doesn't manage to get a decent consign-
ment
of sacrificial cuts to keep us going.

PISTH. Do you mean to tell me the Barbarians
have gods of their own?

PROM.   What about Exekestidês?
Doesn't he have to pray to something?

PISTH.   I see.   31
But these godforsaken gods: what are they called?

PROM. Triballians.

PISTH.   Tribal totems.

PROM.   I suppose so.

—But this is what I have come down to tell you:
Zeus and these Triballians
are sending a delegation to look into
what's going on here. Take my advice:
laugh at every offer they make to you
until they swear to restore the Birds to power

and give you Basileia*° for a wife.   40

PISTH. Basileia? Who is this Basileia?

PROM. She's the prettiest girl you ever saw:
manages Zeus, takes care of his thunderbolts
and all the rest of his weapons—sagacity,
legislation, rearmament, ideology, ultimatums,
revenue officers, jurymen—

PISTH.   She does all that?

PROM. That's only an outline. When you get
Basileia,
you've got everything.

                            I thought I ought to tell you:
I have a certain stake in humanity.

PISTH. A well-broiled one,° thanks to your
foresightedness.   50

PROM. And I hate the gods.

PISTH.   And the gods hate
you.

PROM. Yes. I'm a regular Timôn.*

                                —But it's late.
I must be getting back.

                          Give me my umbrella:
Zeus will think I'm a Virgin of the Escort.

PISTH. Take this footstool° with you; it will make
a better effect.   [*Exeunt.*]

CHORIKON:⁵ CHORAL INTERLUDE

CHORUS.   [*Strophe.*]

    There is a mystic river
        In the land of the Shadowfeet
    Where Sokratês the Bathless calls
        The souls of men to meet.

    There Chickenheart Peisandros*
        Made sacrifice one day
    To conjure up his own dim soul
        And hear what it would say.

40. Basileia: Her name means Sovereignty, Imperium. She has no place in the official Pantheon, but is an *ad hoc* creation to provide Pisthetairos with a mate equivalent to Zeus' Hêra. The final mockery of this drama, of course, is the apotheosis of the bungling Hero.   **50. a well-broiled one:** Prometheus first taught men the use of fire.   **55. take this footstool:** At the Panathenaia Festival the daughters of Athenian aristocrats were attended by wealthy girls of foreign ancestry who carried ceremonial footstools and parasols. Prometheus hopes that Zeus, looking down from Olympos, will mistake him for one of these attendants.

⁵ The Birds' travel lecture proceeds. The Shadowfeet were a remarkable tribe, said to live in Libya, who enjoyed feet so large that they could be used as parasols during siesta time. This is a fit setting for the deplorable Sokratês, who is represented as "leading the souls of men"—leading them, that is to say, as Odysseus* did the souls in Hadês, but also misleading them by perverse teaching, a charge that Aristophanes constantly makes against this philosopher. The Strophe is a comic *Nekuia*, parodying the eleventh book of the *Odyssey*. The fainthearted Peisandros, having lost his own soul, goes to the land of the Shadowfeet to conjure it back.

Odysseus-like he cut the throat
  Of a kind of camel-cat;   10
But all he raised was the squeaking ghost
  Of Chairephôn* the Bat.

SCENE

[*Enter the Ambassadors from Olympos:*[6] POSEIDON, HERAKLES, *and a* TRIBALLIAN GOD. *The first wears a sea-weed crown, a cloak embroidered with large horse-heads, and carries a trident and a rigid stuffed fish; the second wears a lion skin and carries a club; the third, blackface, wears a stovepipe hat and is desperately entangled in a multicoloured cloak.*]

POSEIDON. So this is Cloudcuckooland. Very well,
let us proceed to act like a Delegation.
                  [*to the* TRIBALLIAN.]
You, there,
what are you up to now? Don't you know better
than to drape your cloak on the left side? Look,
you celestial rustic, it ought to hang on the right,
gracefully, like this. Do you want these people
to take you for Laispodias?* Hold still,
can't you? There!
Democracy, what sins are committed in thy name!°
Damn it, of all the barbarous gods I've met 11
you're the barbarousest.
         —What's your plan, Heraklês?
HERAKLES. You heard what I said. Just croak
    the guy
what shut the gods out with this here Stone Curtain.
POS. Yes, my good fellow; but we're supposed
    to discuss peace.
HER. All the more reason for croaking him, I
    say.
[*Enter* PISTHETAIROS *attended by various birds in kitchen costume; he elaborately disregards the Ambassadors.*]
PISTH. Quick, now,
let's have the cheesegrater. Where's the horse-
    radish?
Grate that cheese, somebody. Keep the fire hot.
POS. In the name of the Divine Authority,
three gods greet thee, O Man.
PISTH.   The horseradish. 20
HER. Say, Mac, what kind of a roast is that?
PISTH. Bird roast. Subjects condemned for
    subversion
of the Authority of the Birds.

HER.   And you use
horseradish?
PISTH.   Why, it's Heraklês! Good
afternoon, Heraklês.
POS.   The Divine Authority
empowers three gods to consider conciliation.
A COOK. Oil's out. What do I do now?
HER.   No oil?
Damn bad. You can't barbecue without oil.
POS. Regarded disinterestedly, this war
subserves no aim of the Divine Authority. 30
Similarly, your Delegates should reflect
how much you have to gain from a friendly
    Olympos:
I instance only
fresh rain water for your swamps, and halcyon
    days.
Shall we initiate talks?
PISTH.   I don't see why.
In the first place, we were not the ones
who started hostilities. But let that pass.
As for peace, we are perfectly willing to agree
if the gods will meet our terms. We demand
restoration of our ancient sovereignty 40
and the return of the sceptre to the Birds.
Let Zeus accept that much, and I'll invite
all three of you to dinner.
HER.   I vote Yes.
POS. You gastric monomaniac, would you vote
    away
your own Father's crown?
PISTH.   That's a silly question.
Do you gods imagine that you will be losing power
by delegating the imperium of the skies?
Surely you know that all over the earth
men are hiding under clouds and breaking your
    laws
with impunity. Suppose you had the Birds 50
on your side: then if a man swore
by Zeus and the Crow, say, and broke his oath,
we'd simply have a Crow swoop down upon him
and peck out his right eye.
POS.   Good, by Myself!°
HER. I think so too.
PISTH. [*to* TRIBALLIAN]
             What do *you* say?
TRIBALLIAN.   Wockle.°
HER. The poor fish says Yes.
PISTH.   And here's some-
    thing else.

---

[6] This theophany seems outrageous to us, but our ideas of what constitutes blasphemy are different from the Greeks', who would find Aristophanes brilliantly but conventionally comic. **10. Democracy, what sins . . .:** Zeus, to be fair, has decided that even the Barbarians should be represented in this embassage.

54. by Myself . . : Poseidôn swears "By Poseidôn!" **55. Wockle:** The Triballian speaks a murky language rather like that of Muta and Juva in *Finnegans Wake*. Much needless ingenuity has been expended by Professors attempting to reduce it to sense.

Suppose a man promises an offering
to some god or other, and maybe greed
gets the better of him, and he thinks: *Well,
the gods are used to waiting:*
                              we birds   60
will know how to handle him.

POS.   How? Instruct me.

PISTH. Well, say that man's
sitting in his office some day, counting his money,
or say he's in the tub enjoying a nice hot bath:
down comes one of the Kites when he isn't looking
and zooms off to Olympos with a couple of his
    sheep.

HER. I say it again: give the Birds what they ask
    for.

POS. What do *you* think?

PISTH.   Speak, you divine Mistake.

TRIB. Treeballs beetee gnaw ouch, Glapp.

HER.   He says Yes.

POS. If you say so. I suppose I must say so too.
Very well. Divine Authority cedes the Sceptre.   71

PISTH. Hold on! I nearly forgot.
The Birds are prepared to confirm Zeus' right to
    Hêra,
but in return
they insist upon my having Basileia.

POS. I can see that you are not interested in peace.
Good-bye.

PISTH.   It makes no difference to me.
—Now this gravy, cook: see that it's thick enough.

HER. Hey, damn it, Admiral, hold on, what the
    hell?
Who wants to fight a war for a damn woman?°

POS. What else can we do?

HER.   Damn it, make peace!   81

POS. Idiot, can't you see he's trying to ruin you?
And you walk right into the trap.
                              Think a
    moment: if Zeus
gives the Birds what they ask for, and then dies—
Where are you then? Where's your inheritance?

PISTH. Heraklês, don't listen to the man.
Every word he speaks is a delusion.
              [*Beckons him aside.*]
Step over here a minute.
                    —My poor fellow,
that Ancient Mariner is just leading you on.
You inherit from Zeus? You couldn't, not a penny.
You, being a bastard—

HER.   Me, a bastard?   91
Say, listen, you—

PISTH.   Well, your mother

was an alien, wasn't she? Besides, Athenê
is heir apparent, and how could she be that
if she had legitimate brothers?

HER.   What if the Boss
says I'm his heir, bastard or no bastard?

PISTH. Illegal. And suppose he does:
Poseidôn will be the first to contest the will,
as the decedent's brother.
                    Here is the law,
straight from Solôn:*   100
A BASTARD SHALL NOT INHERIT IF
THERE BE LEGITIMATE ISSUE. IF
THERE BE NO LEGITIMATE ISSUE,
THE PROPERTY SHALL PASS TO THE
NEXT OF KIN.

HER. So I can't get nothing out of the Old Man's
    estate?

PISTH. Nothing at all.
                    —For that matter,
has your Father enrolled you yet?°

HER.   No. I guess I
    know why.

PISTH. Come, what's the use of snapping at
    empty wind?
Join the Birds: 110
you'll live like a king and feed on pie in the
    sky.°
              [*They return to the others.*]

HER. About that dame we were beating our gums
    about:
I said, and I say it again: Give him what he wants.

PISTH. You, Poseidôn?

POS.   No.

PISTH.   Then the Triballian
must break the tie. Vote, heavenly Hayseed!

TRIB. Quiffing gamsel cockitty, gotta tweet
    tweet.

HER. He says Yes.

POS.   I doubt very much if he says
    Yes
or anything else that matters. But let it pass.

HER. He's ready to pass her over, anyhow.

POS. Have it your way, you two. Make your
    peace,   120
and I'll hold mine.

HER.   These here top-level talks
are all over, and we say he gets the green light.
Come on, man, you got a date up in the sky
with Basileia and any other damn thing you want.

PISTH. It's a lucky thing that I had these roasts
    ready.

108. has your Father . . . ?: In the register of citizens; as the illegitimate son of a foreign woman, Heraklês would be ineligible.   **111. pie in the sky:** The Greek phrase was "birds' milk," but this seems too esoteric.

80. Who wants . . . ?: As the Trojan War was fought for Helen.

They'll do for the wedding.

HER.   You birds run along:
I'll stick around here and keep an eye on the cook.

POS. Can't you rise superior to food? You come
with us.

PISTH. And somebody bring along my wedding
clothes.   [*Exeunt omnes; manet* CHORUS.]

CHORIKON:[7] CHORAL INTERLUDE

CHORUS.   [*Antistrophe.*]
> Phonéya* is that far country
>   Where the Englottogasters* dwell:
> They plough the fields there with
>   their tongues
> And sow and reap as well.
>
> Oh blest Englottogasters!
>   And yet we need not roam
> In search of tongues as versatile—
>   They twitch for us at home:
>
> The tongue that tells for ready cash,
>   The slimy tongue that smiles,   10
> The paid, applauded, patriot tongue
>   That guards us, and defiles.

ÉXODOS[8]

[*Enter* THIRD MESSENGER.]
MESS. Thrice happy generation of Birds, O
winged
with joy beyond word's contriving: receive
your great Prince in his palace of delight!
His glory burns: no star
flames brighter in the wheeling vault, no sun
has ever blazed so pure. He comes,
and beauty walks beside him crowned
with lightning from God's hand, his divine
Bride, veiled i' th' smoke of incense rising.
Your King, your Queen!   10
Sing them a song of the Nine Sisters' devising.
[*Re-enter* PISTHETAIROS, *splendidly gowned, with newly*

gilded wings; he is accompanied by BASILEIA, *in cloth
of gold, crowned, her face hidden by a veil.*]

CHORUS. Back!
                          Make way there!
                                   Circle them!
                                            Dance!
Beat on the bright ground with quick feet
For the Prince of Luck, for his Bride—
    Oh sweet! Oh fair!—
Dance, dance the marriage in the air.

    CHORAG. Dance in the sky,
                          joy in the sky!
Dance in the reign of the Birds,
                          dance in
The augury of his polity:
Dance Hymen*
          the wedding chorus
                          dance   20

CHORUS.   [*Strophe.*]
> When heavenly Hêra was the bride
>   Of Zeus in his high hall,
> The Fatal Ladies danced and sang
>   This for their festival:
>   *Round the royal pair we go:*
>   *Hymen O! The wedding O!*
>
> Erôs flicked his golden wings   [*Antistrophe.*]
>   To be their charioteer,
> And through the swaying skies their car
>   Darted in sweet career.   30
>   *Round the royal pair we go:*
>   *Hymen O! The wedding O!*

PISTH. For your songs, for your good wishes,
thanks:
I am gratified, and I am sure
that I speak for my wife as well. I should be
even more gratified to hear you perform
two or three odes in honour of my triumph
over the dangerous thunderbolts of Zeus,
the difficult lightning.

CHORUS.   [*Epode.*]
> O fire lancing the black night,   40
>   O rage of voices under ground,
> Thunder, hurly of rain, bright
>   Tempest of sound:
> Sing, sing his audacity
>   Who draws down from God's throne
> God's Basileia, Sovereignty,
>   And crowns her his own.
>   *Round the royal pair we go:*
>   *Hymen O! The wedding O!*

---

[7] The travelogue resumed. The Englottogasters, "men who
live by their tongues," are nearer home than the Shadowfeet:
they are to be found wherever men make money by informing
on their fellows, and are particularly flagrant in times of political
uncertainty.

[8] The conclusion of the play is dictated not only by dramatic
appropriateness—the marriage and deification of the Hero—
but by ritual inheritance. Comedy culminates in marriage, and
the final scene (cf. the *Pax* and, though slightly different in vein,
the *Lysistrata*) has overtones of an ancestral fertility rite. The
Chorus sings of the wedding of Zeus and Hêra, thus equating
Pisthetairos and Basileia with the King and Queen of Heaven.
The ordinary man has found Cloudcuckooland, his Utopia, and
now becomes God. Like God, he insists upon the recital of his
own meritorious exploits.

PISTH. Follow the bridal, follow, fortunate
      friends,   50
to the high lands of God, to the happy bed.
And oh my darling, take
my wings in your shining hands, and I
will lift you, lift you above the sky
in the Birds' dance, the whirring dance.

CHORUS. *Iô! Iô!*
          I Paián!° Alalaí!
      See the conquering hero go!
      Hymen O! The wedding O!

INDEX OF PROPER NAMES

AESOP, AISOPOS: A semi-legendary writer of fables.

AGAMEMNON: Commander of the Greeks in the Trojan
    War.

AISCHINES: An impoverished braggart politician; his
    "castles" are what we should call "castles in Spain."

AITNA: A town on the slope of the Sicilian mountain,
    founded by Hiero of Syracuse.

AKROPOLIS: The Citadel of Athens, sacred to Athenê;
    here the inner fortress of Cloudcuckooland.

ALKMENE: A mistress of Zeus; mother of Heraklês.

ALOPE: A mistress of Poseidôn.

AMMON: A famous temple and oracle of Zeus in Libya.

AMPHION: Husband of Niobê; the quotation is an ab-
    surdly jumbled parody of a passage in the [lost]
    Niobê of Aischylos.

APHRODITE: Goddess of love.

APOLLO: God of healing, of prophecy, of the sun.

ARES: God of war.

ARTEMIS: Goddess of the chase.

ATHENE: Daughter of Zeus; tutelary goddess of Athens.

ATHENS: Chief city of the district of Attika.

BABYLON: The Assyrian capital, on the Euphratês
    River; Herodotos (I:178 *sqq.*) describes its enormous
    and complex walls.

BAKIS: A celebrated and indefatigable Boiotian sooth-
    sayer.

BASILEIA: "Sovereignty," or "Empery," personified as a
    housekeeper of Zeus and, later, the bride of Pis-
    thetairos.

BOIOTIA: A country north of Attika.

CHAIREPHON: An Athenian friend of Sokratês, nick-
    named "Bat" because of his squeaky voice and sallow
    complexion.

CHAIRIS: A musician, "somewhat frigid" according to Σ,
    who seems to have offended Aristophanes' sense of
    propriety; here, a crow accompanying the Chorus.

CHAOS: A pre-Olympian* deity; primal matter.

56. Iê Paián!: The play ends with a volley of ritual phrases,
among which rings the Athenian battle-cry, *Alalaí!*, which
had been *Eleleú!* among the Birds.

CHIANS: The Island of Chios supported Athens early in
    the Peloponnesian War, and a clause for the Chians
    was accordingly added to prayers for the public good.
    After the Sicilian Expedition, Chios defected to
    Sparta.

DAREIOS: King of Persia (549–485 B.C.).

DELPHOI: A famous oracle of Apollo, in Phokis.

DEMETER: Sister of Zeus; goddess of agriculture and
    vegetation.

DIAGORAS: A native of Mêlos, professor of Philosophy
    in Athens, accused and condemned *in absentia* for
    atheism.

DIEITREPHES: A self-made man, manufacturer of wicker
    baskets, who bought his way into the upper echelons
    of the Government.

DIONYSOS: God of wine.

DODONA: A notable oracle of Zeus.

ENGLOTTOGASTERS: "Belly-tongued"; used of political
    informers and the officials who employ them.

EPOPS: The Hoopoe, *Upupa epops.*

EREBOS: A pre-Olympian* deity; usually, son of Night
    and Chaos; the infernal depths.

EROS: Son of Aphroditê; god of love.

EURIPIDES: Tragic poet (484–406 B.C.).

EXEKESTIDES: A parvenu alien living in Athens.

GRACES: Aglaia, Thaleia, and Euphrosynê, daughters
    of Zeus and Aphroditê, goddesses of delight.

HALIMOS: A town in Attika, south of Athens.

HEBROS: A river in Thrace.

HERA: Sister and wife of Zeus.

HERAKLES: Son of Zeus and Alkmenê; most famous of
    the legendary Heroes, often represented by Aristoph-
    anes as a glutton and braggart.

HERMES: The winged Messenger of the gods.

HESTIA: Goddess of the hearth; as "Nestiarch," absurdly
    assimilated to the Birds.

HIPPONIKOS: An illustrative name

HOMER: The epic poet.

HYMEN: God of marriage.

IRIS: The rainbow goddess; confidential messenger of
    Hêra.

KALLIAS: A wealthy and dissolute Athenian amateur of
    philosophy. Here, the name is illustrative.

KARIAN: A native of Karia, a country of Asia Minor.
    The Karians were said to prefer fighting on mountain
    tops as offering better opportunities for flight; hence
    the pun on "crests."

KINESIAS: A dithyrambic poet of Thebes in Boiotia; he
    is amusingly attacked by Aristophanes in *Lysistrata.*

KLEISTHENES: An Athenian bravo noted for his effemi-
    nacy.

KLEOKRITOS: An effeminate fat man with large feet who
    looked like an ostrich (Σ).

KLEONYMOS: A cowardly officer who became famous for having thrown away his shield in battle.

KOLONOS: A small town, suburb of Athens.

KORINTH: A city on the isthmus between Attika and the Peloponnesos; Aristophanes affects to believe that it is inhabited exclusively by lewd wantons.

KORKYRA: The modern Corfù; the "first-class goods" are whips, which were manufactured there.

KRANAOS: One of the mythical founder-kings of Athens.

KRIOA: A deme of Attika.

KRONOS: Father of Zeus.

KYBELE: An Asiatic goddess worshiped as *Magna Mater*, the Mother of gods; here, she is the Great Ostrich.

LAISPODIAS: An Athenian general with a limp (Σ), or possibly the reference is to his sexual incapacity (Σ). The Triballian has draped his cloak as though to conceal his left leg—most inelegant behavior.

LAKONIA: A country of the Peloponnesos; chief city, Sparta.

LAMPON: A noted soothsayer.

LAUREION: A town in Attika famous for its goldmines; the Owl of Athenê was stamped on coins: hence, here, we should say "coals to Newcastle."

LEPREON: A town in Elis; the name suggests leprosy.

LEOTROPHIDES: A dithyrambic poet, thin and corpselike in appearance (Σ).

LIBYA: A region of Africa.

LOKRIS: A district of Greece, extending from Thessaly to Boiotia.

LYKOURGOS: "Called Ibis either because of his Egyptian extraction or because of his skinny legs. There is a redundancy of the ibis in Egypt" (Σ).

LYSIKRATES: A venal Athenian official.

MANES: Name for a servant.

MANODOROS: Name for a servant.

MEGABAZOS: A Persian nobleman, general in the service of King Dareios.*

MEIDIAS: A corrupt and perverse politician; "Quail" seems to have been a cant word in boxing, as we might say "Punchy," and apparently refers to Meidias' dazed and glazed expression.

MELANTHIOS: A tragic poet, effete and afflicted with leprosy (Σ) or some disease resembling it.

MELIANS: Inhabitants of Mêlos, which, in the year preceding this play, had been blockaded by Nikias and starved into submission.

MENELAOS: Brother of Agamemnon; husband of Helen; one of the Greek commanders at Troy.

METON: A famous astronomer and architect. He opposed the Sicilian Expedition and feigned insanity in order to avoid serving on it.

MUSES: Nine goddesses presiding over the arts and sciences; daughters of Zeus and Mnemosynê ("Memory").

NIKIAS: A prominent and disastrous Athenian commander in the Peloponnesian War.

ODYSSEUS: Wiliest of the Greek chieftains at Troy, and hero of Homer's *Odyssey;* here the allusion is to his performing the sacrificial rites necessary for summoning up the dead in Hadês (*Od.* XI).

OLOPHYXOS: A town near Mt. Athos, in Makedonia. The name was chosen for the sake of a heavy pun.

OLYMPIANS: The gods, as living upon Mt. Olympos.

OLYMPIC: Pertaining to the great athletic contests at Olympia.

OLYMPOS: A mountain in Thessaly; seat of the gods.

OPOUNTIOS: A one-eyed grafter; the word is also the proper adjective from Opoûs.

OPOUS: A town in Lokris.*

ORESTES: Not the long-suffering son of Agamemnon, but a foot-pad who assumed the heroic name.

PAN: An Arkadian rural god.

PANDORA: "The Earth, since it gives us everything necessary to life" (Σ); not to be confused, at any rate, with the Greek equivalent of Eve.

PARIS: Prince of Troy, son of Priam; Aphroditê bribed him to award her the prize in the most notable of all beauty contests.

PEISANDROS: A notoriously craven politician.

PEISIAS' SON: Apparently a traitorous citizen; but the evidence is very vague, in spite of lurid hints by Σ.

PELARGIC WALL: The Stork Wall, *Pelargikon,* of the Akropolis at Athens.

PHALERON: A port of Athens, notable for its sea food.

PHARNAKES: A Persian nobleman operating as an "enemy agent" in Athens; the Inspector is in his pay.

PHILEMON: "Lampooned as a foreigner, and a Phrygian one into the bargain" (Σ).

PHILOKLES: A tragic poet, nicknamed "Lark"; he wrote a play called *Tereus, or, the Hoopoe,* much of it plagiarized from Sophoklês.

PHILOKRATES: The proprietor of the shop where Euelpidês and Pisthetairos bought their bird guides.

PHOIBOS: An epithet of Apollo.

PHOINIKIA: Phoenicia, a country in Asia Minor.

PHONEYA: An invented name. The Greek is *Phanês,* the root of which suggests the pseudo-patriot Informers who are supposed to live in that country.

PHRYGIA: A country in Asia Minor.

PHRYNICHOS: A tragic poet (*fl.* 500 B.C.).

PINDAR: Lyric poet (522–442 B.C.).

PORPHYRION: One of the Titans in the conflict with Zeus; the Purple Waterhen, *Porphyrio veterum.*

POSEIDON: God of the sea.

PRIAM: King of Troy.

PRODIKOS: A prominent sophist, reputedly a teacher of Euripidês and Sokratês.

PROKNE: The Nightingale, wife of Tereus.*

PROMETHEUS: A son of the Titan Iapetos, and hence a semi-divine being; reputed to have created man and to have stolen fire from Heaven for the comfort of his creation: for both of which acts he was persecuted by Zeus.

PROXENIDES: An irresponsible boaster; he comes from the wholly imaginary town of Kompasai, a word derived from the verb κομπάζω, "shoot off the mouth."

PYTHODELIAN: The Swan, sacred to Apollo, takes Apollo's epithets: Pythian, as god of the Delphic Oracle, and Dêlian, as native of Dêlos.

SABAZIOS: A Phrygian god, assimilated to Dionysos.

SAKAS: Popular name for a foreigner aspiring to Athenian citizenship.

"SALAMINIA": A state galley in the Athenian service; here, a kind of glorified police boat.

SARDANAPALOS: A lavish and splendidly dissolute king of Assyria.

SEMELE: A mistress of Zeus; mother of Dionysos.

SIMONIDES: An Ionian poet (556–467 B.C.).

SOKRATES: Philosopher and teacher (469–399 B.C.).

SOLON: The lawgiver (639–559 B.C.).

SOPHOKLES: Tragic poet (497–405 B.C.).

SOUNION: An Attic promontory and town, site of a temple of Poseidôn.

SPARTA: Chief city of Lakonia.

SPINTHAROS: Lampooned for the same reason as Philêmon;* otherwise unknown.

SPORGILOS: An Athenian barber.

SYRAKOSIOS: A politician; author of a law forbidding the comic poets to introduce real persons into their plays.

TARTAROS: The infernal and punitive depths.

TELEAS: An unstable Athenian, adequately described here in his own words.

TEREUS: A king of Thrace, transformed, for his outrageous behaviour, into a Hoopoe.

THALES: Mathematician and philosopher (fl. 590 B.C.).

THEOGENES: A boastful, showy man of largely imaginary wealth.

THESMOPHORIA: A festival of Deméter, celebrated in November; the fourth day was a fast.

THRACE: Roughly, the territory north of the Black Sea.

TIMON: A celebrated Athenian misanthrope.

TITANS: Pre-Olympian divinities who revolted against Zeus and were defeated by him in a battle on the Phlegraian Plain; here the great combat is reduced to a riot of boasters.

TRIBALLIANS: A savage Thracian tribe.

XANTHIAS: Name for a servant.

ZEUS: Father of gods and men.

William Shakespeare # Twelfth Night
Or, What You Will

Generally recognized as Shakespeare's greatest romantic comedy, *Twelfth Night*, probably written in 1600 or 1601, was first printed in the folio of 1623.

Shakespeare had a number of possible sources for this play; they include: Plautus' *Menaechmi* (which he had mined earlier for *The Comedy of Errors*), two Italian plays called *Inganni*, and the tale of *Apolonius and Silla* which the English writer Barnabe Riche had included in his collection, *Riche His Farewell to the Military Profession* (1581); a full discussion of these and other sources will be found in the selection from Kenneth Muir's book reprinted in Part II (pp. 185–90).

But Shakespeare transformed all the borrowed material and added a great deal of his own inventing. Particularly rich is the subplot in which the malcontent, Malvolio, is chastened for his "self-love." In truth, the whole play is a series of variations on the themes of love and music. These two values of life are represented sentimentally, realistically and vigorously, and satirically. In addition, one must not ignore the true comedians, the "allowed" fool, Feste, and the "natural" one, Sir Andrew Aguecheek. Finally, there is the poetry, which is used with typically effortless Shakespearean prodigality, to convey all the nuances of mood. Indeed, readers of the text and viewers in the theatre are encouraged to enjoy themselves in accordance with their best imaginative powers, for Shakespeare's invitation is a generous one, expressed in his subtitle, "What You Will."

Joseph Summers has approached the play by analyzing the device of masking; his provocative essay is reprinted in Part IV (pp. 258–62). Another exciting theory about Shakespearean comedy has recently been set forth by C. L. Barber in *Shakespeare's Festive Comedy* (1959). His thesis is that Shakespeare wrote comedy that was basically "festive" rather than "romantic" or "satiric." Further, Barber shows how this festive comedy depends upon a "saturnalian pattern," grounded in folk and courtly holiday customs. He contends that the specific focus of *Twelfth Night* is upon "the folly of misrule"; the play exhibits as well the proper "use" and "abuse" of "social liberty."

The text of the play used here and all of the footnotes have been taken by kind permission from *Shakespeare: The Complete Plays*, edited by G. B. Harrison (N. Y.: Harcourt, Brace, 1948). The line numbers of the play follow the Globe edition.

DRAMATIS PERSONAE

ORSINO, *Duke of Illyria*
SEBASTIAN, *brother to Viola*
ANTONIO, *a sea captain, friend to Sebastian*
A SEA CAPTAIN, *friend to Viola*
VALENTINE ⎫
CURIO ⎬ *gentlemen attending on the Duke*
SIR TOBY BELCH, *uncle to Olivia*
SIR ANDREW AGUECHEEK

MALVOLIO, *steward to Olivia*
FABIAN ⎫
FESTE, *a clown* ⎬ *servants to Olivia*
OLIVIA
VIOLA
MARIA, *Olivia's woman*
LORDS, PRIESTS, SAILORS, OFFICERS, MUSICIANS, *and other* ATTENDANTS

SCENE— *A city in Illyria, and the seacoast near it.*

ACT I

SCENE I. *An apartment in the* DUKE's *palace.*

[*Enter* DUKE, CURIO, *and other* LORDS; MUSICIANS *attending.*]

DUKE. If music be the food of love, play on.
Give me excess of it, that, surfeiting,°
The appetite may sicken, and so die.
That strain again! It had a dying fall.°
Oh, it came o'er my ear like the sweet sound
That breathes upon a bank of violets,
Stealing and giving odor! Enough, no more.
'Tis not so sweet now as it was before.
O spirit of love, how quick and fresh art thou!
That, notwithstanding thy capacity   10
Receiveth as the sea, naught enters there,
Of what validity and pitch soe'er,
But falls into abatement and low price,

Act I, Sc. i: 2. surfeiting: being overfull.   **4. dying fall:** cadence which falls away.

10-14. capacity . . . minute: i.e., though the spirit of love is as wide and deep as the sea, yet whatever falls into it, no matter how valuable and lofty, becomes worthless in a moment. **pitch:** lit., the soaring flight of a hawk.

Even in a minute!° So full of shapes is fancy
That it alone is high fantastical.°
  CUR. Will you go hunt, my lord?
  DUKE.   What, Curio?
  CUR. The hart.
  DUKE. Why, so I do, the noblest that I have.
Oh, when mine eyes did see Olivia first,
Methought she purged the air of pestilence!°   20
That instant was I turned into a hart,
And my desires, like fell° and cruel hounds,
E'er since pursue me.
  [Enter VALENTINE.]   How now! What news from
    her?
  VAL. So please my lord, I might not be admitted,
But from her handmaid do return this answer:
The element° itself, till seven years' heat,°
Shall not behold her face at ample view;°
But, like a cloistress,° she will veilèd walk
And water once a day her chamber round
With eye-offending brine—all this to season°   30
A brother's dead love, which she would keep fresh
And lasting in her sad remembrance.
  DUKE. Oh, she that hath a heart of that fine frame
To pay this debt of love but to a brother,
How will she love when the rich golden shaft°
Hath killed the flock of all affections° else
That live in her; when liver, brain, and heart,°
These sovereign thrones, are all supplied, and filled
Her sweet perfections with one self king!°
Away before me to sweet beds of flowers.   40
Love thoughts lie rich when canopied with bowers.
                                    [Exeunt.]

SCENE II. *The seacoast.*

  [Enter VIOLA, *a* CAPTAIN, *and* SAILORS.]
  VIO. What country, friends, is this?
  CAP. This is Illyria,° lady.
  VIO. And what should I do in Illyria?
My brother he is in Elysium.°
Perchance he is not drowned. What think you,
    sailors?
  CAP. It is perchance that you yourself were saved.

  VIO. Oh, my poor brother! And so perchance
    may he be.
  CAP. True, madam. And to comfort you with
    chance,
Assure yourself, after our ship did split,
When you and those poor number saved with
    you   10
Hung on our driving° boat, I saw your brother,
Most provident in peril, bind himself,
Courage and hope both teaching him the practice,
To a strong mast that lived upon the sea;
Where, like Arion° on the dolphin's back,
I saw him hold acquaintance with the waves
So long as I could see.
  VIO. For saying so, there's gold.
Mine own escape unfoldeth to my hope,
Whereto thy speech serves for authority,   20
The like of him.° Know'st thou this country?
  CAP. Aye, madam, well, for I was bred and born
Not three hours' travel from this very place.
  VIO. Who governs here?
  CAP. A noble Duke, in nature as in name.
  VIO. What is his name?
  CAP. Orsino.
  VIO. Orsino! I have heard my father name him.
He was a bachelor then.
  CAP. And so is now, or was so very late.   30
For but a month ago I went from hence,
And then 'twas fresh in murmur—as, you know,
What great ones do the less will prattle of—
That he did seek the love of fair Olivia.
  VIO. What's she?
  CAP. A virtuous maid, the daughter of a Count
That died some twelvemonth since, then leaving
    her
In the protection of his son, her brother,
Who shortly also died. For whose dear love,
They say, she hath abjured the company   40
And sight of men.
  VIO.   Oh, that I served that lady,
And might not be delivered to the world
Till I had made mine own occasion mellow,
What my estate is!°
  CAP.   That were hard to compass,
Because she will admit no kind of suit,
No, not the Duke's.
  VIO. There is a fair behavior in thee, Captain.

14-15. **So ... fantastical:** love (*fancy*) is so full of imagination
(*shapes*) that above all others (*alone*) it is overflowing with
fantasies (*high fantastical*).   **20. purged . . . pestilence:**
The plague was believed by many to be caused by foul air.
22. fell: fierce.   **26. element:** sky. **seven . . . heat:** till
seven years have passed.   **27. ample view:** fully.   **28.
cloistress:** nun in a cloister.   **30. season:** keep fresh.
35. golden shaft: Cupid has two arrows; the golden causes
love, the leaden dislike.   **36. affections:** desires.   **37. liver
. . . heart:** These parts were believed to be the seat of the
passions, intelligence, and affection.   **39. self king:** sole
object of adoration.
  Sc. ii:2. Illyria: actually on the west coast of the Adriatic sea,
but Shakespeare has in fact chosen a picturesque name for
an imaginary kingdom.   **4. Elysium:** Paradise.

11. **driving:** driven before the wind.   **15. Arion:** for the
F1 reading "Orion." Arion was a singer. He was captured
by pirates who were about to kill him. He asked to be allowed
to sing for the last time. Then he jumped into the sea, where
a dolphin, charmed by his song, carried him safe to land.
19-21. Mine . . . him: i.e., my escape and your speech give
me hope that he is still alive.   **43-44. mine . . . is:** i.e., until
the time is ripe for me to reveal my own affair.

And though that Nature with a beauteous wall
Doth oft close in pollution, yet of thee
I will believe thou hast a mind that suits   50
With this thy fair and outward character.°
I prithee, and I'll pay thee bounteously,
Conceal me what I am, and be my aid
For such disguise as haply shall become
The form of my intent. I'll serve this Duke.
Thou shalt present me as a eunuch° to him.
It may be worth thy pains, for I can sing,°
And speak to him in many sorts of music,
That will allow me very worth his service.°
What else may hap to time I will commit,   60
Only shape thou thy silence to my wit.

CAP. Be you his eunuch, and your mute I'll be.
When my tongue blabs, then let mine eyes not see.

VIO. I thank thee. Lead me on.   [*Exeunt.*]

SCENE III. OLIVIA'S *house.*

[*Enter* SIR TOBY BELCH *and* MARIA.]

SIR TO. What a plague means my niece, to take
the death of her brother thus? I am sure care's an
enemy to life.

MAR. By my troth, Sir Toby, you must come in
earlier o' nights. Your cousin, my lady, takes great
exceptions to your ill hours.

SIR TO. Why, let her except, before excepted.°

MAR. Aye, but you must confine yourself within
the modest limits of order.   9

SIR TO. Confine! I'll confine myself no finer than
I am. These clothes are good enough to drink in,
and so be these boots too. An° they be not, let them
hang themselves in their own straps.

MAR. That quaffing and drinking will undo you.
I heard my lady talk of it yesterday, and of a foolish
knight that you brought in one night here to be her
wooer.

SIR TO. Who, Sir Andrew Aguecheek?

MAR. Aye, he.

SIR TO. He's as tall° a man as any's in Illyria.

MAR. What's that to the purpose?   21

SIR TO. Why, he has three thousand ducats a year.

MAR. Aye, but he'll have but a year in all these
ducats. He's a very fool and a prodigal.

SIR TO. Fie that you'll say so! He plays o' the viol

de gamboys,° and speaks three or four languages
word for word without book, and hath all the good
gifts of nature.   29

MAR. He hath indeed, almost natural,° for besides
that he's a fool, he's a great quarreler. And but that
he hath the gift of a coward to allay the gust° he
hath in quarreling, 'tis thought among the prudent
he would quickly have the gift of a grave.

SIR TO. By this hand, they are scoundrels and
substractors° that say so of him. Who are they?

MAR. They that add, moreover, he's drunk
nightly in your company.   39

SIR TO. With drinking healths to my niece. I'll
drink to her as long as there is a passage in my
throat and drink in Illyria. He's a coward and a
coystrill° that will not drink to my niece till his
brains turn o' the toe like a parish top.° What,
wench! *Castiliano vulgo;*° for here comes Sir Andrew
Agueface.

[*Enter* SIR ANDREW AGUECHEEK.]

SIR AND. Sir Toby Belch! How now, Sir Toby
Belch!

SIR TO. Sweet Sir Andrew!

SIR AND. Bless you, fair shrew.   50

MAR. And you too, sir.

SIR TO. Accost, Sir Andrew, accost.°

SIR AND. What's that?

SIR TO. My niece's chambermaid.

SIR AND. Good Mistress Accost, I desire better acquaintance.

MAR. My name is Mary, sir.

SIR AND. Good Mistress Mary Accost——

SIR TO. You mistake, knight. "Accost" is front
her, board her, woo her, assail her.   60

SIR AND. By my troth, I would not undertake her
in this company. Is that the meaning of "accost"?

MAR. Fare you well, gentlemen.

SIR TO. An thou let part so, Sir Andrew, would
thou mightst never draw sword again.

SIR AND. An you part so, mistress, I would I
might never draw sword again. Fair lady, do you
think you have fools in hand?

MAR. Sir, I have not you by the hand.   70

SIR AND. Marry,° but you shall have, and here's
my hand.

MAR. Now, sir, "thought is free." I pray you,

---

51. character: face—an outward indication of the nature
within.   **56. eunuch:** boy singer.   **57. I . . . sing:** The
part of Viola was originally written for a boy with a good voice,
but later small alterations were made and the songs were
given to the Clown.   **59. allow . . . service:** approve me as
worth employing.
    Sc. iii: 6. except . . . excepted: Toby caps Maria's "excep-
tion" with a common legal phrase *exceptis excipiendis* (with the
exceptions already excepted).   **12. An:** if.   **20. tall:** Andrew
is tall and thin, but Toby implies that he is also "tall" in the
common meaning of "brave."

26-27. viol de gamboys: base viol, viola da gamba, so called
because, like the cello, it was held between the legs.   **30.
natural:** with a pun on "natural," meaning born fool.   **33.
allay . . . gust:** water down the taste.   **37. substractors:**
detractors.   **43. coystrill:** knave.   **44. parish top:** a large
spinning top used by villagers on frosty days when it was too
cold to work.   **45. Castiliano vulgo:** i.e., keep a straight
face; lit., a Castilian face. The origin of the phrase is disputed.
52. accost: introduce yourself.   **71. Marry:** Mary, by the
Virgin.

bring your hand to the buttery bar° and let it drink.

SIR AND. Wherefore, sweetheart? What's your metaphor?

MAR. It's dry,° sir.

SIR AND. Why, I think so. I am not such an ass but I can keep my hand dry. But what's your jest? 80

MAR. A dry jest, sir.

SIR AND. Are you full of them?

MAR. Aye, sir, I have them at my fingers' ends. Marry, now I let go your hand, I am barren. [*Exit.*]

SIR TO. O knight, thou lackest a cup of canary.° When did I see thee so put down?

SIR AND. Never in your life, I think, unless you see canary put me down. Methinks sometimes I have no more wit than a Christian or an ordinary man has. But I am a great eater of beef° and I believe that does harm to my wit. 91

SIR TO. No question.

SIR AND. An I thought that, I'd forswear it. I'll ride home tomorrow, Sir Toby.

SIR TO. *Pourquoi*,° my dear knight?

SIR AND. What is "*pourquoi*"? Do or not do? I would I had bestowed that time in the tongues that I have in fencing, dancing and bearbaiting. Oh, had I but followed the arts!

SIR TO. Then hadst thou had an excellent head of hair. 101

SIR AND. Why, would that have mended my hair?

SIR TO. Past question, for thou seest it will not curl by nature.°

SIR AND. But it becomes me well enough, does 't not?

SIR TO. Excellent. It hangs like flax on a distaff,° and I hope to see a housewife take thee between her legs and spin it off.° 110

SIR AND. Faith, I'll home tomorrow, Sir Toby. Your niece will not be seen, or if she be, it's four to one she'll none of me. The Count himself here hard by woos her.

SIR TO. She'll none o' the Count. She'll not match above her degree,° neither in estate, years, nor wit. I have heard her swear 't. Tut, there's life in 't, man.

SIR AND. I'll stay a month longer. I am a fellow o' the strangest mind i' the world. I delight in masques and revels° sometimes altogether. 121

SIR TO. Art thou good at these kickshawses,° knight?

SIR AND. As any man in Illyria, whatsoever he be, under the degree of my betters. And yet I will not compare with an old man.°

SIR TO. What is thy excellence in a galliard,° knight?

SIR AND. Faith, I can cut a caper.°

SIR TO. And I can cut the mutton° to 't. 130

SIR AND. And I think I have the backtrick° simply as strong as any man in Illyria.

SIR TO. Wherefore are these things hid? Wherefore have these gifts a curtain before 'em? Are they like to take dust, like Mistress Mall's picture?° Why dost thou not go to church in a galliard and come home in a coranto?° My very walk should be a jig,° I would not so much as make water but in a sinkapace.° What dost thou mean? Is it a world to hide virtues in? I did think, by the excellent constitution of thy leg, it was formed under the star of a galliard. 142

SIR AND. Aye, 'tis strong, and it does indifferent well in a flame-colored stock. Shall we set about some revels?

SIR TO. What shall we do else? Were we not born under Taurus?°

SIR AND. Taurus! That's sides and heart.

SIR TO. No, sir, it is legs and thighs. Let me see thee caper. Ha! higher. Ha, ha! excellent! 150

[*Exeunt.*]

SCENE IV. *The* DUKE's *palace.*

[*Enter* VALENTINE, *and* VIOLA *in man's attire.*]

VAL. If the Duke continue these favors toward you, Cesario, you are like to be much advanced. He hath known you but three days, and already you are no stranger.

VIO. You either fear his humor° or my negligence,

---

74. **buttery bar:** ledge on the half-door of the buttery on which tankards were rested. "Bar" is still used in this sense in "cocktail bar." The phrase "bring your hand to the buttery bar" is an invitation to a flirtation which Andrew is too simple to understand. 77. **dry:** A dry hand denoted lack of generosity and desire. 85. **canary:** wine from the Canary Isles. 90. **eater of beef:** Diet was believed to have considerable influence on bodily and mental health. 95. **Pourquoi:** why. 104-05. **curl by nature:** emendation for the F1 reading "cool my nature." 108. **distaff:** used in spinning. 110. **spin it off:** cause you to lose your hair as a result of venereal disease. 116. **degree:** rank

120-21. **masques . . . revels:** courtly and fashionable entertainments. 122. **kickshawses:** trifles. 126. **old man:** expert. 127. **galliard:** a quick, lively, and popular dance. 129. **caper:** jump into the air. 130. **cut . . . mutton:** Mutton was often served with caper sauce. 131. **backtrick:** a movement in dancing. 135. **Mistress . . . picture:** a topical allusion now lost. Mall or Moll was a common nickname for a prostitute. This Mall may have been one Mall Newberry who figured in a scandalous trial in 1600. 137. **coranto:** a running dance. 138. **jig:** a lively dance. 139. **sinkapace:** "cinque pace," a dance of five steps. 146-47. **born . . . Taurus:** The common penny almanac of the time printed the figure of a naked man surrounded by the signs of the zodiac with lines pointing to the parts of the body governed by each. Both Andrew and Toby are wrong, as Taurus governed the neck and throat.

Sc. iv: 5. humor: whim, inclination, temper.

that you call in question the continuance of his
love. Is he inconstant, sir, in his favors?

VAL. No, believe me.

VIO. I thank you. Here comes the Count.

   [*Enter* DUKE, CURIO, *and* ATTENDANTS.]

DUKE. Who saw Cesario, ho?   10

VIO. On your attendance, my lord. Here.

DUKE. Stand you a while aloof. Cesario,
Thou know'st no less but all. I have unclasped
To thee the book even of my secret soul.
Therefore, good youth, address thy gait unto her.
Be not denied access, stand at her doors,
And tell them there thy fixèd foot shall grow
Till thou have audience.

VIO.   Sure, my noble lord,
If she be so abandoned to her sorrow
As it is spoke, she never will admit me.   20

DUKE. Be clamorous and leap all civil bounds°
Rather than make unprofited return.

VIO. Say I do speak with her, my lord, what then?

DUKE. Oh, then unfolk the passion of my love,
Surprise her with discourse of my dear faith.
It shall become thee well to act my woes.
She will attend it better in thy youth
Than in a nuncio's° of more grave aspéct.°

VIO. I think not so, my lord.

DUKE.   Dear lad, believe it,
For they shall yet belie thy happy years   30
That say thou art a man. Diana's lip
Is not more smooth and rubious;° thy small pipe°
Is as the maiden's organ, shrill and sound,
And all is semblative° a woman's part.
I know thy constellation is right apt°
For this affair. Some four or five attend him,
All, if you will; for I myself am best
When least in company. Prosper well in this,
And thou shalt live as freely as thy lord,
To call his fortunes thine.

VIO.   I'll do my best   40
To woo your lady. [*Aside.*] Yet, a barful° strife!
Whoe'er I woo, myself would be his wife. [*Exeunt.*]

SCENE V. OLIVIA'S *house.*

   [*Enter* MARIA *and* CLOWN.]

MAR. Nay, either tell me where thou hast been, or
I will not open my lips so wide as a bristle may
enter in way of thy excuse. My lady will hang thee
for thy absence.

CLO. Let her hang me. He that is well hanged in
this world needs to fear no colors.°

MAR. Make that good.°

CLO. He shall see none to fear.

MAR. A good lenten° answer. I can tell thee
where that saying was born, of "I fear no colors."

CLO. Where, good Mistress Mary?   11

MAR. In the wars, and that may you be bold to
say in your foolery.

CLO. Well, God give them wisdom that have it,
and those that are fools, let them use their talents.

MAR. Yet you will be hanged for being so long
absent—or to be turned away, is not that as good
as a hanging to you?

CLO. Many a good hanging prevents a bad   20
marriage, and for turning away, let summer bear it
out.°

MAR. You are resolute, then?

CLO. Not so, neither, but I am resolved on two
points.°

MAR. That if one break, the other will hold, or if
both break, your gaskins° fall.

CLO. Apt, in good faith, very apt. Well, go thy
way. If Sir Toby would leave drinking, thou wert
as witty a piece of Eve's flesh° as any in Illyria.   31

MAR. Peace, you rogue, no more o' that. Here
comes my lady. Make your excuse wisely, you
were best.   [*Exit.*]

CLO. Wit, an 't be thy will, put me into good fooling! Those wits that think they have thee do very
oft prove fools, and I that am sure I lack thee may
pass for a wise man. For what says Quinapalus?°
"Better a witty fool than a foolish wit."   40

[*Enter* LADY OLIVIA *with* MALVOLIO.] God bless thee,
lady!

OLI. Take the fool away.

CLO. Do you not hear, fellows? Take away the
lady.

OLI. Go to, you're a dry fool, I'll no more of you.
Besides, you grow dishonest.

CLO. Two faults,° madonna, that drink and good
counsel will amend. For give the dry fool drink,
then is the fool not dry. Bid the dishonest man mend
himself; if he mend, he is no longer dishonest;   50

Sc. v: 6. fear no colors: proverbial phrase meaning "I
dare anyone." Since "collar," "color," and "choler" were pronounced alike, puns on these words were endless.   7. Make...
good: prove it.   9. lenten: fasting, lean.   21-22. let...out:
have the upper hand; i.e., if I have to go, I hope it's good
weather.   25. points: laces used to attach the hose to the
doublet.   27. gaskins: breeches.   31. Eve's flesh: erring
woman—the first hint that there is something between Toby
and Maria.   39. Quinapalus: a character invented by
Rabelais. The clown specializes in mock learning.   47. Two
faults: The fool is in disgrace and to cajole Olivia into good
humor rattles out mock learned nonsense.

---

21. civil bounds: restraints of good manners.   28. nuncio:
messenger. grave aspect: sober countenance.   32. rubious:
ruby-red. small pipe: little throat.   34. semblative: resembling.   35. constellation . . . apt: you are born under
a lucky star.   41. barful: full of bars, impediments.

if he cannot, let the botcher° mend him. Anything that's mended is but patched. Virtue that transgresses is but patched with sin, and sin that amends is but patched with virtue. If that this simple syllogism° will serve, so. If it will not, what remedy? As there is no true cuckold° but calamity, so beauty's a flower. The lady bade take away the fool, therefore I say again, take her away.

OLI. Sir, I bade them take away you.   60

CLO. Misprision° in the highest degree! Lady, *cucullus non facit monachum.*° That's as much to say as I wear not motley° in my brain. Good madonna, give me leave to prove you a fool.

OLI. Can you do it?

CLO. Dexteriously, good madonna.

OLI. Make your proof.

CLO. I must catechize you for it, madonna. Good my mouse° of virtue, answer me.

OLI. Well, sir, for want of other idleness, I'll bide your proof.   71

CLO. Good madonna, why mournest thou?

OLI. Good fool, for my brother's death.

CLO. I think his soul is in Hell, madonna.

OLI. I know his soul is in Heaven, fool.

CLO. The more fool, madonna, to mourn for your brother's soul being in Heaven. Take away the fool, gentlemen.

OLI. What think you of this fool, Malvolio? Doth he not mend?   80

MAL. Yes, and shall do till the pangs of death shake him. Infirmity, that decays the wise, doth ever make the better fool.

CLO. God send you, sir, a speedy infirmity, for the better increasing your folly! Sir Toby will be sworn that I am no fox, but he will not pass his word for twopence that you are no fool.

OLI. How say you to that, Malvolio?

MAL. I marvel your ladyship takes delight in such a barren rascal.° I saw him put down the other day with an ordinary fool that has no more brain   90 than a stone. Look you now, he's out of his guard already. Unless you laugh and minister occasion° to him, he is gagged. I protest, I take these wise men that crow so at these set kind of fools no better than the fools' zanies.°

OLI. Oh, you are sick of self-love, Malvolio, and taste with a distempered appetite. To be generous, guiltless, and of free° disposition is to take those things for bird bolts° that you deem cannon   100 bullets. There is no slander in an allowed° fool, though he do nothing but rail; nor no railing in a known discreet man, though he do nothing but reprove.

CLO. Now Mercury° endue thee with leasing,° for thou speakest well of fools!

[*Re-enter* MARIA.]

MAR. Madam, there is at the gate a young gentleman much desires to speak with you.

OLI. From the Count Orsino, is it?

MAR. I know not, madam. 'Tis a fair young man, and well attended.   111

OLI. Who of my people hold him in delay?

MAR. Sir Toby, madam, your kinsman.

OLI. Fetch him off, I pray you. He speaks nothing but madman, fie on him! [*Exit* MARIA.] Go you, Malvolio. If it be a suit from the Count, I am sick, or not at home—what you will, to dismiss it. [*Exit* MALVOLIO.] Now you see, sir, how your fooling grows old, and people dislike it.   119

CLO. Thou hast spoke for us, madonna, as if thy eldest son should be a fool, whose skull Jove cram with brains! For—here he comes°—one of thy kin has a most weak pia mater.°

[*Enter* SIR TOBY.]

OLI. By mine honor, half-drunk. What is he at the gate, Cousin?

SIR TO. A gentleman.

OLI. A gentleman! What gentleman?

SIR TO. 'Tis a gentleman here—a plague o' these pickle-herring!° How now, sot!

CLO. Good Sir Toby!   130

OLI. Cousin, Cousin, how have you come so early by this lethargy?°

SIR TO. Lechery! I defy lechery. There's one at the gate.

OLI. Aye, marry, what is he?

SIR TO. Let him be the Devil an he will, I care not. Give me faith, say I. Well, it's all one.   [*Exit.*]

OLI. What's a drunken man like, fool?

CLO. Like a drowned man, a fool, and a madman. One draught above heat makes him a fool, the

51. botcher: an unskillful mender of old garments. **55. syllogism:** learned argument. **56. cuckold:** husband deceived by his wife. **61. Misprision:** error. **62. cucullus ... monachum:** a cowl does not make a monk. **63. motley:** the professional fool's particolored costume. **69. mouse:** a term of endearment, like "duck." **89. barren rascal:** By this remark Malvolio rouses the malice of the fool, and so ultimately brings about his own downfall. **92. minister occasion:** i.e., give him a lead. **96. zanies:** stooges; the zany was the clown's assistant who tried to copy his tricks.

99. free: innocent. **100. bird bolts:** short, blunt headed arrows used in a crossbow for killing small birds. **101. allowed:** licensed. **105. Mercury:** the god of thieves and rascals. **endue ... leasing:** endow you with lying. **122. here he comes:** i.e., Toby. This is the usual phrase to draw attention to a character entering at the back of the stage. **123. pia mater:** outer covering of the brain. **129. pickle-herring:** very salty and indigestible, and so causing thirst and wind. **132. lethargy:** lack of sense.

second mads him, and a third drowns him.   141

OLI. Go thou and seek the crowner,° and let him sit o' my coz,° for he's in the third degree of drink, he's drowned. Go look after him.

CLO. He is but mad yet, madonna, and the fool shall look to the madman.   [*Exit.*]

[*Re-enter* MALVOLIO.]

MAL. Madam, yond young fellow swears he will speak with you. I told him you were sick; he takes on him to understand so much, and therefore   150 comes to speak with you. I told him you were asleep; he seems to have a foreknowledge of that too, and therefore comes to speak with you. What is to be said to him, lady? He's fortified against any denial.

OLI. Tell him he shall not speak with me.

MAL. Has been told so, and he says he'll stand at your door like a sheriff's post,° and be the supporter° to a bench, but he'll speak with you.

OLI. What kind o' man is he?

MAL. Why, of mankind.   160

OLI. What manner of man?

MAL. Of very ill manner. He'll speak with you, will you or no.

OLI. Of what personage and years is he?

MAL. Not yet old enough for a man, nor young enough for a boy, as a squash° is before 'tis a peascod, or a codling when 'tis almost an apple. 'Tis with him in standing water,° between boy and man. He is very well-favored° and he speaks very shrewishly.° One would think his mother's milk were scarce out of him.   171

OLI. Let him approach. Call in my gentlewoman.

MAL. Gentlewoman, my lady calls.   [*Exit.*]

[*Re-enter* MARIA.]

OLI. Give me my veil. Come, throw it o'er my face. We'll once more hear Orsino's embassy.

[*Enter* VIOLA *and* ATTENDANTS.]

VIO. The honorable lady of the house, which is she?

OLI. Speak to me, I shall answer for her. Your will?   180

VIO. Most radiant, exquisite, and unmatchable beauty, I pray you tell me if this be the lady of the house, for I never saw her. I would be loath to cast away my speech, for besides that it is excellently

well penned, I have taken great pains to con° it. Good beauties, let me sustain no scorn. I am very comptible,° even to the least sinister° usage.

OLI. Whence came you, sir?

VIO. I can say little more than I have studied, and that question's out of my part. Good gentle one, give me modest assurance if you be the lady of the house, that I may proceed in my speech.   192

OLI. Are you a comedian?°

VIO. No, my profound heart. And yet, by the very fangs of malice I swear, I am not that I play.° Are you the lady of the house?

OLI. If I do not usurp myself, I am.

VIO. Most certain, if you are she, you do usurp yourself; for what is yours to bestow is not yours to reserve. But this is from my commission.° I   200 will on with my speech in your praise, and then show you the heart of my message.

OLI. Come to what is important in 't. I forgive you the praise.

VIO. Alas, I took great pains to study it, and 'tis poetical.

OLI. It is the more like to be feigned. I pray you keep it in. I heard you were saucy at my gates, and allowed your approach rather to wonder° at you than to hear you. If you be not mad, be gone.   211 If you have reason, be brief. 'Tis not that time of moon° with me to make one in so skipping° a dialogue.

MAR. Will you hoist sail, sir? Here lies your way.

VIO. No, good swabber,° I am to hull° here a little longer. Some mollification for your giant,° sweet lady. Tell me your mind. I am a messenger.   220

OLI. Sure, you have some hideous matter to deliver when the courtesy of it is so fearful.° Speak your office.

VIO. It alone concerns your ear. I bring no overture° of war, no taxation of° homage. I hold the olive in my hand, my words are as full of peace as matter.

---

185. **con:** learn by heart.   187. **comptible:** susceptible. **sinister:** left-handed, unkind   193. **comedian:** actor. 195. **that I play:** i.e., the part I act, that of a man   200. **from my commission:** not included in my instructions.   210. **allowed . . . wonder:** I allowed you to come in so that I might look at you—not to listen to your prepared speeches.   212-13. **time of moon:** lucky end of the month.   213. **skipping:** frivolous.   218. **swabber:** one who swabs the decks. Viola retorts to Maria's "hoist sail" with a series of nautical metaphors. **hull:** lie at anchor.   219. **mollification . . . giant:** Viola apologizes for the interruption—"I had to pacify your little lady." Maria's size is stressed. The company had a small boy actor at this time.   222. **courtesy . . . fearful:** you must have some dreadful message to deliver if it need such elaborate introduction.   225. **overture:** declaration. **taxation of:** demand for.

---

142. **crowner:** coroner, whose function is to hold an inquest on the bodies of those who die unnaturally.   143. **coz:** cousin —used for any near relation.   157. **sheriff's post:** painted post set up before the house of the sheriff as a sign of office. 158. **supporter:** support.   166. **squash:** unripe peapod. 168. **standing water:** the moment at the change of the tide when the water neither ebbs nor flows.   169. **well-favored:** good-looking.   170. **shrewishly:** like a shrew, shrill.

OLI. Yet you began rudely. What are you? What would you? 229

VIO. The rudeness that hath appeared in me have I learned from my entertainment. What I am, and what I would, are as secret as maidenhead—to your ears, divinity; to any other's, profanation.

OLI. Give us the place alone. We will hear this divinity.° [*Exeunt* MARIA *and* ATTENDANTS.] Now, sir, what is your text?

VIO. Most sweet lady——

OLI. A comfortable doctrine, and much may be said of it. Where lies your text? 240

VIO. In Orsino's bosom.

OLI. In his bosom! In what chapter of his bosom?

VIO. To answer by the method,° in the first of his heart.

OLI. Oh, I have read it. It is heresy. Have you no more to say?

VIO. Good madam, let me see your face.

OLI. Have you any commission from your lord to negotiate with my face? You are now out of 250 your text. But we will draw the curtain and show you the picture. Look you, sir, [*Unveiling*] such a one I was this present°—is 't not well done?

VIO. Excellently done, if God did all.

OLI. 'Tis in grain,° sir, 'twill endure wind and weather.

VIO. 'Tis beauty truly blent,° whose red and white
Nature's own sweet and cunning hand laid on.
Lady, you are the cruel'st she alive
If you will lead these graces to the grave 260
And leave the world no copy.°

OLI. Oh, sir, I will not be so hardhearted, I will give out divers schedules of my beauty. It shall be inventoried, and every particle and utensil labeled to my will—as, item, two lips, indifferent red; item, two gray eyes, with lids to them; item, one neck, one chin, and so forth. Were you sent hither to praise me?

VIO. I see what you are, you are too proud;
But if you were the Devil, you are fair. 270
My lord and master loves you. Oh, such love
Could be but recompensed, though you were crowned
The nonpareil° of beauty!

OLI.   How does he love me?

VIO. With adorations, fertile tears,
With groans that thunder love, with sighs of fire.

OLI. Your lord does know my mind. I cannot love him.
Yet I suppose him virtuous, know him noble,
Of great estate, of fresh and stainless youth;
In voices well divulged,° free, learned, and valiant;
And in dimension° and the shape of nature 280
A gracious person. But yet I cannot love him.
He might have took his answer long ago.

VIO. If I did love you in my master's flame,
With such a suffering, such a deadly life,
In your denial I would find no sense.
I would not understand it.

OLI.   Why, what would you?

VIO. Make me a willow cabin° at your gate,
And call upon my soul within the house;
Write loyal cantons° of contemnèd° love
And sing them loud even in the dead of night; 290
Halloo your name to the reverberate hills,
And make the babbling gossip of the air
Cry out "Olivia!" Oh, you should not rest
Between the elements of air and earth,
But you should pity me!

OLI.   You might do much.
What is your parentage?

VIO. Above my fortunes, yet my state is well.
I am a gentleman.

OLI.   Get you to your lord.
I cannot love him. Let him send no more,
Unless, perchance, you come to me again 300
To tell me how he takes it. Fare you well.
I thank you for your pains. Spend this for me.

VIO. I am no fee'd post,° lady, keep your purse.
My master, not myself, lacks recompense.
Love make his heart of flint that you shall love;
And let your fervor, like my master's, be
Placed in contempt! Farewell, fair cruelty. [*Exit.*]

OLI. "What is your parentage?"
"Above my fortunes, yet my state is well.
I am a gentleman." I'll be sworn thou art. 310
Thy tongue, thy face, thy limbs, actions, and spirit,
Do give thee fivefold blazon.° Not too fast. Soft, soft!
Unless the master were the man. How now!
Even so quickly may one catch the plague?
Methinks I feel this youth's perfections
With an invisible and subtle stealth

---

236. divinity: Olivia takes up Viola's *divinity*, and the two follow up the metaphor in their conversation.   **244. To . . . method:** to keep up the metaphor.   **252-53. such . . . present:** This is the F1 reading, and has been much emended. The general meaning is "This is what I really am."   **255. in grain:** i.e., the colors are fast, they will not wash out.   **257. blent:** blended.   **261. leave . . . copy:** die without children to carry on the pattern. Cf. Sonnets 1–17.   **273. nonpareil:** without an equal.

279. voices . . . divulged: spoken well of.   **280. dimension:** bodily form.   **287. willow cabin:** an arbor of willow—the unhappy lover's tree.   **289. cantons:** songs. **contemned:** despised.   **303. fee'd post:** paid messenger.   **312. blazon:** coat of arms denoting a gentleman.

To creep in at mine eyes. Well, let it be.   317
What ho, Malvolio!

[*Re-enter* MALVOLIO.]

MAL.   Here, madam, at your service.

OLI. Run after that same peevish messenger,
The County's° man. He left this ring behind him,
Would I or not. Tell him I'll none of it.
Desire him not to flatter with his lord,
Nor hold him up with hopes. I am not for him.
If that the youth will come this way tomorrow,
I'll give him reasons for 't. Hie thee,° Malvolio.

MAL. Madam, I will.   [*Exit.*]

OLI. I do I know not what, and fear to find
Mine eye too great a flatterer for my mind.   328
Fate, show thy force, ourselves we do not owe.°
What is decreed must be, and be this so.   [*Exit.*]

ACT II

SCENE I. *The seacoast.*

[*Enter* ANTONIO *and* SEBASTIAN.]

ANT. Will you stay no longer? Nor will you not
that I go with you?

SEB. By your patience, no. My stars shine darkly
over me. The malignancy° of my fate might perhaps distemper° yours, therefore I shall crave of you
your leave that I may bear my evils alone. It were
a bad recompense for your love to lay any of them
on you.

ANT. Let me yet know of you whither you are
bound.   10

SEB. No, sooth, sir. My determinate voyage is
mere extravagancy.° But I perceive in you so excellent a touch of modesty that you will not extort
from me what I am willing to keep in; therefore it
charges me in manners the rather to express myself.° You must know of me then, Antonio, my
name is Sebastian, which I called Roderigo.° My
father was that Sebastian of Messaline° whom I
know you have heard of. He left behind him myself
and a sister, both born in an hour. If the   20
Heavens had been pleased, would we had so
ended! But you, sir, altered that, for some hour
before you took me from the breach° of the sea was
my sister drowned.

ANT. Alas the day!

SEB. A lady, sir, though it was said she much resembled me, was yet of many accounted beautiful.
But though I could not with such estimable won-
der° overfar believe that, yet thus far I will boldly
publish° her—she bore a mind that envy could   30
not but call fair. She is drowned already, sir, with
salt water, though I seem to drown her remembrance again with more.

ANT. Pardon me, sir, your bad entertainment.°

SEB. O good Antonio, forgive me your trouble.

ANT. If you will not murder me for my love, let
me be your servant.

SEB. If you will not undo what you have done—
that is, kill him whom you have recovered—desire
it not. Fare ye well at once. My bosom is full of   40
kindness,° and I am yet so near the manners of my
mother that upon the least occasion more mine eyes
will tell tales of me. I am bound to the Count Orsino's Court. Farewell.   [*Exit.*]

ANT. The gentleness of all the gods go with thee!
I have many enemies in Orsino's Court,
Else would I very shortly see thee there.
But, come what may, I do adore thee so
That danger shall seem sport, and I will go.

[*Exit.*]

SCENE II. *A street.*

[*Enter* VIOLA, MALVOLIO *following.*]

MAL. Were not you even now with the Countess
Olivia?

VIO. Even now, sir. On a moderate pace I have
since arrived but hither.

MAL. She returns this ring to you, sir. You might
have saved me my pains, to have taken it away
yourself. She adds, moreover, that you should put
your lord into a desperate assurance° she will none
of him. And one thing more, that you be never so
hardy to come again in his affairs, unless it be to report your lord's taking of this. Receive it so.   12

VIO. She took the ring of me. I'll none of it.

MAL. Come, sir, you peevishly threw it to her;
and her will is, it should be so returned. If it be
worth stooping for, there it lies in your eye. If not,
be it his that finds it.   [*Exit.*]

VIO. I left no ring with her. What means this
lady?
Fortune forbid my outside have not charmed her!
She made good view of me;° indeed, so much   20
That sure methought her eyes had lost her tongue,

---

320. **County:** Count.   325. **Hie thee:** hasten.   329. **owe:** own.

Act II, Sc. i: 4. **malignancy:** evil disposition of the stars.
5. **distemper:** disturb.   11-12. **determinate . . . extravagancy:** the journey I have determined is mere wandering.
There is a touch of affectation in Sebastian's language.
14-15. **it . . . myself:** good manners demand that I tell you who
I am.   17. **I . . . Roderigo:** hitherto I have pretended that my
name was Roderigo.   18. **Messaline:** Messina in Sicily.
24. **breach:** where the waves break.

28-29. **estimable wonder:** admiring judgment.   30. **publish:** proclaim.   34. **your . . . entertainment:** looking after
you so badly.   41. **kindness:** tender feeling.
Sc. ii: 9. **desperate assurance:** certainty that there is no
hope.   20. **made . . . me:** took a good look at me.

For she did speak in starts distractedly.
She loves me, sure, the cunning of her passion
Invites me in this churlish messenger.
None of my lord's ring! Why, he sent her none.
I am the man. If it be so, as 'tis,
Poor lady, she were better love a dream.
Disguise, I see thou art a wickedness,
Wherein the pregnant° enemy does much.
How easy is it for the proper-false°   30
In women's waxen hearts to set their forms!
Alas, our frailty is the cause, not we!
For such as we are made of, such we be.
How will this fadge?° My master loves her dearly;
And I, poor monster, fond as much on him,
And she, mistaken, seems to dote on me.
What will become of this? As I am man,
My state is desperate for my master's love;
As I am woman—now alas the day!—
What thriftless° sighs shall poor Olivia breathe!
O Time, thou must untangle this, not I!   41
It is too hard a knot for me to untie!   [Exit.]

SCENE III. OLIVIA's *house*.

[*Enter* SIR TOBY *and* SIR ANDREW.]

SIR TO. Approach, Sir Andrew. Not to be abed
after midnight is to be up betimes; and "*diluculo
surgere*,"° thou know'st——
    SIR AND. Nay, by my troth,° I know not. But I
know to be up late is to be up late.
    SIR TO. A false conclusion. I hate it as an unfilled
can.° To be up after midnight, and to go to bed
then, is early, so that to go to bed after midnight is
to go to bed betimes. Does not our life consist of the
four elements?°   10
    SIR AND. Faith, so they say, but I think it rather
consists of eating and drinking.
    SIR TO. Thou 'rt a scholar. Let us therefore eat
and drink. Marian, I say, a stoup° of wine!
        [*Enter* CLOWN.]
    SIR AND. Here comes the fool, i' faith.
    CLO. How now, my hearts! Did you never see the
picture of "we three"?°
    SIR TO. Welcome, ass. Now let's have a catch.°
    SIR AND. By my troth, the fool has an excellent
breast.° I had rather than forty shillings I had   20

such a leg, and so sweet a breath to sing, as the fool
has. In sooth, thou wast in very gracious fooling
last night, when thou spokest of Pigrogromitus, of
the Vapians passing the equinoctial of Queubus.°
'Twas very good, i' faith. I sent thee sixpence for
thy leman.° Hadst it?
    CLO. I did impeticos thy gratillity,° for Malvo-
lio's nose is no whipstock. My lady has a white
hand, and the Myrmidons are no bottle-ale houses.
    SIR AND. Excellent! Why, this is the best fooling,
when all is done. Now, a song.   31
    SIR TO. Come on, there is sixpence for you—let's
have a song.
    SIR AND. There's a testril° of me too. If one
knight give a——
    CLO. Would you have a love song, or a song of
good life?
    SIR TO. A love song, a love song.
    SIR AND. Aye, aye. I care not for good life.
    CLO. [*Sings.*]
        O mistress mine, where are you roaming?   40
        Oh, stay and hear, your truelove's coming,
            That can sing both high and low.
        Trip no further, pretty sweeting,
        Journeys end in lovers meeting,
            Every wise man's son doth know.
    SIR AND. Excellent good, i' faith.
    SIR TO. Good, good.
    CLO. [*Sings.*]
        What is love? 'Tis not hereafter,
        Present mirth hath present laughter,
            What's to come is still unsure.   50
        In delay there lies no plenty,
        Then come kiss me, sweet and twenty,°
            Youth's a stuff will not endure.
    SIR AND. A mellifluous° voice, as I am a true
knight.
    SIR TO. A contagious breath.
    SIR AND. Very sweet and contagious, i' faith.
    SIR TO. To hear by the nose, it is dulcet in con-
tagion.° But shall we make the welkin° dance indeed? Shall we rouse the night owl in a catch°   60
that will draw three souls out of one weaver?° Shall
we do that?

29. pregnant: resourceful. 30. proper-false: men who are
handsome but deceitful. 34. fadge: turn out. 40. thrift-
less: useless.
    Sc. iii: 2-3. diluculo surgere: early to rise—a tag from the
schoolboy's Latin grammar. 4. troth: truth. 7. can: pot.
10. four elements: earth, air, fire, water. 14. stoup: large
pot. 17. we three: a picture of two asses, the spectator
making the third member of the party. 18. catch: rowdy
song, where each singer in turn catches up the song a few words
after the others. 20. breast: voice.

23-24. Pigrogromitus . . . Queubus: more mock learned
foolery. 26. leman: sweetheart. 27. impeticos . . . gratil-
lity: pocket your tip. The rest of the fool's profundity is un-
explained; but as both knights are growing more and more
fuddled, it is not important. 34. testril: coin worth sixpence.
52. sweet . . . twenty: gay girl. 54. mellifluous: honey-
sweet. 58-59. dulcet in contagion: sweetly catching.
59. welkin: sky. 60. catch: See l. 18, n. The words of the
catch which they sing at l. 75 are "Hold thy peace, thou knave."
61. three . . . weaver: Weavers, mostly Puritan refugees from
the Netherlands, were noted psalm singers. It will need a
powerful song to draw out three souls.

SIR AND. An you love me, let's do 't. I am dog at a catch.

CLO. By 'r lady, sir, and some dogs will catch well.

SIR AND. Most certain. Let our catch be "Thou knave."

CLO. "Hold thy peace, thou knave," knight?   69
I shall be constrained in 't to call thee knave, knight.

SIR AND. 'Tis not the first time I have constrained one to call me knave. Begin, fool. It begins "Hold thy peace."

CLO. I shall never begin if I hold my peace.

SIR AND. Good, i' faith. Come, begin.
                                            [Catch sung.]

[Enter MARIA.]

MAR. What a caterwauling do you keep here! If my lady have not called up her steward Malvolio and bid him turn you out of doors, never trust me.

SIR TO. My lady's a Cataian,° we are politi-   80
cians,° Malvolio's a Peg-a-Ramsey,° and "Three merry men be we." Am not I consanguineous?°
Am I not of her blood? Tillyvally.° Lady! [Sings.]
"There dwelt a man in Babylon, lady, lady!"

CLO. Beshrew me,° the knight's in admirable fool-ing.

SIR AND. Aye, he does well enough if he be dis-posed, and so do I too. He does it with a better grace, but I do it more natural.   89

SIR TO. [Sings.] "Oh, the twelfth day of Decem-ber"——

MAR. For the love o' God, peace!

[Enter MALVOLIO.]

MAL. My masters, are you mad? Or what are you? Have you no wit, manners, nor honesty, but to gabble like tinkers at this time of night? Do ye make an alehouse of my lady's house, that ye squeak out your coziers'° catches without any mit-igation or remorse of voice? Is there no respect of place, persons, nor time in you?   99

SIR TO. We did keep time, sir, in our catches. Sneck up!°

MAL. Sir Toby, I must be round° with you. My lady bade me tell you that though she harbors you as her kinsman, she's nothing allied to your dis-orders. If you can separate yourself and your mis-demeanors, you are welcome to the house. If not, an it would please you to take leave of her, she is very willing to bid you farewell.

SIR TO. "Farewell,° dear heart, since I must needs be gone."   110

MAR. Nay, good Sir Toby.

CLO. "His eyes do show his days are almost done."

MAL. Is 't even so?

SIR TO. "But I will never die."

CLO. Sir Toby, there you lie.

MAL. This is much credit to you.

SIR TO. "Shall I bid him go?"

CLO. "What an if you do?"

SIR TO. "Shall I bid him go, and spare not?"   120

CLO. "Oh, no, no, no, no, you dare not."

SIR TO. Out o' tune, sir. Ye lie. Art any more than a steward? Dost thou think because thou art virtu-ous, there shall be no more cakes and ale?

CLO. Yes, by Saint Anne, and ginger shall be hot i' the mouth too.

SIR TO. Thou 'rt i' the right. Go, sir, rub your chain° with crumbs.° A stoup of wine, Maria!

MAL. Mistress Mary, if you prized my   130
lady's favor at anything more than contempt, you would not give means for this uncivil rule.° She shall know of it, by this hand.   [Exit.]

MAR. Go shake your ears.

SIR AND. 'Twere as good a deed as to drink when a man's a-hungry, to challenge him the field, and then to break promise with him and make a fool of him.

SIR TO. Do 't, knight. I'll write thee a challenge, or I'll deliver thy indignation to him by word of mouth.

MAR. Sweet Sir Toby, be patient for to-   142
night. Since the youth of the Count's was today with my lady, she is much out of quiet. For Mon-sieur Malvolio, let me alone with him. If I do not gull him into a nayword,° and make him a common recreation,° do not think I have wit enough to lie straight in my bed. I know I can do it.

SIR TO. Possess us, possess us. Tell us something of him.   150

MAR. Marry, sir, sometimes he is a kind of Puritan.

SIR AND. Oh, if I thought that, I'd beat him like a dog!

SIR TO. What, for being a Puritan? Thy exquisite reason, dear knight?

SIR AND. I have no exquisite reason for 't, but I have reason good enough.

MAR. The devil a Puritan that he is, or anything constantly, but a timepleaser;° an affec-   160

---

80. **Cataian:** Chinaman. **politicians:** deep ones.   81. **Peg-a-Ramsey:** It is not known who this lady was or why Malvolio resembled her.   82. **consanguineous:** related by blood. Toby's mind has now strayed to Olivia.   83. **Tillyvally:** "hoity-toity."   85: **Beshrew me:** lit., ill luck take me.   96. **coziers:** cobblers.   101. **Sneck up:** be hanged.   102. **round:** direct.   109-21. **Farewell . . . not:** Toby and the Clown here indulge in an impromptu duet.

129. **chain:** i.e., of office as a steward. **with crumbs:** used for polishing silver.   132. **uncivil rule:** disorderly conduct.   146. **nayword:** byword.   146-47. **common recreation:** general laughing-stock.   160. **timepleaser:** one who suits his behavior to his advantage.

tioned° ass, that cons state° without book and utters it by great swarths—the best persuaded of himself, so crammed, as he thinks, with excellencies, that it is his grounds of faith that all that look on him love him. And on that vice in him will my revenge find notable cause to work.

SIR TO. What wilt thou do?

MAR. I will drop in his way some obscure epistles of love, wherein, by the color of his beard, the shape of his leg, the manner of his gait, the expres- 170 sure of his eye, forehead, and complexion, he shall find himself most feelingly° personated. I can write very like my lady your niece. On a forgotten matter we can hardly make distinction of our hands.

SIR TO. Excellent! I smell a device.

SIR AND. I have 't in my nose too.

SIR TO. He shall think, by the letters that thou wilt drop, that they come from my niece, and that she's in love with him.   180

MAR. My purpose is indeed a horse of that color.

SIR AND. And your horse now would make him an ass.

MAR. Ass, I doubt not.

SIR AND. Oh, 'twill be admirable!

MAR. Sport royal, I warrant you. I know my physic will work with him. I will plant you two, and let the fool make a third, where he shall find the letter. Observe his construction of it. For 190 this night, to bed, and dream on the event. Fare-well.   [Exit.]

SIR TO. Good night, Penthesilea.°

SIR AND. Before me, she's a good wench.

SIR TO. She's a beagle,° true-bred, and one that adores me. What o' that?

SIR AND. I was adored once too.

SIR TO. Let's to bed, knight. Thou hadst need send for more money.

SIR AND. If I cannot recover° your niece, I am a foul way out.°   201

SIR TO. Send for money, knight. If thou hast her not i' the end, call me cut.°

SIR AND. If I do not, never trust me, take it how you will.

SIR TO. Come, come, I'll go burn some sack.° 'Tis too late to go to bed now. Come, knight, come, knight.   [Exeunt.]

SCENE IV. *The* DUKE'S *palace.*

[*Enter* DUKE, VIOLA, CURIO, *and others.*]

DUKE. Give me some music. Now, good morrow, friends.

Now, good Cesario, but that piece of song,°
That old and antique song we heard last night.
Methought it did relieve my passion much,
More than light airs and recollected terms°
Of these most brisk and giddy-pacèd° times.
Come, but one verse.

CUR. He is not here, so please your lordship, that should sing it.

DUKE. Who was it?   10

CUR. Feste, the jester, my lord, a fool that the Lady Olivia's father took much delight in. He is about the house.

DUKE. Seek him out, and play the tune the while.
                    [*Exit* CURIO. *Music plays.*]
Come hither, boy. If ever thou shalt love,
In the sweet pangs of it remember me;
For such as I am all true lovers are,
Unstaid and skittish in all motions else
Save in the constant image of the creature
That is beloved. How dost thou like this tune?   20

VIO. It gives a very echo to the seat
Where Love is throned.

DUKE.   Thou dost speak masterly.
My life upon 't, young though thou art, thine eye
Hath stayed upon some favor° that it loves.
Hath it not, boy?

VIO.   A little, by your favor.

DUKE. What kind of woman is 't?

VIO.   Of your complexion.

DUKE. She is not worth thee, then. What years, i' faith?

VIO. About your years, my lord.

DUKE. Too old, by Heaven. Let still° the woman take   30
An elder than herself, so wears she to him,
So sways she level in her husband's heart.
For, boy, however we do praise ourselves,
Our fancies are more giddy and unfirm,
More longing, wavering, sooner lost and worn,
Than women's are.

VIO.   I think it well, my lord.

DUKE. Then let thy love be younger than thyself,
Or thy affection cannot hold the bent.°

---

affectioned: affected.   161. cons state: learns courtly behavior by heart.   172. feelingly: exactly.   192. Penthesilea: Queen of the Amazons, a large muscular lady—an ironical description of the little gentlewoman.   195. beagle: a small hound.   200. recover: win.   201. foul...out: have wasted a lot of money.   203. cut: gelded.   206. burn... sack: warm some sack. Sack (Falstaff's favorite drink; see *II Hen IV*, IV.iii. 103–35) was a Spanish wine. It was sometimes sweetened and drunk warm.

Sc. iv: 2. piece of song: another indication that Viola was originally intended to be the singer. See I.ii.57,n.   5. recollected terms: artificial phrases.   6. giddy-paced: frivolous.   25. favor: face. Viola (l. 26) in the safety of disguise takes up the word "by your favor," which Orsino interprets as "by your leave."   30. still: always.   38. hold...bent: keep the tension; the image is of a strung bow.

For women are as roses, whose fair flower
Being once displayed, doth fall that very hour.   40
   VIO. And so they are. Alas, that they are so—
To die, even when they to perfection grow!
        [*Re-enter* CURIO *and* CLOWN.]
   DUKE. Oh, fellow, come, the song we had last
   night.
Mark it, Cesario, it is old and plain.
The spinsters and the knitters in the sun
And the free maids that weave their thread with
   bones°
Do use to chant it. It is silly sooth,°
And dallies with the innocence of love,
Like the old age.
   CLO. Are you ready, sir?   50
   DUKE. Aye, prithee sing.   [*Music.*]
   CLO. [*Sings.*]
Come away, come away, death,
   And in sad cypress° let me be laid.
Fly away, fly away, breath,
   I am slain by a fair cruel maid.
My shroud° of white, stuck all with yew,
   Oh, prepare it!
My part of death, no one so true
   Did share it!

Not a flower, not a flower sweet,   60
   On my black coffin let there be strown.
Not a friend, not a friend greet
   My poor corpse, where my bones shall be
     thrown.
A thousand thousand sighs to save,
   Lay me, oh, where
Sad true lover never find my grave,
   To weep there!
   DUKE. There's for thy pains.   69
   CLO. No pains, sir. I take pleasure in singing, sir.
   DUKE. I'll pay thy pleasure then.
   CLO. Truly, sir, and pleasure will be paid, one
time or another.
   DUKE. Give me now leave to leave thee.
   CLO. Now, the melancholy god protect thee, and
the tailor make thy doublet° of changeable° taffeta,
for thy mind is a very opal. I would have men of
such constancy° put to sea, that their business might
be everything and their intent everywhere; for
that's it that always makes a good voyage of   80
nothing. Farewell.   [*Exit.*]
   DUKE. Let all the rest give place.

[CURIO *and* ATTENDANTS *retire.*]
              Once more, Cesario,
Get thee to yond same sovereign cruelty.
Tell her my love, more noble than the world,
Prizes not quantity of dirty lands.
The parts° that fortune hath bestowed upon her,
Tell her I hold as giddily as fortune.°
But 'tis that miracle and queen of gems
That nature pranks° her in attracts my soul.
   VIO. But if she cannot love you, sir?   90
   DUKE. I cannot be so answered.
   VIO.   Sooth, but you must.
Say that some lady, as perhaps there is,
Hath for your love as great a pang of heart
As you have for Olivia. You cannot love her,
You tell her so. Must she not then be answered?
   DUKE. There is no woman's sides
Can bide the beating of so strong a passion
As love doth give my heart, no woman's heart
So big to hold so much. They lack retention.
Alas, their love may be called appetite—   100
No motion of the liver,° but the palate—
That suffer surfeit, cloyment, and revolt;
But mine is all as hungry as the sea,
And can digest as much. Make no compare
Between that love a woman can bear me
And that I owe Olivia.
   VIO.   Aye, but I know——
   DUKE. What dost thou know?
   VIO. Too well what love women to men may
   owe.
In faith, they are as true of heart as we.
My father had a daughter loved a man,
As it might be, perhaps, were I a woman,   110
I should your lordship.
   DUKE.   And what's her history?
   VIO. A blank, my lord. She never told her love,
But let concealment, like a worm i' the bud,
Feed on her damask° cheek. She pined in thought,
And with a green and yellow melancholy
She sat like Patience on a monument,°
Smiling at grief. Was not this love indeed?
We men may say more, swear more, but indeed
Our shows are more than will,° for still we prove
Much in our vows, but little in our love.   121
   DUKE. But died thy sister of her love, my boy?
   VIO. I am all the daughters of my father's house,
And all the brothers too. And yet I know not.
Sir, shall I to this lady?

---

46. **weave . . . bones:** i.e., make lace with bone bobbins.
47. **silly sooth:** simple truth.   53. **cypress:** coffin of cypress
wood.   56. **shroud:** burial dress.   76. **doublet:** short jacket,
often made of silk.   **changeable:** changing its color as the light
falls.   78. **such constancy:** The fool is ironical, for Orsino
hitherto has been "to one thing constant never."

86. **parts:** wealth.   87. **giddily as fortune:** i.e., I am not
interested in her wealth.   89. **pranks:** adorns.   101. **liver:**
true passion, as in I.i.37.   115. **damask:** color of the damask
rose, pink and white.   117. **Patience . . . monument:** a
statue of Patience.   120. **Our . . . will:** our outward appearances are greater than our feelings.

DUKE.   Aye, that's the theme.
To her in haste. Give her this jewel. Say
My love can give no place, bide no denay.°

                                    [*Exeunt.*]

SCENE V. OLIVIA'S *garden.*

[*Enter* SIR TOBY, SIR ANDREW, *and* FABIAN.]
SIR TO. Come thy ways, Signior Fabian.
FAB. Nay, I'll come. If I lose a scruple° of this
sport, let me be boiled to death with melancholy.
SIR TO. Wouldst thou not be glad to have the nig-
gardly rascally sheepbiter° come by some notable
shame?
FAB. I would exult, man. You know he brought
me out o' favor with my lady about a bearbaiting°
here.   10
SIR TO. To anger him we'll have the bear again,
and we will fool him black and blue. Shall we not
Sir Andrew?
SIR AND. An we do not, it is pity of our lives.
SIR TO. Here comes the little villain. [*Enter* MARIA.]
How now, my metal of India!°
MAR. Get ye all three into the box tree.° Malvolio's coming down this walk. He has been yonder i'
the sun practicing behavior to his own shadow   20
this half-hour. Observe him, for the love of mockery, for I know this letter will make a contemplative
idiot° of him. Close, in the name of jesting! Lie thou
there, [*throws down a letter*] for here comes the trout
that must be caught with tickling.°   [*Exit.*]
[*Enter* MALVOLIO.]
MAL. 'Tis but fortune, all is fortune. Maria once
told me she did affect me.° And I have heard herself come thus near, that, should she fancy, it should
be one of my complexion. Besides, she uses me   30
with a more exalted respect than anyone else that
follows her. What should I think on 't?
SIR TO. Here's an overweening rogue!
FAB. Oh, peace! Contemplation makes a rare
turkeycock of him. How he jets under his advanced
plumes!°
SIR AND. 'Slight,° I could so beat the rogue!
SIR TO. Peace, I say.
MAL. To be Count Malvolio!   40
SIR TO. Ah, rogue!

SIR AND. Pistol him, pistol him.
SIR TO. Peace, peace!
MAL. There is example for 't. The lady of the
Strachy° married the yeoman of the wardrobe.°
SIR AND. Fie on him, Jezebel!°
FAB. Oh, peace! Now he's deeply in. Look how
imagination blows him.
MAL. Having been three months married to her,
sitting in my state°——   50
SIR TO. Oh, for a stonebow,° to hit him in the eye!
MAL. Calling my officers about me, in my
branched° velvet gown, having come from a day
bed,° where I have left Olivia sleeping——
SIR TO. Fire and brimstone!
FAB. Oh, peace, peace!
MAL. And then to have the humor of state.° And
after a demure travel of regard,° telling them I
know my place as I would they should do theirs,
to ask for my kinsman Toby——   61
SIR TO. Bolts and shackles!
FAB. Oh, peace, peace, peace! Now, now.
MAL. Seven of my people, with an obedient start,
make out for him. I frown the while, and perchance
wind up my watch, or play with my—some
rich jewel.° Toby approaches, curtsies there to
me——
SIR TO. Shall this fellow live?
FAB. Though our silence be drawn from us with
cars,° yet peace.   71
MAL. I extend my hand to him thus, quenching
my familiar smile with an austere regard of con-
trol°——
SIR TO. And does not Toby take you a blow o' the
lips then?
MAL. Saying, "Cousin Toby, my fortunes having
cast me on your niece, give me this prerogative° of
speech——"
SIR TO. What, what?   80
MAL. "You must amend your drunkenness."
SIR TO. Out, scab!
FAB. Nay, patience, or we break the sinews of our
plot.

44-45. lady ... Strachy: She has not been identified.   45. yeoman . . . wardrobe: in a great household each department
was under the control of a *yeoman*, or upper servant, and a
"gentleman servingman."   46. Jezebel: Andrew's knowledge
of the Bible is weak, but at least he does know that Jezebel was
a shameless person. See I Kings 34; II Kings 9:30–37.   50. state:
chair of state.   51. stonebow: crossbow for shooting stones.
54. branched: embroidered with a pattern of leaves and
branches.   55. day bed: couch.   58. humor of state:
dignified manner of some statesman.   59. demure...regard:
glancing gravely from one to the other.   66-67. my—some
rich jewel: Malvolio inadvertently touches his steward's
chain.   71. drawn ... cars: though we should be torn
to pieces by chariots and wild horses.   73-74. austere . . .
control: severe look of authority.   78. prerogative: privilege.

127. denay: denial.
Sc. v: 2. scruple: minute part.   5. sheepbiter: sheepstealer.
9. bearbaiting: a popular and cruel sport, detested by the
Puritans.   17. metal of India: fine gold.   18. box tree: an
evergreen shrub much used by Elizabethan gardeners for
ornamental hedges.   22. contemplative idiot: pompous ass.
26. caught . . . tickling: a poacher's method of catching trout
with the bare hand.   28. she . . . me: Olivia liked me.
36-37. jets . . . plumes: struts with his tail feathers up.
38. 'Slight: by God's light.

MAL. "Besides, you waste the treasure of your time with a foolish knight——"

SIR AND. That's me, I warrant you.

MAL. "One Sir Andrew——"

SIR AND. I knew 'twas I, for many do call me fool.

MAL. What employment have we here?   91

[*Taking up the letter.*]

FAB. Now is the woodcock° near the gin.°

SIR TO. Oh, peace! And the spirit of humors° intimate reading aloud to him!

MAL. By my life, this is my lady's hand. These be her very C's, her U's, and her T's; and thus makes she her great P's. It is, in contempt of question,° her hand.

SIR AND. Her C's, her U's and her T's. Why that?   100

MAL. [*Reads.*] "To the unknown beloved, this, and my good wishes:—" Her very phrases! By your leave, wax.° Soft, and the impressure her Lucrece,° with which she uses to seal. 'Tis my lady. To whom should this be?

FAB. This wins, him, liver and all.

MAL. [*Reads.*] "Jove knows I love.

But who?

Lips, do not move.

No man must know."   110

"No man must know." What follows? The numbers° altered! "No man must know." If this should be thee, Malvolio?

SIR TO. Marry, hang thee, brock!°

MAL. [*Reads.*]

"I may command where I adore,

But silence, like a Lucrece knife,°

With bloodless stroke my heart doth gore.

M, O, A, I, doth sway my life."

FAB. A fustian° riddle!

SIR TO. Excellent wench, say I.   120

MAL. "M, O, A, I, doth sway my life." Nay, but first, let me see, let me see, let me see.

FAB. What dish o' poison has she dressed him!

SIR TO. And with what wing the staniel° checks at it!

MAL. "I may command where I adore." Why, she may command me. I serve her, she is my lady. Why, this is evident to any formal capacity,° there is no obstruction in this. And the end—what should that alphabetical position portend? If I   130

could make that resemble something in me—— Softly! M, O, A, I——

SIR TO. Oh, aye, make up that. He is now at a cold scent.

FAB. Sowter° will cry upon 't for all this, though it be as rank as a fox.°

MAL. M—Malvolio. M—why, that begins my name.

FAB. Did not I say he would work it out? The cur is excellent at faults.°   140

MAL. M—but then there is no consonancy° in the sequel, that suffers under probation.° A should follow, but O does.

FAB. And O shall end, I hope.

SIR TO. Aye, or I'll cudgel him and make him cry O!

MAL. And then I comes behind.

FAB. Aye, an you had any eye behind you, you might see more detraction at your heels than fortunes before you.   150

MAL. M, O, A, I. This simulation° is not as the former. And yet, to crush° this a little, it would bow to me,° for every one of these letters are in my name. Soft! Here follows prose. [*Reads.*]

"If this fall into thy hand, revolve.° In my stars° I am above thee; but be not afraid of greatness. Some are born great, some achieve greatness, and some have greatness thrust upon 'em. Thy Fates open their hands. Let thy blood and spirit embrace them, and to inure thyself to what thou art like to be,   160 cast thy humble slough° and appear fresh. Be opposite with a kinsman, surly with servants, let thy tongue tang° arguments of state, put thyself into the trick of singularity.° She thus advises thee that sighs for thee. Remember who commended thy yellow stockings, and wished to see thee ever cross-gartered.° I say, remember. Go to, thou art made, if thou desirest to be so. If not, let me see thee a steward still, the fellow of servants, and not worthy to touch Fortune's fingers. Farewell. She that   170 would alter services with thee,

THE FORTUNATE-UNHAPPY"

Daylight and champain° discovers not more. This is open. I will be proud, I will read politic authors,°

92. **woodcock:** regarded as a very simple bird. **gin:** trap. 93. **spirit of humors:** i.e., of mockery, as in a Comedy of Humors, fashionable at this time. 97. **contempt of question:** without any doubt.   103. **wax:** used to seal. **her Lucrece:** the head of Lucrece, the device on her seal.   112. **numbers:** meter.   114. **brock:** badger.   116. **Lucrece knife:** the knife with which Lucrece killed herself.   119. **fustian:** coarse cloth, so "common."   124. **staniel:** kestrel, an inferior kind of hunting hawk.   128. **formal capacity:** normal intelligence.

135. **Sowter:** lit., cobbler, nickname for a clumsy hound. 135-36. **cry . . . fox:** he'll make a great cry, and follow it up, for the scent is as strong as a fox's.   140. **excellent at faults:** will follow the scent, however bad. **fault:** a break in scent. 141. **consonancy:** consistency.   142. **suffers . . . probation:** fails when tested.   151. **simulation:** disguised meaning. 152. **crush:** force.   152-53. **bow . . . me:** incline my way. 155. **revolve:** ponder. **stars:** fate.   161. **slough:** snakeskin. 163. **tang:** resound.   164. **trick of singularity:** unusual behavior.   166-67. **cross-gartered:** The garter was passed round the leg beneath the knee, crossed at the back, and tied above the knee. 174. **champain:** open country.   175-76. **politic authors:** books on statecraft.

I will baffle° Sir Toby, I will wash off gross acquaintance, I will be point-device° the very man. I do not now fool myself, to let imagination jade me,° for every reason excites to this, that my lady loves me. She did commend my yellow stock-   180 ings of late, she did praise my leg being cross-gartered; and in this she manifests herself to my love, and with a kind of injunction drives me to these habits of her liking. I thank my stars I am happy. I will be strange,° stout,° in yellow stockings, and cross-gartered, even with the swiftness of putting on. Jove and my stars be praised! Here is yet a postscript.   [*Reads.*]

"Thou canst not choose but know who I am. If thou entertainest my love, let it appear in thy   190 smiling. Thy smiles become thee well, therefore in my presence still smile, dear my sweet, I prithee." Jove, I thank thee. I will smile, I will do everything that thou wilt have me.   [*Exit.*]

FAB. I will not give my part of this sport for a pension of thousands to be paid from the Sophy.°

SIR TO. I could marry this wench for this de-vice——   200

SIR AND. So could I too.

SIR TO. And ask no other dowry with her but such another jest.

SIR AND. Nor I neither.

FAB. Here comes my noble gull-catcher.°

[*Re-enter* MARIA.]

SIR TO. Wilt thou set thy foot o' my neck?

SIR AND. Or o' mine either?

SIR TO. Shall I play my freedom at trey-trip,° and become thy bondslave?

SIR AND. I' faith, or I either?   210

SIR TO. Why, thou hast put him in such a dream that when the image of it leaves him he must run mad.

MAR. Nay, but say true. Does it work upon him?

SIR TO. Like aqua vitae° with a midwife.

MAR. If you will then see the fruits of the sport, mark his first approach before my lady. He will come to her in yellow stockings, and 'tis a color she abhors, and cross-gartered, a fashion she de-   220 tests. And he will smile upon her, which will now be so unsuitable to her disposition, being addicted to a melancholy as she is, that it cannot but turn him into a notable contempt. If you will see it, follow me.

SIR TO. To the gates of Tartar, thou most excellent devil of wit!

SIR AND. I'll make one too.   [*Exeunt.*]

ACT III

SCENE I. OLIVIA'S *garden.*

[*Enter* VIOLA, *and* CLOWN *with a tabor.°*]

VIO. Save thee, friend, and thy music. Dost thou live by thy tabor?

CLO. No, sir, I live by the church.

VIO. Art thou a churchman?°

CLO. No such matter, sir. I do live by the church, for I do live at my house, and my house doth stand by° the church.

VIO. So thou mayst say the King lies by a beggar, if a beggar dwell near him, or the church stands by thy tabor, if thy tabor stand by the church.   11

CLO. You have said, sir. To see this age! A sentence is but a cheveril° glove to a good wit. How quickly the wrong side may be turned outward!

VIO. Nay, that's certain. They that dally° nicely with words may quickly make them wanton.

CLO. I would, therefore, my sister had had no name, sir.   20

VIO. Why, man?

CLO. Why, sir, her name's a word, and to dally with that word might make my sister wanton. But indeed words are very rascals since bonds disgraced them.°

VIO. Thy reason, man?

CLO. Troth, sir, I can yield you none without words, and words are grown so false I am loath to prove reason with them.   29

VIO. I warrant thou art a merry fellow and carest for nothing.

CLO. Not so, sir. I do care for something, but in my conscience, sir, I do not care for you. If that be to care for nothing, sir, I would it would make you invisible.

VIO. Art not thou the Lady Olivia's fool?

CLO. No indeed, sir. The Lady Olivia has no folly. She will keep no fool, sir, till she be married, and fools are as like husbands as pilchards° are to herrings—the husband's the bigger. I am indeed not her fool, but her corrupter of words.   41

VIO. I saw thee late at the Count Orsino's.

CLO. Foolery, sir, does walk about the orb like

---

176. **baffle:** bring into disgrace.   177. **point-device:** exactly. 178. **jade me:** play me a dirty trick.   185. **strange:** distant. **stout:** haughty.   198. **Sophy:** Shah of Persia.   205. **gull-catcher:** fool-catcher.   208. **trey-trip:** game played with cards and dice.   216. **aqua vitae:** spirits especially favored by old women such as Juliet's Nurse. See *R & J.* IV.v.16.

Act. III, Sc. i: s.d., **tabor:** small drum.   4. **churchman:** cleric.   7. **by:** near.   14. **cheveril:** kidskin.   16. **dally:** play.   23-25. **sister . . . them:** an allusion not certainly identified.   39. **pilchard:** a smaller variety of herring.

the sun. It shines everywhere. I would be sorry,
sir, but the fool should be as oft with your master as
with my mistress. I think I saw your wisdom there.

VIO. Nay, an thou pass upon° me. I'll no more
with thee. Hold, there's expenses for thee.

CLO. Now Jove, in his next commodity° of hair,
send thee a beard!   51

VIO. By my troth, I'll tell thee, I am almost sick
for one—[Aside] though I would not have it grow
on my chin. Is thy lady within?

CLO. Would not a pair of these° have bred, sir?

VIO. Yes, being kept together and put to use.

CLO. I would play Lord Pandarus° of Phrygia,°
sir, to bring a Cressida to this Troilus.

VIO. I understand you, sir. 'Tis well begged.   60

CLO. The matter, I hope, is not great, sir, begging
but a beggar.° Cressida was a beggar. My lady is
within, sir. I will construe to them whence you
come; who you are and what you would are out of
my welkin— I might say "element,"° but the word
is overworn.   [Exit.]

VIO. This fellow° is wise enough to play the fool,
And to do that well craves° a kind of wit.
He must observe their mood on whom he jests,
The quality of persons, and the time,   70
And, like the haggard,° check at° every feather
That comes before his eye. This is a practice
As full of labor as a wise man's art.
For folly that he wisely shows is fit,
But wise men, folly-fall'n, quite taint their wit.

              [Enter SIR TOBY, and SIR ANDREW.]

SIR TO. Save° you, gentleman.

VIO. And you, sir.

SIR AND. Dieu vous garde, monsieur.

VIO. Et vous aussi. Votre serviteur.

SIR AND. I hope, sir, you are, and I am yours.   81

SIR TO. Will you encounter° the house? My niece
is desirous you should enter, if your trade be to her.

VIO. I am bound to your niece, sir. I mean she is
the list° of my voyage.

SIR TO. Taste your legs, sir, put them to motion.

VIO. My legs do better understand me, sir, than I
understand what you mean by bidding me taste my
legs.   91

SIR TO. I mean to go, sir, to enter.

VIO. I will answer you with gait and entrance.
But we are prevented.° [Enter OLIVIA and MARIA.]
Most excellent accomplished lady, the heavens
rain odors on you!

SIR AND. That youth's a rare courtier. "Rain
odors," well.

VIO. My matter hath no voice, lady, but to your
own most pregnant° and vouchsafed° ear.   100

SIR AND. "Odors," "pregnant," and "vouchsafed." I'll get 'em all three all ready.

OLI. Let the garden door be shut, and leave me
to my hearing. [Exeunt SIR TOBY, SIR ANDREW, and
MARIA.] Give me your hand, sir.

VIO. My duty, madam, and most humble service.

OLI. What is your name?

VIO. Cesario is your servant's name, fair Princess.

OLI. My servant, sir! 'Twas never merry world
Since lowly feigning was called compliment.   110
You're servant to the Count Orsino, youth.

VIO. And he is yours, and his must needs be yours.
Your servant's servant is your servant, madam.

OLI. For him, I think not on him. For his
        thoughts,
Would they were blanks rather than filled with me!

VIO. Madam, I come to whet your gentle
        thoughts
On his behalf.

OLI.   Oh, by your leave, I pray you,
I bade you never speak again of him.
But would you undertake another suit,
I had rather hear you to solicit that   120
Than music from the spheres.°

VIO.   Dear lady——

OLI. Give me leave, beseech you. I did send,
After the last enchantment you did here,
A ring in chase of you. So did I abuse°
Myself, my servant, and, I fear me, you.
Under your hard construction° must I sit,
To force that on you, in a shameful cunning,
Which you knew none of yours. What might you
        think?
Have you not set mine honor at the stake
And baited it with all the unmuzzled thoughts°
That tyrannous heart can think? To one of your
        receiving°   131

48. pass upon: make a thrust at.   50. commodity: consign
ment.   55. pair of these: i.e., wouldn't you like to give me
another coin?   57. Pandarus: the go-between in the love
affair of Cressida and Troilus. See Tr & Cr. Phrygia: the
district of Asia Minor in which Troy stood.   61-62. The . . .
beggar: the Clown is himself an incorrigible beggar. See
V.i.31-42.   65. welkin . . . element: both words mean sky.
Element is still overworn by writers of textbooks who cannot
avoid the "supernatural element," the "pastoral element," etc.
67. This fellow: i.e., Robert Armin, the Company's new
clown.   68. craves: calls for.   71. haggard: wild hawk. As
this line seems to contradict the preceding, some editors
emend "And" to "But." check at: go after.   76. Save: God
save.   82. encounter: lit., go to meet. Toby addresses this
young courtier with the extravagant terms fashionable at the
time.   86. list: boundary, objective.

94. prevented: forestalled.   100. pregnant: receptive.
vouchsafed: condescending.   121. music . . . spheres:
sweet and perfect harmony.   124. abuse: wrong.   126. construction: interpretation, judgment.   129. at . . . thoughts:
An image from bearbaiting. See II.v.9.   131. receiving:
understanding.

Enough is shown. A cypress,° not a bosom,
Hides my heart. So let me hear you speak.

VIO. I pity you.

OLI.   That's a degree to love.

VIO. No, not a grize,° for 'tis a vulgar proof°
That very oft we pity enemies.

OLI. Why, then, methinks 'tis time to smile again.
O world, how apt the poor are to be proud!
If one should be a prey, how much the better
To fall before the lion than the wolf!   140

[Clock strikes.]

The clock upbraids me with the waste of time.
Be not afraid, good youth, I will not have you.
And yet, when wit and youth is come to harvest,
Your wife is like to reap a proper man.
There lies your way, due west.

VIO.   Then westward ho!°

Grace and good disposition attend your ladyship!
You'll nothing, madam, to my lord by me?

OLI. Stay.
I prithee tell me what thou think'st of me.   150

VIO. That you do think you are not what you are.

OLI. If I think so, I think the same of you.

VIO. Then think you right. I am not what I am.

OLI. I would you were as I would have you be!

VIO. Would it be better, madam, than I am?
I wish it might, for now I am your fool.

OLI. Oh, what a deal of scorn looks beautiful
In the contempt and anger of his lip!
A murderous guilt shows not itself more soon
Than love that would seem hid. Love's night is
     noon.   160
Cesario, by the roses of the spring,
By maidhood, honor, truth, and everything,
I love thee so, that, mauger° all thy pride,
Nor wit nor reason can my passion hide.
Do not extort thy reasons from this clause,
But rather reason thus with reason fetter,
Love sought is good, but given unsought is better.°

VIO. By innocence I swear, and by my youth,
I have one heart, one bosom, and one truth,   170
And that no woman has; nor never none
Shall mistress be of it, save I alone.
And so adieu, good madam. Nevermore
Will I my master's tears to you deplore.

OLI. Yet come again, for thou perhaps mayst
     move

That heart which now abhors to like his love.

[Exeunt.]

SCENE II. OLIVIA's *house.*

[*Enter* SIR TOBY, SIR ANDREW, *and* FABIAN.]

SIR AND. No, faith, I'll not stay a jot longer.

SIR TO. Thy reason, dear venom,° give thy reason.

FAB. You must needs yield your reason, Sir Andrew.

SIR AND. Marry, I saw your niece do more favors
to the Count's servingman° than ever she bestowed
upon me. I saw't i' the orchard.

SIR TO. Did she see thee the while, old boy? Tell
me that.   10

SIR AND. As plain as I see you now.

FAB. This was a great argument of love in her toward you.

SIR AND. 'Slight, will you make an ass o' me?

FAB. I will prove it legitimate, sir, upon the oaths
of judgment and reason.

SIR TO. And they have been grand jurymen° since
before Noah was a sailor.

FAB. She did show favor to the youth in your
sight only to exasperate you, to awake your   20
dormouse valor, to put fire in your heart and brimstone in your liver. You should then have accosted
her, and with some excellent jests, fire-new from
the mint,° you should have banged the youth into
dumbness. This was looked for at your hand, and
this was balked. The double gilt° of this opportunity you let time wash off, and you are now sailed
into the north of my lady's opinion, where you will
hang like an icicle on a Dutchman's beard unless
you do redeem it by some laudable attempt either
of valor or policy.   31

SIR AND. An 't be any way, it must be with valor
for policy I hate. I had as lief be a Brownist° as a
politician.

SIR TO. Why then, build me thy fortunes upon the
basis of valor. Challenge me the Count's youth to
fight with him. Hurt him in eleven places. My niece
shall take note of it, and assure thyself there is no
love broker° in the world can more prevail in

---

132. **cypress:** a sheer material.   135. **grize:** step. **vulgar
proof:** common experience.   145. **westward ho:** the cry
of the Thames watermen, who carried passengers up or down
the river.   163. **mauger:** in spite of.   165-68. **Do...better:**
i.e., do not argue to yourself that because I (the woman) am the
wooer, you should therefore have no reason to return my love;
rather rebut that argument by this—it is good for a man to ask
for a woman's love, but better still to receive it without asking.

Sc. ii: 2. **venom:** poison, because Andrew is full of hate.
7. **servingman:** attendant.   17. **grand juryman:** The
grand jury was chosen from the most respectable citizens.
Fabian means "Judgment and Reason have been a most
highly respected pair since the Flood."   23. **fire-new ...
mint:** i.e., as bright as new pennies.   26. **double gilt:** The
best gold plate was twice dipped. Fabian amuses himself and
Toby by puzzling Andrew with this metaphorical talk.
33. **Brownist:** The Brownists were one of the most extreme
sects of Puritans.   39. **love broker:** go-between in making a
marriage, an important office when marriages were arranged.

man's commendation with woman than report of valor. 41

FAB. There is no way but this, Sir Andrew.

SIR AND. Will either of you bear me a challenge to him?

SIR TO. Go, write it in a martial hand. Be curst° and brief. It is no matter how witty, so it be eloquent and full of invention.° Taunt him with the license of ink. If thou thou'st° him some thrice, it shall not be amiss. And as many lies as will lie 49 in thy sheet of paper, although the sheet were big enough for the bed of Ware° in England, set 'em down. Go, about it. Let there be gall° enough in thy ink, though thou write a goose pen,° no matter. About it.

SIR AND. Where shall I find you?

SIR TO. We'll call thee at the cubiculo.° Go.

[*Exit* SIR ANDREW.]

FAB. This is a dear manikin to you, Sir Toby.

SIR TO. I have been dear to him, lad, some two thousand strong, or so.°

FAB. We shall have a rare letter from him. But you'll not deliver 't? 61

SIR TO. Never trust me, then, and by all means stir on the youth to an answer. I think oxen and wainropes° cannot hale them together. For Andrew, if he were opened and you find so much blood in his liver as will clog the foot of a flea, I'll eat the rest of the anatomy.

FAB. And his opposite, the youth, bears in his visage no great presage of cruelty.

[*Enter* MARIA.]

SIR TO. Look where the youngest wren of nine° comes. 71

MAR. If you desire the spleen, and will laugh yourself into stitches, follow me. Yond gull Malvolio is turned heathen, a very renegado,° for there is no Christian that means to be saved by believing rightly can ever believe such impossible passages of grossness. He's in yellow stockings.

SIR TO. And cross-gartered? 79

MAR. Most villainously, like a pedant that keeps a school i' the church. I have dogged him like his

murderer. He does obey every point of the letter that I dropped to betray him. He does smile his face into more lines than is in the new map° with the augmentation of the Indies. You have not seen such a thing as 'tis. I can hardly forbear hurling things at him. I know my lady will strike him. If she do, he'll smile and take 't for a great favor.

SIR TO. Come, bring us, bring us where he is. 90

[*Exeunt.*]

SCENE III. *A street.*

[*Enter* SEBASTIAN *and* ANTONIO.]

SEB. I would not by my will have troubled you,
But since you make your pleasure of your pains,
I will no further chide you.

ANT. I could not stay behind you. My desire,
More sharp than filèd steel, did spur me forth;
And not all love to see you, though so much
As might have drawn one to a longer voyage,
But jealousy what might befall your travel,
Being skill-less in these parts, which to a stranger,
Unguided and unfriended, often prove 10
Rough and unhospitable. My willing love,
The rather by these arguments of fear,
Set forth in your pursuit.

SEB. My kind Antonio,
I can no other answer make but thanks,
And thanks, and everoft° good turns
Are shuffled off with such uncurrent° pay.
But were my worth as is my conscience firm,
You should find better dealing. What's to do?
Shall we go see the reliques° of this town?

ANT. Tomorrow, sir. Best first go see your lodging. 20

SEB. I am not weary, and 'tis long to night.
I pray you, let us satisfy our eyes
With the memorials and the things of fame
That do renown this city.

ANT. Would you'd pardon me.
I do not without danger walk these streets.
Once, in a sea fight, 'gainst the Count his galleys
I did some service, of such note indeed
That were I ta'en here it would scarce be answered.

SEB. Belike you slew great number of his people.

ANT. The offense is not of such a bloody nature,
Albeit the quality° of the time and quarrel 31
Might well have given us bloody argument.
It might have since been answered in repaying
What we took from them, which, for traffic's sake,°

---

46. **curst:** vicious. 47. **invention:** wit. 48. **thou thou'st:** to call a stranger "thou" was a considerable insult, as it implied that he was an inferior. 51. **bed of Ware:** a famous and enormous four-poster bed, formerly in an inn at Ware. It could hold 7 couples at a time. It is now in the Victoria and Albert Museum in London. 52. **gall:** "oak apple," produced in the branches of an oak by a parasite, and used for making ink. Toby puns on "gall," meaning bitterness. 53. **goose pen:** the pen used at this time was made of a goose quill. 56. **cubiculo:** bedchamber. 58-59. **I . . . so:** I've cost him some 2,000 ducats. 64. **wainropes:** cart ropes. 70. **youngest . . . nine:** the youngest of the brood, sometimes called the "rickling," is often smaller than the rest. The wren is the smallest of English birds. 74. **renegado:** Christian turned heathen.

84. **new map:** first published in 1600.

Sc. iii: 15. **and . . . oft:** Two words have apparently been omitted in this line. Some editors read "ever *thanks, and* oft." 16. **uncurrent:** worthless. 19. **reliques:** antiquities. 31. **quality:** nature. 34. **traffic's sake:** for the sake of business.

Most of our city did. Only myself stood out,
For which, if I be lapsèd° in this place,
I shall pay dear.

SEB.   Do not then walk too open.

ANT. It doth not fit me. Hold, sir, here's my
    purse.
In the south suburbs, at the Elephant,°
Is best to lodge. I will bespeak our diet°   40
While you beguile the time and feed your knowl-
    edge
With viewing of the town. There shall you have me.

SEB. Why I your purse?

ANT. Haply° your eye shall light upon some toy°
You have desire to purchase, and your store,
I think, is not for idle markets,° sir.

SEB. I'll be your purse bearer and leave you
For an hour.

ANT.   To the Elephant.

SEB. I do remember.   [*Exeunt.*]

SCENE IV. OLIVIA's *garden*.

[*Enter* OLIVIA *and* MARIA.]

OLI. I have sent after him. He says he'll come.
How shall I feast him? What bestow of him?°
For youth is bought more oft than begged or bor-
    rowed.
I speak too loud.
Where is Malvolio? He is sad and civil,°
And suits well for a servant with my fortunes.
Where is Malvolio?

MAR. He's coming, madam, but in very strange
manner. He is sure possessed,° madam.

OLI. Why, what's the matter? Does he rave?   10

MAR. No, madam, he does nothing but smile.
Your ladyship were best to have some guard about
you if he come, for sure the man is tainted in 's wits.

OLI. Go call him hither. [*Exit* MARIA.] I am as
    mad as he,
If sad and merry madness equal be.

[*Re-enter* MARIA, *with* MALVOLIO.]   How now,
    Malvolio!

MAL. Sweet lady, ho, ho.

OLI. Smilest thou?
I sent for thee upon a sad occasion.   20

MAL. Sad, lady? I could be sad. This does make
some obstruction in the blood, this cross-gartering,
but what of that? If it please the eye of one, it is

with me as the very true sonnet is, "Please one,
and please all."°

OLI. Why, how dost thou, man? What is the matter with thee?

MAL. Not black in my mind, though yellow in
my legs. It did come to his hands, and commands
shall be executed. I think we do know the sweet
Roman hand.°   31

OLI. Wilt thou go to bed, Malvolio?

MAL. To bed! Aye, sweetheart, and I'll come to
    thee.

OLI. God comfort thee! Why dost thou smile so
and kiss thy hand so oft?

MAR. How do you, Malvolio?

MAL. At your request! Yes, nightingales answer
daws.°

MAR. Why appear you with this ridiculous boldness before my lady?   41

MAL. "Be not afraid of greatness." 'Twas well
writ.

OLI. What meanest thou by that, Malvolio?

MAL. "Some are born great——"

OLI. Ha!

MAL. "Some achieve greatness——"

OLI. What sayest thou?

MAL. "And some have greatness thrust upon
them."   50

OLI. Heaven restore thee!

MAL. "Remember who commended thy yellow
stockings."

OLI. Thy yellow stockings!

MAL. "And wished to see thee cross-gartered."

OLI. Cross-gartered!

MAL. "Go to, thou art made, if thou desirest to
be so."

OLI. Am I made?   59

MAL. "If not, let me see thee a servant still."

OLI. Why, this is very midsummer madness.

[*Enter* SERVANT.]

SERV. Madam, the young gentleman of the
Count Orsino's is returned. I could hardly entreat
him back. He attends your ladyship's pleasure.

OLI. I'll come to him. [*Exit* SERVANT.] Good
Maria, let this fellow be looked to. Where's my
cousin Toby? Let some of my people have a special
care of him. I would not have him miscarry° for
the half of my dowry.   70

[*Exeunt* OLIVIA *and* MARIA.]

24-25. Please . . . all: The ditty is not a sonnet but a ballad, called "The crow sits upon the wall, Please one and please all." It was not at all the kind of song suitable for Malvolio.   **31. Roman hand:** The Italian handwriting (from which modern handwriting and *italic* type derives) was coming into fashion among aristocratic writers, and superseding the old English "Court" or "secretary" hand.   **38-39. nightingales . . . daws:** songbirds answer jackdaws.   **69. miscarry:** come to harm.

36. lapsed: taken.   **39. Elephant:** There was a famous London Inn of this name on the south side of the Thames; it is now known as the Elephant and Castle.   **40. bespeak . . . diet:** order our dinner.   **44. Haply:** perchance. **toy:** trifle. **46. idle markets:** unnecessary purchases.
  Sc. iv: 2. of him: on him.   **5. civil:** sober, serious.   **9. possessed:** i.e., with an evil spirit.

MAL. Oh, ho! Do you come near me now? No worse man than Sir Toby to look to me! This concurs directly with the letter. She sends him on purpose, that I may appear stubborn to him, for she incites me to that in the letter. "Cast thy humble slough," says she. "Be opposite with a kinsman, surly with servants, let thy tongue tang with arguments of state, put thyself into the trick of singularity"—and consequently sets down the manner how, as a sad face, a reverend carriage, a slow tongue, in the habit of some sir of note,° and   81 so forth. I have limed° her, but it is Jove's doing, and Jove make me thankful! And when she went away now, "Let this fellow be looked to." Fellow! Not Malvolio, nor after my degree, but fellow.° Why, everything adheres together, that no dram of a scruple,° no scruple of a scruple, no obstacle, no incredulous or unsafe circumstance——What can be said? Nothing that can be can come between me and the full prospect of my hopes.   90 Well, Jove, not I, is the doer of this, and he is to be thanked.

[*Re-enter* MARIA, *with* SIR TOBY *and* FABIAN.]

SIR TO. Which way is he, in the name of sanctity? If all the devils of Hell be drawn in little,° and Legion himself° possessed him, yet I'll speak to him.

FAB. Here he is, here he is. How is 't with you, sir? How is 't with you, man?

MAL. Go off, I discard you. Let me enjoy my private. Go off.   100

MAR. Lo, how hollow the fiend speaks within him! Did not I tell you? Sir Toby, my lady prays you to have a care of him.

MAL. Ah, ha! Does she so?

SIR TO. Go to, go to; peace, peace. We must deal gently with him. Let me alone. How do you, Malvolio? How is 't with you? What, man! defy the Devil. Consider, he's an enemy to mankind.

MAL. Do you know what you say?   110

MAR. La you, an you speak ill of the Devil, how he takes it at heart! Pray God he be not bewitched!

FAB. Carry his water° to the wise woman.

MAR. Marry, and it shall be done tomorrow

morning, if I live. My lady would not lose him for more than I'll say.

MAL. How now, mistress!

MAR. Oh Lord!   119

SIR TO. Prithee, hold thy peace, this is not the way. Do you not see you move him? Let me alone with him.

FAB. No way but gentleness—gently, gently. The fiend is rough, and will not be roughly used.

SIR TO. Why, how now, my bawcock!° How dost thou, chuck?°

MAL. Sir!

SIR TO. Aye, biddy,° come with me. What, man! 'Tis not for gravity to play at cherry pit° with Satan. Hang him, foul collier!°   130

MAR. Get him to say his prayers, good Sir Toby, get him to pray.

MAL. My prayers, minx!

MAR. No, I warrant you, he will not hear of godliness.°

MAL. Go, hang yourselves all! You are idle shallow things. I am not of your element. You shall know more hereafter.   [*Exit.*]

SIR TO. Is 't possible?

FAB. If this were played upon a stage now, I could condemn it as an improbable fiction.   141

SIR TO. His very genius° hath taken the infection° of the device,° man.

MAR. Nay, pursue him now, lest the device take air and taint.°

FAB. Why, we shall make him mad indeed.

MAR. The house will be the quieter.

SIR TO. Come, we'll have him in a dark room and bound. My niece is already in the belief that he's mad. We may carry it thus, for our pleasure   150 and his penance, till our very pastime, tired out of breath, prompt us to have mercy on him, at which time we will bring the device to the bar° and crown thee for a finder of madmen. But see, but see.

[*Enter* SIR ANDREW.]

FAB. More matter for a May morning.°

SIR AND. Here's the challenge, read it. I warrant there's vinegar and pepper in 't.

FAB. Is 't so saucy?   159

SIR AND. Aye, is 't, I warrant him. Do but read

81. sir of note: great man.   **82. limed:** caught, as with birdlime.   **86. fellow:** the word has a double meaning. The fellow of a college or learned society is a man of dignity; the word is also used of an inferior.   **87. dram . . . scruple:** minutest part.   **94. in little:** into a small space.   **95. Legion himself:** the name given to the devils cast out of the man from the tombs (Mark 5: 1–19). Toby pretends that Malvolio is possessed and treats him accordingly. Witches (who could be of either sex) were often accused of causing possession by evil spirits.   **114. his water:** diagnosis of diseases by inspection of the urine was practiced by qualified doctors as well as by quacks. Cf. the gloomy report on Falstaff's health (*II Hen IV,* I.ii.1–6).

125. bawcock: fine fellow. Toby humors Malvolio by talking baby talk to him.   **126. chuck:** chick.   **128. biddy:** child's name for a chick.   **129. cherry pit:** a game of throwing cherry stones into a hole.   **130. foul collier:** The Devil is a collier (coalman) because he is black.   **134-35. will . . . godliness:** One of the tests usually applied to a witch was to ask him to say the Lord's Prayer. If he could not, or would not, it was a most suspicious sign of guilt.   **142. genius:** guardian angel. **taken . . . infection:** caught the plague.   **143. device:** plan. **144-45. take . . . taint:** be spoiled and go bad.   **154. device . . . bar:** bring to public trial.   **156. May morning:** Mayday was a general holiday.

SIR TO. Give me. [*Reads.*] "Youth, whatsoever thou art, thou art but a scurvy fellow."

FAB. Good, and valiant.

SIR TO. [*Reads.*] "Wonder not, nor admire° not in thy mind, why I do call thee so, for I will show thee no reason for 't."

FAB. A good note. That keeps you from the blow of the law.   169

SIR TO. [*Reads.*] "Thou comest to the Lady Olivia, and in my sight she uses thee kindly; but thou liest in thy throat.° That is not the matter I challenge thee for."

FAB. Very brief, and to exceeding good sense—less.

SIR TO. [*Reads.*] "I will waylay thee going home, where if it be thy chance to kill me——"

FAB. Good.

SIR TO. [*Reads.*] "Thou killest me like a rogue and a villain."   180

FAB. Still you keep o' the windy side° of the law. Good.

SIR TO. [*Reads.*] "Fare thee well, and God have mercy upon one of our souls! He may have mercy upon mine, but my hope is better, and so look to thyself. Thy friend, as thou usest him, and thy sworn enemy,   ANDREW AGUECHEEK."
If this letter move him not, his legs cannot. I'll give 't him.   189

MAR. You may have very fit occasion for 't. He is now in some commerce with my lady, and will by and by depart.

SIR TO. Go, Sir Andrew. Scout me for him at the corner of the orchard like a bumbaily.° So soon as ever thou seest him, draw, and, as thou drawest, swear horrible; for it comes to pass oft that a terrible oath, with a swaggering accent sharply twanged off, gives manhood more approbation than ever proof itself would have earned him. Away!   200

SIR AND. Nay, let me alone for swearing.° [*Exit.*]

SIR TO. Now will not I deliver his letter, for the behavior of the young gentleman gives him out to be of good capacity and breeding. His employment between his lord and my niece confirms no less. Therefore this letter, being so excellently ignorant, will breed no terror in the youth. He will find it comes from a clodpole.° But, sir, I will deliver his challenge by word of mouth, set upon Aguecheek a notable report of valor, and drive the gentle- 210 man, as I know his youth will aptly receive it, into

a most hideous opinion of his rage, skill, fury, and impetuosity. This will so fright them both that they will kill one another by the look, like cocka-trices.°

[Re-enter OLIVIA, *with* VIOLA.]

FAB. Here he comes with your niece. Give them way till he take leave, and presently after him.

SIR TO. I will meditate the while upon some horrid message for a challenge.   220

[Exeunt SIR TOBY, FABIAN, *and* MARIA.]

OLI. I have said too much unto a heart of stone,
And laid mine honor too unchary° out.
There's something in me that reproves my fault,
But such a headstrong potent fault it is
That it but mocks reproof.

VIO.   With the same 'havior that your passion
        bears
Goes on my master's grief.

OLI. Here, wear this jewel for me, 'tis my picture.
Refuse it not, it hath no tongue to vex you.
And I beseech you come again tomorrow.   230
What shall you ask of me that I'll deny,
That honor saved may upon asking give?

VIO. Nothing but this—your true love for my
        master.

OLI. How with mine honor may I give him that
Which I have given to you?

VIO.   I will acquit° you.

OLI. Well, come again tomorrow. Fare thee well.
A fiend like thee might bear my soul to Hell. [*Exit.*]

[Re-enter SIR TOBY *and* FABIAN.]

SIR TO. Gentleman, God save thee.

VIO. And you, sir.   239

SIR TO. That defense thou hast, betake thee to 't. Of what nature the wrongs are thou hast done him, I know not, but thy interceptor, full of despite,° bloody as the hunter, attends thee at the orchard end. Dismount thy tuck,° be yare° in thy preparation, for thy assailant is quick, skillful, and deadly.

VIO. You mistake, sir. I am sure no man hath any quarrel to me. My remembrance is very free and clear from any image of offense done to any man.   250

SIR TO. You'll find it otherwise, I assure you. Therefore, if you hold your life at any price, betake you to your guard; for your opposite hath in him what youth, strength, skill, and wrath can furnish man withal.

VIO. I pray you, sir, what is he?

---

164. admire: be amazed.   **171-72. liest . . . throat:** This was the bitterest insult possible.   **181. windy side:** safe side.   **195. bumbaily:** sheriff's officer who made arrests for debt.   **201. let . . . swearing:** i. e., I'm an expert at swearing.   **208. clodpole:** blockhead.

215. cockatrice: a fabulous serpent, able to kill by its mere look.   **222. unchary:** heedlessly.   **235. acquit:** release from a payment.   **243. despite:** spite.   **244. tuck:** sword. **yare:** handy.

SIR TO. He is knight, dubbed° with unhatched° rapier and on carpet consideration,° but he is a devil in private brawl. Souls and bodies hath he divorced three, and his incensement at this moment is so implacable that satisfaction can be   260 none but by pangs of death and sepulcher. Hob, nob,° is his word, give 't or take 't.

VIO. I will return again into the house and desire some conduct of the lady. I am no fighter. I have heard of some kind of men that put quarrels purposely on others, to taste their valor. Belike this is a man of that quirk.°

SIR TO. Sir, no, his indignation derives itself out of a very competent° injury. Therefore get   270 you on and give him his desire. Back you shall not to the house, unless you undertake that with me which with as much safety you might answer him. Therefore on, or strip your sword stark-naked, for meddle you must, that's certain, or forswear° to wear iron about you.

VIO. This is as uncivil as strange. I beseech you, do me this courteous office, as to know of the knight what my offense to him is. It is something of my negligence, nothing of my purpose.   280

SIR TO. I will do so. Signior Fabian, stay you by this gentleman till my return.   [Exit.]

VIO. Pray you, sir, do you know of this matter?

FAB. I know the knight is incensed against you, even to a mortal arbitrament,° but nothing of the circumstance more.

VIO. I beseech you, what manner of man is he?

FAB. Nothing of that wonderful promise, to   290 read him by his form, as you are like to find him in the proof of his valor. He is, indeed, sir, the most skillful, bloody, and fatal opposite that you could possibly have found in any part of Illyria. Will you walk toward him? I will make your peace with him if I can.

VIO. I shall be much bound to you for 't. I am one that had rather go with sir priest° than sir knight. I care not who knows so much of my   299 mettle.   [Exeunt.]

_____ [Re-enter SIR TOBY, with SIR ANDREW.]

SIR TO. Why, man, he's a very devil. I have not seen such a firago.° I had a pass with him, rapier, scabbard, and all, and he gives me the stuck-in°

with such a mortal motion that it is inevitable; and on the answer, he pays you as surely as your feet hit the ground they step on. They say he has been fencer to the Sophy.

SIR AND. Pox on 't, I'll not meddle with him.

SIR TO. Aye, but he will not now be pacified. Fabian can scarce hold him yonder.   310

SIR AND. Plague on 't, an I thought he had been valiant and so cunning in fence, I'd have seen him damned ere I'd have challenged him. Let him let the matter slip, and I'll give him my horse, gray Capilet.

SIR TO. I'll make the motion. Stand here, make a good show on 't. This shall end without the perdition of souls. [Aside] Marry, I'll ride your horse as well as I ride you.   319

[Re-enter FABIAN and VIOLA.]

[To FABIAN] I have his horse to take up the quarrel. I have persuaded him the youth's a devil.

FAB. He is as horribly conceited° of him, and pants and looks pale, as if a bear were at his heels.

SIR TO. [To VIOLA] There's no remedy, sir, he will fight with you for 's oath sake. Marry, he hath better bethought him of his quarrel, and he finds that now scarce to be worth talking of. Therefore draw, for the supportance of his vow. He protests he will not hurt you.   330

VIO. [Aside.] Pray God defend me! A little thing would make me tell them how much I lack of a man.

FAB. Give ground, if you see him furious.

SIR TO. Come, Sir Andrew, there's no remedy. The gentleman will, for his honor's sake, have one bout with you. He cannot by the duello° avoid it. But he has promised me, as he is a gentleman and a soldier, he will not hurt you. Come on—to 't.   340

SIR AND. Pray God he keep his oath!

VIO. I do assure you 'tis against my will.

[They draw.]

[Enter ANTONIO.]

ANT. Put up your sword. If this young gentleman Have done offense, I take the fault on me. If you offend him, I for him defy you.

SIR TO. You, sir! Why, what are you?

ANT. One, sir, that for his love dares yet do more Than you have heard him brag to you he will.

SIR TO. Nay, if you be an undertaker,° I am   349 for you.   [They draw.]

[Enter OFFICERS.]

FAB. O good Sir Toby, hold! Here come the officers.

---

257. dubbed: knighted. **unhatched:** unhacked, not dented by use in battle.   **258. carpet consideration:** kneeling on a carpet, and not on the battlefield.   **262. Hob, nob:** hit or miss. **268. quirk:** whim.   **270. competent:** considerable. **275. forswear:** swear not to.   **286. mortal arbitrament:** decision by deadly combat.   **298. sir priest:** a Bachelor of Arts was termed "Dominus" (= Sir); in the class lists at Cambridge University the B.A.'s are still noted as "Ds." As most priests were graduates, they were called "Sir."   **302. firago:** for virago, a mannish woman.   **303. stuck-in:** thrust.

323. as . . . conceited: has as horrible ideas of.   **338. duello:** the rules of duelling, a matter of great importance to a man of honor.   **349. undertaker:** meddler.

SIR TO. To him, Sir Topas.   20

CLO. What ho,° I say! Peace in this prison!

SIR TO. The knave counterfeits well—a good knave.

MAL. [*Within*] Who calls there?

CLO. Sir Topas the curate, who comes to visit Malvolio the lunatic.

MAL. Sir Topas, Sir Topas, good Sir Topas, go to my lady.

CLO. Out, hyperbolical° fiend! How vexest thou this man! Talkest thou nothing but of ladies?   30

SIR TO. Well said, Master Parson.

MAL. Sir Topas, never was man thus wronged. Good Sir Topas, do not think I am mad. They have laid me here in hideous darkness.

CLO. Fie, thou dishonest Satan! I call thee by the most modest terms, for I am one of those gentle ones that will use the Devil himself with courtesy. Sayest thou that house is dark?

MAL. As Hell, Sir Topas.   39

CLO. Why, it hath bay windows transparent as barricadoes,° and the clerestories° toward the south-north are as lustrous as ebony—and yet complainest thou of obstruction?

MAL. I am not mad, Sir Topas. I say to you, this house is dark.

CLO. Madman, thou errest. I say, there is no darkness but ignorance, in which thou art more puzzled than the Egyptians in their fog.°

MAL. I say, this house is as dark as ignorance, though ignorance were as dark as Hell. And I   50 say there was never man thus abused. I am no more mad than you are. Make the trial of it in any constant question.°

CLO. What is the opinion of Pythagoras° concerning wild fowl?

MAL. That the soul of our grandam might haply inhabit a bird.

CLO. What thinkest thou of his opinion?

MAL. I think nobly of the soul, and no way approve his opinion.   60

CLO. Fare thee well. Remain thou still in darkness. Thou shalt hold the opinion of Pythagoras ere I will allow of thy wits, and fear to kill a woodcock° lest thou dispossess the soul of thy grandam. Fare thee well.

MAL. Sir Topas, Sir Topas!

SIR TO. My most exquisite Sir Topas!

CLO. Nay, I am for all waters.°

MAR. Thou mightst have done this without thy beard and gown. He sees thee not.   70

SIR TO. To him in thine own voice, and bring me word how thou findest him. I would we were well rid of this knavery. If he may be conveniently delivered, I would he were, for I am now so far in offense with my niece that I cannot pursue with any safety this sport to the upshot.° Come by and by to my chamber.   [*Exeunt* SIR TOBY *and* MARIA.]

CLO. [*Sings.*] Hey, Robin, jolly Robin,
                    Tell me how thy lady does.   79

MAL. Fool——

CLO. "My lady is unkind, perdy."°

MAL. Fool——

CLO. "Alas, why is she so?"

MAL. Fool, I say——

CLO. "She loves another——" Who calls, ha?

MAL. Good fool, as ever thou wilt deserve well at my hand, help me to a candle, and pen, ink, and paper. As I am a gentleman, I will live to be thankful to thee for 't.

CLO. Master Malvolio!   90

MAL. Aye, good fool.

CLO. Alas, sir, how feel you besides your five wits?°

MAL. Fool, there was never man so notoriously abused. I am as well in my wits, fool, as thou art.

CLO. But as well? Then you are mad indeed, if you be no better in your wits than a fool.

MAL. They have here propertied° me, keep me in darkness, send ministers to me, asses, and do all they can to face me out of my wits.   101

CLO. Advise you what you say. The minister is here. Malvolio, Malvolio, thy wits the Heavens restore! Endeavor thyself to sleep, and leave thy vain bibble-babble.

MAL. Sir Topas——

CLO. Maintain no words° with him, good fellow. Who, I, sir? Not I, sir. God be wi' you, good Sir Topas. Marry, amen. I will, sir, I will.

MAL. Fool, fool, fool, I say——   110

CLO. Alas, sir, be patient. What say you, sir? I am shent° for speaking to you.

MAL. Good fool, help me to some light and some paper. I tell thee I am as well in my wits as any man in Illyria.

---

21. **What ho:** Here the fool assumes a ministerial voice. 29. **hyperbolical:** extravagant.   41. **barricadoes:** barricades. **clerestories:** the upper part of the inner wall of a church, above the arches, containing a row of windows.   48. **fog:** darkness; i.e., the ninth of the plagues of Egypt. See Exodus 10: 21–23.   52-53. **constant question:** coherent argument. 54. **Pythagoras:** Pythagoras held that the human soul after death could pass into a beast or a bird.   63. **woodcock:** regarded as a foolish bird.

68. **for . . . waters:** i.e., can turn my hand to anything. 76. **upshot:** conclusion.   81. **perdy:** by God.   92-93. **five wits:** i.e., full possession of your senses. The five were common wit, imagination, fantasy, estimation, and memory.   99. **propertied:** treated like a property; i.e., "thrust me into the attic." 107. **Maintain no words:** Here the fool resumes his assumed voice as he keeps up a dialogue with himself as Sir Topas addressing the Clown.   112. **shent:** rebuked.

CLO. Welladay° that you were, sir!

MAL. By this hand, I am. Good fool, some ink, paper, and light; and convey what I will set down to my lady. It shall advantage thee more than ever the bearing of letter did. 120

CLO. I will help you to 't. But tell me true, are you not mad indeed? Or do you but counterfeit?

MAL. Believe me, I am not, I tell thee true.

CLO. Nay, I'll ne'er believe a madman till I see his brains. I will fetch you light and paper and ink.

MAL. Fool, I'll requite it in the highest degree. I prithee be gone.

CLO. [Sings.] I am gone, sir, 130
    And anon, sir,
  I'll be with you again,
    In a trice,
    Like to the old vice,
  Your need to sustain,
  Who, with dagger of lath,°
  In his rage and his wrath,
    Cries, ah, ha! to the Devil.
  Like a mad lad,
  Pare thy nails, dad. 140
Adieu, Goodman Devil. [Exit.]

SCENE III. OLIVIA's garden.

[Enter SEBASTIAN.]

SEB. This is the air, that is the glorious sun,
This pearl she gave me, I do feel 't and see 't.
And though 'tis wonder that enwraps me thus,
Yet 'tis not madness. Where's Antonio, then?
I could not find him at the Elephant.
Yet there he was, and there I found this credit,°
That he did range° the town to seek me out.
His counsel now might do me golden service.
For though my soul disputes well with my sense,
That this may be some error, but no madness, 10
Yet doth this accident and flood of fortune
So far exceed all instance,° all discourse,
That I am ready to distrust mine eyes
And wrangle with my reason, that persuades me
To any other trust but that I am mad,
Or else the lady's mad—yet, if 'twere so,
She could not sway her house, command her fol-
    lowers,
Take and give back affairs and their dispatch
With such a smooth, discreet, and stable bearing

116. **Welladay:** alas. **134–36. vice . . . lath:** the clown's part in the old Morality plays. He was armed with a wooden dagger (*dagger of lath*), with which he attacked the Devil and tried to cut his nails. **Sc. iii: 6. credit:** report. **7. range:** traverse. **12. exceed . . . instance:** go beyond anything recorded.

As I perceive she does. There's something in 't 20
That is deceivable.° But here the lady comes.

[Enter OLIVIA and PRIEST.]

OLI. Blame not this haste of mine. If you mean
    well,
Now go with me and with this holy man
Into the chantry° by. There, before him,
And underneath that consecrated roof,
Plight° me the full assurance of your faith,
That my most jealous and too doubtful soul
May live at peace. He shall conceal it
While you are willing it shall come to note,
What time we will our celebration keep 30
According to my birth. What do you say?

SEB. I'll follow this good man, and go with you,
And, having sworn truth, ever will be true.

OLI. Then lead the way, good Father, and
    Heavens so shine,
That they may fairly note this act of mine!

[Exeunt.]

ACT V

SCENE I. Before OLIVIA's house.

[Enter CLOWN and FABIAN.]

FAB. Now, as thou lovest me, let me see his letter.

CLO. Good Master Fabian, grant me another request.

FAB. Anything.

CLO. Do not desire to see this letter.

FAB. This is to give a dog,° and in recompense desire my dog again.

[Enter DUKE, VIOLA, CURIO, and LORDS.]

DUKE. Belong you to the Lady Olivia, friends?

CLO. Aye, sir, we are some of her trappings.° 10

DUKE. I know thee well. How dost thou, my good fellow?

CLO. Truly, sir, the better for my foes and the worse for my friends.

DUKE. Just the contrary — the better for thy friends.

CLO. No, sir, the worse.

DUKE. How can that be?

21. **deceivable:** deceptive. **24. chantry** chapel. **26. Plight:** promise. Olivia is proposing not full marriage but formal betrothal, which will legally bind Sebastian.
Act V, Sc. i: 7. give a dog: This was a contemporary anecdote recorded in Manningham's diary: "Dr. Bullein, the Queen's kinsman, had a dog which he doted on, so much that the Queen understanding of it requested he would grant her one desire, and he should have whatsoever she should ask. She demanded his dog; he gave it, and, 'Now, Madam,' quoth he, 'you promised to give me my desire.' 'I will,' quoth she. 'Then I pray you give me my dog again.'" **10. trappings:** ornamental accessories.

CLO. Marry, sir, they praise me and make an ass of me. Now my foes tell me plainly I am an ass,   20 so that by my foes, sir, I profit in the knowledge of myself, and by my friends I am abused. So that, conclusions to be as kisses,° if your four negatives make your two affirmatives, why then, the worse for my friends, and the better for my foes.

DUKE. Why, this is excellent.

CLO. By my troth, sir, no, though it please you to be one of my friends.

DUKE. Thou shalt not be the worse for me. There's gold.   31

CLO. But that it would be double-dealing,° sir, I would you could make it another.

DUKE. Oh, you give me ill counsel.

CLO. Put your grace in your pocket,° sir, for this once, and let your flesh and blood obey it.

DUKE. Well, I will be so much a sinner, to be a double-dealer. There's another.

CLO. Primo, secundo, tertio, is a good play, and the old saying is, the third pays for all. The   40 triplex, sir, is a good tripping measure, or the bells of Saint Bennet,° sir, may put you in mind—one, two, three.

DUKE. You can fool no more money out of me at this throw. If you will let your lady know I am here to speak with her, and bring her along with you, it may awake my bounty further.

CLO. Marry, sir, lullaby to your bounty till I come again. I go, sir, but I would not have you to think that my desire of having is the sin of   50 covetousness. But, as you say, sir, let your bounty take a nap. I will awake it anon.   [Exit.]

VIO. Here comes the man, sir, that did rescue me.

[Enter ANTONIO and OFFICERS.]

DUKE. That face of his I do remember well, Yet when I saw it last it was besmeared As black as Vulcan° in the smoke of war. A bawbling° vessel was he captain of, For shallow draught and bulk unprizable,° With which such scathful grapple° did he make With the most noble bottom° of our fleet   60 That very envy and the tongue of loss Cried fame and honor on him. What's the matter?

I. OFF. Orsino, this is that Antonio That took the *Phoenix* and her fraught° from Candy,° And this is he that did the *Tiger* board,

When your young nephew Titus lost his leg. Here in the streets, desperate° of shame and state,° In private brabble° did we apprehend him.

VIO. He did me kindness, sir, drew on my side, But in conclusion put strange speech upon me.   70 I know not what 'twas but distraction.°

DUKE. Notable pirate! Thou salt-water thief! What foolish boldness brought thee to their mercies Whom thou, in terms so bloody and so dear, Hast made thine enemies?

ANT.   Orsino, noble sir, Be pleased that I shake off these names you give me. Antonio never yet was thief or pirate, Though I confess, on base and ground enough, Orsino's enemy. A witchcraft drew me hither. That most ingrateful boy there by your side   80 From the rude sea's enragèd and foamy mouth Did I redeem—a wreck past hope he was. His life I gave him and did thereto add My love, without retention or restraint, All his in dedication. For his sake Did I expose myself, pure for his love, Into the danger of this adverse° town, Drew to defend him when he was beset, Where being apprehended, his false cunning, Not meaning to partake with me in danger,   90 Taught him to face me out of his acquaintance, And grew a twenty years' removèd thing While one would wink—denied me mine own purse, Which I had recommended to his use Not half an hour before.

VIO.   How can this be?

DUKE. When came he to this town?

ANT. Today, my lord, and for three months before, No interim, not a minute's vacancy, Both day and night did we keep company.

[Enter OLIVIA and ATTENDANTS.]

DUKE. Here comes the Countess. Now Heaven walks on earth.   100 But for thee, fellow—fellow, thy words are madness. Three months this youth hath tended upon me. But more of that anon. Take him aside.

OLI. What would my lord, but that he may not have, Wherein Olivia may seem serviceable? Cesario, you do not keep promise with me.

VIO. Madam!

DUKE. Gracious Olivia——

OLI. What do you say, Cesario? Good my
  lord——

VIO. My lord would speak, my duty hushes me.

OLI. If it be aught to the old tune, my lord,   111
It is as fat° and fulsome° to mine ear
As howling after music.

    DUKE.   Still so cruel?

OLI. Still so constant, lord.

    DUKE. What, to perverseness? You uncivil lady,
To whose ingrate° and unauspicious altars
My soul the faithful'st offerings hath breathed out
That e'er devotion tendered! What shall I do?

    OLI. Even what it please my lord that shall be-
    come him.

    DUKE. Why should I not, had I the heart to do it,
Like to the Egyptian thief° at point of death, 121
Kill what I love?—A savage jealousy
That sometime savors nobly. But hear me this.
Since you to nonregardance cast my faith,
And that I partly know the instrument
That screws° me from my true place in your favor,
Live you the marble-breasted tyrant still.
But this your minion,° whom I know you love,
And whom, by Heaven I swear, I tender dearly,
Him will I tear out of that cruel eye,   130
Where he sits crownèd in his master's spite.°
Come, boy, with me. My thoughts are ripe in mis-
    chief.
I'll sacrifice the lamb that I do love,
To spite a raven's heart within a dove.

    VIO. And I, most jocund, apt, and willingly,
To do you rest, a thousand deaths would die.

    OLI. Where goes Cesario?

    VIO.   After him I love
More than I love these eyes, more than my life,
More, by all mores, than e'er I shall love wife.
If I do feign, you witnesses above   140
Punish my life for tainting of my love!

    OLI. Aye me, detested! How am I beguiled!

    VIO. Who does beguile you? Who does do you
    wrong?

    OLI. Hast thou forgot thyself? Is it so long?
Call forth the holy Father.

    DUKE.   Come, away!

OLI. Whither, my lord? Cesario, husband, stay.

DUKE. Husband!

OLI.   Aye, husband. Can he that deny?

DUKE. Her husband, sirrah!

VIO.   No, my lord, not I.

OLI. Alas, it is the baseness of thy fear
That makes thee strangle thy propriety.°   151
Fear not, Cesario. Take thy fortunes up.
Be that thou know'st thou art, and then thou art
As great as that thou fear'st.

[*Enter* PRIEST.]   Oh, welcome, Father!
Father, I charge thee, by thy reverence,
Here to unfold, though lately we intended
To keep in darkness what occasion now
Reveals before 'tis ripe, what thou dost know
Hath newly passed between this youth and me.

    PRIEST. A contract of eternal bond of love,
Confirmed by mutual joinder of your hands,   160
Attested by the holy close of lips,
Strengthened by interchangement of your rings.
And all the ceremony of this compáct°
Sealed in my function, by my testimony.
Since when, my watch hath told me, toward my
    grave
I have travelèd but two hours.

    DUKE. O thou dissembling cub! What wilt
    thou be
When time hath sowed a grizzle on thy case?°
Or will not else thy craft so quickly grow
That thine own trip shall be thine overthrow?°
Farewell, and take her, but direct thy feet   171
Where thou and I henceforth may never meet.

    VIO. My lord, I do protest——

    OLI.   Oh, do not swear!
Hold little faith, though thou hast too much fear.

         [*Enter* SIR ANDREW.]

    SIR AND. For the love of God, a surgeon! Send one
presently° to Sir Toby.

    OLI. What's the matter?

    SIR AND. He has broke my head across and has
given Sir Toby a bloody coxcomb° too. For the love
of God, your help! I had rather than forty pound I
were at home.   181

    OLI. Who has done this, Sir Andrew?

    SIR AND. The Count's gentleman, one Cesario.
We took him for a coward, but he's the very Devil
incardinate.°

    DUKE. My gentleman, Cesario?

    SIR AND. 'Od's lifelings,° here he is! You broke
my head for nothing, and that that I did, I was set
on to do 't by Sir Toby.

---

112. **fat:** gross. **fulsome:** nauseous.   116. **ingrate:** ungrateful.   121. **Egyptian thief:** Thyamis, an Egyptian robber,
captured Chariclea and shut her in a cave. Being attacked by
other robbers, he rushed into the cave intending to slay her
rather than that she should fall into other hands. 125-26. **instrument . . . screws:** a jack that forces. 128. **minion:**
darling. 131. **in . . . spite:** to the vexation of his master.

150. **strangle . . . propriety:** lit., choke your proper self; i.e.,
behave like a coward. 163. **compact:** agreement. 168. **hath
. . . case:** has brought you gray hairs. 170. **thine . . .
overthrow:** your trickery will overthrow you. 176. **presently:** immediately. 179. **bloody coxcomb:** broken head.
185. **incardinate:** incarnate. 187. **'Od's lifelings:** by God's
little life.

VIO. Why do you speak to me? I never hurt you.
You drew your sword upon me without 191
  cause,
But I bespake you fair, and hurt you not.

SIR AND. If a bloody coxcomb be a hurt, you have
hurt me. I think you set nothing by a bloody coxcomb. [*Enter* SIR TOBY *and* CLOWN.] Here comes
Sir Toby halting.° You shall hear more. But if he
had not been in drink, he would have tickled you
othergates° than he did.

DUKE. How now, gentleman! How is 't with
you? 200

SIR TO. That's all one. Has hurt me, and there's
the end on 't. Sot, didst see Dick surgeon, sot?

CLO. Oh, he's drunk, Sir Toby, an hour agone.
His eyes were set at eight i' the morning.°

SIR TO. Then he's a rogue, and a passy measures
pavin.° I hate a drunken rogue.

OLI. Away with him! Who hath made this havoc
with them?

SIR AND. I'll help you, Sir Toby, because we'll be
dressed together. 211

SIR TO. Will you help? An asshead and a coxcomb and a knave, a thin-faced knave, a gull!

OLI. Get him to bed, and let his hurt be looked to.
[*Exeunt* CLOWN, FABIAN, SIR TOBY, *and* SIR ANDREW.]
[*Enter* SEBASTIAN.]

SEB. I am sorry, madam, I have hurt your kins-
man,
But had it been the brother of my blood,
I must have done no less with wit and safety.
You throw a strange regard° upon me, and by that
I do perceive it hath offended you. 220
Pardon me, sweet one, even for the vows
We made each other but so late ago.

DUKE. One face, one voice, one habit, and two
  persons,
A natural perspective,° that is and is not!

SEB. Antonio, O my dear Antonio!
How have the hours racked and tortured me
Since I have lost thee!

ANT. Sebastian are you?

SEB.   Fear'st thou that, Antonio?

ANT. How have you made division of yourself?
An apple, cleft in two, is not more twin 230
Than these two creatures. Which is Sebastian?

OLI. Most wonderful!

SEB. Do I stand there? I never had a brother,
Nor can there be that deity in my nature,
Of here and everywhere.° I had a sister,
Whom the blind waves and surges have devoured.
Of charity, what kin are you to me?
What countryman? What name? What parent-
  age?

VIO. Of Messaline. Sebastian was my father.
Such a Sebastian was my brother too, 240
So went he suited° to his watery tomb.
If spirits can assume both form and suit,
You come to fright us.

SEB.   A spirit I am indeed,
But am in that dimension grossly clad°
Which from the womb I did participate.
Were you a woman, as the rest goes even,
I should my tears let fall upon your cheek,
And say "Thrice welcome, drownèd Viola!"

VIO. My father had a mole upon his brow.

SEB. And so had mine. 250

VIO. And died that day when Viola from her
  birth
Had numbered thirteen years.

SEB. Oh, that recórd is lively in my soul!
He finishèd indeed his mortal act
That day that made my sister thirteen years.

VIO. If nothing lets° to make us happy both
But this my masculine usurped attire,
Do not embrace me till each circumstance
Of place, time, fortune, do cohere and jump°
That I am Viola. Which to confirm, 260
I'll bring you to a captain in this town,
Where lie my maiden weeds,° by whose gentle help
I was preserved to serve this noble Count.
All the occurrence of my fortune since
Hath been between this lady and this lord.

SEB. [*To* OLIVIA] So comes it, lady, you have been
  mistook.
But nature to her bias° drew in that.
You would have been contracted to a maid,
Nor are you therein, by my life, deceived,
You are betrothed both to a maid and man. 270

DUKE. Be not amazed. Right noble is his blood.
If this be so, as yet the glass° seems true,
I shall have share in this most happy wreck.
[*To* VIOLA] Boy, thou hast said to me a thousand
  times
Thou never shouldst love woman like to me.

VIO. And all those sayings will I overswear,

---

195. halting: limping. **196-97. othergates:** otherwise.
205. Set . . . morning: dimmed by drink (*set*) since eight in the
morning. **206-07. passy . . . pavin:** The folio reads "passy
measures panyn" (misprint for "pauyn"). Toby is very drunk.
The fool's words "set at eight" stir in his fuddled head the
memory that there were eight strains in the "passa measures
pavan," a slow, stately measured dance. **219. regard:** look.
224. perspective: a picture which shows one image when seen
in front and another when viewed from an angle. See *Rich II*,
II.ii.18–20.

234-35. Nor . . . everywhere: I cannot be a god to be in two
places at once. **241. suited:** clothed. **244. in . . . clad:**
enclosed in bodily form. **256. lets:** hinders. **259. jump:**
agree. **262. weeds:** garments. **267. bias:** natural inclination. **272. glass:** reflection.

And all those swearings keep as true in soul
As doth that orbèd continent the fire°
That severs day from night.
  DUKE.   Give me thy hand,
And let me see thee in thy woman's weeds. 280
  VIO. The captain that did bring me first on shore
Hath my maid's garments. He upon some action
Is now in durance,° at Malvolio's suit,
A gentleman, and follower of my lady's.
  OLI. He shall enlarge him. Fetch Malvolio hither.
And yet, alas, now I remember me,
They say, poor gentleman, he's much distract.
  [*Re-enter* CLOWN *with a letter, and* FABIAN.]
A most extracting frenzy° of mine own
From my remembrance clearly banished his.
How does he, sirrah?   290
  CLO. Truly, madam, he holds Belzebub at the
stave's end° as well as a man in his case may do.
Has here writ a letter to you. I should have given 't
you today morning, but as a madman's epistles are
no gospels, so it skills° not much when they are de-
livered.
  OLI. Open 't, and read it.
  CLO. Look then to be well edified when the fool
delivers° the madman. [*Reads.*] "By the Lord,
madam"——   300
  OLI. How now! Art thou mad?
  CLO. No, madam, I do but read madness. An
your ladyship will have it as it ought to be, you must
allow Vox.°
  OLI. Prithee, read i' thy right wits.
  CLO. So I do, madonna, but to read his right wits
is to read thus. Therefore perpend,° my Princess,
and give ear.
  OLI. [*To* FABIAN] Read it you, sirrah. 309
  FAB. [*Reads.*] "By the Lord, madam, you wrong
me, and the world shall know it. Though you have
put me into darkness and given your drunken
cousin rule over me, yet have I the benefit of my
senses as well as your ladyship. I have your own letter that induced me to the semblance I put on, with
the which I doubt not but to do myself much right,
or you much shame. Think of me as you please. I
leave my duty a little unthought-of,° and speak out
of my injury. THE MADLY USED MALVOLIO"
  OLI. Did he write this?   320
  CLO. Aye, madam.

DUKE. This savors not much of distraction.
  OLI. See him delivered, Fabian. Bring him hither.
            [*Exit* FABIAN.]
My lord, so please you, these things further thought
  on,
To think me as well a sister as a wife,
One day shall crown the alliance on 't, so please you,
Here at my house and at my proper° cost.
DUKE. Madam, I am most apt to embrace your
  offer.
[*To* VIOLA] Your master quits° you, and for your
  service done him,
So much against the mettle° of your sex, 330
So far beneath your soft and tender breeding,
And since you called me master for so long,
Here is my hand. You shall from this time be
Your master's mistress.
  OLI.   A sister! You are she.
  [*Re-enter* FABIAN, *with* MALVOLIO.]
  DUKE. Is this the madman?
  OLI.   Aye, my lord, this same.
How now, Malvolio!
  MAL.   Madam, you have done me wrong,
Notorious wrong.
  OLI.   Have I, Malvolio? No.
  MAL. Lady, you have. Pray you peruse that letter.
You must not now deny it is your hand.
Write from° it, if you can, in hand or phrase, 340
Or say 'tis not your seal, not your invention.
You can say none of this. Well, grant it then
And tell me, in the modesty of honor,
Why you have given me such clear lights of favor,
Bade me come smiling and cross-gartered to you,
To put on yellow stockings and to frown
Upon Sir Toby and the lighter people.
And, acting this in an obedient hope,
Why have you suffered me to be imprisoned,
Kept in a dark house, visited by the priest, 350
And made the most notorious geck° and gull
That e'er invention played on? Tell me why.
  OLI. Alas, Malvolio, this is not my writing,
Though, I confess, much like the character°
But out of question 'tis Maria's hand.
And now I do bethink me it was she
First told me thou wast mad, then camest in smiling,
And in such forms which here were presupposed
Upon thee in the letter. Prithee, be content. 359
This practice° hath most shrewdly passed upon thee,
But when we know the grounds and authors of it,
Thou shalt be both the plaintiff and the judge
Of thine own cause.

---

278. **orbed . . . fire:** the sun. **283. durance:** confinement.
288. frenzy: madness. **291-92. holds . . . end:** he keeps the
fiend at bay; i.e., he is putting up a fight against Belzebub, who
possesses him. **295. skills:** makes little difference. **299. de-
livers:** utters the words of. **304. allow Vox:** the proper tone
of voice. **307. perpend:** consider. **318. duty . . .
unthought-of:** i.e., I do not write with the formal phrases
that a steward should use to his mistress.

327. **proper:** own. **329. quits:** releases. **330. mettle:**
material, nature. **340. Write from:** deny. **351. geck:**
fool. **354. character:** handwriting. **360. practice:** plot.

FAB.   Good madam, hear me speak,
And let no quarrel nor no brawl to come
Taint the condition° of this present hour,
Which I have wondered at. In hope it shall not,
Most freely I confess, myself and Toby
Set this device against Malvolio here,
Upon some stubborn and uncourteous parts
We had conceived° against him. Maria writ   370
The letter at Sir Toby's great importance,°
In recompense whereof he hath married her.
How with a sportful malice it was followed
May rather pluck on laughter than revenge,
If that the injuries be justly weighed
That have on both sides passed.

OLI. Alas, poor fool, how have they baffled° thee!

CLO. Why, "some are born great, some achieve
greatness, and some have greatness thrown upon
them." I was one, sir, in this interlude; one   380
Sir Topas, sir. But that's all one. "By the Lord,
fool, I am not mad." But do you remember?
"Madam, why laugh you at such a barren rascal?
An you smile not, he's gagged." And thus the
whirligig of time brings in his revenges.°

MAL. I'll be revenged on the whole pack of you.
                                              [Exit.]

OLI. He hath been most notoriously abused.

DUKE. Pursue him, and entreat him to a peace.
He hath not told us of the captain yet.   390
When that is known, and golden time convents,°

A solemn combination shall be made
Of our dear souls. Meantime, sweet sister,
We will not part from hence. Cesario, come—
For so you shall be, while you are a man,
But when in other habits you are seen,
Orsino's mistress and his fancy's Queen.
                      [Exeunt all, except CLOWN.]

CLO. [Sings.]
    When that I was and a little tiny boy,
        With hey, ho, the wind and the rain,
    A foolish thing was but a toy,   400
        For the rain it raineth every day.

    But when I came to man's estate,
        With hey, ho, the wind and the rain,
    'Gainst knaves and thieves men shut their gate,
        For the rain it raineth every day.

    But when I came, alas! to wive,
        With hey, ho, the wind and the rain,
    By swaggering could I never thrive,
        For the rain it raineth every day.

    But when I came unto my beds,°   410
        With hey, ho, the wind and the rain,
    With tosspots° still had drunken heads,
        For the rain it raineth every day.

    A great while ago the world begun,
        With hey, ho, the wind and the rain,
    But that's all one, our play is done,
        And we'll strive to please you every day.
                                              [Exit.]

---

365. Taint . . . condition: spoil the harmony.   **370. conceived:** perceived.   **371. importance:** importunity, insistence.   **377. baffled:** disgraced.   **385. brings . . . revenges:** i.e., now I have my own back. See I.v.88.   **391. golden . . . convents:** happy time summons.

410. unto my beds: a difficult phrase, meaning probably "when I came to the end of my life."   **412. tosspots:** drunkards.

Molière The Misanthrope

in a Translation by Richard Wilbur

Probably the greatest and certainly the most complex of all Molière's comedies, *The Misanthrope* was first produced in 1666. Molière (born Jean-Baptiste Poquelin) was at the height of his career as actor, producer, and dramatist; indeed, his royal patron, Louis XIV, had himself taken part in some of Molière's magnificent court productions. *The Misanthrope* was initially presented at Richelieu's theatre in the Palais-Royal in Paris, but unlike other comedies of Molière, it had only a mild success. Perhaps because it was too provocative; the piece has been called Molière's *Hamlet.*

The meaning of the play is the problem. To his own age—the "splendid century" it has been called—Alceste was without doubt a comic figure, somewhat grotesque in his high-principled rigidity and in his blunt rejection of accepted social patterns of behavior. Succeeding ages have reversed this judgment: society has become the object of derision, for its absurdities, its facile compromises. Today, we are inclined to see both sides of the argument presented in this comedy and to enjoy the consequent ambiguity.

A helpful approach to the play, and to Molière's theatre in general, is by way of theatrical history. We know that the great French dramatist was much interested in, as well as influenced by, the Italian *commedia dell'arte* productions, which had become so popular in Paris, indeed in all France. Allardyce Nicoll's account of this type of theatre (see Part II, pp. 181–85) throws light upon Molière's plays for it explains one of the traditions upon which the dramatist depended. In particular, Molière was enchanted with the vitality of this Italian style, the professional dash and deftness of its stage business, and the brilliance of the grotesque characterizations.

The translation reprinted here is by the American poet, Richard Wilbur (N. Y.: Harcourt, Brace, 1955). In his introduction, Mr. Wilbur has indicated the rationale behind his verse rendition: "to control the tone" (including the parody-tragic effect discussed in Turnell's essay in Part IV, pp. 268–80), to bridge by means of rhythm and rhyme "the great gaps between high comedy and farce, lofty diction and ordinary talk, deep character and shallow," to maintain the play's "musical" intricacy and, finally, to preserve both the "redundancy" and the "logic" of the dialogue.

CHARACTERS

ALCESTE, *in love with Célimène*
PHILINTE, *Alceste's friend*
ORONTE, *in love with Célimène*
CELIMENE, *Alceste's beloved*

ELIANTE, *Célimène's cousin*
ARSINOE, *a friend of Célimène's*
ACASTE ⎫
CLITANDRE ⎭ *marquesses*

BASQUE, *Célimène's servant*
A GUARD *of the Marshalsea*
DUBOIS, *Alceste's valet*

The scene throughout is in Célimène's house at Paris.

ACT I

SCENE I. PHILINTE, ALCESTE.

PHILINTE. Now, what's got into you?

ALCESTE. [*seated*]   Kindly leave me alone.

PHIL. Come, come, what is it? This lugubrious tone . . .

ALC. Leave me, I said; you spoil my solitude.

PHIL. Oh, listen to me, now, and don't be rude.

ALC. I choose to be rude, Sir, and to be hard of hearing.

PHIL. These ugly moods of yours are not endearing;

Friends though we are, I really must insist . . .

    ALC. [*abruptly rising*] Friends? Friends, you say? Well, cross me off your list.

I've been your friend till now, as you well know;

But after what I saw a moment ago   10

I tell you flatly that our ways must part.

I wish no place in a dishonest heart.

    PHIL. Why, what have I done, Alceste? Is this quite just?

    ALC. My God, you ought to die of self-disgust.

I call your conduct inexcusable, Sir,

And every man of honor will concur.

I see you almost hug a man to death,

Exclaim for joy until you're out of breath,

And supplement these loving demonstrations
With endless offers, vows, and protestations;   20
Then when I ask you "Who was that?", I find
That you can barely bring his name to mind!
Once the man's back is turned, you cease to love
   him,
And speak with absolute indifference of him!
By God, I say it's base and scandalous
To falsify the heart's affections thus;
If I caught myself behaving in such a way,
I'd hang myself for shame, without delay.
   PHIL. It hardly seems a hanging matter to me;
I hope that you will take it graciously   30
If I extend myself a slight reprieve,
And live a little longer, by your leave.
   ALC. How dare you joke about a crime so grave?
   PHIL. What crime? How else are people to
   behave?
   ALC. I'd have them be sincere, and never part
With any word that isn't from the heart.
   PHIL. When someone greets us with a show of
   pleasure
It's but polite to give him equal measure,
Return his love the best that we know how,
And trade him offer for offer, vow for vow.   40
   ALC. No, no, this formula you'd have me follow,
However fashionable, is false and hollow,
And I despise the frenzied operations
Of all these barterers of protestations,
These lavishers of meaningless embraces,
These utterers of obliging commonplaces,
Who court and flatter everyone on earth
And praise the fool no less than the man of worth.
Should you rejoice that someone fondles you,
Offers his love and service, swears to be true,   50
And fills your ears with praises of your name,
When to the first damned fop he'll say the same?
No, no: no self-respecting heart would dream
Of prizing so promiscuous an esteem;
However high the praise, there's nothing worse
Than sharing honors with the universe.
Esteem is founded on comparison:
To honor all men is to honor none.
Since you embrace this indiscriminate vice,
Your friendship comes at far too cheap a price;   60
I spurn the easy tribute of a heart
Which will not set the worthy man apart:
I choose, Sir, to be chosen; and in fine,
The friend of mankind is no friend of mine.
   PHIL. But in polite society, custom decrees
That we show certain outward courtesies. . . .
   ALC. Ah, no! we should condemn with all our
   force
Such false and artificial intercourse.

Let men behave like men; let them display
Their inmost hearts in everything they say;   70
Let the heart speak, and let our sentiments
Not mask themselves in silly compliments.
   PHIL. In certain cases it would be uncouth
And most absurd to speak the naked truth;
With all respect for your exalted notions,
It's often best to veil one's true emotions.
Wouldn't the social fabric come undone
If we were wholly frank with everyone?
Suppose you met with someone you couldn't bear;
Would you inform him of it then and there?   80
   ALC. Yes.
   PHIL.   Then you'd tell old Emilie it's pathetic
The way she daubs her features with cosmetic
And plays the gay coquette at sixty-four?
   ALC. I would.
   PHIL.   And you'd call Dorilas a bore,
And tell him every ear at court is lame
From hearing him brag about his noble name?
   ALC. Precisely.
   PHIL.   Ah, you're joking.
   ALC.   *Au contraire:*
In this regard there's none I'd choose to spare.
All are corrupt; there's nothing to be seen
In court or town but aggravates my spleen.   90
I fall into deep gloom and melancholy
When I survey the scene of human folly,
Finding on every hand base flattery,
Injustice, fraud, self-interest, treachery. . . .
Ah, it's too much; mankind has grown so base,
I mean to break with the whole human race.
   PHIL. This philosophic rage is a bit extreme;
You've no idea how comical you seem;
Indeed, we're like those brothers in the play
Called *School for Husbands*, one of whom was
   prey . . .   100
   ALC. Enough, now! None of your stupid similes.
   PHIL. Then let's have no more tirades, if you
   please.
The world won't change, whatever you say or do;
And since plain speaking means so much to you,
I'll tell you plainly that by being frank
You've earned the reputation of a crank,
And that you're thought ridiculous when you rage
And rant against the manners of the age.
   ALC. So much the better; just what I wish to hear.
No news could be more grateful to my ear.   110
All men are so detestable in my eyes,
I should be sorry if they thought me wise.
   PHIL. Your hatred's very sweeping, is it not?
   ALC. Quite right: I hate the whole degraded lot.
   PHIL. Must all poor human creatures be
   embraced,

Without distinction, by your vast distaste?
Even in these bad times, there are surely a few . . .
   ALC. No, I include all men in one dim view:
Some men I hate for being rogues; the others
I hate because they treat the rogues like brothers,
And, lacking a virtuous scorn for what is vile,   121
Receive the villain with a complaisant smile.
Notice how tolerant people choose to be
Toward that bold rascal who's at law with me.
His social polish can't conceal his nature;
One sees at once that he's a treacherous creature;
No one could possibly be taken in
By those soft speeches and that sugary grin.
The whole world knows the shady means by which
The low-brow's grown so powerful and rich,   130
And risen to a rank so bright and high
That virtue can but blush, and merit sigh.
Whenever his name comes up in conversation,
None will defend his wretched reputation;
Call him knave, liar, scoundrel, and all the rest,
Each head will nod, and no one will protest.
And yet his smirk is seen in every house,
He's greeted everywhere with smiles and bows,
And when there's any honor that can be got
By pulling strings, he'll get it, like as not.   140
My God! It chills my heart to see the ways
Men come to terms with evil nowadays;
Sometimes, I swear, I'm moved to flee and find
Some desert land unfouled by humankind.
   PHIL. Come, let's forget the follies of the times
And pardon mankind for its petty crimes;
Let's have an end of rantings and of railings,
And show some leniency toward human failings.
This world requires a pliant rectitude;
Too stern a virtue makes one stiff and rude;   150
Good sense views all extremes with detestation,
And bids us to be noble in moderation.
The rigid virtues of the ancient days
Are not for us; they jar with all our ways
And ask of us too lofty a perfection.
Wise men accept their times without objection,
And there's no greater folly, if you ask me,
Than trying to reform society.
Like you, I see each day a hundred and one
Unhandsome deeds that might be better done,
But still, for all the faults that meet my view,   161
I'm never known to storm and rave like you.
I take men as they are, or let them be,
And teach my soul to bear their frailty;
And whether in court or town, whatever the scene,
My phlegm's as philosophic as your spleen.
   ALC. This phlegm which you so eloquently
      commend,
Does nothing ever rile it up, my friend?

Suppose some man you trust should treacherously
Conspire to rob you of your property,   170
And do his best to wreck your reputation?
Wouldn't you feel a certain indignation?
   PHIL. Why, no. These faults of which you so
      complain
Are part of human nature, I maintain,
And it's no more a matter for disgust
That men are knavish, selfish and unjust,
Than that the vulture dines upon the dead,
And wolves are furious, and apes ill-bred.
   ALC. Shall I see myself betrayed, robbed, torn
      to bits,
And not . . . Oh, let's be still and rest our wits.   180
Enough of reasoning, now. I've had my fill.
   PHIL. Indeed, you would do well, Sir, to be still.
Rage less at your opponent, and give some thought
To how you'll win this lawsuit that he's brought.
   ALC. I assure you I'll do nothing of the sort.
   PHIL. Then who will plead your case before the
      court?
   ALC. Reason and right and justice will plead for
      me.
   PHIL. Oh, Lord. What judges do you plan to see?
   ALC. Why, none. The justice of my cause is clear.
   PHIL. Of course, man; but there's politics to
      fear. . . .   190
   ALC. No, I refuse to lift a hand. That's flat.
I'm either right, or wrong.
   PHIL.   Don't count on that.
   ALC. No, I'll do nothing.
   PHIL.   Your enemy's influence
Is great, you know . . .
   ALC.   That makes no difference.
   PHIL. It will; you'll see.
   ALC.   Must honor bow to guile?
If so, I shall be proud to lose the trial.
   PHIL. Oh, really . . .
   ALC.   I'll discover by this case
Whether or not men are sufficiently base
And impudent and villainous and perverse
To do me wrong before the universe.   200
   PHIL. What a man!
   ALC.   Oh, I could wish, whatever the cost,
Just for the beauty of it, that my trial were lost
   PHIL. If people heard you talking so, Alceste,
They'd split their sides. Your name would be a jest.
   ALC. So much the worse for jesters.
   PHIL.   May I enquire
Whether this rectitude you so admire,
And these hard virtues you're enamored of
Are qualities of the lady whom you love?
It much surprises me that you, who seem
To view mankind with furious disesteem,   210

Have yet found something to enchant your eyes
Amidst a species which you so despise.
And what is more amazing, I'm afraid,
Is the most curious choice your heart has made.
The honest Eliante is fond of you,
Arsinoé, the prude, admires you too;
And yet your spirit's been perversely led
To choose the flighty Célimène instead,
Whose brittle malice and coquettish ways
So typify the manners of our days.   220
How is it that the traits you most abhor
Are bearable in this lady you adore?
Are you so blind with love that you can't find them?
Or do you contrive, in her case, not to mind them?

ALC. My love for that young widow's not the
    kind
That can't perceive defects; no, I'm not blind.
I see her faults, despite my ardent love,
And all I see I fervently reprove.
And yet I'm weak; for all her falsity,
That woman knows the art of pleasing me,   230
And though I never cease complaining of her,
I swear I cannot manage not to love her.
Her charm outweighs her faults; I can but aim
To cleanse her spirit in my love's pure flame.

PHIL. That's no small task; I wish you all success.
You think then that she loves you?

ALC.   Heavens, yes!
I wouldn't love her did she not love me.

PHIL. Well, if her taste for you is plain to see,
Why do these rivals cause you such despair?

ALC. True love, Sir, is possessive, and cannot bear
To share with all the world. I'm here today   241
To tell her she must send that mob away.

PHIL. If I were you, and had your choice to make,
Eliante, her cousin, would be the one I'd take;
That honest heart, which cares for you alone,
Would harmonize far better with your own.

ALC. True, true: each day my reason tells me so;
But reason doesn't rule in love, you know.

PHIL. I fear some bitter sorrow is in store;
This love . . .

SCENE II. ORONTE, ALCESTE, PHILINTE.

ORONTE. [*to* ALCESTE] The servants told me at
    the door   250
That Eliante and Célimène were out,
But when I heard, dear Sir, that you were about,
I came to say, without exaggeration,
That I hold you in the vastest admiration,
And that it's always been my dearest desire
To be the friend of one I so admire.
I hope to see my love of merit requited,
And you and I in friendship's bond united.

I'm sure you won't refuse—if I may be frank—
A friend of my devotedness—and rank.   260
[*During this speech of* ORONTE'S, ALCESTE *is abstracted,
and seems unaware that he is being spoken to. He only
breaks off his reverie when* ORONTE *says:*]
It was for you, if you please, that my words were
    intended.

ALC. For me, Sir?

OR.   Yes, for you. You're not offended?

ALC. By no means. But this much surprises me. . . .
The honor comes most unexpectedly. . . .

OR. My high regard should not astonish you;
The whole world feels the same. It is your due.

ALC. Sir . . .

OR.   Why, in all the State there isn't one
Can match your merits; they shine, Sir, like the sun.

ALC. Sir . . .

OR.   You are higher in my estimation
Than all that's most illustrious in the nation.   270

ALC. Sir . . .

OR. If I lie, may heaven strike me dead!
To show you that I mean what I have said,
Permit me, Sir, to embrace you most sincerely,
And swear that I will prize our friendship dearly.
Give me your hand. And now, Sir, if you choose,
We'll make our vows.

ALC.   Sir . . .

OR.   What! You refuse?

ALC. Sir, it's a very great honor you extend:
But friendship is a sacred thing, my friend;
It would be profanation to bestow
The name of friend on one you hardly know.   280
All parts are better played when well-rehearsed;
Let's put off friendship, and get acquainted first.
We may discover it would be unwise
To try to make our natures harmonize.

OR. By heaven! You're sagacious to the core;
This speech has made me admire you even more.
Let time, then, bring us closer day by day;
Meanwhile, I shall be yours in every way.
If, for example, there should be anything
You wish at court, I'll mention it to the King.   290
I have his ear, of course; it's quite well known
That I am much in favor with the throne.
In short, I am your servant. And now, dear friend,
Since you have such fine judgment, I intend
To please you, if I can, with a small sonnet
I wrote not long ago. Please comment on it,
And tell me whether I ought to publish it.

ALC. You must excuse me, Sir; I'm hardly fit
To judge such matters.

OR.   Why not?

ALC.   I am, I fear,
Inclined to be unfashionably sincere.   300

OR. Just what I ask; I'd take no satisfaction
In anything but your sincere reaction.
I beg you not to dream of being kind.
    ALC. Since you desire it, Sir, I'll speak my mind.
    OR. *Sonnet.* It's a sonnet. . . . *Hope* . . . The poem's
    addressed
To a lady who wakened hopes within my breast.
Hope . . . this is not the pompous sort of thing,
Just modest little verses, with a tender ring.
    ALC. Well, we shall see.
    OR.   *Hope* . . . I'm anxious to hear
Whether the style seems properly smooth and
    clear,   310
And whether the choice of words is good or bad.
    ALC. We'll see, we'll see.
    OR.   Perhaps I ought to add
That it took me only a quarter-hour to write it.
    ALC. The time's irrelevant, Sir: kindly recite it.
    OR. [*reading*]
        Hope comforts us awhile, 'tis true,
        Lulling our cares with careless laughter,
        And yet such joy is full of rue,
        My Phyllis, if nothing follows after.
    PHIL. I'm charmed by this already; the style's
    delightful.
    ALC. [*sotto voce, to* PHILINTE] How can you say
    that? Why, the thing is frightful.   320
    OR.
        Your fair face smiled on me awhile,
        But was it kindness so to enchant me?
        'Twould have been fairer not to smile,
        If hope was all you meant to grant me.
    PHIL. What a clever thought! How handsomely
    you phrase it!
    ALC. [*sotto voce, to* PHILINTE] You know the thing
    is trash. How dare you praise it?
    OR.   *If it's to be my passion's fate*
        Thus everlastingly to wait,
        Then death will come to set me free:
        For death is fairer than the fair;   330
        Phyllis, to hope is to despair
        When one must hope eternally.
    PHIL. The close is exquisite—full of feeling and
    grace.
    ALC. [*sotto voce, aside*] Oh, blast the close, you'd
    better close your face
Before you send your lying soul to hell.
    PHIL. I can't remember a poem I've liked so well.
    ALC. [*sotto voce, aside*] Good Lord!
    OR. [*to* PHILINTE]   I fear you're
    flattering me a bit.
    PHIL. Oh, no!
    ALC. [*sotto voce, aside*] What else d'you call it, you
    hypocrite?

OR. [*to* ALCESTE] But you, Sir, keep your promise
    now: don't shrink
From telling me sincerely what you think.   340
    ALC. Sir, these are delicate matters; we all desire
To be told that we've the true poetic fire.
But once, to one whose name I shall not mention,
I said, regarding some verse of his invention,
That gentlemen should rigorously control
That itch to write which often afflicts the soul;
That one should curb the heady inclination
To publicize one's little avocation;
And that in showing off one's works of art
One often plays a very clownish part.   350
    OR. Are you suggesting in a devious way
That I ought not . . .
    ALC.   Oh, that I do not say.
Further, I told him that no fault is worse
Than that of writing frigid, lifeless verse,
And that the merest whisper of such a shame
Suffices to destroy a man's good name.
    OR. D'you mean to say my sonnet's dull and
    trite?
    ALC. I don't say that. But I went on to cite
Numerous cases of once-respected men
Who came to grief by taking up the pen.   360
    OR. And am I like them? Do I write so poorly?
    ALC. I don't say that. But I told this person,
    "Surely
You're under no necessity to compose;
Why you should wish to publish, heaven knows.
There's no excuse for printing tedious rot
Unless one writes for bread, as you do not.
Resist temptation, then, I beg of you;
Conceal your pastimes from the public view;
And don't give up, on any provocation,
Your present high and courtly reputation,   370
To purchase at a greedy printer's shop
The name of silly author and scribbling fop."
These were the points I tried to make him see.
    OR. I sense that they are also aimed at me;
But now—about my sonnet—I'd like to be told . . .
    ALC. Frankly, that sonnet should be pigeonholed.
You've chosen the worst models to imitate.
The style's unnatural. Let me illustrate:
    For example, *Your fair face smiled on me awhile,*
    Followed by, *'Twould have been fairer not to smile!*
    Or this: *such joy is full of rue;*   381
    Or this: *For death is fairer than the fair;*
    Or, *Phyllis, to hope is to despair*
        When one must hope eternally!
This artificial style, that's all the fashion,
Has neither taste, nor honesty, nor passion;
It's nothing but a sort of wordy play,
And nature never spoke in such a way.

What, in this shallow age, is not debased?
Our fathers, though less refined, had better taste;
I'd barter all that men admire today   391
For one old love-song I shall try to say:

> *If the King had given me for my own*
> *Paris, his citadel,*
> *And I for that must leave alone*
> *Her whom I love so well,*
> *I'd say then to the Crown,*
> *Take back your glittering town;*
> *My darling is more fair, I swear,*
> *My darling is more fair.*   400

The rhyme's not rich, the style is rough and old,
But don't you see it's the purest gold
Beside the tinsel nonsense now preferred,
And that there's passion in its every word?

> *If the King had given me for my own*
> *Paris, his citadel,*
> *And I for that must leave alone*
> *Her whom I love so well,*
> *I'd say then to the Crown,*
> *Take back your glittering town;*   410
> *My darling is more fair, I swear,*
> *My darling is more fair.*

There speaks a loving heart. [*to* PHILINTE] You're
    laughing, eh?
Laugh on, my precious wit. Whatever you say,
I hold that song's worth all the bibelots
That people hail today with ah's and oh's.
  OR. And I maintain my sonnet's very good.
  ALC. It's not at all surprising that you should.
You have your reasons; permit me to have mine
For thinking that you cannot write a line.   420
  OR. Others have praised my sonnet to the skies.
  ALC. I lack their art of telling pleasant lies.
  OR. You seem to think you've got no end of wit.
  ALC. To praise your verse, I'd need still more of it.
  OR. I'm not in need of your approval, Sir.
  ALC. That's good; you couldn't have it if you
    were.
  OR. Come now, I'll lend you the subject of my
    sonnet;
I'd like to see you try to improve upon it.
  ALC. I might, by chance, write something just
    as shoddy;
But then I wouldn't show it to everybody.   430
  OR. You're most opinionated and conceited.
  ALC. Go find your flatterers, and be better
    treated.
  OR. Look here, my little fellow, pray watch
    your tone.
  ALC. My great big fellow, you'd better watch
    your own.
  PHIL. [*stepping between them*] Oh, please, please,

gentlemen! This will never do.
  OR. The fault is mine, and I leave the field to you.
I am your servant, Sir, in every way.
  ALC. And I, Sir, am your most abject valet.

SCENE III. PHILINTE, ALCESTE.

  PHIL. Well, as you see, sincerity in excess
Can get you into a very pretty mess;   440
Oronte was hungry for appreciation. . . .
  ALC. Don't speak to me.
  PHIL.   What?
  ALC.   No more conversation.
  PHIL. Really, now . . .
  ALC.   Leave me alone.
  PHIL.   If I . . .
  ALC.   Out
    of my sight!
  PHIL. But what . . .
  ALC.   I won't listen.
  PHIL.   But . . .
  ALC.   Silence!
  PHIL.   Now, is it
    polite . . .
  ALC. By heaven, I've had enough. Don't follow
    me.
  PHIL. Ah, you're just joking. I'll keep you
    company.

ACT II

SCENE I. ALCESTE, CELIMENE.

  ALC. Shall I speak plainly, Madam? I confess
Your conduct gives me infinite distress,
And my resentment's grown too hot to smother.
Soon, I foresee, we'll break with one another.
If I said otherwise, I should deceive you;
Sooner or later, I shall be forced to leave you,
And if I swore that we shall never part,
I should misread the omens of my heart.
  CELIMENE. You kindly saw me home, it would
    appear,
So as to pour invectives in my ear.   10
  ALC. I've no desire to quarrel. But I deplore
Your inability to shut the door
On all these suitors who beset you so.
There's what annoys me, if you care to know.
  CEL. Is it my fault that all these men pursue me?
Am I to blame if they're attracted to me?
And when they gently beg an audience,
Ought I to take a stick and drive them hence?
  ALC. Madam, there's no necessity for a stick;

A less responsive heart would do the trick.   20
Of your attractiveness I don't complain;
But those your charms attract, you then detain
By a most melting and receptive manner,
And so enlist their hearts beneath your banner.
It's the agreeable hopes which you excite
That keep these lovers round you day and night;
Were they less liberally smiled upon,
That sighing troop would very soon be gone.
But tell me, Madam, why it is that lately
This man Clitandre interests you so greatly?   30
Because of what high merits do you deem
Him worthy of the honor of your esteem?
Is it that your admiring glances linger
On the splendidly long nail of his little finger?
Or do you share the general deep respect
For the blond wig he chooses to affect?
Are you in love with his embroidered hose?
Do you adore his ribbons and his bows?
Or is it that this paragon bewitches
Your tasteful eye with his vast German breeches?
Perhaps his giggle, or his falsetto voice,   41
Makes him the latest gallant of your choice?

CEL. You're much mistaken to resent him so.
Why I put up with him you surely know:
My lawsuit's very shortly to be tried,
And I must have his influence on my side.

ALC. Then lose your lawsuit, Madam, or let it
     drop;
Don't torture me by humoring such a fop.

CEL. You're jealous of the whole world, Sir.

ALC.   That's true
Since the whole world is well-received by you.   50

CEL. That my good nature is so unconfined
Should serve to pacify your jealous mind;
Were I to smile on one, and scorn the rest,
Then you might have some cause to be distressed.

ALC. Well, if I mustn't be jealous, tell me, then,
Just how I'm better treated than other men.

CEL. You know you have my love. Will that
     not do?

ALC. What proof have I that what you say is true?

CEL. I would expect, Sir, that my having said it
Might give the statement a sufficient credit   60

ALC. But how can I be sure that you don't tell
The selfsame thing to other men as well?

CEL. What a gallant speech! How flattering to
     me!
What a sweet creature you make me out to be!
Well then, to save you from the pangs of doubt,
All that I've said I hereby cancel out;
Now, none but yourself shall make a monkey
     of you:
Are you content?

ALC.   Why, why am I doomed to love you?
I swear that I shall bless the blissful hour
When this poor heart's no longer in your power!
I make no secret of it: I've done my best   71
To exorcise this passion from my breast;
But thus far all in vain; it will not go;
It's for my sins that I must love you so.

CEL. Your love for me is matchless, Sir; that's
     clear.

ALC. Indeed, in all the world it has no peer;
Words can't describe the nature of my passion,
And no man ever loved in such a fashion.

CEL. Yes, it's a brand-new fashion, I agree:
You show your love by castigating me,   80
And all your speeches are enraged and rude.
I've never been so furiously wooed.

ALC. Yet you could calm that fury, if you chose.
Come, shall we bring our quarrels to a close?
Let's speak with open hearts, then, and begin . . .

SCENE II. CELIMENE, ALCESTE, BASQUE.

CEL. What is it?

BASQUE.   Acaste is here.

CEL.   Well, send him in.

SCENE III. CELIMENE, ALCESTE.

ALC. What! Shall we never be alone at all?
You're always ready to receive a call,
And you can't bear, for ten ticks of the clock,
Not to keep open house for all who knock.   90

CEL. I couldn't refuse him: he'd be most put out.

ALC. Surely that's not worth worrying about.

CEL. Acaste would never forgive me if he guessed
That I consider him a dreadful pest.

ALC. If he's a pest, why bother with him then?

CEL. Heavens! One can't antagonize such men;
Why, they're the chartered gossips of the court,
And have a say in things of every sort.
One must receive them, and be full of charm;
They're no great help, but they can do you harm,
And though your influence be ever so great,   101
They're hardly the best people to alienate.

ALC. I see, dear lady, that you could make a case
For putting up with the whole human race;
These friendships that you calculate so nicely . . .

SCENE IV. ALCESTE, CELIMENE, BASQUE.

BAS. Madam, Clitandre is here as well.

ALC.   Precisely.

CEL. Where are you going?

ALC.   Elsewhere.

CEL.   Stay.
ALC.   No, no.
CEL. Stay, Sir.
ALC.   I can't.
CEL.   I wish it.
ALC.   No, I must go.
I beg you, Madam, not to press the matter;
You know I have no taste for idle chatter.   110
CEL. Stay: I command you.
ALC.   No, I cannot stay.
CEL. Very well; you have my leave to go away.

SCENE V. ELIANTE, PHILINTE, ACASTE,
CLITANDRE, ALCESTE, CELIMENE, BASQUE.

ELIANTE [to CELIMENE] The Marquesses have
    kindly come to call.
Were they announced?
CEL.   Yes. Basque, bring chairs for all.
    [BASQUE provides the chairs, and exits.]
[to ALCESTE] You haven't gone?
ALC.   No; and I shan't depart
Till you decide who's foremost in your heart.
CEL. Oh, hush.
ALC.   It's time to choose; take them, or me.
CEL. You're mad.
ALC.   I'm not, as you shall shortly see.
CEL. Oh?
ALC.   You'll decide.
CEL.   You're joking now, dear
    friend.
ALC. No, no; you'll choose; my patience is at
    an end.   120
CLITANDRE. Madam, I come from court, where
    poor Cléonte
Behaved like a perfect fool, as is his wont.
Has he no friend to counsel him, I wonder,
And teach him less unerringly to blunder?
CEL. It's true, the man's most accomplished
    dunce;
His gauche behavior strikes the eye at once;
And every time one sees him, on my word,
His manner's grown a trifle more absurd.
ACASTE. Speaking of dunces, I've just now con-
    versed
With old Damon, who's one of the very worst;
I stood a lifetime in the broiling sun   131
Before his dreary monologue was done.
CEL. Oh, he's a wondrous talker, and has the
    power
To tell you nothing hour after hour:
If, by mistake, he ever came to the point,
The shock would put his jawbone out of joint.

EL. [to PHILINTE] The conversation takes its
    usual turn,
And all our dear friends' ears will shortly burn.
CLIT. Timante's a character, Madam.
CEL.   Isn't he, though?
A man of mystery from top to toe,   140
Who moves about in a romantic mist
On secret missions which do not exist.
His talk is full of eyebrows and grimaces;
How tired one gets of his momentous faces;
He's always whispering something confidential
Which turns out to be quite inconsequential;
Nothing's too slight for him to mystify;
He even whispers when he says "good-by."
ACAS. Tell us about Géralde.
CEL.   That tiresome ass.
He mixes only with the titled class,   150
And fawns on dukes and princes, and is bored
With anyone who's not at least a lord.
The man's obsessed with rank, and his discourses
Are all of hounds and carriages and horses;
He uses Christian names with all the great,
And the word Milord, with him, is out of date.
CLIT. He's very taken with Bélise, I hear.
CEL. She is the dreariest company, poor dear.
Whenever she comes to call, I grope about
To find some topic which will draw her out,   160
But, owing to her dry and faint replies,
The conversation wilts, and droops, and dies.
In vain one hopes to animate her face
By mentioning the ultimate commonplace;
But sun or shower, even hail or frost
Are matters she can instantly exhaust.
Meanwhile her visit, painful though it is,
Drags on and on through mute eternities,
And though you ask the time, and yawn, and yawn,
She sits there like a stone and won't be gone. 170
ACAS. Now for Adraste.
CEL.   Oh, that conceited elf
Has a gigantic passion for himself;
He rails against the court, and cannot bear it
That none will recognize his hidden merit;
All honors given to others give offense
To his imaginary exellence.
CLIT. What about young Cléon? His house,
    they say,
Is full of the best society, night and day.
CEL. His cook has made him popular, not he:
It's Cléon's table that people come to see.   180
EL. He gives a spendid dinner, you must admit.
CEL. But must he serve himself along with it?
For my taste, he's a most insipid dish
Whose presence sours the wine and spoils the fish.
PHIL. Damis, his uncle, is admired no end.

What's your opinion, Madam?
CEL.   Why, he's my friend.
    PHIL. He seems a decent fellow, and rather
        clever.
    CEL. He works too hard at cleverness, however.
I hate to see him sweat and struggle so
To fill his conversation with bons mots.   190
Since he's decided to become a wit
His taste's so pure that nothing pleases it;
He scolds at all the latest books and plays,
Thinking that wit must never stoop to praise,
That finding fault's a sign of intellect,
That all appreciation is abject,
And that by damning everything in sight
One shows oneself in a distinguished light.
He's scornful even of our conversations:
Their trivial nature sorely tries his patience;   200
He folds his arms, and stands above the battle,
And listens sadly to our childish prattle.
    ACAS. Wonderful, Madam! You've hit him off
        precisely.
    CLIT. No one can sketch a character so nicely.
    ALC. How bravely, Sirs, you cut and thrust at all
These absent fools, till one by one they fall:
But let one come in sight, and you'll at once
Embrace the man you lately called a dunce,
Telling him in a tone sincere and fervent
How proud you are to be his humble servant.   210
    CLIT. Why pick on us? Madame's been speaking,
        Sir,
And you should quarrel, if you must, with her.
    ALC. No, no, by God, the fault is yours, because
You lead her on with laughter and applause,
And make her think that she's the more delightful
The more her talk is scandalous and spiteful.
Oh, she would stoop to malice far, far less
If no such claque approved her cleverness.
It's flatterers like you whose foolish praise
Nourishes all the vices of these days.   220
    PHIL. But why protest when someone ridicules
Those you'd condemn, yourself, as knaves or fools?
    CEL. Why, Sir? Because he loves to make a fuss.
You don't expect him to agree with us,
When there's an opportunity to express
His heaven-sent spirit of contrariness?
What other people think, he can't abide;
Whatever they say, he's on the other side;
He lives in deadly terror of agreeing;
'Twould make him seem an ordinary being.   230
Indeed, he's so in love with contradiction,
He'll turn against his most profound conviction
And with a furious eloquence deplore it,
If only someone else is speaking for it.
    ALC. Go on, dear lady, mock me as you please;

You have your audience in ecstasies.
    PHIL. But what she says is true: you have a way
Of bridling at whatever people say;
Whether they praise or blame, your angry spirit
Is equally unsatisfied to hear it.   240
    ALC. Men, Sir, are always wrong, and that's the
        reason
That righteous anger's never out of season;
All that I hear in all their conversation
Is flattering praise or reckless condemnation.
    CEL. But . . .
    ALC.   No, no, Madam, I am forced to state
That you have pleasures which I deprecate,
And that these others, here, are much to blame
For nourishing the faults which are your shame.
    CLIT. I shan't defend myself, Sir; but I vow
I'd thought this lady faultless until now.   250
    ACAS. I see her charms and graces, which are
        many;
But as for faults, I've never noticed any.
    ALC. I see them, Sir; and rather than ignore
        them,
I strenuously criticize her for them.
The more one loves, the more one should object
To every blemish, every least defect.
Were I this lady, I would soon get rid
Of lovers who approved of all I did,
And by their slack indulgence and applause
Endorsed my follies and excused my flaws.   260
    CEL. If all hearts beat according to your measure,
The dawn of love would be the end of pleasure;
And love would find its perfect consummation
In ecstasies of rage and reprobation.
    EL. Love, as a rule, affects men otherwise,
And lovers rarely love to criticize.
They see their lady as a charming blur,
And find all things commendable in her.
If she has any blemish, fault, or shame,
They will redeem it by a pleasing name.   270
The pale-faced lady's lily-white, perforce;
The swarthy one's a sweet brunette, of course;
The spindly lady has a slender grace;
The fat one has a most majestic pace;
The plain one, with her dress in disarray,
They classify as *beauté négligée*;
The hulking one's a goddess in their eyes,
The dwarf, a concentrate of Paradise;
The haughty lady has a noble mind;
The mean one's witty, and the dull one's kind;
The chatterbox has liveliness and verve,   281
The mute one has a virtuous reserve.
So lovers manage, in their passion's cause,
To love their ladies even for their flaws.
    ALC. But I still say . . .

CEL.   I think it would be nice
To stroll around the gallery once or twice.
What! You're not going, Sirs?
    CLIT. and ACAS.   No, Madam, no.
    ALC. You seem to be in terror lest they go.
Do what you will, Sirs; leave, or linger on,
But I shan't go till after you are gone.   290
    ACAS. I'm free to linger, unless I should perceive
Madame is tired, and wishes me to leave.
    CLIT. And as for me, I needn't go today
Until the hour of the King's *coucher.*
    CEL. [*to* ALCESTE] You're joking, surely?
    ALC.   Not in
        the least; we'll see
Whether you'd rather part with them, or me.

SCENE VI. ALCESTE, CELIMENE, ELIANTE, ACASTE, PHILINTE, CLITANDRE, BASQUE.

    BAS. [*to* ALCESTE] Sir, there's a fellow here who
        bids me state
That he must see you, and that it can't wait.   298
    ALC. Tell him that I have no such pressing affairs.
    BAS. It's a long tailcoat that this fellow wears,
With gold all over.
    CEL. [*to* ALCESTE] You'd best go down and see.
Or—have him enter.

SCENE VII. ALCESTE, CELIMENE, ELIANTE, ACASTE, PHILINTE, CLITANDRE, A GUARD *of the Marshalsea.*

    ALC. [*confronting the* GUARD] Well, what do you
        want with me?
Come in, Sir.
    GUARD.   I've a word, Sir, for your ear.
    ALC. Speak it aloud, Sir; I shall strive to hear.
    GUARD. The Marshals have instructed me to say
You must report to them without delay.
    ALC. Who? Me, Sir?
    GUARD.   Yes, Sir; you.
    ALC.   But what do
        they want?
    PHIL. [*to* ALCESTE] To scotch your silly quarrel
        with Oronte.
    CEL. [*to* PHILINTE] What quarrel?
    PHIL.   Oronte and
        he have fallen out
Over some verse he spoke his mind about;   310
The Marshals wish to arbitrate the matter.
    ALC. Never shall I equivocate or flatter!
    PHIL. You'd best obey their summons; come,
        let's go.
    ALC. How can they mend our quarrel, I'd like
        to know?

Am I to make a cowardly retraction,
And praise those jingles to his satisfaction?
I'll not recant; I've judged that sonnet rightly.
It's bad.
    PHIL. But you might say so more politely. . . .
    ALC. I'll not back down; his verses make me sick.
    PHIL. If only you could be more politic!   320
But come, let's go.
    ALC.   I'll go, but I won't unsay
A single word.
    PHIL.   Well, let's be on our way.
    ALC. Till I am ordered by my lord the King
To praise that poem, I shall say the thing
Is scandalous, by God, and that the poet
Ought to be hanged for having the nerve to show
        it. [*to* CLITANDRE *and* ACASTE, *who are laughing*]
By heaven, Sirs, I really didn't know
That I was being humorous.
    CEL.   Go, Sir, go;
Settle your business.
    ALC.   I shall, and when I'm through,
I shall return to settle things with you.   330

ACT III

SCENE I. CLITANDRE, ACASTE.

    CLIT. Dear Marquess, how contented you
        appear;
All things delight you, nothing mars your cheer.
Can you, in perfect honesty, declare
That you've a right to be so debonair?
    ACAS. By Jove, when I survey myself, I find
No cause whatever for distress of mind.
I'm young and rich; I can in modesty
Lay claim to an exalted pedigree;
And owing to my name and my condition
I shall not want for honors and position.   10
Then as to courage, that most precious trait,
I seem to have it, as was proved of late
Upon the field of honor, where my bearing,
They say, was very cool and rather daring.
I've wit, of course; and taste in such perfection
That I can judge without the least reflection,
And at the theater, which is my delight,
Can make or break a play on opening night,
And lead the crowd in hisses or bravos,
And generally be known as one who knows.   20
I'm clever, handsome, gracefully polite;
My waist is small, my teeth are strong and white;
As for my dress, the world's astonished eyes
Assure me that I bear away the prize.
I find myself in favor everywhere,
Honored by men, and worshiped by the fair;

And since these things are so, it seems to me
I'm justified in my complacency.
    CLIT. Well, if so many ladies hold you dear,
Why do you press a hopeless courtship here?   30
    ACAS. Hopeless, you say? I'm not the sort of fool
That likes his ladies difficult and cool.
Men who are awkward, shy, and peasantish
May pine for heartless beauties, if they wish,
Grovel before them, bear their cruelties,
Woo them with tears and sighs and bended knees,
And hope by dogged faithfulness to gain
What their poor merits never could obtain.
For men like me, however, it makes no sense
To love on trust, and foot the whole expense.   40
Whatever any lady's merits be,
I think, thank God, that I'm as choice as she;
That if my heart is kind enough to burn
For her, she owes me something in return;
And that in any proper love affair
The partners must invest an equal share.
    CLIT. You think, then, that our hostess favors
        you?
    ACAS. I've reason to believe that that is true.
    CLIT. How did you come to such a mad conclu-
        sion?
You're blind, dear fellow. This is sheer delusion.
    ACAS. All right, then: I'm deluded and I'm
        blind.   51
    CLIT. Whatever put the notion in your mind?
    ACAS. Delusion.
    CLIT.   What persuades you that you're right?
    ACAS. I'm blind.
    CLIT.   But have you any proofs to cite?
    ACAS. I tell you I'm deluded.
    CLIT.   Have you, then,
Received some secret pledge from Célimène?
    ACAS. Oh, no: she scorns me.
    CLIT.   Tell me the truth, I beg.
    ACAS. She just can't bear me.
    CLIT.   Ah, don't pull my leg.
Tell me what hope she's given you, I pray.
    ACAS. I'm hopeless, and it's you who win the
        day.   60
She hates me thoroughly, and I'm so vexed
I mean to hang myself on Tuesday next.
    CLIT. Dear Marquess, let us have an armistice
And make a treaty. What do you say to this?
If ever one of us can plainly prove
That Célimène encourages his love,
The other must abandon hope, and yield,
And leave him in possession of the field.
    ACAS. Now, there's a bargain that appeals to me;
With all my heart, dear Marquess, I agree.   70
But hush.

SCENE II. CELIMENE, ACASTE, CLITANDRE.

    CEL. Still here?
    CLIT.   'Twas love that stayed our feet.
    CEL. I think I heard a carriage in the street.
Whose is it? D'you know?

SCENE III. CELIMENE, ACASTE, CLITANDRE, BASQUE.

    BAS.   Arsinoé is here,
Madame.
    CEL. Arsinoé, you say? Oh, dear.
    BAS. Eliante is entertaining her below.
    CEL. What brings the creature here, I'd like to
        know?
    ACAS. They say she's dreadfully prudish, but in
        fact
I think her piety . . .
    CEL.   It's all an act.
At heart she's wordly, and her poor success
In snaring men explains her prudishness.   80
It breaks her heart to see the beaux and gallants
Engrossed by other women's charms and talents,
And so she's always in a jealous rage
Against the faulty standards of the age.
She lets the world believe that she's a prude
To justify her loveless solitude,
And strives to put a brand of moral shame
On all the graces that she cannot claim.
But still she'd love a lover; and Alceste
Appears to be the one she'd love the best.   90
His visits here are poison to her pride;
She seems to think I've lured him from her side;
And everywhere, at court or in the town,
The spiteful, envious woman runs me down.
In short, she's just as stupid as can be,
Vicious and arrogant in the last degree,
And . . .

SCENE IV. ARSINOE, CELIMENE, CLITANDRE, ACASTE.

    CEL. Ah! What happy chance has brought you
        here?
I've thought about you ever so much, my dear.
    ARSINOE. I've come to tell you something you
        should know.
    CEL. How good of you to think of doing so!   100
        [CLITANDRE *and* ACASTE *go out, laughing.*]

SCENE V. ARSINOE, CELIMENE.

    ARSIN. It's just as well those gentlemen didn't
        tarry.
    CEL. Shall we sit down?

ARSIN.   That won't be necessary.
Madam, the flame of friendship ought to burn
Brightest in matters of the most concern,
And as there's nothing which concerns us more
Than honor, I have hastened to your door
To bring you, as your friend, some information
About the status of your reputation.
I visited, last night, some virtuous folk,
And, quite by chance, it was of you they spoke;   110
There was, I fear, no tendency to praise
Your light behavior and your dashing ways.
The quantity of gentlemen you see
And your by now notorious coquetry
Were both so vehemently criticized
By everyone, that I was much surprised.
Of course, I needn't tell you where I stood;
I came to your defense as best I could,
Assured them you were harmless, and declared
Your soul was absolutely unimpaired.   120
But there are some things, you must realize,
One can't excuse, however hard one tries,
And I was forced at last into conceding
That your behavior, Madam, is misleading,
That it makes a bad impression, giving rise
To ugly gossip and obscene surmise,
And that if you were more *overtly* good,
You wouldn't be so much misunderstood.
Not that I think you've been unchaste—no! no!
The saints preserve me from a thought so low!   130
But mere good conscience never did suffice:
One must avoid the outward show of vice.
Madam, you're too intelligent, I'm sure,
To think my motives anything but pure
In offering you this counsel—which I do
Out of a zealous interest in you.
     CEL. Madam, I haven't taken you amiss;
I'm very much obliged to you for this;
And I'll at once discharge the obligation
By telling you about *your* reputation.   140
You've been so friendly as to let me know
What certain people say of me, and so
I mean to follow your benign example
By offering you a somewhat similar sample.
The other day, I went to an affair
And found some most distinguished people there
Discussing piety, both false and true.
The conversation soon came round to you.
Alas! Your prudery and bustling zeal
Appeared to have a very slight appeal.   150
Your affectation of a grave demeanor,
Your endless talk of virtue and of honor,
The aptitude of your suspicious mind
For finding sin where there is none to find,
Your towering self-esteem, that pitying face

With which you contemplate the human race,
Your sermonizings and your sharp aspersions
On people's pure and innocent diversions—
All these were mentioned, Madam, and, in fact,
Were roundly and concertedly attacked.   160
"What good," they said, "are all these outward
     shows,
When everything belies her pious pose?
She prays incessantly; but then, they say,
She beats her maids and cheats them of their pay;
She shows her zeal in every holy place,
But still she's vain enough to paint her face;
She holds that naked statues are immoral,
But with a naked *man* she'd have no quarrel."
Of course, I said to everybody there
That they were being viciously unfair;   170
But still they were disposed to criticize you,
And all agreed that someone should advise you
To leave the morals of the world alone,
And worry rather more about your own.
They felt that one's self-knowledge should be great
Before one thinks of setting others straight;
That one should learn the art of living well
Before one threatens other men with hell,
And that the Church is best equipped, no doubt,
To guide our souls and root our vices out.   180
Madam, you're too intelligent, I'm sure,
To think my motives anything but pure
In offering you this counsel—which I do
Out of a zealous interest in you.
     ARSIN. I dared not hope for gratitude, but I
Did not expect so acid a reply;
I judge, since you've been so extremely tart,
That my good counsel pierced you to the heart.
     CEL. Far from it, Madam. Indeed, it seems to me
We ought to trade advice more frequently.   190
One's vision of oneself is so defective
That it would be an excellent corrective.
If you are willing, Madam, let's arrange
Shortly to have another frank exchange
In which we'll tell each other, *entre nous*,
What you've heard tell of me, and I of you.
     ARSIN. Oh, people never censure you, my dear;
It's me they criticize. Or so I hear.
     CEL. Madam, I think we either blame or praise
According to our taste and length of days.   200
There is a time of life for coquetry,
And there's a season, too, for prudery.
When all one's charms are gone, it is, I'm sure,
Good strategy to be devout and pure:
It makes one seem a little less forsaken.
Some day, perhaps, I'll take the road you've taken:
Time brings all things. But I have time aplenty,
And see no cause to be a prude at twenty.

ARSIN. You give your age in such a gloating tone
That one would think I was an ancient crone;   210
We're not so far apart, in sober truth,
That you can mock me with a boast of youth!
Madam, you baffle me. I wish I knew
What moves you to provoke me as you do.

CEL. For my part, Madam, I should like to know
Why you abuse me everywhere you go.
Is it my fault, dear lady, that your hand
Is not, alas, in very great demand?
If men admire me, if they pay me court
And daily make me offers of the sort   220
You'd dearly love to have them make to you,
How can I help it? What would you have me do?
If what you want is lovers, please feel free
To take as many as you can from me.

ARSIN. Oh, come. D'you think the world is losing
   sleep
Over that flock of lovers which you keep,
Or that we find it difficult to guess
What price you pay for their devotedness?
Surely you don't expect us to suppose
Mere merit could attract so many beaux?   230
It's not your virtue that they're dazzled by;
Nor is it virtuous love for which they sigh.
You're fooling no one, Madam; the world's not
   blind;
There's many a lady heaven has designed
To call men's noblest, tenderest feeling out,
Who has no lovers dogging her about;
From which it's plain that lovers nowadays
Must be acquired in bold and shameless ways,
And only pay one court for such reward
As modesty and virtue can't afford.   240
Then don't be quite so puffed up, if you please,
About your tawdry little victories;
Try, if you can, to be a shade less vain,
And treat the world with somewhat less disdain.
If one were envious of your amours,
One soon could have a following like yours;
Lovers are no great trouble to collect
If one prefers them to one's self-respect.

CEL. Collect them then, my dear; I'd love to see
You demonstrate that charming theory;   250
Who knows, you might . . .

ARSIN.   Now, Madam, that
   will do;
It's time to end this trying interview.
My coach is late in coming to your door,
Or I'd have taken leave of you before.

CEL. Oh, please don't feel that you must rush
   away;
I'd be delighted, Madam, if you'd stay.
However, lest my conversation bore you,

Let me provide some better company for you;
This gentleman, who comes most apropos,
Will please you more than I could do, I know.   260

SCENE VI. ALCESTE, CELIMENE, ARSINOE.

CEL. Alceste, I have a little note to write
Which simply must go out before tonight;
Please entertain *Madame;* I'm sure that she
Will overlook my incivility.

SCENE VII. ALCESTE, ARSINOE.

ARSIN. Well, Sir, our hostess graciously contrives
For us to chat until my coach arrives;
And I shall be forever in her debt
For granting me this little tête-à-tête.
We women very rightly give our hearts
To men of noble character and parts,   270
And your especial merits, dear Alceste,
Have roused the deepest sympathy in my breast.
Oh, how I wish they had sufficient sense
At court, to recognize your excellence!
They wrong you greatly, Sir. How it must hurt you
Never to be rewarded for your virtue!

ALC. Why, Madam, what cause have I to feel
   aggrieved?
What great and brilliant thing have I achieved?
What service have I rendered to the King
That I should look to him for anything?   280

ARSIN. Not everyone who's honored by the State
Has done great services. A man must wait
Till time and fortune offer him the chance.
Your merit, Sir, is obvious at a glance,
And . . .

ALC. Ah, forget my merit; I'm not neglected.
The court, I think, can hardly be expected
To mine men's souls for merit, and unearth
Our hidden virtues and our secret worth.

ARSIN. *Some* virtues, though, are far too bright
   to hide;
Yours are acknowledged, Sir, on every side.   290
Indeed, I've heard you warmly praised of late
By persons of considerable weight.

ALC. This fawning age has praise for everyone,
And all distinctions, Madam, are undone.
All things have equal honor nowadays,
And no one should be gratified by praise.
To be admired, one only need exist,
And every lackey's on the honors list.

ARSIN. I only wish, Sir, that you had your eye
On some position at court, however high;   300
You'd only have to hint at such a notion
For me to set the proper wheels in motion;

I've certain friendships I'd be glad to use
To get you any office you might choose.

    ALC. Madam, I fear that any such ambition
Is wholly foreign to my disposition.
The soul God gave me isn't of the sort
That prospers in the weather of a court.
It's all too obvious that I don't possess
The virtues necessary for success.   310
My one great talent is for speaking plain;
I've never learned to flatter or to feign;
And anyone so stupidly sincere
Had best not seek a courtier's career.
Outside the court, I know, one must dispense
With honors, privilege, and influence;
But still one gains the right, foregoing these,
Not to be tortured by the wish to please.
One needn't live in dread of snubs and slights,
Nor praise the verse that every idiot writes,   320
Nor humor silly Marquesses, nor bestow
Politic sighs on Madam So-and-So.

    ARSIN. Forget the court, then; let the matter rest.
But I've another cause to be distressed
About your present situation, Sir.
It's to your love affair that I refer.
She whom you love, and who pretends to love you,
Is, I regret to say, unworthy of you.

    ALC. Why, Madam! Can you seriously intend
To make so grave a charge against your friend? 330

    ARSIN. Alas, I must. I've stood aside too long
And let that lady do you grievous wrong;
But now my debt to conscience shall be paid:
I tell you that your love has been betrayed.

    ALC. I thank you, Madam; you're extremely
      kind.
Such words are soothing to a lover's mind.

    ARSIN. Yes, though she *is* my friend, I say again
You're very much too good for Célimène.
She's wantonly misled you from the start.

    ALC. You may be right; who knows another's
      heart?   340
But ask yourself if it's the part of charity
To shake my soul with doubts of her sincerity.

    ARSIN. Well, if you'd rather be a dupe than
      doubt her,
That's your affair. I'll say no more about her.

    ALC. Madam, you know that doubt and vague
      suspicion
Are painful to a man in my position;
It's most unkind to worry me this way
Unless you've some real proof of what you say.

    ARSIN. Sir, say no more: all doubt shall be
      removed,
And all that I've been saying shall be proved. 350
You've only to escort me home, and there

We'll look into the heart of this affair.
I've ocular evidence which will persuade you
Beyond a doubt, that Célimène's betrayed you.
Then, if you're saddened by that revelation,
Perhaps I can provide some consolation.

ACT IV

SCENE I. ELIANTE, PHILINTE.

    PHIL. Madam, he acted like a stubborn child;
I thought they never would be reconciled;
In vain we reasoned, threatened, and appealed;
He stood his ground and simply would not yield.
The Marshals, I feel sure, have never heard
An argument so splendidly absurd.
"No, gentlemen," said he, "I'll not retract.
His verse is bad: extremely bad, in fact.
Surely it does the man no harm to know it.
Does it disgrace him, not to be a poet?   10
A gentleman may be respected still,
Whether he writes a sonnet well or ill.
That I dislike his verse should not offend him;
In all that touches honor, I commend him;
He's noble, brave, and virtuous—but I fear
He can't in truth be called a sonneteer.
I'll gladly praise his wardrobe; I'll endorse
His dancing, or the way he sits a horse;
But, gentlemen, I cannot praise his rhyme.
In fact, it ought to be a capital crime   20
For anyone so sadly unendowed
To write a sonnet, and read the thing aloud."
At length he fell into a gentler mood
And, striking a concessive attitude,
He paid Oronte the following courtesies:
"Sir, I regret that I'm so hard to please,
And I'm profoundly sorry that your lyric
Failed to provoke me to a panegyric."
After these curious words, the two embraced,
And then the hearing was adjourned—in haste. 30

    EL. His conduct has been very singular lately;
Still, I confess that I respect him greatly.
The honesty in which he takes such pride
Has—to my mind—its noble, heroic side.
In this false age, such candor seems outrageous;
But I could wish that it were more contagious.

    PHIL. What most intrigues me in our friend
      Alceste
Is the grand passion that rages in his breast.
The sullen humors he's compounded of
Should not, I think, dispose his heart to love; 40
But since they do, it puzzles me still more
That he should choose your cousin to adore.

EL. It does, indeed, belie the theory
That love is born of gentle sympathy,
And that the tender passion must be based
On sweet accords of temper and of taste.
    PHIL. Does she return his love, do you suppose?
    EL. Ah, that's a difficult question, Sir. Who
      knows?
How can we judge the truth of her devotion?
Her heart's a stranger to its own emotion.   50
Sometimes it thinks it loves, when no love's there;
At other times it loves quite unaware.
    PHIL. I rather think Alceste is in for more
Distress and sorrow than he's bargained for;
Were he of my mind, Madam, his affection
Would turn in quite a different direction,
And we would see him more responsive to
The kind regard which he receives from you.
    EL. Sir, I believe in frankness, and I'm inclined,
In matters of the heart, to speak my mind.   60
I don't oppose his love for her; indeed,
I hope with all my heart that he'll succeed,
And were it in my power, I'd rejoice
In giving him the lady of his choice.
But if, as happens frequently enough
In love affairs, he meets with a rebuff—
If Célimène should grant some rival's suit—
I'd gladly play the role of substitute;
Nor would his tender speeches please me less
Because they'd once been made without success. 70
    PHIL. Well, Madam, as for me, I don't oppose
Your hopes in this affair; and heaven knows
That in my conversations with the man
I plead your cause as often as I can.
But if those two should marry, and so remove
All chance that he will offer you his love,
Then I'll declare my own, and hope to see
Your gracious favor pass from him to me.
In short, should you be cheated of Alceste,
I'd be most happy to be second best.   80
    EL. Philinte, you're teasing.
    PHIL.   Ah, Madam, never
    fear;
No words of mine were ever so sincere,
And I shall live in fretful expectation
Till I can make a fuller declaration.

SCENE II. ALCESTE, ELIANTE, PHILINTE.

    ALC. Avenge me, Madam! I must have
    satisfaction,
Or this great wrong will drive me to distraction!
    EL. Why, what's the matter? What's upset you
    so?
    ALC. Madam, I've had a mortal, mortal blow.

If Chaos repossessed the universe,
I swear I'd not be shaken any worse.   90
I'm ruined. . . . I can say no more. . . . My soul . . .
    EL. Do try, Sir, to regain your self-control.
    ALC. Just heaven! Why were so much beauty and
    grace
Bestowed on one so vicious and so base?
    EL. Once more, Sir, tell us. . . .
    ALC.   My world has
    gone to wrack;
I'm—I'm betrayed; she's stabbed me in the back:
Yes, Célimène (who would have thought it of her?)
Is false to me, and has another lover.
    EL. Are you quite certain? Can you prove these
    things?
    PHIL. Lovers are prey to wild imaginings   100
And jealous fancies. No doubt there's some
    mistake. . . .
    ALC. Mind your own business, Sir, for heaven's
    sake.
    [to ELIANTE] Madam, I have the proof that
    you demand
Here in my pocket, penned by her own hand.
Yes, all the shameful evidence one could want
Lies in this letter written to Oronte—
Oronte! whom I felt sure she couldn't love,
And hardly bothered to be jealous of.
    PHIL. Still, in a letter, appearances may deceive;
This may not be so bad as you believe.   110
    ALC. Once more I beg you, Sir, to let me be;
Tend to your own affairs; leave mine to me.
    EL. Compose yourself; this anguish that you
    feel . . .
    ALC. Is something, Madam, you alone can heal.
My outraged heart, beside itself with grief,
Appeals to you for comfort and relief.
Avenge me on your cousin, whose unjust
And faithless nature has deceived my trust;
Avenge a crime your pure soul must detest.
    EL. But how, Sir?
    ALC.   Madam, this heart within my
    breast   120
Is yours; pray take it; redeem my heart from her,
And so avenge me on my torturer.
Let her be punished by the fond emotion,
The ardent love, the bottomless devotion,
The faithful worship which this heart of mine
Will offer up to yours as to a shrine.
    EL. You have my sympathy, Sir, in all you
    suffer;
Nor do I scorn the noble heart you offer;
But I suspect you'll soon be mollified,
And this desire for vengeance will subside.   130
When some beloved hand has done us wrong

We thirst for retribution—but not for long;
However dark the deed that she's committed,
A lovely culprit's very soon acquitted.
Nothing's so stormy as an injured lover,
And yet no storm so quickly passes over.

ALC. No, Madam, no—this is no lovers' spat;
I'll not forgive her; it's gone too far for that;
My mind's made up; I'll kill myself before
I waste my hopes upon her any more.   140
Ah, here she is. My wrath intensifies.
I shall confront her with her tricks and lies,
And crush her utterly, and bring you then
A heart no longer slave to Célimène.

SCENE III. CELIMENE, ALCESTE.

ALC. [aside] Sweet heaven, help me to control
   my passion.
CEL. [aside to ALCESTE] Oh, Lord. Why stand
   there staring in that fashion?
And what d'you mean by those dramatic sighs,
And that malignant glitter in your eyes?
ALC. I mean that sins which cause the blood to
   freeze
Look innocent beside your treacheries;   150
That nothing Hell's or Heaven's wrath could do
Ever produced so bad a thing as you.
CEL. Your compliments were always sweet and
   pretty.
ALC. Madam, it's not the moment to be witty.
No, blush and hang your head; you've ample
   reason,
Since I've the fullest evidence of your treason.
Ah, this is what my sad heart prophesied;
Now all my anxious fears are verified;
My dark suspicion and my gloomy doubt
Divined the truth, and now the truth is out. 160
For all your trickery, I was not deceived;
It was my bitter stars that I believed.
But don't imagine that you'll go scot-free;
You shan't misuse me with impunity.
I know that love's irrational and blind;
I know the heart's not subject to the mind,
And can't be reasoned into beating faster;
I know each soul is free to choose its master;
Therefore had you but spoken from the heart,
Rejecting my attentions from the start,   170
I'd have no grievance, or at any rate
I could complain of nothing but my fate.
Ah, but so falsely to encourage me—
That was a treason and a treachery
For which you cannot suffer too severely,
And you shall pay for that behavior dearly.
Yes, now I have no pity, not a shred;
My temper's out of hand; I've lost my head;

Shocked by the knowledge of your double-dealings,
My reason can't restrain my savage feelings; 180
A righteous wrath deprives me of my senses,
And I won't answer for the consequences.
CEL. What does this outburst mean? Will you
   please explain?
Have you, by any chance, gone quite insane?
ALC. Yes, yes, I went insane the day I fell
A victim to your black and fatal spell,
Thinking to meet with some sincerity
Among the treacherous charms that beckoned me.
CEL. Pooh. Of what treachery can you complain?
ALC. How sly you are, how cleverly you feign!
But you'll not victimize me any more.   191
Look: here's a document you've seen before.
This evidence, which I acquired today,
Leaves you, I think, without a thing to say.
CEL. Is this what sent you into such a fit?
ALC. You should be blushing at the sight of it.
CEL. Ought I to blush? I truly don't see why.
ALC. Ah, now you're being bold as well as sly;
Since there's no signature, perhaps you'll claim . . .
CEL. I wrote it, whether or not it bears my name.
ALC. And you can view with equanimity   201
This proof of your disloyalty to me!
CEL. Oh, don't be so outrageous and extreme.
ALC. You take this matter lightly, it would seem.
Was it no wrong to me, no shame to you,
That you should send Oronte this billet-doux?
CEL. Oronte! Who said it was for him?
ALC.   Why, those
Who brought me this example of your prose.
But what's the difference? If you wrote the letter
To someone else, it pleases me no better.   210
My grievance and your guilt remain the same.
CEL. But need you rage, and need I blush for
   shame,
If this was written to a *woman* friend?
ALC. Ah! Most ingenious. I'm impressed no end;
And after that incredible evasion
Your guilt is clear. I need no more persuasion.
How dare you try so clumsy a deception?
D'you think I'm wholly wanting in perception?
Come, come, let's see how brazenly you'll try
To bolster up so palpable a lie: 220
Kindly construe this ardent closing section
As nothing more than sisterly affection!
Here, let me read it. Tell me, if you dare to,
That this is for a woman . . .
CEL.   I don't care to.
What right have you to badger and berate me,
And so highhandedly interrogate me?
ALC. Now, don't be angry; all I ask of you
Is that you justify a phrase or two . . .

CEL. No, I shall not. I utterly refuse,   229
And you may take those phrases as you choose.
  ALC. Just show me how this letter could be
    meant
For a woman's eyes, and I shall be content.
  CEL. No, no, it's for Oronte; you're perfectly
    right.
I welcome his attentions with delight,
I prize his character and his intellect,
And everything is just as you suspect.
Come, do your worst now; give your rage free rein;
But kindly cease to bicker and complain.
  ALC. [aside] Good God! Could anything be more
    inhuman?
Was ever a heart so mangled by a woman?   240
When I complain of how she has betrayed me,
She bridles, and commences to upbraid me!
She tries my tortured patience to the limit;
She won't deny her guilt; she glories in it!
And yet my heart's too faint and cowardly
To break these chains of passion, and be free,
To scorn her as it should, and rise above
This unrewarded, mad, and bitter love.
[to CELIMENE] Ah, traitress, in how confident a
    fashion
You take advantage of my helpless passion,   250
And use my weakness for your faithless charms
To make me once again throw down my arms!
But do at least deny this black transgression;
Take back that mocking and perverse confession;
Defend this letter and your innocence,
And I, poor fool, will aid in your defense.
Pretend, pretend, that you are just and true,
And I shall make myself believe in you.
  CEL. Oh, stop it. Don't be such a jealous dunce,
Or I shall leave off loving you at once.   260
Just why should I *pretend*? What could impel me
To stoop so low as that? And kindly tell me
Why, if I loved another, I shouldn't merely
Inform you of it, simply and sincerely!
I've told you where you stand, and that admission
Should altogether clear me of suspicion;
After so generous a guarantee,
What right have you to harbor doubts of me?
Since women are (from natural reticence)
Reluctant to declare their sentiments,   270
And since the honor of our sex requires
That we conceal our amorous desires,
Ought any man for whom such laws are broken
To question what the oracle has spoken?
Should he not rather feel an obligation
To trust that most obliging declaration?
Enough, now. Your suspicions quite disgust me;
Why should I love a man who doesn't trust me?

I cannot understand why I continue,
Fool that I am, to take an interest in you.   280
I ought to choose a man less prone to doubt,
And give you something to be vexed about.
  ALC. Ah, what a poor enchanted fool I am;
These gentle words, no doubt, were all a sham;
But destiny requires me to entrust
My happiness to you, and so I must.
I'll love you to the bitter end, and see
How false and treacherous you dare to be.
  CEL. No, you don't really love me as you ought.
  ALC. I love you more than can be said or thought;
Indeed, I wish you were in such distress   291
That I might show my deep devotedness.
Yes, I could wish that you were wretchedly poor,
Unloved, uncherished, utterly obscure;
That fate had set you down upon the earth
Without possessions, rank, or gentle birth;
Then, by the offer of my heart, I might
Repair the great injustice of your plight;
I'd raise you from the dust, and proudly prove
The purity and vastness of my love.   300
  CEL. This is a strange benevolence indeed!
God grant that I may never be in need. . . .
Ah, here's Monsieur Dubois, in quaint disguise.

SCENE IV. CELIMENE, ALCESTE, DUBOIS.

  ALC. Well, why this costume? Why those
    frightened eyes?
What ails you?
  DUBOIS.   Well, Sir, things are most mysterious.
  ALC. What do you mean?
  DUB.   I fear they're very serious.
  ALC. What?
  DUB.   Shall I speak more loudly?
  ALC.   Yes; speak out.
  DUB. Isn't there someone here, Sir?
  ALC.   Speak, you lout!
Stop wasting time.
  DUB.   Sir, we must slip away.
  ALC. How's that?
  DUB.   We must decamp without delay.
  ALC. Explain yourself.
  DUB.   I tell you we must fly.   311
  ALC. What for?
  DUB.   We mustn't pause to say good-by.
  ALC. Now what d'you mean by all of this, you
    clown?
  DUB. I mean, Sir, that we've got to leave this
    town.
  ALC. I'll tear you limb from limb and joint from
    joint
If you don't come more quickly to the point.

DUB. Well, Sir, today a man in a black suit,
Who wore a black and ugly scowl to boot,
Left us a document scrawled in such a hand
As even Satan couldn't understand.   320
It bears upon your lawsuit, I don't doubt;
But all hell's devils couldn't make it out.

ALC. Well, well, go on. What then? I fail to see
How this event obliges us to flee.

DUB. Well, Sir: an hour later, hardly more,
A gentleman who's often called before
Came looking for you in an anxious way.
Not finding you, he asked me to convey
(Knowing I could be trusted with the same)
The following message. . . . Now, what *was* his
    name?   330

ALC. Forget his name, you idiot. What did he
    say?

DUB. Well, it was one of your friends, Sir, anyway.
He warned you to begone, and he suggested
That if you stay, you may well be arrested.

ALC. What? Nothing more specific? Think,
    man, think!

DUB. No, Sir. He had me bring him pen and ink,
And dashed you off a letter which, I'm sure,
Will render things distinctly less obscure.

ALC. Well—let me have it!

CEL.   What *is* this all about?

ALC. God knows; but I have hopes of finding out.
How long am I to wait, you blitherer?   341

DUB. [*after a protracted search for the letter*] I must
    have left it on your table, Sir.

ALC. I ought to . . .

CEL.   No, no, keep your self-control;
Go find out what's behind his rigmarole.

ALC. It seems that fate, no matter what I do,
Has sworn that I may not converse with you;
But, Madam, pray permit your faithful lover
To try once more before the day is over.

ACT V

SCENE I. ALCESTE, PHILINTE.

ALC. No, it's too much. My mind's made up, I
    tell you.

PHIL. Why should this blow, however hard,
    compel you . . .

ALC. No, no, don't waste your breath in
    argument;
Nothing you say will alter my intent;
This age is vile, and I've made up my mind
To have no further commerce with mankind.
Did not truth, honor, decency, and the laws

Oppose my enemy and approve my cause?
My claims were justified in all men's sight;
I put my trust in equity and right;   10
Yet, to my horror and the world's disgrace,
Justice is mocked, and I have lost my case!
A scoundrel whose dishonesty is notorious
Emerges from another lie victorious!
Honor and right condone his brazen fraud,
While rectitude and decency applaud!
Before his smirking face, the truth stands charmed,
And virtue conquered, and the law disarmed!
His crime is sanctioned by a court decree!
And not content with what he's done to me,   20
The dog now seeks to ruin me by stating
That I composed a book now circulating,
A book so wholly criminal and vicious
That even to speak its title is seditious!
Meanwhile Oronte, my rival, lends his credit
To the same libelous tale, and helps to spread it!
Oronte! a man of honor and of rank,
With whom I've been entirely fair and frank;
Who sought me out and forced me, willy-nilly,
To judge some verse I found extremely silly;   30
And who, because I properly refused
To flatter him, or see the truth abused,
Abets my enemy in a rotten slander!
There's the reward of honesty and candor!
The man will hate me to the end of time
For failing to commend his wretched rhyme!
And not this man alone, but all humanity
Do what they do from interest and vanity;
They prate of honor, truth, and righteousness,
But lie, betray, and swindle nonetheless.   40
Come then: man's villainy is too much to bear;
Let's leave this jungle and this jackal's lair.
Yes! treacherous and savage race of men,
You shall not look upon my face again.

PHIL. Oh, don't rush into exile prematurely;
Things aren't as dreadful as you make them, surely.
It's rather obvious, since you're still at large,
That people don't believe your enemy's charge,
Indeed, his tale's so patently untrue
That it may do more harm to him than you.   50

ALC. Nothing could do that scoundrel any harm:
His frank corruption is his greatest charm,
And, far from hurting him, a further shame
Would only serve to magnify his name.

PHIL. In any case, his bald prevarication
Has done no injury to your reputation,
And you may feel secure in that regard.
As for your lawsuit, it should not be hard
To have the case reopened, and contest
This judgment . . .

ALC.   No, no, let the verdict rest.   60

Whatever cruel penalty it may bring,
I wouldn't have it changed for anything.
It shows the time's injustice with clarity
That I shall pass it down to our posterity
As a great proof and signal demonstration
Of the black wickedness of this generation.
It may cost twenty thousand francs; but I
Shall pay their twenty thousand, and gain thereby
The right to storm and rage at human evil,
And send the race of mankind to the devil.   70

   PHIL. Listen to me. . . .

   ALC.   Why? What can you
     possibly say?

Don't argue, Sir; your labor's thrown away.
Do you propose to offer lame excuses
For men's behavior and the time's abuses?

   PHIL. No, all you say I'll readily concede:
This is a low, conniving age indeed;
Nothing but trickery prospers nowadays,
And people ought to mend their shabby ways.
Yes, man's a beastly creature; but must we then
Abandon the society of men?   80
Here in the world, each human frailty
Provides occasion for philosophy,
And that is virtue's noblest exercise;
If honesty shone forth from all men's eyes,
If every heart were frank and kind and just,
What could our virtues do but gather dust
(Since their employment is to help us bear
The villainies of men without despair)?
A heart well-armed with virtue can endure. . . .

   ALC. Sir, you're a matchless reasoner, to be sure;
Your words are fine and full of cogency;   91
But don't waste time and eloquence on me.
My reason bids me go, for my own good.
My tongue won't lie and flatter as it should;
God knows what frankness it might next commit,
And what I'd suffer on account of it.
Pray let me wait for Célimène's return
In peace and quiet. I shall shortly learn,
By her response to what I have in view,
Whether her love for me is feigned or true.   100

   PHIL. Till then, let's visit Eliante upstairs.

   ALC. No, I am too weighed down with somber
    cares.
Go to her, do; and leave me with my gloom
Here in the darkened corner of this room.

   PHIL. Why, that's no sort of company, my friend;
I'll see if Eliante will not descend.

SCENE II. CELIMENE, ORONTE, ALCESTE.

   OR. Yes, Madam, if you wish me to remain
Your true and ardent lover, you must deign

To give me some more positive assurance.
All this suspense is quite beyond endurance.   110
If your heart shares the sweet desires of mine,
Show me as much by some convincing sign;
And here's the sign I urgently suggest:
That you no longer tolerate Alceste,
But sacrifice him to my love, and sever
All your relations with the man forever.

   CEL. Why do you suddenly dislike him so?
You praised him to the skies not long ago.

   OR. Madam, that's not the point. I'm here to find
Which way your tender feelings are inclined.   120
Choose, if you please, between Alceste and me,
And I shall stay or go accordingly.

   ALC. [*emerging from the corner*] Yes, Madam,
    choose; this gentleman's demand
Is wholly just, and I support his stand.
I too am true and ardent; I too am here
To ask you that you make your feelings clear.
No more delays, now; no equivocation;
The time has come to make your declaration.

   OR. Sir, I've no wish in any way to be
An obstacle to your felicity.   130

   ALC. Sir, I've no wish to share her heart with you;
That may sound jealous, but at least it's true.

   OR. If, weighing us, she leans in your direction . . .

   ALC. If she regards you with the least affection . . .

   OR. I swear I'll yield her to you there and then.

   ALC. I swear I'll never see her face again.

   OR. Now, Madam, tell us what we've come to
    hear.

   ALC. Madam, speak openly and have no fear.

   OR. Just say which one is to remain your lover.

   ALC. Just name one name, and it will all be
    over.   140

   OR. What! Is it possible that you're undecided?

   ALC. What! Can your feelings possibly be
    divided?

   CEL. Enough: this inquisition's gone too far:
How utterly unreasonable you are!
Not that I couldn't make the choice with ease;
My heart has no conflicting sympathies;
I know full well which one of you I favor,
And you'd not see me hesitate or waver.
But how can you expect me to reveal
So cruelly and bluntly what I feel?   150
I think it altogether too unpleasant
To choose between two men when both are
    present;
One's heart has means more subtle and more kind
Of letting its affections be divined,
Nor need one be uncharitably plain
To let a lover know he loves in vain.

   OR. No, no, speak plainly; I for one can stand it.

I beg you to be frank.
    ALC.   And I demand it.
The simple truth is what I wish to know,
And there's no need for softening the blow. 160
You've made an art of pleasing everyone,
But now your days of coquetry are done:
You have no choice now, Madam, but to choose,
For I'll know what to think if you refuse;
I'll take your silence for a clear admission
That I'm entitled to my worst suspicion.
  OR. I thank you for this ultimatum, Sir,
And I may say I heartily concur.
  CEL. Really, this foolishness is very wearing:
Must you be so unjust and overbearing? 170
Haven't I told you why I must demur?
Ah, here's Eliante; I'll put the case to her.

SCENE III. ELIANTE, PHILINTE, CELIMENE,
ORONTE, ALCESTE.

  CEL. Cousin, I'm being persecuted here
By these two persons, who, it would appear,
Will not be satisfied till I confess
Which one I love the more, and which the less,
And tell the latter to his face that he
Is henceforth banished from my company.
Tell me, has ever such a thing been done?
  EL. You'd best not turn to me; I'm not the one
To back you in a matter of this kind: 181
I'm all for those who frankly speak their mind.
  OR. Madam, you'll search in vain for a defender.
  ALC. You're beaten, Madam, and may as well
    surrender.
  OR. Speak, speak, you must; and end this awful
    strain.
  ALC. Or don't, and your position will be plain.
  OR. A single word will close this painful scene.
  ALC. But if you're silent, I'll know what you
    mean.

SCENE IV. ARSINOE, CELIMENE, ELIANTE, ALCESTE,
PHILINTE, ACASTE, CLITANDRE, ORONTE.

  ACAS. [to CELIMENE] Madam, with all due
    deference, we two
Have come to pick a little bone with you. 190
  CLIT. [to ORONTE and ALCESTE] I'm glad you're
    present, Sirs; as you'll soon learn,
Our business here is also your concern.
  ARSIN. [to CELIMENE] Madam, I visit you so soon
    again
Only because of these two gentlemen,
Who came to me indignant and aggrieved
About a crime too base to be believed.
Knowing your virtue, having such confidence in it,
I couldn't think you guilty for a minute,

In spite of all their telling evidence;
And, rising above our little difference, 200
I've hastened here in friendship's name to see
You clear yourself of this great calumny.
  ACAS. Yes, Madam, let us see with what compo-
    sure
You'll manage to respond to this disclosure.
You lately sent Clitandre this tender note.
  CLIT. And this one, for Acaste, you also wrote.
  ACAS. [to ORONTE and ALCESTE] You'll
    recognize this writing, Sirs, I think;
The lady is so free with pen and ink
That you must know it all too well, I fear.
But listen: this is something you should hear. 210

"How absurd you are to condemn my lightheartedness in society, and to accuse me of being
happiest in the company of others. Nothing could
be more unjust; and if you do not come to me
instantly and beg pardon for saying such a thing,
I shall never forgive you as long as I live. Our big
bumbling friend the Viscount . . ."
What a shame that he's not here.

"Our big bumbling friend the Viscount, whose
name stands first in your complaint, is hardly 220
a man to my taste; and ever since the day I
watched him spend three-quarters of an hour
spitting into a well, so as to make circles in the
water, I have been unable to think highly of him.
As for the little Marquess . . ."
In all modesty, gentlemen, that is I.

"As for the little Marquess, who sat squeezing
my hand for such a long while yesterday, I find
him in all respects the most trifling creature alive;
and the only things of value about him are 230
his cape and his sword. As for the man with the
green ribbons . . ."
[to ALCESTE] It's your turn now, Sir.

"As for the man with the green ribbons, he
amuses me now and then with his bluntness and
his bearish ill-humor; but there are many times
indeed when I think him the greatest bore in the
world. And as for the sonneteer . . ."
[to ORONTE] Here's your helping.

"And as for the sonneteer, who has taken it into
his head to be witty, and insists on being an author
in the teeth of opinion, I simply cannot be bothered
to listen to him, and his prose wearies me 243
quite as much as his poetry. Be assured that I am
not always so well-entertained as you suppose;
that I long for your company, more than I dare
to say, at all these entertainments to which people
drag me; and that the presence of those one loves
is the true and perfect seasoning to all one's
pleasures."

CLIT. And now for me.

"Clitandre, whom you mention, and who so
pesters me with his saccharine speeches, is the last
man on earth for whom I could feel any affection.
He is quite mad to suppose that I love him,   255
and so are you, to doubt that you are loved. Do
come to your senses; exchange your suppositions
for his; and visit me as often as possible, to help me
bear the annoyance of his unwelcome attentions."

It's a sweet character that these letters show,
And what to call it, Madam, you well know.
Enough. We're off to make the world acquainted
With this sublime self-portrait that you've painted.

ACAS. Madam, I'll make you no farewell oration;
No, you're not worthy of my indignation.   265
Far choicer hearts than yours, as you'll discover,
Would like this little Marquess for a lover.

SCENE V. CELIMENE, ELIANTE, ARSINOE, ALCESTE, ORONTE, PHILINTE.

OR. So! After all those loving letters you wrote,
You turn on me like this, and cut my throat!
And your dissembling, faithless heart, I find,
Has pledged itself by turns to all mankind!
How blind I've been! But now I clearly see;
I thank you, Madam, for enlightening me.
My heart is mine once more, and I'm content;
The loss of it shall be your punishment.
[to ALCESTE] Sir, she is yours; I'll seek no more to
    stand
Between your wishes and this lady's hand.   277

SCENE VI. CELIMENE, ELIANTE, ARSINOE, ALCESTE, PHILINTE.

ARSIN. [to CELIMENE] Madam, I'm forced to
    speak. I'm far too stirred
To keep my counsel, after what I've heard.
I'm shocked and staggered by your want of morals.
It's not my way to mix in others' quarrels;
But really, when this fine and noble spirit,
This man of honor and surpassing merit,
Laid down the offering of his heart before you,
How could you . . .
ACAS.   Madam, permit me, I implore you,
To represent myself in this debate.
Don't bother, please, to be my advocate.   287
My heart, in any case, could not afford
To give your services their due reward;
And if I chose, for consolation's sake,
Some other lady, 'twould not be you I'd take.
ARSIN. What makes you think you could, Sir?

And how dare you
Imply that I've been trying to ensnare you?
If you can for a moment entertain
Such flattering fancies, you're extremely vain.
I'm not so interested as you suppose
In Célimène's discarded gigolos.   297
Get rid of that absurd illusion, do.
Women like me are not for such as you.
Stay with this creature, to whom you're so at-
    tached;
I've never seen two people better matched.

SCENE VII. CELIMENE, ELIANTE, ALCESTE, PHILINTE.

ALC. [to CELIMENE] Well, I've been still through-
    out this exposé,
Till everyone but me has said his say.
Come, have I shown sufficient self-restraint?
And may I now . . .
CEL.   Yes, make your just complaint.
Reproach me freely, call me what you will;   306
You've every right to say I've used you ill.
I've wronged you, I confess it; and in my shame
I'll make no effort to escape the blame.
The anger of those others I could despise;
My guilt toward you I sadly recognize.
Your wrath is wholly justified, I fear;
I know how culpable I must appear,
I know all things bespeak my treachery,
And that, in short, you've grounds for hating me.
Do so; I give you leave.
ALC.   Ah, traitress—how,
How should I cease to love you, even now?   317
Though mind and will were passionately bent
On hating you, my heart would not consent.
[to ELIANTE and PHILINTE] Be witness to my mad-
    ness, both of you;
See what infatuation drives one to;
But wait; my folly's only just begun,
And I shall prove to you before I'm done
How strange the human heart is, and how far
From rational we sorry creatures are.
[to CELIMENE] Woman, I'm willing to forget your
    shame   325
And clothe your treacheries in a sweeter name;
I'll call them youthful errors, instead of crimes,
And lay the blame on these corrupting times.
My one condition is that you agree
To share my chosen fate, and fly with me
To that wild, trackless, solitary place
In which I shall forget the human race.
Only by such a course can you atone
For those atrocious letters; by that alone

Can you remove my present horror of you,   335
And make it possible for me to love you.
 CEL. What! *I* renounce the world at my young
  age,
And die of boredom in some hermitage?
 ALC. Ah, if you really loved me as you ought,
You wouldn't give the world a moment's thought;
Must you have me, and all the world beside?
 CEL. Alas, at twenty one is terrified
Of solitude. I fear I lack the force
And depth of soul to take so stern a course.   344
But if my hand in marriage will content you,
Why, there's a plan which I might well consent to,
And . . .
 ALC. No, I detest you now. I could excuse
Everything else, but since you thus refuse
To love me wholly, as a wife should do,
And see the world in me, as I in you,
Go! I reject your hand, and disenthrall
My heart from your enchantments, once for all.

SCENE VIII. ELIANTE, ALCESTE, PHILINTE.

 ALC. [*to* ELIANTE] Madam, your virtuous beauty
  has no peer;
Of all this world, you only are sincere;

I've long esteemed you highly, as you know;
Permit me ever to esteem you so,   356
And if I do not now request your hand,
Forgive me, Madam, and try to understand.
I feel unworthy of it; I sense that fate
Does not intend me for the married state,
That I should do you wrong by offering you
My shattered heart's unhappy residue,
And that in short . . .
 EL.   Your argument's well taken:
Nor need you fear that I shall feel forsaken.
Were I to offer him this hand of mine,
Your friend Philinte, I think, would not decline.
 PHIL. Ah, Madam, that's my heart's most cher-
  ished goal,   367
For which I'd gladly give my life and soul.
 ALC. [*to* ELIANTE *and* PHILINTE] May you be true
  to all you now profess,
And so deserve unending happiness.
Meanwhile, betrayed and wronged in everything,
I'll flee this bitter world where vice is king,
And seek some spot unpeopled and apart
Where I'll be free to have an honest heart.
 PHIL. Come, Madam, let's do everything we can
To change the mind of this unhappy man.   376

The Critic
Or, A Tragedy Rehearsed

Richard Brinsley Sheridan

Richard Brinsley Sheridan (1751–1816) was one of those rare individuals who succeeded in two distinct professions. The son of an actor and of an author—his mother, Mrs. Frances Sheridan, wrote both plays and novels—he was first attracted to the theatre. While still in his twenties he achieved a phenomenal success: in a five-year span (1775–1779) he had a series of six dramatic triumphs, beginning with *The Rivals* and culminating in *The School for Scandal* and *The Critic*. Then, in 1780, he became a Member of Parliament, where, in the company of Burke, Fox, and Pitt the Younger, he achieved fame as a distinguished speaker in an age of great oratory.

The Rivals and *The School for Scandal* are social comedies, exhibiting and heightening the manners of the day. They are polished and witty, inventive but not profound. Sheridan had, says Louis Kronenberger, "only worldly tastes, not—like Congreve or Molière—an incorruptibly worldly mind." However, in *The Critic*, Sheridan's talent shows up at its most brilliant. Burlesque always is a difficult form; because it mocks the immediate, it consequently tends to disappear with its object, a victim of changing tastes. Sheridan avoided that fate by satirizing what is permanent, poking fun at the absurdities of certain kinds of playwriting as well as

certain ways of producing and criticizing plays. He makes fun of a great number of things permanently with us.

As a theatrical burlesque, *The Critic* belongs to a distinguished tradition in the English theatre. One links it with the dazzling parody which Shakespeare created by inserting the tragedy of Pyramus and Thisbe into *A Midsummer Night's Dream*. Closer in style and manner was the Duke of Buckingham's *The Rehearsal* (1671) which satirized Dryden and the heroic verse play. The vogue for this kind of literary burlesque may be said to have reached its peak with Sheridan's play.

The Critic is also remarkable for its dramaturgy. The shifting back and forth between the stage and the sidelines, all placed in turn within the confines of the theatre, is masterly; the characters, especially Puff, are conceived and drawn with skill; the literary as well as the personal satire, imaginative and keen though it is, in no way limits the theatrical effectiveness of this play, the stage history of which has been a series of triumphs even into our own day.

The Critic was first produced at Drury Lane Theatre on October 30, 1779; the text was subsequently published by T. Becket in London in 1781.

DRAMATIS PERSONAE

SIR FRETFUL PLAGIARY	SIGNOR PASTICCIO RITORNELLO	MRS. DANGLE
PUFF	INTERPRETER	SIGNORE PASTICCIO RITORNELLO
DANGLE	UNDER PROMPTER	
SNEER	MR. HOPKINS	SCENEMEN, MUSICIANS, *and* SERVANTS

Characters of the Tragedy

Lord Burleigh	Beefeater	Justice's Lady
Governor of Tilbury Fort	Justice	First Niece
Earl of Leicester	Son	Second Niece
Sir Walter Raleigh	Constable	
Sir Christopher Hatton	Thames	Knights, Guards, Constables,
Master of the Horse	Tilburina	Sentinels, Servants, Chorus,
Don Ferolo Whiskerandos	Confidant	Rivers, Attendants, &c., &c.

SCENE—*London: in* DANGLE'S *House during the First Act,
and throughout the rest of the Play in Drury Lane Theatre.*

TO MRS. GREVILLE

MADAM,—In requesting your permission to address the following pages to you, which, as they aim themselves to be critical, require every protection and allowance that approving taste or friendly prejudice can give them, I yet ventured to mention no other motive than the gratification of private friendship and esteem. Had I suggested a hope that your implied approbation would give a sanction to their defects, your particular reserve, and dislike to the reputation of critical taste, as well as of poetical talent, would have made you refuse the protection of your name to such a purpose. However, I am not so ungrateful as now to attempt to combat this disposition in you. I shall not here presume to argue that the present state of poetry claims and expects every assistance that taste and example can afford it; nor endeavour to prove that a fastidious concealment of the most elegant productions of judgment and fancy is an ill return for the possession of those endowments. Continue to deceive yourself in the idea that you are known only to be eminently admired and regarded for the valuable qualities that attach private friendships, and the graceful talents that adorn conversation. Enough of what you have written has stolen into full public notice to answer my purpose; and you will, perhaps, be the only person, conversant in elegant literature, who shall read this address and not perceive that by publishing your particular approbation of the following drama, I have a more interested object than to boast the true respect and regard with which I have the honour to be, Madam, your very sincere and obedient humble servant,

R. B. SHERIDAN

PROLOGUE

By the Honourable Richard Fitzpatrick

The sister Muses, whom these realms obey,
Who o'er the drama hold divided sway,
Sometimes by evil counsellors, 'tis said,
Like earth-born potentates have been misled.
In those gay days of wickedness and wit,
When Villiers criticised what Dryden writ,
The tragic queen, to please a tasteless crowd,
Had learn'd to bellow, rant, and roar so loud,
That frighten'd Nature, her best friend before,
The blustering beldam's company foreswore;
Her comic sister, who had wit 'tis true,
With all her merits, had her failings too:
And would sometimes in mirthful moments use
A style too flippant for a well-bred muse;
Then female modesty abash'd began
To seek the friendly refuge of the fan,
Awhile behind that slight intrenchment stood,
Till driven from thence, she left the stage for good.
In our more pious, and far chaster times,
These sure no longer are the Muse's crimes!
But some complain that, former faults to shun,

The reformation to extremes has run.
The frantic hero's wild delirium past,
Now insipidity succeeds bombast:
So slow Melpomene's cold numbers creep,
Here dulness seems her drowsy court to keep,
And we are scarce awake, whilst you are fast asleep.
Thalia, once so ill-behaved and rude,
Reform'd, is now become an arrant prude;
Retailing nightly to the yawning pit
The purest morals, undefiled by wit!
Our author offers, in these motley scenes,
A slight remonstrance to the drama's queens:
Nor let the goddesses be over nice;
Free-spoken subjects give the best advice.
Although not quite a novice in his trade,
His cause to-night requires no common aid.
To this, a friendly, just, and powerful court,
I come ambassador to beg support.
Can he undaunted brave the critic's rage?
In civil broils with brother bards engage?
Hold forth their errors to the public eye,
Nay more, e'en newspapers themselves defy?
Say, must his single arm encounter all?
By number vanquish'd, e'en the brave may fall;
And though no leader should success distrust,
Whose troops are willing, and whose cause is just;
To bid such hosts of angry foes defiance,
His chief dependence must be, your alliance.

ACT I

SCENE I. *A Room in* DANGLE'S *House.*

[MR. *and* MRS. DANGLE *discovered at breakfast, and reading newspapers.*]

DANGLE. [*reading*] Brutus to Lord North.—*Letter the second on the State of the Army*—Psha! *To the first L dash D of the A dash Y.—Genuine extract of a Letter from St. Kitt's.— Coxheath Intelligence.—It is now confidently asserted that Sir Charles Hardy*—Psha! nothing but about the fleet and the nation!—and I hate all politics but theatrical politics.—Where's the Morning Chronicle?

MRS. D. Yes, that's your Gazette.

DANG. So, here we have it.— [*Reads.*] *Theatrical intelligence extraordinary.—We hear there is a new tragedy in rehearsal at Drury Lane Theatre, called the Spanish Armada, said to be written by Mr. Puff, a gentleman well-known in the theatrical world. If we may allow ourselves to give credit to the report of the performers, who, truth to say, are in general but indifferent judges, this piece abounds with the most striking and received beauties of modern composition.*—So! I am very glad

my friend Puff's tragedy is in such forwardness.—
Mrs. Dangle, my dear, you will be very glad to
hear that Puff's tragedy——

MRS. D. Lord, Mr. Dangle, why will you plague
me about such nonsense?—Now the plays are
begun I shall have no peace.—Isn't it sufficient to
make yourself ridiculous by your passion for the
theatre, without continually teasing me to join
you? Why can't you ride your hobby-horse without
desiring to place me on a pillion behind you, Mr.
Dangle?

DANG. Nay, my dear, I was only going to
read——

MRS. D. No, no; you will never read anything
that's worth listening to. You hate to hear about
your country; there are letters every day with
Roman signatures, demonstrating the certainly of
an invasion, and proving that the nation is utterly
undone. But you never will read anything to
entertain one.

DANG. What has a woman to do with politics,
Mrs. Dangle?

MRS. D. And what have you to do with the
theatre, Mr. Dangle? Why should you affect the
character of a critic? I have no patience with
you!—haven't you made yourself the jest of all
your acquaintance by your interference in matters
where you have no business? Are you not called a
theatrical Quidnunc, and a mock Mæcenas to
second-hand authors?

DANG. True; my power with the managers is
pretty notorious. But is it no credit to have appli-
cations from all quarters for my interest—from
lords to recommend fiddlers, from ladies to get
boxes, from authors to get answers, and from
actors to get engagements?

MRS. D. Yes, truly; you have contrived to get a
share in all the plague and trouble of theatrical
property, without the profit, or even the credit of
the abuse that attends it.

DANG. I am sure, Mrs. Dangle, you are no loser
by it, however; you have all the advantages of it.
Mightn't you, last winter, have had the reading of
the new pantomime a fortnight previous to its
performance? And doesn't Mr. Fosbrook let you
take places for a play before it is advertised, and set
you down for a box for every new piece through the
season? And didn't my friend, Mr. Smatter, ded-
icate his last farce to you at my particular request,
Mrs. Dangle?

MRS. D. Yes; but wasn't the farce damned, Mr.
Dangle? And to be sure it is extremely pleasant to
have one's house made the motley rendezvous of
all the lackeys of literature; the very high 'Change

of trading authors and jobbing critics!—Yes, my
drawing-room is an absolute register-office for
candidate actors, and poets without character.—
Then to be continually alarmed with misses and
ma'ams piping hysteric changes on Juliets and
Dorindas, Pollys and Ophelias; and the very
furniture trembling at the probationary starts and
unprovoked rants of would-be Richards and Hamlets!—And what is worse than all, now that the
manager has monopolized the Opera House,
haven't we the signors and signoras calling here,
sliding their smooth semibreves and gargling glib
divisions in their outlandish throats—with foreign
emissaries and French spies, for aught I know,
disguised like fiddlers and figure dancers?

DANG. Mercy! Mrs. Dangle!

MRS. D. And to employ yourself so idly at such
an alarming crisis as this too—when, if you had
the least spirit, you would have been at the head
of one of the Westminster associations—or trailing
a volunteer pike in the Artillery Ground! But
you—o' my conscience, I believe, if the French
were landed to-morrow, your first inquiry would
be, whether they had brought a theatrical troop
with them.

DANG. Mrs. Dangle, it does not signify—I say
the stage is *the mirror of Nature*, and the actors are
the Abstract and brief Chronicles of the Time: and pray
what can a man of sense study better?—Besides,
you will not easily persuade me that there is no
credit or importance in being at the head of a
band of critics, who take upon them to decide for
the whole town, whose opinion and patronage all
writers solicit, and whose recommendation no
manager dares refuse.

MRS. D. Ridiculous!—Both managers and authors
of the least merit laugh at your pretensions.—The
public is their critic—without whose fair approbation they know no play can rest on the stage,
and with whose applause they welcome such
attacks as yours, and laugh at the malice of them,
where they can't at the wit.

DANG. Very well, madam—very well!

[*Enter* SERVANT.]

SERVANT. Mr. Sneer, sir, to wait on you.

DANG. Oh, show Mr. Sneer up.—[*Exit* SERVANT.]
—Plague on't, now we must appear loving and
affectionate, or Sneer will hitch us into a story.

MRS. D. With all my heart; you can't be more
ridiculous than you are.

DANG. You are enough to provoke——[*Enter*
SNEER.] Ha! my dear Sneer, I am vastly glad to
see you.—My dear, here's Mr. Sneer.

MRS. D. Good-morning to you, sir.

DANG. Mrs. Dangle and I have been diverting ourselves with the papers. Pray, Sneer, won't you go to Drury Lane Theatre the first night of Puff's tragedy?

SNEER. Yes; but I suppose one shan't be able to get in, for on the first night of a new piece they always fill the house with orders to support it. But here, Dangle, I have brought you two pieces, one of which you must exert yourself to make the managers accept, I can tell you that; for 'tis written by a person of consequence.

DANG. So! now my plagues are beginning.

SNEER. Ay, I am glad of it, for now you'll be happy. Why, my dear Dangle, it is a pleasure to see how you enjoy your volunteer fatigue, and your solicited solicitations.

DANG. It's a great trouble—yet, egad, it's pleasant too.—Why, sometimes of a morning I have a dozen people call on me at breakfast-time, whose faces I never saw before, nor ever desire to see again.

SNEER. That must be very pleasant indeed!

DANG. And not a week but I receive fifty letters, and not a line in them about any business of my own.

SNEER. An amusing correspondence!

DANG. [Reading.] Bursts into tears and exit.—What, is this a tragedy?

SNEER. No, that's a genteel comedy, not a translation—only taken from the French: it is written in a style which they have lately tried to run down; the true sentimental, and nothing ridiculous in it from the beginning to the end.

MRS. D. Well, if they had kept to that, I should not have been such an enemy to the stage; there was some edification to be got from those pieces, Mr. Sneer!

SNEER. I am quite of your opinion, Mrs. Dangle: the theatre, in proper hands, might certainly be made the school of morality; but now, I am sorry to say it, people seem to go there principally for their entertainment!

MRS. D. It would have been more to the credit of the managers to have kept it in the other line.

SNEER. Undoubtedly, madam; and hereafter perhaps to have had it recorded, that in the midst of a luxurious and dissipated age, they preserved two houses in the capital, where the conversation was always moral at least, if not entertaining!

DANG. Now, egad, I think the worst alteration is in the nicety of the audience!—No *double-entendre*, no smart innuendo admitted; even Vanbrugh and Congreve obliged to undergo a bungling reformation!

SNEER. Yes, and our prudery in this respect is just on a par with the artificial bashfulness of a courtesan, who increases the blush upon her cheek in an exact proportion to the diminution of her modesty.

DANG. Sneer can't even give the public a good word! But what have we here?—This seems a very odd——

SNEER. Oh, that's a comedy on a very new plan; replete with wit and mirth, yet of a most serious moral! You see it is called *The Reformed House-breaker;* where, by the mere force of humour, house-breaking is put in so ridiculous a light, that if the piece has its proper run, I have no doubt but that bolts and bars will be entirely useless by the end of the season.

DANG. Egad, this is new indeed!

SNEER. Yes; it is written by a particular friend of mine, who has discovered that the follies and foibles of society are subjects unworthy the notice of the comic muse, who should be taught to stoop only to the greater vices and blacker crimes of humanity—gibbeting capital offences in five acts, and pillorying petty larcenies in two.—In short, his idea is to dramatize the penal laws, and make the stage a court of ease to the Old Bailey.

DANG. It is truly moral.

[*Re-enter* SERVANT.]

SERV. Sir Fretful Plagiary, sir.

DANG. Beg him to walk up.—[*Exit* SERVANT.] Now, Mrs. Dangle, Sir Fretful Plagiary is an author to your own taste.

MRS. D. I confess he is a favourite of mine, because everybody else abuses him.

SNEER. Very much to the credit of your charity, madam, if not of your judgment.

DANG. But, egad, he allows no merit to any author but himself, that's the truth on't—though he's my friend.

SNEER. Never.—He is as envious as an old maid verging on the desperation of six and thirty; and then the insidious humility with which he seduces you to give a free opinion on any of his works, can be exceeded only by the petulant arrogance with which he is sure to reject your observations.

DANG. Very true, egad—though he's my friend.

SNEER. Then his affected contempt of all newspaper strictures; though, at the same time, he is the sorest man alive, and shrinks like scorched parchment from the fiery ordeal of true criticism: yet he is so covetous of popularity, that he had rather be abused than not mentioned at all.

DANG. There's no denying it—though he is my friend.

SNEER. You have read the tragedy he has just

finished, haven't you?

DANG. Oh, yes; he sent it to me yesterday.

SNEER. Well, and you think it execrable, don't you?

DANG. Why, between ourselves, egad, I must own—though he is my friend—that it is one of the most——He's here—[aside]—finished and most admirable perform——

SIR FRET. [without] Mr. Sneer with him did you say?   [Enter SIR FRETFUL PLAGIARY.]

DANG. Ah, my dear friend!—Egad, we were just speaking of your tragedy.—Admirable, Sir Fretful, admirable!

SNEER. You never did anything beyond it, Sir Fretful—never in your life.

SIR FRET. You make me extremely happy; for without a compliment, my dear Sneer, there isn't a man in the world whose judgment I value as I do yours and Mr. Dangle's.

MRS. D. They are only laughing at you, Sir Fretful; for it was but just now that——

DANG. Mrs. Dangle!—Ah, Sir Fretful, you know Mrs. Dangle.—My friend Sneer was rallying just now:—he knows how she admires you, and——

SIR FRET. O Lord, I am sure Mr. Sneer has more taste and sincerity than to   [aside] A damned double-faced fellow!

DANG. Yes, yes—Sneer will jest—but a better humoured——

SIR FRET. Oh, I know——

DANG. He has a ready turn for ridicule—his wit costs him nothing.

SIR FRET. No, egad—[aside] or I should wonder how he came by it.

MRS. D. [aside] Because his jest is always at the expense of his friend.

DANG. But, Sir Fretful, have you sent your play to the managers yet?—or can I be of any service to you?

SIR FRET. No, no, I thank you: I believe the piece had sufficient recommendation with it.—I thank you though.—I sent it to the manager of Covent Garden Theatre this morning.

SNEER. I should have thought now, that it might have been cast (as the actors call it) better at Drury Lane.

SIR FRET. O Lud! no—never send a play there while I live—hark'ee!   [Whispers SNEER.]

SNEER. Writes himself!—I know he does.

SIR FRET. I say nothing—I take away from no man's merit—am hurt at no man's good fortune —I say nothing.—But this I will say—through all my knowledge of life, I have observed—that there is not a passion so strongly rooted in the human heart as envy.

SNEER. I believe you have reason for what you say, indeed.

SIR FRET. Besides—I can tell you it is not always so safe to leave a play in the hands of those who write themselves.

SNEER. What, they may steal from them, hey, my dear Plagiary?

SIR FRET. Steal!—to be sure they may; and, egad, serve your best thoughts as gypsies do stolen children, disfigure them to make 'em pass for their own.

SNEER. But your present work is a sacrifice to Melpomene, and he, you know, never——

SIR FRET. That's no security: a dexterous plagiarist may do anything. Why, sir, for aught I know, he might take out some of the best things in my tragedy, and put them into his own comedy.

SNEER. That might be done, I dare be sworn.

SIR FRET. And then, if such a person gives you the least hint or assistance, he is devilish apt to take the merit of the whole——

DANG. If it succeeds.

SIR FRET. Ay, but with regard to this piece, I think I can hit that gentleman, for I can safely swear he never read it.

SNEER. I'll tell you how you may hurt him more.

SIR FRET. How?

SNEER. Swear he wrote it.

SIR FRET. Plague on't now, Sneer, I shall take it ill!—I believe you want to take away my character as an author.

SNEER. Then I am sure you ought to be very much obliged to me.

SIR FRET. Hey!—sir!——

DANG. Oh, you know, he never means what he says.

SIR FRET. Sincerely then—do you like the piece?

SNEER. Wonderfully!

SIR FRET. But come, now, there must be something that you think might be mended, hey?—Mr. Dangle, has nothing struck you?

DANG. Why, faith, it is but an ungracious thing for the most part, to——

SIR FRET. With most authors it is just so, indeed; they are in general strangely tenacious! But, for my part, I am never so well pleased as when a judicious critic points out any defect to me; for what is the purpose of showing a work to a friend, if you don't mean to profit by his opinion?

SNEER. Very true.—Why, then, though I seriously admire the piece upon the whole, yet there is one small objection; which, if you'll give me leave, I'll mention.

SIR FRET. Sir, you can't oblige me more.

SNEER. I think it wants incident.

SIR FRET. Good God! you surprise me!—wants incident!

SNEER. Yes; I own I think the incidents are too few.

SIR FRET. Good God! Believe me, Mr. Sneer, there is no person for whose judgment I have a more implicit deference. But I protest to you, Mr. Sneer, I am only apprehensive that the incidents are too crowded.—My dear Dangle, how does it strike you?

DANG. Really I can't agree with my friend Sneer. I think the plot quite sufficient; and the four first acts by many degrees the best I ever read or saw in my life. If I might venture to suggest anything, it is that the interest rather falls off in the fifth.

SIR FRET. Rises, I believe you mean, sir.

DANG. No, I don't, upon my word.

SIR FRET. Yes, yes, you do, upon my soul!—it certainly don't fall off, I assure you.—No, no; it don't fall off.

DANG. Now, Mrs. Dangle, didn't you say it struck you in the same light?

MRS. D. No, indeed, I did not.—I did not see a fault in any part of the play, from the beginning to the end.

SIR FRET. Upon my soul, the women are the best judges after all!

MRS. D. Or, if I made any objection, I am sure it was to nothing in the piece; but that I was afraid it was on the whole, a little too long.

SIR FRET. Pray, madam, do you speak as to duration of time; or do you mean that the story is tediously spun out?

MRS. D. O Lud! no.—I speak only with reference to the usual length of acting plays.

SIR FRET. Then I am very happy—very happy indeed—because the play is a short play, a remarkably short play. I should not venture to differ with a lady on a point of taste; but on these occasions, the watch, you know, is the critic.

MRS. D. Then, I suppose, it must have been Mr. Dangle's drawling manner of reading it to me.

SIR FRET. Oh, if Mr. Dangle read it, that's quite another affair!—But I assure you, Mrs. Dangle, the first evening you can spare me three hours and a half, I'll undertake to read you the whole, from beginning to end, with the prologue and epilogue, and allow time for the music between the acts.

MRS. D. I hope to see it on the stage next.

DANG. Well, Sir Fretful, I wish you may be able to get rid as easily of the newspaper criticisms as you do of ours.

SIR FRET. The newspapers! Sir, they are the most villainous—licentious—abominable—infernal.— Not that I ever read them—no—I make it a rule never to look into a newspaper.

DANG. You are quite right; for it certainly must hurt an author of delicate feelings to see the liberties they take.

SIR FRET. No, quite the contrary! their abuse is, in fact, the best panegyric—I like it of all things. An author's reputation is only in danger from their support.

SNEER. Why, that's true—and that attack, now, on you the other day——

SIR FRET. What? where?

DANG. Ay, you mean in a paper of Thursday: it was completely ill-natured, to be sure.

SIR FRET. Oh so much the better.—Ha! Ha! Ha! I wouldn't have it otherwise.

DANG. Certainly it is only to be laughed at; for ——

SIR FRET. You don't happen to recollect what the fellow said, do you?

SNEER. Pray, Dangle—Sir Fretful seems a little anxious——

SIR FRET. O Lud, no!—anxious!—not I—not the least.—I—but one may as well hear, you know.

DANG. Sneer, do you recollect?—[aside to SNEER] Make out something.

SNEER. [aside to DANGLE] I will.—[aloud] Yes, yes, I remember perfectly.

SIR FRET. Well, and pray now—not that it signifies—what might the gentleman say?

SNEER. Why, he roundly asserts that you have not the slightest invention or original genius whatever; though you are the greatest traducer of all other authors living.

SIR FRET. Ha! ha! ha!—very good!

SNEER. That as to comedy, you have not one idea of your own, he believes, even in your common-place-book—where stray jokes and pilfered witticisms are kept with as much method as the ledger of the lost and stolen office.

SIR FRET. Ha! ha! ha!—very pleasant!

SNEER. Nay, that you are so unlucky as not to have the skill even to steal with taste:—but that you glean from the refuse of obscure volumes, where more judicious plagiarists have been before you; so that the body of your work is a composition of dregs and sentiments—like a bad tavern's worst wine.

SIR FRET. Ha! ha!

SNEER. In your more serious efforts, he says, your bombast would be less intolerable, if the thoughts were ever suited to the expression; but the homeliness of the sentiment stares through the fantastic encumbrance of its fine language, like a clown in one of the new uniforms!

SIR FRET. Ha! ha!

SNEER. That your occasional tropes and flowers suit the general coarseness of your style, as tambour sprigs would a ground of linsey-woolsey; while your imitations of Shakespeare resemble the mimicry of Falstaff's page, and are about as near the standard as the original.

SIR FRET. Ha!

SNEER. In short, that even the finest passages you steal are of no service to you; for the poverty of your own language prevents their assimilating; so that they lie on the surface like lumps of marl on a barren moor, encumbering what it is not in their power to fertilize!

SIR FRET. [after great agitation] Now, another person would be vexed at this!

SNEER. Oh! but I wouldn't have told you—only to divert you.

SIR FRET. I know it—I am diverted.—Ha! ha! ha!—not the least invention!—Ha! ha! ha!—very good!—very good!

SNEER. Yes—no genius! ha! ha! ha!

DANG. A severe rogue! ha! ha! ha! But you are quite right, Sir Fretful, never to read such nonsense.

SIR FRET. To be sure—for if there is anything to one's praise, it is a foolish vanity to be gratified at it; and, if it is abuse—why one is always sure to hear of it from one damned good-natured friend or other!

[Enter SERVANT.]

SERV. Sir, there is an Italian gentleman, with a French interpreter, and three young ladies, and a dozen musicians, who say they are sent by Lady Rondeau and Mrs. Fugue.

DANG. Gadso! they come by appointment!—Dear Mrs. Dangle, do let them know I'll see them directly.

MRS. D. You know, Mr. Dangle, I shan't understand a word they say.

DANG. But you hear there's an interpreter.

MRS. D. Well, I'll try to endure their complaisance till you come.   [Exit.]

SERV. And Mr. Puff, sir, has sent word that the last rehearsal is to be this morning, and that he'll call on you presently.

DANG. That's true—I shall certainly be at home. —[Exit SERVANT.]—Now, Sir Fretful, if you have a mind to have justice done you in the way of answer, egad, Mr. Puff's your man.

SIR FRET. Psha! sir, why should I wish to have it answered, when I tell you I am pleased at it?

DANG. True, I had forgot that. But I hope you are not fretted at what Mr. Sneer——

SIR FRET. Zounds! no, Mr. Dangle; don't I tell you these things never fret me in the least?

DANG. Nay, I only thought——

SIR FRET. And let me tell you, Mr. Dangle, 'tis damned affronting in you to suppose that I am hurt when I tell you I am not.

SNEER. But why so warm, Sir Fretful?

SIR FRET. Gad's life! Mr. Sneer, you are as absurd as Dangle: how often must I repeat it to you, that nothing can vex me but your supposing it possible for me to mind the damned nonsense you have been repeating to me!—and, let me tell you, if you continue to believe this, you must mean to insult me, gentlemen—and, then, your disrespect will affect me no more than the newspaper criticisms—and I shall treat it with exactly the same calm indifference and philosophic contempt—and so your servant.   [Exit.]

SNEER. Ha! ha! ha! poor Sir Fretful! Now will he go and vent his philosophy in anonymous abuse of all modern critics and authors.—But, Dangle, you must get your friend Puff to take me to the rehearsal of his tragedy.

DANG. I'll answer for't, he'll thank you for desiring it. But come and help me to judge of this musical family: they are recommended by people of consequence, I assure you.

SNEER. I am at your disposal the whole morning! —but I thought you had been a decided critic in music as well as in literature.

DANG. So I am—but I have a bad ear. I'faith, Sneer, though, I am afraid we were a little too severe on Sir Fretful—though he is my friend.

SNEER. Why, 'tis certain, that unnecessarily to mortify the vanity of any writer is a cruelty which mere dullness never can deserve, but where a base and personal malignity usurps the place of literary emulation, the aggressor deserves neither quarter nor pity.

DANGLE. That's true, egad!—though he's my friend!

SCENE II. *A drawing-room in* DANGLE's *House.*

[MRS. DANGLE, SIGNOR PASTICCIO RITORNELLO, SIGNORE PASTICCIO RITORNELLO, INTERPRETER, *and* MUSICIANS *discovered.*]

INTERPRETER. Je dis, madame, j'ai l'honneur *to introduce* et de vous demander votre protection pour le Signor Pasticcio Ritornello et pour sa charmante famille.

SIGNOR PASTICCIO. Ah! vosignoria, noi vi preghiamo di favoritevi colla vostra protezione.

I SIGNORA P. Vosignoria fatevi questi grazie.

2 SIGNORA P. Si, signora.

INTERP. Madame—*me interpret.*—C'est à dire—*in English*—qu'ils vous prient de leur faire l'honneur——

MRS. D. I say again, gentlemen, I don't understand a word you say.

SIGNOR P. Questo signore spiegheró——

INTERP. Oui—*me interpret.*—Nous avons les lettres de recommendation pour Monsieur Dangle de——

MRS. D. Upon my word, sir, I don't understand you.

SIGNOR P. La Contessa Rondeau è nostra padrona.

3 SIGNORA P. Si, padre, et Miladi Fugue.

INTERP. O!—*me interpret.*—Madame, ils disent—*in English*—Qu'ils ont l'honneur d'être protégés de ces dames.—*You understand?*

MRS. D. No, sir,—no understand!

[*Enter* DANGLE *and* SNEER.]

INTERP. Ah, voici, Monsieur Dangle!

ALL ITALIANS. Ah! Signor Dangle!

MRS. D. Mr. Dangle, here are two very civil gentlemen trying to make themselves understood, and I don't know which is the interpreter.

DANG. Eh, bien!

[*The* INTERPRETER *and* SIGNOR PASTICCIO *here speak at the same time.*]

INTERP. Monsieur Dangle, le grand bruit de vos talents pour la critique, et de votre intérêt avec messieurs les directeurs à tous les théâtres——

SIGNOR P. Vosignoria siete si famoso par la vostra conoscenza, e vostra interessa colla le direttore da

DANG. Egad, I think the interpreter is the hardest to be understood of the two!

SNEER. Why, I thought, Dangle, you had been an admirable linguist!

DANG. So I am, if they would not talk so damned fast.

SNEER. Well, I'll explain that—the less time we lose in hearing them the better—for that, I suppose, is what they are brought here for.

[*Speaks to* SIGNOR PASTICCIO—*they sing trios, &c.,* DANGLE *beating out of time.*]

[*Enter* SERVANT *and whispers* DANGLE.]

DANG. Show him up.—[*Exit* SERVANT.] Bravo! admirable! bravissimo! admirablissimo!—Ah! Sneer! where will you find voices such as these in England?

SNEER. Not easily.

DANG. But Puff is coming.—Signor and little signoras obligatissimo!—Sposa Signora Danglena.—Mrs. Dangle, shall I beg you to offer them some refreshments, and take their address in the next room.

[*Exit* MRS. DANGLE *with* SIGNOR PASTICCIO, SIGNORE PASTICCIO, MUSICIANS, *and* INTERPRETER, *ceremoniously.*]

[*Re-enter* SERVANT.]

SERV. Mr. Puff, sir.   [*Exit.*]

[*Enter* PUFF.]

DANG. My dear Puff!

PUFF. My dear Dangle, how is it with you?

DANG. Mr. Sneer, give me leave to introduce Mr. Puff to you.

PUFF. Mr. Sneer is this?—Sir, he is a gentleman whom I have long panted for the honour of knowing—a gentleman whose critical talents and transcendent judgment——

SNEER. Dear sir——

DANG. Nay, don't be modest, Sneer; my friend Puff only talks to you in the style of his profession.

SNEER. His profession.

PUFF. Yes, sir; I make no secret of the trade I follow: among friends and brother authors, Dangle knows I love to be frank on the subject, and to advertise myself *vivâ voce.*—I am, sir, a practitioner in panegyric, or, to speak more plainly, a professor of the art of puffing, at your service—or anybody else's.

SNEER. Sir, you are very obliging!—I believe, Mr. Puff, I have often admired your talents in the daily prints.

PUFF. Yes, sir, I flatter myself I do as much business in that way as any six of the fraternity in town.—Devilish hard work all the summer, friend Dangle,—never worked harder! But, hark'ee,—the winter managers were a little sore, I believe.

DANG. No; I believe they took it all in good part.

PUFF. Ay! then that must have been affectation in them: for, egad, there were some of the attacks which there was no laughing at!

SNEER. Ay, the humorous ones.—But I should think, Mr. Puff, that authors would in general be able to do this sort of work for themselves.

PUFF. Why, yes—but in a clumsy way. Besides, we look on that as an encroachment, and so take the opposite side. I dare say, now, you conceive half the very civil paragraphs and advertisements you see to be written by the parties concerned, or their friends? No such thing: nine out of ten manufactured by me in the way of business.

SNEER. Indeed!

PUFF. Even the auctioneers now—the auctioneers, I say—though the rogues have lately got some credit for their language—not an article of the merit theirs: take them out of their pulpits, and they are as dull as catalogues!—No, sir; 'twas I first enriched their style—'twas I first taught them to crowd their advertisements with panegyrical superlatives, each epithet rising above the other, like the bidders in their own auction rooms! From me they learned to inlay their phraseology with variegated chips of exotic metaphor: by me too their inventive faculties were called forth:—yes, sir, by me they were instructed to clothe ideal walls with gratuitous fruits—to insinuate obsequious rivulets into visionary groves—to teach courteous shrubs to nod their approbation of the grateful soil, or on emergencies to raise upstart oaks, where there never had been an acorn; to create a delightful vicinage without the assistance of a neighbour; or fix the temple of Hygeia in the fens of Lincolnshire!

DANG. I am sure you have done them infinite service; for now, when a gentleman is ruined, he parts with his house with some credit.

SNEER. Service! if they had any gratitude, they would erect a statue to him; they would figure him as a presiding Mercury, the god of traffic and fiction, with a hammer in his hand instead of a caduceus.—But pray, Mr. Puff, what first put you on exercising your talents in this way?

PUFF. Egad, sir, sheer necessity!—the proper parent of an art so nearly allied to invention. You must know, Mr. Sneer, that from the first time I tried my hand at an advertisement, my success was such, that for some time after I led a most extraordinary life indeed!

SNEER. How, pray?

PUFF. Sir, I supported myself two years entirely by my misfortunes.

SNEER. By your misfortunes!

PUFF. Yes, sir, assisted by long sickness, and other occasional disorders: and a very comfortable living I had of it.

SNEER. From sickness and misfortunes! You practised as a doctor and an attorney at once?

PUFF. No, egad; both maladies and miseries were my own.

SNEER. Hey! what the plague!

DANG. 'Tis true, i'faith.

PUFF. Hark'ee!—By advertisements—*To the charitable and humane!* and *To those whom Providence hath blessed with affluence!*

SNEER. Oh, I understand you.

PUFF. And, in truth, I deserved what I got! for, I suppose never man went through such a series of calamities in the same space of time. Sir, I was five times made a bankrupt, and reduced from a state of affluence, by a train of unavoidable misfortunes: then, sir, though a very industrious tradesman, I was twice burned out, and lost my little all both times: I lived upon those fires a month. I soon after was confined by a most excruciating disorder, and lost the use of my limbs: that told very well; for I had the case strongly attested, and went about to collect the subscriptions myself.

DANG. Egad, I believe that was when you first called on me.

PUFF. In November last?—O no; I was at that time a close prisoner in the Marshalsea, for a debt benevolently contracted to serve a friend. I was afterwards twice tapped for a dropsy, which declined into a very profitable consumption. I was then reduced to—O no—then, I became a widow with six helpless children, after having had eleven husbands pressed, and being left every time eight months gone with child, and without money to get me into an hospital!

SNEER. And you bore all with patience, I make no doubt?

PUFF. Why yes; though I made some occasional attempts at *felo de se*, but as I did not find those rash actions answer, I left off killing myself very soon. Well, sir, at last, what with bankruptcies, fires, gout, dropsies, imprisonments, and other valuable calamities, having got together a pretty handsome sum, I determined to quit a business which had always gone rather against my conscience, and in a more liberal way still to indulge my talents for fiction and embellishment, through my favourite channels of diurnal communication—and so, sir, you have my history.

SNEER. Most obligingly communicative indeed! and your confession, if published, might certainly serve the cause of true charity, by rescuing the most useful channels of appeal to benevolence from the cant of imposition. But surely, Mr. Puff, there is no great mystery in your present profession?

PUFF. Mystery, sir! I will take upon me to say the matter was never scientifically treated nor reduced to rule before.

SNEER. Reduced to rule!

PUFF. O Lud, sir, you are very ignorant, I am afraid!—Yes, sir, puffing is of various sorts; the principal are, the puff direct, the puff preliminary, the puff collateral, the puff collusive, and the puff oblique, or puff by implication. These all assume, as circumstances require, the various forms of Letter to the Editor, Occasional Anecdote, Impartial Critique, Observation from Correspondent, or Advertisement from the Party.

SNEER. The puff direct, I can conceive——

PUFF. O yes, that's simple enough! For instance, —a new comedy or farce is to be produced at one of the theatres (though by-the-by they don't bring out half what they ought to do)—the author, suppose Mr. Smatter, or Mr. Dapper, or any particular friend of mine—very well; the day before it is to be performed, I write an account of the manner in which it was received; I have the plot from the author, and only add—"characters strongly drawn —highly coloured—hand of a master—fund of genuine humour—mine of invention—neat dialogue—Attic salt." Then for the performance— "Mr. Dodd was astonishingly great in the character of Sir Harry. That universal and judicious actor, Mr. Palmer, perhaps never appeared to more advantage than in the colonel;—but it is not in the power of language to do justice to Mr. King: indeed he more than merited those repeated bursts of applause which he drew from a most brilliant and judicious audience. As to the scenery—the miraculous powers of Mr. De Loutherbourg's pencil are universally acknowledged. In short, we are at a loss which to admire most, the unrivalled genius of the author, the great attention and liberality of the managers, the wonderful abilities of the painter, or the incredible exertions of all the performers."

SNEER. That's pretty well indeed, sir.

PUFF. Oh, cool!—quite cool!—to what I sometimes do.

SNEER. And do you think there are any who are influenced by this?

PUFF. O Lud, yes, sir! the number of those who undergo the fatigue of judging for themselves is very small indeed.

SNEER. Well, sir, the puff preliminary.

PUFF. O, that, sir, does well in the form of a caution. In a matter of gallantry now—Sir Flimsy Gossamer wishes to be well with Lady Fanny Fête —he applies to me—I open trenches for him with a paragraph in the Morning Post.—"It is recommended to the beautiful and accomplished Lady F four stars F dash E to be on her guard against that dangerous character, Sir F dash G; who, however pleasing and insinuating his manners may be, is certainly not remarkable for the *constancy of his attachments!*"—in italics. Here, you see, Sir Flimsy Gossamer is introduced to the particular notice of Lady Fanny, who perhaps never thought of him before—she finds herself publicly cautioned to avoid him, which naturally

makes her desirous of seeing him; the observation of their acquaintance causes a pretty kind of mutual embarrassment; this produces a sort of sympathy of interest, which if Sir Flimsy is unable to improve effectually, he at least gains the credit of having their names mentioned together, by a particular set, and in a particular way—which nine times out of ten is the full accomplishment of modern gallantry.

DANG. Egad, Sneer, you will be quite an adept in the business.

PUFF. Now, Sir, the puff collateral is much used as an appendage to advertisements, and may take the form of anecdote.—"Yesterday, as the celebrated George Bonmot was sauntering down St. James's Street, he met the lively Lady Mary Myrtle coming out of the park:—'Good God, Lady Mary, I'm surprised to meet you in a white jacket,— for I expected never to have seen you, but in a full-trimmed uniform and a light horseman's cap!' —'Heavens, George, where could you have learned that?'—'Why,' replied the wit, 'I just saw a print of you, in a new publication called the Camp Magazine; which, by-the-by, is a devilish clever thing, and is sold at No. 3, on the right hand of the way, two doors from the printing-office, the corner of Ivy Lane, Paternoster Row, price only one shilling.' "

SNEER. Very ingenious indeed!

PUFF. But the puff collusive is the newest of any; for it acts in the disguise of determined hostility. It is much used by bold booksellers and enterprising poets.—"An indignant correspondent observes, that the new poem called *Beelzebub's Cotillon, or Proserpine's Fête Champêtre*, is one of the most unjustifiable performances he ever read. The severity with which certain characters are handled is quite shocking: and as there are many descriptions in it too warmly coloured for female delicacy, the shameful avidity with which this piece is bought by all people of fashion is a reproach on the taste of the times, and a disgrace to the delicacy of the age." Here you see the two strongest inducements are held forth; first, that nobody ought to read it; and secondly, that everybody buys it: on the strength of which the publisher boldly prints the tenth edition, before he had sold ten of the first; and then establishes it by threatening himself with the pillory, or absolutely indicting himself for *scan. mag.*

DANG. Ha! ha! ha!—gad, I know it is so.

PUFF. As to the puff oblique, or puff by implication, it is too various and extensive to be illustrated by an instance: it attracts in titles and presumes in patents; it lurks in the limitation of a subscription, and invites in the assurance of crowd and in-commodation at public places; it delights to draw forth concealed merit, with a most disinterested assiduity; and sometimes wears a countenance of smiling censure and tender reproach. It has a wonderful memory for parliamentary debates, and will often give the whole speech of a favoured member with the most flattering accuracy. But, above all, it is a great dealer in reports and sup-positions. It has the earliest intelligence of in-tended preferments that will reflect honour on the patrons; and embryo promotions of modest gentle-men, who know nothing of the matter themselves. It can hint a ribbon for implied services in the air of a common report; and with the carelessness of a casual paragraph, suggest officers into commands, to which they have no pretension but their wishes. This, sir, is the last principal class of the art of puffing—an art which I hope you will now agree with me is of the highest dignity, yielding a tablature of benevolence and public spirit; be-friending equally trade, gallantry, criticism, and politics: the applause of genius—the register of charity—the triumph of heroism—the self-defense of contractors—the fame of orators—and the gazette of ministers.

SNEER. Sir, I am completely a convert both to the importance and ingenuity of your profession; and now, sir, there is but one thing which can possibly increase my respect for you, and that is, your permitting me to be present this morning at the rehearsal of your new trage——

PUFF. Hush, for heaven's sake!—*My* tragedy! Egad, Dangle, I take this very ill: you know how apprehensive I am of being known to be the author.

DANG. I'faith I would not have told—but it's in the papers, and your name at length in the Morn-ing Chronicle.

PUFF. Ah! those damned editors never can keep a secret!—Well, Mr. Sneer, no doubt you will do me great honour—I shall be infinitely happy—highly flattered——

DANG. I believe it must be near the time—shall we go together?

PUFF. No; it will not be yet this hour, for they are always late at that theatre: besides, I must meet you there, for I have some little matters here to send to the papers, and a few paragraphs to scribble before I go.—[*Looking at memorandums.*] Here is *A conscientious Baker, on the subject of the Army Bread;* and *a Detester of visible Brickwork, in favour of the new invented Stucco;* both in the style of Junius, and promised for to-morrow. The Thames naviga-tion too is at a stand. Misomud or Anti-shoal must

go to work again directly.—Here too are some political memorandums—I see; ay—*To take Paul Jones and get the Indiamen out of the Shannon—reinforce Byron—compel the Dutch to*—so!—I must do that in the evening papers, or reserve it for the Morning Herald; for I know that I have undertaken to-morrow, besides, to establish the unanimity of the fleet in the Public Advertiser, and to shoot Charles Fox in the Morning Post.—So, egad, I ha'n't a moment to lose.

DANG. Well, we'll meet in the Green Room.

[*Exeunt severally.*]

ACT II

SCENE I. *The Theatre, before the Curtain.*

[*Enter* DANGLE, PUFF, *and* SNEER.]

PUFF. No, no, sir; what Shakespeare says of actors may be better applied to the purpose of plays; they ought to be *the abstract and brief chron-icles of the time.* Therefore when history, and particularly the history of our own country, fur-nishes anything like a case in point, to the time in which an author writes, if he knows his own in-terest, he will take advantage of it; so, sir, I call my tragedy *The Spanish Armada;* and have laid the scene before Tilbury Fort.

SNEER. A most happy thought, certainly!

DANG. Egad it was—I told you so. But pray now, I don't understand how you have contrived to introduce any love into it.

PUFF. Love! oh, nothing so easy! for it is a received point among poets, that where history gives you a good heroic outline for a play, you may fill up with a little love at your own discretion: in doing which, nine times out of ten, you only make up a deficiency in the private history of the times. Now, I rather think I have done this with some success.

SNEER. No scandal about Queen Elizabeth, I hope?

PUFF. O Lud! no, no; I only suppose the governor of Tilbury Fort's daughter to be in love with the son of the Spanish admiral.

SNEER. Oh, is that all!

DANG. Excellent, i'faith! I see at once. But won't this appear rather improbable?

PUFF. To be sure it will—but what the plague! a play is not to show occurrences that happen every day, but things just so strange, that though they never did, they might happen.

SNEER. Certainly nothing is unnatural, that is not physically impossible.

PUFF. Very true—and for that matter Don Ferolo Whiskerandos, for that's the lover's name, might have been over here in the train of the Spanish ambassador, or Tilburina, for that is the lady's name, might have been in love with him, from having heard his character, or seen his picture; or from knowing that he was the last man in the world she ought to be in love with—or for any other good female reason.—However, sir, the fact is, that though she is but a knight's daughter, egad! she is in love like any princess!

DANG. Poor young lady! I feel for her already! for I can conceive how great the conflict must be between her passion and her duty; her love for her country, and her love for Don Ferolo Whiskerandos!

PUFF. Oh, amazing!—her poor susceptible heart is swayed to and fro by contending passions like——

[Enter UNDER PROMPTER.]

UNDER PROMPTER. Sir, the scene is set, and everything is ready to begin, if you please.

PUFF. Egad, then we'll lose no time.

UNDER P. Though, I believe, sir, you will find it very short, for all the performers have profited by the kind permission you granted them.

PUFF. Hey! what?

UNDER P. You know, sir, you gave them leave to cut out or omit whatever they found heavy or unnecessary to the plot, and I must own they have taken very liberal advantage of your indulgence.

PUFF. Well, well.—They are in general very good judges, and I know I am luxuriant.—Now, Mr. Hopkins, as soon as you please.

UNDER P. [to the Orchestra] Gentlemen, will you play a few bars of something, just to——

PUFF. Ay, that's right; for as we have the scenes and dresses, egad, we'll go to't, as if it was the first night's performance;—but you need not mind stopping between the acts—[Exit UNDER PROMP-TER.—Orchestra play—then the bell rings.] So! stand clear, gentlemen. Now you know there will be a cry of Down! down!—Hats off!—Silence!—Then up curtain, and let us see what our painters have done for us.   [Curtain rises.]

SCENE II. *Tilbury Fort.*
["*Two* SENTINELS *discovered asleep.*"]

DANG. Tilbury Fort!—very fine indeed!
PUFF. Now, what do you think I open with?
SNEER. Faith, I can't guess——

PUFF. A clock.—Hark!—[*Clock strikes.*] I open with a clock striking, to beget an awful attention in the audience: it also marks the time, which is four o'clock in the morning, and saves a description of the rising sun, and a great deal about gilding the eastern hemisphere.

DANG. But pray, are the sentinels to be asleep?
PUFF. Fast as watchmen.
SNEER. Isn't that odd though at such an alarming crisis?

PUFF. To be sure it is,—but smaller things must give way to a striking scene at the opening; that's a rule. And the case is, that two great men are coming to this very spot to begin the piece; now it is not to be supposed they would open their lips, if these fellows were watching them; so, egad, I must either have sent them off their posts, or set them asleep.

SNEER. Oh, that accounts for it. But tell us, who are these coming?

PUFF. These are they—Sir Walter Raleigh, and Sir Christopher Hatton. You'll know Sir Christopher by his turning out his toes—famous, you know, for his dancing. I like to preserve all the little traits of character.—Now attend.

["*Enter* SIR WALTER RALEIGH *and* SIR CHRISTOPHER HATTON."]
Sir Christopher. True, gallant Raleigh!

DANG. What, they had been talking before?
PUFF. O yes; all the way as they came along.—[*to the actors*] I beg pardon, gentlemen, but these are particular friends of mine, whose remarks may be of great service to us.—[*to* SNEER *and* DANGLE] Don't mind interrupting them whenever anything strikes you.

Sir Christopher. True, gallant Raleigh!
But oh, thou champion of thy country's fame,
There is a question which I yet must ask:
A question which I never ask'd before—
What mean these mighty armaments?
This general muster? and this throng of chiefs?

SNEER. Pray, Mr. Puff, how came Sir Christopher Hatton never to ask that question before?

PUFF. What before the play began?—how the plague could he?

DANG. That's true, i'faith!

PUFF. But you will hear what he thinks of the matter.

Sir Christopher. Alas! my noble friend, when I behold
Yon tented plains in martial symmetry

Array'd; when I count o'er yon glittering lines
Of crested warriors, where the proud steeds'
   neigh,
And valour-breathing trumpet's shrill appeal,
Responsive vibrate on my listening ear;
When virgin majesty herself I view,
Like her protecting Pallas, veil'd in steel,
With graceful confidence exhort to arms!
When, briefly, all I hear or see bears stamp
Of martial vigilance and stern defence,
I cannot but surmise—forgive, my friend,
If the conjecture's rash—I cannot but
Surmise the state some danger apprehends!

SNEER. A very cautious conjecture that.

PUFF. Yes, that's his character; not to give an
opinion but on secure grounds.—Now then.

    Sir Walter. O most accomplish'd Chris-
topher!——

PUFF. He calls him by his christian name, to
show that they are on the most familiar terms.

    Sir Walter. O most accomplish'd Christopher!
    I find
Thy staunch sagacity still tracks the future,
In the fresh print of the o'ertaken past.

PUFF. Figurative!

    Sir Walter. Thy fears are just.
    Sir Christopher. But where? whence? when?
    and what?
The danger is,—methinks I fain would learn.
    Sir Walter. You know, my friend, scarce two
    revolving suns,
And three revolving moons, have closed their
    course
Since haughty Philip, in despite of peace,
With hostile hand hath struck at England's
    trade.
    Sir Christopher. I know it well.
    Sir Walter. Philip, you know, is proud Iberia's
    king!
    Sir Christopher. He is.
    Sir Walter.   His subjects in base bigotry
And Catholic oppression held;—while we,
You know, the Protestant persuasion hold.
    Sir Christopher. We do.
    Sir Walter. You know, beside, his boasted
    armament,
The famed Armada, by the Pope baptized,
With purpose to invade these realms——
    Sir Christopher.   Is sailed,
Our last advices so report.

    Sir Walter. While the Iberian admiral's chief
    hope,
His darling son——
    Sir Christopher.   Ferolo Whiskerandos hight
—

    Sir Walter. The same—by chance a prisoner
    hath been ta'en,
And in this fort of Tilbury——
    Sir Christopher.   Is now
Confined—'tis true, and oft from yon tall turret's
    top
I've mark'd the youthful Spaniard's haughty
    mien—
Unconquer'd, though in chains.
    Sir Walter.   You also know——

DANG. Mr. Puff, as he knows all this, why does
Sir Walter go on telling him?

PUFF. But the audience are not supposed to know
anything of the matter, are they?

SNEER. True; but I think you manage ill: for
there certainly appears no reason why Sir Walter
should be so communicative.

PUFF. 'Fore Gad, now, that is one of the most
ungrateful observations I ever heard!—for the
less inducement he has to tell all this, the more, I
think, you ought to be obliged to him; for I am
sure you'd know nothing of the matter without it.

DANG. That's very true, upon my word.

PUFF. But you will find he was not going on.

    Sir Christopher. Enough, enough —'tis plain—
    and I no more
Am in amazement lost!——

PUFF. Here, now you see, Sir Christopher did not
in fact ask any one question for his own information.

SNEER. No, indeed: his has been a most disinterested curiosity!

DANG. Really, I find that we are very much
obliged to them both.

PUFF. To be sure you are. Now then for the
commander-in-chief, the Earl of Leicester, who,
you know, was no favourite but of the queen's.—
We left off—*in amazement lost!*

    Sir Christopher.   Am in amazement lost.
But, see where noble Leicester comes! supreme
In honours and command.
    Sir Walter.   And yet, methinks,
At such a time, so perilous, so fear'd,
That staff might well become an abler grasp.
    Sir Christopher. And so, by Heaven! think I;
    but soft, he's here!

PUFF. Ay, they envy him!

SNEER. But who are these with him?

PUFF. Oh! very valiant knights: one is the governor of the fort, the other the master of the horse. And now, I think, you shall hear some better language: I was obliged to be plain and intelligible in the first scene, because there was so much matter of fact in it; but now, i'faith, you have trope, figure, and metaphor, as plenty as noun-substantives.

["*Enter* EARL OF LEICESTER, GOVERNOR, MASTER OF THE HORSE, KNIGHTS, &c."]

Leicester. How's this, my friends! is't thus your new-fledged zeal,
And plumed valour moulds in roosted sloth?
Why dimly glimmers that heroic flame,
Whose reddening blaze, by patriot spirit fed,
Should be the beacon of a kindling realm?
Can the quick current of a patriot heart
Thus stagnate in a cold and weedy converse,
Or freeze in tideless inactivity?
No! rather let the fountain of your valour
Spring through each stream of enterprise,
Each petty channel of conducive daring,
Till the full torrent of your foaming wrath
O'erwhelm the flats of sunk hostility!

PUFF. There it is—followed up!

Sir Walter. No more!—the freshening breath of thy rebuke
Hath fill'd the swelling canvas of our souls!
And thus, though fate should cut the cable of
                                    [*All take hands.*]
Our topmost hopes, in friendship's closing line
We'll grapple with despair, and if we fall,
We'll fall in glory's wake!
Leicester. There spoke old England's genius!
Then, are we all resolved?
All. We are—all resolved.
Leicester. To conquer—or be free?
All. To conquer, or be free.
Leicester. All?
All. All.

DANG. *Nem. con.* egad!
PUFF. O yes!—where they do agree on the stage, their unanimity is wonderful!

Leicester. Then let's embrace—and now——
                                    [*Kneels.*]

SNEER. What the plague, is he going to pray?
PUFF. Yes; hush!—in great emergencies, there is nothing like a prayer.

Leicester. O mighty Mars!

DANG. But why should he pray to Mars?

PUFF. Hush!

Leicester.   If in thy homage bred,
Each point of discipline I've still observed;
Nor but by due promotion, and the right
Of service, to the rank of major-general
Have risen; assist thy votary now!
  Governor. Yet do not rise—hear me! [*Kneels.*]
  Master. And me!   [*Kneels.*]
  Knight. And me!   [*Kneels.*]
  Sir Walter. And me!   [*Kneels.*]
  Sir Christopher. And me!   [*Kneels.*]

PUFF. Now pray altogether.

All. Behold thy votaries submissive beg,
That thou wilt deign to grant them all they ask;
Assist them to accomplish all their ends,
And sanctify whatever means they use
To gain them!

SNEER. A very orthodox quintetto!
PUFF. Vastly well, gentlemen!—Is that well managed or not? Have you such a prayer as that on the stage?
SNEER. Not exactly.
LEICESTER. [*to* PUFF] But, sir, you haven't settled how we are to get off here.
PUFF. You could not go off kneeling, could you?
SIR WALTER. [*to* PUFF] O no, sir; impossible!
PUFF. It would have a good effect i'faith, if you could exeunt praying!—Yes, and would vary the established mode of springing off with a glance at the pit.
SNEER. Oh, never mind, so as you get them off!— I'll answer for it, the audience won't care how.
PUFF. Well, then, repeat the last line standing, and go off the old way.

All. And sanctify whatever means we use
To gain them.   [*Exeunt.*]

DANG. Bravo! a fine exit.
SNEER. Well, really, Mr. Puff——
PUFF. Stay a moment!

["*The* SENTINELS *get up.*"]
  1 *Sentinel.* All this shall to Lord Burleigh's ear.
  2 *Sentinel.* 'Tis meet it should.   [*Exeunt.*]

DANG. Hey!—why, I thought those fellows had been asleep?
PUFF. Only a pretence; there's the art of it: they were spies of Lord Burleigh's.
SNEER. But isn't it odd they never were taken notice of, not even by the commander-in-chief?
PUFF. O Lud, sir! if people who want to listen, or overhear, were not always connived at in a

tragedy, there would be no carrying on any plot in the world.

DANG. That's certain.

PUFF. But take care, my dear Dangle! the morning gun is going to fire.   [*Cannon fires.*]

DANG. Well, that will have a fine effect!

PUFF. I think so, and helps to realize the scene.—[*Cannon twice.*] What the plague! three morning guns! there never is but one!—Ay, this is always the way at the theatre: give these fellows a good thing, and they never know when to have done with it.—You have no more cannon to fire?

UNDER P. [*within*] No, sir.

PUFF. Now, then, for soft music.

SNEER. Pray, what's that for?

PUFF. It shows that Tilburina is coming!—nothing introduces you a heroine like soft music. Here she comes!

DANG. And her confidant, I suppose?

PUFF. To be sure! Here they are—inconsolable to the minuet in Ariadne!   [*Soft music.*]

["*Enter* TILBURINA *and* CONFIDANT."]

Tilburina. Now has the whispering breath of gentle morn

Bid Nature's voice and Nature's beauty rise;
While orient Phœbus, with unborrow'd hues,
Clothes the waked loveliness which all night slept
In heavenly drapery! Darkness is fled.
Now flowers unfold their beauties to the sun,
And, blushing, kiss the beam he sends to wake them—
The striped carnation, and the guarded rose,
The vulgar wallflower, and smart gillyflower,
The polyanthus mean—the dapper daisy,
Sweet-William, and sweet marjoram—and all
The tribe of single and of double pinks!
Now, too, the feather'd warblers tune their notes
Around, and charm the listening grove. The lark!
The linnet! chaffinch! bulfinch! goldfinch! greenfinch!
But O, to me no joy can they afford!
Nor rose, nor wallflower, nor smart gilly-flower,
Nor polyanthus mean, nor dapper daisy,
Nor William sweet, nor marjoram—nor lark,
Linnet nor all the finches of the grove!

PUFF. Your white handkerchief, madam!——

TILBURINA. I thought, sir, I wasn't to use that till *heart-rending woe.*

PUFF. O yes, madam, at *the finches of the grove,* if you please.

Tilburina.   Nor lark,
Linnet, nor all the finches of the grove! [*Weeps.*]

PUFF. Vastly well, madam!

DANG. Vastly well, indeed!

Tilburina. For, O, too sure, heart-rending woe is now
The lot of wretched Tilburina!

DANG. Oh!—it's too much.

SNEER. Oh!—it is indeed.

Confidant. Be comforted, sweet lady; for who knows,
But Heaven has yet some milk-white day in store?

Tilburina. Alas! my gentle Nora,
Thy tender youth as yet hath never mourn'd
Love's fatal dart. Else wouldst thou know, that when
The soul is sunk in comfortless despair,
It cannot taste of merriment.

DANG. That's certain.

Confidant. But see where your stern father comes:
It is not meet that he should find you thus.

PUFF. Hey, what the plague!— what a cut is here! Why, what is become of the description of her first meeting with Don Whiskerandos—his gallant behavior in the sea-fight—and the simile of the canary-bird?

TILBURINA. Indeed, sir, you'll find they will not be missed.

PUFF. Very well, very well!

TILBURINA. [*to* CONFIDANT] The cue, ma'am, if you please.

Confidant. It is not meet that he should find you thus.

Tilburina. Thou counsel'st right; but 'tis no easy task
For barefaced grief to wear a mask of joy.
["*Enter* GOVERNOR."]

Governor. How's this!—in tears? O Tilburina, shame!
Is this a time for maudling tenderness,
And Cupid's baby woes?—Hast thou not heard
That haughty Spain's pope-consecrated fleet
Advances to our shores, while England's fate,
Like a clipp'd guinea, trembles in the scale?

Tilburina. Then is the crisis of my fate at hand!
I see the fleets approach—I see——

PUFF. Now, pray, gentlemen, mind. This is one of the most useful figures we tragedy writers have, by which a hero or heroine, in consideration of their being often obliged to overlook things that are on the stage, is allowed to hear and see a number of things that are not.

SNEER. Yes; a kind of poetical second-sight!

PUFF. Yes.—Now then, madam.

Tilburina.   I see their decks
Are clear'd!—I see the signal made!
The line is form'd!—a cable's length asunder!
I see the frigates station'd in the rear;
And now, I hear the thunder of the guns!
I hear the victor's shouts—I also hear
The vanquish'd groan!—and now 'tis smoke—
    and now
I see the loose sails shiver in the wind!
I see!—I see—what soon you'll see——
    Governor. Hold, daughter! peace! this love
    hath turn'd thy brain:
The Spanish fleet thou canst not see—because
—It is not yet in sight!

DANG. Egad, though, the governor seems to make no allowance for this poetical figure you talk of.

PUFF. No, a plain matter-of-fact man;—that's his character.

Tilburina. But will you then refuse his offer?
Governor. I must—I will—I can—I ought—
    I do.
Tilburina. Think what a noble price.
Governor. No more—you urge in vain.
Tilburina. His liberty is all he asks.

SNEER. All who asks, Mr. Puff? Who is——

PUFF. Egad, sir, I can't tell! Here has been such cutting and slashing, I don't know where they have got to myself.

TILBURINA. Indeed, sir, you will find it will connect very well.

    —And your reward secure.

PUFF. Oh, if they hadn't been so devilish free with their cutting here, you would have found that Don Whiskerandos has been tampering for his liberty, and has persuaded Tilburina to make this proposal to her father. And now, pray observe the conciseness with which the argument is conducted. Egad, the *pro* and *con* goes as smart as hits in a fencing match. It is indeed a sort of small-sword-logic, which we have borrowed from the French.

Tilburina. A retreat in Spain!
Governor. Outlawry here!
Tilburina. Your daughter's prayer!
Governor. Your father's oath!
Tilburina. My lover!

Governor. My country!
Tilburina. Tilburina!
Governor. England!
Tilburina. A title!
Governor. Honour!
Tilburina. A pension!
Governor. Conscience!
Tilburina. A thousand pounds!
Governor. Ha! thou hast touch'd me nearly!

PUFF. There you see—she threw in *Tilburina.* Quick, parry quarte with *England!* Ha! thrust in tierce *a title!*—parried by *honour.* Ha! *a pension* over the arm!—put by by *conscience.* Then flankonade with *a thousand pounds*—and a palpable hit, egad!

Tilburina. Canst thou—
Reject the suppliant, and the daughter too?
    Governor. No more; I would not hear thee
    plead in vain:
The father softens—but the governor
Is fix'd!   [*Exit.*]

DANG. Ay, that antithesis of persons is a most established figure.

Tilburina. 'Tis well,—hence then, fond hopes,
    —fond passion hence;
Duty, behold I am all over thine——
    Whiskerandos. [*without*] Where is my love—
    my——
    Tilburina. Ha!
    ["*Enter* DON FEROLO WHISKERANDOS."]
    Whiskerandos. My beauteous enemy!——

PUFF. O dear, ma'am, you must start a great deal more than that! Consider, you had just determined in favour of duty—when, in a moment, the sound of his voice revives your passion—overthrows your resolution—destroys your obedience. If you don't express all that in your start, you do nothing at all.

TILBURINA. Well, we'll try again.

DANG. Speaking from within has always a fine effect.

SNEER. Very.

Whiskerandos. My conquering Tilburina!
    How! is't thus
We meet? why are thy looks averse? what means
That falling tear—that frown of boding woe?
Ha! now indeed I am a prisoner!
Yes, now I feel the galling weight of these
Disgraceful chains—which, cruel Tilburina!
Thy doting captive gloried in before.—
But thou art false, and Whiskerandos is undone!
    Tilburina. O no! how little dost thou know thy
    Tilburina!

Whiskerandos. Art thou then true?—Begone
  cares, doubts, and fears,
I make you all a present to the winds;
And if the winds reject you—try the waves.

PUFF. The wind, you know, is the established
receiver of all stolen sighs, and cast-off griefs and
apprehensions.

Tilburina. Yet must we part!—stern duty seals
  our doom:
Though here I call yon conscious clouds to
  witness,
Could I pursue the bias of my soul,
All friends, all right of parents, I'd disclaim,
And thou, my Whiskerandos, shouldst be father
And mother, brother, cousin, uncle, aunt,
And friend to me!
  Whiskerandos. Oh, matchless excellence! and
  must we part?
Well, if—we must—we must—and in that case
The less is said the better.

PUFF. Heyday! here's a cut!—What, are all the
mutual protestations out?

TILBURINA. Now, pray, sir, don't interrupt us
just here: you ruin our feelings.

PUFF. Your feelings!—but, zounds, my feelings,
ma'am!

SNEER. No, pray don't interrupt them.

Whiskerandos. One last embrace.
Tilburina. Now,— farewell, for ever.
Whiskerandos, For ever!
Tilburina. Ay, for ever!   [*Going*.]

PUFF. 'Sdeath and fury!—Gad's life!—sir!
madam! if you go out without the parting look,
you might as well dance out. Here, here!

CONFIDANT. But pray, sir, how am I to get off
here?

PUFF. You! pshaw! what the devil signifies how
you get off! edge away at the top, or where you
will— [*Pushes the* CONFIDANT *off*.] Now, ma'am, you
see——

TILBURINA. We understand you, sir.

Ay, for ever.
  Both. Oh! [*Turning back, and exeunt. —Scene
  closes*.]

DANG. Oh, charming!

PUFF. Hey!—'tis pretty well, I believe: you see I
don't attempt to strike out anything new—but I
take it I improve on the established modes.

SNEER. You do, indeed! But pray is not Queen
Elizabeth to appear?

PUFF. No, not once—but she is to be talked of for

ever; so that, egad, you'll think a hundred times
that she is on the point of coming in.

SNEER. Hang it, I think it's a pity to keep her in
the green-room all the night.

PUFF. O no, that always has a fine effect—it
keeps up expectation.

DANG. But are we not to have a battle?

PUFF. Yes, yes, you will have a battle at last: but,
egad, it's not to be by land, but by sea—and that is
the only quite new thing in the piece.

DANG. What, Drake at the Armada, hey?

PUFF. Yes, i'faith—fire-ships and all; then we
shall end with the procession. Hey, that will do, I
think?

SNEER. No doubt on't.

PUFF. Come, we must not lose time; so now for
the under-plot.

SNEER. What the plague, have you another plot?

PUFF. O Lord, yes; ever while you live have two
plots to your tragedy. The grand point in manag-
ing them is only to let your under-plot have as little
connection with your main-plot as possible.—I
flatter myself nothing can be more distinct than
mine; for as in my chief plot the characters are all
great people, I have laid my under-plot in low life,
and as the former is to end in deep distress, I make
the other end as happy as a farce.—Now, Mr.
Hopkins, as soon as you please.

[*Enter* UNDER PROMPTER.]

UNDER P. Sir, the carpenter says it is impossible
you can go to the park scene yet.

PUFF. The park scene! no! I mean the description scene here, in the wood.

UNDER P. Sir, the performers have cut it out.

PUFF. Cut it out!

UNDER P. Yes, sir.

PUFF. What! the whole account of Queen
Elizabeth?

UNDER P. Yes, sir.

PUFF. And the description of her horse and side-
saddle?

UNDER P. Yes, sir.

PUFF. So, so; this is very fine indeed!— Mr. Hopkins, how the plague could you suffer this?

MR. HOPKINS. [*within*] Sir, indeed the pruning-
knife——

PUFF. The pruning-knife—zounds!—the axe!
Why, here has been such lopping and topping, I
shan't have the bare trunk of my play left presently!
—Very well, sir—the performers must do as they
please; but, upon my soul, I'll print it every word.

SNEER. That I would, indeed.

PUFF. Very well, sir; then we must go on.—
Zounds! I would not have parted with the descrip-

tion of the horse!—Well, sir, go on.—Sir, it was one of the finest and most laboured things.—Very well, sir; let them go on.—There you had him and his accoutrements, from the bit to the crupper.— Very well, sir; we must go to the park scene.

UNDER P. Sir, there is the point: the carpenters say, that unless there is some business put in here before the drop, they sha'n't have time to clear away the fort, or sink Gravesend and the river.

PUFF. So! this is a pretty dilemma, truly!— Gentlemen, you must excuse me—these fellows will never be ready, unless I go and look after them myself.

SNEER. O dear, sir, these little things will happen.

PUFF. To cut out this scene!—but I'll print it— egad, I'll print it every word!   [*Exeunt.*]

ACT III

SCENE I. *The Theatre, before the Curtain.*

[*Enter* PUFF, SNEER, *and* DANGLE.]

PUFF. Well, we are ready; now then for the justices.   [*Curtain rises.*]

["JUSTICES, CONSTABLES, &C., *discovered.*"]

SNEER. This, I suppose, is a sort of senate scene.

PUFF. To be sure; there has not been one yet.

DANG. It is the under-plot, isn't it?

PUFF. Yes.—What, gentlemen, do you mean to go at once to the discovery scene?

JUSTICE. If you please, sir.

PUFF. Oh, very well!—Hark'ee, I don't choose to say anything more; but, i'faith they have mangled my play in a most shocking manner.

DANG. It's a great pity!

PUFF. Now, then, Mr. Justice, if you please.

Justice. Are all the volunteers without?
Constable.   They are.
Some ten in fetters, and some twenty drunk.
Justice. Attends the youth, whose most op-
     probrious fame
And clear convicted crimes have stamp'd him
     soldier?
Constable. He waits your pleasure; eager to
     repay
The best reprieve that sends him to the fields
Of glory, there to raise his branded hand
In honour's cause.
Justice.   'Tis well—'tis justice arms him!
Oh! may he now defend his country's laws
With half the spirit he has broke them all!
If 'tis your worship's pleasure, bid him enter.

Constable. I fly, the herald of your will. [*Exit.*]

PUFF. Quick, sir.

SNEER. But, Mr. Puff, I think not only the Justice, but the clown seems to talk in as high a style as the first hero among them.

PUFF. Heaven forbid they should not in a free country!—Sir, I am not for making slavish distinc- tions, and giving all the fine language to the upper sort of people.

DANG. That's very noble in you, indeed.

["*Enter* JUSTICE'S LADY."]

PUFF. Now, pray mark this scene.

Lady. Forgive this interruption, good my love;
But as I just now pass'd a prisoner youth,
Whom rude hands hither lead, strange bodings
     seized
My fluttering heart, and to myself I said,
An' if our Tom had lived, he'd surely been
This stripling's height!
Justice. Ha! sure some powerful sympathy
     directs
Us both——
          ["*Enter* CONSTABLE *with* SON."]
               What is thy name?
Son. My name is Tom Jenkins—*alias* have I
     none—
Though orphan'd, and without a friend
     Justice.   Thy parents?
Son. My father dwelt in Rochester—and was,
As I have heard—a fishmonger—no more.

PUFF. What, sir, do you leave out the account of your birth, parentage, and education?

SON. They have settled it so, sir, here.

PUFF. Oh! oh!

Lady. How loudly nature whispers to my heart
Had he no other name?
     Son.   I've seen a bill
Of his sign'd Tomkins, creditor.
     Justice. This does indeed confirm each circum-
     stance
The gipsy told!—Prepare!
     Son.   I do.
Justice. No orphan, nor without a friend art
     thou—
I am thy father; here's thy mother; there
Thy uncle—this thy first cousin, and those
Are all your near relations!
Lady. O ecstasy of bliss!
Son. O most unlook'd for happiness!
Justice. O wonderful event!
     [*They faint alternately in each other's arms.*]

PUFF. There, you see, relationship, like murder, will out.

> *Justice.* Now let's revive—else were this joy too
> much!
> But come—and we'll unfold the rest within;
> And thou, my boy, must needs want rest and
> food.
> Hence may each orphan hope, as chance directs,
> To find a father—where he least expects!
> [*Exeunt.*]

PUFF. What do you think of that?

DANG. One of the finest discovery-scenes I ever saw!—Why, this under-plot would have made a tragedy itself.

SNEER. Ay, or a comedy either.

PUFF. And keeps quite clear you see of the other.

[*"Enter* SCENEMEN, *taking away the seats."*]

PUFF. The scene remains, does it?

SCENEMAN. Yes, sir.

PUFF. You are to leave one chair, you know.—But it is always awkward in a tragedy, to have your fellows coming in in your play-house liveries to remove things.—I wish that could be managed better.—So now for my mysterious yeoman.

[*"Enter* BEEFEATER.*"*]

Beefeater. Perdition catch my soul, but I do love thee.

SNEER. Haven't I heard that line before?

PUFF. No, I fancy not.—Where, pray?

DANG. Yes, I think there is something like it in Othello.

PUFF. Gad! now you put me in mind on't, I believe there is—but that's of no consequence; all that can be said is, that two people happened to hit upon the same thought—and Shakespeare made use of it first, that's all.

SNEER. Very true.

PUFF. Now, sir, your soliloquy—but speak more to the pit, if you please—the soliloquy always to the pit, that's a rule.

> *Beefeater.* Though hopeless love finds comfort
> in despair,
> It never can endure a rival's bliss!
> But soft—I am observed.   [*Exit.*]

DANG. That's a very short soliloquy.

PUFF. Yes—but it would have been a great deal longer if he had not been observed.

SNEER. A most sentimental Beefeater that, Mr. Puff!

PUFF. Hark'ee—I would not have you be too sure that he is a Beefeater.

SNEER. What, a hero in disguise?

PUFF. No matter—I only give you a hint. But now for my principal character. Here he comes—Lord Burleigh in person! Pray, gentlemen, step this way—softly—I only hope the Lord High Treasurer is perfect—if he is but perfect!

[*"Enter* LORD BURLEIGH, *goes slowly to a chair, and sits."*]

SNEER. Mr. Puff!

PUFF. Hush!—Vastly well, sir! vastly well! a most interesting gravity.

DANG. What, isn't he to speak at all?

PUFF. Egad, I thought you'd ask me that!—Yes, it is a very likely thing—that a minister in his situation, with the whole affairs of the nation on his head, should have time to talk!—But hush! or you'll put him out.

SNEER. Put him out; how the plague can that be, if he's not going to say anything?

PUFF. There's the reason! why, his part is to think; and how the plague do you imagine he can think if you keep talking?

DANG. That's very true, upon my word!

[*"*LORD BURLEIGH *comes forward, shakes his head, and exit."*]

SNEER. He is very perfect indeed! Now, pray what did he mean by that?

PUFF. You don't take it?

SNEER. No, I don't, upon my soul.

PUFF. Why, by that shake of the head, he gave you to understand that even though they had more justice in their cause, and wisdom in their measures—yet, if there was not a greater spirit shown on the part of the people, the country would at last fall a sacrifice to the hostile ambition of the Spanish monarchy.

SNEER. The devil! did he mean all that by shaking his head?

PUFF. Every word of it—if he shook his head as I taught him.

DANG. Ah! there certainly is a vast deal to be done on the stage by dumb show and expressions of face; and a judicious author knows how much he may trust to it.

SNEER. Oh, here are some of our old acquaintance.

[*"Enter* SIR CHRISTOPHER HATTON *and* SIR WALTER RALEIGH.*"*]

> *Sir Christopher.* My niece and your niece too!

By Heaven! there's witchcraft in't.—He could not else
Have gain'd their hearts.—But see where they approach:
Some horrid purpose lowering on their brows!
Sir Walter. Let us withdraw and mark them.
                                    [*They withdraw.*]
SNEER. What is all this?
PUFF. Ah! here has been more pruning!—but the fact is, these two young ladies are also in love with Don Whiskerandos.—Now, gentlemen, this scene goes entirely for what we call situation and stage effect, by which the greatest applause may be obtained, without the assistance of language, sentiment, or character: pray mark!

["*Enter the two* NIECES."]
   1st Niece. Ellena here!
She is his scorn as much as I—that is
Some comfort still!
PUFF. O dear, madam, you are not to say that to her face!—Aside, ma'am, aside.—The whole scene is to be aside.
   1st Niece. [*aside*] She is his scorn as much as I—that is
Some comfort still.
   2nd Niece. [*aside*] I know he prizes not Pollina's love;
But Tilburina lords it o'er his heart.
   1st Niece. [*aside*] But see the proud destroyer of my peace.
Revenge is all the good I've left.
   2nd Niece. [*aside*] He comes, the false disturber of my quiet.
Now vengeance do thy worst.
   ["*Enter* DON FEROLO WHISKERANDOS."]
   Whiskerandos. O hateful liberty—if thus in vain
I seek my Tilburina!
   Both Nieces.   And ever shalt!
[SIR CHRISTOPHER HATTON *and* SIR WALTER RALEIGH *come forward.*]
   Sir Christopher and Sir Walter. Hold! we will avenge you.
   Whiskerandos. Hold *you*—or see your nieces bleed!
[*The two* NIECES *draw their two daggers to strike* WHISKERANDOS: *the two* UNCLES *at the instant, with their two swords drawn, catch their two* NIECES' *arms, and turn the points of their swords to* WHISKERANDOS, *who immediately draws two daggers, and holds them to the two* NIECES' *bosoms.*]
PUFF. There's situation for you! there's an heroic group!—You see the ladies can't stab Whisker-

andos—he durst not strike them, for fear of their uncles—the uncles durst not kill him, because of their nieces.—I have them all at a deadlock!—for every one of them is afraid to let go first.
SNEER. Why, then they must stand there for ever!
PUFF. So they would, if I hadn't a very fine contrivance for't.—Now mind——

   ["*Enter* BEEFEATER, *with his halbert.*"]
   Beefeater. In the queen's name I charge you all to drop
Your swords and daggers!
      [*They drop their swords and daggers.*]

SNEER. That is a contrivance indeed!
PUFF. Ay—in the queen's name.

   Sir Christopher. Come, niece!
   Sir Walter. Come, niece! [*Exeunt with the two* NIECES.]
   Whiskerandos. What's he, who bids us thus renounce our guard?
   Beefeater. Thou must do more—renounce thy love!
   Whiskerandos. Thou liest—base Beefeater!
   Beefeater.   Ha! hell! the lie!
By Heaven thou'st roused the lion in my heart!
Off, yeoman's habit!—base disguise! off! off!
[*Discovers himself by throwing off his upper dress, and appearing in a very fine waistcoat.*]
Am I a Beefeater now?
Or beams my crest as terrible as when
In Biscay's Bay I took thy captive sloop?

PUFF. There, egad! he comes out to be the very captain of the privateer who had taken Whiskerandos prisoner—and was himself an old lover of Tilburina's.
DANG. Admirably managed, indeed!
PUFF. Now, stand out of their way.

   Whiskerandos. I thank thee, Fortune, that hast thus bestowed
A weapon to chastise this insolent. [*Takes up one of the swords.*]
   Beefeater. I take thy challenge, Spaniard, and I thank thee,
Fortune, too! [*Takes up the other sword.*]

DANG. That's excellently contrived!—It seems as if the two uncles had left their swords on purpose for them.
PUFF. No, egad, they could not help leaving them.

   Whiskerandos. Vengeance and Tilburina!
   Beefeater.   Exactly so——
[*They fight—and after the usual number of wounds given,* WHISKERANDOS *falls.*]

Whiskerandos. O cursed parry!—that last thrust in tierce

Was fatal.—Captain, thou hast fenced well! And Whiskerandos quits this bustling scene For all eter——

Beefeater.   ——nity—he would have added, but stern death

Cut short his being, and the noun at once!

PUFF. Oh, my dear sir, you are too slow: now mind me.—Sir, shall I trouble you to die again?

Whiskerandos. And Whiskerandos quits this bustling scene

For all eter——

Beefeater.   ——nity—he would have added,——

PUFF. No, sir—that's not it—once more, if you please.

WHISKERANDOS. I wish, sir, you would practise this without me—I can't stay dying here all night.

PUFF. Very well; we'll go over it by-and-by.— [*Exit* WHISKERANDOS.] I must humour these gentlemen!

Beefeater. Farewell, brave Spaniard! and when next——

PUFF. Dear sir, you needn't speak that speech, as the body has walked off.

BEEFEATER. That's true, sir—then I'll join the fleet.

PUFF. If you please.—[*Exit* BEEFEATER.] Now, who comes on?

["*Enter* GOVERNOR, *with his hair properly disordered.*"]
Governor. A hemisphere of evil planets reign! And every planet sheds contagious frenzy! My Spanish prisoner is slain! my daughter, Meeting the dead corse borne along, has gone Distract! [*A loud flourish of trumpets.*]
          But hark! I am summoned to the fort: Perhaps the fleets have met! amazing crisis! O Tilburina! from thy aged father's beard Thou'st pluck'd the few brown hairs which time had left!   [*Exit.*]

SNEER. Poor gentleman!

PUFF. Yes—and no one to blame but his daughter!

DANG. And the planets——

PUFF. True.—Now enter Tilburina!

SNEER. Egad, the business comes on quick here.

PUFF. Yes, sir—now she comes in stark mad in white satin.

SNEER. Why in white satin?

PUFF. O Lord, sir—when a heroine goes mad, she always goes into white satin.—Don't she, Dangle?

DANG. Always—it's a rule.

PUFF. Yes—here it is—[*Looking at the book.*] "Enter Tilburina stark mad in white satin, and her confidant stark mad in white linen."

["*Enter* TILBURINA *and* CONFIDANT, *mad, according to custom.*"]

SNEER. But, what the deuce! is the confidant to be mad too?

PUFF. To be sure she is: the confidant is always to do whatever her mistress does; weep when she weeps, smile when she smiles, go mad when she goes mad.—Now, Madam Confidant—but keep your madness in the background, if you please

Tilburina. The wind whistles—the moon rises—see,

They have kill'd my squirrel in his cage: Is this a grasshopper?—Ha! no; it is my Whiskerandos—you shall not keep him— I know you have him in your pocket— An oyster may be cross'd in love!—who says A whale's a bird?—Ha! did you call, my love?— He's here! he's there!—He's everywhere! Ah me! he's nowhere!   [*Exit.*]

PUFF. There, do you ever desire to see anybody madder than that?

SNEER. Never, while I live!

PUFF. You observed how she mangled the metre?

DANG. Yes,—egad, it was the first thing made me suspect she was out of her senses!

SNEER. And pray what becomes of her?

PUFF. She is gone to throw herself into the sea, to be sure—and that brings us at once to the scene of action and so to my catastrophe—my sea-fight, I mean.

SNEER. What, you bring that in at last?

PUFF. Yes, yes—you know my play is called *The Spanish Armada;* otherwise, egad, I have no occasion for the battle at all.—Now then for my magnificence!—my battle!—my noise!—and my procession!—You are all ready?

UNDER P. [*within*] Yes, sir.

PUFF. Is the Thames dressed?

["*Enter* THAMES *with two* ATTENDANTS."]

THAMES. Here I am, sir.

PUFF. Very well, indeed!—See, gentlemen, there's a river for you!—This is blending a little of the masque with my tragedy—a new fancy, you know—and very useful in my case; for as there must be a procession, I suppose Thames, and all his tributary rivers, to compliment Britannia with a fête in honour of the victory.

SNEER. But pray, who are these gentlemen in green with him?

PUFF. Those?—those are his banks.

SNEER. His banks?

PUFF. Yes, one crowned with alders, and the other with a villa!—you take the allusions?—But hey! what the plague!—you have got both your banks on one side.—Here, sir, come round.—Ever while you live, Thames, go between your banks.— [*Bell rings.*] There, so! now for't!—Stand aside, my dear friends!—Away, Thames!

[*Exit* THAMES *between his banks.*]
[*Flourish of drums, trumpets, cannon, &c., &c. Scene changes to the sea—the fleets engage—the music plays— "Britons strike home."—Spanish fleet destroyed by fire-ships, &c.—English fleet advances—music plays, "Rule Britannia."—The procession of all the English rivers, and their tributaries, with their emblems, &c., begins with Handel's water music, ends with a chorus to the march in Judas Maccabæus.—During this scene,* PUFF *directs and applauds everything—then:*]

PUFF. Well, pretty well—but not quite perfect. So ladies and gentlemen, if you please, we'll re-hearse this piece again to-morrow. [*Curtain drops.*]

Anton Chekhov # A Wedding
Or, A Joke in One Act

in an English version by Eric Bentley

No one now doubts the genius of Anton Pavlovich Chekhov (1860–1904). But this was not always the case. He first started to write—stories and articles—as a means of financing his medical education; although his sketches were successful, he devoted himself to his medical practice until forced by tuberculosis to give it up. Then he turned to playwriting as well as to fiction, at first with disastrous results. Success came slowly— only in 1899, with a revival of *The Sea-Gull* by Stanislavsky at the newly organized Moscow Art Theatre.

Meanwhile, in the 1880's, Chekhov had written a number of short farces, or "jokes" as he called them, apprentice pieces, perhaps, but nonetheless positive exercises in a search to create a kind of drama in which, as Eric Bentley puts it, "tragic and comic elements lose their separate identities in a new, if nameless, unity." These farces, although minor, are not unimportant for, as Mr. Bentley continues, they have "something in them of the seriousness, pathos, and even subtlety of the greatest plays. In some ways simple, they are not one-sided but dialectical. The critic who judges them and the director who stages them must have a dialectical mind in order to grasp the constant conflict and synthesis of elements. In its fine balance of contrasts—particularly of the pathetic and the ridiculous—a Chekhov farce might be regarded as a full-fledged Chekhov drama in miniature."

A Wedding (1889) is based on some humorous captions, describing "The Marriage Season," a series of cartoons drawn by the dramatist's brother and published in 1881, and on two short stories of 1884, "A Wedding with a General" and "A Marriage of Convenience" (two English translations of the second are available, one by Frances H. Jones, the other by Nora Gottlieb), all of which contain incidents about which Chekhov had heard or read. In addition, as David Magarshack points out in *Chekhov the Dramatist* (1952), "the flat above the one in which the Chekhov family lived in 1885 in Moscow was hired out for weddings and Chekhov had an excellent opportunity of being an unseen witness of such occasions." The link between stories and plays is also an aesthetic one according to Magarshack: "the remarkable fact about a Chekhov short story is that it possesses the three indispensable elements of drama: compactness of structure (Chekhov's term for it was 'architecture'); movement, that is, dramatic development of plot; and action."

Chekhov loved gaiety. "To write a good vaudeville," Magarshack quotes him as saying, "requires a special kind of mood, a mood full of high spirits." But it also is "far from easy." The skillful dramatist must be able to "speak" the language of his characters, he must see the total work as an organic whole, and he must have an impeccable sense of timing. All these qualities are displayed in *A Wedding*. The English version used here is by Eric Bentley and is from *The Brute and other Farces by Anton Chekhov* (N. Y.: Grove Press, 1958).

CHARACTERS

MADAM ZMEYUKIN, *a midwife.*
YAT, *a telegraph clerk*
THE BEST MAN.
MRS. ZIGALOV, *the bride's mother.*
APLOMBOV, *the bridegroom.*

A WAITER.
DASHENKA, *the bride.*
MR. ZIGALOV, *the bride's father,*
  civil servant, retired.
DIMBA, *a Greek confectioner.*

A SAILOR.
NYUNIN, *an insurance man.*
"GENERAL," REVUNOV.
WEDDING GUESTS.

[*The scene is a private room in a second-rate restaurant. Brilliantly lit. Large table laid for supper.* WAITERS *in tails busy at this and other tables. Behind the scenes, a band playing the last figure of a quadrille.*]

Three figures cross the stage: MADAM ZMEYUKIN, *a midwife;* YAT, *a telegraph clerk; and the* BEST MAN. *The* MIDWIFE *is crying "No, no, no!"*]

TELEGRAPH CLERK. [*on her heels*] Have pity on me! [*But she keeps on crying "No, no, no!"*]

BEST MAN. [*following*] Now look, you can't carry on like that! Where are you going? What about the *Grand Rond? Grand Rond, s'il vous plaît!*
[*All three are off stage.*]
[*Enter* APLOMBOV, *the bridegroom and* MRS. ZIGALOV, *the bride's mother.*]

BRIDE'S MOTHER. Now, instead of bothering me with all this talk, why don't you just go and dance?

BRIDEGROOM. I can't make figure eights with my feet, I'm no Spinoza, I'm a practical man, a man of character, I find nothing amusing in idle pursuits. But dancing is not the point. Forgive me, mother dear, but there's a great deal in your conduct that I can't figure out. For example, quite apart from furniture, utensils, miscellaneous effects, you promised to give me, with your daughter, two lottery tickets. Where are they?

BRIDE'S M. My poor head, it's aching again, it must be the weather, they say it's going to thaw.

BRIDEGR. Don't try to wriggle out of it. You pawned those tickets. I found out only this afternoon. You're an exploiter, mother dear. Excuse the expression, but you are. I speak without prejudice. I don't want the confounded tickets. It's a matter of principle. And I don't like being gypped. I am making your daughter the happiest of women and if you don't get those tickets back I'll make mincemeat of her into the bargain. I'm a man of honour, don't forget.

BRIDE'S M. [counting the places at table] One, two, three, four, five . . .

WAITER. The cook says how would you like the ice cream, ma'am?

BRIDE'S M. How do you mean: how would I like the ice cream?

WAITER. With rum, with Madeira, or with nothing, ma'am?

BRIDEGR. With rum, you fool. And tell the head waiter there isn't enough wine. We need some Haut Sauterne as well. [to BRIDE'S MOTHER] There was another agreement: you promised me a general. You swore to deliver a general as a wedding guest. Where is he?

BRIDE'S M. It's not my fault, my dear.

BRIDEGR. Whose fault is it, for heaven's sake?

BRIDE'S M. Nyunin's. The insurance man. He was here yesterday, he swore he'd dig up a general, but I suppose he just couldn't find one. We're as sorry as you are. There's nothing we wouldn't do for you. When you say a general, a general it should be . . .

BRIDEGR. Another thing. Everyone knows that telegraph clerk courted Dashenka before me. Why must you invite him to our wedding? Have you no consideration for my feelings?

BRIDE'S M. Well, er . . . what's your name again? Yes: Aplombov. My dear Aplombov, you have been married just two hours, and already you have us both worn out—me and my daughter—with your incessant talk, talk, talk. How will it be a year

from now? Think of that.

BRIDEGR. So you don't like to hear the truth. I see. But that's no excuse for having no sense of honour. I want you to have a sense of honour! [Couples cross the stage, dancing the Grand Rond. The first couple are the BRIDE and the BEST MAN. THE MIDWIFE and the TELEGRAPH CLERK come last and stay behind. Enter ZIGALOV, the bride's father and DIMBA, a Greek confectioner. During the cross and afterwards in the wings, the BEST MAN is shouting: "Promenade! Promenade Messieurs-dames! Promenade!"]

TEL. CL. [to the MIDWIFE] Have pity on me, enchanting one!

MIDW. Listen to him . . . My dear fellow, I've told you: I am not in good voice today!

TEL. CL. Just a couple of notes! One! One note! Have pity on me!

MIDW. You bother me [She sits down and vigorously uses her fan.]

TEL. CL. But you have no pity. A monster of cruelty, if I may so express myself, with the voice of a goddess! You've no right being a midwife with a voice like that. You should be a concert singer. Your rendering of that phrase—how does it go?—yes, um: [He sings.]
I loved you though 'twas all in vain!
Exquisite!

MIDW. [Singing.]
I loved you—and may do again!
Is that the bit you mean?

TEL. CL. That's it. Exquisite!

MIDW. But I am not in voice today. Fan me. It's hot. [to BRIDEGROOM] Why are you so sad, Aplombov? On your wedding day? What are you thinking of?

BRIDEGR. It's a serious step—marriage. Must be given serious thought—from every angle.

MIDW. What sceptics you all are! Unbelievers! I can't breathe among you. Give me air! Air! [She practises a few notes of song.]

TEL. CL. Exquisite!

MIDW. Fan me! My heart's about to burst! Answer me one question: why am I suffocating?

TEL. CL. You've been sweating such a lot—

MIDW. Such a word in my presence!

TEL. CL. Many apologies. I was forgetting you move in aristocratic circles, if I may so express myself.

MIDW. Oh, stop it. Give me poetry! Heavenly raptures! And fan me, fan me.

BRIDE'S FATHER. [In tipsy conversation with the GREEK.] Another? [Fill his glass.] Every time is the right time for a drink. As long as your work gets done, eh, Dimba? Drink and . . . drink and . . .

drink again. [*They drink.*] Do you have tigers—in Greece?

GREEK. [*Showing the whites of his eyes.*] I'll say!

BRIDE'S F. And lions?

GREEK. Lions, tigers, everything! In Russia—nothing. In Greece—everything. That's the whole difference between Russia and Greece.

BRIDE'S F. Everything?

GREEK. Everything: my father, my uncle, all my brothers . . .

BRIDE'S F. You have whales too—in Greece?

GREEK. Everything. Whales, sharks . . .

BRIDE'S M. [*to her husband*] Time to sit down, my dear. And hands off the canned lobster— it's for the General—I still think there'll be a General—

BRIDE'S F. You have lobsters—in Greece?

GREEK. Everything! Everything I tell you—

BRIDE'S F. Civil servants too?

MIDW. The air must be divine—in Greece.

BRIDE'S F. Have another.

BRIDE'S M. No time for another! It's past eleven. Time to sit down!

BRIDE'S F. Sit down? Good idea! Sit down! Sit down, everyone!

[*And his wife joins him in calling to all the guests, on stage and off, to take their places at table.*]

MIDW. [*Sitting.*] Give me poetry!

His quest for storms will never cease
For only storms can bring him peace!

Give me storms!

TEL. CL. [*aside*] Isn't she remarkable? I'm head over heels in love with her.

[*Enter the BRIDE, a SAILOR, the BEST MAN, other wedding guests. They sit down noisily. Pause. The band plays a march.*]

SAILOR. [*Rising.*] Ladies and gentlemen, as we have a great many toasts and speeches ahead of us, I propose we start at once—with the greatest toast of them all. I give you: the bride and groom!

[*ALL cry: "The bride and groom" and clink glasses and drink. The band plays a flourish.*]

SAIL. And now: it needs sweetening!

ALL. It needs sweetening.

[*The BRIDE and GROOM kiss.*]

TEL. CL. Exquisite! Ladies and gentlemen: credit where credit is due! Let us give thanks for a splendid party in a splendid setting! What a magnificent establishment this is! Only one thing lacking: electric light—if I may so express myself. They have it all over the world. Everywhere but Mother Russia. [*He sits, sadly.*]

BRIDE'S F. Yes, um, electric light. Come to think of it, electric light is a hoax. They slip a piece of coal in when no one's looking. So, my good man, if you want to give us light, give us good old-fashioned light, none of these superintellectual notions.

TEL. CL. Take a look at a battery some time. That's no superintellectual notion.

BRIDE'S F. Certainly not! I've no wish to be caught looking at such a thing. [*Severely.*] And I'm sorry to find you sympathizing with tricksters and swindlers, young man, when you should be having a drink and handing the bottle round!

BRIDEGR. I quite agree, father dear. Not that I object to scientific discoveries on principle. But there's a time for everything. [*to his bride*] What do you say, *ma chère?*

BRIDE. Some people like to show off and talk so no one can understand a word.

BRIDE'S M. Don't worry, my dear, your father and I never got mixed up in this education business, not in all our lives. And you're the third daughter we've found a good Russian husband for. [*to TELEGRAPH CLERK*] Why do you have to come here if you think we're so uneducated? Why not go to your educated friends?

TEL. CL. I respect you and your family very much, Mrs. Zigalov. I wasn't trying to show off, mentioning electric light. I've always wished Dashenka would find a good husband. And it isn't easy these days, with everyone marrying for money . . .

BRIDEGR. A dig at me.

TEL. CL. [*Scared.*] That's not true! That was a . . . general observation . . . present company always excepted, if I may so express myself. Heavens, everyone knows *you're* marrying for love. The dowry isn't worth talking about.

BRIDE'S M. What? Not worth talking about, isn't it? You'd better watch your tongue. A thousand rubles in cash, three fur coats, complete furniture and linen. Try and find a dowry to match that!

TEL. CL. But I didn't mean . . . The furniture's splendid of course . . . I wasn't getting in any digs!

BRIDE'S M. Well, don't! We invited you on your parents' account, so don't go sticking *your* oar in. If you knew Aplombov was marrying her for money, why couldn't you have said so before? [*Tearfully.*] I nursed her, I raised her, if she'd been a diamond I couldn't have treasured her more, my child, my emerald . . .

BRIDEGR. So you believe him! Thank you so much, thank you *so* much! [*to TELEGRAPH CLERK*] As for you, Mr. Yat, friend of the family as you are, I cannot permit you to carry on like this in other folks' houses. Kindly take yourself off.

TEL. CL. How do you mean?

BRIDEGR. What a pity you're not a real gentleman—like myself! That being so, however, take yourself off.

[*The band plays a flourish.*]

VARIOUS GENTLEMEN. [*to* BRIDEGROOM] Come off it, Aplombov, old boy! Leave him alone, old man, don't spoil the fun. Take your seat. [*Etc.*]

TEL. CL. But I never . . . why, I . . . I honestly don't understand . . . Certainly, I'll go . . . But first give me the five rubles you borrowed a year ago to buy yourself a *piqué* waistcoat, if I may so express myself. Then I'll have one more drink and, um, go. But first give me the money.

GENTLEMEN. Take your seats. Drop it now. Much ado about nothing. [*Etc.*]

BEST M. [*Shouting.*] To the bride's parents, Mr. and Mrs. Zigalov!

[*The cry is taken up by the others who clink and drink. The band plays a flourish.*]

ZIGALOV. [*Touched, bowing in all directions.*] Thank you, my friends, thank you, for not forgetting us, for not snubbing us. I don't put it this way from false modesty, I have no ulterior motive, I'm not planning to cheat you in any way, I speak as I feel, in the simplicity of my heart, I begrudge you nothing, you are my friends, and I . . . I thank you! [*He kisses those near him.*]

BRIDE. [*to her mother*] Mama, you're crying! Why is that? I'm so happy.

BRIDEGR. Your mother's upset at the approaching separation from you. But I wouldn't advise her to forget our little talk.

TEL. CL. Don't cry, Mrs. Zigalov! What *are* tears, scientifically speaking? Nothing but neurotic weakness!

BRIDE'S F. You have mushrooms—in Greece?

GREEK. Everything. We have everything.

BRIDE'S F. Bet you don't have brown mushrooms. Like ours.

GREEK. Every kind! Every kind!

BRIDE'S F. All right, Dimba, old man, now it's your turn to make a speech. Ladies and gentlemen, Mr. Dimba is going to make a speech!

ALL. A speech! Mr. Dimba! Come on, Dimba! [*Etc.*]

GREEK. But why? What for? I don't see it!

MIDW. It's your turn! Make it snappy!

GREEK. [*Stands, confused.*] All I can say is . . . There's Russia . . . and there's Greece . . . In Russia, there are many people . . . In Greece . . . there are many people . . . On the sea, there are ships . . . In Russia, that is . . . On land, railways . . . You are Russians, we are Greeks, I want nothing for myself. There's Russia, and there's Greece . . .

[*Enter* NYUNIN, *the aforementioned insurance man.*]

INSURANCE MAN. One moment, ladies and gentlemen, just one moment! Mrs. Zigalov, may I have your attention? [*He takes her on one side.*] You shall have your general. He's on his way over. A real live general aged eighty. Or maybe ninety.

BRIDE'S M. When will he get here?

INS. M. Any minute. You'll be grateful to me till your dying day.

BRIDE'S M. A real general.

INS. M. Well, almost real. Actually, he was in the navy. They called him Captain. That's naval lingo for General.

BRIDE'S M. You couldn't be deceiving me, could you?

INS. M. Am I a swindler?

BRIDE'S M. Oh, no!

INS. M. Thank you.

BRIDE'S M. It's just that I don't like to spend money for nothing.

INS. M. Rest easy. He's a model general. [*Raising his voice for all to hear.*] "General," I said, "general, you've been forgetting us lately!" [*Sits down at table among the guests.*] "Pon my soul, Nyunin, my boy," said the general to me, "how can I go to a wedding when I don't even know the bridegroom?" "What's wrong with the bridegroom?" I rejoined. "Splendid, open-hearted fellow that he is!" "What does he do?" says the general. "Do?" says I, "do? Why he's the valuer in a pawnshop." "Oh!" says the general. "Oh what?" says I, "the best of men work in pawnshops these days, also the best of women." At this he clapped me on the shoulder, we smoked a Havana together, and . . .

BRIDEGR. When will he get here?

INS. M. Any minute. He was putting his rubbers on when I left.

BRIDEGR. We must have them play a military march.

INS. M. Bandmaster! *Marche militaire!*

WAITER. General Re

[*As the band strikes up with a march,* "GENERAL" REVUNOV *enters.* NYUNIN *and both* ZIGALOVS *rush to greet him.*]

BRIDE'S M. General Revunov, welcome to our home!

"GENERAL." Delighted I'm sure.

BRIDE'S F. We aren't celebrities, General, we aren't millionaires, but don't think the worse of us on that account. We won't cheat you. We begrudge you nothing. You are welcome.

"GENERAL." Delighted I'm sure.

INS. M. General Revunov, allow me to present the bridegroom, Mr. Aplombov, along with his newly born, I mean newly married, bride, the former Miss Zigalov. Mr. Yat of the Telegraph Office. Mr. Dimba, noted confectioner of Greek descent . . . And so forth. The rest aren't worth much. Why don't you sit down, General?

"GENERAL." Delighted I'm sure. [*But he doesn't sit down. He takes* NYUNIN *on one side.*] One moment, ladies and gentlemen, a confidential conference! [*Whispering.*] What do you mean: General? There are no generals in the navy! I was captain of the smallest ship in the fleet. The rank is equivalent to colonel!

INS. M. [*Speaking over-distinctly into his ear as to a deaf man.*] Let us call you General. It's simpler. These folks respect their betters. Resign yourself to being their betters!

"GENERAL." Oh. Oh, I see. [*Goes meekly back to table.*] Delighted I'm sure.

BRIDE'S M. Take a seat, General. We can't give you the dainty food you're used to, but if our simple fare should take your fancy . . .

"GENERAL." [*Not following this.*] What? What's that? Oh, yes. [*Long silence.*] I live plainly, ma'am. Everyone lived plainly in the old days. [*Another silence.*] When Nyunin invited me here, I said to him: "That could be awkward, I don't know them." "What of it" said Nyunin. "These folk respect their betters!" "They do?" I replied, "well, that's different. And it's awfully boring at home."

BRIDE'S F. So you came out of pure generosity, General. How much I respect that! We're plain folks. We won't cheat you. Have something to eat, General.

BRIDEGR. Have you been out of the service long, General?

"GENERAL." What? Oh, yes. Very true. Yes. But what's this? This herring is bitter. This bread is bitter . . .

ALL. It needs sweetening!

[BRIDE *and* GROOM *kiss.*]

"GENERAL." [*Chuckling.*] Your health, your health! [*Silence.*] In the old days, everything was plain. I like that. Of course, I'm getting on. Seventy-two. Retired from the service in sixty-five. [*Silence.*] On occasion, of course, they used to make a bit of a splash—in the old days . . . [*His eye lights on the sailor.*] Aren't you a sailor?

SAIL. Yes, sir.

"GENERAL." [*Relaxing considerably.*] Ah! Yes. The navy. Not an easy life. Always something to think about. Every word has a special meaning. "Top-sheets and main-sail, mast-hands aloft!" Isn't that good? And what does it mean? Your sailor knows! He, he, he!

INS. M. To General Revunov!

[*The band plays a flourish. All cheer.*]

TEL. CL. Thanks for telling us about the problems of the navy, General. But what about the telegraph service? You can't go in for modern telegraphy without French and German. Transmitting telegrams is no easy matter. Listen.

[*He taps out code with his fork on the table.*]

"GENERAL." What does it mean?

TEL. CL. It means: "Oh, how I respect all your noble qualities, General!" D'you think that's easy? Now.

[*He taps again.*]

"GENERAL." Louder. I can't hear.

TEL. CL. [*Loudly.*] "How happy am I, dear madam, to hold you in my arms!"

"GENERAL." What madam is that? Oh. Oh yes. [*Turning to the* SAILOR.] In the face of a hundred-mile-an-hour headwind, always hoist your foretop halyards, my boy, and your topsail halyards too! When the sails get loose, take hold of the foresail and foretopsail halyards and the topgallant braces . . .

INS. M. Our guests are bored, Revunov, they don't understand.

"GENERAL." I'll explain. If the ship is lying with the wind on the starboard tack under full sail, and you want to bring her round before the wind, pipe all hands on deck, and as soon as they've run up, give the command: "To your places! Round before the wind!" The men pull the stays and braces and, oh, what a life it is, in spite of yourself you leap up and shout: "Bravo! Bravo, brave lads!" [*He breaks off in a fit of coughing.*]

BEST M. [*Taking advantage of this pause.*] Ladies and gentlemen, we are gathered together, are we not, to do honour to our beloved . . .

"GENERAL." "Let out the foretopsail-sheet, the topgallantsail-sheet!"

BEST M. I was making a speech!

BRIDE'S M. We are only ignorant people, General. Tell us something funny!

BEST M. And brief.

"GENERAL." [*Not hearing.*] Thank you, I've had some. Did you say beef? Er, no, thanks. The old days, yes. The life on the ocean wave. [*In a voice laden with emotion.*] Tacking! Is there any joy like the joy of . . . tacking? What sailor's heart doesn't thrill to it? "Pipe all hands on deck," goes the cry. An electric shock runs through the crew. From captain to cabin boy . . .

MIDW. I'm bored!

BEST M. So am I.

"GENERAL." Thank you, I've had some. Did

you say pie? Er, no, thanks. [*In an exalted tone.*] All eyes on the senior officer. "Foretopsails and mainsail braces to starboard," he cries, "mizzen-braces to larboard, counter-braces to port!" [*He leaps up.*] The ship rolls to the wind! "Look alive, ye lubbers," the officer cries, and fixes his eye on the topsail. Seconds of unbearable suspense. Then, it begins to flap! The ship begins to turn! "Loose the stays, let go the braces," yells the officer at the top of his voice. Then it's the tower of Babel. Things flying through the air, the old ship creaking in all its joints. [*Roaring.*] The ship is turned! [*Silence.*]

BRIDE'S M. [*Furious.*] You may be a General, but you ought to be ashamed of yourself, so there! "GENERAL." A pear? Yes please!

BRIDE'S M. [*Louder.*] You ought to be ashamed of yourself, General or no General. [*In some confusion.*] Now, friends . . .

"GENERAL." [*Drawing himself up after hearing the* BRIDE'S MOTHER'S *second effort.*] No general. I am no general. I am a ship's captain. Equivalent to a colonel.

BRIDE'S M. No general! And you took our money! Let me tell you, sir: we don't pay good money to get ourselves insulted!

"GENERAL." [*Bewildered.*] Money? What money's that?

BRIDE'S M. You know what money. The money you took from Nyunin here. Nyunin, you made a mess of things. Engaged *this* sort of general.

INS. M. Let's drop it. Why make a fuss?

"GENERAL." Engaged . . . money from Nyunin . . .

BRIDEGR. Excuse me. Didn't you accept twenty-five rubles from Mr. Nyunin here?

"GENERAL." Twenty-five rubles from Nyunin . . . [*He realizes.*] Ah! So that's it. I see it all. [*Shaking his head sorrowfully.*] What a dirty trick, what a dirty trick!

BRIDEGR. At least you got paid for it.

"GENERAL." Got paid? I did NOT get paid! [*He rises from the table.*] What a trick—to insult an old man this way, a sailor, an officer who has served his country! . . . [*Muttering to himself.*] If these were gentlemen, I could challenge someone to a duel, but as things are . . . [*He is distracted.*] Where is the door? Waiter, show me out, waiter! [*He is leaving.*] What a dirty trick! [*He has left.*]

[*Pause*]

BRIDE'S M. [*to the* INSURANCE MAN] So where's that twenty-five rubles?

INS. M. The way you carry on about trifles when people are enjoying themselves! [*Loudly.*] To the happy pair! Bandmaster, a march! [*The band plays a march.*] To the happy pair!

MIDW. Give me air, air! I'm suffocating here!

TEL. CL. [*Delighted.*] Exquisite creature!

[*Plenty of noise.*]

BEST M. [*Trying to outshout the rest.*] Ladies and gentlemen, we are gathered together, are we not, to do honour . . .

The Man of Destiny

George Bernard Shaw

George Bernard Shaw (1856–1950) is a figure of magnificence in the theatre. Critic, dramatist, philosopher, he delighted in crushing idols, in challenging beliefs, in reviewing history. Never content, he wrote plays and prefaces and criticism and books of advice. His works are numerous, his opinions many, his position somewhere between that of Diogenes and Puck, with more than a dash of both; upsetter of apple-carts, a Fabian social critic who wrote and spoke with passion, a historian of insight and originality, he was, above all, prodigal and provocative.

Shaw delighted in inverting current theatrical patterns of which *The Man of Destiny* is an early and stunning example. Here he is debunking the Victorian heroic play, the romantic concept of the larger-than-life figure in which Sir Henry Irving inevitably starred and which Shaw, as dramatic critic, just as inevitably damned. In a more positive way, Shaw is also dramatizing an idea: the relationship between the ideal, as we human beings romantically imagine it, and the real, especially the real as actually embodied in a historical personage. Shaw does not debunk history, nor heroes. He exposes what is unchanging in human affairs; in the process, his historical figures—Napoleon, Caesar and, to a degree, Saint Joan—become very much like George Bernard Shaw.

Shaw himself once said, "My plays contain not so much humour and wit as fun." This is his contribution to the theatre: an exuberance of spirit, a continual inventiveness, an audacious topsy-turvy mocking of accepted views and attitudes. These practices are all neatly and characteristically embodied in *The Man of Destiny*, which was first produced in 1897 and first printed in *Plays: Pleasant and Unpleasant* (Chicago and N. Y.: Herbert S. Stone and Co., 1898).

CAST OF CHARACTERS

GIUSEPPE GRANDI, *innkeeper in Tavazzano*
GENERAL NAPOLEON BONAPARTE

THE STRANGE LADY
THE LIEUTENANT

[The twelfth of May, 1796, in north Italy, at Tavazzano, on the road from Lodi to Milan. The afternoon sun is blazing serenely over the plains of Lombardy, treating the Alps with respect and the anthills with indulgence, not incommoded by the basking of the swine and oxen in the villages nor hurt by its cool reception in the churches, but fiercely disdainful of two hordes of mischievous insects which are the French and Austrian armies. Two days before, at Lodi, the Austrians tried to prevent the French from crossing the river by the narrow bridge there; but the French, commanded by a general aged 27, Napoleon Bonaparte, who does not understand the art of war, rushed the fireswept bridge, supported by a tremendous cannonade in which the young general assisted with his own hands. Cannonading is his technical specialty; he has been trained in the artillery under the old régime, and made perfect in the military arts of shirking his duties, swindling the paymaster over travelling expenses, and dignifying war with the noise and smoke of cannon, as depicted in all military portraits. He is, however, an original observer, and has perceived, for the first time since the invention of gunpowder, that a cannon ball, if it strikes a man, will kill him. To a thorough grasp of this remarkable discovery, he adds a highly evolved faculty for physical geography and for the calculation of times and distances. He has prodigious powers of work, and a clear, realistic knowledge of human nature in public affairs, having seen it exhaustively tested in that department during the French Revolution. He is imaginative without illusions, and creative without religion, loyalty, patriotism or any of the common ideals. Not that he is incapable of these ideals: on the contrary, he has swallowed them all in his boyhood, and now, having a keen dramatic faculty, is extremely clever at playing upon them by the arts of the actor and stage manager. Withal, he is no spoiled child. Poverty, ill-luck, the shifts of impecunious shabby-gentility, repeated failure as a would-be author, humiliation as a rebuffed time server, reproof and punishment as an incompetent and dishonest officer, an escape from dismissal from the service so narrow that if the emigration of the nobles had not raised the value of even the most rascally lieutenant to the famine price of a general he would have been swept contemptuously from the army: these trials have ground the conceit out of him, and forced him to be self-sufficient and to understand that to such men as he is the world will give nothing that he cannot take from it by force. In this the world is not free from cowardice and folly; for Napoleon, as a merciless cannonader of political rubbish, is making himself useful: indeed, it is even now impossible to live in England without sometimes feeling how much that country lost in not being conquered by him as well as by Julius Caesar.

However, on this May afternoon in 1796, it is early days with him. He is only 26, and has but recently become a general, partly by using his wife to seduce the Directory (then governing France) partly by the scarcity of officers caused by the emigration as aforesaid; partly by his faculty of knowing a country, with all its roads, rivers, hills and valleys, as he knows the palm of his hand; and largely by that new faith of his in the efficacy of firing cannons at people. His army is, as to discipline, in a state which has so greatly shocked some modern writers before whom the following story has been enacted, that they, impressed with the later glory of "L'Empereur," have altogether refused to credit it. But Napoleon is not "L'Empereur" yet: he has only just been dubbed "Le Petit Caporal," and is in the stage of gaining influence over his men by displays of pluck. He is not in a position to force his will on them, in orthodox military fashion, by the cat o' nine tails. The French Revolution which has escaped suppression solely through the monarchy's habit of being at least four years in arrear with its soldiers in the matter of pay, has substituted for that habit, as far as possible, the habit of not paying at all, except in promises and patriotic flatteries which are not compatible with martial law of the Prussian type. Napoleon has therefore approached the Alps in command of men without money, in rags, and consequently indisposed to stand much discipline, especially from upstart generals. This circumstance, which would have embarrassed an idealist soldier, has been worth a thousand cannon to Napoleon. He has said to his army, "You have patriotism and courage; but you have no money, no clothes, and deplorably indifferent food. In Italy there are all these things, and glory as well, to be gained by a devoted army led by a general who regards loot as the natural right of the soldier. I am such a general. En avant, mes enfants!" The result has entirely justified him. The army conquers Italy as the locusts conquered Cyprus. They fight all day and march all night, covering impossible distances and appearing in incredible places, not because every soldier carries a field marshal's baton in his knapsack, but because he hopes to carry at least half a dozen silver forks there next day.

It must be understood, by the way, that the French army does not make war on the Italians. It is there to rescue them from the tyranny of their Austrian conquerors, and confer republican institutions on them; so that in incidentally looting them, it merely makes free with the property of its friends, who ought to grateful to it, and perhaps would be if ingratitude were not the proverbial failing of their country. The Austrians, whom it fights, are a throughly respectable regular army, well disciplined, commanded by gentlemen trained and versed in the art of war: at the head of them Beaulieu, practising the classic art of war under orders from Vienna, and getting horribly beaten by Napoleon, who acts on his own responsibility in defiance of professional precedents or orders from Paris. Even when the Austrians win a battle, all that is necessary is to wait until their routine obliges them to return to their quarters for afternoon tea, so to speak, and win it back again from them: a course pursued later on with brilliant success at Marengo. On the whole, with his foe handicapped by Austrian statesmanship, classic generalship, and the exigencies of the aristocratic social structure of Viennese society, Napoleon finds it possible to be irresistible without working heroic miracles. The world, however, likes miracles and heroes, and is quite incapable of conceiving the action of such forces as academic militarism or Viennese drawing-roomism. Hence it has already begun to manufacture "L'Empereur," and thus to make it difficult for the romanticists of a hundred years later to credit the little scene now in question at Tavazzano as aforesaid.

The best quarters at Tavazzano are at a little inn, the first house reached by travellers passing through the place from Milan to Lodi. It stands in a vineyard; and its principal room, a pleasant refuge from the summer heat, is open so widely at the back to this vineyard that it is almost a large veranda. The bolder children, much excited by the alarums and excursions of the past few days, and by an irruption of French troops at six o'clock, know that the French commander has quartered himself in this room, and are divided between a craving to peep in the front windows, and a mortal terror of the sentinel, a young gentleman-soldier, who, having no natural moustache, has had a most ferocious one painted on his face with boot blacking by his sergeant. As his heavy uniform, like all the uniforms of that day, is designed for parade without the least reference to his health or comfort, he perspires profusely in the sun; and his painted moustache has run in little streaks down his chin and round his neck except where it has dried in stiff japanned flakes, and had its sweeping outline chipped off in grotesque little bays and headlands, making him unspeakably ridiculous in the eye of History a hundred years later, but monstrous and horrible to the contemporary north Italian infant, to whom nothing would seem more natural than that he should relieve the monotony of his guard by pitchforking a stray child up on his bayonet, and eating it uncooked. Nevertheless one girl of bad character, in whom an instinct of privilege with soldiers is already dawning, does peep in at the safest window for a moment, before a glance and a clink from the sentinel sends her flying. Most of what she sees she has seen before: the vineyard at the back, with the old winepress and a cart among the vines; the door close down on her right leading to the inn entry; the landlord's best sideboard, now in full action for dinner, further back on the same side; the fireplace on the other side, with a couch near it, and another door, leading to the inner rooms, between it and the vineyard; and the table in the middle with its repast of Milanese risotto, cheese, grapes, bread, olives, and a big wickered flask of red wine.

The landlord, Giuseppe Grandi, is also no novelty. He is a swarthy, vivacious, shrewdly cheerful, black-curled, bullet-headed, grinning little man of 40. Naturally an excellent host, he is in quite special spirits this evening at his good fortune in having the French commander as his guest to protect him against the license of the troops, and actually sports a pair of gold earrings which he would otherwise have hidden carefully under the winepress with his little equipment of silver plate.

Napoleon, sitting facing her on the further side of the table, and Napoleon's hat, sword and riding whip lying on the couch, she sees for the first time. He is working hard, partly at his meal, which he has discovered how to dispatch, by attacking all the courses simultaneously, in ten minutes (this practice is the beginning of his downfall), and partly at a map which he is correcting from memory, occasionally marking the position of the forces by taking a grapeskin from his mouth and planting it on the map with his thumb like a wafer. He has a supply of writing materials before him mixed up in disorder with the dishes and cruets; and his long hair gets sometimes into the risotto gravy and sometimes into the ink.]

GIUSEPPE. Will your excellency—

NAPOLEON. [*Intent on his map, but cramming himself mechanically with his left hand.*] Don't talk. I'm busy.

GIUS. [*With perfect goodhumor.*] Excellency: I obey.

NAP. Some red ink.

GIUS. Alas! excellency, there is none.

NAP. [*With Corsican facetiousness.*] Kill something and bring me its blood.

GIUS. [*Grinning.*] There is nothing but your excellency's horse, the sentinel, the lady upstairs, and my wife.

NAP. Kill your wife.

GIUS. Willingly, your excellency; but unhappily I am not strong enough. She would kill me.

NAP. That will do equally well.

GIUS. Your excellency does me too much honor. [*Stretching his hand toward the flask.*] Perhaps some wine will answer your excellency's purpose.

NAP. [*Hastily protecting the flask, and becoming quite serious.*] Wine! No: that would be waste. You are all the same: waste! waste! waste! [*He marks the map with gravy, using his fork as a pen.*] Clear away. [*He finishes his wine; pushes back his chair; and uses his napkin, stretching his legs and leaning back, but still frowning and thinking.*]

GIUS. [*Clearing the table and removing the things to a tray on the sideboard.*] Every man to his trade, excellency. We innkeepers have plenty of cheap wine: we think nothing of spilling it. You great generals have plenty of cheap blood: you think nothing of spilling it. Is it not so, excellency?

NAP. Blood costs nothing: wine costs money. [*He rises and goes to the fireplace.*]

GIUS. They say you are careful of everything except human life, excellency.

NAP. Human life, my friend, is the only thing that takes care of itself. [*He throws himself at his ease on the couch.*]

GIUS. [*Admiring him.*] Ah, excellency, what fools we all are beside you! If I could only find out the secret of your success!

NAP. You would make yourself Emperor of Italy, eh?

GIUS. Too troublesome, excellency: I leave all that to you. Besides, what would become of my inn if I were Emperor? See how you enjoy looking on at me whilst I keep the inn for you and wait on you! Well, I shall enjoy looking on at you whilst you become Emperor of Europe, and govern the country for me. [*Whilst he chatters, he takes the cloth off without removing the map and inkstand, and takes the corners in his hands and the middle of the edge in his mouth, to fold it up.*]

NAP. Emperor of Europe, eh? Why only Europe?

GIUS. Why, indeed? Emperor of the world, excellency! Why not? [*He folds and rolls up the cloth, emphasizing his phrases by the steps of the process.*] One man is like another [*fold*]: one country is like another [*fold*]: one battle is like another. [*At the last fold, he slaps the cloth on the table and deftly rolls it up, adding, by way of peroration.*] Conquer one: conquer all. [*He takes the cloth to the sideboard, and puts it in a drawer.*]

NAP. And govern for all; fight for all; be everybody's servant under cover of being everybody's master. Giuseppe.

GIUS. [*At the sideboard.*] Excellency.

NAP. I forbid you to talk to me about myself.

GIUS. [*Coming to the foot of the couch.*] Pardon. Your excellency is so unlike other great men. It is the subject they like best.

NAP. Well, talk to me about the subject they like next best, whatever that may be.

GIUS. [*Unabashed.*] Willingly, your excellency. Has your excellency by any chance caught a glimpse of the lady upstairs? [*Napoleon promptly sits up and looks at him with an interest which entirely justifies the implied epigram.*]

NAP. How old is she?

GIUS. The right age, excellency.

NAP. Do you mean seventeen or thirty?

GIUS. Thirty, excellency.

NAP. Goodlooking?

GIUS. I cannot see with your excellency's eyes: every man must judge that for himself. In my opinion, excellency, a fine figure of a lady. [*Slyly.*] Shall I lay the table for her collation here?

NAP. [*Brusquely, rising.*] No: lay nothing here until the officer for whom I am waiting comes back. [*He looks at his watch, and takes to walking to and fro between the fireplace and the vineyard.*]

GIUS. [*With conviction.*] Excellency: believe me, he has been captured by the accursed Austrians. He dare not keep you waiting if he were at liberty.

NAP. [*Turning at the edge of the shadow of the veranda.*] Giuseppe: if that turns out to be true, it will put me into such a temper that nothing short of hanging you and your whole household, including the lady upstairs, will satisfy me.

GIUS. We are all cheerfully at your excellency's disposal, except the lady. I cannot answer for her; but no lady could resist you, General.

NAP. [*Sourly, resuming his march.*] Hm! You will never be hanged. There is no satisfaction in hanging a man who does not object to it.

GIUS. [*Sympathetically.*] Not the least in the world, excellency: is there? [*Napoleon again looks at his watch, evidently growing anxious.*] Ah, one can see that you are a great man, General: you know how to wait. If it were a corporal now, or a sub-lieutenant, at the end of three minutes he would be swearing, fuming, threatening, pulling the house about our ears.

NAP. Giuseppe: your flatteries are insufferable. Go and talk outside. [*He sits down again at the table, with his jaws in his hands, and his elbows propped on the map, poring over it with a troubled expression.*]

GIUS. Willingly, your excellency. You shall not be disturbed. [*He takes up the tray and prepares to withdraw.*]

NAP. The moment he comes back, send him to me.

GIUS. Instantaneously, your excellency.

A LADY'S VOICE. [*Calling from some distant part of the inn.*] Giusep-pe! [*The voice is very musical, and the two final notes make an ascending interval.*]

NAP. [*Startled.*] What's that? What's that?

GIUS. [*Resting the end of his tray on the table and leaning over to speak the more confidentially.*] The lady, excellency.

NAP. [*Absently.*] Yes. What lady? Whose lady?

GIUS. The strange lady, excellency.

NAP. What strange lady?

GIUS. [*With a shrug.*] Who knows? She arrived here half an hour before you in a hired carriage belonging to the Golden Eagle at Borghetto. Actually by herself, excellency. No servants. A dressing bag and a trunk: that is all. The postillion says she left a horse—a charger, with military trappings, at the Golden Eagle.

NAP. A woman with a charger! That's extraordinary.

THE LADY'S VOICE. [*The two final notes now making a peremptory descending interval.*] Giuseppe!

NAP. [*Rising to listen.*] That's an interesting voice.

GIUS. She is an interesting lady, excellency. [*Calling.*] Coming, lady, coming. [*He makes for the inner door.*]

NAP. [*Arresting him with a strong hand on his shoulder.*] Stop. Let her come.

VOICE. Giuseppe!! [*Impatiently.*]

GIUS. [*Pleadingly.*] Let me go, excellency. It is my point of honor as an innkeeper to come when I am called. I appeal to you as a soldier.

A MAN'S VOICE. [*Outside, at the inn door, shouting.*] Here, someone. Hollo! Landlord. Where are you? [*Somebody raps vigorously with a whip handle on a bench in the passage.*]

NAP. [*Suddenly becoming the commanding officer again and throwing Giuseppe off.*] There he is at last. [*Pointing to the inner door.*] Go. Attend to your business: the lady is calling you. [*He goes to the fireplace and stands with his back to it with a determined military air.*]

GIUS. [*With bated breath, snatching up his tray.*] Certainly, excellency. [*He hurries out by the inner door.*]

THE MAN'S VOICE. [*Impatiently.*] Are you all asleep here?

[*The door opposite the fireplace is kicked rudely open; and a dusty sub-lieutenant bursts into the room. He is a chuckleheaded young man of 24, with the fair, delicate, clear skin of a man of rank, and a self-assurance on that ground which the French Revolution has failed to shake in the smallest degree. He has a thick silly lip, an eager credulous eye, an obstinate nose, and a loud confident voice. A young man without fear, without reverence, without imagination, without sense, hopelessly insusceptible to the Napoleonic or any other idea, stupendously egotistical, eminently qualified to rush in where angels fear to tread, yet of a vigorous babbling vitality which bustles him into the thick of things. He is just now boiling with vexation, attributable by a superficial observer to his impatience at not being promptly attended to by the staff of the inn, but in which a more discerning eye can perceive a certain moral depth, indicating a more permanent and momentous grievance. On seeing Napoleon, he is sufficiently taken aback to check himself and salute; but he does not betray by his manner any of that prophetic consciousness of Marengo and Austerlitz, Waterloo and St. Helena, or the Napoleonic pictures of Delaroche and Meissonier, which modern culture will instinctively expect from him.*]

NAP. [*Sharply.*] Well, sir, here you are at last. Your instructions were that I should arrive here at six, and that I was to find you waiting for me with my mail from Paris and with despatches. It is now twenty minutes to eight. You were sent on this service as a hard rider with the fastest horse in the camp. You arrive a hundred minutes late, on foot. Where is your horse!

LIEUTENANT. [*Moodily pulling off his gloves and dashing them with his cap and whip on the table.*] Ah! where indeed? That's just what I should like to know, General. [*With emotion.*] You don't know how fond I was of that horse.

NAP. [*Angrily sarcastic.*] Indeed! [*With sudden misgiving.*] Where are the letters and despatches?

LIEUT. [*Importantly, rather pleased than otherwise at having some remarkable news.*] I don't know.

NAP. [*Unable to believe his ears.*] You don't know!

LIEUT. No more than you do, General. Now I suppose I shall be court-martialled. Well, I don't mind being court-martialled; but [*with solemn determination*] I tell you, General, if ever I catch that innocent looking youth, I'll spoil his beauty, the slimy little liar! I'll make a picture of him. I'll——

NAP. [*Advancing from the hearth to the table.*] What innocent looking youth? Pull yourself together, sir, will you; and give an account of yourself.

LIEUT. [*Facing him at the opposite side of the table, leaning on it with his fists.*] Oh, I'm all right, General: I'm perfectly ready to give an account of myself. I shall make the court-martial thoroughly understand that the fault was not mine. Advantage has been taken of the better side of my nature; and I'm not ashamed of it. But with all respect to you as my commanding officer, General, I say again that if ever I set eyes on that son of Satan, I'll—

NAP. [*Angrily.*] So you said before.

LIEUT. [*Drawing himself upright.*] I say it again. Just wait until I catch him. Just wait: that's all. [*He folds his arms resolutely, and breathes hard, with compressed lips.*]

NAP. I am waiting, sir—for your explanation.

LIEUT. [*Confidently.*] You'll change your tone, General, when you hear what has happened to me.

NAP. Nothing has happened to you, sir: you are alive and not disabled. Where are the papers entrusted to you?

LIEUT. Nothing! Nothing! Oho! Well, we'll see. [*Posing himself to overwhelm Napoleon with his news.*] He swore eternal brotherhood with me. Was that nothing? He said my eyes reminded him of his sister's eyes. Was that nothing? He cried—actually cried—over the story of my separation from Angelica. Was that nothing? He paid for both bottles of wine, though he only ate bread and grapes himself. Perhaps you call that nothing! He gave me his pistols and his horse and his despatches—most important despatches—and let me go away with them. [*Triumphantly, seeing that he has reduced Napoleon to blank stupefaction.*] Was that nothing?

NAP. [*Enfeebled by astonishment.*] What did he do that for?

LIEUT. [*As if the reason were obvious.*] To shew his confidence in me. [*Napoleon's jaw does not exactly drop; but its hinges become nerveless. The Lieutenant proceeds with honest indignation.*] And I was worthy of his confidence: I brought them all back honorably. But would you believe it?—when I trusted him with my pistols, and my horse, and my despatches—

NAP. [*Enraged.*] What the devil did you do that for?

LIEUT. Why, to shew my confidence in him, of course. And he betrayed it—abused it—never came back. The thief! the swindler! the heartless, treacherous little blackguard! You call that nothing, I suppose. But look here, General: [*again resorting to the table with his fist for greater emphasis*] you may put up with this outrage from the Austrians if you like; but speaking for myself personally, I tell you that if ever I catch—

NAP. [*Turning on his heel in disgust and irritably resuming his march to and fro.*] Yes: you have said that more than once already.

LIEUT. [*Excitedly.*] More than once! I'll say it fifty times; and what's more, I'll do it. You'll see, General. I'll shew my confidence in him, so I will. I'll—

NAP. Yes, yes, sir: no doubt you will. What kind of man was he?

LIEUT. Well, I should think you ought to be able to tell from his conduct the sort of man he was.

NAP. Psh! What was he like?

LIEUT. Like! He's like—well, you ought to have just seen the fellow: that will give you a notion of what he was like. He won't be like it five minutes after I catch him; for I tell you that if ever—

NAP. [*Shouting furiously for the innkeeper.*] Giuseppe! [*to the Lieutenant, out of all patience*] Hold your tongue, sir, if you can.

LIEUT. I warn you it's no use to try to put the blame on me. [*Plaintively.*] How was I to know the sort of fellow he was? [*He takes a chair from between the sideboard and the outer door; places it near the table; and sits down.*] If you only knew how hungry and tired I am, you'd have more consideration.

GIUS. [*Returning.*] What is it, excellency?

NAP. [*Struggling with his temper.*] Take this—this officer. Feed him; and put him to bed, if necessary. When he is in his right mind again, find out what has happened to him and bring me word. [*to the Lieutenant*] Consider yourself under arrest, sir.

LIEUT. [*With sulky stiffness.*] I was prepared for that. It takes a gentleman to understand a gentleman. [*He throws his sword on the table. Giuseppe takes it up and politely offers it to Napoleon, who throws it violently on the couch.*]

GIUS. [*With sympathetic concern.*] Have you been attacked by the Austrians, lieutenant? Dear, dear, dear!

LIEUT. [*Contemptuously.*] Attacked! I could have broken his back between my finger and thumb. I wish I had, now. No: it was by appealing to the better side of my nature: that's what I can't get

over. He said he'd never met a man he liked so much as me. He put his handkerchief round my neck because a gnat bit me, and my stock was chafing it. Look! [*He pulls a handkerchief from his stock. Giuseppe takes it and examines it.*]

GIUS. [*to Napoleon*] A lady's handkerchief, excellency. [*He smells it.*] Perfumed!

NAP. Eh? [*He takes it and looks at it attentively.*] Hm! [*He smells it.*] Ha! [*He walks thoughtfully across the room, looking at the handkerchief, which he finally sticks in the breast of his coat.*]

LIEUT. Good enough for him, anyhow. I noticed that he had a woman's hands when he touched my neck, with his coaxing, fawning ways, the mean, effeminate little hound. [*Lowering his voice with thrilling intensity.*] But mark my words, General. If ever—

THE LADY'S VOICE. [*Outside, as before.*] Giuseppe!

LIEUT. [*Petrified.*] What was that?

GIUS. Only a lady upstairs, lieutenant, calling me.

LIEUT. Lady!

VOICE. Giuseppe, Giuseppe: where are you?

LIEUT. [*Murderously.*] Give me that sword. [*He strides to the couch; snatches the sword; and draws it.*]

GIUS. [*Rushing forward and seizing his right arm.*] What are you thinking of, lieutenant? It's a lady: don't you hear that it's a woman's voice?

LIEUT. It's his voice, I tell you. Let me go.

[*He breaks away, and rushes to the inner door. It opens in his face; and the Strange Lady steps in. She is a very attractive lady, tall and extraordinarily graceful, with a delicately intelligent, apprehensive, questioning face—perception in the brow, sensitiveness in the nostrils, character in the chin: all keen, refined, and original. She is very feminine, but by no means weak: the lithe, tender figure is hung on a strong frame: the hands and feet, neck and shoulders, are no fragile ornaments, but of full size in proportion to her stature, which considerably exceeds that of Napoleon and the innkeeper, and leaves her at no disadvantage with the lieutenant. Only, her elegance and radiant charm keep the secret of her size and strength. She is not, judging by her dress, an admirer of the latest fashions of the Directory; or perhaps she uses up her old dresses for travelling. At all events she wears no jacket with extravagant lapels, no Greco-Tallien sham chiton, nothing, indeed, that the Princesse de Lamballe might not have worn. Her dress of flowered silk is long waisted, with a Watteau pleat behind, but with the paniers reduced to mere rudiments, as she is too tall for them. It is cut low in the neck, where it is eked out by a creamy fichu. She is fair, with golden brown hair and grey eyes.*]

She enters with the self-possession of a woman accustomed to the privileges of rank and beauty. The innkeeper, who has exellent natural manners, is highly appreciative of her. Napoleon, on whom her eyes first fall, is instantly smitten self-conscious. His color deepens: he becomes stiffer and less at ease than before. She perceives this instantly, and, not to embarrass him, turns in an infinitely well bred manner to pay the respect of a glance to the other gentleman, who is staring at her dress, as at the earth's final masterpiece of treacherous dissimulation, with feelings altogether inexpressible and indescribable. As she looks at him, she becomes deadly pale. There is no mistaking her expression: a revelation of some fatal error, utterly unexpected, has suddenly appalled her in the midst of tranquillity, security and victory. The next moment a wave of color rushes up from beneath the creamy fichu and drowns her whole face. One can see that she is blushing all over her body. Even the lieutenant, ordinarily incapable of observation, and just now lost in the tumult of his wrath, can see a thing when it is painted red for him. Interpreting the blush as the involuntary confession of black deceit confronted with its victim, he points to it with a loud crow of retributive triumph, and then, seizing her by the wrist, pulls her past him into the room as he claps the door to, and plants himself with his back to it.]

LIEUT. So I've got you, my lad. So you've disguised yourself, have you? [*In a voice of thunder.*] Take off that skirt.

GIUS. [*Remonstrating.*] Oh, lieutenant!

LADY. [*Affrighted, but highly indignant at his having dared to touch her.*] Gentlemen: I appeal to you. Giuseppe. [*Making a movement as if to run to Giuseppe.*]

LIEUT. [*Interposing, sword in hand.*] No you don't.

LADY. [*Taking refuge with Napoleon.*] Oh, sir, you are an officer—a general. You will protect me, will you not?

LIEUT. Never you mind him, General. Leave me to deal with him.

NAP. With him! With whom, sir? Why do you treat this lady in such a fashion?

LIEUT. Lady! He's a man! the man I shewed my confidence in. [*Advancing threateningly.*] Here you—

LADY. [*Running behind Napoleon and in her agitation embracing the arm which he instinctively extends before her as a fortification.*] Oh, thank you, General. Keep him away.

NAP. Nonsense, sir. This is certainly a lady [*she suddenly drops his arm and blushes again*]; and you are under arrest. Put down your sword, sir, instantly.

LIEUT. General: I tell you he's an Austrian spy. He passed himself off on me as one of General Masséna's staff this afternoon; and now he's passing himself off on you as a woman. Am I to believe my own eyes or not?

LADY. General: it must be my brother. He is on

General Masséna's staff. He is very like me.

LIEUT. [*His mind giving way.*] Do you mean to say that you're not your brother, but your sister?— the sister who was so like me?—who had my beautiful blue eyes? It was a lie: your eyes are not like mine: they're exactly like your own. What perfidy!

NAP. Lieutenant: will you obey my orders and leave the room, since you are convinced at last that this is no gentleman?

LIEUT. Gentleman! I should think not. No gentleman would have abused my confi

NAP. [*Out of all patience.*] Enough, sir, enough. Will you leave the room. I order you to leave the room.

LADY. Oh, pray let me go instead.

NAP. [*Drily.*] Excuse me, madame. With all respect to your brother, I do not yet understand what an officer on General Masséna's staff wants with my letters. I have some questions to put to you.

GIUS. [*Discreetly.*] Come, lieutenant. [*He opens the door.*]

LIEUT. I'm off. General: take warning by me: be on your guard against the better side of your nature. [*to the lady*] Madame: my apologies. I thought you were the same person, only of the opposite sex; and that naturally misled me.

LADY. [*Sweetly.*] It was not your fault, was it? I'm so glad you're not angry with me any longer, lieutenant. [*She offers her hand.*]

LIEUT. [*Bending gallantly to kiss it.*] Oh, madam, not the lea—[*Checking himself and looking at it.*] You have your brother's hand. And the same sort of ring.

LADY. [*Sweetly.*] We are twins.

LIEUT. That accounts for it. [*He kisses her hand.*] A thousand pardons. I didn't mind about the despatches at all: that's more the General's affair than mine: it was the abuse of my confidence through the better side of my nature. [*Taking his cap, gloves, and whip from the table and going.*] You'll excuse my leaving you, General, I hope. Very sorry, I'm sure. [*He talks himself out of the room. Giuseppe follows him and shuts the door.*]

NAP. [*Looking after them with concentrated irritation.*] Idiot! [*The Strange Lady smiles sympathetically. He comes frowning down the room between the table and the fireplace, all his awkwardness gone now that he is alone with her.*]

LADY. How can I thank you, General, for your protection?

NAP. [*Turning on her suddenly.*] My despatches: come! [*He puts out his hand for them.*]

LADY. General! [*She involuntarily puts her hands on her fichu as if to protect something there.*]

NAP. You tricked that blockhead out of them. You disguised yourself as a man. I want my despatches. They are there in the bosom of your dress, under your hands.

LADY. [*Quickly removing her hands.*] Oh, how unkindly you are speaking to me! [*She takes her handkerchief from her fichu.*] You frighten me. [*She touches her eyes as if to wipe away a tear.*]

NAP. I see you don't know me madam, or you would save yourself the trouble of pretending to cry.

LADY. [*Producing an effect of smiling through her tears.*] Yes, I do know you. You are the famous General Buonaparte. [*She gives the name a marked Italian pronunciation— Bwaw-na-parr-te.*]

NAP. [*Angrily, with the French pronunciation.*] Bonaparte, madame, Bonaparte. The papers, if you please.

LADY. But I assure you—[*He snatches the handkerchief rudely from her.*] General! [*Indignantly.*]

NAP. [*Taking the other handkerchief from his breast.*] You were good enough to lend one of your handkerchiefs to my lieutenant when you robbed him. [*He looks at the two handkerchiefs.*] They match one another. [*He smells them.*] The same scent. [*He flings them down on the table.*] I am waiting for the despatches. I shall take them, if necessary, with as little ceremony as the handkerchief. [*This historical incident was used eighty years later, by M. Victorien Sardou, in his drama entitled "Dora."*]

LADY. [*In dignified reproof.*] General: do you threaten women?

NAP. [*Bluntly.*] Yes.

LADY. [*Disconcerted, trying to gain time.*] But I don't understand. I—

NAP. You understand perfectly. You came here because your Austrian employers calculated that I was six leagues away. I am always to be found where my enemies don't expect me. You have walked into the lion's den. Come: you are a brave woman. Be a sensible one: I have no time to waste. The papers. [*He advances a step ominously.*]

LADY. [*Breaking down in the childish rage of impotence, and throwing herself in tears on the chair left beside the table by the Lieutenant.*] I brave! How little you know! I have spent the day in an agony of fear. I have a pain here from the tightening of my heart at every suspicious look, every threatening movement. Do you think every one is as brave as you? Oh, why will not you brave people do the brave things? Why do you leave them to us, who have no courage at all? I'm not brave: I shrink from violence: danger makes me miserable.

NAP. [*Interested.*] Then why have you thrust yourself into danger?

LADY. Because there is no other way: I can trust nobody else. And now it is all useless—all because of you, who have no fear, because you have no heart, no feeling, no—[*She breaks off, and throws herself on her knees.*] Ah, General, let me go: let me go without asking any questions. You shall have your despatches and letters: I swear it.

NAP. [*Holding out his hand.*] Yes: I am waiting for them. [*She gasps, daunted by his ruthless promptitude into despair of moving him by cajolery; but as she looks up perplexedly at him, it is plain that she is racking her brains for some device to outwit him. He meets her regard inflexibly.*]

LADY. [*Rising at last with a quiet little sigh.*] I will get them for you. They are in my room. [*She turns to the door.*]

NAP. I shall accompany you, madame.

LADY. [*Drawing herself up with a noble air of offended delicacy.*] I cannot permit you, General, to enter my chamber.

NAP. Then you shall stay here, madame, whilst I have your chamber searched for my papers.

LADY. [*Spitefully, openly giving up her plan.*] You may save yourself the trouble. They are not there.

NAP. No: I have already told you where they are. [*Pointing to her breast.*]

LADY. [*With pretty piteousness.*] General: I only want to keep one little private letter. Only one. Let me have it.

NAP. [*Cold and stern.*] Is that a reasonable demand, madam?

LADY. [*Encouraged by his not refusing point blank.*] No; but that is why you must grant it. Are your own demands reasonable? thousands of lives for the sake of your victories, your ambitions, your destiny! And what I ask is such a little thing. And I am only a weak woman, and you a brave man. [*She looks at him with her eyes full of tender pleading and is about to kneel to him again.*]

NAP. [*Brusquely.*] Get up, get up. [*He turns moodily away and takes a turn across the room, pausing for a moment to say, over his shoulder.*] You're talking nonsense; and you know it. [*She gets up and sits down in almost listless despair on the couch. When he turns and sees her there, he feels that his victory is complete, and that he may now indulge in a little play with his victim. He comes back and sits beside her. She looks alarmed and moves a little away from him; but a ray of rallying hope beams from her eye. He begins like a man enjoying some secret joke.*] How do you know I am a brave man?

LADY. [*Amazed.*] You! General Buonaparte. [*Italian pronunciation.*]

NAP. Yes, I, General Bonaparte. [*Emphasizing the French pronunciation.*]

LADY. Oh, how can you ask such a question? you! who stood only two days ago at the bridge at Lodi, with the air full of death, fighting a duel with cannons across the river! [*Shuddering.*] Oh, you do brave things.

NAP. So do you.

LADY. I! [*With a sudden odd thought.*] Oh! Are you a coward?

NAP. [*Laughing grimly and pinching her cheek.*] That is the one question you must never ask a soldier. The sergeant asks after the recruit's height, his age, his wind, his limb, but never after his courage. [*He gets up and walks about with his hands behind him and his head bowed, chuckling to himself.*]

LADY. [*As if she had found it no laughing matter.*] Ah, you can laugh at fear. Then you don't know what fear is.

NAP. [*Coming behind the couch.*] Tell me this. Suppose you could have got that letter by coming to me over the bridge at Lodi the day before yesterday! Suppose there had been no other way, and that this was a sure way—if only you escaped the cannon! [*She shudders and covers her eyes for a moment with her hands.*] Would you have been afraid?

LADY. Oh, horribly afraid, agonizingly afraid. [*She presses her hands on her heart.*] It hurts only to imagine it.

NAP. [*Inflexibly.*] Would you have come for the despatches?

LADY. [*Overcome by the imagined horror.*] Don't ask me. I must have come.

NAP. Why?

LADY. Because I must. Because there would have been no other way.

NAP. [*With conviction.*] Because you would have wanted my letter enough to bear your fear. There is only one universal passion: fear. Of all the thousand qualities a man may have, the only one you will find as certainly in the youngest drummer boy in my army as in me, is fear. It is fear that makes men fight: it is indifference that makes them run away: fear is the mainspring of war. Fear!—I know fear well, better than you, better than any woman. I once saw a regiment of good Swiss soldiers massacred by a mob in Paris because I was afraid to interfere: I felt myself a coward to the tips of my toes as I looked on at it. Seven months ago I revenged my shame by pounding that mob to death with cannon balls. Well, what of that? Has fear ever held a man back from anything he really wanted—or a woman either? Never. Come with me; and I will shew you twenty thousand cowards who will risk death every day for the price of a glass of brandy. And do you think there are no women in the army, braver than the men, because their lives are worth less? Psha! I think nothing of your fear or your bravery. If you had had to come across to me at Lodi, you would not have been afraid: once on the bridge, every other feeling would have gone down before the necessity—the necessity—for making your way to my side and getting what you wanted.

And now, suppose you had done all this—suppose you had come safely out with that letter in your hand, knowing that when the hour came, your fear had tightened, not your heart, but your grip of your own purpose—that it had ceased to be fear, and had become strength, penetration, vigilance, iron resolution—how would you answer then if you were asked whether you were a coward?

LADY. [*Rising.*] Ah, you are a hero, a real hero.

NAP. Pooh! there's no such thing as a real hero. [*He strolls down the room, making light of her enthusiasm, but by no means displeased with himself for having evoked it.*]

LADY. Ah, yes, there is. There is a difference between what you call my bravery and yours. You wanted to win the battle of Lodi for yourself and not for anyone else, didn't you?

NAP. Of course. [*Suddenly recollecting himself.*] Stop: no. [*He pulls himself piously together, and says, like a man conducting a religious service.*] I am only the servant of the French republic, following humbly in the footsteps of the heroes of classical antiquity. I win battles for humanity—for my country, not for myself.

LADY. [*Disappointed.*] Oh, then you are only a womanish hero, after all. [*She sits down again, all her enthusiasm gone, her elbow on the end of the couch, and her cheek propped on her hand.*]

NAP. [*Greatly astonished.*] Womanish!

LADY. [*Listlessly.*] Yes, like me. [*With deep melancholy.*] Do you think that if I only wanted those despatches for myself, I dare venture into a battle for them? No: if that were all, I should not have the courage to ask to see you at your hotel, even. My courage is mere slavishness: it is of no use to me for my own purpose. It is only through love, through pity, through the instinct to save and protect someone else, that I can do the things that terrify me.

NAP. [*Contemptuously.*] Pshaw! [*He turns slightingly away from her.*]

LADY. Aha! now you see that I'm not really brave. [*Relapsing into petulant listlessness.*] But what right have you to despise me if you only win your battles for others? for your country! through patriotism! That is what I call womanish: it is so like a Frenchman!

NAP. [*Furiously.*] I am no Frenchman.

LADY. [*Innocently.*] I thought you said you won the battle of Lodi for your country, General Bu— shall I pronounce it in Italian or French?

NAP. You are presuming on my patience, madam. I was born a French subject, but not in France.

LADY. [*Folding her arms on the end of the couch, and leaning on them with a marked access of interest in him.*] You were not born a subject at all, I think.

NAP. [*Greatly pleased, starting on a fresh march.*] Eh? Eh? You think not.

LADY. I am sure of it.

NAP. Well, well, perhaps not. [*The self-complacency of his assent catches his own ear. He stops short, reddening. Then, composing himself into a solemn attitude, modelled on the heroes of classical antiquity, he takes a high moral tone.*] But we must not live for ourselves alone, little one. Never forget that we should always think of others, and work for others, and lead and govern them for their own good. Self-sacrifice is the foundation of all true nobility of character.

LADY. [*Again relaxing her attitude with a sigh.*] Ah, it is easy to see that you have never tried it, General.

NAP. [*Indignantly, forgetting all about Brutus and Scipio.*] What do you mean by that speech, madam?

LADY. Haven't you noticed that people always exaggerate the value of the things they haven't got? The poor think they only need riches to be quite happy and good. Everybody worships truth, purity, unselfishness, for the same reason—because they have no experience of them. Oh, if they only knew!

NAP. [*With angry derision.*] If they only knew! Pray, do you know?

LADY. [*With her arms stretched down and her hands clasped on her knees, looking straight before her.*] Yes. I had the misfortune to be born good. [*Glancing up at him for a moment.*] And it is a misfortune, I can tell you, General. I really am truthful and unselfish and all the rest of it; and it's nothing but cowardice; want of character; want of being really, strongly, positively oneself.

NAP. Ha? [*Turning to her quickly with a flash of strong interest.*]

LADY. [*Earnestly, with rising enthusiasm.*] What is the secret of your power? Only that you believe in yourself. You can fight and conquer for yourself and for nobody else. You are not afraid of your own destiny. You teach us what we all might be if we had the will and courage; and that [*Suddenly sinking on her knees before him.*] is why we all begin to worship you. [*She kisses his hands.*]

NAP. [*Embarrassed.*] Tut, tut! Pray rise, madam.

LADY. Do not refuse my homage: it is your right. You will be emperor of France—

NAP. [*Hurriedly.*] Take care. Treason!

LADY. [*Insisting.*] Yes, emperor of France; then of Europe; perhaps of the world. I am only the first subject to swear allegiance. [*Again kissing his hand.*] My Emperor!

NAP. [*Overcome, raising her.*] Pray, pray. No, no, little one: this is folly. Come: be calm, be calm. [*Petting her.*] There, there, my girl.

LADY. [*Struggling with happy tears.*] Yes, I know it is an impertinence in me to tell you what you must know far better than I do. But you are not angry with me, are you?

NAP. Angry! No, no: not a bit, not a bit. Come: you are a very clever and sensible and interesting little woman. [*He pats her on the check.*] Shall we be friends?

LADY. [*Enraptured.*] Your friend! You will let me be your friend! Oh! [*She offers him both her hands with a radiant smile.*] You see: I shew my confidence in you.

NAP. [*With a yell of rage, his eyes flashing.*] What!

LADY. What's the matter?

NAP. Shew your confidence in me! So that I may shew my confidence in you in return by letting you give me the slip with the despatches, eh? Ah, Dalila, Dalila, you have been trying your tricks on me; and I have been as great a gull as my jackass of a lieutenant. [*He advances threateningly on her.*] Come: the despatches. Quick: I am not to be trifled with now.

LADY. [*Flying round the couch.*] General—

NAP. Quick, I tell you. [*He passes swiftly up the middle of the room and intercepts her as she makes for the vineyard.*]

LADY. [*At bay, confronting him.*] You dare address me in that tone.

NAP. Dare!

LADY. Yes, dare. Who are you that you should presume to speak to me in that coarse way? Oh, the vile, vulgar Corsican adventurer comes out in you very easily.

NAP. [*Beside himself.*] You she devil! [*Savagely.*] Once more, and only once, will you give me those papers or shall I tear them from you—by force?

LADY. [*Letting her hands fall.*] Tear them from me—by force! [*As he glares at her like a tiger about to spring, she crosses her arms on her breast in the attitude of a martyr. The gesture and pose instantly awaken his theatrical instinct: he forgets his rage in the desire to shew her that in acting, too, she has met her match. He keeps her a moment in suspense; then suddenly clears up his countenance; puts his hands behind him with provoking coolness; looks at her up and down a couple of times; takes a pinch of snuff; wipes his fingers carefully and puts up his handkerchief, her heroic pose becoming more and more ridiculous all the time.*]

NAP. [*At last.*] Well?

LADY. [*Disconcerted, but with her arms still crossed devotedly.*] Well: what are you going to do?

NAP. Spoil your attitude.

LADY. You brute! [*Abandoning the attitude, she comes to the end of the couch, where she turns with her back to it, leaning against it and facing him with her hands behind her.*]

NAP. Ah, that's better. Now listen to me. I like you. What's more, I value your respect.

LADY. You value what you have not got, then.

NAP. I shall have it presently. Now attend to me. Suppose I were to allow myself to be abashed by the respect due to your sex, your beauty, your heroism and all the rest of it? Suppose I, with nothing but such sentimental stuff to stand between these muscles of mine and those papers which you have about you, and which I want and mean to have: suppose I, with the prize within my grasp, were to falter and sneak away with my hands empty; or, what would be worse, cover up my weakness by playing the magnanimous hero, and sparing you the violence I dared not use, would you not despise me from the depths of your woman's soul? Would any woman be such a fool? Well, Bonaparte can rise to the situation and act like a woman when it is necessary. Do you understand?

[*The lady, without speaking, stands upright, and takes a packet of papers from her bosom. For a moment she has an intense impulse to dash them in his face. But her good breeding cuts her off from any vulgar method of relief. She hands them to him politely, only averting her head. The moment he takes them, she hurries across to the other side of the room; covers her face with her hands; and sits down, with her body turned away to the back of the chair.*]

NAP. [*Gloating over the papers.*] Aha! That's right. That's right. [*Before opening them he looks at her and says.*] Excuse me. [*He sees that she is hiding her face.*] Very angry with me, eh? [*He unties the packet, the seal of which is already broken, and puts it on the table to examine its contents.*]

LADY. [*Quietly, taking down her hands and shewing that she is not crying, but only thinking.*] No. You were

right. But I am sorry for you.

NAP. [*Pausing in the act of taking the uppermost paper from the packet.*] Sorry for me! Why?

LADY. I am going to see you lose your honor.

NAP. Hm! Nothing worse than that? [*He takes up the paper.*]

LADY. And your happiness.

NAP. Happiness, little woman, is the most tedious thing in the world to me. Should I be what I am if I cared for happiness? Anything else?

LADY. Nothing— [*He interrupts her with an exclamation of satisfaction. She proceeds quietly.*] except that you will cut a very foolish figure in the eyes of France.

NAP. [*Quickly.*] What? [*The hand holding the paper involuntarily drops. The lady looks at him enigmatically in tranquil silence. He throws the letter down and breaks out into a torrent of scolding.*] What do you mean? Eh? Are you at your tricks again? Do you think I don't know what these papers contain? I'll tell you. First, my information as to Beaulieu's retreat. There are only two things he can do—leatherbrained idiot that he is!—shut himself up in Mantua or violate the neutrality of Venice by taking Peschiera. You are one of old Leatherbrain's spies: he has discovered that he has been betrayed, and has sent you to intercept the information at all hazards—as if that could save him from me, the old fool! The other papers are only my usual correspondence from Paris, of which you know nothing.

LADY. [*Prompt and businesslike.*] General: let us make a fair division. Take the information your spies have sent you about the Austrian army; and give me the Paris correspondence. That will content me.

NAP. [*His breath taken away by the coolness of the proposal.*] A fair di— [*He gasps.*] It seems to me, madame, that you have come to regard my letters as your own property, of which I am trying to rob you.

LADY. [*Earnestly.*] No: on my honor I ask for no letter of yours—not a word that has been written by you or to you. That packet contains a stolen letter: a letter written by a woman to a man—a man not her husband—a letter that means disgrace, infamy—

NAP. A love letter?

LADY. [*Bitter-sweetly.*] What else but a love letter could stir up so much hate?

NAP. Why is it sent to me? To put the husband in my power, eh?

LADY. No, no: it can be of no use to you: I swear that it will cost you nothing to give it to me. It has been sent to you out of sheer malice—solely to injure the woman who wrote it.

NAP. Then why not send it to her husband instead of to me?

LADY. [*Completely taken aback.*] Oh! [*Sinking back into the chair.*] I—I don't know. [*She breaks down.*]

NAP. Aha! I thought so: a little romance to get the papers back. [*He throws the packet on the table and confronts her with cynical goodhumor.*] Per Bacco, little woman, I can't help admiring you. If I could lie like that, it would save me a great deal of trouble.

LADY. [*Wringing her hands.*] Oh, how I wish I really had told you some lie! You would have believed me then. The truth is the one thing that nobody will believe.

NAP. [*With coarse familiarity, treating her as if she were a vivandière.*] Capital! Capital! [*He puts his hands behind him on the table, and lifts himself on to it, sitting with his arms akimbo and his legs wide apart.*] Come: I am a true Corsican in my love for stories. But I could tell them better than you if I set my mind to it. Next time you are asked why a letter compromising a wife should not be sent to her husband, answer simply that the husband would not read it. Do you suppose, little innocent, that a man wants to be compelled by public opinion to make a scene, to fight a duel, to break up his household, to injure his career by a scandal, when he can avoid it all by taking care not to know?

LADY. [*Revolted.*] Suppose that packet contained a letter about your own wife?

NAP. [*Offended, coming off the table.*] You are impertinent, madame.

LADY. [*Humbly.*] I beg your pardon. Caesar's wife is above suspicion.

NAP. [*With a deliberate assumption of superiority.*] You have committed an indiscretion. I pardon you. In future, do not permit yourself to introduce real persons in your romances.

LADY. [*Politely ignoring a speech which is to her only a breach of good manners, and rising to move towards the table.*] General: there really is a woman's letter there. [*Pointing to the packet.*] Give it to me.

NAP. [*With brute conciseness, moving so as to prevent her getting too near the letters.*] Why?

LADY. She is an old friend: we were at school together. She has written to me imploring me to prevent the letter falling into your hands.

NAP. Why has it been sent to me?

LADY. Because it compromises the director Barras.

NAP. [*Frowning, evidently startled.*] Barras! [*Haughtily.*] Take care, madame. The director Barras is my attached personal friend.

LADY. [*Nodding placidly.*] Yes. You became friends through your wife.

NAP. Again! Have I not forbidden you to speak of my wife? [*She keeps looking curiously at him, taking no account of the rebuke. More and more irritated, he drops his haughty manner, of which he is himself somewhat impatient, and says suspiciously, lowering his voice.*] Who is this woman with whom you sympathize so deeply?

LADY. Oh, General! How could I tell you that?

NAP. [*Ill-humoredly, beginning to walk about again in angry perplexity.*] Ay, ay: stand by one another. You are all the same, you women.

LADY. [*Indignantly.*] We are not all the same, any more than you are. Do you think that if *I* loved another man, I should pretend to go on loving my husband, or be afraid to tell him or all the world? But this woman is not made that way. She governs men by cheating them; and [*With disdain.*] they like it, and let her govern them. [*She sits down again, with her back to him.*]

NAP. [*Not attending to her.*] Barras, Barras! [*Turning very threateningly to her, his face darkening.*] Take care, take care: do you hear? You may go too far.

LADY. [*Innocently turning her face to him.*] What's the matter?

NAP. What are you hinting at? Who is this woman?

LADY. [*Meeting his angry searching gaze with tranquil indifference as she sits looking up at him with her right arm resting lightly along the back of her chair, and one knee crossed over the other.*] A vain, silly, extravagant creature, with a very able and ambitious husband who knows her through and through— knows that she has lied to him about her age, her income, her social position, about everything that silly women lie about—knows that she is incapable of fidelity to any principle or any person; and yet could not help loving her—could not help his man's instinct to make use of her for his own advancement with Barras.

NAP. [*In a stealthy, coldly furious whisper.*] This is your revenge, you she cat, for having had to give me the letters.

LADY. Nonsense! Or do you mean that you are that sort of man?

NAP. [*Exasperated, clasps his hands behind him, his fingers twitching, and says, as he walks irritably away from her to the fireplace.*] This woman will drive me out of my senses. [*to her*] Begone.

LADY. [*Seated immovably.*] Not without that letter.

NAP. Begone, I tell you. [*Walking from the fireplace to the vineyard and back to the table.*] You shall have no letter. I don't like you. You're a detestable woman, and as ugly as Satan. I don't choose to be pestered by strange women. Be off. [*He turns his back on her. In quiet amusement, she leans her cheek on her hand and laughs at him. He turns again, angrily mocking her.*] Ha! ha! ha! What are you laughing at?

LADY. At you, General. I have often seen persons of your sex getting into a pet and behaving like children; but I never saw a really great man do it before.

NAP. [*Brutally, flinging the words in her face.*] Pooh: flattery! flattery! coarse, impudent flattery!

LADY. [*Springing up with a bright flush in her cheeks.*] Oh, you are too bad. Keep your letters. Read the story of your own dishonor in them; and much good may they do you. Good-bye. [*She goes indignantly towards the inner door.*]

NAP. My own——! Stop. Come back. Come back, I order you. [*She proudly disregards his savagely peremptory tone and continues on her way to the door. He rushes at her; seizes her by the wrist; and drags her back.*] Now, what do you mean? Explain. Explain, I tell you, or— [*Threatening her. She looks at him with unflinching defiance.*] Rrrr! you obstinate devil, you. Why can't you answer a civil question?

LADY. [*Deeply offended by his violence.*] Why do you ask me? You have the explanation.

NAP. Where?

LADY. [*Pointing to the letters on the table.*] There. You have only to read it. [*He snatches the packet up, hesitates; looks at her suspiciously; and throws it down again.*]

NAP. You seem to have forgotten your solicitude for the honor of your old friend.

LADY. She runs no risk now: she does not quite understand her husband.

NAP. I am to read the letter, then? [*He stretches out his hand as if to take up the packet again, with his eye on her.*]

LADY. I do not see how you can very well avoid doing so now. [*He instantly withdraws his hand.*] Oh, don't be afraid. You will find many interesting things in it.

NAP. For instance?

LADY. For instance, a duel—with Barras, a domestic scene, a broken household, a public scandal, a checked career, all sorts of things.

NAP. Hm! [*He looks at her; takes up the packet and looks at it, pursing his lips and balancing it in his hand; looks at her again; passes the packet into his left hand and puts it behind his back, raising his right to scratch the back of his head as he turns and goes up to the edge of the vineyard, where he stands for a moment looking out into the vines, deep in thought. The Lady watches him in silence,* somewhat slightingly. *Suddenly he turns and comes back again, full of force and decision.*] I grant your request, madame. Your courage and resolution deserve to succeed. Take the letters for which you have fought so well; and remember henceforth that you found the vile, vulgar Corsican adventurer as generous to the vanquished after the battle as he was resolute in the face of the enemy before it. [*He offers her the packet.*]

LADY. [*Without taking it, looking hard at him.*] What are you at now, I wonder? [*He dashes the packet furiously to the floor.*] Aha! I've spoiled that attitude, I think. [*She makes him a pretty mocking curtsey.*]

NAP. [*Snatching it up again.*] Will you take the letters and begone [*advancing and thrusting them upon her*]?

LADY. [*Escaping round the table.*] No: I don't want your letters.

NAP. Ten minutes ago, nothing else would satisfy you.

LADY. [*Keeping the table carefully between them.*] Ten minutes ago you had not insulted me past all bearing.

NAP. I—[*swallowing his spleen*] I apologize.

LADY. [*Coolly.*] Thanks. [*With forced politeness he offers her the packet across the table. She retreats a step out of its reach and says*] But don't you want to know whether the Austrians are at Mantua or Peschiera?

NAP. I have already told you that I can conquer my enemies without the aid of spies, madame.

LADY. And the letter! don't you want to read that?

NAP. You have said that it is not addressed to me. I am not in the habit of reading other people's letters. [*He again offers the packet.*]

LADY. In that case there can be no objection to your keeping it. All I wanted was to prevent your reading it. [*Cheerfully.*] Good afternoon, General. [*She turns coolly towards the inner door.*]

NAP. [*Furiously flinging the packet on the couch.*] Heaven grant me patience! [*He goes up determinedly and places himself before the door.*] Have you any sense of personal danger? Or are you one of those women who like to be beaten black and blue?

LADY. Thank you, General: I have no doubt the sensation is very voluptuous; but I had rather not. I simply want to go home: that's all. I was wicked enough to steal your despatches; but you have got them back; and you have forgiven me, because [*delicately reproducing his rhetorical cadence*] you are as generous to the vanquished after the battle as you are resolute in the face of the enemy before it. Won't you say good-bye to me? [*She offers her hand sweetly.*]

NAP. [*Repulsing the advance with a gesture of concentrated rage, and opening the door to call fiercely.*] Giuseppe! [*Louder.*] Giuseppe! [*He bangs the door to, and comes to the middle of the room. The lady goes a little way into the vineyard to avoid him.*]

GIUS. [*Appearing at the door.*] Excellency?

NAP. Where is that fool?

GIUS. He has had a good dinner, according to your instructions, excellency, and is now doing me the honor to gamble with me to pass the time.

NAP. Send him here. Bring him here. Come with him. [*Giuseppe, with unruffled readiness, hurries off. Napoleon turns curtly to the lady, saying*] I must trouble you to remain some moments longer, madame. [*He comes to the couch. She comes from the vineyard down the opposite side of the room to the sideboard, and posts herself there, leaning against it, watching him. He takes the packet from the couch and deliberately buttons it carefully into his breast pocket, looking at her meanwhile with an expression which suggests that she will soon find out the meaning of his proceedings, and will not like it. Nothing more is said until the lieutenant arrives followed by Giuseppe, who stands modestly in attendance at the table. The lieutenant, without cap, sword or gloves, and much improved in temper and spirits by his meal, chooses the Lady's side of the room, and waits, much at his ease, for Napoleon to begin.*]

NAP. Lieutenant.

LIEUT. [*Encouragingly.*] General.

NAP. I cannot persuade this lady to give me much information; but there can be no doubt that the man who tricked you out of your charge was, as she admitted to you, her brother.

LIEUT. [*Triumphantly.*] What did I tell you, General! What did I tell you!

NAP. You must find that man. Your honor is at stake; and the fate of the campaign, the destiny of France, of Europe, of humanity, perhaps, may depend on the information those despatches contain.

LIEUT. Yes, I suppose they really are rather serious [*as if this had hardly occurred to him before*].

NAP. [*Energetically.*] They are so serious, sir, that if you do not recover them, you will be degraded in the presence of your regiment.

LIEUT. Whew! The regiment won't like that, I can tell you.

NAP. Personally, I am sorry for you. I would willingly conceal the affair if it were possible. But I shall be called to account for not acting on the despatches. I shall have to prove to all the world that I never received them, no matter what the consequences may be to you. I am sorry; but you see that I cannot help myself.

LIEUT. [*Goodnaturedly.*] Oh, don't take it to heart, General: it's really very good of you. Never mind what happens to me: I shall scrape through somehow; and we'll beat the Austrians for you, despatches or no despatches. I hope you won't insist on my starting off on a wild goose chase after the fellow now. I haven't a notion where to look for him.

GIUS. [*Deferentially.*] You forget, Lieutenant: he has your horse.

LIEUT. [*Starting.*] I forgot that. [*Resolutely.*] I'll go after him, General: I'll find that horse if it's alive anywhere in Italy. And I shan't forget the despatches: never fear. Giuseppe: go and saddle one of those mangy old posthorses of yours, while I get my cap and sword and things. Quick march. Off with you [*bustling him*].

GIUS. Instantly, Lieutenant, instantly. [*He disappears in the vineyard, where the light is now reddening with the sunset.*]

LIEUT. [*Looking about him on his way to the inner door.*] By the way, General, did I give you my sword or did I not? Oh, I remember now. [*Fretfully.*] It's all that nonsense about putting a man under arrest: one never knows where to find— [*Talks himself out of the room.*]

LADY. [*Still at the sideboard.*] What does all this mean, General?

NAP. He will not find your brother.

LADY. Of course not. There's no such person.

NAP. The despatches will be irrecoverably lost.

LADY. Nonsense! They are inside your coat.

NAP. You will find it hard, I think, to prove that wild statement. [*The Lady starts. He adds, with clinching emphasis.*] Those papers are lost.

LADY. [*Anxiously, advancing to the corner of the table.*] And that unfortunate young man's career will be sacrificed.

NAP. His career! The fellow is not worth the gunpowder it would cost to have him shot. [*He turns contemptuously and goes to the hearth, where he stands with his back to her.*]

LADY. [*Wistfully.*] You are very hard. Men and women are nothing to you but things to be used, even if they are broken in the use.

NAP. [*Turning on her.*] Which of us has broken this fellow—I or you? Who tricked him out of the despatches? Did you think of his career then?

LADY. [*Naively concerned about him.*] Oh, I never thought of that. It was brutal of me; but I couldn't help it, could I? How else could I have got the papers? [*Supplicating.*] General: you will save him from disgrace.

NAP. [*Laughing sourly.*] Save him yourself, since

you are so clever: it was you who ruined him. [*With savage intensity.*] I hate a bad soldier.

[*He goes out determinedly through the vineyard. She follows him a few steps with an appealing gesture, but is interrupted by the return of the lieutenant, gloved and capped, with his sword on, ready for the road. He is crossing to the outer door when she intercepts him.*]

LADY. Lieutenant.

LIEUT. [*Importantly.*] You mustn't delay me, you know. Duty, madame, duty.

LADY. [*Imploringly.*] Oh, sir, what are you going to do to my poor brother?

LIEUT. Are you very fond of him?

LADY. I should die if anything happened to him. You must spare him. [*The lieutenant shakes his head gloomily.*] Yes, yes: you must: you shall: he is not fit to die. Listen to me. If I tell you where to find him—if I undertake to place him in your hands a prisoner, to be delivered up by you to General Bonaparte—will you promise me on your honor as an officer and a gentleman not to fight with him or treat him unkindly in any way?

LIEUT. But suppose he attacks me. He has my pistols.

LADY. He is too great a coward.

LIEUT. I don't feel so sure about that. He's capable of anything.

LADY. If he attacks you, or resists you in any way, I release you from your promise.

LIEUT. My promise! I didn't mean to promise. Look here: you're as bad as he is: you've taken an advantage of me through the better side of my nature. What about my horse?

LADY. It is part of the bargain that you are to have your horse and pistols back.

LIEUT. Honor bright?

LADY. Honor bright. [*She offers her hand.*]

LIEUT. [*Taking it and holding it.*] All right: I'll be as gentle as a lamb with him. His sister's a very pretty woman. [*He attempts to kiss her.*]

LADY. [*Slipping away from him.*] Oh, Lieutenant! You forget: your career is at stake—the destiny of Europe—of humanity.

LIEUT. Oh, bother the destiny of humanity. [*Making for her.*] Only a kiss.

LADY. [*Retreating round the table.*] Not until you have regained your honor as an officer. Remember: you have not captured my brother yet.

LIEUT. [*Seductively.*] You'll tell me where he is, won't you?

LADY. I have only to send him a certain signal; and he will be here in quarter of an hour.

LIEUT. He's not far off, then.

LADY. No: quite close. Wait here for him: when he gets my message he will come here at once and surrender himself to you. You understand?

LIEUT. [*Intellectually overtaxed.*] Well, it's a little complicated; but I daresay it will be all right.

LADY. And now, whilst you're waiting, don't you think you had better make terms with the General?

LIEUT. Oh, look here, this is getting frightfully complicated. What terms?

LADY. Make him promise that if you catch my brother he will consider that you have cleared your character as a soldier. He will promise anything you ask on that condition.

LIEUT. That's not a bad idea. Thank you: I think I'll try it.

LADY. Do. And mind, above all things, don't let him see how clever you are.

LIEUT. I understand. He'd be jealous.

LADY. Don't tell him anything except that you are resolved to capture my brother or perish in the attempt. He won't believe you. Then you will produce my brother—

LIEUT. [*Interrupting as he masters the plot.*] And have the laugh at him! I say: what a clever little woman you are! [*Shouting.*] Giuseppe!

LADY. Sh! Not a word to Giuseppe about me. [*She puts her finger on her lips. He does the same. They look at one another warningly. Then, with a ravishing smile, she changes the gesture into wafting him a kiss, and runs out through the inner door. Electrified, he bursts into a volley of chuckles. Giuseppe comes back by the outer*]

GIUS. The horse is ready, Lieutenant.

LIEUT. I'm not going just yet. Go and find the General, and tell him I want to speak to him.

GIUS. [*Shaking his head.*] That will never do, Lieutenant.

LIEUT. Why not?

GIUS. In this wicked world a general may send for a lieutenant; but a lieutenant must not send for a general.

LIEUT. Oh, you think he wouldn't like it. Well, perhaps you're right: one has to be awfully particular about that sort of thing now we've got a republic.

[*Napoleon reappears, advancing from the vineyard, buttoning the breast of his coat, pale and full of gnawing thoughts.*]

GIUS. [*Unconscious of Napoleon's approach.*] Quite true, Lieutenant, quite true. You are all like innkeepers now in France: you have to be polite to everybody.

NAP. [*Putting his hand on Giuseppe's shoulder.*] And that destroys the whole value of politeness, eh?

LIEUT. The very man I wanted! See here, General: suppose I catch that fellow for you!

NAP. [*With ironical gravity.*] You will not catch him, my friend.

LIEUT. Aha! you think so; but you'll see. Just wait. Only, if I do catch him and hand him over to you, will you cry quits? Will you drop all this about degrading me in the presence of my regiment? Not that *I* mind, you know; but still no regiment likes to have all the other regiments laughing at it.

NAP. [*A cold ray of humor striking pallidly across his gloom.*] What shall we do with this officer, Giuseppe? Everything he says is wrong.

GIUS. [*Promptly.*] Make him a general, excellency; and then everything he says will be right.

LIEUT. [*Crowing.*] How-aw! [*He throws himself ecstatically on the couch to enjoy the joke.*]

NAPOLEON. [*Laughing and pinching Giuseppe's ear.*] You are thrown away in this inn, Giuseppe. [*He sits down and places Giuseppe before him like a schoolmaster with a pupil.*] Shall I take you away with me and make a man of you?

GIUS. [*Shaking his head rapidly and repeatedly.*] No, thank you, General. All my life long people have wanted to make a man of me. When I was a boy, our good priest wanted to make a man of me by teaching me to read and write. Then the organist at Melegnano wanted to make a man of me by teaching me to read music. The recruiting sergeant would have made a man of me if I had been a few inches taller. But it always meant making me work; and I am too lazy for that, thank Heaven! So I taught myself to cook and became an innkeeper; and now I keep servants to do the work, and have nothing to do myself except talk, which suits me perfectly.

NAP. [*Looking at him thoughtfully.*] You are satisfied?

GIUS. [*With cheerful conviction.*] Quite, excellency.

NAP. And you have no devouring devil inside you who must be fed with action and victory—gorged with them night and day—who makes you pay, with the sweat of your brain and body, weeks of Herculean toil for ten minutes of enjoyment—who is at once your slave and your tyrant, your genius and your doom—who brings you a crown in one hand and the oar of a galley slave in the other—who shews you all the kingdoms of the earth and offers to make you their master on condition that you become their servant!—have you nothing of that in you?

GIUS. Nothing of it! Oh, I assure you, excellency, my devouring devil is far worse than that. He offers me no crowns and kingdoms: he expects to get everything for nothing—sausages, omelettes, grapes, cheese, polenta, wine—three times a day, excellency; nothing less will content him.

LIEUT. Come, drop it, Giuseppe: you're making me feel hungry again.

[*Giuseppe, with an apologetic shrug, retires from the conversation, and busies himself at the table, dusting it, setting the map straight, and replacing Napoleon's chair, which the lady has pushed back.*]

NAP. [*Turning to the lieutenant with sardonic ceremony.*] I hope *I* have not been making you feel ambitious.

LIEUT. Not at all: I don't fly so high. Besides: I'm better as I am: men like me are wanted in the army just now. The fact is, the Revolution was all very well for civilians; but it won't work in the army. You know what soldiers are, General: they will have men of family for their officers. A subaltern must be a gentleman, because he's so much in contact with the men. But a general, or even a colonel, may be any sort of riff-raff if he understands the shop well enough. A lieutenant is a gentleman: all the rest is chance. Why, who do you suppose won the battle of Lodi? I'll tell you. My horse did.

NAP. [*Rising.*] Your folly is carrying you too far, sir. Take care.

LIEUT. Not a bit of it. You remember all that red-hot cannonade across the river: the Austrians blazing away at you to keep you from crossing, and you blazing away at them to keep them from setting the bridge on fire? Did you notice where I was then?

NAP. [*With menacing politeness.*] I am sorry. I am afraid I was rather occupied at the moment.

GIUS. [*With eager admiration.*] They say you jumped off your horse and worked the big guns with your own hands, General.

LIEUT. That was a mistake: an officer should never let himself down to the level of his men. [*Napoleon looks at him dangerously, and begins to walk tigerishly to and fro.*] But you might have been firing away at the Austrians still, if we cavalry fellows hadn't found the ford and got across and turned old Beaulieu's flank for you. You know you daren't have given the order to charge the bridge if you hadn't seen us on the other side. Consequently, I say that whoever found that ford won the battle of Lodi. Well, who found it? I was the first man to cross: and I know. It was my horse that found it. [*With conviction, as he rises from the couch.*] That horse is the true conqueror of the Austrians.

NAP. [*Passionately.*] You idiot: I'll have you shot for losing those despatches: I'll have you blown from the mouth of a cannon: nothing less could make any impression on you. [*Baying at him.*] Do you hear? Do you understand?

[*A French officer enters unobserved, carrying his sheathed sabre in his hand.*]

LIEUT. [*Unabashed.*] If I don't capture him, General. Remember the if.

NAP. If! If!! Ass: there is no such man.

OFFICER. [*Suddenly stepping between them and speaking in the unmistakable voice of the Strange Lady.*] Lieutenant: I am your prisoner. [*She offers him her sabre. They are amazed. Napoleon gazes at her for a moment thunderstruck; then seizes her by the wrist and drags her roughly to him, looking closely and fiercely at her to satisfy himself as to her identity; for it now begins to darken rapidly into night, the red glow over the vineyard giving way to clear starlight.*]

NAP. Pah! [*He flings her hand away with an exclamation of disgust, and turns his back on her with his hand in his breast and his brow lowering.*]

LIEUT. [*Triumphantly, taking the sabre.*] No such man: eh, General? [*to the Lady*] I say: where's my horse?

LADY. Safe at Borghetto, waiting for you, Lieutenant.

NAP. [*Turning on them.*] Where are the despatches?

LADY. You would never guess. They are in the most unlikely place in the world. Did you meet my sister here, any of you?

LIEUT. Yes. Very nice woman. She's wonderfully like you; but of course she's better looking.

LADY. [*Mysteriously.*] Well, do you know that she is a witch?

GIUS. [*Running down to them in terror, crossing himself.*] Oh, no, no, no. It is not safe to jest about such things. I cannot have it in my house, excellency.

LIEUT. Yes, drop it. You're my prisoner, you know. Of course I don't believe in any such rubbish; but still it's not a proper subject for joking.

LADY. But this is very serious. My sister has bewitched the General. [*Giuseppe and the Lieutenant recoil from Napoleon.*] General: open your coat: you will find the despatches in the breast of it. [*She puts her hand quickly on his breast.*] Yes: there they are: I can feel them. Eh? [*She looks up into his face half coaxingly, half mockingly.*] Will you allow me, General? [*She takes a button as if to unbutton his coat, and pauses for permission.*]

NAP. [*Inscrutably.*] If you dare.

LADY. Thank you. [*She opens his coat and takes out the despatches.*] There! [*To Giuseppe, shewing him the despatches.*] See!

GIUS. [*Flying to the outer door.*] No, in heaven's name! They're bewitched.

LADY. [*Turning to the Lieutenant.*] Here, Lieutenant: you're not afraid of them.

LIEUT. [*Retreating.*] Keep off. [*Seizing the hilt of the sabre.*] Keep off, I tell you.

LADY. [*to Napoleon.*] They belong to you, General. Take them.

GIUS. Don't touch them, excellency. Have nothing to do with them.

LIEUTENANT. Be careful, General: be careful.

GIUS. Burn them. And burn the witch, too.

LADY. [*to Napoleon*] Shall I burn them?

NAP. [*Thoughtfully.*] Yes, burn them. Giuseppe: go and fetch a light.

GIUS. [*Trembling and stammering.*] Do you mean go alone—in the dark—with a witch in the house?

NAP. Psha! You're a poltroon. [*to the Lieutenant.*] Oblige me by going, Lieutenant.

LIEUT. [*Remonstrating.*] Oh, I say, General! No, look here, you know: nobody can say I'm a coward after Lodi. But to ask me to go into the dark by myself without a candle after such an awful conversation is a little too much. How would you like to do it yourself?

NAP. [*Irritably.*] You refuse to obey my order?

LIEUT. [*Resolutely.*] Yes, I do. It's not reasonable. But I'll tell you what I'll do. If Giuseppe goes, I'll go with him and protect him.

NAP. [*to Giuseppe*] There! will that satisfy you? Be off, both of you.

GIUS. [*Humbly, his lips trembling.*] W-willingly, your excellency. [*He goes reluctantly towards the inner door.*] Heaven protect me! [*to the Lieutenant*] After you, Lieutenant.

LIEUT. You'd better go first: I don't know the way.

GIUS. You can't miss it. Besides [*imploringly, laying his hand on his sleeve*], I am only a poor innkeeper; and you are a man of family.

LIEUT. There's something in that. Here: you needn't be in such a fright. Take my arm. [*Giuseppe does so.*] That's the way. [*They go out, arm in arm. It is now starry night. The lady throws the packet on the table and seats herself at her ease on the couch enjoying the sensation of freedom from petticoats.*]

LADY. Well, General: I've beaten you.

NAP. [*Walking about.*] You have been guilty of indelicacy—of unwomanliness. Do you consider that costume a proper one to wear?

LADY. It seems to me much the same as yours.

NAP. Psha! I blush for you.

LADY. [*Naively.*] Yes: soldiers blush so easily! [*He growls and turns away. She looks mischievously at him, balancing the despatches in her hand.*] Wouldn't you like to read these before they're burnt, General? You must be dying with curiosity. Take a peep. [*She throws the packet on the table, and turns her face away from it.*] I won't look.

NAP. I have no curiosity whatever, madame. But since you are evidently burning to read them, I give you leave to do so.

LADY. Oh, I've read them already.

NAP. [*Starting.*] What!

LADY. I read them the first thing after I rode away on that poor lieutenant's horse. So you see I know what's in them; and you don't.

NAP. Excuse me: I read them when I was out there in the vineyard ten minutes ago.

LADY. Oh! [*Jumping up.*] Oh, General: I've not beaten you. I do admire you so. [*He laughs and pats her cheek.*] This time really and truly without shamming, I do you homage. [*Kissing his hand.*]

NAP. [*Quickly withdrawing it.*] Brr! Don't do that. No more witchcraft.

LADY. I want to say something to you—only you would misunderstand it.

NAP. Need that stop you?

LADY. Well, it is this. I adore a man who is not afraid to be mean and selfish.

NAP. [*Indignantly.*] I am neither mean nor selfish.

LADY. Oh, you don't appreciate yourself. Besides, I don't really mean meanness and selfishness.

NAP. Thank you. I thought perhaps you did.

LADY. Well, of couse I do. But what I mean is a certain strong simplicity about you.

NAP. That's better.

LADY. You didn't want to read the letters; but you were curious about what was in them. So you went into the garden and read them when no one was looking, and then came back and pretended you hadn't. That's the meanest thing I ever knew any man do; but it exactly fulfilled your purpose; and so you weren't a bit afraid or ashamed to do it.

NAP. [*Abruptly.*] Where did you pick up all these vulgar scruples—this [*with contemptuous emphasis*] conscience of yours? I took you for a lady—an aristocrat. Was your grandfather a shopkeeper, pray?

LADY. No: he was an Englishman.

NAP. That accounts for it. The English are a nation of shopkeepers. Now I understand why you've beaten me.

LADY. Oh, I haven't beaten you. And I'm not English.

NAP. Yes, you are—English to the backbone. Listen to me: I will explain the English to you.

LADY. [*Eagerly.*] Do. [*With a lively air of anticipating an intellectual treat, she sits down on the couch and composes herself to listen to him. Secure of his audience, he at once nerves himself for a performance.*

He considers a little before he begins; so as to fix her attention by a moment of suspense. His style is at first modelled on Talma's in Corneille's "Cinna"; but it is somewhat lost in the darkness, and Talma presently gives way to Napoleon, the voice coming through the gloom with startling intensity.]

NAP. There are three sorts of people in the world, the low people, the middle people, and the high people. The low people and the high people are alike in one thing: they have no scruples, no morality. The low are beneath morality, the high above it. I am not afraid of either of them: for the low are unscrupulous without knowledge, so that they make an idol of me; whilst the high are unscrupulous without purpose, so that they go down before my will. Look you: I shall go over all the mobs and all the courts of Europe as a plough goes over a field. It is the middle people who are dangerous: they have both knowledge and purpose. But they, too, have their weak point. They are full of scruples—chained hand and foot by their morality and respectability.

LADY. Then you will beat the English; for all shopkeepers are middle people.

NAP. No, because the English are a race apart. No Englishman is too low to have scruples: no Englishman is high enough to be free from their tyranny. But every Englishman is born with a certain miraculous power that makes him master of the world. When he wants a thing, he never tells himself that he wants it. He waits patiently until there comes into his mind, no one knows how, a burning conviction that it is his moral and religious duty to conquer those who have got the thing he wants. Then he becomes irresistible. Like the aristocrat, he does what pleases him and grabs what he wants: like the shopkeeper, he pursues his purpose with the industry and steadfastness that come from strong religious conviction and deep sense of moral responsibility. He is never at a loss for an effective moral attitude. As the great champion of freedom and national independence, he conquers and annexes half the world, and calls it Colonization. When he wants a new market for his adulterated Manchester goods, he sends a missionary to teach the natives the gospel of peace. The natives kill the missionary: he flies to arms in defence of Christianity; fights for it; conquers for it; and takes the market as a reward from heaven. In defence of his island shores, he puts a chaplain on board his ship; nails a flag with a cross on it to his top-gallant mast; and sails to the ends of the earth, sinking, burning and destroying all who dispute the empire of the seas with him. He boasts that a slave is free the moment his foot touches British soil; and he sells the children of his poor at six years of age to work under the lash in his factories for sixteen hours a day. He makes two revolutions, and then declares war on our one in the name of law and order. There is nothing so bad or so good that you will not find Englishmen doing it; but you will never find an Englishman in the wrong. He does everything on principle. He fights you on patriotic principles; he robs you on business principles; he enslaves you on imperial principles; he bullies you on manly principles; he supports his king on loyal principles, and cuts off his king's head on republican principles. His watchword is always duty; and he never forgets that the nation which lets its duty get on the opposite side to its interest is lost. He—

LADY. W-w-w-w-w-wh! Do stop a moment. I want to know how you make me out to be English at this rate.

NAP. [*Dropping his rhetorical style.*] It's plain enough. You wanted some letters that belonged to me. You have spent the morning in stealing them —yes, stealing them, by highway robbery. And you have spent the afternoon in putting me in the wrong about them—in assuming that it was *I* who wanted to steal y o u r letters—in explaining that it all came about through my meanness and selfishness, and your goodness, your devotion, your self-sacrifice. That's English.

LADY. Nonsense. I am sure I am not a bit English. The English are a very stupid people.

NAP. Yes, too stupid sometimes to know when they're beaten. But I grant that your brains are not English. You see, though your grandfather was an Englishman, your grandmother was— what? A Frenchwoman?

LADY. Oh, no. An Irishwoman.

NAP. [*Quickly.*] Irish! [*Thoughtfully.*] Yes: I forgot the Irish. An English army led by an Irish general: that might be a match for a French army led by an Italian general.[*He pauses, and adds, half jestingly, half moodily.*] At all events, you have beaten me; and what beats a man first will beat him last. [*He goes meditatively into the moonlit vineyard and looks up. She steals out after him. She ventures to rest her hand on his shoulder, overcome by the beauty of the night and emboldened by its obscurity.*]

LADY. [*Softly.*] What are you looking at?

NAP. [*Pointing up.*] My star.

LADY. You believe in that?

NAP. I do. [*They look at it for a moment, she leaning a little on his shoulder.*]

LADY. Do you know that the English say that a man's star is not complete without a woman's garter?

NAP. [*Scandalized—abruptly shaking her off and coming back into the room.*] Pah! The hypocrites! If the French said that, how they would hold up their hands in pious horror! [*He goes to the inner door and holds it open, shouting.*] Hallo! Giuseppe. Where's that light, man. [*He comes between the table and the sideboard, and moves the chair to the table, beside his own*] We have still to burn the letter. [*He takes up the packet. Giuseppe comes back, pale and still trembling, carrying a branched candlestick with a couple of candles alight, in one hand, and a broad snuffers tray in the other.*]

GIUS. [*Piteously, as he places the light on the table.*] Excellency: what were you looking up at just now —out there? [*He points across his shoulder to the vineyard, but is afraid to look round.*]

NAP. [*Unfolding the packet.*] What is that to you?

GIUS. [*Stammering.*] Because the witch is gone— vanished; and no one saw her go out.

LADY. [*Coming behind him from the vineyard.*] We were watching her riding up to the moon on your broomstick, Giuseppe. You will never see her again.

GIUS. Gesu Maria! [*He crosses himself and hurries out.*]

NAP. [*Throwing down the letters in a heap on the table.*] Now. [*He sits down at the table in the chair which he has just placed.*]

LADY. Yes; but you know you have t h e letter in your pocket. [*He smiles; take a letter from his pocket; and tosses it on the top of the heap. She holds it up and looks at him, saying.*] About Caesar's wife.

NAP. Caesar's wife is above suspicion. Burn it.

LADY. [*Taking up the snuffers and holding the letter to the candle flame with it.*] I wonder would Caesar's wife be above suspicion if she saw us here together!

NAP. [*Echoing her, with his elbows on the table and his cheeks on his hands, looking at the letter.*] I wonder! [*The Strange Lady puts the letter down alight on the snuffers tray, and sits down beside Napoleon, in the same attitude, elbows on table, cheeks on hands, watching it burn. When it is burnt, they simultaneously turn their eyes and look at one another. The curtain steals down and hides them.*]

The Importance of Being Earnest

Oscar Wilde

One of the wittiest of all stage comedies, *The Importance of Being Earnest* (1895) was the last of the seven plays written by the brilliant and eccentric Oscar Wilde (1854–1900). Like Sheridan and Shaw, Wilde was an Irishman; he shares with them a talent for comic dialogue and a feeling for dramatic timing, characteristics which have made his plays and many of his glittering quips disappear into the language. This is the ultimate accolade which time accords fame.

The basic structure of *The Importance of Being Earnest* is that of melodrama, most obvious in the contrived ending. Wilde has been able to make the most even of this prosaic device, for the play becomes an effective satire not only upon the social conventions it portrays and upon the human beings who make up that society, but upon the literary modes of the times as well. Wilde has indeed made his point: life imitates art.

The playwright's method is the use of paradox in every detail: in the characters and in the situations, but above all in the dialogue, which sparkles with life even after more than half a century. The balance seen within the character of Jack, for instance (Jack as man-about-town versus Jack as country gentleman), or between two such characters as Lady Bracknell and Miss Prism, is repeated in the language in sally after sally of stunning repartee. Social conventions are turned upside down as the whole world laughs. As has more than once been

suggested, this kind of farce is very close to the musical comedy of Gilbert and Sullivan, who caricatured Wilde as the fleshly poet, Bunthorne, in *Patience* (1881)—just the kind of notoriety which the dramatist thoroughly enjoyed.

When *The Importance of Being Earnest* was first produced, Shaw, as drama critic of *The Saturday Review*, reviewed it. He found the comedy amusing but contrived. "I go to the theatre to be moved to laughter, not to be tickled or bustled into it," he wrote. For Shaw the predominance of farcical elements was the play's major characteristic—and major defect. When the piece was revived in 1902, Max Beerbohm, "the incomparable Max" as Shaw called him, had taken over Shaw's old assignment on *The Saturday Review*. He termed the play "fresh and exquisite," a true "classic" of the theatre. The quality which distinguishes *The Importance of Being Earnest*, according to Max, is "the humorous contrast between its style and matter." And the only way "to preserve its style fully" is to see that "the sound and the sense of the words must be taken seriously, treated beautifully." The shift in point of view from Shaw to Beerbohm is instructive. A further position, that of a twentieth-century critic, may be consulted in Part IV (pp. 280–84) where Otto Reinert's essay on the play's "strategy" is reprinted.

THE PERSONS OF THE PLAY

JOHN WORTHING, J.P.	MERRIMAN, *Butler*	HON. GWENDOLEN FAIRFAX
ALGERNON MONCRIEFF	LANE, *Manservant*	CECILY CARDEW
REV. CANON CHASUBLE, D.D.	LADY BRACKNELL	MISS PRISM, *Governess*

THE SCENES OF THE PLAY

ACT I— ALGERNON MONCRIEFF's *Flat in Half-Moon Street, W.*
ACT II— *The Garden at the Manor House, Woolton.*
ACT III— *Drawing-room at the Manor House, Woolton.*
TIME—*The Present.*

ACT I

[SCENE—*Morning-room in Algernon's flat in Half-Moon Street. The room is luxuriously and artistically furnished. The sound of a piano is heard in the adjoining room.*]
[LANE *is arranging afternoon tea on the table, and after the music has ceased,* ALGERNON *enters.*]

ALGERNON. Did you hear what I was playing, Lane?

LANE. I didn't think it polite to listen, sir.

ALGER. I'm sorry for that, for your sake. I don't play accurately—any one can play accurately—but I play with wonderful expression. As far as the piano is concerned, sentiment is my forte. I keep science for Life.

LANE. Yes, sir.

ALGER. And, speaking of the science of Life, have you got the cucumber sandwiches cut for Lady Bracknell?

LANE. Yes, sir. [*Hands them on a salver.*]

ALGER. [*Inspects them, takes two, and sits down on the sofa.*] Oh! . . . by the way, Lane, I see from your book that on Thursday night, when Lord Shoreman and Mr. Worthing were dining with me, eight bottles of champagne are entered as having been consumed.

LANE. Yes, sir; eight bottles and a pint.

ALGER. Why is it that at a bachelor's establishment the servants invariably drink the champagne? I ask merely for information.

LANE. I attribute it to superior quality of the wine, sir. I have often observed that in married households the champagne is rarely of a first-rate brand.

ALGER. Good heavens! Is marriage so demoralizing as that?

LANE. I believe It *is* a very pleasant state, sir. I have had very little experience of it myself up to the present. I have only been married once. That was in consequence of a misunderstanding between myself and a young person.

ALGER. [*Languidly.*] I don't know that I am much interested in your family life, Lane.

LANE. No, sir; it is not a very interesting subject. I never think of it myself.

ALGER. Very natural, I am sure. That will do, Lane, thank you.

LANE. Thank you, sir.

[LANE *goes out.*]

ALGER. Lane's views on marriage seem somewhat lax. Really, if the lower orders don't set us a good example, what on earth is the use of them? They seem, as a class, to have absolutely no sense of moral responsibility.

[*Enter* LANE.]

LANE. Mr. Ernest Worthing.

[*Enter* JACK. LANE *goes out.*]

ALGER. How are you, my dear Ernest? What brings you up to town?

JACK. Oh, pleasure, pleasure! What else should bring one anywhere? Eating as usual, I see, Algy!

ALGER. [*Stiffly.*] I believe it is customary in good society to take some slight refreshment at five o'clock. Where have you been since last Thursday?

JACK. [*Sitting down on the sofa*]: In the country.

ALGER. What on earth do you do there?

JACK. [*Pulling off his gloves.*] When one is in town one amuses oneself. When one is in the country one amuses other people. It is excessively boring.

ALGER. And who are the people you amuse?

JACK. [*Airily.*] Oh, neighbours, neighbours.

ALGER. Got nice neighbours in your part of Shropshire?

JACK. Perfectly horrid! Never speak to one of them.

ALGER. How immensely you must amuse them! [*Goes over and takes sandwich.*] By the way, Shropshire is your county, is it not?

JACK. Eh? Shropshire? Yes, of course. Hallo! Why all these cups? Why cucumber sandwiches? Why such reckless extravagance in one so young? Who is coming to tea?

ALGER. Oh! merely Aunt Augusta and Gwendolen.

JACK. How perfectly delightful!

ALGER. Yes, that is all very well; but I am afraid Aunt Augusta won't quite approve of your being here.

JACK. May I ask why?

ALGER. My dear fellow, the way you flirt with Gwendolen is perfectly disgraceful. It is almost as bad as the way Gwendolen flirts with you.

JACK. I am in love with Gwendolen. I have come up to town expressly to propose to her.

ALGER. I thought you had come up for pleasure? . . . I call that business.

JACK. How utterly unromantic you are!

ALGER. I really don't see anything romantic in proposing. It is very romantic to be in love. But there is nothing romantic about a definite proposal. Why, one may be accepted. One usually is, I believe. Then the excitement is all over. The very essence of romance is uncertainty. If ever I get married, I'll certainly try to forget the fact.

JACK. I have no doubt about that, dear Algy. The Divorce Court was specially invented for people whose memories are so curiously constituted.

ALGER. Oh! there is no use speculating on that subject. Divorces are made in Heaven—[JACK *puts out his hand to take a sandwich.* ALGERNON *at once interferes.*] Please don't touch the cucumber sandwiches. They are ordered specially for Aunt Augusta. [*Takes one and eats it.*]

JACK. Well, you have been eating them all the time.

ALGER. That is quite a different matter. She is my aunt. [*Takes plate from below.*] Have some bread and butter. The bread and butter is for Gwendolen. Gwendolen is devoted to bread and butter.

JACK. [*Advancing to table and helping himself.*] And very good bread and butter it is too.

ALGER. Well, my dear fellow, you need not eat as

if you were going to eat it all. You behave as if you were married to her already. You are not married to her already, and I don't think you ever will be.

JACK. Why on earth do you say that?

ALGER. Well, in the first place, girls never marry the men they flirt with. Girls don't think it right.

JACK. Oh, that is nonsense!

ALGER. It isn't. It is a great truth. It accounts for the extraordinary number of bachelors that one sees all over the place. In the second place, I don't give my consent.

JACK. Your consent!

ALGER. My dear fellow, Gwendolen is my first cousin. And before I allow you to marry her, you will have to clear up the whole question of Cecily. [*Rings bell.*]

JACK. Cecily! What on earth do you mean? What do you mean, Algy, by Cecily! I don't know any one of the name of Cecily.

[*Enter* LANE.]

ALGER. Bring me that cigarette case Mr. Worthing left in the smoking-room the last time he dined here.

LANE. Yes, sir.   [LANE *goes out.*]

JACK. Do you mean to say you have had my cigarette case all this time? I wish to goodness you had let me know. I have been writing frantic letters to Scotland Yard about it. I was very nearly offering a large reward.

ALGER. Well, I wish you would offer one. I happen to be more than usually hard up.

JACK. There is no good offering a large reward now that the thing is found.

[*Enter* LANE *with the cigarette case on a salver.* ALGERNON *takes it at once.* LANE *goes out.*]

ALGER. I think that is rather mean of you, Ernest, I must say. [*Opens case and examines it.*] However, it makes no matter, for, now that I look at the inscription inside, I find that the thing isn't yours after all.

JACK. Of course it's mine. [*Moving to him.*] You have seen me with it a hundred times, and you have no right whatsoever to read what is written inside. It is a very ungentlemanly thing to read a private cigarette case.

ALGER. Oh! it is absurd to have a hard and fast rule about what one should read and what one shouldn't. More than half of modern culture depends on what one shouldn't read.

JACK. I am quite aware of the fact, and I don't propose to discuss modern culture. It isn't the sort of thing one should talk of in private. I simply want my cigarette case back.

ALGER. Yes; but this isn't your cigarette case.

This cigarette case is a present from someone of the name of Cecily, and you said you didn't know anyone of that name.

JACK. Well, if you want to know, Cecily happens to be my aunt.

ALGER. Your aunt!

JACK. Yes. Charming old lady she is, too. Lives at Tunbridge Wells. Just give it back to me, Algy.

ALGER. [*Retreating to back of sofa.*] But why does she call herself little Cecily if she is your aunt and lives at Tunbridge Wells? [*Reading.*] "From little Cecily with her fondest love."

JACK. [*Moving to sofa and kneeling upon it.*] My dear fellow, what on earth is there in that? Some aunts are tall, some aunts are not tall. That is a matter that surely an aunt may be allowed to decide for herself. You seem to think that every aunt should be exactly like your aunt! That is absurd. For Heaven's sake give me back my cigarette case. [*Follows* ALGERNON *round the room.*]

ALGER. Yes. But why does your aunt call you her uncle? "From little Cecily, with her fondest love to her dear Uncle Jack." There is no objection, I admit, to an aunt being a small aunt, but why an aunt, no matter what her size may be, should call her own nephew her uncle, I can't quite make out. Besides, your name isn't Jack at all; it is Ernest.

JACK. It isn't Ernest; it's Jack.

ALGER. You have always told me it was Ernest. I have introduced you to every one as Ernest. You answer to the name of Ernest. You look as if your name was Ernest. You are the most earnest-looking person I ever saw in my life. It is perfectly absurd your saying that your name isn't Ernest. It's on your cards. Here is one of them. [*Taking it from case.*] "Mr. Ernest Worthing, B.4, The Albany." I'll keep this as a proof that your name is Ernest if ever you attempt to deny it to me, or to Gwendolen, or to any else. [*Puts the card in his pocket.*]

JACK. Well, my name is Ernest in town and Jack in the country, and the cigarette case was given to me in the country.

ALGER. Yes, but that does not account for the fact that your small Aunt Cecily, who lives at Tunbridge Wells, calls you her dear uncle. Come, old boy, you had much better have the thing out at once.

JACK. My dear Algy, you talk exactly as if you were a dentist. It is very vulgar to talk like a dentist when one isn't a dentist. It produces a false impression.

ALGER. Well, that is exactly what dentists always do. Now, go on! Tell me the whole thing. I may mention that I have always suspected you of being a confirmed and secret Bunburyist; and I am quite sure of it now.

JACK. Bunburyist? What on earth do you mean by a Bunburyist?

ALGER. I'll reveal to you the meaning of that incomparable expression as soon as you are kind enough to inform me why you are Ernest in town and Jack in the country.

JACK. Well, produce my cigarette case first.

ALGER. Here it is. [*Hands cigarette case.*] Now produce your explanation, and pray make it improbable. [*Sits on sofa.*]

JACK. My dear fellow, there is nothing improbable about my explanation at all. In fact it's perfectly ordinary. Old Mr. Thomas Cardew, who adopted me when I was a little boy, made me in his will guardian to his granddaughter, Miss Cecily Cardew. Cecily, who addresses me as her uncle from motives of respect that you could not possibly appreciate, lives at my place in the country under the charge of her admirable governess, Miss Prism.

ALGER. Where is that place in the country, by the way?

JACK. That is nothing to you, dear boy. You are not going to be invited. . . . I may tell you candidly that the place is not in Shropshire.

ALGER. I suspected that, my dear fellow! I have Bunburyed all over Shropshire on two separate occasions. Now, go on. Why are you Ernest in town and Jack in the country?

JACK. My dear Algy, I don't know whether you will be able to understand my real motives. You are hardly serious enough. When one is placed in the position of guardian, one has to adopt a very high moral tone on all subjects. It's one's duty to do so. And as a high moral tone can hardly be said to conduce very much to either one's health or one's happiness, in order to get up to town I have always pretended to have a younger brother of the name of Ernest, who lives in the Albany, and gets into the most dreadful scrapes. That, my dear Algy, is the whole truth pure and simple.

ALGER. The truth is rarely pure and never simple. Modern life would be very tedious if it were either, and modern literature a complete impossibility!

JACK. That wouldn't be at all a bad thing.

ALGER. Literary criticism is not your forte, my dear fellow. Don't try it. You should leave that to people who haven't been at a University. They do it so well in the daily papers. What you really are is a Bunburyist. I was quite right in saying you were a Bunburyist. You are one of the most advanced Bunburyists I know.

JACK. What on earth do you mean?

ALGER. You have invented a very useful younger brother called Ernest, in order that you may be able to come up to town as often as you like. I have invented an invaluable permanent invalid called Bunbury, in order that I may be able to go down into the country whenever I choose. Bunbury is perfectly invaluable. If it wasn't for Bunbury's extraordinary bad health, for instance, I wouldn't be able to dine with you at Willis's to-night, for I have been really engaged to Aunt Augusta for more than a week.

JACK. I haven't asked you to dine with me anywhere to-night.

ALGER. I know. You are absurdly careless about sending out invitations. It is very foolish of you. Nothing annoys people so much as not receiving invitations.

JACK. You had much better dine with your Aunt Augusta.

ALGER. I haven't the smallest intention of doing anything of the kind. To begin with, I dined there on Monday, and once a week is quite enough to dine with one's own relations. In the second place, whenever I do dine there I am always treated as a member of the family, and sent down with either no woman at all, or two. In the third place, I know perfectly well whom she will place me next to, to-night. She will place me next Mary Farquhar, who always flirts with her own husband across the dinner-table. That is not very pleasant. Indeed, it is not even decent. . . and that sort of thing is enormously on the increase. The amount of women in London who flirt with their own husbands is perfectly scandalous. It looks so bad. It is simply washing one's clean linen in public. Besides, now that I know you to be a confirmed Bunburyist I naturally want to talk to you about Bunburying. I want to tell you the rules.

JACK. I'm not a Bunburyist at all. If Gwendolen accepts me, I am going to kill my brother, indeed I think I'll kill him in any case. Cecily is a little too much interested in him. It is rather a bore. So I am going to get rid of Ernest. And I strongly advise you to do the same with Mr. . . with your invalid friend who has the absurd name.

ALGER. Nothing will induce me to part with Bunbury, and if you ever get married, which seems to me extremely problematic, you will be very glad to know Bunbury. A man who marries without knowing Bunbury has a very tedious time of it.

JACK. That is nonsense. If I marry a charming girl like Gwendolen, and she is the only girl I ever saw in my life that I would marry, I certainly won't want to know Bunbury.

ALGER. Then your wife will. You don't seem to realize, that in married life three is company and two is none.

JACK. [*Sententiously.*] That, my dear young friend, is the theory that the corrupt French Drama has been propounding for the last fifty years.

ALGER. Yes, and that the happy English home has proved in half the time.

JACK. For heaven's sake, don't try to be cynical. It's perfectly easy to be cynical.

ALGER. My dear fellow, it isn't easy to be anything nowadays. There's such a lot of beastly competition about. [*The sound of an electric bell is heard.*] Ah! that must be Aunt Augusta. Only relatives, or creditors, ever ring in that Wagnerian manner. Now, if I get her out of the way for ten minutes, so that you can have an opportunity for proposing to Gwendolen, may I dine with you to-night at Willis's?

JACK. I suppose so, if you want to.

ALGER. Yes, but you must be serious about it. I hate people who are not serious about meals. It is so shallow of them.

[*Enter* LANE.]

LANE. Lady Bracknell and Miss Fairfax.

[ALGERNON *goes forward to meet them. Enter* LADY BRACKNELL *and* GWENDOLEN.]

LADY BRACKNELL. Good afternoon, dear Algernon, I hope you are behaving very well.

ALGER. I'm feeling very well, Aunt Augusta.

LADY B. That's not quite the same thing. In fact the two things rarely go together. [*Sees* JACK *and bows to him with icy coldness.*]

ALGER. [*to* GWENDOLEN] Dear me, you are smart!

GWENDOLEN. I am always smart! Am I not, Mr. Worthing?

JACK. You're quite perfect, Miss Fairfax.

GWEN. Oh! I hope I am not that. It would leave no room for developments, and I intend to develop in many directions. [GWENDOLEN *and* JACK *sit down together in the corner.*]

LADY B. I'm sorry if we are a little late, Algernon, but I was obliged to call on dear Lady Harbury. I hadn't been there since her poor husband's death. I never saw a woman so altered; she looks quite twenty years younger. And now I'll have a cup of tea, and one of those nice cucumber sandwiches you promised me.

ALGER. Certainly, Aunt Augusta. [*Goes over to tea-table.*]

LADY B. Won't you come and sit here, Gwendolen?

GWEN. Thanks, mamma, I'm quite comfortable where I am.

ALGER. [*Picking up empty plate in horror.*] Good heavens! Lane! Why are there no cucumber sandwiches? I ordered them specially.

LANE. [*Gravely.*] There were no cucumbers in the market this morning, sir. I went down twice.

ALGER. No cucumbers!

LANE. No, sir. Not even for ready money.

ALGER. That will do, Lane, thank you.

LANE. Thank you, sir. [*Goes out.*]

ALGER. I am greatly distressed, Aunt Augusta, about there being no cucumbers, not even for ready money.

LADY B. It really makes no matter, Algernon. I had some crumpets with Lady Harbury, who seems to me to be living entirely for pleasure now.

ALGER. I hear her hair has turned quite gold from grief.

LADY B. It certainly has changed its colour. From what cause I, of course, cannot say. [ALGERNON *crosses and hands tea.*] Thank you. I've quite a treat for you to-night, Algernon. I am going to send you down with Mary Farquhar. She is such a nice woman, and so attentive to her husband. It's delightful to watch them.

ALGER. I am afraid, Aunt Augusta, I shall have to give up the pleasure of dining with you to-night after all.

LADY B. [*Frowning.*] I hope not, Algernon. It would put my table completely out. Your uncle would have to dine upstairs. Fortunately he is accustomed to that.

ALGER. It is a great bore, I need hardly say, a terrible disappointment to me, but the fact is I have just had a telegram to say that my poor friend Bunbury is very ill again. [*Exchanges glances with* JACK.] They seem to think I should be with him.

LADY B. It is very strange. This Mr. Bunbury seems to suffer from curiously bad health.

ALGER. Yes; poor Bunbury is a dreadful invalid.

LADY B. Well, I must say, Algernon, that I think it is high time that Mr. Bunbury made up his mind whether he was going to live or to die. This shilly-shallying with the question is absurd. Nor do I in any way approve of the modern sympathy with invalids. I consider it morbid. Illness of any kind is hardly a thing to be encouraged in others. Health is the primary duty of life. I am always telling that to your poor uncle, but he never seems to take much notice. . . as far as any improvement in his ailment goes. I should be much obliged if you would ask Mr. Bunbury, from me, to be kind enough not to have a relapse on Saturday, for I rely on you to arrange my music for me. It is my last reception, and one wants something that will encourage conversation, particularly at the end of the season when every one has practically said whatever they had to say, which in most cases, was probably not much.

ALGER. I'll speak to Bunbury, Aunt Augusta, if he is still conscious, and I think I can promise you he'll be all right by Saturday. Of course the music is a great difficulty. You see, if one plays good music, people don't listen, and if one plays bad music people don't talk. But I'll run over the programme I've drawn out, if you will kindly come into the next room for a moment.

LADY B. Thank you, Algernon. It is very thoughtful of you. [*Rising, and following* ALGERNON.] I'm sure the programme will be delightful, after a few expurgations. French songs I cannot possibly allow. People always seem to think that they are improper, and either look shocked, which is vulgar, or laugh, which is worse. But German sounds a thoroughly respectable language, and, indeed I believe is so. Gwendolen, you will accompany me.

GWEN. Certainly, mamma.

[LADY BRACKNELL *and* ALGERNON *go into the music-room,* GWENDOLEN *remains behind.*]

JACK. Charming day it has been, Miss Fairfax.

GWEN. Pray don't talk to me about the weather, Mr. Worthing. Whenever people talk to me about the weather, I always feel quite certain that they mean something else. And that makes me so nervous.

JACK. I do mean something else.

GWEN. I thought so. In fact, I am never wrong.

JACK. And I would like to be allowed to take advantage of Lady Bracknell's temporary absence . . . .

GWEN. I would certainly advise you to do so. Mamma has a way of coming back suddenly into a room that I have often had to speak to her about.

JACK. [*Nervously.*] Miss Fairfax, ever since I met you I have admired you more than any girl. . . I have ever met since. . . I met you.

GWEN. Yes, I am quite well aware of the fact. And I often wish that in public, at any rate, you had been more demonstrative. For me you have always had an irresistible fascination. Even before I met you I was far from indifferent to you. [JACK *looks at her in amazement.*] We live, as I hope you know, Mr. Worthing, in an age of ideals. The fact is constantly mentioned in the more expensive monthly magazines, and has reached the provincial pulpits, I am told; and my ideal has always been to love some one of the name of Ernest.

There is something in that name that inspires absolute confidence. The moment Algernon first mentioned to me that he had a friend called Ernest, I knew I was destined to love you.

JACK. You really love me, Gwendolen?

GWEN. Passionately!

JACK. Darling! You don't know how happy you've made me.

GWEN. My own Ernest!

JACK. But you don't really mean to say that you couldn't love me if my name wasn't Ernest?

GWEN. But your name is Ernest.

JACK. Yes, I know it is. But supposing it was something else? Do you mean to say you couldn't love me then?

GWEN. [*Glibly.*] Ah! that is clearly a metaphysical speculation, and like most metaphysical speculations has very little reference at all to the actual facts of real life, as we know them.

JACK. Personally, darling, to speak quite candidly, I don't much care about the name of Ernest. . . . I don't think the name suits me at all.

GWEN. It suits you perfectly. It is a divine name. It has music of its own. It produces vibrations.

JACK. Well, really, Gwendolen, I must say that I think there are lots of other much nicer names. I think Jack, for instance, a charming name.

GWEN. Jack? . . . No, there is very little music in the name Jack, if any at all, indeed. It does not thrill. It produces absolutely no vibrations. . . . I have known several Jacks, and they all, without exception, were more than usually plain. Besides, Jack is a notorious domesticity for John! And I pity any woman who is married to a man called John. She would probably never be allowed to know the entrancing pleasure of a single moment's solitude. The only really safe name is Ernest.

JACK. Gwendolen, I must get christened at once —I mean we must get married at once. There is no time to be lost.

GWEN. Married, Mr. Worthing?

JACK. [*Astounded.*] Well . . . surely. You know that I love you, and you led me to believe, Miss Fairfax, that you were not absolutely indifferent to me.

GWEN. I adore you. But you haven't proposed to me yet. Nothing has been said at all about marriage. The subject has not even been touched on.

JACK. Well . . . may I propose to you now?

GWEN. I think it would be an admirable opportunity. And to spare you any possible disappointment, Mr. Worthing, I think it only fair to tell you quite frankly beforehand that I am fully determined to accept you.

JACK. Gwendolen!

GWEN. Yes, Mr. Worthing, what have you got to say to me?

JACK. You know what I have got to say to you.

GWEN. Yes, but you don't say it.

JACK. Gwendolen, will you marry me? [*Goes on his knees.*]

GWEN. Of course I will, darling. How long you have been about it! I am afraid you have had very little experience in how to propose.

JACK. My own one, I have never loved any one in the world but you.

GWEN. Yes, but men often propose for practice. I know my brother Gerald does. All my girl-friends tell me so. What wonderfully blue eyes you have, Ernest! They are quite, quite blue. I hope you will always look at me just like that, especially when there are other people present.

[*Enter* LADY BRACKNELL.]

LADY B. Mr. Worthing! Rise, sir, from this semi-recumbent posture. It is most indecorous.

GWEN. Mamma! [*He tries to rise; she restrains him.*] I must beg you to retire. This is no place for you. Besides, Mr. Worthing has not quite finished yet.

LADY B. Finished what, may I ask?

GWEN. I am engaged to Mr. Worthing, mamma. [*They rise together.*]

LADY B. Pardon me, you are not engaged to any one. When you do become engaged to some one, I, or your father, should his health permit him, will inform you of the fact. An engagement should come on a young girl as a surprise, pleasant or unpleasant, as the case may be. It is hardly a matter that she could be allowed to arrange for herself. . . . And now I have a few questions to put to you, Mr. Worthing. While I am making these inquiries, you, Gwendolen, will wait for me below in the carriage.

GWEN. [*Reproachfully.*] Mamma!

LADY B. In the carriage, Gwendolen! [GWEN-DOLEN *goes to the door. She and* JACK *blow kisses to each other behind* LADY BRACKNELL'S *back.* LADY BRACK-NELL *looks vaguely about as if she could not understand what the noise was. Finally turns round.*] Gwendolen, the carriage!

GWEN. Yes, mamma. [*Goes out, looking back at* JACK.]

LADY B. [*Sitting down.*] You can take a seat, Mr. Worthing.

[*Looks in her pocket for note-book and pencil.*]

JACK. Thank you, Lady Bracknell, I prefer standing.

LADY B. [*Pencil and note-book in hand.*] I feel bound to tell you that you are not down on my list of eligible young men, although I have the same list as the dear Duchess of Bolton has. We work together, in fact. However, I am quite ready to enter your name, should your answers be what a really affectionate mother requires. Do you smoke?

JACK. Well, yes, I must admit I smoke.

LADY B. I am glad to hear it. A man should always have an occupation of some kind. There are far too many idle men in London as it is. How old are you?

JACK. Twenty-nine.

LADY B. A very good age to be married at. I have always been of opinion that a man who desires to get married should know either everything or nothing. Which do you know?

JACK. [*After some hesitation.*] I know nothing, Lady Bracknell.

LADY B. I am pleased to hear it. I do not approve of anything that tampers with natural ignorance. Ignorance is like a delicate exotic fruit; touch it and the bloom is gone. The whole theory of modern education is radically unsound. Fortunately in England, at any rate, education produces no effect whatsoever. If it did, it would prove a serious danger to the upper classes, and probably lead to acts of violence in Grosvenor Square. What is your income?

JACK. Between seven and eight thousand a year.

LADY B. [*Makes a note in her book.*] In land, or in investments?

JACK. In investments chiefly.

LADY B. That is satisfactory. What between the duties expected of one during one's lifetime, and the duties exacted from one after one's death, land has ceased to be either a profit or a pleasure. It gives one position, and prevents one from keeping it up. That's all that can be said about land.

JACK. I have a country house with some land, of course, attached to it, about fifteen hundred acres, I believe; but I don't depend on that for my real income. In fact, as far as I can make out, the poachers are the only people who make anything out of it.

LADY B. A country house! How many bedrooms? Well, that point can be cleared up afterwards. You have a town house, I hope? A girl with a simple, unspoiled nature, like Gwendolen, could hardly be expected to reside in the country.

JACK. Well, I own a house in Belgrave Square, but it is let by the year to Lady Bloxham. Of course, I can get it back whenever I like, at six months' notice.

LADY B. Lady Bloxham? I don't know her.

JACK. Oh, she goes about very little. She is a lady considerably advanced in years.

LADY B. Ah, nowadays that is no guarantee of respectability of character. What number in Belgrave Square?

JACK. 149.

LADY B. [*Shaking her head.*] The unfashionable side. I thought there was something. However, that could easily be altered.

JACK. Do you mean the fashion, or the side?

LADY B. [*Sternly.*] Both, if necessary, I presume. What are your politics?

JACK. Well, I am afraid I really have none. I am a Liberal Unionist.

LADY B. Oh, they count as Tories. They dine with us. Or come in the evening, at any rate. Now to minor matters. Are your parents living?

JACK. I have lost both my parents.

LADY B. To lose one parent, Mr. Worthing, may be regarded as a misfortune; to lose both looks like carelessness. Who was your father? He was evidently a man of some wealth. Was he born in what the Radical papers call the purple of commerce, or did he rise from the ranks of the aristocracy?

JACK. I am afraid I really don't know. The fact is, Lady Bracknell, I said I had lost my parents. It would be nearer the truth to say that my parents seem to have lost me. . . . I don't actually know who I am by birth. I was . . . well, I was found.

LADY B. Found!

JACK. The late Mr. Thomas Cardew, an old gentleman of a very charitable and kindly disposition, found me, and gave me the name of Worthing, because he happened to have a first-class ticket for Worthing in his pocket at the time. Worthing is a place in Sussex. It is a seaside resort.

LADY B. Where did the charitable gentleman who had a first-class ticket for this seaside resort find you?

JACK. [*Gravely.*] In a hand-bag.

LADY B. A hand-bag?

JACK. [*Very seriously.*] Yes, Lady Bracknell. I was in a hand-bag—a somewhat large, black leather hand-bag, with handles to it—an ordinary hand-bag in fact.

LADY B. In what locality did this Mr. James, or Thomas, Cardew come across this ordinary hand-bag?

JACK. In the cloak-room at Victoria Station. It was given to him in mistake for his own.

LADY B. The cloak-room at Victoria Station?

JACK. Yes. The Brighton line.

LADY B. The line is immaterial. Mr. Worthing, I confess I feel somewhat bewildered by what you have just told me. To be born, or at any rate bred, in a hand-bag, whether it had handles or not, seems to me to display a contempt for the ordinary decencies of family life that reminds one of the worst excesses of the French Revolution. And I presume you know what that unfortunate movement led to? As for the particular locality in which the hand-bag was found, a cloak-room at a railway station might serve to conceal a social indiscretion—has probably, indeed, been used for that purpose before now—but it could hardly be regarded as an assured basis for a recognized position in good society.

JACK. May I ask you then what you would advise me to do? I need hardly say I would do anything in the world to ensure Gwendolen's happiness.

LADY B. I would strongly advise you, Mr. Worthing, to try and acquire some relations as soon as possible, and to make a definite effort to produce at any rate one parent, of either sex, before the season is quite over.

JACK. Well, I don't see how I could possibly manage to do that. I can produce the hand-bag at any moment. It is in my dressing-room at home. I really think that should satisfy you, Lady Bracknell.

LADY B. Me, sir! What has it to do with me? You can hardly imagine that I and Lord Bracknell would dream of allowing our only daughter—a girl brought up with the utmost care—to marry into a cloak-room, and form an alliance with a parcel. Good morning, Mr. Worthing!

[LADY BRACKNELL *sweeps out in majestic indignation.*]

JACK. Good morning! [ALGERNON, *from the other room, strikes up the Wedding March.* JACK *looks perfectly furious, and goes to the door.*] For goodness' sake don't play that ghastly tune, Algy! How idiotic you are!

[*The music stops and* ALGERNON *enters cheerily.*]

ALGER. Didn't it go off all right, old boy? You don't mean to say Gwendolen refused you? I know it is a way she has. She is always refusing people. I think it is most ill-natured of her.

JACK. Oh, Gwendolen is as right as a trivet. As far as she is concerned, we are engaged. Her mother is perfectly unbearable. Never met such a Gorgon. . . . I don't really know what a Gorgon is like, but I am quite sure that Lady Bracknell is one. In any case, she is a monster, without being a myth, which is rather unfair. . . . I beg your pardon, Algy, I suppose I shouldn't talk about your own aunt in that way before you.

ALGER. My dear boy, I love hearing my relations

abused. It is the only thing that makes me put up with them at all. Relations are simply a tedious pack of people, who haven't got the remotest knowledge of how to live, nor the smallest instinct about when to die.

JACK. Oh, that is nonsense!

ALGER. It isn't!

JACK. Well, I won't argue about the matter. You always want to argue about things.

ALGER. That is exactly what things were originally made for.

JACK. Upon my word, if I thought that, I'd shoot myself. . . . [*A pause.*] You don't think there is any chance of Gwendolen becoming like her mother in about a hundred and fifty years, do you, Algy?

ALGER. All women become like their mothers. That is their tragedy. No man does. That's his.

JACK. Is that clever?

ALGER. It is perfectly phrased! and quite as true as any observation in civilized life should be.

JACK. I am sick to death of cleverness. Everybody is clever nowadays. You can't go anywhere without meeting clever people. The thing has become an absolute public nuisance. I wish to goodness we had a few fools left.

ALGER. We have.

JACK. I should extremely like to meet them. What do they talk about?

ALGER. The fools? Oh! about the clever people, of course.

JACK. What fools.

ALGER. By the way, did you tell Gwendolen the truth about your being Ernest in town, and Jack in the country?

JACK. [*In a very patronizing manner.*] My dear fellow, the truth isn't quite the sort of thing one tells to a nice, sweet, refined girl. What extraordinary ideas you have about the way to behave to a woman!

ALGER. The only way to behave to a woman is to make love to her, if she is pretty, and to someone else, if she is plain.

JACK. Oh, that is nonsense.

ALGER. What about your brother? What about the profligate Ernest?

JACK. Oh, before the end of the week I shall have got rid of him. I'll say he died in Paris of apoplexy. Lots of people die of apoplexy, quite suddenly, don't they?

ALGER. Yes, but it's hereditary, my dear fellow. It's a sort of thing that runs in families. You had much better say a severe chill.

JACK. You are sure a severe chill isn't hereditary, or anything of that kind?

ALGER. Of course it isn't!

JACK. Very well, then. My poor brother Ernest is carried off suddenly, in Paris, by a severe chill. That gets rid of him.

ALGER. But I thought you said that . . . Miss Cardew was a little too much interested in your poor brother Ernest? Won't she feel his loss a good deal?

JACK. Oh, that is all right. Cecily is not a silly romantic girl, I am glad to say. She has got a capital appetite, goes long walks, and pays no attention at all to her lessons.

ALGER. I would rather like to see Cecily.

JACK. I will take very good care you never do. She is excessively pretty, and she is only just eighteen.

ALGER. Have you told Gwendolen yet that you have an excessively pretty ward who is only just eighteen?

JACK. Oh! one doesn't blurt these things out to people. Cecily and Gwendolen are perfectly certain to be extremely great friends. I'll bet you anything you like that half an hour after they have met, they will be calling each other sister.

ALGER. Women only do that when they have called each other a lot of other things first. Now, my dear boy, if we want to get a good table at Willis's, we really must go and dress. Do you know it is nearly seven?

JACK. [*Irritably.*] Oh! it always is nearly seven.

ALGER. I'm hungry.

JACK. I never knew you when you weren't. . . .

ALGER. What shall we do after dinner? Go to a theatre?

JACK. Oh no! I loathe listening.

ALGER. Well, let us go to the Club?

JACK. Oh, no! I hate talking.

ALGER. Well, we might trot round to the Empire at ten?

JACK. Oh, no! I can't bear looking at things. It is so silly.

ALGER. Well, what shall we do?

JACK. Nothing!

ALGER. It is awfully hard work doing nothing. However, I don't mind hard work where there is no definite object of any kind.

[*Enter* LANE.]

LANE. Miss Fairfax.

[*Enter* GWENDOLEN. LANE *goes out.*]

ALGER. Gwendolen, upon my word!

GWEN. Algy, kindly turn your back. I have something very particular to say to Mr. Worthing.

ALGER. Really, Gwendolen, I don't think I can allow this at all.

GWEN. Algy, you always adopt a strictly immoral attitude towards life. You are not quite old enough to do that. [ALGERNON *retires to the fire-place.*]

JACK. My own darling!

GWEN. Ernest, we may never be married. From the expression on mamma's face I fear we never shall. Few parents nowadays pay any regard to what their children say to them. The old-fashioned respect for the young is fast dying out. Whatever influence I ever had over mamma, I lost at the age of three. But although she may prevent us from becoming man and wife, and I may marry someone else, and marry often, nothing that she can possibly do can alter my eternal devotion to you.

JACK. Dear Gwendolen!

GWEN. The story of your romantic origin, as related to me by mamma, with unpleasing comments, has naturally stirred the deeper fibres of my nature. Your Christian name has an irresistible fascination. The simplicity of your character makes you exquisitely incomprehensible to me. Your town address at the Albany I have. What is your address in the country?

JACK. The Manor House, Woolton, Herfordshire.

[ALGERNON, *who has been carefully listening, smiles to himself, and writes the address on his shirt-cuff. Then picks up the Railway Guide.*]

GWEN. There is a good postal service, I suppose? It may be necessary to do something desperate. That of course will require serious consideration. I will communicate with you daily.

JACK. My own one!

GWEN. How long do you remain in town?

JACK. Till Monday.

GWEN. Good! Algy, you may turn round now.

ALGER. Thanks, I've turned round already.

GWEN. You may also ring the bell.

JACK. You will let me see you to your carriage, my own darling?

GWEN. Certainly.

JACK. [*To* LANE, *who now enters.*] I will see Miss Fairfax out.

LANE. Yes, sir. [JACK *and* GWENDOLEN *go off.*]

[LANE *presents several letters on a salver to* ALGERNON. *It is to be surmised that they are bills, as* ALGERNON, *after looking at the envelopes, tears them up.*]

ALGER. A glass of sherry, Lane.

LANE. Yes, sir.

ALGER. To-morrow, Lane, I'm going Bunburying.

LANE. Yes, sir.

ALGER. I shall probably not be back till Monday. You can put up my dress clothes, my smoking jacket, and all the Bunbury suits . . .

LANE. Yes, sir. [*Handing sherry.*]

ALGER. I hope to-morrow will be a fine day, Lane.

LANE. It never is, sir.

ALGER. Lane, you're a perfect pessimist.

LANE. I do my best to give satisfaction, sir.

[*Enter* JACK. LANE *goes off.*]

JACK. There's a sensible, intellectual girl! the only girl I ever cared for in my life. [ALGERNON *is laughing immoderately.*] What on earth are you so amused at?

ALGER. Oh, I'm a little anxious about poor Bunbury, that is all.

JACK. If you don't take care, your friend Bunbury will get you into a serious scrape some day.

ALGER. I love scrapes. They are the only things that are never serious.

JACK. Oh, that's nonsense, Algy. You never talk anything but nonsense.

ALGER. Nobody ever does.

[JACK *looks indignantly at him, and leaves the room.* ALGERNON *lights a cigarette, reads his shirt-cuff, and smiles.*]

ACT DROP

ACT II

[SCENE—*Garden at the Manor House. A flight of grey stone steps leads up to the house. The garden, an old-fashioned one, full of roses. Time of year, July. Basket chairs, and a table covered with books, are set under a large yew-tree.*]

[MISS PRISM *discovered seated at the table.* CECILY *is at the back, watering flowers.*]

MISS PRISM. [*Calling.*] Cecily, Cecily! Surely such a utilitarian occupation as the watering of flowers is rather Moulton's duty than yours? Especially at a moment when intellectual pleasures await you. Your German grammar is on the table. Pray open it at page fifteen. We will repeat yesterday's lesson.

CECILY. [*Coming over very slowly.*] But I don't like German. It isn't at all a becoming language. I know perfectly well that I look quite plain after my German lesson.

MISS P. Child, you know how anxious your guardian is that you should improve yourself in every way. He laid particular stress on your German, as he was leaving for town yesterday. Indeed, he always lays stress on your German when he is leaving for town.

CEC. Dear Uncle Jack is so very serious! Sometimes he is so serious that I think he cannot be quite well.

MISS P. [*Drawing herself up.*] Your guardian enjoys the best of health, and his gravity of demeanour is especially to be commended in one so comparatively young as he is. I know no one who has a higher sense of duty and responsibility.

CEC. I suppose that is why he often looks a little bored when we three are together.

MISS P. Cecily! I am surprised at you. Mr. Worthing has many troubles in his life. Idle merriment and triviality would be out of place in his conversation. You must remember his constant anxiety about that unfortunate young man his brother.

CEC. I wish Uncle Jack would allow that unfortunate young man, his brother, to come down here sometimes. We might have a good influence over him, Miss Prism. I am sure you certainly would. You know German, and geology, and things of that kind influence a man very much. [CECILY *begins to write in her diary.*]

MISS P. [*Shaking her head.*] I do not think that even I could produce any effect on a character that according to his own brother's admission is irretrievably weak and vacillating. Indeed I am not sure that I would desire to reclaim him. I am not in favour of this modern mania for turning bad people into good people at a moment's notice. As a man sows so let him reap. You must put away your diary, Cecily. I really don't see why you should keep a diary at all.

CEC. I keep a diary in order to enter the wonderful secrets of my life. If I didn't write them down, I should probably forget all about them.

MISS P. Memory, my dear Cecily, is the diary that we all carry about with us.

CEC. Yes, but it usually chronicles the things that have never happened, and couldn't possibly have happened. I believe that Memory is responsible for nearly all the three-volume novels that Mudie sends us.

MISS P. Do not speak slightingly of the three-volume novel, Cecily. I wrote one myself in earlier days.

CEC. Did you really, Miss Prism? How wonderfully clever you are! I hope it did not end happily? I don't like novels that end happily. They depress me so much.

MISS P. The good ended happily, and the bad unhappily. That is what Fiction means.

CEC. I suppose so. But it seems very unfair. And was your novel ever published?

MISS P. Alas! no. The manuscript unfortunately was abandoned. [CECILY *starts.*] I used the word in the sense of lost or mislaid. To your work, child,

these speculations are profitless.

CEC. [*Smiling.*] But I see dear Dr. Chasuble coming up through the garden.

MISS P. [*Rising and advancing.*] Dr. Chasuble! This is indeed a pleasure.

[*Enter* CANON CHASUBLE.]

CHASUBLE. And how are we this morning? Miss Prism, you are, I trust, well?

CEC. Miss Prism has just been complaining of a slight headache. I think it would do her so much good to have a short stroll with you in the Park, Dr. Chasuble.

MISS P. Cecily, I have not mentioned anything about a headache.

CEC. No, dear Miss Prism, I know that, but I felt instinctively that you had a headache. Indeed I was thinking about that, and not about my German lesson, when the Rector came in.

CHAS. I hope, Cecily, you are not inattentive.

CEC. Oh, I am afraid I am.

CHAS. That is strange. Were I fortunate enough to be Miss Prism's pupil, I would hang upon her lips. [MISS PRISM *glares.*] I spoke metaphorically.—My metaphor was drawn from bees. Ahem! Mr. Worthing, I suppose, has not returned from town yet?

MISS P. We do not expect him till Monday afternoon.

CHAS. Ah yes, he usually likes to spend his Sunday in London. He is not one of those whose sole aim is enjoyment, as, by all accounts, that unfortunate young man his brother seems to be. But I must not disturb Egeria and her pupil any longer.

MISS P. Egeria? My name is Laetitia, Doctor.

CHAS. [*Bowing.*] A classical allusion merely, drawn from the Pagan authors. I shall see you both no doubt at Evensong?

MISS P. I think, dear Doctor, I will have a stroll with you. I find I have a headache after all, and a walk might do it good.

CHAS. With pleasure, Miss Prism, with pleasure. We might go as far as the schools and back.

MISS P. That would be delightful. Cecily, you will read your Political Economy in my absence. The chapter on the Fall of the Rupee you may omit. It is somewhat too sensational. Even these metallic problems have their melodramatic side.

[*Goes down the garden with* DR. CHASUBLE.]

CEC. [*Picks up books and throws them back on table.*] Horrid Political Economy! Horrid Geography! Horrid, horrid German!

[*Enter* MERRIMAN *with a card on a salver.*]

MERRIMAN. Mr. Ernest Worthing has just driven

over from the station. He has brought his luggage with him.

CEC. [*Takes the card and reads it.*] "Mr. Ernest Worthing, B.4, The Albany, W." Uncle Jack's brother! Did you tell him Mr. Worthing was in town?

MERRIMAN. Yes, Miss. He seemed very much disappointed. I mentioned that you and Miss Prism were in the garden. He said he was anxious to speak to you privately for a moment.

CEC. Ask Mr. Ernest Worthing to come here. I suppose you had better talk to the housekeeper about a room for him.

MERRIMAN. Yes, Miss. [MERRIMAN *goes off.*]

CEC. I have never met any really wicked person before. I feel rather frightened. I am so afraid he will look just like every one else.

[*Enter* ALGERNON, *very gay and debonair.*]
He does!

ALGER. [*Raising his hat.*] You are my little cousin Cecily, I'm sure.

CEC. You are under some strange mistake. I am not little. In fact, I believe I am more than usually tall for my age. [ALGERNON *is rather taken aback.*] But I am your cousin Cecily. You, I see from your card, are Uncle Jack's brother, my cousin Ernest, my wicked cousin Ernest.

ALGER. Oh! I am not really wicked at all, cousin Cecily. You mustn't think that I am wicked.

CEC. If you are not, then you have certainly been deceiving us all in a very inexcusable manner. I hope you have not been leading a double life, pretending to be wicked and being really good all the time. That would be hypocrisy.

ALGER. [*Looks at her in amazement.*] Oh! Of course I have been rather reckless.

CEC. I am glad to hear it.

ALGER. In fact, now you mention the subject, I have been very bad in my own small way.

CEC. I don't think you should be so proud of that, though I am sure it must have been very pleasant.

ALGER. It is much pleasanter being here with you.

CEC. I can't understand how you are here at all. Uncle Jack won't be back till Monday afternoon.

ALGER. That is a great disappointment. I am obliged to go up by the first train on Monday morning. I have a business appointment that I am anxious . . . to miss!

CEC. Couldn't you miss it anywhere but in London?

ALGER. No: the appointment is in London.

CEC. Well, I know, of course, how important it is not to keep a business engagement, if one wants to retain any sense of the beauty of life, but still I think you had better wait till Uncle Jack arrives. I know he wants to speak to you about your emigrating.

ALGER. About my what?

CEC. Your emigrating. He has gone up to buy your outfit.

ALGER. I certainly wouldn't let Jack buy my outfit. He has no taste in neckties at all.

CEC. I don't think you will require neckties. Uncle Jack is sending you to Australia.

ALGER. Australia! I'd sooner die.

CEC. Well, he said at dinner on Wednesday night, that you would have to choose between this world, the next world, and Australia.

ALGER. Oh, well! The accounts I have received of Australia and the next world are not particularly encouraging. This world is good enough for me, cousin Cecily.

CEC. Yes, but are you good enough for it?

ALGER. I'm afraid I'm not that. That is why I want you to reform me. You might make that your mission, if you don't mind, Cousin Cecily.

CEC. I'm afraid I've no time, this afternoon.

ALGER. Well, would you mind my reforming myself this afternoon?

CEC. It is rather Quixotic of you. But I think you should try.

ALGER. I will. I feel better already.

CEC. You are looking a little worse.

ALGER. That is because I am hungry.

CEC. How thoughtless of me. I should have remembered that when one is going to lead an entirely new life, one requires regular and wholesome meals. Won't you come in?

ALGER. Thank you. Might I have a buttonhole first? I have never any appetite unless I have a buttonhole first.

CEC. A Maréchal Niel? [*Picks up scissors.*]

ALGER. No, I'd sooner have a pink rose.

CEC. Why? [*Cuts a flower.*]

ALGER. Because you are like a pink rose, Cousin Cecily.

CEC. I don't think it can be right for you to talk to me like that. Miss Prism never says such things to me.

ALGER. Then Miss Prism is a short-sighted old lady. [CECILY *puts the rose in his buttonhole.*] You are the prettiest girl I ever saw.

CEC. Miss Prism says that all good looks are a snare.

ALGER. They are a snare that every sensible man would like to be caught in.

CEC. Oh, I don't think I would care to catch a

sensible man. I shouldn't know what to talk to him about.

[*They pass into the house.* MISS PRISM *and* DR. CHASUBLE *return.*]

MISS P. You are too much alone, dear Dr. Chasuble. You should get married. A misanthrope I can understand—a womanthrope, never!

CHAS. [*With a scholar's shudder.*] Believe me, I do not deserve so neologistic a phrase. The precept as well as the practice of the Primitive Church was distinctly against matrimony.

MISS P. [*Sententiously.*] That is obviously the reason why the Primitive Church has not lasted up to the present day. And you do not seem to realize, dear Doctor, that by persistently remaining single, a man converts himself into a permanent public temptation. Men should be more careful; this very celibacy leads weaker vessels astray.

CHAS. But is a man not equally attractive when married?

MISS P. No married man is ever attractive except to his wife.

CHAS. And often, I've been told, not even to her.

MISS P. That depends on the intellectual sympathies of the woman. Maturity can always be depended on. Ripeness can be trusted. Young women are green. [DR. CHASUBLE *starts.*] I spoke horticulturally. My metaphor was drawn from fruits. But where is Cecily?

CHAS. Perhaps she followed us to the schools.

[*Enter* JACK *slowly from the back of the garden. He is dressed in the deepest mourning, with crepe hatband and black gloves.*]

MISS P. Mr. Worthing!

CHAS. Mr. Worthing?

MISS P. This is indeed a surprise. We did not look for you till Monday afternoon.

JACK. [*Shakes* MISS PRISM's *hand in a tragic manner.*] I have returned sooner than I expected. Dr. Chasuble, I hope you are well?

CHAS. Dear Mr. Worthing, I trust this garb of woe does not betoken some terrible calamity?

JACK. My brother.

MISS P. More shameful debts and extravagance?

CHAS. Still leading his life of pleasure?

JACK. [*Shaking his head.*] Dead!

CHAS. Your brother Ernest dead?

JACK. Quite dead.

MISS P. What a lesson for him! I trust he will profit by it.

CHAS. Mr. Worthing, I offer you my sincere condolence. You have at least the consolation of knowing that you were always the most generous and forgiving of brothers.

JACK. Poor Ernest! He had many faults, but it is a sad, sad blow.

CHAS. Very sad indeed. Were you with him at the end?

JACK. No. He died abroad; in Paris, in fact. I had a telegram last night from the manager of the Grand Hotel.

CHAS. Was the cause of death mentioned?

JACK. A severe chill, it seems.

MISS P. As a man sows, so shall he reap.

CHAS. [*Raising his hand.*] Charity, dear Miss Prism, charity! None of us are perfect. I myself am peculiarly susceptible to draughts. Will the interment take place here?

JACK. No. He seems to have expressed a desire to be buried in Paris.

CHAS. In Paris! [*Shakes his head.*] I fear that hardly points to any very serious state of mind at the last. You would no doubt wish me to make some slight allusion to this tragic domestic affliction next Sunday. [JACK *presses his hand convulsively.*] My sermon on the meaning of the manna in the wilderness can be adapted to almost any occasion, joyful, or, as in the present case, distressing. [*All sigh.*] I have preached it at harvest celebrations, christenings, confirmations, on days of humiliation and festal days. The last time I delivered it was in the Cathedral, as a charity sermon on behalf of the Society for the Prevention of Discontent among the Upper Orders. The Bishop, who was present, was much struck by some of the analogies I drew.

JACK. Ah! that reminds me, you mentioned christenings I think, Dr. Chasuble? I suppose you know how to christen all right? [DR. CHASUBLE *looks astounded.*] I mean, of course, you are continually christening, aren't you?

MISS P. It is, I regret to say, one of the Rector's most constant duties in this parish. I have often spoken to the poorer classes on the subject. But they don't seem to know what thrift is.

CHAS. But is there any particular infant in whom you are interested, Mr. Worthing? Your brother was, I believe, unmarried, was he not?

JACK. Oh yes.

MISS P. [*Bitterly.*] People who live entirely for pleasure usually are.

JACK. But it is not for any child, dear Doctor. I am very fond of children. No! the fact is, I would like to be christened myself, this afternoon, if you have nothing better to do.

CHAS. But surely, Mr. Worthing, you have been christened already?

JACK. I don't remember anything about it.

CHAS. But have you any grave doubts on the subject?

JACK. I certainly intend to have. Of course I don't know if the thing would bother you in any way, or if you think I am a little too old now.

CHAS. Not at all. The sprinkling, and, indeed, the immersion of adults is a perfectly canonical practice.

JACK. Immersion!

CHAS. You need have no apprehensions. Sprinkling is all that is necessary, or indeed I think advisable. Our weather is so changeable. At what hour would you wish the ceremony performed?

JACK. Oh, I might trot round about five if that would suit you.

CHAS. Perfectly, perfectly! In fact I have two similar ceremonies to perform at that time. A case of twins that occurred recently in one of the outlying cottages on your own estate. Poor Jenkins the carter, a most hard-working man.

JACK. Oh! I don't see much fun in being christened along with other babies. It would be childish. Would half-past five do?

CHAS. Admirably! Admirably! [*Takes out watch.*] And now, dear Mr. Worthing, I will not intrude any longer into a house of sorrow. I would merely beg you not to be too much bowed down by grief. What seem to us bitter trials are often blessings in disguise.

MISS P. This seems to me a blessing of an extremely obvious kind.

[*Enter CECILY from the house.*]

CEC. Uncle Jack! Oh, I am pleased to see you back. But what horrid clothes you have got on. Do go and change them.

MISS P. Cecily!

CHAS. My child! my child. [CECILY *goes towards* JACK; *he kisses her brow in a melancholy manner.*]

CEC. What is the matter, Uncle Jack? Do look happy! You look as if you had toothache, and I have got such a surprise for you. Who do you think is in the dining-room? Your brother!

JACK. Who?

CEC. Your brother Ernest. He arrived about half an hour ago.

JACK. What nonsense! I haven't got a brother.

CEC. Oh, don't say that. However badly he may have behaved to you in the past he is still your brother. You couldn't be so heartless as to disown him. I'll tell him to come out. And you will shake hands with him, won't you, Uncle Jack? [*Runs back into the house.*]

CHAS. These are very joyful tidings.

MISS P. After we had all been resigned to his loss, his sudden return seems to me peculiarly distressing.

JACK. My brother is in the dining-room? I don't know what it all means. I think it is perfectly absurd.

[*Enter ALGERNON and CECILY hand in hand. They come slowly up to JACK.*]

JACK. Good heavens! [*Motions ALGERNON away.*]

ALGER. Brother John, I have come down from town to tell you that I am very sorry for all the trouble I have given you, and I intend to lead a better life in the future. [JACK *glares at him and does not take his hand.*]

CEC. Uncle Jack, you are not going to refuse your own brother's hand?

JACK. Nothing will induce me to take his hand. I think his coming down here disgraceful. He knows perfectly well why.

CEC. Uncle Jack, do be nice. There is some good in everyone. Ernest has just been telling me about his poor invalid friend Mr. Bunbury whom he goes to visit so often. And surely there must be much good in one who is kind to an invalid, and leaves the pleasures of London to sit by a bed of pain.

JACK. Oh! he has been talking about Bunbury, has he?

CEC. Yes, he has told me all about poor Mr. Bunbury, and his terrible state of health.

JACK. Bunbury! Well, I won't have him talk to you about Bunbury or about anything else. It is enough to drive one perfectly frantic.

ALGER. Of course I admit that the faults were all on my side. But I must say that I think that Brother John's coldness to me is peculiarly painful. I expected a more enthusiatic welcome, especially considering it is the first time I have come here.

CEC. Uncle Jack, if you don't shake hands with Ernest I will never forgive you.

JACK. Never forgive me?

CEC. Never, never, never!

JACK. Well, this is the last time I shall ever do it. [*Shakes hands with ALGERNON and glares.*]

CHAS. It's pleasant, is it not, to see so perfect a reconciliation? I think we might leave the two brothers together.

MISS P. Cecily, you will come with us.

CEC. Certainly, Miss Prism. My little task of reconciliation is over.

CHAS. You have done a beautiful action to-day, dear child.

MISS P. We must not be premature in our judgements.

CEC. I feel very happy. [*They all go off except* JACK *and* ALGERNON.]

JACK. You young scoundrel, Algy, you must get out of this place as soon as possible. I don't allow any Bunburying here.

[*Enter* MERRIMAN.]

MERRIMAN. I have put Mr. Ernest's things in the room next to yours, sir. I suppose that is all right?

JACK. What?

MERRIMAN. Mr. Ernest's luggage, sir. I have unpacked it and put it in the room next to your own.

JACK. His luggage?

MERRIMAN. Yes, sir. Three portmanteaus, a dressing-case, two hatboxes, and a large luncheon-basket.

ALGER. I am afraid I can't stay more than a week this time.

JACK. Merriman, order the dog-cart at once. Mr. Ernest has been suddenly called back to town.

MERRIMAN. Yes, sir. [*Goes back into the house.*]

ALGER. What a fearful liar you are, Jack. I have not been called back to town at all.

JACK. Yes, you have.

ALGER. I haven't heard any one call me.

JACK. Your duty as a gentleman calls you back.

ALGER. My duty as a gentleman has never interfered with my pleasures in the smallest degree.

JACK. I can quite understand that.

ALGER. Well, Cecily is a darling.

JACK. You are not to talk of Miss Cardew like that. I don't like it.

ALGER. Well, I don't like your clothes. You look perfectly ridiculous in them. Why on earth don't you go up and change? It is perfectly childish to be in deep mourning for a man who is actually staying for a whole week with you in your house as a guest. I call it grotesque.

JACK. You are certainly not staying with me for a whole week as a guest or anything else. You have got to leave . . . by the four-five train.

ALGER. I certainly won't leave you so long as you are in mourning. It would be most unfriendly. If I were in mourning you would stay with me, I suppose. I should think it very unkind if you didn't.

JACK. Well, will you go if I change my clothes?

ALGER. Yes, if you are not too long. I never saw anybody take so long to dress, and with such little result.

JACK. Well, at any rate, that is better than being always over-dressed as you are.

ALGER. If I am occasionally a little over-dressed, I make up for it by being always immensely over-educated.

JACK. Your vanity is ridiculous, your conduct an outrage, and your presence in my garden utterly absurd. However, you have got to catch the four-five, and I hope you will have a pleasant journey back to town. This Bunburying, as you call it, has not been a great success for you.

[*Goes into the house.*]

ALGER. I think it has been a great success. I'm in love with Cecily, and that is everything. [*Enter* CECILY *at the back of the garden. She picks up the can and begins to water the flowers.*] But I must see her before I go, and make arrangements for another Bunbury. Ah, there she is.

CEC. Oh, I merely came back to water the roses. I though you were with Uncle Jack.

ALGER. He's gone to order the dog-cart for me.

CEC. Oh, is he going to take you for a nice drive?

ALGER. He's going to send me away.

CEC. Then have we got to part?

ALGER. I am afraid so. It's very painful parting.

CEC. It is always painful to part from people whom one has known for a very brief space of time. The absence of old friends one can endure with equanimity. But even a momentary separation from any one to whom one has just been introduced is almost unbearable.

ALGER. Thank you.

[*Enter* MERRIMAN.]

MERRIMAN. The dog-cart is at the door, sir.

[ALGERNON *looks appealingly at* CECILY.]

CEC. It can wait, Merriman . . . for . . . five minutes.

MERRIMAN. Yes, miss.   [*Exit* MERRIMAN.]

ALGER. I hope, Cecily, I shall not offend you if I state quite frankly and openly that you seem to me to be in every way the visible personification of absolute perfection.

CEC. I think your frankness does you great credit, Ernest. If you will allow me, I will copy your remarks into my diary. [*Goes over to table and begins writing in diary.*]

ALGER. Do you really keep a diary? I'd give anything to look at it. May I?

CEC. Oh no. [*Puts her hand over it.*] You see, it is simply a very young girl's record of her own thoughts and impressions, and consequently meant for publication. When it appears in volume form I hope you will order a copy. But pray, Ernest, don't stop. I delight in taking down from dictation. I have reached "absolute perfection." You can go on. I am quite ready for more.

ALGER. [*Somewhat taken aback.*] Ahem! Ahem!

CEC. Oh, don't cough, Ernest. When one is dictating one should speak fluently and not cough.

Besides, I don't know how to spell a cough. [*Writes as* ALGERNON *speaks.*]

ALGER. [*Speaking very rapidly.*] Cecily, ever since I first looked upon your wonderful and incomparable beauty, I have dared to love you wildly, passionately, devotedly, hopelessly.

CEC. I don't think that you should tell me that you love me wildly, passionately, devotedly, hopelessly. Hopelessly doesn't seem to make much sense, does it?

ALGER. Cecily.

[*Enter* MERRIMAN.]

MERRIMAN. The dog-cart is waiting, sir.

ALGER. Tell it to come round next week, at the same hour.

MERRIMAN. [*Looks at* CECILY, *who makes no sign.*] Yes, sir.   [MERRIMAN *retires.*]

CEC. Uncle Jack would be very much annoyed if he knew you were staying on till next week, at the same hour.

ALGER. Oh, I don't care about Jack. I don't care for anybody in the whole world but you. I love you, Cecily. You will marry me, won't you?

CEC. You silly boy! Of course. Why, we have been engaged for the last three months.

ALGER. For the last three months?

CEC. Yes, it will be exactly three months on Thursday.

ALGER. But how did we become engaged?

CEC. Well, ever since dear Uncle Jack first confessed to us that he had a younger brother who was very wicked and bad, you of course have formed the chief topic of conversation between myself and Miss Prism. And of course a man who is much talked about is always very attractive. One feels there must be something in him, after all. I daresay it was foolish of me, but I fell in love with you, Ernest.

ALGER. Darling. And when was the engagement actually settled?

CEC. On the 14th of February last. Worn out by your entire ignorance of my existence, I determined to end the matter one way or the other, and after a long struggle with myself I accepted you under this dear old tree here. The next day I bought this little ring in your name, and this is the little bangle with the true lover's knot I promised you always to wear.

ALGER. Did I give you this? It's very pretty, isn't it?

CEC. Yes, you've wonderfully good taste, Ernest. It's the excuse I've always given for your leading such a bad life. And this is the box in which I keep all your dear letters. [*Kneels at table, opens box, and produces letters tied up with blue ribbon.*]

ALGER. My letters! But, my own sweet Cecily, I have never written you any letters.

CEC. You need hardly remind me of that, Ernest. I remember only too well that I was forced to write your letters for you. I wrote always three times a week, and sometimes oftener.

ALGER. Oh, do let me read them, Cecily?

CEC. Oh, I couldn't possibly. They would make you far too conceited. [*Replaces box.*] The three you wrote me after I had broken off the engagement are so beautiful, and so badly spelled, that even now I can hardly read them without crying a little.

ALGER. But was our engagement ever broken off?

CEC. Of course it was. On the 22nd of last March. You can see the entry if you like. [*Shows diary.*] "To-day I broke off my engagement with Ernest. I feel it is better to do so. The weather still continues charming."

ALGER. But why on earth did you break it off? What had I done? I had done nothing at all. Cecily, I am very much hurt indeed to hear you broke it off. Particularly when the weather was so charming.

CEC. It would hardly have been a really serious engagement if it hadn't been broken off at least once. But I forgave you before the week was out.

ALGER. [*Crossing to her, and kneeling.*] What a perfect angel you are, Cecily.

CEC. You dear romantic boy. [*He kisses her, she puts her fingers through his hair.*] I hope your hair curls naturally, does it?

ALGER. Yes, darling, with a little help from others.

CEC. I am so glad.

ALGER. You'll never break off our engagement again, Cecily?

CEC. I don't think I could break it off now that I have actually met you. Besides, of course, there is the question of your name.

ALGER. Yes, of course. [*Nervously.*]

CEC. You must not laugh at me, darling, but it had always been a girlish dream of mine to love some one whose name was Ernest. [ALGERNON *rises,* CECILY *also.*] There is something in that name that seems to inspire absolute confidence. I pity any poor married woman whose husband is not called Ernest.

ALGER. But, my dear child, do you mean to say you could not love me if I had some other name?

CEC. But what name?

ALGER. Oh, any name you like—Algernon—for instance . . .

CEC. But I don't like the name of Algernon.

ALGER. Well, my own dear, sweet, loving little darling, I really can't see why you should object to the name of Algernon. It is not at all a bad name. In fact, it is rather an aristocratic name. Half of the chaps who get into the Bankruptcy Court are called Algernon. But seriously, Cecily . . . [*Moving to her*] if my name was Algy, couldn't you love me?

CEC. [*Rising.*] I might respect you, Ernest, I might admire your character, but I fear that I should not be able to give you my undivided attention.

ALGER. Ahem! Cecily! [*Picking up hat.*] Your Rector here is, I suppose, thoroughly experienced in the practice of all the rites and ceremonials of the Church?

CEC. Oh, yes. Dr. Chasuble is a most learned man. He has never written a single book, so you can imagine how much he knows.

ALGER. I must see him at once on a most important christening—I mean on most important business.

CEC. Oh!

ALGER. I shan't be away more than half an hour.

CEC. Considering that we have been engaged since February the 14th, and that I only met you to-day for the first time, I think it is rather hard that you should leave me for so long a period as half an hour. Couldn't you make it twenty minutes?

ALGER. I'll be back in no time. [*Kisses her and rushes down the garden.*]

CEC. What an impetuous boy he is! I like his hair so much. I must enter his proposal in my diary.   [*Enter* MERRIMAN.]

MERRIMAN. A Miss Fairfax has just called to see Mr. Worthing. On very important business, Miss Fairfax states.

CEC. Isn't Mr. Worthing in his library?

MERRIMAN. Mr. Worthing went over in the direction of the Rectory some time ago.

CEC. Pray ask the lady to come out here; Mr. Worthing is sure to be back soon. And you can bring tea.

MERRIMAN. Yes, Miss.   [*Goes out.*]

CEC. Miss Fairfax! I suppose one of the many good elderly women who are associated with Uncle Jack in some of his philantropic work in London. I don't quite like women who are interested in philanthropic work. I think it is so forward of them.

[*Enter* MERRIMAN.]

MERRIMAN. Miss Fairfax.

[*Enter* GWENDOLEN. *Exit* MERRIMAN.]

CEC. [*Advancing to meet her.*] Pray let me introduce myself to you. My name is Cecily Cardew.

GWEN. Cecily Cardew? [*Moving to her and shaking hands.*] What a very sweet name! Something tells me that we are going to be great friends. I like you already more than I can say. My first impressions of people are never wrong.

CEC. How nice of you to like me so much after we have known each other such a comparatively short time. Pray sit down.

GWEN. [*Still standing up.*] I may call you Cecily, may I not?

CEC. With pleasure!

GWEN. And you will always call me Gwendolen, won't you?

CEC. If you wish.

GWEN. Then that is all quite settled, is it not?

CEC. I hope so. [*A pause. They both sit down together.*]

GWEN. Perhaps this might be a favourable opportunity for my mentioning who I am. My father is Lord Bracknell. You have never heard of papa, I suppose?

CEC. I don't think so.

GWEN. Outside the family circle, papa, I am glad to say, is entirely unknown. I think that is quite as it should be. The home seems to me to be the proper sphere for the man. And certainly once a man begins to neglect his domestic duties he becomes painfully effeminate, does he not? And I don't like that. It makes men so very attractive. Cecily, mamma, whose views on education are remarkably strict, has brought me up to be extremely shortsighted; it is part of her system; so do you mind my looking at you through my glasses?

CEC. Oh! not at all, Gwendolen. I am very fond of being looked at.

GWEN. [*After examining* CECILY *carefully through a lorgnette.*] You are here on a short visit, I suppose.

CEC. Oh no! I live here.

GWEN. [*Severely.*] Really? Your mother, no doubt, or some female relative of advanced years, resides here also?

CEC. Oh no! I have no mother, nor, in fact, any relations.

GWEN. Indeed?

CEC. My dear guardian, with the assistance of Miss Prism, has the arduous task of looking after me.

GWEN. Your guardian?

CEC. Yes, I am Mr. Worthing's ward.

GWEN. Oh! It is strange he never mentioned to me that he had a ward. How secretive of him! He grows more interesting hourly. I am not sure, however, that the news inspires me with feelings of unmixed delight. [*Rising and going to her.*] I am very fond of you, Cecily; I have liked you ever since I met you! But I am bound to state that now that I know that you are Mr. Worthing's ward, I cannot help expressing a wish you were – well, just a little older than you seem to be – and not quite so very alluring in appearance. In fact, if I may speak candidly——

CEC. Pray do! I think that whenever one has anything unpleasant to say, one should always be quite candid.

GWEN. Well, to speak with perfect candour, Cecily, I wish that you were fully forty-two, and more than usually plain for your age. Ernest has a strong upright nature. He is the very soul of truth and honor. Disloyalty would be as impossible to him as deception. But even men of the noblest possible moral character are extremely susceptible to the influence of the physical charms of others. Modern, no less than Ancient History, supplies us with many most painful examples of what I refer to. If it were not so, indeed, History would be quite unreadable.

CEC. I beg your pardon, Gwendolen, did you say Ernest?

GWEN. Yes.

CEC. Oh, but it is not Mr. Ernest Worthing who is my guardian. It is his brother—his elder brother.

GWEN. [*Sitting down again.*] Ernest never mentioned to me that he had a brother.

CEC. I am sorry to say they have not been on good terms for a long time.

GWEN. Ah! that accounts for it. And now that I think of it I have never heard any man mention his brother. The subject seems distasteful to most men. Cecily, you have lifted a load from my mind. I was growing almost anxious. It would have been terrible if any cloud had come across a friendship like ours, would it not? Of course you are quite, quite sure that it is not Mr. Ernest Worthing who is your guardian?

CEC. Quite sure. [*A pause.*] In fact, I am going to be his.

GWEN. [*Inquiringly.*] I beg your pardon?

CEC. [*Rather shy and confidingly.*] Dearest Gwendolen, there is no reason why I should make a secret of it to you. Our little country newspaper is sure to chronicle the fact next week. Mr. Ernest Worthing and I are engaged to be married.

GWEN. [*Quite politely, rising.*] My darling Cecily, I think there must be some slight error. Mr. Ernest Worthing is engaged to me. The announcement will appear in the *Morning Post* on Saturday at the latest.

CEC. [*Very politely, rising.*] I am afraid you must be under some misconception. Ernest proposed to me exactly ten minutes ago. [*Shows diary.*]

GWEN. [*Examines diary through her lorgnette carefully.*] It is very curious, for he asked me to be his wife yesterday afternoon at 5:30. If you would care to verify the incident, pray do so. [*Produces diary of her own.*] I never travel without my diary. One should always have something sensational to read in the train. I am so sorry, dear Cecily, if it is any disappointment to you, but I am afraid I have the prior claim.

CEC. It would distress me more than I can tell you, dear Gwendolen, if it caused you any mental or physical anguish, but I feel bound to point out that since Ernest proposed to you he clearly has changed his mind.

GWEN. [*Meditatively.*] If the poor fellow has been entrapped into any foolish promise I shall consider it my duty to rescue him at once, and with a firm hand.

CEC. [*Thoughtfully and sadly.*] Whatever unfortunate entanglement my dear boy may have got into, I will never reproach him with it after we are married.

GWEN. Do you allude to me, Miss Cardew, as an entanglement? You are presumptuous. On an occasion of this kind it becomes more than a moral duty to speak one's mind. It becomes a pleasure.

CEC. Do you suggest, Miss Fairfax, that I entrapped Ernest into an engagement? How dare you? This is no time for wearing the shallow mask of manners. When I see a spade I call it a spade.

GWEN. [*Satirically.*] I am glad to say that I have never seen a spade. It is obvious that our social spheres have been widely different.

[*Enter* MERRIMAN, *followed by the footman. He carries a salver, table cloth, and plate stand.* CECILY *is about to retort. The presence of the servants exercises a restraining influence, under which both girls chafe.*]

MERRIMAN. Shall I lay tea here as usual, Miss?

CEC. [*Sternly, in a calm voice.*] Yes, as usual.

[MERRIMAN *begins to clear table and lay cloth. A long pause.* CECILY *and* GWENDOLEN *glare at each other.*]

GWEN. Are there many interesting walks in the vicinity, Miss Cardew?

CEC. Oh! yes! a great many. From the top of one of the hills quite close one can see five counties.

GWEN. Five counties! I don't think I should like that; I hate crowds.

CEC. [*Sweetly.*] I suppose that is why you live in town? [GWENDOLEN *bites her lip, and beats her foot nervously with her parasol.*]

GWEN. [*Looking round.*] Quite a well-kept garden this is, Miss Cardew.

CEC. So glad you like it, Miss Fairfax.

GWEN. I had no idea there were any flowers in the country.

CEC. Oh, flowers are as common here, Miss Fairfax, as people are in London.

GWEN. Personally I cannot understand how anybody manages to exist in the country, if anybody who is anybody does. The country always bores me to death.

CEC. Ah! This is what the newspapers call agricultural depression, is it not? I believe the aristocracy are suffering very much from it just at present. It is almost an epidemic amongst them, I have been told. May I offer you some tea, Miss Fairfax?

GWEN. [*With elaborate politeness.*] Thank you. [*aside*] Detestable girl! But I require tea!

CEC. [*Sweetly.*] Sugar?

GWEN. [*Superciliously.*] No, thank you. Sugar is not fashionable any more. [CECILY *looks angrily at her, takes up the tongs and puts four lumps of sugar into the cup.*]

CEC. [*Severely.*] Cake or bread and butter?

GWEN. [*In a bored manner.*] Bread and butter, please. Cake is rarely seen at the best houses nowadays.

CEC. [*Cuts a very large slice of cake and puts it on the tray.*] Hand that to Miss Fairfax.

[MERRIMAN *does so, and goes out with footman.* GWENDOLEN *drinks the tea and makes a grimace. Puts down cup at once, reaches out her hand to the bread and butter, looks at it, and finds it is cake. Rises in indignation.*]

GWEN. You have filled my tea with lumps of sugar, and though I asked most distinctly for bread and butter, you have given me cake. I am known for the gentleness of my disposition, and the extraordinary sweetness of my nature, but I warn you, Miss Cardew, you may go too far.

CEC. [*Rising.*] To save my poor, innocent, trusting boy from the machinations of any other girl there are no lengths to which I would not go.

GWEN. From the moment I saw you I distrusted you. I felt that you were false and deceitful. I am never deceived in such matters. My first impressions of people are invariably right.

CEC. It seems to me, Miss Fairfax, that I am trespassing on your valuable time. No doubt you have many other calls of a similar character to make in the neighbourhood.

[*Enter* JACK.]

GWEN. [*Catching sight of him.*] Ernest! My own Ernest!

JACK. Gwendolen! Darling! [*Offers to kiss her.*]

GWEN. [*Drawing back.*] A moment! May I ask if you are engaged to be married to this young lady? [*Points to* CECILY.]

JACK. [*Laughing.*] To dear little Cecily! Of course not! What could have put such an idea into your pretty little head?

GWEN. Thank you. You may! [*Offers her cheek.*]

CEC. [*Very sweetly.*] I knew there must be some misunderstanding, Miss Fairfax. The gentleman whose arm is at present round your waist is my guardian, Mr. John Worthing.

GWEN. I beg your pardon?

CEC. This is Uncle Jack.

GWEN. [*Receding.*] Jack! Oh!

[*Enter* ALGERNON.]

CEC. Here is Ernest.

ALGER. [*Goes straight over to* CECILY *without noticing anyone else.*] My own love! [*Offers to kiss her.*]

CEC. [*Drawing back.*] A moment, Ernest! May I ask you—are you engaged to be married to this young lady?

ALGER. [*Looking round.*] To what young lady? Good heavens! Gwendolen!

CEC. Yes: to good heavens, Gwendolen, I mean to Gwendolen.

ALGER. [*Laughing.*] Of course not! What could have put such an idea into your pretty little head.

CEC. Thank you. [*Presenting her cheek to be kissed.*] You may. [ALGERNON *kisses her.*]

GWEN. I felt there was some slight error, Miss Cardew. The gentleman who is now embracing you is my cousin, Mr. Algernon Moncrieff.

CEC. [*Breaking away from Algernon.*] Algernon Moncrieff! Oh!

[*The two girls move towards each other and put their arms round each other's waists as if for protection.*]

CEC. Are you called Algernon?

ALGER. I cannot deny it.

CEC. Oh!

GWEN. Is your name really John?

JACK. [*Standing rather proudly.*] I could deny it if I liked. I could deny anything if I liked. But my name certainly is John. It has been John for years.

CEC. [*to* GWENDOLEN] A gross deception has been practised on both of us.

GWEN. My poor wounded Cecily!

CEC. My sweet wronged Gwendolen!

GWEN. [*Slowly and seriously.*] You will call me sister, will you not? [*They embrace.* JACK *and* ALGERNON *groan and walk up and down.*]

CEC. [*Rather brightly.*] There is just one question I would like to be allowed to ask my guardian.

GWEN. An admirable idea! Mr. Worthing, there is just one question I would like to be permitted to put to you. Where is your brother Ernest? We are both engaged to be married to your brother Ernest, so it is a matter of some importance to us to know where your brother Ernest is at present.

JACK. [*Slowly and hesitatingly.*] Gwendolen – Cecily – it is very painful for me to be forced to speak the truth. It is the first time in my life that I have ever been reduced to such a painful position, and I am really quite inexperienced in doing anything of the kind. However, I will tell you quite frankly that I have no brother Ernest. I have no brother at all. I never had a brother in my life, and I certainly have not the smallest intention of ever having one in the future.

CEC. [*Surprised.*] No brother at all?

JACK. [*Cheerily.*] None!

GWEN. [*Severely.*] Had you never a brother of any kind?

JACK [*Pleasantly.*] Never. Not even of any kind.

GWEN. I am afraid it is quite clear, Cecily, that neither of us is engaged to be married to anyone.

CEC. It is not a very pleasant position for a young girl suddenly to find herself in. Is it?

GWEN. Let us go into the house. They will hardly venture to come after us there.

CEC. No, men are so cowardly, aren't they?

[*They retire into the house with scornful looks.*]

JACK. This ghastly state of things is what you call Bunburying, I suppose?

ALGER. Yes, and a perfectly wonderful Bunbury it is. The most wonderful Bunbury I have ever had in my life.

JACK. Well, you've no right whatsoever to Bunbury here.

ALGER. That is absurd. One has a right to Bunbury anywhere one chooses. Every serious Bunburyist knows that.

JACK. Serious Bunburyist? Good heavens!

ALGER. Well, one must be serious about something, if one wants to have any amusement in life. I happen to be serious about Bunburying. What on earth you are serious about I haven't got the remotest idea. About everything, I should fancy. You have such an absolutely trivial nature.

JACK. Well, the only small satisfaction I have in the whole of this wretched business is that your friend Bunbury is quite exploded. You won't be able to run down to the country quite so often as you used to do, dear Algy. And a very good thing too.

ALGER. Your brother is a little off colour, isn't he, dear Jack? You won't be able to disappear to London quite so frequently as your wicked custom was. And not a bad thing either.

JACK. As for your conduct towards Miss Cardew, I must say that your taking in a sweet, simple, innocent girl like that is quite inexcusable. To say nothing of the fact that she is my ward.

ALGER. I can see no possible defence at all for your deceiving a brilliant, clever, thoroughly experienced young lady like Miss Fairfax. To say nothing of the fact that she is my cousin.

JACK. I wanted to be engaged to Gwendolen, that is all. I love her.

ALGER. Well, I simply wanted to be engaged to Cecily. I adore her.

JACK. There is certainly no chance of your marrying Miss Cardew.

ALGER. I don't think there is much likelihood, Jack, of you and Miss Fairfax being united.

JACK. Well, that is no business of yours.

ALGER. If it was my business, I wouldn't talk about it. [*Begins to eat muffins.*] It is very vulgar to talk about one's business. Only people like stockbrokers do that, and then merely at dinner parties.

JACK. How you can sit there, calmly eating muffins when we are in this horrible trouble, I can't make out. You seem to me to be perfectly heartless.

ALGER. Well, I can't eat muffins in an agitated manner. The butter would probably get on my cuffs. One should always eat muffins quite calmly. It is the only way to eat them.

JACK. I say it's perfectly heartless your eating muffins at all, under the circumstances.

ALGER. When I am in trouble, eating is the only thing that consoles me. Indeed, when I am in really great trouble, as any one who knows me intimately will tell you, I refuse everything except food and drink. At the present moment I am eating muffins because I am unhappy. Besides, I am particularly fond of muffins. [*Rising.*]

JACK. [*Rising.*] Well, there is no reason why you should eat them all in that greedy way. [*Takes muffins from Algernon.*]

ALG. [*Offering tea-cake.*] I wish you would have tea-cake instead. I don't like tea-cake.

JACK. Good heavens! I suppose a man may eat his own muffins in his own garden.

ALGER. But you have just said it was perfectly heartless to eat muffins.

JACK. I said it was perfectly heartless of you, under the circumstances. That is a very different thing.

ALGER. That may be. But the muffins are the same. [*He seizes the muffin-dish from JACK.*]

JACK. Algy, I wish to goodness you would go.

ALGER. You can't possibly ask me to go without having some dinner. It's absurd. I never go without my dinner. No one ever does, except vegetarians and people like that. Besides I have just made arrangements with Dr. Chasuble to be christened at a quarter to six under the name of Ernest.

JACK. My dear fellow, the sooner you give up that nonsense the better. I made arrangements this morning with Dr. Chasuble to be christened myself at 5:30, and I naturally will take the name of Ernest. Gwendolen would wish it. We can't both be christened Ernest. It's absurd. Besides, I have a perfect right to be christened if I like. There is no evidence at all that I have ever been christened by anybody. I should think it extremely probable I never was, and so does Dr. Chasuble. It is entirely different in your case. You have been christened already.

ALGER. Yes, but I have not been christened for years.

JACK. Yes, but you have been christened. That is the important thing.

ALGER. Quite so. So I know my constitution can stand it. If you are not quite sure about your ever having been christened, I must say I think it rather dangerous your venturing on it now. It might make you very unwell. You can hardly have forgotten that someone very closely connected with you was very nearly carried off this week in Paris by a severe chill.

JACK. Yes, but you said yourself that a severe chill was not hereditary.

ALGER. It usen't to be, I know—but I daresay it is now. Science is always making wonderful improvements in things.

JACK. [*Picking up the muffin-dish.*] Oh, that is nonsense; you are always talking nonsense.

ALGER. Jack, you are at the muffins again! I wish you wouldn't. There are only two left. [*Takes them.*] I told you I was particularly fond of muffins.

JACK. But I hate tea-cake.

ALGER. Why on earth then do you allow tea-cake to be served up for your guests? What ideas you have of hospitality!

JACK. Algernon! I have already told you to go. I don't want you here. Why don't you go!

ALGER. I haven't quite finished my tea yet! and there is still one muffin left. [JACK *groans, and sinks into a chair.* ALGERNON *continues eating.*]

ACT DROP

ACT III

[SCENE—*Drawing-room at the Manor House.*]
[GWENDOLEN *and* CECILY *are at the window, looking out into the garden.*]

GWEN. The fact that they did not follow us at once into the house, as any one else would have done, seems to me to show that they have some sense of shame left.

CEC. They have been eating muffins. That looks like repentance.

GWEN. [*After a pause.*] They don't seem to notice us at all. Couldn't you cough?

CEC. But I haven't got a cough.

GWEN. They're looking at us. What effrontery!

CEC. They're approaching. That's very forward of them.

GWEN. Let us preserve a dignified silence.

CEC. Certainly. It's the only thing to do now.

[*Enter* JACK *followed by* ALGERNON. *They whistle some dreadful popular air from a British Opera.*]

GWEN. This dignified silence seems to produce an unpleasant effect.

CEC. A most distasteful one.

GWEN. But we will not be the first to speak.

CEC. Certainly not

GWEN. Mr. Worthing, I have something very particular to ask you. Much depends on your reply.

CEC. Gwendolen, your common sense is invaluable. Mr. Moncrieff, kindly answer me the following question. Why did you pretend to be my guardian's brother?

ALGER. In order that I might have an opportunity of meeting you.

CEC. [*to* GWENDOLEN] That certainly seems a satisfactory explanation, does it not?

GWEN. Yes, dear, if you can believe him.

CEC. I don't. But that does not affect the wonderful beauty of his answer.

GWEN. True. In matters of grave importance, style, not sincerity, is the vital thing. Mr. Worthing, what explanation can you offer to me for pretending to have a brother? Was it in order that you might have an opportunity of coming up to town to see me as often as possible?

JACK. Can you doubt it, Miss Fairfax?

GWEN. I have the gravest doubts upon the subject. But I intend to crush them. This is not the moment for German scepticism. [*Moving to* CECILY.] Their explanations appear to be quite satisfactory, especially Mr. Worthing's. That seems to me to have the stamp of truth upon it.

CEC. I am more than content with what Mr. Moncrieff said. His voice alone inspires one with absolute credulity.

GWEN. Then you think we should forgive them?

CEC. Yes. I mean no.

GWEN. True! I had forgotten. There are principles at stake that one cannot surrender. Which of us should tell them? The task is not a pleasant one.

CEC. Could we not both speak at the same time?

GWEN. An excellent idea! I nearly always speak at the same time as other people. Will you take the time from me?

CEC. Certainly [GWENDOLEN *beats time with uplifted finger.*]

GWEN and CEC. [*Speaking together.*] Your Christian names are still an insuperable barrier. That is all!

JACK and ALGER. [*Speaking together.*] Our Christian names! Is that all? But we are going to be christened this afternoon.

GWEN. [*to* JACK] For my sake you are prepared to do this terrible thing?

JACK. I am.

CEC. [*to* ALGERNON] To please me you are ready to face this fearful ordeal?

ALGER. I am!

GWEN. How absurd to talk of the equality of the sexes! Where questions of self-sacrifice are concerned, men are infinitely beyond us.

JACK. We are. [*Clasps hands with* ALGERNON.]

CEC. They have moments of physical courage of which we women know absolutely nothing.

GWEN. [*to* JACK] Darling!

ALGER. [*to* CECILY] Darling! [*They fall into each other's arms.*]

[*Enter* MERRIMAN. *When he enters he coughs loudly, seeing the situation.*]

MERRIMAN. Ahem! Ahem! Lady Bracknell.

JACK. Good heavens!

[*Enter* LADY BRACKNELL. *The couples separate in alarm. Exit* MERRIMAN.]

LADY B. Gwendolen! What does this mean?

GWEN. Merely that I am engaged to be married to Mr. Worthing, mamma.

LADY B. Come here. Sit down. Sit down immediately. Hesitation of any kind is a sign of mental decay in the young, of physical weakness in the old. [*Turns to* JACK.] Apprised, sir, of my daughter's sudden flight by her trusty maid, whose confidence I purchased by means of a small coin, I followed her at once by a luggage train. Her unhappy father is, I am glad to say, under the impression that she is attending a more than usually lengthy lecture by the University Extension Scheme on the Influence of a permanent income on Thought. I do not propose to undeceive him. Indeed I have never undeceived him on any question. I would consider it wrong. But of course, you will clearly understand that all communication between yourself and my daughter must cease immediately from this moment. On this point, as indeed on all points, I am firm.

JACK. I am engaged to be married to Gwendolen, Lady Bracknell!

LADY B. You are nothing of the kind, sir. And now as regards Algernon! . . . Algernon!

ALGER. Yes, Aunt Augusta.

LADY B. May I ask if it is in this house that your invalid friend Mr. Bunbury resides?

ALGER. [*Stammering.*] Oh! No! Bunbury doesn't live here. Bunbury is somewhere else at present. In fact, Bunbury is dead.

LADY B. Dead! When did Mr. Bunbury die? His death must have been extremely sudden.

ALGER. [*Airily.*] Oh! I killed Bunbury this afternoon. I mean poor Bunbury died this afternoon.

LADY B. What did he die of?

ALGER. Bunbury? Oh, he was quite exploded.

LADY B. Exploded! Was he the victim of a revolutionary outrage? I was not aware that Mr. Bunbury was interested in social legislation. If so, he is well punished for his morbidity.

ALGER. My dear Aunt Augusta, I mean he was found out! The doctors found out that Bunbury could not live, that is what I mean—so Bunbury died.

LADY B. He seems to have had great confidence in the opinion of his physicians. I am glad, however, that he made up his mind at the last to some definite course of action, and acted under proper medical advice. And now that we have finally got rid of this Mr. Bunbury, may I ask, Mr. Worthing, who is that young person whose hand my nephew Algernon is now holding in what seems to me a peculiarly unnecessary manner?

JACK. That lady is Miss Cecily Cardew, my ward. [LADY BRACKNELL *bows coldly to* CECILY.]

ALGER. I am engaged to be married to Cecily, Aunt Augusta.

LADY B. I beg your pardon?

CEC. Mr. Moncrieff and I are engaged to be married, Lady Bracknell.

LADY B. [*With a shiver, crossing to the sofa and sitting down.*] I do not know whether there is anything peculiarly exciting in the air of this particular part of Hertfordshire, but the number of engagements that go on seems to me considerably above the proper average that statistics have laid down for our guidance. I think some preliminary inquiry on my part would not be out of place. Mr. Worthing, is Miss Cardew at all connected with any of the larger railway stations in London? I merely desire information. Until yesterday I had no idea that there were any families or persons whose origin was a Terminus. [JACK *looks perfectly furious, but restrains himself.*]

JACK. [*In a cold, clear voice.*] Miss Cardew is the granddaughter of the late Mr. Thomas Cardew of 149 Belgrave Square, S.W.; Gervase Park, Dorking, Surrey; and the Sporran, Fifeshire, N.B.

LADY B. That sounds not unsatisfactory. Three addresses always inspire confidence, even in tradesmen. But what proof have I of their authenticity?

JACK. I have carefully preserved the Court Guides of the period. They are open to your inspection, Lady Bracknell.

LADY B. [*Grimly.*] I have known strange errors in that publication.

JACK. Miss Cardew's family solicitors are Messrs. Markby, Markby, and Markby.

LADY B. Markby, Markby, and Markby? A firm of the very highest position in their profession. Indeed I am told that one of the Mr. Markbys is occasionally to be seen at dinner parties. So far I am satisfied.

JACK [*Very irritably.*] How extremely kind of you, Lady Bracknell! I have also in my possession, you will be pleased to hear, certificates of Miss Cardew's birth, baptism, whooping cough, registration, vaccination, confirmation, and the measles; both the German and the English variety.

LADY B. Ah! A life crowded with incident, I see; though perhaps somewhat too exciting for a young girl. I am not myself in favour of premature experiences. [*Rises, looks at her watch.*] Gwendolen! the time approaches for our departure. We have not a moment to lose. As a matter of form, Mr. Worthing, I had better ask you if Miss Cardew has any little fortune?

JACK. Oh! about a hundred and thirty thousand pounds in the Funds. That is all. Good-bye, Lady Bracknell. So pleased to have seen you.

LADY B. [*Sitting down again.*] A moment, Mr. Worthing. A hundred and thirty thousand pounds! And in the Funds! Miss Cardew seems to me a most attractive young lady, now that I look at her. Few girls of the present day have any really solid qualities, any of the qualities that last, and improve with time. We live, I regret to say, in an age of surfaces. [*to* CECILY] Come over here, dear. [*CECILY goes across.*] Pretty child! your dress is sadly simple, and your hair seems almost as Nature might have left it. But we can soon alter all that. A thoroughly experienced French maid produces a really marvellous result in a very brief space of time. I remember recommending one to young Lady Lancing, and after three months her own husband did not know her.

JACK. And after six months nobody knew her.

LADY B. [*Glares at* JACK *for a few moments. Then bends, with a practised smile, to* CECILY.] Kindly turn round, sweet child. [CECILY *turns completely round.*] No, the side view is what I want. [CECILY *presents her profile.*] Yes, quite as I expected. There are distinct social possibilities in your profile. The two weak points in our age are its want of principle and its want of profile. The chin a little higher, dear. Style largely depends on the way the chin is worn. They are worn very high, just at present. Algernon!

ALGER. Yes, Aunt Augusta!

LADY B. There are distinct social possibilities in Miss Cardew's profile.

ALGER. Cecily is the sweetest, dearest, prettiest girl in the whole world. And I don't care twopence about social possibilities.

LADY B. Never speak disrespectfully of Society, Algernon. Only people who can't get into it do that. [*to* CECILY] Dear child, of course you know that Algernon has nothing but his debts to depend upon. But I do not approve of mercenary marriages. When I married Lord Bracknell I had no fortune of any kind. But I never dreamed for a moment of allowing that to stand in my way. Well, I suppose I must give my consent.

ALGER. Thank you, Aunt Augusta.

LADY B. Cecily, you may kiss me!

CEC. [*Kisses her.*] Thank you, Lady Bracknell.

LADY B. You may also address me as Aunt Augusta for the future.

CEC. Thank you, Aunt Augusta.

LADY B. The marriage, I think, had better take place quite soon.

ALGER. Thank you, Aunt Augusta.

CEC. Thank you, Aunt Augusta.

LADY B. To speak frankly, I am not in favour of long engagements. They give people the opportunity of finding out each other's character before marriage, which I think is never advisable.

JACK. I beg your pardon for interrupting you, Lady Bracknell, but this engagement is quite out of the question. I am Miss Cardew's guardian, and she cannot marry without my consent until she comes of age. That consent I absolutely decline to give.

LADY B. Upon what grounds, may I ask? Algernon is an extremely, I may almost say an ostentatiously, eligible young man. He has nothing, but he looks everything. What more can one desire?

JACK. It pains me very much to have to speak frankly to you, Lady Bracknell, about your nephew, but the fact is that I do not approve at all of his moral character. I suspect him of being untruthful. [ALGERNON *and* CECILY *look at him in indignant amazement.*]

LADY B. Untruthful! My nephew Algernon? Impossible! He is an Oxonian.

JACK. I fear there can be no possible doubt about the matter. This afternoon during my temporary absence in London on an important question of romance, he obtained admission to my house by means of the false pretence of being my brother. Under an assumed name he drank, I've just been informed by my butler, an entire pint bottle of my Perrier-Jouet, Brut, '89, wine I was specially reserving for myself. Continuing his disgraceful deception, he succeeded in the course of the afternoon in alienating the affections of my only ward. He subsequently stayed to tea, and devoured every single muffin. And what makes his conduct all the more heartless is, that he was perfectly well aware from the first that I have no brother, that I never had a brother, and that I don't intend to have a brother, not even of any kind. I distinctly told him so myself yesterday afternoon.

LADY B. Ahem! Mr. Worthing, after careful consideration I have decided entirely to overlook my nephew's conduct to you.

JACK. That is very generous of you, Lady Bracknell. My own decision, however, is unalterable. I decline to give my consent.

LADY B. [*to* CECILY] Come here, sweet child. [CECILY *goes over.*] How old are you, dear?

CEC. Well, I am really only eighteen, but I always admit to twenty when I go to evening parties.

LADY B. You are perfectly right in making some slight alteration. Indeed, no woman should ever be quite accurate about her age. It looks so calculating. . . . [*In a meditative manner.*] Eighteen, but admitting to twenty at evening parties. Well, it will not be very long before you are of age and free from the restraints of tutelage. So I don't think your guardian's consent is, after all, a matter of any importance.

JACK. Pray excuse me, Lady Bracknell, for interrupting you again, but it is only fair to tell you that according to the terms of her grandfather's will Miss Cardew does not come legally of age till she is thirty-five.

LADY B. That does not seem to me to be a grave objection. Thirty-five is a very attractive age. London society is full of women of the very highest birth who have, of their own free choice, remained thirty-five for years. Lady Dumbleton is an instance in point. To my own knowledge she has been thirty-five ever since she arrived at the age of forty, which was many years ago now. I see no reason why our dear Cecily should not be even still more attractive at the age you mention than she is at present. There will be a large accumulation of property.

CEC. Algy, could you wait for me till I was thirty-five?

ALGER. Of course I could, Cecily. You know I could.

CEC. Yes, I felt instinctively, but I couldn't wait all that time. I hate waiting even five minutes for anybody. It always makes me rather cross. I am not punctual myself, I know, but I do like punctuality in others, and waiting, even to be married, is quite out of the question.

ALGER. Then what is to be done, Cecily?

CEC. I don't know, Mr. Moncrieff.

LADY B. My dear Mr. Worthing, as Miss Cardew states positively that she cannot wait till she is thirty-five—a remark which I am bound to say seems to me to show a somewhat impatient nature—I would beg of you to reconsider your decision.

JACK. But my dear Lady Bracknell, the matter is entirely in your own hands. The moment you consent to my marriage with Gwendolen, I will most gladly allow your nephew to form an alliance with my ward.

LADY B. [*Rising and drawing herself up.*] You must be quite aware that what you propose is out of the question.

JACK. Then a passionate celibacy is all that any of us can look forward to.

LADY B. That is not the destiny I propose for Gwendolen. Algernon, of course, can choose for himself. [*Pulls out her watch.*] Come, dear [GWENDOLEN *rises*], we have already missed five, if not six, trains. To miss any more might expose us to comment on the platform.

[*Enter* DR. CHASUBLE.]

CHAS. Everything is quite ready for the christenings.

LADY B. The christenings, sir! Is not that somewhat premature?

CHAS. [*Looking rather puzzled, and pointing to* JACK *and* ALGERNON.] Both these gentlemen have expressed a desire for immediate baptism.

LADY B. At their age? The idea is grotesque and irreligious! Algernon, I forbid you to be baptized. I will not hear of such excesses. Lord Bracknell would be highly displeased if he learned that that was the way in which you wasted your time and money.

CHAS. Am I to understand then that there are to be no christenings at all this afternoon?

JACK. I don't think that, as things are now, it would be of much practical value to either of us, Dr. Chasuble.

CHAS. I am grieved to hear such sentiments from you, Mr. Worthing. They savour of the heretical views of the Anabaptists, views that I have completely refuted in four of my unpublished sermons. However, as your present mood seems to be one peculiarly secular, I will return to the church at once. Indeed, I have just been informed by the pew-opener that for the last hour and a half Miss Prism has been waiting for me in the vestry.

LADY B. [*Starting.*] Miss Prism! Did I hear you mention a Miss Prism?

CHAS. Yes, Lady Bracknell. I am on my way to join her.

LADY B. Pray allow me to detain you for a moment. This matter may prove to be one of vital importance to Lord Bracknell and myself. Is this Miss Prism a female of repellent aspect, remotely connected with education?

CHAS. [*Somewhat indignantly.*] She is the most cultivated of ladies, and the very picture of respectability.

LADY B. It is obviously the same person. May I ask what position she holds in your household?

CHAS. [*Severely.*] I am a celibate, madam.

JACK [*Interposing.*] Miss Prism, Lady Bracknell, has been for the last three years Miss Cardew's esteemed governess and valued companion.

LADY B. In spite of what I hear of her, I must see her at once. Let her be sent for.

CHAS. [*Looking off.*] She approaches; she is nigh.

[*Enter* MISS PRISM *hurriedly.*]

MISS P. I was told you expected me in the vestry, dear Canon. I have been waiting for you there for an hour and three-quarters. [*Catches sight of* LADY BRACKNELL, *who has fixed her with a stony glare.* MISS PRISM *grows pale and quails. She looks anxiously round as if desirous to escape.*]

LADY B. [*In a severe, judicial voice.*] Prism! [MISS PRISM *bows her head in shame.*] Come here, Prism! [MISS PRISM *approaches in a humble manner.*] Prism! Where is that baby? [*General consternation. The Canon starts back in horror.* ALGERNON *and* JACK *pretend to be anxious to shield* CECILY *and* GWENDOLEN *from hearing the details of a terrible scandal.*] Twenty-eight years ago, Prism, you left Lord Bracknell's house, Number 104, Upper Grosvenor Square, in charge of a perambulator that contained a baby of the male sex. You never returned. A few weeks later, through the elaborate investigations of the Metropolitan police, the perambulator was discovered at midnight standing by itself in a remote corner of Bayswater. It contained the manuscript of a three-volume novel of more than usually revolting sentimentality. [MISS PRISM *starts in involuntary indignation.*] But the baby was not there. [*Every one looks at* MISS PRISM.] Prism! Where is that baby? [*A pause.*]

MISS P. Lady Bracknell, I admit with shame that I do not know. I only wish I did. The plain facts of the case are these. On the morning of the day you mention, a day that is for ever branded on my memory, I prepared as usual to take the baby out in its perambulator. I had also with me a somewhat old, but capacious hand-bag in which I had intended to place the manuscript of a work of fiction that I had written during my few unoccupied hours. In a moment of mental abstraction, for which I can never forgive myself, I deposited the manuscript in the bassinette and placed the baby in the hand-bag.

JACK. [*Who has been listening attentively.*] But where did you deposit the hand-bag?

MISS PRISM. Do not ask me, Mr. Worthing.

JACK. Miss Prism, this is a matter of no small importance to me. I insist on knowing where you deposited the hand-bag that contained that infant.

MISS P. I left it in the cloak-room of one of the larger railway stations in London.

JACK. What railway station?

MISS P. [*Quite crushed.*] Victoria. The Brighton line. [*Sinks into a chair.*]

JACK. I must retire to my room for a moment. Gwendolen, wait here for me.

GWEN. If you are not too long, I will wait here for you all my life. [*Exit* JACK *in great excitement.*]

CHAS. What do you think this means, Lady Bracknell?

LADY B. I dare not even suspect, Dr. Chasuble. I need hardly tell you that in families of high position strange coincidences are not supposed to occur. They are hardly considered the thing.

[*Noises heard overhead as if some one was throwing trunks about. Every one looks up.*]

CEC. Uncle Jack seems strangely agitated.

CHAS. Your guardian has a very emotional nature.

LADY B. This noise is extremely unpleasant. It sounds as if he was having an argument. I dislike arguments of any kind. They are always vulgar, and often convincing.

CHAS. [*Looking up.*] It has stopped now. [*The noise is redoubled.*]

LADY B. I wish he would arrive at some conclusion.

GWEN. This suspense is terrible. I hope it will last.

[*Enter* JACK *with a hand-bag of black leather in his hand.*]

JACK [*Rushing over to* MISS PRISM.] Is this the hand-bag, Miss Prism? Examine it carefully before you speak. The happiness of more than one life depends on your answer.

MISS P. [*Calmly.*] It seems to be mine. Yes, here is the injury it received through the upsetting of a Gower Street omnibus in younger and happier days. Here is the stain on the lining caused by the explosion of a temperance beverage, an incident that occurred at Leamington. And here, on the lock, are my initials. I had forgotten that in an extravagant mood I had had them placed there. The bag is undoubtedly mine. I am delighted to have it so unexpectedly restored to me. It has been a great inconvenience being without it all these years.

JACK. [*In a pathetic voice.*] Miss Prism, more is restored to you than this hand-bag. I was the baby you placed in it.

MISS P. [*Amazed.*] You?

JACK. [*Embracing her.*] Yes . . . mother!

MISS P. [*Recoiling in indignant astonishment.*] Mr. Worthing. I am unmarried!

JACK. Unmarried! I do not deny that is a serious blow. But after all, who has the right to cast a stone against one who has suffered? Cannot repentance wipe out an act of folly? Why should there be one law for men, and another for women? Mother, I forgive you. [*Tries to embrace her again.*]

MISS P. [*Still more indignant.*] Mr. Worthing, there is some error. [*Pointing to* LADY BRACKNELL.] There is the lady who can tell you who you really are.

JACK. [*After a pause.*] Lady Bracknell, I hate to seem inquisitive, but would you kindly inform me who I am?

LADY B. I am afraid that the news I have to give you will not altogether please you. You are the son of my poor sister, Mrs. Moncrieff, and consequently Algernon's elder brother.

JACK. Algy's elder brother! Then I have a brother after all. I knew I had a brother! I always said I had a brother! Cecily—how could you have ever doubted that I had a brother? [*Seizes hold of* ALGERNON.] Dr. Chasuble, my unfortunate brother. Miss Prism, my unfortunate brother. Gwendolen, my unfortunate brother. Algy, you young scoundrel, you will have to treat me with more respect in the future. You have never behaved to me like a brother in all your life.

ALGER. Well, not till to-day, old boy, I admit. I did my best, however, though I was out of practice.

[*Shakes hands.*]

GWEN. [*to* JACK] My own! But what own are you? What is your Christian name, now that you have become some one else?

JACK. Good heavens! . . . I had quite forgotten that point. Your decision on the subject of my name is irrevocable, I suppose?

GWEN. I never change, except in my affections.

CEC. What a noble nature you have, Gwendolen!

JACK. Then the question had better be cleared up at once. Aunt Augusta, a moment. At the time when Miss Prism left me in the hand-bag, had I been christened already?

LADY B. Every luxury that money could buy, including christening, had been lavished on you by your fond and doting parents.

JACK. Then I was christened! That is settled. Now, what name was I given? Let me know the worst.

LADY B. Being the eldest son you were naturally christened after your father.

JACK. [*Irritably.*] Yes, but what was my father's Christian name?

LADY B. [*Meditatively.*] I cannot at the present moment recall what the General's Christian name was. But I have no doubt he had one. He was eccentric, I admit. But only in later years. And that was the result of the Indian climate, and marriage, and indigestion, and other things of that kind.

JACK. Algy! Can't you recollect what our father's Christian name was?

ALGER. My dear boy, we were never even on speaking terms. He died before I was a year old.

JACK. His name would appear in the Army Lists of the period, I suppose, Aunt Augusta?

LADY B. The General was essentially a man of peace, except in his domestic life. But I have no doubt his name would appear in any military directory.

JACK. The Army Lists of the last forty years are here. These delightful records should have been my constant study. [*Rushes to bookcase and tears the books out.*] M. Generals . . . Mallam, Maxbohm, Magley—what ghastly names they have—Markby, Migsby, Mobbs, Moncrieff! Lieutenant 1840, Captain, Lieutenant-Colonel, Colonel, General 1869, Christian names, Ernest John. [*Puts book very quietly down and speaks quite calmly.*] I always told you, Gwendolen, my name was Ernest, didn't I? Well, it is Ernest after all. I mean it naturally is Ernest.

LADY B. Yes, I remember now that the General was called Ernest. I knew I had some particular reason for disliking the name.

GWEN. Ernest! My own Ernest! I felt from the first that you could have no other name!

JACK. Gwendolen, it is a terrible thing for a man to find out suddenly that all his life he has been speaking nothing but the truth. Can you forgive me?

GWEN. I can. For I feel that you are sure to change.

JACK. My own one!

CHAS. [*to* MISS PRISM] Laetitia! [*Embraces her.*]

MISS P. [*Enthusiastically.*] Frederick! At last!

ALGER. Cecily! [*Embraces her.*] At last!

JACK. Gwendolen! [*Embraces her.*] At last!

LADY B. My nephew, you seem to be displaying signs of triviality.

JACK. On the contrary, Aunt Augusta, I've now realized for the first time in my life the vital Importance of Being Earnest.

TABLEAU

CURTAIN

Christopher Fry # A Phoenix Too Frequent

There has been a notable revival of poetic drama in the twentieth century. Many of our most distinguished poets—Yeats and Eliot, Cummings, Auden and Mac-Leish—have contributed to this movement. Among the genuine poetic dramatists who have appeared, no name is brighter than that of Christopher Fry, whose jeweled pieces have been the delight of two continents.

Born in 1907, Fry served in a number of capacities—schoolteacher, actor, director of a repertory theatre, and member of a Pioneer Corps (as a Quaker, he refused to bear arms) cleaning up bomb damage in London—while he developed his skills as poetic dramatist. Looking back over his brilliant success in the theatre—his first published play was *The Boy with a Cart* (1936) and he first achieved fame with *The Lady's Not for Burning* (1949); in 1950, he had four plays running concurrently in London—one can divide his career into three main segments: one group of plays is religious; in addition to *The Boy with a Cart*, there are *The Firstborn*, a tragedy (1947), *Thor, with Angels* (1948), and the imaginative, provocative *A Sleep of Prisoners* (1951). Fry is also a remarkable translator from the French; his touch has provided just the right rendition for two plays by Anouilh, *Ring Round the Moon* and *The Lark*, and one by Giraudoux, *Tiger at the Gates*. But his major work has been in comedy; after *The Lady's Not for Burning*, which

starred Sir John Gielgud and Pamela Brown, he wrote *Venus Observed* (1950) for Sir Laurence Olivier. His most recent plays are *The Dark Is Light Enough* and *Curtmantle* (1961).

A Phoenix Too Frequent is one of his most charming and typical plays. It was first produced at the Mercury Theatre, London, in April, 1946, and was revived in November of that year at the Arts Theatre. Like others of his works, it is set in the past. But its most distinctive characteristic is the magnificent language, particularly the dazzling metaphors. It also incorporates Fry's comic vision, which he once (in the *Adelphi* magazine for November, 1950) set forth in prose: "Comedy is an escape, not from truth but from despair: a narrow escape into faith. It believes in a universal cause for delight, even though knowledge of the cause is always twitched away from under us. . . . Somehow the characters have . . . to affirm life and assimilate death and persevere in joy . . . not by a vulnerable optimism but by a hard-won maturity of delight." To Fry, "Life itself is the real and most miraculous miracle of all," and this celebration of life fills his comedies.

The text of the play was first published by Hollis & Carter; it was reissued by the Oxford University Press (N.Y. and London) in 1949 and has been reprinted many times.

CHARACTERS

DYNAMENE   DOTO   TEGEUS-CHROMIS

SCENE—*The tomb of Virilius, near Ephesus ; night.*
NOTE—*The story was got from Jeremy Taylor[1]*
who had it from Petronius.

"To whom conferr'd a peacock's undecent,
A squirrel's harsh, a phoenix too frequent."
Robert Burton quoting Martial

[1] Jeremy Taylor (1613-1667) was a churchman and writer. A chaplain to Charles I, he was taken prisoner during the Civil War. After the Restoration, he was made a Bishop. His literary reputation rests largely upon his simple but splendid style best illustrated in his *Holy Living* and *Holy Dying* (1650-1651). In the latter work, to illustrate the evil of excessive passion, Taylor

retold the story from Petronius (cf. Section II). Taylor's point was that "stormy passions do so spend the whole stock of grief, that they presently admit a comfort and contrary affection." His lesson: "When thou hast wept awhile, compose the body to burial; . . . that it [can] be done gravely, decently, and charitably, we have the example of all nations. . . ."

[*An underground tomb, in darkness except for the very low light of an oil-lamp. Above ground the starlight shows a line of trees on which hang the bodies of several men. It also penetrates a gate and falls on to the first of the steps which descend into the darkness of the tomb.* DOTO *talks to herself in the dark.*]

DOTO. Nothing but the harmless day gone into black

Is all the dark is. And so what's my trouble?
Demons is so much wind. Are so much wind.
I've plenty to fill my thoughts. All that I ask
Is don't keep turning men over in my mind,
Venerable Aphrodite. I've had my last one
And thank you. I thank thee. He smelt of sour grass
And was likeable. He collected ebony quoits.

[*An owl hoots near at hand.*]

O Zeus! O some god or other, where is the oil?
Fire's from Prometheus. I thank thee. If I   10
Mean to die I'd better see what I'm doing.

[*She fills the lamp with oil. The flame burns up brightly and shows* DYNAMENE, *beautiful and young, leaning asleep beside a bier.*]

Honestly, I would rather have to sleep
With a bald bee-keeper who was wearing his boots
Than spend more days fasting and thirsting and crying
In a tomb. I shouldn't have said that. Pretend
I didn't hear myself. But life and death
Is cat and dog in this double-bed of a world.
My master, my poor master, was a man
Whose nose was as straight as a little buttress,
And now he has taken it into Elysium   20
Where it won't be noticed among all the other straightness.

[*The owl cries again and wakens* DYNAMENE.]

Oh, them owls. Those owls. It's woken her.

DYNAMENE. Ah! I'm breathless. I caught up with the ship
But it spread its wings, creaking a cry of *Dew,
Dew!* and flew figurehead foremost into the sun.

DOTO. How crazy, madam.

DYN.   Doto, draw back the curtains.
I'll take my barley-water.

DOTO.   We're not at home
Now, madam. It's the master's tomb.

DYN.   Of course!
Oh, I'm wretched. Already I have disfigured   29
My vigil. My cynical eyelids have soon dropped me
In a dream.

DOTO.   But then it's possible, madam, you might

Find yourself in bed with him again
In a dream, madam. Was he on the ship?

DYN. He was the ship.

DOTO.   Oh. That makes it different.

DYN. He was the ship. He had such a deck, Doto,
Such a white, scrubbed deck. Such a stern prow,
Such a proud stern, so slim from port to starboard.
If ever you meet a man with such fine masts
Give your life to him, Doto. The figurehead
Bore his own features, so serene in the brow   40
And hung with a little seaweed. O Virilius,
My husband, you have left a wake in my soul.
You cut the glassy water with a diamond keel.
I must cry again.

DOTO.   What, when you mean to join him?
Don't you believe he will be glad to see you, madam?
Thankful to see you, I should imagine, among
Them shapes and shades; all shapes of shapes and all
Shades of shades, from what I've heard. I know
I shall feel odd at first with Cerberus,
Sop or no sop. Still, I know how you feel, madam.
You think he may find a temptation in Hades   51
I shouldn't worry. It would help him to settle down.

[DYNAMENE *weeps.*]

It would only be *fun*, madam. He couldn't go far
With a shade.

DYN.   He was one of the coming men.
He was certain to have become the most well-organized provost
The town has known, once they had made him provost.
He was so punctual, you could regulate
The sun by him. He made the world succumb
To his daily revolution of habit. But who,
In the world he has gone to, will appreciate that?
O poor Virilius! To be a coming man   61
Already gone—it must be distraction.
Why did you leave me walking about our ambitions
Like a cat in the ruins of a house? Promising husband,
Why did you insult me by dying? Virilius,
Now I keep no flower, except in the vase
Of the tomb.

DOTO.   O poor madam! O poor master!
I presume so far as to cry somewhat for myself
As well. I know you won't mind, madam. It's two
Days not eating makes me think of my uncle's   70
Shop in the country, where he has a hardware business,
Basins, pots, ewers, and alabaster birds.
He makes you die of laughing. O madam,
Isn't it sad?

CRY

[*They both weep.*]

DYN.   How could I have allowed you
To come and die of my grief? Doto, it puts
A terrible responsibility on me. Have you
No grief of your own you could die of?
    DOTO.   Not really,
    madam.
    DYN. Nothing?
    DOTO.   Not really. They was all one to me.
Well, all but two was all one to me. And they,
Strange enough, was two who kept recurring.   80
I could never be sure if they had gone for good
Or not; and so that kept things cheerful, madam.
One always gave a wink before he deserted me,
The other slapped me as it were behind, madam;
Then they would be away for some months.
    DYN.   Oh Doto,
What an unhappy life you were having to lead.
    DOTO. Yes, I'm sure. But never mind, madam,
It seemed quite lively then. And now I know
It's what you say; life is more big than a bed
And full of miracles and mysteries like   90
One man made for one woman, etcetera, etcetera.
Lovely. I feel sung, madam, by a baritone
In mixed company with everyone pleased.
And so I had to come with you here, madam,
For the last sad chorus of me. It's all
Fresh to me. Death's a new interest in life,
If it doesn't disturb you, madam, to have me
    crying.
It's because of us not having breakfast again.
And the master, of course. And the beautiful world.
And you crying too, madam. Oh—Oh!   100
    DYN. I can't forbid your crying; but you must cry
On the other side of the tomb. I'm becoming con-
    fused.

Rise
walk
center
stage

This is my personal grief and my sacrifice
Of self, solus. Right over there, darling girl.
    DOTO. What here?
    DYN.   Now, if you wish, you may
    cry, Doto.
But our tears are very different. For me
The world is all with Charon, all, all,
Even the metal and plume of the rose garden,
And the forest where the sea fumes overhead
In vegetable tides, and particularly   110

walk
upstage

The entrance to the warm baths in Arcite Street
Where we first met;—all!—the sun itself
Trails an evening hand in the sultry river

to
coffin

Far away down by Acheron. I am lonely,
Virilius. Where is the punctual eye

sit

And where is the cautious voice which made
Balance-sheets sound like Homer and Homer
    sound

Like balance-sheets? The precision of limbs, the
    amiable
Laugh, the exact festivity? Gone from the world.
You were the peroration of nature, Virilius.   120
You explained everything to me, even the ex-
    tremely
Complicated gods. You wrote them down
In seventy columns. Dear curling calligraphy!
Gone from the world, once and for all. And I taught
    you

Rise

In your perceptive moments to appreciate me.

move @ circular move

You said I was harmonious, Virilius,
Moulded and harmonious, little matronal
Ox-eye, your package. And then I would walk

nov coffin

Up and down largely, as it were making my own
Sunlight. What a mad blacksmith creation is   130

more pt.

Who blows his furnaces until the stars fly upward
And iron Time is hot and politicians glow
And bulbs and roots sizzle into hyacinth
And orchis, and the sand puts out the lion,
Roaring yellow, and oceans bud with porpoises,
Blenny, tunny and the almost unexisting
Blindfish; throats are cut, the masterpiece
Looms out of labour; nations and rebellions

down plyn

Are spat out to hang on the wind—and all is gone
In one Virilius, wearing his office tunic,   140
Checking the pence column as he went.
Where's animation now? What is there that
    stays
To dance? The eye of the one-eyed world is out.

Kneel @ coffin

    [*She weeps.*]
    DOTO. I shall try to grieve a little, too.
It would take lessons, I imagine, to do it out loud
For long. If I could only remember
Any one of those fellows without wanting to laugh.
Hopeless, I am. Now those good pair of shoes
I gave away without thinking, that's a different—
Well, I've cried enough about *them*, I suppose   150
Poor madam, poor master.
[*TEGEUS comes through the gate to the top of the steps.*]
    TEGEUS.   What's your trouble?
    DOTO.   Oh!
Oh! Oh, a man. I thought for a moment it was
    something
With harm in it. Trust a man to be where it's dark.
What is it? Can't you sleep?
    TEG.   Now, listen—
    DOTO.   Hush!
Remember you're in the grave. You must go away.
Madam is occupied.
    TEG.   What, here?
    DOTO.   Becoming
Dead. We both are.
    TEG.   What's going on here?

DOTO.   Grief.
Are you satisfied now?
TEG.   Less and less. Do you know
What the time is?
DOTO.   I'm not interested.
We've done with all that. Go away. Be a gentle-
    man.   160
If we can't be free of men in a grave
Death's a dead loss.
TEG.   It's two in the morning. All
I ask is what are women doing down here
At two in the morning?
DOTO.   Can't you see she's crying?
Or is she sleeping again? Either way
She's making arrangements to join her husband.
TEG.   Where?
DOTO. Good god, in the Underworld, dear man.
Haven't you learnt
About life and death?
TEG.   In a manner, yes; in a
    manner;
The rudiments. So the lady means to die?
DOTO. For love; beautiful, curious madam.
TEG.   Not
    curious;   170
I've had thoughts like it. Death is a kind of love.
Not anything I can explain.
DOTO.   You'd better come in
And sit down.
TEG.   I'd be grateful.
DOTO.   Do. It will be my last
Chance to have company, in the flesh.
TEG.   Do you mean
You're going too?
DOTO.   Oh, certainly I am.
Not anything I can explain.
It all started with madam saying a man
Was two men really, and I'd only noticed one,
One each, I mean. It seems he has a soul
As well as his other troubles. And I like to know
What I'm getting with a man. I'm inquisitive, 181
I suppose you'd call me.
TEG.   It takes some courage.
DOTO.   Well, yes
And no. I'm fond of change.
TEG.   Would you object
To have me eating my supper here?
DOTO.   Be careful
Of the crumbs. We don't want a lot of squeaking
    mice
Just when we're dying.
TEG.   What a sigh she gave then.
Down the air like a slow comet.
And now she's all dark again. Mother of me.

How long has this been going on?
DOTO.   Two days.
It should have been three by now, but at first   190
Madam had difficulty with the Town Council.
    They said
They couldn't have a tomb used as a private
    residence.
But madam told them she wouldn't be eating here,
Only suffering, and they thought that would be all
    right.
TEG. Two of you. Marvellous. Who would have
    said
I should ever have stumbled on anything like this?
Do you have to cry? Yes, I suppose so. It's all
Quite reasonable.
DOTO.   Your supper and your knees.
That's what's making me cry. I can't bear sym-
    pathy
And they're sympathetic.
TEG.   Please eat a bit of some-
    thing.   200
I've no appetite left.
DOTO.   And see her go ahead of me?
Wrap it up; put it away. You sex of wicked beards!
It's no wonder you have to shave off your black
    souls
Every day as they push through your chins.
I'll turn my back on you. It means utter
Contempt. Eat? Utter contempt. Oh, little new
    rolls!
TEG. Forget it, forget it; please forget it. Remem-
    ber
I've had no experience of this kind of thing before.
Indeed I'm as sorry as I know how to be. Ssh,
We'll disturb her. She sighed again. O Zeus,   210
It's terrible! Asleep, and still sighing.
Mourning has made a warren in her spirit,
All that way below. Ponos! the heart
Is the devil of a medicine.
DOTO.   And I don't intend
To turn round.
TEG.   I understand how you must feel.
Would it be   have you any objection
To my having a drink? I have a little wine here.
And, you probably see how it is: grief's in order,
And death's in order, and women—I can usually
Manage that too; but not all three together   220
At this hour of the morning. So you'll excuse me.
How about you? It would make me more com-
    fortable
If you'd take a smell of it.
DOTO.   One for the road?
TEG. One for the road.
DOTO.   It's the dust in my throat.

The tomb
Is so dusty. Thanks, I will. There's no point in
dying
Of everything, simultaneous.
    TEG.   It's lucky
I brought two bowls. I was expecting to keep
A drain for my relief when he comes in the morning.
    DOTO. Are you on duty?
    TEG.   Yes.
    DOTO.   It looks like it.
    TEG.   Well,
Here's your good health.
    DOTO.   What good is that going
        to do me?   230
Here's to an easy crossing and not too much wait-
        ing
About on the bank. Do you have to tremble like
        that?
    TEG. The idea—I can't get used to it.
    DOTO.   For a
        member
Of the forces, you're peculiarly queasy. I wish
Those owls were in Hades—oh no; let them stay
        where they are.
Have you never had nothing to do with corpses
        before?
    TEG. I've got six of them outside.
    DOTO.   Morpheus,
        that's plenty.
What are they doing there?
    TEG. Hanging.
    DOTO.   Hanging?
    TEG.   On trees.
Five plane trees and a holly. The holly-berries
Are just reddening. Another drink?
    DOTO.   Why not?
    TEG. It's from Samos. Here's—   241
    DOTO.   All right. Let's
        just drink it.
—How did they get in that predicament?
    TEG. The sandy-haired fellow said we should
        collaborate
With everybody; the little man said he wouldn't
Collaborate with anybody; the old one
Said that the Pleiades weren't sisters but cousins
And anyway were manufactured in Lacedaemon.
The fourth said that we hanged men for nothing.
The other two said nothing. Now they hang
About at the corner of the night, they're present
And absent, horribly obsequious to every   251
Move in the air, and yet they keep me standing
For five hours at a stretch.
    DOTO.   The wine has gone
Down to my knees.

    TEG.   And up to your cheeks. You're
        looking
Fresher. If only—
    DOTO.   Madam? She never would.
Shall I ask her?
    TEG.   No; no, don't dare, don't breathe it.
This is privilege, to come so near
To what is undeceiving and uncorrupt
And undivided; this is the clear fashion
For all souls, a ribbon to bind the unruly   260
Curls of living, a faith, a hope, Zeus
Yes, a fine thing. I am human, and this
Is human fidelity, and we can be proud
And unphilosophical.
    DOTO.   I need to dance
But I haven't the use of my legs.
    TEG.   No, no, don't
        dance,
Or, at least, only inwards; don't dance; cry
Again. We'll put a moat of tears
Round her bastion of love, and save
The world. It's something, it's more than some-
        thing,
It's regeneration, to see how a human cheek   270
Can become as pale as a pool.
    DOTO.   Do you love me,
        handsome?
    TEG. To have found life, after all, unambiguous!
    DOTO. Did you say Yes?
    TEG.   Certainly; just now I
        love all men.
    DOTO. So do I.
    TEG.   And the world is a good creature
        again.
I'd begun to see it as mildew, verdigris,
Rust, woodrot, or as though the sky had uttered
An oval twirling blasphemy with occasional vistas
In country districts. I was within an ace
Of volunteering for overseas service. Despair
Abroad can always nurse pleasant thoughts of
        home.   280
Integrity, by god!
    DOTO.   I love all the world
And the movement of the apple in your throat.
So shall you kiss me? It would be better, I should
        think,
To go moistly to Hades.
    TEG.   Her's is the way,
Luminous with sorrow.
    DOTO.   Then I'll take
Another little swiggy. I love all men,
Everybody, even you, and I'll pick you
Some outrageous honeysuckle for your helmet,
If only it lived here. Pardon.

DYN.   Doto. Who is it?

DOTO. Honeysuckle, madam. Because of the bees.
Go back to sleep, madam.

DYN.   What person is it?   291

DOTO. Yes, I see what you mean, madam. It's a
    kind of
Corporal talking to his soul, on a five-hour shift,
Madam, with six bodies. He's been having his
    supper.

TEG. I'm going. It's terrible that we should have
    disturbed her.

DOTO. He was delighted to see you so sad,
    madam.
It has stopped him going abroad.

DYN.   One with six bodies?
A messenger, a guide to where we go.
It is possible he has come to show us the way
Out of these squalid suburbs of life, a shade,   300
A gorgon, who has come swimming up, against
The falls of my tears (for which in truth he would
    need
Many limbs) to guide me to Virilius.
I shall go quietly.

TEG.   I do assure you—
Such clumsiness, such a vile and unforgivable
Intrusion. I shall obliterate myself
Immediately.

DOTO.   Oblit—oh, what a pity
To oblit. Pardon. Don't let him, the nice fellow.

DYN. Sir: your other five bodies: where are they?

TEG.   Madam—
Outside; I have them outside. On trees.

DYN.   Quack!

TEG. What do I reply?   311

DYN.   Quack, charlatan!
You've never known the gods. You came to mock me.
Doto, this never was a gorgon, never.
Nor a gentleman either. He's completely spurious.
Admit it, you creature. Have you even a feather
Of the supernatural in your system? Have you?

TEG. Some of my relations—

DYN.   Well?

TEG.   Are dead, I think;
That is to say I have connexions—

DYN.   Connexions
With pickpockets. It's a shameless imposition.
Does the army provide you with no amusements?
If I were still of the world, and not cloistered   321
In a colourless landscape of winter thought
Where the approaching Spring is desired oblivion,
I should write sharply to your commanding officer.
It should be done, it should be done. If my fingers
Weren't so cold I would do it now. But they are,
Horribly cold. And why should insolence matter

When my colour of life is unreal, a blush on death,
A partial mere diaphane? I don't know
Why it should matter. Oafish, non-commissioned
Young man! The boots of your conscience   331
    will pinch for ever
If life's dignity has any self-protection.
Oh, I have to sit down. The tomb's going round.

DOTO. Oh, madam, don't give over. I can't
    remember
When things were so lively. He looks marvellously
Marvellously uncomfortable. Go on, madam.
Can't you, madam? Oh, madam, don't you feel
    up to it?
There, do you see her, you acorn-chewing
    infantryman?
You've made her cry, you square-bashing
    barbarian.

TEG. O history, my private history, why   340
Was I led here? What stigmatism has got
Into my stars? Why wasn't it my brother?
He has a tacit misunderstanding with everybody
And washes in it. Why wasn't it my mother?
She makes a collection of other people's tears
And dries them all. Let them forget I came;
And lie in the terrible black crystal of grief
Which held them, before I broke it. Outside,
    Tegeus.

DOTO. Hey, I don't think so, I shouldn't say so.
    Come
Down again, uniform. Do you think you're going
To half kill an unprotected lady and then   351
Back out upwards? Do you think you can leave her
    like this?

TEG. Yes, yes, I'll leave her. O directorate of gods,
How can I? Beauty's bit is between my teeth.
She has added another torture to me. Bottom
Of Hades' bottom.

DOTO.   Madam. Madam, the corporal
Has some wine here. It will revive you, madam.
And then you can go at him again, madam.

TEG. It's the opposite of everything you've said,
I swear, I swear by Horkos and the Styx,   360
I swear by the nine acres of Tityos,
I swear the Hypnotic oath, by all the Titans
By Koeos, Krios, Iapetos, Kronos, and so on—
By the three Hekatoncheires, by the insomnia
Of Tisiphone, by Jove, by jove, and the dew
On the feet of my boyhood, I am innocent
Of mocking you. Am I a Salmoneus
That, seeing such a flame of sorrow—

DYN.   You needn't
Labour to prove your secondary education.
Perhaps I jumped to a wrong conclusion, perhaps
I was hasty.   371

DOTO.   How easy to swear if you're properly educated.

Wasn't it pretty, madam? Pardon.

DYN.   If I misjudged you
I apologize, I apologize. Will you please leave us?
You were wrong to come here. In a place of mourning
Light itself is a trespasser; nothing can have
The right of entrance except those natural symbols
Of mortality, the jabbing, funeral, sleek-
With-omen raven, the death-watch beetle which mocks
Time: particularly, I'm afraid, the spider
Weaving his home with swift self-generated   380
Threads of slaughter; and, of course, the worm.
I wish it could be otherwise. Oh dear,
They aren't easy to live with.

DOTO.   Not even a *little* wine, madam?

DYN. Here, Doto?

DOTO.   Well, on the steps perhaps,
Except it's so draughty.

DYN.   Doto! Here?

DOTO   No, madam;
I quite see.

DYN.   I might be wise to strengthen myself
In order to fast again; it would make me abler
For grief. I will breathe a little of it, Doto.

DOTO. Thank god. Where's the bottle?

DYN.   What an exquisite bowl.

TEG. Now that it's peacetime we have pottery classes.   390

DYN. You made it yourself?

TEG.   Yes. Do you see the design?
The corded god, tied also by the rays
Of the sun, and the astonished ship erupting
Into vines and vine-leaves, inverted pyramids
Of grapes, the uplifted hands of the men (the raiders),
And here the headlong sea, itself almost
Venturing into leaves and tendrils, and Proteus
With his beard braiding the wind, and this
Held by other hands is a drowned sailor—

DYN. Always, always.

DOTO.   Hold the bowl steady, madam.   400
Pardon.

DYN. Doto, have you been drinking?

DOTO.   Here, madam?
I coaxed some a little way towards my mouth, madam,
But I scarcely swallowed except because I had to. The hiccup
Is from no breakfast, madam, and not meant to be funny.

DYN. You may drink this too. Oh, how the inveterate body,
Even when cut from the heart, insists on leaf,
Puts out, with a separate meaningless will,
Fronds to intercept the thankless sun.
How it does, oh, how it does. And how it confuses
The nature of the mind.

TEG.   Yes, yes, the confusion;   410
That's something I understand better than anything.

DYN. When the thoughts would die, the instincts will set sail
For life. And when the thoughts are alert for life
The instincts will rage to be destroyed on the rocks.
To Virilius it was not so; his brain was an ironing-board
For all crumpled indecision: and I follow him,
The hawser of my world. You don't belong here,
You see; you don't belong here at all.

TEG.   If only
I did. If only you knew the effort it costs me
To mount those steps again into an un-trustworthy,   420
Unpredictable, unenlightened night,
And turn my back on—on a state of affairs,
I can only call it a vision, a hope, a promise,
A—By that I mean loyalty, enduring passion,
Unrecking bravery and beauty all in one.

DOTO. He means you, or you and me; or me, madam.

TEG. It only remains for me to thank you, and to say
That whatever awaits me and for however long
I may be played by this poor musician, existence,
Your person and sacrifice will leave their trace   430
As clear upon me as the shape of the hills
Around my birthplace. Now I must leave you to your husband.

DOTO. Oh! You, madam.

DYN.   I'll tell you what I will do.
I will drink with you to the memory of my husband,
Because I have been curt, because you are kind,
And because I'm extremely thirsty. And then we will say
Good-bye and part to go to our opposite corruptions,
The world and the grave.

TEG.   The climax to the vision.

DYN. [*Drinking.*] My husband, and all he stood for.

TEG. Stands for.

DYN.   Stands for.

TEG. Your husband.

DOTO. The master.
DYN. How good it is, 440
How it sings to the throat, purling with summer.
TEG. It has a twin nature, winter and warmth in one,
Moon and meadow. Do you agree?
DYN. Perfectly;
A cold bell sounding in a golden month.
TEG. Crystal in harvest.
DYN. Perhaps a nightingale
Sobbing among the pears.
TEG. In an old autumnal midnight.
DOTO. Grapes.—Pardon. There's some more here.
TEG. Plenty.
I drink to the memory of your husband.
DYN. My husband.
DOTO. The master.
DYN. He was careless in his choice of wines.
TEG. And yet
Rendering to living its rightful poise is not 450
Unimportant.
DYN. A mystery's in the world
Where a little liquid, with flavour, quality, and fume
Can be as no other, can hint and flute our senses
As though a music played in harvest hollows
And a movement was in the swathes of our memory.
Why should scent, why should flavor come
With such wings upon us? Parsley, for instance.
TEG. Seaweed.
DYN. Lime trees.
DOTO. Horses.
TEG. Fruit in the fire.
DYN. Do I know your name?
TEG. Tegeus.
DYN. That's very thin for you,
It hardly covers your bones. Something quite different, 460
Altogether other, I shall think of it presently.
TEG. Darker vowels, perhaps.
DYN. Yes, certainly darker vowels.
And your consonants should have a slight angle,
And a certain temperature. Do you know what I mean?
It will come to me.
TEG. Now *your* name—
DYN. It is nothing
To any purpose. I'll be to you the She
In the tomb. You have the air of a natural-historian
As though you were accustomed to handling birds' eggs,

Or tadpoles, or putting labels on moths. You see?
The genius of dumb things, that they are nameless. 470
Have I found the seat of the weevil in human brains?
Our names. They make us broody; we sit and sit
To hatch them into reputation and dignity.
And then they set upon us and become despair,
Guilt and remorse. We go where they lead. We dance
Attendance on something wished upon us by the wife
Of our mother's physician. But insects meet and part
And put the woods about them, fill the dusk
And freckle the light and go and come without
A name among them, without the wish of a name 480
And very pleasant too. Did I interrupt you?
TEG. I forget. We'll have no names then.
DYN. I should like
You to have a name, I don't know why; a small one
To fill out the conversation.
TEG. I should like
You to have a name too, if only for something
To remember. Have you still some wine in your bowl?
DYN. Not altogether.
TEG. We haven't come to the end
By several inches. Did I splash you?
DYN. It doesn't matter.
Well, here's to my husband's name.
TEG. Your husband's name.
DOTO. The master.
DYN. It was kind of you to come. 490
TEG. It was more than coming. I followed my future here,
As we all do if we're sufficiently inattentive
And don't vex ourselves with questions; or do I mean
Attentive? If so, attentive to what? Do I sound Incoherent?
DYN. You're wrong. There isn't a future here,
Not here, not for you.
TEG. You name's Dynamene.
DYN. Who—Have I been utterly irreverent?
Are you—
Who made you say that? Forgive me the question,
But are you dark or light? I mean which shade
Of the supernatural? Or if neither, what prompted you? 500
TEG. Dynamene——
DYN. No, but I'm sure you're the friend of nature,

It must be so, I think I see little Phoebuses
Rising and setting in your eyes.

DOTO   They're not little Phoebuses,
They're hoodwinks, madam. Your name is on
    your brooch.
No little Phoebuses to-night.

DYN.   That's twice
You've played me a trick. Oh, I know practical
    jokes
Are common on Olympus, but haven't we at all
Developed since the gods were born? Are gods
And men both to remain immortal adolescents?
How tiresome it all is.

TEG.   It was you, each time,   510
Who said I was supernatural. When did I say so?
You're making me into whatever you imagine
And then you blame me because I can't live up
    to it.

DYN. I shall call you Chromis. It has a bread-
    like sound.
I think of you as a crisp loaf.

TEG.   And now
You'll insult me because I'm not sliceable.

DYN. I think drinking is harmful to our tempers.

TEG. If I seem to be frowning, that is only be-
    cause
I'm looking directly into your light: I must look
Angrily, or shut my eyes.

DYN.   Shut them.—Oh,   520
You have eyelashes! A new perspective of you.
Is that how you look when you sleep?

TEG.   My jaw drops down.

DYN. Show me how.

TEG.   Like this.

DYN.   It makes an irresistible
Moron of you. Will you waken now?
It's morning; I see a thin dust of daylight
Blowing on to the steps.

TEG.   Already? Dynamene,
You're tricked again. This time by the moon.

DYN.   Oh, well,
Moon's daylight, then. Doto is asleep.

TEG.   Doto
Is asleep . . .

DYN.   Chromis, what made you walk about
In the night? What, I wonder, made you not
    stay   530
Sleeping wherever you slept? Was it the friction
Of the world on your mind? Those two are
    difficult
To make agree. Chromis—now try to learn
To answer your name. I won't say Tegeus.

TEG.   And I
Won't say Dynamene.

DYN.   Not?

TEG.   It makes you real.
Forgive me, a terrible thing has happened. Shall I
Say it and perhaps destroy myself for you?
Forgive me first, or, more than that, forgive
Nature who winds her furtive stream all through
Our reason. Do you forgive me?

DYN.   I'll forgive   540
Anything, if it's the only way I can know
What you have to tell me.

TEG.   I felt us to be alone;
Here in a grave, separate from any life,
I and the only one of beauty, the only
Persuasive key to all my senses,
In spite of my having lain day after day
And pored upon the sepals, corolla, stamen, and
    bracts
Of the yellow bog-iris. Then my body ventured
A step towards interrupting your perfection of
    purpose
And my own renewed faith in human nature.
Would you have believed that possible?   551

DYN.   I have never
Been greatly moved by the yellow bog-iris. Alas,
It's as I said. This place is for none but the spider,
Raven and worms, not for a living man.

TEG. It has been a place of blessing to me. It
    will always
Play in me, a fountain of confidence
When the world is arid. But I know it is true
I have to leave it, and though it withers my soul
I must let you make your journey.

DYN.   No.

TEG.   Not true?

DYN. We can talk of something quite different.

TEG.   Yes, we can!
Oh yes, we will! Is it your opinion   561
That no one believes who hasn't learned to doubt?
Or, another thing, if we persuade ourselves
To one particular Persuasion, become Sophist,
Stoic, Platonist, anything whatever,
Would you say that there must be areas of soul
Lying unproductive therefore, or dishonoured
Or blind?

DYN.   No, I don't know.

TEG.   No. It's impossible
To tell. Dynamene, if only I had
Two cakes of pearl-barley and hydromel   570
I could see you to Hades, leave you with your
    husband
And come back to the world.

DYN.   Ambition, I suppose,
Is an appetite particular to man.
What is your definition?

TEG.   The desire to find
A reason for living.
    DYN.   But then, suppose it leads,
As often, one way or another, it does, to death.
    TEG. Then that may be life's reason. Oh, but how
Could I bear to return, Dynamene? The earth's
Daylight would be my grave if I had left you
In that unearthly night.
    DYN.   O Chromis——
    TEG.   Tell me,   580
What is your opinion of Progress? Does it, for
    example,
Exist? Is there ever progression without retrogres-
    sion?
Therefore is it not true that mankind
Can more justly be said increasingly to Gress?
As the material improves, the craftsmanship
    deteriorates
And honour and virtue remain the same. I love
    you,
Dynamene.
    DYN. Would you consider we go round and
    round?
    TEG. We concertina, I think; taking each time
A larger breath, so that the farther we go out
The farther we have to go in.
    DYN.   There'll come a time   590
When it will be unbearable to continue.
    TEG. Unbearable.
    DYN.   Perhaps we had better have something
To eat. The wine has made your eyes so quick
I am breathless beside them. It is
Your eyes, I think; or your intelligence
Holding my intelligence up above you
Between its hands. Or the cut of your uniform.
    TEG. Here's a new roll with honey. In the gods'
    names
Let's sober ourselves.
    DYN.   As soon as possible.
    TEG.   Have you
Any notion of algebra?
    DYN.   We'll discuss you, Chromis.   600
We will discuss you, till you're nothing but words
    TEG. I? There is nothing, of course, I would
    rather discuss,
Except—if it would be no intrusion—you,
    Dynamene.
    DYN. No, you couldn't want to. But your
    birthplace, Chromis,
With the hills that placed themselves in you for
    ever
As you say, where was it?
    TEG.   My father's farm at Pyxa.

    DYN. There? Could it be there?
    TEG.   I was born in the hills
Between showers, a quarter of an hour before
    milking time.
Do you know Pyxa? It stretches to the crossing
    of two
Troublesome roads, and buries its back in
    beechwood,   610
From which come the white owls of our nights
And the mulling and cradling of doves in the day.
I attribute my character to those shadows
And heavy roots; and my interest in music
To the sudden melodious escape of the young river
Where it breaks from nosing through the cresses
    and kingcups.
That's honestly so.
    DYN.   You used to climb about
Among the windfallen tower of Phrasidemus
Looking for bees' nests.
    TEG.   What? When have I
Said so?
    DYN. Why, all the children did.   620
    TEG. Yes: but, in the name of light, how do
    you *know* that?
    DYN. I played there once, on holiday.
    TEG.   O Klotho,
Lachesis and Atropos!
    DYN.   It's the strangest chance:
I may have seen, for a moment, your boyhood.
    TEG.   I may
Have seen something like an early flower
Something like a girl. If I only could remember
    how I must
Have seen you. Were you after the short white
    violets?
Maybe I blundered past you, taking your look,
And scarcely acknowledged how a star
Ran through me, to live in the brooks of my
    blood for ever.   630
Or I saw you playing at hiding in the cave
Where the ferns are and the water drips.
    DYN. I was quite plain and fat and I was
    usually
Hitting someone. I wish I could remember you.
I'm envious of the days and children who saw you
Then. It is curiously a little painful
Not to share your past.
    TEG.   How did it come
Our stars could mingle for an afternoon
So long ago, and then forget us or tease us
Or helplessly look on the dark high seas   640
Of our separation, while time drank
The golden hours? What hesitant fate is that?
    DYN. Time? Time? Why—how old are we?

TEG.   Young,
Thank both our mothers, but still we're older than
    to-night
And so older than we should be. Wasn't I born
In love with what, only now, I have grown to meet?
I'll tell you something else. I was born entirely
For this reason. I was born to fill a gap
In the world's experience, which had never known
Chromis loving Dynamene.
    DYN.   You are so   650
Excited, poor Chromis. What is it? Here you sit
With a woman who has wept away all claims
To appearance, unbecoming in her oldest clothes,
With not a trace of liveliness, a drab
Of melancholy, entirely shadow without
A smear of sun. Forgive me if I tell you
That you fall easily into superlatives.
    TEG. Very well. I'll say nothing, then. I'll fume
With feeling.
    DYN.   Now you go to the extreme. Certainly
You must speak. You may have more to say.
    Besides   660
You might let your silence run away with you
And not say something that you should. And how
Should I answer you then? Chromis, you boy,
I can't look away from you. You use
The lamplight and the moon so skilfully,
So arrestingly, in and around your furrows.
A humorous ploughman goes whistling to a team
Of sad sorrow, to and fro in your brow
And over your arable cheek. Laugh for me. Have
    you
Cried for women, ever?
    TEG.   In looking about for you.
But I have recognized them for what they were.
    DYN. What were they?   672
    TEG.   Never you: never,
    although
They could walk with bright distinction into all
    men's
Longest memories, never you, by a hint
Or a faint quality, or at least not more
Than reflectively, stars lost and uncertain
In the sea, compared with the shining salt, the
    shiners,
The galaxies, the clusters, the bright grain whirling
Over the black threshing-floor of space.
Will you make some effort to believe that?
    DYN.   No, no
    effort.   680
It lifts me and carries me. It may be wild
But it comes to me with a charm, like trust indeed,
And eats out of my heart, dear Chromis,
Absurd, disconcerting Chromis. You make me

Feel I wish I could look my best for you.
I wish, at least, that I could believe myself
To be showing some beauty for you, to put in the
    scales
Between us. But they dip to you, they sink
With masculine victory.
    TEG.   Eros, no! No!
If this is less than your best, then never, in my
    presence,   690
Be more than your less: never! If you should bring
More to your mouth or to your eyes, a moisture
Or a flake of light, anything, anything fatally
More, perfection would fetch her unsparing rod
Out of pickle to flay me, and what would have been
    love
Will be the end of me. O Dynamene,
Let me unload something of my lips' longing
On to yours receiving. Oh, when I cross
Like this the hurt of the little space between us
I come a journey from the wrenching ice   700
To walk in the sun. That is the feeling.
    DYN.   Chromis,
Where am I going? No, don't answer. It's death
I desire, not you. *move left*
    TEG.   Where is the difference? Call me
Death instead of Chromis. I'll answer to anything.
It's desire all the same, of death in me, or me
In death, but Chromis either way. Is it so?
Do you not love me, Dynamene?
    DYN.   How could it
    happen?
I'm going to my husband. I'm too far on the way
To admit myself to life again. Love's in Hades.
    TEG. Also here. And here are we, not there   710
In Hades. Is your husband expecting you?
    DYN. Surely, surely? *Look at coffin*
    TEG.   Not necessarily. I,
If I had been your husband, would never dream
Of expecting you. I should remember your body
Descending stairs in the floating light, but not
Descending in Hades. I should say "I have left
My wealth warm on the earth, and, hell, earth
    needs it."
"Was all I taught her of love," I should say, "so
    poor
That she will leave her flesh and become shadow?"
"Wasn't our love for each other" (I should
    continue)   720
"Infused with life, and life infused with our love?
Very well; repeat me in love, repeat me in life,
And let me sing in your blood for ever."
    DYN. Stop, stop, I shall be dragged apart! *center stage*
Why should the fates do everything to keep me
From dying honourably? They must have got

Tired of honour in Elysium. Chromis, it's terrible
To be susceptible to two conflicting norths.
I have the constitution of a whirlpool.
Am I actually twirling, or is it just sensation?   730
   TEG. You're still; still as the darkness.
   DYN.   What
    appears
Is so unlike what is. And what is madness
To those who only observe, is often wisdom
To those to whom it happens.
   TEG.   Are we compelled
To go into all this?
   DYN.   Why, how could I return
To my friends? Am I to be an entertainment?
   TEG. That's for to-morrow. To-night I need to
    kiss you,
Dynamene. Let's see what the whirlpool does
Between my arms; let it whirl on my breast. O
    love,
Come in.
DYN.   I am there before I reach you; my body
Only follows to join my longing which   741
Is holding you already.—Now I am
All one again.
   TEG.   I feel as the gods feel:
This is their sensation of life, not a man's.
Their suspension of immortality, to enrich
Themselves with time. O life, O death, O body,
O spirit, O Dynamene.
   DYN.   O all
In myself; it so covets all in you,
My care, my Chromis. Then I shall be
Creation.
   TEG.   You have the skies already;   750
Out of them you are buffeting me with your gales
Of beauty. Can we be made of dust, as they tell us?
What! dust with dust releasing such a light
And such an apparition of the world
Within one body? A thread of your hair has stung
    me.
Why do you push me away?
   DYN.   There's so much
    metal
About you. Do I have to be imprisoned
In an armoury?
   TEG.   Give your hand to the buckles and
    then
To me.
   DYN. Don't help; I'll do them all myself.
   TEG. O time and patience! I want you back
    again.   760
   DYN. We have a lifetime. O Chromis, think,
    think
Of that. And even unfastening a buckle

loving. And not easy. Very well,
You can help me. Chromis, what zone of miracle
Did you step into to direct you in the dark
To where I waited, not knowing I waited?
   TEG.   I saw
The lamplight. That was only the appearance
Of some great gesture in the bed of fortune.
I saw the lamplight.
   DYN.   But here? So far from life?
What brought you near enough to see lamplight?
   TEG.   Zeus,
That reminds me.
   DYN.   What is it, Chromis?
   TEG.   I'm on duty.
   DYN. Is it warm enough to do without your
    greaves?   772
   TEG. Darling loom of magic, I must go back
To take a look at those boys. The whole business
Of guard had gone out of my mind.
   DYN.   What boys,
    my heart?
   TEG. My six bodies.
   DYN.   Chromis, not that joke
Again.
   TEG. No joke, sweet. To-day our city
Held a sextuple hanging. I'm minding the bodies
Until five o'clock. Already I've been away
For half an hour.
   DYN.   What can they do, poor bodies,
In half an hour, or half a century?   781
You don't really mean to go?
   TEG.   Only to make
My conscience easy. Then, Dynamene,
No cloud can rise on love, no hovering thought
Fidget, and the night will be only to *us*.
   DYN. But if every half-hour——
   TEG.   Hush, smile of
    my soul,
My sprig, my sovereign: this is to hold your eyes,
I sign my lips on them both: this is to keep
Your forehead—do you feel the claim of my kiss
Falling into your thought? And now your throat
Is a white branch and my lips two singing birds—
They are coming to rest. Throat, remember me
Until I come back in five minutes. Over all   793
Here is my parole: I give it to your mouth
To give me again before it's dry. I promise.
Before it's dry, or not long after.
   DYN.   Run,
Run all the way. You needn't be afraid of stum-
    bling.
There's plenty of moon. The fields are blue. Oh,
    wait,
Wait! My darling. No, not now: it will keep

Until I see you; I'll have it here at my lips.   800
Hurry.
  TEG. So long, my haven.
  DYN.   Hurry, hurry!
                    [*Exit* TEGEUS.]
  DOTO. Yes, madam, hurry; of course. Are we there
Already? How nice. Death doesn't take
Any doing at all. We were gulped into Hades
As easy as an oyster.
  DYN.   Doto!
  DOTO.   Hurry, hurry,
Yes, madam.—But they've taken out all my bones.
I haven't a bone left. I'm a Shadow: wonderfully shady
In the legs. We shall have to sit out eternity, madam,
If they've done the same to you.
  DYN.   You'd better
    wake up.   809
If you can't go to sleep again, you'd better wake up.
Oh dear.—We're still alive, Doto, do you hear me?
  DOTO. You must speak for yourself, madam. I'm quite dead.
I'll tell you how I know. I feel
Invisible. I'm a wraith, madam; I'm only
Waiting to be wafted.
  DYN.   If only you *would* be.
Do you see where you are? Look. Do you see?
  DOTO. Yes. You're right, madam. We're still alive.
Isn't it enough to make you swear?
Here we are, dying to be dead,
And where does it get us?
  DYN.   Perhaps you should try to die   820
In some other place. Yes! Perhaps the air here
Suits you too well. You were sleeping very heavily.
  DOTO. And all the time you alone and dying.
I shouldn't have. Has the corporal been long gone, Madam?
  DYN. He came and went, came and went,
You know the way.
  DOTO.   Very well I do. And went
He should have, come he should never. Oh dear, he must
Have disturbed you, madam.
  DYN.   He could be said
To've disturbed me. Listen; I have something to say to you.
  DOTO. I expect so, madam. Maybe I *could* have kept him out   830
But men are in before I wish they wasn't.
I think quickly enough, but I get behindhand

With what I ought to be saying. It's a kind of stammer
In my way of life, madam.
  DYN.   I have been unkind,
I have sinfully wronged you, Doto
  DOTO.   Never, madam.
  DYN. Oh yes. I was letting you die with me, Doto, without
Any fair reason. I was drowning you
In grief that wasn't yours. That was wrong. Doto.
  DOTO. But I haven't got anything against dying, madam.
I may *like* the situation, as far as I like   840
Any situation, madam. Now if you'd said mangling.
A lot of mangling, I might have thought twice about staying,
We all have our dislikes, madam.
  DYN.   I'm asking you
To leave me, Doto, at once, as quickly as possible,
Now, before—now, Doto, and let me forget
My bad mind which confidently expected you
To companion me to Hades. Now good-bye,
Good-bye.
  DOTO.   No, it's not good-bye at all.
I shouldn't know another night of sleep, wondering
How you got on, or what I was missing, come to that.   850
I should be anxious about you, too. When you belong
To an upper class, the netherworld might come strange.
Now I was born nether, madam, though not
As nether as some. No, it's not good-bye, madam.
  DYN. Oh Doto, go; you must, you must! And if I seem
Without gratitude, forgive me. It isn't so,
It is far, far from so. But I can only
Regain my peace of mind if I know you're gone.
  DOTO. Besides, look at the time, madam. Where should I go
At three in the morning? Even if I was to think
Of going; and think of it I never shall.   861
  DYN. Think of the unmatchable world, Doto.
  DOTO.   I do
Think of it, madam. And when I think of it, what
Have I thought? Well, it depends, madam.
  DYN.   I insist,
Obey me! At once! Doto!
  DOTO.   Here I sit.
  DYN. What shall I do with you?
  DOTO.   Ignore me, madam.
I know my place. I shall die quite unobtrusive.

Oh look, the corporal's forgotten to take his
   equipment.
   DYN. Could he be so careless?
   DOTO.   I shouldn't hardly
   have thought so.
Poor fellow. They'll go and deduct it off his
   credits.   870
I suppose, madam, I suppose he couldn't be
   thinking
Of coming back?
   DYN.   He'll think of these. He will notice
He isn't wearing them. He'll come; he is sure to
   come.
   DOTO. Oh.
   DYN.   I know he will.
   DOTO.   Oh, oh.
Is that all for to-night, madam? May I go now,
   madam?
   DYN. Doto! Will you?
   DOTO.   Just you try to stop me,
   madam.
Sometimes going is a kind of instinct with me.
I'll leave death to some other occasion.
   DYN.   Do,
Doto. Any other time. Now you must hurry.
I won't delay you from life another moment.   880
Oh, Doto, good-bye.
   DOTO.   Good-bye. Life is unusual,
Isn't it, madam? Remember me to Cerberus.
   [*Re-enter* TEGEUS. DOTO *passes him on the steps.*]
   DOTO. [*As she goes.*] You left something behind.
   Ye gods, what a moon!
   DYN. Chromis, it's true; my lips are hardly dry.
Time runs again; the void is space again;
Space has life again; Dynamene has Chromis.
   TEG. It's over.
   DYN.   Chromis, you're sick. As white as
   wool.
Come, you covered the distance too quickly.
Rest in my arms; get your breath again.
   TEG. I've breathed one night too many. Why did
   I see you,   890
Why in the name of life did I see you?
   DYN.   Why?
Weren't we gifted with each other? O heart,
What do you mean?
   TEG.   I mean that joy is nothing
But the parent of doom. Why should I have found
Your constancy such balm to the world and yet
Find, by the same vision, its destruction
A necessity? We're set upon by love
To make us incompetent to steer ourselves,
To make us docile to fate. I should have known:
Indulgences, not fulfilment, is what the world   900

Permits us.
   DYN.   Chromis, is this intelligible?
Help me to follow you. What did you meet in the
   fields
To bring about all this talk? Do you still love me?
   TEG. What good will it do us? I've lost a body.
   DYN.   A body?
One of the six? Well, it isn't with them you propose
To love me; and you couldn't keep it for ever.
Are we going to allow a body that isn't there
To come between us?
   TEG.   But I'm responsible for it.
I have to account for it in the morning. Surely
You see, Dynamene, the horror we're faced with?
The relatives have had time to cut him down   911
And take him away for burial. It means
A court martial. No doubt about the sentence.
I shall take the place of the missing man.
To be hanged, Dynamene! Hanged, Dynamene!
   DYN. No; it's monstrous! Your life is yours,
   Chromis.
   TEG. Anything but. That's why I have to take it.
At the best we live our lives on loan,
At the worst in chains. And I was never born
To have life. Then for what? To be had by it,   920
And so are we all. But I'll make it what it is,
By making it nothing.
   DYN.   Chromis, you're frightening
What are you meaning to do?
   TEG.   I have to die,
Dance of my heart, I have to die, to die,
To part us, to go to my sword and let it part us.
I'll have my free will even if I'm compelled to it.
I'll kill myself.
   DYN.   Oh, no! No, Chromis!
It's all unreasonable—no such horror
Can come of a pure accident. Have you hanged?
How can they hang you for simply not being
   somewhere?   930
How can they hang you for losing a dead man?
They must have wanted to lose him, or they
   wouldn't
Have hanged him. No, you're scaring yourself for
   nothing
And making me frantic.
   TEG.   It's section six, paragraph
Three in the Regulations. That's my doom.
I've read it for myself. And, by my doom,
Since I have to die, let me die here, in love,
Promoted by your kiss to tower, in dying,
High above my birth. For god's sake let me die
On a wave of life, Dynamene, with an action   940
I can take some pride in. How could I settle to
   death

Knowing that you last saw me stripped and strangled
On a holly tree? Demoted first and then hanged!
　DYN. Am I supposed to love the corporal
Or you? It's you I love, from head to foot
And out to the ends of your spirit. What shall I do
If you die? How could I follow you? I should find you
Discussing me with my husband, comparing your feelings,
Exchanging reactions. Where should I put myself?
Or am I to live on alone, or find in life   950
Another source of love, in memory
Of Virilius and of you?
　　TEG.   Dynamene,
Not that! Since everything in the lives of men
Is brief to indifference, let our love at least
Echo and perpetuate itself uniquely
As long as time allows you. Though you go
To the limit of age, it won't be far to contain me.
　　DYN. It will seem like eternity ground into days
　　and days.
　　TEG. Can I be certain of you, for ever?
　　DYN.   But, Chromis,
Surely you said——
　　TEG.   Surely we have sensed   960
Our passion to be greater than mortal? Must I
Die believing it is dying with me?
　　DYN.   Chromis,
You must never die, never! It would be
An offence against truth.
　　TEG.   I cannot live to be hanged.
It would be an offence against life. Give me my sword,
Dynamene. O Hades, when you look pale
You take the heart out of me. I could die
Without a sword by seeing you suffer. Quickly!
Give me my heart back again with your lips
And I'll live the rest of my ambition   970
In a last kiss.
　　DYN.   Oh, no, no, no.
Give my blessing to your desertion of me?
Never, Chromis, never. Kiss you and then
Let you go? Love you, for death to have you?
Am I to be made the fool of courts martial?
Who are they who think they can discipline souls
Right off the earth? What discipline is that?
Chromis, love is the only discipline
And we're the disciples of love. I hold you to that:
Hold you, hold you.
　　TEG.   We have no chance. It's determined   980
In section six, paragraph three, of the Regulations.

That has more power than love. It can snuff the great
Candles of creation. It makes me able
To do the impossible, to leave you, to go from the light
That keeps you.
　　DYN.   No!
　　TEG.   O dark, it does. Good-bye,
My memory of earth, my dear most dear
Beyond every expectation. I was wrong
To want you to keep our vows existent
In the vacuum that's coming. It would make you
A heaviness to the world, when you should be,
As you are, a form of light. Dynamene, turn   991
Your head away. I'm going to let my sword
Solve all the riddles.
　　DYN.   Chromis, I have it! I know!
Virilius will help you.
　　TEG.   Virilius?
　　DYN. My husband. He can be the other body.
　　TEG. Your husband can?
　　DYN.   He has no further use
For what he left of himself to lie with us here.
Is there any reason why he shouldn't hang
On your holly tree? Better, far better, he,
Than you who are still alive, and surely better
Than *idling* into corruption?
　　TEG.   Hang your husband?
Dynamene, it's terrible, horrible.   1002
　　DYN. How little you can understand. I loved
His life not his death. And now we can give his death
The power of life. Not horrible: wonderful!
Isn't it so? That I should be able to feel
He moves again in the world, accomplishing
Our welfare? It's more than my grief could do.
　　TEG. What can I say?
　　DYN.   That you love me; as I love him
And you. Let's celebrate your safety then.   1010
Where's the bottle? There's some wine unfinished in this bowl.
I'll share it with you. Now forget the fear
We were in; look at me, Chromis. Come away
From the pit you nearly dropped us in. My darling,
I give you Virilius.
　　TEG.   Virilius.
And all that follows.
　　DOTO. [*On the steps, with the bottle.*]
　　　　　　　　　　The master. Both the masters.

CURTAIN

II
Source and Supplementary Material

Victor Ehrenberg The Poet and His Audience

The following explanation of the background of *The Birds* has been taken from *The People of Aristophanes* by Victor Ehrenberg (Oxford: Basil Blackwell, 1951, second edition, revised and enlarged). These comments not only present the results of recent research but they are also eminently reasonable and full. Professor Ehrenberg, who has studied at the Universities of Göttingen, Berlin, and Tübingen, left his native Germany in 1939, became a naturalized British subject in 1947, and has taught in the United States. His most recent work is *The Greek State* (1960).

The footnotes are the editor's.

Every performance of a comedy in Athens was based on a number of social facts. The poets of Old Comedy[1] were Athenian citizens. Practically nothing is known of their social /20/ standing, but, as far as we know, none of them belonged to the nobility. On the other hand, from the fact that Euripides alone, and none of the comic poets, was derided because of his alleged low origin, we may assume that none, or at least none of the better known comic poets, came from the lower classes. How far we can generalize when a poet's poverty is mentioned, is less certain. At least one of the comic writers was compelled by poverty to sell some of his

comedies to rich people who performed them as their own. Aristophanes, who had an estate in Aigina and left the production of some of his plays to others who thus received the renumeration for a victory, must have been well off . . . The poets who took part in the tragic or comic *agon* received public remuneration, but we have no idea of the amount, though it was certainly in proportion to the poet's place in the result of the *agon*.

A poet who intended to produce one of his plays, had to ask for a chorus to be assigned to him, and the task of assigning choruses was the function of the chief archon for the Dionysia, of the *archon basileus* for the Lenaia. It might happen that a /21/ good poet went away empty-handed, while some obscure bungler was awarded the chorus; but generally, under the control of public opinion, the better poets were chosen, and the "chatterboxes," the "degraders of their art," only got a chorus once in their lives. The payment of the chorus, which always consisted of citizens, as well as the total cost of the equipment of the play and the festive meal which followed the performance, was the responsibility of the choregus;[2] only the actors were chosen and paid by the archon, that is the State. The duty of the choregus was not confined to the mere payment of money, but involved weeks of painstaking preparation and care. This, however, the choregus left for the most part to the poet and his helpers. Even a choregus who was always victorious did not necessarily understand anything about the technique of the musical part or of producing a play. There were good and bad choregi. "Have you ever seen a choregus meaner than him?" Such a man might well complain that it was no longer possible to give the chorus quite simple clothes and food. A dinner after the performance was due to the members of the chorus: "The meat of the grouse is best to eat after a

---

[1] Comedies in Athens were generally performed at the festivals of Dionysus (Dionysos), called the Dionysia and the Lenaea (Lenaia); the Dionysia were held about December, the Lenaea in January; both were connected with wine-making. Old Comedy was simply the comedy produced before 400 B.C. Five poets usually competed in each festival, producing one play each. We know little of any writer of Old Comedy except Aristophanes. The most successful of all was Cratinus (c. 520 – c. 423) who wrote twenty-three comedies, nine of which won prizes. In general, Old Comedy was characterized by a great deal of scurrility.

There is today widespread agreement that Aristotle (for whose theory of the origin of comedy, see Section III) was wrong and that the word comedy comes from *kômos*, meaning revel. These revels took place at festivals, particularly those of Dionysus, and consisted in part of a procession, singing, dancing, and bantering. However, Aristotle was probably correct in asserting that comedy in Attica originated in the villages (the Greek word for village is *kômê*).

[2] A wealthy private citizen.

victory on the stage." When the chorus of the initiates in the *Frogs* are satisfied with the breakfast they have had, this refers to the men of the chorus rather than to the Athenian procession to Eleusis. It is well known that the choregy was one of the liturgies which were undertaken as a kind of moral obligation, and at the same time regarded as an honour by wealthy men; it was open at the Dionysia to citizens only, at the Lenaia to metics[3] also. As a rule, however, a comic choregy was far cheaper than that of a tragedy. Naturally, the costumes of the chorus were simpler, and the artistic task was probably less difficult, though the comic chorus in its own way would aim /22/ at equal perfection and the comedians claimed that they had to solve more difficult problems than the tragedians. Great statesmen were proud of being victorious with a chorus. But gradually the liturgies became a heavy and unwelcome burden to the rich, and a source of income to at least part of the people.

The chorus, not the actors, not even the plot, was of chief importance. The expressions "to perform a tragedy" and "to dance a chorus" could be synonymous, and the dramatic competition could take its name from the *thymele*, the altar around which the chorus danced. Athens needed the poet, says Dionysos when he has descended to Hades, in order that the city, saved by the poet, "might maintain her choruses." When the chorus declined and eventually became a merely incidental feature of the play, the connection between comedy and the people became increasingly weaker. "The chorus was suited to the Agora,[4] but not to the fireside." The comic mask, "the comic bogey," is a symbol of comedy, and it is significant that such masks—both tragic and comic—were hung in the temple of Dionysos. "The man is dancing, and all is well with the god." Not the "theatre," but the cult made the performance possible, and gave it meaning.

The poet was the *chorodidaskalos*, the teacher and trainer of the chorus; the "comic poet" was the "comedy teacher," and in this quality the true servant of the Muses, just like the "tragedy teacher." This means that he himself wrote the words and /23/ rehearsed the music and the dancing of the chorus. There was a special kind of dance for every chorus, appropriate to the char-

acter it represented in the play, and there were different melodies suited to the various songs, for example, the exit song of the chorus. Thespis and Aischylos are said to have themselves planned the figures of the dances for their choruses; indeed, the drunken old man in the *Wasps* actually challenges the tragic poets to a competition in dancing, and the Muse is warned not to admit certain bad tragedians who were equally bad dancers. The rehearsal of a chorus asked for an almost military discipline, but even so it cannot always have been simple to teach the men who formed the chorus to sing and dance correctly. Some of them may not have been very musical, and it is doubtful whether the wine always had, as the poet hopes, the necessary effect. Sometimes there was considerable strain between poet and chorus; certain tragedians are said to have been hated by the choruses, and Kinesias was called "the chorus-killer." The poet was content if the chorus fulfilled their task sufficiently well. Sometimes the poet himself was his own chief actor, and at least he instructed the actors. These, and perhaps the musicians also, though citizens, were more or less professionals. But the poet was composer, dance-master, producer, probably also the technical manager who gave his orders to the technician about the working of the various stage-devices such as the *ekkyklema*,[5] which occasionally went wrong. Thus, the task and the responsibility of the poet were immense. We can understand that Aristophanes did not produce his first plays, his "maiden's children," himself. Being very young, he /24/ did not feel equal to the task. But he also employed a special "producer" on some later occasions.

In addition to these general tasks, there was the special situation of the political poet. He had to keep in touch with the most recent events, and therefore frequently added to his text and made alterations up to the time of the performance. At the same time, there were particular dangers which a political poet had to fear. Young Aristophanes had a taste of them himself, when Kleon,[6] a year after the punishment of Mytilene, brought him before the council on a charge of slandering the State in the presence of allies and other foreigners. "I do not say *the State*," he therefore emphasized in the next year. A year later he attacked

[3] Resident aliens who assumed the ordinary financial and social obligations of citizens, but who had no political rights nor were allowed to own land.

[4] Originally an assembly of the people; later, the name given to the place (usually an open space) where such meetings were held.

[5] A machine to exhibit an interior.

[6] Kleon (d. 422 B.C.) was an Athenian demagogue, violently attacked both by Aristophanes (in the *Knights*, 424 B.C.) and by Thucydides. In 427 B.C., after the suppression of a revolt by the inhabitants of Mytilene, chief city of the Island of Lesbos, he advocated that all the male population be put to death. Many were killed, the walls of the city were demolished and its fleet confiscated.

Kleon in the strongest and sharpest possible terms, with Kleon himself listening, no doubt, from the front row, for he had the right of *prohedria*[7] since his success at Pylos the year before. The same play, the *Knights*, introduced the Demos, led by Kleon, as an old doddering blockhead. We are told that the Athenians would not tolerate the deriding and slandering of the demos, but encouraged caricatures of individuals. The exact meaning of this passage is much disputed and uncertain. At any rate, it is /25/ important to note that the remarkable comic licence could have its limits. It is somewhat surprising that Perikles seems to have been the first to introduce a kind of censorship; this happened during the dangerous revolt of Samos in 440, and the law remained in force for three years. About the year 415, a similar attempt was made by one Syrakosios, though its operation is obscure. On the other hand, Kleon's treatment of Aristophanes proves that a single citizen or member of the council had the means of bringing before the judges a comedian who is supposed to have offended public interests. Yet such incidents must not conceal the fact that what was really unique was not the occasional limitation and risk, but the unheard-of-liberty of comedy. In no other place or age were men of all classes attacked and ridiculed in public and by name with such freedom as in Old Attic Comedy. The ultimate reason for this, apart from the magnanimity and the sense of humour which were inherent in the Attic character, was the fact that comedy was an internal affair of the sovereign people as a whole, and so there was complete *parrhesia*, freedom of speech. Kleon was therefore justified in calling attention, in his denunciation, to the presence of foreigners.

In a Greek Polis no citizen can be said to have been a private person; this is particularly obvious of the dramatic poet. He was a citizen who, together with a number of his fellow-citizens, presented a play to some thousands of people in the audience who also were for the most part citizens. Furthermore, in an *agon*, a contest with other poets in a single day's performance, he submitted himself to the judgment of his audience and a few specially chosen judges. In a preliminary ceremony, the so-called *proagon*, the chorus and the actors, the choregus and the poet had appeared on the stage of the Odeion;[8] in this way, they were introduced to the people. Although our casual sources which refer to the *proagon* deal

only with tragedy, it is possible that lyric choruses as well as /26/ comedies took part in it. The relation of poet, chorus, and actors to the audience was the same for all these kinds of poetry, but tragedy and in most cases also the choral lyric were too remote in their mythical themes to allow the situation to be expressed in words. It was the privilege of the comedian to make it clear that there were no barriers and no imaginary curtain between stage and audience. Citizens they were on both sides, united and linked together in space and spirit. Comedy is seen to be a social phenomenon, and so to demonstrate most plainly the social character of the Greek theatre.

The audience was the Athenian people, the same people who formed the assembly. There were, at the Dionysia at least, foreigners in the audience, allies, ambassadors, and metics; but these few hundreds were unimportant, compared with the many thousands of Athenian citizens. "I don't fear you," says /27/ Kleon to the sausage-seller and the knights, "as long as the council is alive, and the figure of Demos smiles, sitting on the benches." Kleon means the assembly and perhaps the courts, but he hints at the audience. Even if some people preferred, as they undoubtedly did, the sphere of politics, while others found the excitements of tragedy and comedy more to their liking, the general composition of assembly and theatre was the same. In many ways the playwright, in particular the comedian, worked upon the minds of the people by means similar to those used by the orator in the assembly.

The gap between the play on the stage or in the orchestra and the public is bridged by many utterances. Each year, there came "to the art," that is to see the play, that multitude, the number of which—like "the sand of the sea"—is given as "numberless myriads," or as 13,000; this, though not of course exact, is not without significance. Tragedy and comedy were the concern of the whole people, and part of their common experience. Quite often the dialogue or the song of the chorus alludes in some way to the audience who are thus drawn into the action of the play. Reference to outstanding examples will make this clear. Sometimes a situation is directly explained to the audience to enable them to understand it; or "a pert young witling" will put questions with regard to the play which may be answered by a neighbour; or the spectators are asked to guess what they do not know, though they usually guess wrong. Or on the other hand, the public is represented as the cleverer party, as an "assembly of

---

[7] Front rows reserved for officials.
[8] A theatre built for musical performances and, unlike other Greek theatres, provided with a roof.

all-wise old men," whose judgment is decisive, who know better "whilst all the chorus /28/ stand like idiots by." Euripides can be blamed for dealing with "scenes of common life" which the audience knew something about; a comedian would never be blamed for this.

The connection becomes even closer, when "the house" is given a part in the play. They are told to sing hymns at some good news from the stage, or an old hag complains that she is being abused "in front of so many men." "You see," the chorus asks the sausage-seller, "those people on the benches? —I do—You shall be overlord of all those people." When the goddess of Peace appears, one can guess from the faces of the spectators their different vocations—whether they have gained or lost by the war. But the goddess will not speak one word to the audience; "they have wronged her far too much for that," so that Hermes addresses the people, communicating her questions and complaints. The Just and the Unjust Logos wish to fight their *agon* in front of the many spectators. In another contest one party is asked to gather all his rhetorical force and to "move the theatre."

It is, of course, a favourite joke to abuse the public, the "sink of spectators." As a rule this is done in so general a way (all of them, for instance, are parricides and perjurers), that the joke could only be laughed at, even if it was not particularly funny. Of an old hag we are told that she "has been the sport of these thirteen thousand." In a long list of more or less deformed people the poet seems to be picking out individual spectators. Sometimes real criticism was pronounced. "I know these fellows, voting in hot haste, and straight ignoring the decree they've passed." In their capacity as audience, the people might be offered either criticism or flattery. The statement that the spectators detest hearing or seeing again what /29/ has been said or done before, and want the poet "to make haste," is a criticism directed against some fellow-comedians rather than against the audience; but when a young girl is fond of her singing, because it is amusing and pleasant, though the listeners are bored, then the hit is probably directed at them. Kratinos shows a charming irony in the lines: "Hail, ye throngs that laugh not at once, but the next day, the world's best judges of my art! Your mothers bore you to happiness as the thunder of the tiers." Another poet considers it shameful that the beauty of a play should be judged by the applause of the mob. Pronouncements on the sagacity of the audience, who could be called insane and who, of course, were sagacious only as long as they applauded the poet, culminate in the description of the "clever spectator" as one who is "over-subtle, on the look-out for sententious phrases," and as one who "euripid-aristophan-izes."

All this reappears in an even more striking, though often conventional, manner when the audience is accosted directly, which can equally happen in the course of the dialogue, in the *parabasis* or in a song of the chorus. Frequently the audience is exhorted to listen carefully. The spectators are asked the most varied questions; for instance, whether they like the characters represented on the stage, whether they would share "with the birds a life of pleasure," or whether they can produce for the slave who feeds the dung-beetle a nose with no nostrils. The chorus exhorts the audience to cherish any poet who brings some new saying or device in his plays. An invitation, though hardly a serious one, to participate in the common feast is a /30/ favourite form of address to the audience. An actor's mistake is mentioned with the remark "if you still remember." There is a real unity between "spectators and actors and choruses."

The most striking example of direct apostrophe of this type is the great speech of Dikaiopolis, in which he informs the people about the situation and at the same time criticizes them sharply. Dikaiopolis, the Attic peasant, claims the right to criticize in this manner, "although he is presenting a comedy; for even comedy can tell the truth." Here the poet is clearly speaking in his own character. Like the tragedian, Aristophanes regards himself as entitled to speak "about the State" and to criticize. It is true that the passage which follows, in which he speaks of the causes of the war, is ridiculous and, to some extent, mere comic distortion; but that a serious attack on politics and serious criticism are intended is evident. In particular, the lightheartedness with which the Athenians seized every opportunity for going to war with Sparta was the subject of bitter irony. On the other hand, Dikaiopolis had staked his head on his ability to convince the people of the justice of the cause of peace by telling them unpleasant truths. When finally the warlike chorus is won over to the side of peace, the poet perhaps hoped that he had convinced the greater part of his audience as well.

Another special privilege of comedy is its ability to allude to current events. There was little point in introducing them except for the purpose of making in the end the audience think as well as laugh. The lament that it was beyond comedy to heal so old a disease of the Polis as the foolish passion for serving on juries shows that tasks of this kind were thought to be at least one of the final aims of the comic poets, even if their fulfilment was obviously beyond their power. Comedy became a platform on which political men and events were not only derided, but also discussed. No doubt, the "rolling sea" of the audience took part in this debate by cheering and hissing, by laughing and interrupting, often indeed in a very rude /31/ manner. The appeal of the comic poet to the people continually found new and surprising expression, but his jests and his harshest satire sprang from a profound affection and concern for their welfare.

An outward sign of Old Comedy, although one not altogether indispensable, is the *parabasis*, which had developed from the original *kômos* and had become the centre of the play. The chorus "came forward" or "turned aside"—hence the name *parabasis*—and addressed the audience, usually in the name of the poet. It is not our intention to discuss in detail the various parts of comedy. To us each single comedy, like Old Comedy as a whole, is a literary unit, even though composed of the most different elements. The *parabasis*, however, deserves special mention, because it furnishes the clearest evidence for the relations between the poet and his public.

The *parabasis* is a rather complicated compound of various sections, partly recitative and partly song. Within the lifetime of Aristophanes it went through a process of gradual decay, until it disappeared entirely. The problems of this development do not concern us; but it is of fundamental importance to realize that the "anapaests"[9] as well as the *epirrhema*,[10] "the core of the *parabasis*," contain a direct address to the audience, in which either the chorus or, through their voices, the poet speaks to the people. The address is frequently introduced by an exhortation to pay attention. An early and also a rather late play of Aristophanes lay the same stress on the idea which underlies the *parabasis*. In the *Acharnians* the poet for the first time speaks openly for himself. He prides himself on having /32/ saved the people from the deceptive orators, and on having helped them by his criticism. The man whom the chorus calls its teacher has indeed "taught the things that are best." He was "the best of the poets," because he dared to speak what is just. Again, the chorus of initiates in

the *Frogs* begins its *parabasis* thus: "Well does it suit the holy chorus to exhort the Polis and to teach it what is good." The poet is no longer mentioned; the chorus, as it were, has taken on a responsibility of its own. The form, and soon the contents as well, of comedy are becoming more and more impersonal. The words of the *parabasis* do not always contain so serious an exhortation, nor are they invariably so irrelevant to the story of the play. But it never varies in its essential function of giving expression to the unity of the people in both orchestra and auditorium, a unity in which the poet was certainly included.

This unity is shown in still another way. In spite of everything that makes the comic no less than the tragic poet the "teacher" of his audience and his people, he was, above all, a poet. His personal achievements as a poet are the outstanding theme of most of the *parabasis*. The leader of the chorus sings the praise of the poet, which is thus self-praise. The poet "has cheered you up and then sent you home." He even assures us that there has never been a better comedy than his. There is no need to call for Muses and Charites;[11] they are always present when Aristophanes writes his plays—"thus speaks the poet." The comedian's lot is not an easy one; the public is fickle, and the old poet is often hissed, though not always without justification. To explain this, Aristophanes blames and attacks the older comedians. Such attacks upon /33/ fellow-competitors, those "vulgar people," are found fairly often, and the discrimination of the audience is assessed according as they like Aristophanes better than the other poets. In the main, Aristophanes claims over and over again, though certainly only with a limited justification, that his jokes are not so stupid and coarse as those of others and that he does not try to win the audience by throwing them figs and sweets. Once during a sacrifice corn is thrown to the spectators, but that is done only to provide occasion for an obscene joke. Aristophanes is proud of his great art, of his language and ideas, of his jokes. He demands the gratitude of his audience especially for his unselfish political attacks; what an injustice was done, for instance, by not giving the first prize to the poet of the *Clouds*, who like Herakles tried to cleanse the State from all evils!

The other poets, of course, repaid in like coin. "Wake up, spectators, and shake from your eyelids the nonsense of ephemeral poets," are the

---

[9] A form of meter, each foot consisting of two short and one long syllable, in that order.

[10] A satiric speech on current events.

[11] Goddesses of joy and beauty, also known as the Graces (Euphrosyne, Aglaia, and Thalia); poetry was their special interest, hence their identification with the Muses.

words of Kratinos, who in his *Odysses* declares that he has produced a new kind of play. He derides a tragic poet Gnesippos whose chorus "pulled out their songs" as slave-girls pull out the hairs of their mistress. The chorus has "to undertake and to dare everything," except to use the melodies of certain other comedians. The genuine poet—possibly Kratinos—can claim "to have got his art instead of a wife"; his love belongs to his art, and the comedies he writes are his legitimate offspring. Kratinos' last comedy, the *Wine-bottle* (*Pytine*), was a magnificent effort of the old poet against his detractors, especially Aristophanes, whose *Clouds* he defeated on this occasion. The poet, who had been advised by Aristophanes to sit as an honoured man among the spectators, defended with the same vigour both his poetry and his love of wine: "wine's a swift steed to the bard of true wit; /34/ no water-drinker's work is worth a penny." Eupolis complained to the public that they preferred "foreign poets," and though the Greeks did not know the reproach of plagiarism, Hermippos said that Phrynichos put other people's poetry in his plays. . . . The same is true of the innumerable attacks on Euripides. Occasionally, however, something might be said against tragedy which reflected the envy of a competitor:

> Truly to be clad in feather is the very best of things.
> Only fancy, dear spectators, had you each a brace of wings,
> Never need you, tired and hungry, at a tragic chorus stay,
> You would lightly, when it bored you, spread your wings and fly away,
> Back returning, after luncheon, to enjoy our comic play.

Naturally, every comedian aimed at displaying new and original theatrical ideas, and their competition might be particularly concerned with the *agon* which played such an important part in almost every comedy. The spirit of competition indeed permeated the work of all the comic poets, culminating in their *agon* for the prizes, for "Nike, companion of the choruses." The *agon* within the comedy and that between certain poets are sometimes welded into one. The *Frogs* pro- /35/ vide the outstanding example, the *agon* between Aischylos and Euripides before Dionysos. It is significant for the wide scope of this kind of competition that Euripides reproaches Aischylos with having deceived the spectators after they had been made stupid by Phrynichos.

While it was important in the competition of the plays to win the manifest applause of the masses, the decision was made by the judges who were a few specially elected citizens, real "auditors for the accounts of the choruses going out of office." Individual judges might have been bribed or might have some personal link with one of the poets or might be singled out for an appeal. The judges who at the *Choes* or Pitcher-feast were to give the skin of wine to Dikaiopolis as a reward for the best drinker, were at the same time the judges of the play. The choruses of the *Clouds* and the *Birds* promise the judges the finest rewards if they are victorious, and threaten the worst if they are not. "The judges I warn not to break their oath nor to judge unjustly; else, by the god of friendship, the poet will say other and far more slanderous things against you." The oath of the chorus of the *Birds* becomes strongest when they swear by the wish to win "by the vote of every judge and every spectator." Only those of the audience "who are well disposed," and those judges "who look not otherwards," are invited to the feast; if the wise men among the judges will judge the poet according to his jests, he will get every vote.

It is possible, as we have said, to regard as an almost inevitable result of the *agon* of the comedies the extravagant self-praise of the poets which we might otherwise feel to be overdone, the crude attacks on rival competitors, the flatteries addressed to the judges. But all these features appear only because of the people's liking for such personal and literary references, and the people's insistence on their inclusion. This liking and insistence, however, are nothing but specific expressions of the general interest of the people, their interest in the play, in the poet, in the *agon* of the poets as well as of the actors. Although we are told that a good breakfast and drink /36/ were the usual preparation of the spectators, no time was too early, no distance too great, to prevent punctual arrival at the theatre. The poet was one of the people, the theatre was an affair of theirs, and there was food for their natural delight in every kind of *agon*. The theatre was the Polis. /37/

The Commedia Dell'Arte

Allardyce Nicoll

The influence of *commedia dell'arte*, the improvised but utterly professional comedy which traveling troupes of Italian players spread over Europe from the middle of the sixteenth till about the middle of the eighteenth centuries, while difficult to measure with absolute accuracy, is of great importance in the development of the drama and in the evolution of theatrical traditions of performance. In both forms of influence the precise details are obscure. Insofar as it was improvised, the genius of *commedia dell'arte* disappeared in performance, in the styles of particular players, and in the monologue and dialogue which the players extemporized as they acted out the stock roles assigned them within the skeletal *scenarii*. That the influence was great there can be no doubt. Molière was fascinated by the vigor of *commedia dell'arte*; Shakespeare was not untouched, as the troupe who come to Elsinore in *Hamlet* testify.

There have been many attempts to reconstruct full texts from the large repertory of *commedia dell'arte scenarii*. One of the most recent and most vigorous reconstructions—*The Three Cuckolds*—appears in *The Classic Theatre*, I, *Six Italian Plays*, edited by Eric Bentley (Anchor Books, 1959).

Widely known as one of the foremost living authorities on the theatre, Allardyce Nicoll (born 1894) is Professor of English at Birmingham University and Director of the Shakespeare Institute, Stratford-upon-Avon. Professor Nicoll has lectured throughout the world. His many works on the history of the drama—the most recent of which, *The World of Harlequin* (1962), is a searching study of *commedia dell'arte*—not only are the most authoritative in the field but also have the distinction of being charmingly written. From one of them, *World Drama from Aeschylus to Anouilh* (New York: Harcourt, Brace, 1950), the following excerpt (Chapter II) on the *commedia dell'arte* is reprinted.

... Let us imagine ourselves standing in the great square of Venice about the year 1600.

It is spring-time, and the lazy Italian sun is falling gently on the flagstones, on the roofs of the surrounding buildings, on the gay façade of the Cathedral of San Marco.

At one corner of the square a platform stage has been erected; in front of it are benches for specially privileged spectators; around, in a widely expectant semicircle, stands a jostling, excited crowd. The comedians are about to present a play, announced as *Arcadia incantata* (*Enchanted Arcady*).

Of scenic decoration there is little. Two little boxlike side-wings are set at the sides of the stage,

and at the rear is a backcloth painted with trees to represent a wood.

Suddenly an actor steps forward, and the crowd is silent. His heavy robe is decorated with astrological signs; he bears a heavy, leather-bound volume and leans upon a peculiarly carved staff; obviously he is a magician. Alone on the stage he addresses the audience, declaring that by his art he has become lord of this island of Arcadia and of its silly inhabitants, the shepherds and the nymphs of the woods; but now he has learned by his magic skill that the privacy of his lonely retreat is about to be broken: strangers are approaching.

At this he departs, and the backcloth of the forest is changed to represent a stormy sea with, in the distance, a ship foundering upon rocks. From one of the side-wings staggers in a strangely dressed creature, hump-backed, with a dark half-mask showing a sharply curved nose and a wrinkled receding brow on which a large wart is prominent. There is no doubt about his identity, for he has appeared in countless other plays; his name is Pulcinella. Gaspingly he tells us that he has just escaped from the wreck; alone of all his companions he has been saved.

As he is speaking, from the other side comes in a second character, also masked but even more grotesque, with a long, drooping nose and exaggeratedly large spectacles perched precariously on its /191/ bridge. His dress consists of a jacket, flapping trousers, a short cloak, and a beret with two long, curving feathers. He too is immediately recognizable as Coviello. In a kind of echo of Pulcinella's words, he also relates how he, alone of all his companions, has escaped a watery grave.

Gradually the pair move over towards the centre of the stage until, the one looking to the right and the other to the left, they bump into each other, start back in fear, take one another for ghosts, make as if to run away, then cautiously, timorously, draw near again, put out tremulous fingers, touch each other's arms, and finally, realizing the truth, embrace ecstatically. This done, they move aside in doleful converse over the loss of the others.

Meanwhile the same scene is repeated with another pair—the first, bespectacled like Coviello, and the other, older and ridiculously pompous, dressed like a savant of the University of Padua—Tartaglia and the Dottore. First, these two recognize each other as Coviello and Pulcinella had done, and then the two couples go through the scene of fear as a foursome. The more the crowd laughs at their ridiculous antics the more absurd their gestures become, until at last, the tumult over, they sit down and, talking all at once, gabble excitedly about their adventures. Then the thought of food comes into their minds; they are all hungry, and with one accord they decide to go off on a foraging expedition.

The scene now changes back to the wood, and four pastoral figures enter—the shepherd Silvio, who tells us he is in love with the shepherdess Clori, who tells us she is in love with Fileno, who tells us he is in love with Filli, who tells us she is in love with Silvio. Blundering into the midst of this idyllic tangle comes Pulcinella, and they all run off. Pulcinella has become separated from his companions, and, having failed to stay the shepherds, he is delighted when a company of richly costumed priests enters. He begs them for food, and they ask him to come to their temple—where, they explain to the audience, they intend to sacrifice him.

Again the scene changes, this time to a temple. A great procession of priests and shepherds comes in, with Pulcinella, ludicrously unaware of the fate intended for him, borne on a chair. In a scene of equivoque he asks for food, while they exhort him to make a good end. At last he realizes what is intended; the knife is just descending when the Magician makes an impressive entry, bids them desist, and, when they prove obdurate, calls up two fiery Spirits who drive the whole crowd off the stage.

The first act is now over, and, after a pause, the scene is altered /192/ to the wood again, with a large property fruit-tree set in front of the backcloth. The Dottore, Tartaglia, and Coviello wander in, abjectly miserable, hungry, and lost. Wild beasts have terrified them in the forest, and they fear that Pulcinella has been eaten by one of these. At this moment Pulcinella dashes across the stage convulsed with fear. Forcibly they stay him, and in stammering words he relates his adventures in the temple, while they laugh at his words, thinking he has gone off his mind through lack of food. Suddenly the Dottore spies the fruit-tree and calls the attention of his companions, whereupon, with ridiculously cautious movements, they start to peer into every corner of the stage to see if anyone is looking; satisfied at last, they approach to take the fruit—only to be terrified at the rising of flames, which consume the tree and drive them

back. As they are going a shepherdess, Silvana, enters complaining about a shepherd, Dameta, who, having loved, has left her. All the four comic characters at once fall in love with her, and there is a ridiculous struggle among them, when the Magician enters with words of reproof. Thinking him powerless in the face of their numbers, they are about to attack him, but he charms them into immobility and releases them only if they promise to be good. Off they go with the kind-hearted Silvana to have some supper.

Once more there is a pastoral interlude, Fileno lamenting the cruelty of Filli, Clori suing Fileno, Silvio in despair, and Filli making vain love to him. Now the Magician places a magic garland on a tree, explaining that if anyone puts it on his temples he will seem to be the person beloved by another.

First comes Pulcinella, satisfied after having had a good repast: he sees the garland, puts it on, and is immediately taken for Clori by Silvio. Pulcinella jeers at him, and he goes off; but a moment later Filli enters and takes Pulcinella to be Silvio; then Fileno thinks he is Filli, while Clori deems him Fileno. As Pulcinella stands amazed at this madness his companions enter, assume that he is Silvana, and attempt to embrace him; and matters become more complicated when, in the resultant confusion, the Magician enters invisible and shifts the garland from head to head.

At last he desists and carries the garland away; Silvana comes on stage and, hearing them all woo her, declares she cannot belong to all four, but will marry the one who is the best sleeper—whereupon all settle themselves down to display their prowess in repose, only to be awakened by four Spirits who chase them off the stage. Thus ends the second act amid cries of fear and strange noises. /193/

The third act opens with the pastoral characters, all of whom are bearing gifts to the temple and propose to pray for success in love. Coviello, who has overheard their words, immediately outlines a plan to his companions: the Dottore shall dress as Jove, Tartaglia as Venus, Pulcinella as Cupid, and Coviello as a Priest; seated in the temple, they will be able to appropriate all the rustic sacrifices for themselves. In a richly ludicrous scene this project is realized, and the four conspirators set themselves down for a good feast. Again, however, Pulcinella becomes separated from the other three and, when they depart, remains alone.

The Magician now enters and creates him King

of Arcadia, handing to him the magic book, the crown, and the sceptre. Pulcinella opens the book, and at once a Spirit appears and declares he is at his lord's service. Just at first Pulcinella is terrified, but he soon gains assurance, bids the Spirit bring him a chair, and seats himself royally upon it. Silvio enters, jeers at him, is beaten for his pains by the Spirit, begs for pardon, and is admitted to Pulcinella's retinue: and a similar scene is enacted with Fileno, Clori, Filli, and Silvana. Finally the Dottore, Tartaglia, and Coviello come on stage and mock him unmercifully, until in a rage he opens his book and a Spirit appears. First he orders them to be beaten, and they are duly chastised; then he commands them to be hanged. Ropes are put around their necks, while they weep and implore, and the execution is about to take place when the Magician enters, stops the Spirit, chides Pulcinella, and marries off Silvio to Clori, Fileno to Filli, and Silvana to Dameta.

So the play ends.

THE PROFESSIONAL PLAYERS

Clearly this is something entirely different from the tragedies and comedies, the *intermezzi* and the *opere*, acted at Court. The performers are professionals, not courtly amateurs; and, were we able to go backstage, we should find that their entire method of approach towards the play is different from that familiar in the palace theatres. There a poet composed his drama and the actors learned their lines. Here, search where we will, we shall find no written text. All that the manager of the company has is a brief scenario, specifying entries and exits, with a summary indication of what is to be done in each scene; all that the actors have is a short set of instructions pinned up behind the wings. When, for example, Pulcinella and Coviello are to make their first appearance on the stage they /194/ have as guidance only a general sketch of what they are expected to do and to say:

> *Enter* PULCINELLA, *from the sea; he speaks of the storm, the shipwreck and loss of his master and his companions. At this enter* COVIELLO, *from the other side; he speaks of the same things as* PULCINELLA; *they see one another and make a* lazzi *of fear. At last, after* lazzi *of touching one another, they realize that they have been saved and speak of the loss of their comrades and their master.*

The players, therefore, were expected to be their own authors, providing in their various scenes such dialogue as might appear necessary. Thus the type of performance illustrated by *Arcadia incantata* could be carried out only by men and women trained for long years in a special kind of acting technique; and consequently, in contradistinction to the *commedia erudita*—the "erudite," or "amateur," play of the Court—men were accustomed to speak of this other sort of drama as the *commedia dell'arte*, the play of "the quality" (as the Elizabethans would have said), or, as we say now, of "*the* profession."

Even for well-trained professionals, however, the creation of such scenes could not have been effectively realized without the acceptance of a number of conventions. The *commedia dell'arte* plays were improvised, certainly, so that no two performances of any given scenario could be quite the same in action and in dialogue, but the players were aided in diverse ways towards the successful securing of their ends. While it is true that over eight hundred scenarios have come down to us from the sixteenth, seventeenth, and eighteenth centuries, and that we must presume this number to have been but a small proportion of those originally in existence, we must observe, first, that many of these are almost duplicates, and, second, that any single company would have been content to use only a dozen or score out of the entire list.

Besides this fact, there is another still more important. In play after play of this kind the same characters put in an appearance and similar scenes occur. Each company was made up of a limited number of actors, each of whom, in every play, interpreted the same stock role. Normally there were four lovers, dressed either as gallants and ladies of the day or, as in *Arcadia incantata*, as shepherds and their nymphs. Alongside these were two old men, Pantalone, the Venetian merchant, and Dottore, the Paduan academic. Then came the Capitano, a boasting soldier, and an indeterminate number of so-called *zanni*, servants or clowns, each with his own particular name and characteristics—Pulcinella, Tartaglia, Coviello in *Arcadia* /195/ *incantata*, or elsewhere Arlecchino, Brighella, Bertolino, Fritellino, Pedrolino—together with a clownish maid or two, Colombina or Arlecchina. Occasionally other types appeared; occasionally the Capitano took the role of one of the *zanni* or Pantalone played the part of another old man (as probably he did in *Arcadia incantata*); but generally the dramatic characters were fixed and constant.

This meant that each actor from experience could build up for himself a long range of set speeches suitable for particular occasions: the lover might memorize Petrarchan sonnets for quoting to his lady; the Dottore might at leisure compose and learn long rigmaroles full of Latin tags; the Capitano might rehearse at length his mouth-filling oaths and rhadamontades. Business, too, could be established and used on different occasions. In the scenario of *Arcadia incantata* reference is made to the "*lazzi* of fear," and whenever we come across that word *lazzi* (and no scenario is without it) we recognize that we are in the presence of stock business. If the manager bade two *zanni* to do a scene with the *lazzi* of fear they knew precisely what was required of them; they had enacted this scene together many times before, and their comic tricks were all ready to hand.

In this way a *commedia dell'arte* performance took shape as a repatterning of well-established, familiar stock-types and of well-known "acts" or "turns" similiar to those we associate now with circus clown and music-hall comedian. A modern Christmas pantomime, although the words are here provided for the actors, is not dissimilarly composed: from the music-hall come the players with their diverse turns, and these are incorporated into the framework provided by the theme of a *Cinderella* or a *Puss-in-Boots*.

The performers in these companies set their eyes mainly upon broadly popular audiences. It is true that often, indeed, generally, the larger troupes were attached to particular Courts and that some of the actors were on such familiar terms with the dukes and princes that they might dare to address their lords with impertinent levity: regularly, *commedia dell'arte* productions were given in palace halls, while the time and energy of ambassadors were occupied in trying to persuade the sovereigns to whom they were accredited to grant leave for foreign tours of the troupes acting under their licence. At the same time the roots of even the most famous companies ran deep into the common soil; most of their performances were given before the people of the cities they visited. No doubt they purchased their trinkets out of moneys allotted to them by Court treasurers; but their bread and butter came from the takings at /196/ public performances. And beside the more famous troupes, with skilled actresses, like Isabella Andreini, who were the companions of queens and the stars of poets, with expert *zanni* like Drusiano Martinelli or Guiseppe Domenico Ciancolelli, honoured guests at Court, were dozens of smaller companies, some engaged solely in producing plays, some merely appendages to the booth of some quack or charlatan, eager, through their antics, to gather gaping spectators apt to buy his nostrums.

THE FORTUNES OF THE *Commedia Dell'Arte*

No one knows for certain whence the *commedia dell'arte* arose. It may have been born independently out of the social conditions of sixteenth-century Italy; on the other hand, there seems to be sufficient evidence to suggest that in this Renaissance form of entertainment we may trace the inspiration of medieval *jongleurs*, who themselves were the inheritors of the tradition of the Roman mimes.

All that is sure is that about the middle of the sixteenth century we begin to catch glimpses of dramatic shows which included some of the later stock characters—the Venetian Pantalone, the Bolognese Dottore, and the *zanni*—and that with extraordinary rapidity these small early groups of players expanded into the internationally renowned troupes of the Gelosi, the Confidenti, and the Fedeli.

At first their activities were confined to Italian cities, but before the sixteenth century had drawn to a close they were giving performances in France, while during the following century their fame spread widely over the entirety of Europe, where the various countries welcomed them and gradually modified their stock personages. In German lands Hanswurst is a native type born of Italian inspiration; France created the pathetic Pierrot out of Pedrolino, and refined the early rough Colombina into the dainty Columbine; in England Pulcinella became Punch, and the pantomime clown was born out of the Italian *zanni*. For nearly two hundred years the *commedia dell'arte* was the most popular form of dramatic entertainment in most countries of the Continent.

In itself, of course, it has vanished; these improvised plays have left no record of their original productions such as come from the production of written dramas. Yet the debt of the theatre to the *commedia dell'arte* cannot be exaggerated. Continually, in the pictorial records of the stage during the time of the Renaissance, an /197/ Arlecchino or a Dottore is peering impertinently from the wings, and in the writings of even the greatest authors of the time the spirit of the lost improvised comedies is to be traced. The theme of *Arcadia incantata* is so close to that of *The Tempest* that we are almost bound to assume a connexion between Shakespeare's last comedy and some similar piece played by the Italians; in *The Taming of the Shrew* Gremio is specifically named as the "pantalowne," while the *zanni*, or zany, well known to the English playwright, seems to have left his impress on more than one Elizabethan clown. Nearly a century later Molière was finding his genius stimulated by the *commedia dell'arte*, while a few decades after that Goldoni began his artistic career among these players.

There can be no doubt concerning the influence of the *commedia dell'arte* upon the drama, yet this very influence serves to indicate why the Renaissance in Italy failed to produce great plays. To create worthy tragedies and comedies an age requires to put all its strength into the theatre; part of its effort will not do. In Italy the stage was split. The literary qualities were reserved for the *commedia erudita,* and that remains lifeless and dull. There is a closet atmosphere, a preciousness, a smell of the wax candle, about every one of these Court productions, and their very weakness led to the expenditure of excessive effort upon costly scenic production. The atmosphere they breathe is so heavy with perfume, their surroundings are so stiff with brocade, that one sighs for at least a faint whiff of good honest garlic and the feel of homespun. In exchange for a sincere kersey "yeas" and "noes" we would willingly sacrifice much of their artificial and turgid rhetoric.

Yet when we turn to the popular play we find something instinct with life, no doubt, but like life, mortal. Of the elements making for perma-nence in art there was none. Hence the strange double paradox: that, although the Italian stage has left us virtually no memorable play from this time, it established the form of theatre which still endures today, and that it created a dramatic form which, though evanescent, appealed throughout the whole of Europe not only to popular audiences, but also to the greatest dramatists of the seventeenth and eighteenth centuries. There was no lack of theatrical inspiration in Renaissance Italy, but the delicate balance of forces out of which alone a great dramatic expression can come was absent. Only rarely, and then without the power of a Goldoni, did any Italian author of this time succeed in fusing the literary and the popular. Although Giovan Battista Andreini, the son of the famous actress Isabella Andreini and himself an actor /198/ in the *commedia dell'arte* tradition, essayed the task in such plays as *Amor nello specchio* (*Love in the Looking-Glass;* printed 1622) and *Le due commedia in commedia* (*The Two Plays within a Play;* printed 1623) with spirit and a certain grace, he failed, partly because his own talents were not equal to the occasion, partly because already it was too late to hope for the achieving of an end which, if it were to have proved fruitful, ought to have been secured nearly a century before. /199/

Kenneth Muir Twelfth Night

Where great art is concerned, it is perfectly true that sources are utterly transformed in the masterworks on which—however faintly—they are based. This truth however does not lessen the pleasure which the study of such transformation bestows on the student. There is no firmer guide to such work in Shakespeare than Kenneth Muir (1907-   ) who, since 1951, has been King Alfred Professor of English Literature at the University of Liverpool. He has an international reputation as a scholar and lecturer. His publications, including translations and a collection of original poems, range widely over the whole field of literature but he has achieved particular distinction as a student of Shakespeare. His *Shakespeare's Sources* (Vol. I), from which the essay on *Twelfth Night* has been taken, was published in 1957 (London: Methuen). Professor Muir's footnotes have been retained.

Twelfth Night, it has been said, is a masterpiece of recapitulation.[1] Shakespeare had already used

[1] Barrett Wendell, *William Shakespeare* (1898), p. 209.

the device of mistaken identity of twins in *The Comedy of Errors;* in *Twelfth Night,* as in many Italian plays, the twins were made of opposite sex. In *The Two Gentlemen of Verona* a girl, disguised as a page, had acted as emissary from the man she loves to the woman he loves. In *Love's Labour's Lost* we hear of a woman who died of unrequited /66/ love, and her fate may have suggested the Patience on a monument speech. In *The Merchant of Venice* we have the deep affection of Antonio for Bassanio, which is paralleled by the love of the later Antonio for Sebastian. In *As You Like It* we have a fool and a singer; in *Twelfth Night* we have a singing Fool. In *Much Ado about Nothing* Beatrice and Benedick are tricked into loving each other; Malvolio is tricked into believing that Olivia is in love with him. Sir Toby is a reduced version of Falstaff, and Slender was developed into Sir Andrew Aguecheek.

But there were sources apart from Shakespeare's own work. John Manningham in his diary (unless the passage is a Collier forgery[2]) mentions that he saw the play at the Middle Temple and says that it is "much like the *Commedy of Errores*, or *Menechmi* in Plautus, but most like and neere to that in Italian called *Inganni*." There are at least three. plays of that title, one of them later than *Twelfth Night*. *Gl'Inganni* of Curtzio Gonzaga (1592) has some links with Shakespeare. The disguised woman takes the name of Cesare, and the author's name reminds us of *The Murder of Gonzago*, the play "written in very choice Italian" performed before Claudius. Secchi's play (published 1562) has a woman, Ginevra, disguised as a man, in love with Gostanzo. Gostanzo is told by the disguised Ginevra that a woman is secretly in love with him, and that she is the same age as Ginevra. In a later scene, as Miss Helen A. Kaufman points out,[3] Gostanzo asks his supposed page why he is so upset by the girl's suffering, and Ginevra replies that she loves the girl as much as she does herself. Similarly Viola admits that she is in love. Given the situation of the girl disguised as a page in love with her master, repeated in other plays and stories, I do not find the resemblance in actual dialogue very striking.

Another play by Secchi, *L'Interesse*, also has some resemblances to *Twelfth Night*, though the plot itself is totally different. To win a wager, Pandolfo disguises his daughter as a boy and names her Lelio. Her elder sister, Virginia, is wooed by two men, Fabio and Flaminio. Lelio falls in love with Fabio, disguises herself as her sister, and becomes pregnant by him. As Miss Kaufman points out, we have here, in a different form, the situation of a girl disguised as a man, in love with a man who loves another woman. There is a comic duel in the play, Fabio fighting his own wife, Lelio, whom he thinks to be Virginia's brother. Although /67/ the scene in *Twelfth Night* is totally different, Secchi's may have suggested to Shakespeare the comic possibilities of involving his heroine in a duel. A scrap of dialogue in which Fabio asks Lelio about her love is very close to a similar passage in *Twelfth Night*:

Fabio: Is she young?
Lelio: About your age.
Fabio: Is she beautiful?
Lelio: A sweet face, and comely like yours.

There is also in the same scene an account by Lelio of an unknown girl who is pining away for love, which has a slight resemblance to Cesario's account of her sister. Miss Kaufman claims that Lelio resembles Viola in her wit, her gaiety, and her freedom from sentimentality.

Two other plays, sometimes bound up with *Gl'Inganni*, are of varying importance. In one there is a character called *Orsino innamorato*, but it should be said that Orsino was also the name of the Duke of Bracciano, before whom, on Twelfth Night, 1601, the play was perhaps first performed.[4] The other play, the anonymous *Gl'Ingannati*, resembles *Twelfth Night* so closely that it is usually assumed that Manningham was referring to this when he spoke of *Inganni*. In the introduction to this play mention is made of "Messer Agnol Malevolti," though Malvolio's name may be derived rather from the phrase *mala voglia*, which occurs seven times in Bandello's version of the story. The comedy is in prose. Lelia, the heroine, with the help of the nuns in the convent where she has been living, disguises herself as a man and takes the name of Fabio, for love of Flaminio, in whose household she becomes a page. Flaminio sends her on love embassies to Isabella, who falls in love with her as Olivia falls in love with Viola. Lelia tells Isabella, "Perhaps I may love you, if you dismiss Flaminio." Fabrizio, Lelia's lost brother, comes to Modena with his tutor, who shows him the "remarkable places of the town."[5] Virginio, Lelia's father, learns of her disguise from a nun, and he and Gherardo—her father's choice for her husband and Isabella's father—meet Fabrizio and take him for Lelia. Thinking him mad, they lock him up in Isabella's room. Then Gherardo meets Lelia, and thinking she must have escaped, he returns to his house and finds that Fabrizio and Isabella are betrothed. The play ends with a recognition /68/ scene and the marriages of Fabrizio to Isabella and Flaminio to Lelia.

There is no shipwreck in this play. Fabrizio had been separated from his family at the sack of Rome. There is a farcical element which Luce thought had affinities with *Twelfth Night*.[6] But it is difficult to see any resemblance between the dealings of Stragualcia with Piero and those of Sir Toby with Malvolio, or between the tricking of an old Spaniard, Giglio, by the housekeeper, Pasquella, and the gulling of Malvolio by Maria. Nor is it likely that Malvolio was a combination of Gherardo, Giglio, and Piero.

[2] Cf. S. Race, *N.Q.* (1954), p. 380.
[3] *S.Q.* (1954), pp. 271–80.

[4] Cf. L. Hotson, *The First Night* of "*Twelfth Night*" (1954), *passim*.
[5] *T.N.* III. iii. 41.
[6] M. Luce, *Rich's "Apolonius and Silla"* (1912), p. 11.

A Latin version of this play was revived at Queen's College, Cambridge, in 1595 under the title *Laelia;* Shakespeare may have heard of it, but the evidence that he had read it consists of vague and doubtful parallels. On the other hand, a phrase in the prologue of *Gl'Ingannati*, "la notte di Beffana" (i.e. the night of Epiphany) presumably gave Shakespeare his title, even though it is usually assumed that the play was first performed on Twelfth Night.[7]

The same story of Lelia was told by Bandello[8] and in Belleforest's translation. Shakespeare probably read one of these versions, as he had used one or the other author for *Much Ado about Nothing*. The closest parallel with *Twelfth Night* is the following. Nicuola speaks to Lattanzio of the girl he once loved—herself:[9]

> Who knoweth but this fair damsel yet loveth you and liveth in sore affliction for your sake? More by token that I have many a time heard say that girls, in their first loves, love far more tenderly and with greater fervour than do men. My heart forebodeth me this hapless lass must needs languish for you, and live a life of anguish and misery.

This resembles Orsino's confession that men's fancies are more giddy and unfirm than women's, and Viola's declaration that she knows "Too well what love women to men may owe" and her story of her father's daughter. Bandello's phrase—

> l'amoroso verme veracemente con grandissimo cordoglio le rodena il core—/69/

may have suggested:

> She never told her loue,
> But let concealment, like a worme i' th' bud,
> Feede on her damaske cheeke.

The story of Lelia is to be found also in Giraldi's *Hecatommithi*, the source of *Othello* and one of the probable sources of *Measure for Measure*. This version, like *Twelfth Night*, contains a shipwreck; but there is a shipwreck in the version of the story given in *Riche his Farewell to the Militarie profession* (1581), which is generally regarded as the main source of Shakespeare's play. It may be mentioned that Riche in other parts of his book uses four words—*coisterell*, *garragascoynes* (gaskins), *pavion* (pavin), and *galliarde*—which are to be found in

Twelfth Night and in no other of Shakespeare's plays. In Riche's fifth story a man tries to reform his shrewish wife by treating her as a lunatic:

> he tied her in a darke house that was on his backside, and then callyng his neibours about her, he would seeme with greate sorrowe to lament his wiues distresse, telling them that she was sodainly become Lunatique.

Luce points out that this incident bears some resemblance to the treatment of Malvolio in Act IV, Scene 2, It should be said, however, that the scene may owe something to the story of the exorcisms of Nicholas Starkey's children by John Darrell, who in his *True Narration* (1600) described the behaviour of the children in these words:

> Theis 4, especially 3 of them, vsed much light behauiour and vayn gestures, sundry also filthy scurrilous speaches, but whispering them for the most part among themselues, so as they were no let to that holy exercise we there had in hand. Sometimes also they spake blasphemy calling the word preached, bible bable, he will neuer haue done prating, prittle prattle.

Samuel Harsnett exposed the bogus exorcisms in his *Discovery of the Fraudulent Practises of John Darrell*, though I have not found in this pamphlet the word "bible-bable."[10] Feste as Sir Topas, it will be remembered, urges Malvolio to leave his vain bibble-babble.

Riche in his epistle dedicatory to gentlewomen tells us that he is not a good dancer: /70/

> At firste for Dauncyng, although I like the Measures verie well, yet I could neuer treade them a right, nor to vse measure in any thyng that I went aboute, although I desired to performe all thynges by line and by leauell, what so euer I tooke in hande.
>
> Our Galliardes are so curious, that thei are not for my daunsyng, for thei are so full of trickes and tournes, that he whiche hath no more but the plaine Sinquepace, is no better accoumpted of then a verie bongler, and for my part, thei might assone teache me to make a Capricornus, as a Capre in the right kinde that it should bee.
>
> For a Ieigge my heeles are too heauie: And these braules are so busie, that I loue not to beate my braines about them.
>
> A Rounde is too giddie a daunce for my diet, for let the dauncers runne about with as much speede as thei maie: yet are thei neuer a whit the nier to the ende of their course, vnlesse with often tourning thei hap to catch a fall. And so thei ende the daunce with shame, that was begonne but in sport.

This passage seems to have contributed to the picture we get of Sir Andrew in I. 3. Sir Andrew has

---

[7] Cf. L. Hotson, op. cit., pp. 173 ff.

[8] *Novelle* (1554), ii. 36.

[9] *Histoires Tragiques*, iv. (1571), 59. Belleforest's version of the Bandello quotation runs as follows: "Et que sçavez vous si ceste fille languist encore pour l'amour de vous, et vist en destresse? Car i'ay ouy dire que les filles en leurs premieres apprehensions aiment d'une vehemence tout autre, et plus grande qui ne font les hommes, et que malaisement on estaint ceste flamme ainsi viuement esprise, ayant trouué suiet non occupé en autre chose."

[10] Hunter and Luce say the word is used in this pamphlet.

"the back-trick as strong as any man in Illyria," he can "cut a caper," and Sir Toby asks:

> Why dost thou not goe to Church in a Galliarde and come home in a Carranto? My verie walke should be a Iigge; I would not so much as make water but in a Sink-a-pace.

His later question, "Were we not borne under Taurus?" may likewise have been suggested by Riche's reference to Capricorn.

Even without the evidence that Shakespeare had read Riche's tale of *Apolonius and Silla*, it therefore appears that he had read the book in which that tale occurs. The following is a summary of the story.

Duke Apolonius, after having spent a year's service in the Turkish wars, was driven by a storm to the island of Cyprus, where he was well received by Duke Pontus, the Governor. His daughter, Silla, fell in love with Apolonius, but he sailed away to Constantinople ignorant of her feelings. Silla thereupon asked her servant Pedro to accompany her to Constantinople, and she disguised herself as his sister. The Captain of the ship tried to seduce her, and she was saved from suicide by a providential shipwreck in which Pedro and the Captain were both drowned. Silla was saved by clinging to a chest containing money and apparel belonging /71/ to the Captain. For better safety she disguised herself as a man, calling herself Silvio, the name of her twin brother. She travelled to Constantinople and took service with Apolonius, who employed her to carry love-tokens and letters to a wealthy widow called Julina with whom he had fallen in love. Julina fell in love with Silla and told her: "It is enough that you have saied for your maister; from henceforthe either speake for your self, or sai nothyng at all."

Meanwhile Silvio, returning from the wars, heard of his sister's flight; and, assuming that she had been carried off by Pedro, he went in search of the couple, in due course arriving at Constantinople. Here, "walkyng in an euenyng for his owne recreation, on a pleasaunte greene yarde, without the walles of the citie" he encountered Julina, who invited him to supper on the following night. Surprised at being addressed by his own name by a complete stranger, and attracted by Julina's beauty, he consented. After supper Julina came to share his bed, and in the morning, "for feare of further euilles," Silvio went off to seek for his sister "in the parts of *Grecia*."

After a while Apolonius asked Julina for a direct answer to his suit, and she replied that she was pledged to another, "whose wife I now remaine by faithfull vowe and promise." Soon afterwards Apolonius heard that his page was his successful rival, and he cast Silla into a dungeon. Julina, finding herself with child, and hearing that the supposed Silvio was imprisoned, hastened to the Duke's palace, confessed her love, and asked Apolonius to impute to her charge the fault of which her lover was accused. Apolonius sent for Silla and reproached her for her abuse of his trust and for her perjuries. Silla urged Julina to confess that she had faithfully undertaken her master's behests. Julina replied that it was at her own suggestion that they had been betrothed, and she urged Silla not to be afraid to acknowledge the truth:

> Now is the tyme to manifest the same vnto the worlde, whiche hath been done before God, and betwene our selues.

Silla said she did not understand; and Julina then declared she was with child. Apolonius drew his rapier and threatened to kill Silla if she did not give Julina satisfaction by marrying her. Silla asked permission to speak with Julina alone, and revealed that she was a woman. Julina informed Apolonius, and he forthwith agreed to marry Silla. Hearing of the marriage, Silvio hastened back to Constantinople /72/ and was told the whole story by Apolonius. Silvio, ashamed of his desertion of Julina, at once agreed to marry her.

There appear to be no verbal echoes of Riche's story in *Twelfth Night*, with one possible exception. Julina's words:

> Ah, vnhappie, and, aboue all other, most vnhappie, that haue so charely preserued myne honour, and now am made a praie to satisfie a yong mans lust.

may have suggested Olivia's words to Viola:

> I have said too much vnto a hart of stone,
> And laid mine honour too vnchary out.[1]

But although there are few or no verbal echoes of Riche's story, there is good reason to believe that Shakespeare had read it. Riche's version and Giraldi's are the only ones that introduce a shipwreck; and Silvio's acceptance of Julina's invitation, Julina's revelation of her betrothal, her criticism of Silvio's fearful refusal to acknowledge it, and the Duke's anger with Silla are sufficiently close to the corresponding scenes of *Twelfth Night* to make it certain that Shakespeare knew Riche's version.

Manningham refers to Olivia as a widow; and

[1] But F. reads *on't* for *out*; perhaps we should read *uncharely*.

some critics think that the play he witnessed must have differed in this respect from the one we know. It is possible that the original play followed Riche in this detail, but it is more likely that Manningham's recollection was at fault. He may have remembered the mourning but forgotten the reason; or, indeed, his memory may well have been confused by his knowledge of Riche as Forman's was by his knowledge of Holinshed. In any case the advantages of having Olivia young and inexperienced are obvious; and it would not have suited the atmosphere of the play to have Olivia and Sebastian sharing a bed with the celerity displayed by Julina and Silvio. Shakespeare's lovers are united by a religious ceremony, and Olivia is not deserted as Julina is.

Riche's story has no underplot, nor have the Bandello and Belleforest versions. In complicating his play by the introduction of Sir Andrew's wooing of Olivia, his challenge to Cesario, and the gulling of Malvolio, Shakespeare may have taken a hint from the two absurd suitors in *Gl' Ingannati*—Gherardo and Giglio—but the hint was very small. The Malvolio plot is more likely to have been suggested by the topical story of the Comptroller of the /73/ Household, Sir William Knollys, who demonstrated against a noisy party in the small hours of the morning by walking amongst the revellers dressed only in his shirt, with a copy of Aretine in his hand.[12] Like Malvolio he complained of bear-baiting; he was connected with Banbury, a place noted for its cakes and ale as well as its puritans; and his father is known to have defended the puritans. Malvolio speaks of his "austere regard of *control*." Dr. Hotson suggests, less plausibly, that the name Malvolio is a pun on *Mallvoglio* (I want Mall) and is an allusion to the fact that Knollys at the age of fifty-three had fallen in love with his charge, Mary Fitton, who became pregnant by another man. Dr. Hotson shows that Viola was the flower of faithfulness, and that the *viola da braccia* was Apollo's instrument and the symbol of passion and chastity. He does not, however, suggest that there was a pun on *braccia* and Virginio Orsino, Count of *Bracciano*, before whom the play was probably performed. It should be mentioned that in Emmanuel Forde's *Parismus* (1598) there is a Violetta who is shipwrecked while following her lover in the disguise of a page, and also an Olivia.

Whether because the play was performed on Twelfth Night, or because of the reference to the Epiphany in *Gl' Ingannati*, or for both reasons, Shakespeare introduces references to the message of the Epiphany as expressed in the words "Today we are liberated from darkness and illuminated by the light of divine knowledge." Feste, for example, tells Malvolio that "there is no darkness but ignorance," and the phrases "rain odours" and "sweet south" (if that is the true reading) recall the Epiphany ceremony.[13]

It has been suggested by Mr. F. Pyle[14] and others that Shakespeare drew on Sidney's *Arcadia* for certain details, but the resemblances are slight. Women disguised as men and men who are tricked by forged letters are too common to be significant. Nor is there any evidence that Shakespeare was influenced by the play, formerly ascribed to Peele, entitled *Sir Clyomon and Sir Clamydes*, or by another crude play entitled *Common Conditions*.

These were the materials on which Shakespeare set to work. I find it difficult to accept Dr. Hotson's theory that the play was written, acted, and rehearsed within a fortnight, though it is possible that the poet adapted a play already written, or partly written, /74/ to suit the topical occasion of Orsino's visit. Shakespeare was not enormously prolific, like the Spanish dramatists with whom Dr. Hotson compares him. If he could have written a masterpiece in ten days his company would have expected him to write more than two plays a year.

Shakespeare adopts a new setting for the plot, abandoning both the Italian town of Modena and the city of Constantinople in favour of Illyria. The social *milieu* of his characters is closest to that of Riche's novel, but Olivia's Illyrian household is essentially Elizabethan. From Riche, too, Shakespeare borrowed the shipwreck as a convenient beginning to his play, but he rejected the episode of the lecherous Captain. Viola's Captain has a fair behaviour in him. Silla is disguised first as Pedro's sister and then in the Captain's clothes; Viola disguises herself as much like her brother as possible, and this makes it more plausible that she should be mistaken for him. Silla is journeying to Constantinople for love of Apolonius when she is shipwrecked. Although Viola decides to take service with Orsino—as a eunuch[15]—she does so only after she has been told that she has no chance of serving Olivia. Shakespeare also avoids the situation of *Gl' Ingannati* in which Lelia has been jilted by Flaminio. Viola and Sebastian—we are not

---

[12] Cf. E. K. Chambers, *William Shakespeare*, i. 407, and L. Hotson, op. cit., pp. 93 ff.

[13] Hotson, op. cit., pp. 145 ff.

[14] Cf. F. Pyle, *M.I.R.* 1948, p. 449, and the Variorum *T.N.*

[15] But presumably she changes her mind when it comes to the point, for Orsino assumes that Cesario will eventually marry.

told the purpose of their voyage—are separated by shipwreck, as the twins had been separated in *The Comedy of Errors*. This brings them both to Illyria, each thinking the other drowned. It is dramatically important that Sebastian should think Viola dead, as he would otherwise jump to the conclusion that he had been mistaken for her. Silvio, although he is looking for Silla, never puts two and two together.

Shakespeare wisely dispenses with the parents of Lelia and Isabella and with Lelia's unwelcome suitor, Isabella's father. Sebastian and Viola are orphans, and Olivia is alone in the world. The courage and self-reliance of Viola are thus increased and Olivia's isolation allows both Sir Andrew and Malvolio to aspire to her hand.

In the first act of *Gl' Ingannati* we have the situation presented to us of Isabella falling in love with Lelia, who is in love with Flaminio, who loves Isabella, and Isabella's father wishes to marry Lelia. By cutting out Gherardo, Shakespeare, by the end of his first act, is able to reach the same point in his plot, with Olivia in love /75/ with Viola, Viola in love with Orsino, and Orsino in love with Olivia—too hard a knot for Viola to untie; but in the first act we have also been introduced to the characters of the underplot; Sir Andrew's pretensions to Olivia's hand prepare the way for his duel with Viola, and Malvolio's scorn for Feste makes an enemy of him.

Lelia's brother does not appear till the third act of *Gl' Ingannati*; Shakespeare introduces Sebastian at the beginning of Act II, and in the same act we have the interruption of the revellers, the hatching of the plot against Malvolio, and a scene in which Viola is able indirectly to express her love for Orsino. In the second act of *Gl' Ingannati* Flaminio hears of the favours granted to his page, and he wishes to kill both Isabella and Lelia. In Riche's version Apolonius does not become jealous until after Silvio has been entertained by Julina. Shakespeare does not allow Orsino to hear of Olivia's love for Cesario until just before the end of the play, and he then proposes to sacrifice the lamb he loves (Cesario) to spite Olivia. It is obvious that he is unconsciously fonder of Cesario than of Olivia; and this, together with Viola's willingness to die for love, prepares the way for the sudden transfer of Orsino's affections. To make possible the postponement of Orsino's knowledge of Olivia's love of Cesario it was necessary to postpone her declaration of love until the third act and Sebastian's meeting with her until the fourth. The intervening scenes, which prevent the action from seeming slow, are filled with plenty of matter for a May morning—Malvolio's appearance in yellow stockings and his treatment as a lunatic, Sir Andrew's challenge, the intervention and arrest of Antonio, and Viola's realization that Sebastian is alive. In the second half of the play Shakespeare owes nothing to the complicated intrigue of *Gl' Ingannati*, which, indeed, more resembles the farce of *The Comedy of Errors*; but by having Sir Andrew, Sir Toby, and the Fool all mistake Sebastian for Cesario he makes a similar use of mistaken identity. In *Gl' Ingannati* Lelia and Fabrizio are never on the stage together and they could be played by one actor or actress. In *Apolonius and Silla* Silvio does not discover his lost sister until after her marriage. Shakespeare has the more dramatic confrontation of brother and sister and the revelation of Cesario's sex in the last act of the play.

Professor T. W. Baldwin has shown with what skill *Twelfth Night* was constructed "on the Andria variety of the Terentian formula"; and he suggests that the interest of *Gl' Ingannati* falls off /76/ after the second act when we reach the epitasis of the more interesting story and have to wait for the catastrophe for more than two acts. Shakespeare, on the other hand, delays the epitasis both of the Viola–Olivia situation and of Malvolio's suit to Olivia until the third act.[16] But although we may well admire the art with which Shakespeare has constructed his play, its superiority to all its sources is displayed more obviously in the characterization, in the humour of the prose scenes, and above all in the poetic texture of the play as a whole. /77/

16 Cf. T. W. Baldwin, *Five-Act Structure*, p. 715.

Petronius The Satyricon: The Pleasures of Peace

Petronius Arbiter can probably be identified as both a novelist and a courtier. On the basis of his success as a proconsul, he attracted the attention of Nero, who made him his *elegantiae arbiter* (arbiter of taste); in that capacity, he presided over the distractions of the corrupt Roman court until, denounced by a rival and fearing the Emperor's disfavor, he committed suicide in 66 A.D.

Presumably, this same Petronius is the author of *The Satyricon*, a comic romance, which relates the adventures of three rogues in the villages of southern Italy. The work is distinguished for its range of Latin slang and for its many satirical digressions, the most prominent of which is the famous "Widow of Ephesus" the source for Christopher Fry's *A Phoenix Too Frequent*.

The translation from which this episode has been selected was made by William Arrowsmith and published by The New American Library (New York, 1959). Professor Arrowsmith, former Rhodes Scholar, holder of a Guggenheim Fellowship, and winner of the *Prix de Rome*, teacher at the University of Texas. He has also made numerous translations of Greek dramas.

Meanwhile Eumolpus, our spokesman in the hour of danger and the author of our present reconciliation, anxious that our gaiety should not be broken, began, in a sudden moment of silence, to gibe at the fickleness of women, the wonderful ease with which they became infatuated, their readiness to abandon their children for their lovers, and so forth. In fact, he declared, no woman was so chaste or faithful that she couldn't be seduced; sooner or later she would fall head over heels in love with some passing stranger. Nor, he added, was he thinking so much of the old tragedies and the classics of love betrayed as of something that had happened in our own time; in fact, if we were willing /121/ to hear, he would be delighted to tell the story. All eyes and ears were promptly turned to our narrator, and he began:

"Once upon a time there was a certain married woman in the city of Ephesus whose fidelity to her husband was so famous that the women from all the neighboring towns and villages used to troop into Ephesus merely to stare at this prodigy. It happened, however, that her husband one day died. Finding the normal custom of following the cortege with hair unbound and beating her breast in public quite inadequate to express her grief, the lady insisted on following the corpse right into the tomb, an underground vault of the Greek type, and there set herself to guard the body, weeping and wailing night and day. Although in her extremes of grief she was clearly courting death from starvation, her parents were utterly unable to persuade her to leave, and even the magistrates, after one last supreme attempt, were rebuffed and driven away. In short, all Ephesus had gone into mourning for this extraordinary woman, all the more since the lady was now passing her fifth consecutive day without once tasting food. Beside the failing woman sat her devoted maid, sharing her mistress' grief and relighting the lamp whenever it flickered out. The whole city could speak, in fact, of nothing else: here at last, all classes alike agreed, was the one true example of conjugal fidelity and love.

"In the meantime, however, the governor of the province gave orders that several thieves should be crucified[1] in a spot close by the vault where the lady was mourning her dead husband's corpse. So, on the following night, the soldier who had been assigned to keep watch on the crosses so that nobody could remove the thieves' bodies for burial suddenly noticed a light blazing among the tombs and heard the sounds of groaning. And prompted by a natural human curiosity to know who or what was making those sounds, he descended into the vault.

"But at the sight of a strikingly beautiful woman, he stopped short in terror, thinking he must be seeing some ghostly appari- /122/ tion out of hell. Then, observing the corpse and seeing the tears on the lady's face and the scratches her fingernails had gashed in her cheeks, he realized what it was: a widow, in inconsolable grief. Promptly fetching his little supper back down to the tomb, he implored the lady not to persist in her sorrow or break her heart with useless mourning. All men alike, he reminded her, have the same end; the same

---

[1] Crucifixion was the commonest form of capital punishment in the ancient world, and was usually reserved for the worst types of criminals or the very lowest orders of society.

resting place awaits us all. He used, in short, all those platitudes we use to comfort the suffering and bring them back to life. His consolations, being unwelcome, only exasperated the widow more; more violently than ever she beat her breast, and tearing out her hair by the roots, scattered it over the dead man's body. Undismayed, the soldier repeated his arguments and pressed her to take some food, until the little maid, quite overcome by the smell of the wine, succumbed and stretched out her hand to her tempter. Then, restored by the food and wine, she began herself to assail her mistress' obstinate refusal.

" 'How will it help you,' she asked the lady, 'if you faint from hunger? Why should you bury yourself alive, and go down to death before the Fates have called you? What does Vergil say?

> Do you suppose the shades and ashes of the dead are by such sorrow touched?

No, begin your life afresh. Shake off these woman's scruples; enjoy the light while you can. Look at that corpse of your poor husband: doesn't it tell you more eloquently than any words that you should live?'

"None of us, of course, really dislikes being told that we must eat, that life is to be lived. And the lady was no exception. Weakened by her long days of fasting, her resistance crumbled at last, and she ate the food the soldier offered her as hungrily as the little maid had eaten earlier.

"Well, you know what temptations are normally aroused in a man on a full stomach. So the soldier, mustering all those /123/ blandishments by means of which he had persuaded the lady to live, now laid determined siege to her virtue. And chaste though she was, the lady found him singularly attractive and his arguments persuasive. As for the maid, she did all she could to help the soldier's cause, repeating like a refrain the appropriate line of Vergil:

If love is pleasing, lady, yield yourself to love.

To make the matter short, the lady's body soon gave up the struggle; she yielded and our happy warrior enjoyed a total triumph on both counts. That very night their marriage was consummated, and they slept together the second and the third night too, carefully shutting the door of the tomb so that any passing friend or stranger would have thought the lady of famous chastity had at last expired over her dead husband's body.

"As you can perhaps imagine, our soldier was a very happy man, utterly delighted with his lady's ample beauty and that special charm that a secret love confers. Every night, as soon as the sun had set, he brought what few provisions his slender pay permitted and smuggled them down to the tomb. One night, however, the parents of one of the crucified thieves, noticing that the watch was being badly kept, took advantage of our hero's absence to remove their son's body and bury it. The next morning, of course, the soldier was horror-struck to discover one of the bodies missing from its cross, and ran to tell his mistress of the horrible punishment which awaited him for neglecting his duty. In the circumstances, he told her, he would not wait to be tried and sentenced, but would punish himself then and there with his own sword. All he asked of her was that she make room for another corpse and allow the same gloomy tomb to enclose husband and lover together.

"Our lady's heart, however, was no less tender than pure. 'God forbid,' she cried, 'that I should have to see at one and the same time the dead bodies of the only two men I have ever loved. No, /124/ better far, I say, to hang the dead than kill the living.' With these words, she gave orders that her husband's body should be taken from its bier and strung up on the empty cross. The soldier followed this good advice, and the next morning the whole city wondered by what miracle the dead man had climbed up on the cross." /125/

III
Some Theories of Comedy

Aristotle Poetics: Comedy

The _Poetics_ of Aristotle (384-322 B.C.) was written in the philosopher's late period, about 330 B.C. It is one of the most famous works of literary criticism in the world, inasmuch as its influence has been lasting; in particular, the observations which Aristotle made in it about the structure and nature of drama were accepted as strictures for the composition of plays during the neoclassical periods (sixteenth to eighteenth centuries) in most European countries. Aristotle evidently reserved a section of the _Poetics_ for a consideration of the nature of Comedy; since that part has been lost (perhaps he never completed it), the following words about Comedy have been taken from the section on Tragedy. The text used here is from _The Student's Oxford Aristotle_, translated by Ingram Bywater (N. Y.: Oxford University Press, 1942).

1 Epic poetry and Tragedy, as also Comedy, Dithyrambic poetry,[1] and most flute-playing and lyre-playing, are all, viewed as a whole, modes of imitation. But at the same time they differ from one another in three ways, either by a difference of kind in their means, or by differences in the objects, or in the manner of their imitations.

2 . . . This difference it is that distinguishes Tragedy and Comedy also; the one would make its personages worse, and the other better, than the men of the present day.

3 So that as an imitator Sophocles will be on one side akin to Homer, both portraying good men; and on another to Aristophanes, since both present their personages as acting and doing. This in fact, according to some, is the reason for plays being termed dramas, because in a play the personages act the story. Hence too both Tragedy and Comedy are claimed by the Dorians as their discoveries; Comedy by the Megarians—by those in Greece as having arisen when Megara[2] became a demo-

cracy, and by the Sicilian Megarians on the ground that the poet Epicharmus[3] was of their country, and a good deal earlier than Chionides and Magnes; even Tragedy also is claimed by certain of the Peloponnesian Dorians. In support of this claim they point to the words "comedy" and "drama." Their word for the outlying hamlets, they say, is _comae_, whereas Athenians call them _demes_—thus assuming that comedians got the name not from their _comoe_, or revels, but from their strolling from hamlet to hamlet, lack of appreciation keeping them out of the city.[4]

4 Poetry, however, soon broke up into two kinds according to the differences of character in the individual poets; for the graver among them would represent noble actions, and those of noble personages; and the meaner sort the actions of the ignoble. The latter class produced invectives at first, just as others did hymns and panegyrics. We know of no such poem by any of the pre-Homeric poets, though there were probably many such writers among them; instances, however, may be found from Homer downwards, e.g., his _Margites_,[5] and the similar poems of others. In this poetry of invective its natural fitness brought an iambic metre into use; hence our present term "iambic," because it was the metre of their "iambs" or invectives against one another. The result was that the old poets became some of them writers of heroic and others of iambic verse. Homer's position, however, is peculiar: just as he was in the serious style the poet of poets, standing alone not only through the literary excellence, but also through the dramatic character of his imitations, so too he was the first to outline for us the general

---

[1] Choral hymns sung at the festivals of Dionysus, out of which Greek tragedy evolved.

[2] A Dorian city, near the base of the Isthmus of Corinth, overlooking Salamis.

[3] A comic poet of the fifth century B.C., who wrote in the Dorian dialect.

[4] See the essays on _The Birds_ (pp. 254-58) for other theories about the origins of comedy.

[5] A lost satirical epic poem, which Aristotle attributes to Homer.

forms of Comedy by producing not a dramatic invective, but a dramatic picture of the Ridiculous; his *Margites* in fact stands in the same relation to our comedies as the *Iliad* and *Odyssey* to our tragedies. As soon, however, as Tragedy and Comedy appeared in the field, those naturally drawn to the one line of poetry became writers of comedies instead of iambs, and those naturally drawn to the other, writers of tragedies instead of epics, because these new modes of art were grander and of more esteem than the old.

It [tragedy] certainly began in improvisations—as did also Comedy; the one originating with the authors of the Dithyramb, the other with those of the phallic songs, which still survive as institutions in many of our cities.

5   As for Comedy, it is (as has been observed) an imitation of men worse than the average; worse, however, not as regards any and every sort of fault, but only as regards one particular kind, the Ridiculous, which is a species of the Ugly. The Ridiculous may be defined as a mistake or deformity not productive of pain or harm to others; the mask, for instance, that excites laughter, is something ugly and distorted without causing pain.

Though the successive changes in Tragedy and their authors are not unknown, we cannot say the same of Comedy; its early stages passed unnoticed, because it was not as yet taken up in a serious way. It was only at a late point in its progress that a chorus of comedians was officially granted by the archon;[6] they used to be mere volunteers. It had also already certain definite forms at the time when the record of those termed comic poets begins. Who it was who supplied it with masks, or prologues, or a plurality of actors and the like, has remained unknown. The invented Fable, or Plot, however, originated in Sicily with Epicharmus and Phormis; of Athenian poets Crates was the first to drop the Comedy of invective and frame stories of a general and non-personal nature, in other words, Fables or Plots.

[6] A high civic official who assigned Choruses, trained at the expense of wealthy citizens, to the Athenian dramatists for use in their plays.

Louis Kronenberger   # Some Prefatory Words on Comedy

"Some Prefatory Words on Comedy" is the introductory section of a longer work. Published in 1952, *The Thread of Laughter* (Alfred A. Knopf, New York), subtitled "Chapters on English Stage Comedy from Jonson to Maugham," is one of many critical works by Louis Kronenberger. Mr. Kronenberger, born in 1904 in Cincinnati, Ohio, is a graduate of the municipal university. He got his start in the publishing world with the firm of Boni and Liveright; in 1936, he became an editor of *Fortune;* two years later he moved to *Time* as drama critic. Besides two novels, Mr. Kronenberger has written mainly of the eighteenth century; in recent years he has taught at both Columbia and Brandeis Universities.

Comedy is not just a happy as opposed to an unhappy ending, but a way of surveying life so that happy endings must prevail. But it is not to be confused, on that account, with optimism, any more than a happy ending is to be confused with happiness. Comedy is much more reasonably associated with pessimism—with at any rate a belief in the smallness that survives as against the greatness that is scarred or destroyed. In mortal affairs it is tragedy, like forgiveness, that seems divine; and comedy, like error, that is human.

One might perhaps begin by talking about comedy in its philosophic sense, as an attitude toward life, rather than as a mere technical aspect of the theater. One might begin, in other words, by speaking of the comedy that unites such writers and writings as Lucian and Aristophanes, the *Decameron* and *Candide*, Congreve and Peacock and Sterne, *Pride and Prejudice* and *Le Bourgeois Gentilhomme*, rather than of the comedy that is the official label for such diverse plays as *Measure for Measure* and *The Man of Mode*, or *All's Well That Ends Well* and *The Importance of |3| Being Earnest*, or *The Misanthrope* and *Private Lives*. For obviously—despite immense differences—the same spirit animates an Aristophanes and a Jane Austen; whereas a vastly different spirit separates *Measure for Measure* from *The Importance of Being Earnest. Measure for Measure*, we feel, is not really comedy; and *The Misanthrope*, again, is something more than comedy. But coarse as Aristophanes can be and genteel as Jane Austen, broadly as Aristophanes can clown and exquisitely as Jane Austen can annihilate, the two have much the same vision of life, much the same eye for its absurdities. They have in full measure the comic point of view, as other writers have the tragic point of view. In the theater, comedy and tragedy are forms that can be used with some purity. Much Restoration comedy was indeed written with some purity. Today, when the theater is debased by the naturalistic drama, when the drama itself is three parts play to seven parts production, when the only comedy that most playwrights try for is standing-room comedy—today very little in the theater really expresses the comic sense of life. Far from probing, it seldom even honestly paints the surface. And the real trouble is not that the contemporary stage aims at artifice, but that it professes to aim at naturalness. It was one of the real virtues of the Restoration stage that it never sought—and never managed   to be "natural." It lied its head off about a good many of the appurtenances of life, but it managed to capture a surprising amount of the thing itself; and even its lies squared with the partial truth that life is a masquerade.

Comedy appeals to the laughter, which is in part at least the malice, in us; for comedy is concerned with human imperfection, with people's failure to measure up either to the world's or to their own conception of excellence. All tragedy is idealistic and says in effect, "The pity of it"—that owing to this fault of circumstance or that flaw of character, a man who is essentially good does evil, a man who is essentially great is toppled from the heights. But all comedy tends to be skeptical and says in effect, "The absurdity of it"—that in spite of his fine talk or noble resolutions, a man is the mere creature of pettiness and vanity and folly. Tragedy is always lamenting the Achilles tendon, the /4/ destructive flaw in man; but comedy, in a sense, is always looking for it. Not cheaply, out of malevolence or cynicism; but rather because even at his greatest, man offers some touch of the fatuous and small, just as a murderer, even at his cleverest, usually makes some fatal slip. In tragedy men aspire to more than they can achieve; in comedy, they pretend to more.

The difference, again, between the two is the very question of difference. A great tragic hero— an Oedipus or Lear—strikes us as tremendously far removed from common humanity. But comedy, stripping off the war-paint and the feathers, the college degrees or the military medals, shows how very like at bottom the hero is to everybody else. Tragedy cannot flourish without giving its characters a kind of aura of poetry, or idealism, or doom; comedy scarcely functions till the aura has been dispelled. And as it thrives on a revelation of the true rather than the trumped-up motive, as it is in one way sustained by imposture, so in another it is sustained by incongruity. Here is the celebrated philosopher cursing the universe because he has mislaid a book. Here are all those who, like King Canute, would bid the clock go backward or the waves stand still. Here is not only the cheat, but the victim who but for his own dishonest desires could never be cheated.

Comedy, in brief, is criticism. If through laughing at others we purge ourselves of certain spiteful and ungenerous instincts—as through tragedy we achieve a higher and more publicized catharsis— that is not quite the whole of it. Comedy need not be hostile to idealism; it need only show how far human beings fall short of the ideal. The higher comedy mounts, the airier and more brilliant its forms, the more are we aware of man's capacity for being foolish or self-deluded or complacent; in the very highest comedy, such as the finale of Mozart's *Marriage of Figaro*, we are in a very paradise of self deceptions and misunderstandings and cross-purposes. At the heart of high comedy there is always a strain of melancholy, as round the edges there is all gaiety and ebullience and glitter; and Schiller was perhaps right in regarding high comedy as the greatest of all literary forms.

Comedy is criticism, then, because it exposes human beings /5/ for what they are in contrast to what they profess to be. How much idealism, it asks, shall we find entirely free from self-love? How much beneficence is born of guilt, how much affection is produced by flattery? At its most severe, doubtless, comedy is not just skeptical but cynical; and asks many of the same questions, returning many of the same answers, as that prince— or at any rate duke— of cynics, La Rochefoucauld. "Pride," La Rochefoucauld remarked, "does not wish to owe, and vanity does not wish to pay." Or again: "To establish oneself in the world, one does all one can to seem established there." Of these and many similar maxims, a play or story might easily be written; from each much cold and worldly comedy, or harsh and worldly farce, might be contrived. But comedy need not be so harsh, and seldom is: though it can be harsher still, can be—

as in Ben Jonson—gloating and sardonic. But always it is the enemy, not of virtue or idealism, but of hypocrisy and pretense; and what it does in literature is very much, I suppose, what experience does for most of us in life: it knocks the bloom off the peach, the gilt off the gingerbread.

But though the comic spirit is, in Meredith's phrase, "humanely malign," it is also kindly and even companionable, in the sense that it brings men together as fellow-fools and sinners, and is not only criticism but understanding. Comedy is always jarring us with the evidence that we are no better than other people, and always comforting us with the knowledge that most other people are no better than we are. It makes us more critical but it leaves us more tolerant; and to that extent it performs a very notable social function. Its whole character, indeed—quite aside from that point—is rather social than individual.

The social basis rests in the very subject-matter of comedy—in all that has to do with one's life as part of a group; with one's wish to charm or persuade or deceive or dazzle others. Thus no exhibitionist can exist in solitude, no hypocrite or poseur can work without an audience. There are indeed so many social situations that engender comedy that many of them are notably hackneyed. There are all kinds of classic family jokes—the mother-in-law joke preëminently; but equally the rich-uncle /6/ theme, or the country cousin, or the visiting relative who forgets to leave, or the one that proffers advice, or the one that prophesies disaster. Right in the home there is the precocious brat or the moping adolescent; there are countless varieties of comic servants; and there is finally the question, though it perhaps belongs in a different category, of who heads the family—the husband or the wife.

The idea of husband and wife more likely belongs with the social aspects of sex, with the War Between the Sexes as it is fought out in the drawing room. As a purely sexual conflict, this war would not be social; but by the same token it would not be comedy. The question whether man really makes the decisions—including the decision to marry—or is merely permitted to think he does, is, whatever the answer, thoroughly social in nature. Or there is the business of how men and women perform in society for one another's benefit; being the fearless protector or the clinging vine, the woman who always understands or the man who is never understood. We have social comedy again when we pit one nationality as well as one sex against another, when the American puritan is ensnared by a continental siren, or when the suitor is German and humorless, and the besought one is French and amused. There is still another social aspect when we add a third person to the situation, a mistress as well as a wife, or a lover as well as a husband; or—for the situation need not be illicit, it need only be triangular—when the wife's old beau or the husband's old flame reappears on the scene. Or there is the man who does not know which of two sisters, or two heiresses, or two widows to marry; or the girl which of a half dozen suitors.

Comedy, indeed, must gain admittance into any part of the world—including prisons and sickrooms and funerals—where people are thrown together. Any institution involving hierarchies and rivalries—for example, a university—is a perfect hotbed of it. There will be everybody's relation to the President or the President's wife; or the President's relation to the President's wife; or to his trustees; all the struggles for precedence and the problems of protocol; the progressives on the faculty /7/ and the die-hards; the wives who can't help looking dowdy, the wives who suppose they look chic. For obviously any institution, whether a college or a department store, an artist colony or a country club, provides a cross-section of social types and traits, and brings us face to face with a hundred things out of which comedy is distilled: ambition and pride, arrogance and obsequiousness; a too-slavish following or a too-emphatic flouting of convention; all the stratagems men use in order to outwit or get their way.

And of course comedy becomes purely social in that best known and perhaps best liked of all its higher forms—the comedy of manners. Here we have hardly less than a picture of society itself; here the men and women are but parts of a general whole, and what survives—if we have it from the past—is likely to be known as the Restoration Scene, or Regency London, or Victorian Family Life. Here the drawing room is not merely the setting of the play or novel, but the subject and even the hero; here enter all the prejudices, the traditions, the taboos, the aspirations, the absurdities, the snobberies, of a group. The group, to constitute itself one, must partake of a common background and accept a similar view of life: though there will usually exist some outsider, some rebel, some nonconformist who, as the case may be, is ringing the doorbell or shattering the window panes; trying desperately to get in or desperately to get out; bending the knee or thumbing his nose. Or the comedy of manners will contrast one social milieu with another—the urban and the rustic, the capital and the provinces, Philistia and Bohemia, America and Europe. And in the comedy of manners, ignorance of good form has much the same value that, in straight drama, ignorance of some vital fact has.

And with ignorance of one kind or another we begin coming close to the very mainspring of comedy, or at any rate of comedy in action. For most comedy is born of ignorance or false knowledge; is based on misunderstanding. (Obviously not knowing the truth—though here one might add "until it is too late"—applies to much tragedy also.) At the level of ordinary farce or romantic comedy, the lovers are estranged until a quarter of /8/ eleven because the young man misunderstood why the young lady was walking with Sir Robert in the garden. At a higher level, it will not be mere circumstance or coincidence, but qualities of character that block the way. Envy proves an obstruction, or arrogance; or a too-great tendency to be suspicious or to take offense. In *Pride and Prejudice* the very title makes this clear. In Jane Austen's finest novel, *Emma*, there is every variety of misunderstanding, but the greatest misunderstanding of all, and the one that leads to so many of the others, is Emma's concerning her own nature. Emma—so high-handed and so wrongheaded, so often reasonable and so seldom right—is herself a wonderfully modulated comic character. And what matters is not so much the realistic consequences of her mistakes as the assured and benevolent air with which she commits them. And now moving higher still, to Meredith's *The Egoist*, we see self-deluded character constituting, really, the whole book. Sir Willoughby Patterne is the supreme example of self-centeredness in literature—the man who, in his absorption with the creature he is and the role he plays and the impression he makes, can care about nobody else. He tramples on the emotions and even the liberties of all who come his way, only cherishing such people so far as they cherish or pay homage to him. He is stunned by what seems to him *their* selfishness when, appalled by his, they walk out or turn away. And as we watch Meredith's great demonstration of human egoism, as we see with what comic flourishes and farcical leaps and wild extravagant motions it proceeds—as we smile and even laugh— we become increasingly uncomfortable. The more monstrous Sir Willoughby seems, the more we realize that in some sense this man is ourselves. If no one ever misunderstood his own nature worse, no one has ever pointed a moral better. Comedy at its greatest is criticism indeed; is nothing less, in fact, than a form of moral enlightenment.

The Egoist is sometimes declared to be comedy in name only, to be at bottom tragic. I would myself disagree—Meredith carries his theme to so extreme a length as to transform his hero from a man into a sort of sublime caricature, and gives him a purely comic intensity, an intensity quite disproportionate to /9/ what it is intense about. If just this is the "tragedy" of most human beings, it must yet serve to expose rather than exalt them; otherwise what shall we call genuine tragedy when we encounter it? Malvolio in *Twelfth Night*, who has also been looked upon as tragic, comes somewhat closer to being so. For pretension with him does partake a little of aspiration; his vanity, moreover, is stung because he is a servant, and stimulated by the mischievousness of others. But Malvolio, like Sir Willoughby, is really too trivial for tragedy, as he is also too priggish. What happens to him seems painful rather than tragic; it is not quite our modern idea of fun.

And this brings up the point that though Comedy has its permanent subject-matter and even its body of laws, it is liable, like everything else, to changes in fashion and taste, to differences of sensibility. One generation's pleasure is the next generation's embarrassment; much that the Victorians shuddered at merely makes us laugh, much that they laughed at might well make us shudder. One always reacts—and quite fortunately—from the vantage-point of one's own age; and it is probably a mistake, and certainly a waste of breath, to be arrogant or snobbish or moral about what amuses or does not amuse one: we may fancy we are less callous than our grandfathers and only be less callous about different things. The cuckold was clearly, in Restoration comedy, a figure to hoot at. Simply for being cuckolded we do not today find a man so comic, or even comic at all: though the moment we add an extra element to his role, such as his elation over cuckolding others, he becomes a comic figure for us. To what extent sex itself is a comic theme must naturally vary with the morality of a particular age: there are times when it seems shocking for a man ever to have a mistress; there are times when it seems even more shocking for a man never to have one. Right in the same age, what is considered virtue by the parson may be termed repression by the psychiatrist; and in such an age, which is usually one of moral transition, we may well find conflicting comedy values. The pendulum-swing of taste always makes it hard for people to know what they really like: if they are in revolt against gentility, they are /10/ likely to confuse what is funny with what is merely bold or obscene; if they are converts to gentility, they will be too much outraged by the indecent to inquire whether it is funny. There is nothing at which the Comic Spirit must smile more than our fickle and inconstant notions as to what constitutes comedy. We need not always look back to Shakespeare's drearier clowns as an instance of how tastes change: sometimes we need only attend a revival of what convulsed us ten years before. /11/

William Congreve `Concerning Humour in Comedy

William Congreve (1670-1729) was one of the chief Restoration dramatists; his works are distinguished not alone by wit, but by a brilliant sense of theatre. Commended in his own time by Dryden as one "whom ev'ry Muse and Grace adorn," he has, through the repeated revivals of such plays as *Love for Love* (1695) and *The Way of the World* (1700), maintained his distinguished place in the history of English comedy. Congreve's letter to John Dennis (1657-1734), a fellow dramatist and critic, shows his own as well as his age's position; it has been, quite rightly, called a "happy piece of constructive criticism." The text used here is from the original edition, *Letters upon Several Occasions Written by and between Mr. Dryden, Mr. Wycherly, Mr. Congreve, and Mr. Dennis* (London: Printed for Sam. Briscoe, at the Corner-Shop of Charles-Street in Russel-Street in Covent Garden. 1696).

DEAR SIR,

You write to me, that you have Entertained your self two or three days, with reading several Comedies, of several Authors; and your Observation is, that there is more of *Humour* in our English Writers, than in any of the other Comick Poets, Ancient or Modern. You desire to know my Opinion, and at the same time my Thought, of that which is generally call'd *Humour* in Comedy.

I agree with you, in an Impartial Preference of our English Writers, in that Particular. But if I tell you my Thoughts of *Humour*, I must at the same time confess, that what I take for true *Humour*, has not been so often written even by them, as is generally believed: And some who have valued themselves, and have been esteem'd by /80/ others, for that kind of Writing, have seldom touch'd upon it. To make this appear to the World, would require a long and labour'd Discourse, and such as I neither am able nor willing to undertake. But such little Remarks, as may be continued within the Compass of a Letter, and

such unpremeditated Thoughts, as may be Communicated between Friend and Friend, without incurring the Censure of the World, or setting up for a *Dictator*, you shall have from me, since you have enjoyn'd it.

To Define *Humour*, perhaps, were as difficult, as to Define *Wit;* for like that, it is of infinite variety. To Enumerate the several *Humours* of Men, were a Work as endless, as to sum up their several Opinions. And in my mind the *Quot homines tot Sententiæ,*[1] might have been more properly interpreted of *Humour;* since there are many Men, of the same Opinion in many things, who are yet quite different in Humours. But thô we cannot certainly tell what *Wit* is, or, what *Humour* is, yet we may go near to shew something, which is not *Wit* or not *Humour;* and yet often mistaken for both. And since I have mentioned *Wit* and *Humour* together, let me make the first Distinction between them, and observe to you that *Wit is often mistaken for Humour.* /81/

I have observed, that when a few things have been Wittily and Pleasantly spoken by any Character in a Comedy; it has been very usual for those, who make their Remarks on a Play, while it is acting, to say, *Such a thing is very Humorously spoken: There is a great Deal of Humour in that Part.* Thus the Character of the Person speaking, may be, Surprizingly and Pleasantly, is mistaken for a Character of *Humour;* which indeed is a Character of *Wit.* But there is great Difference between a Comedy, wherein there are many things *Humorously*, as they call it, which is *Pleasantly* spoken; and one, where there are several Characters of *Humour*, distinguish'd by the Particular and Different Humours, appropriated to the several Persons represented, and which naturally arise, from the

---

[1] As many opinions as there are men.

different Constitutions, Complexions, and Dispositions of Men. The saying of Humorous Things, does not distinguish Characters; For every Person in a Comedy may be allow'd to speak them. From a Witty Man they are expected; and even a *Fool* may be permitted to stumble on 'em by chance. Thô I make a Difference betwixt *Wit* and *Humour;* yet I do not think that Humorous Characters exclude *Wit*: No, but the Manner of *Wit* should be a- /82/ dapted to the *Humour*. As for Instance, a Character of a Splenetick and Peevish *Humour*, should have a Satyrical Wit. A Jolly and Sanguine *Humour*, should have a Facetious Wit. The Former should speak Positively; the Latter, Carelessly; For the former Observes, and shews things as they are; the latter, rather overlooks Nature, and speaks things as he would have them; and his *Wit* and *Humour* have both of them a less Alloy of Judgment than the others.

As *Wit*, so, its opposite, *Folly, is sometimes mistaken for Humour.*

When a Poet brings a *Character* on the Stage, committing a thousand Absurdities, and talking Impertinencies, roaring Aloud, and Laughing immoderately, on every, or rather upon no occasion; this is a Character of Humour.

Is any thing more common, than to have a pretended Comedy, stuff'd with such Grotesques, Figures, and Farce Fools? Things, that either are not in Nature, or if they are, are Monsters, and Births of Mischance; and consequently as such, should be stifled, and huddled out of the way, like *Sooterkins;*[2] that Mankind may not be shock'd with an appearing Possibility of the Degeneration of a God-like *Species*. For my part, I am as willing to Laugh, as /83/ any body, and as easily diverted with an Object truly ridiculous: but at the same time, I can never care for seeing things, that force me to entertain low thoughts of my Nature. I don't know how it is with others, but I confess freely to you, I could never look long upon a Monkey, without very Mortifying Reflections; thô I never heard any thing to the Contrary, why that Creature is not Originally of a Distinct *Species*. As I dont think *Humour* exclusive of *Wit*, neither do I think it inconsistent with *Folly;* but I think the Follies should be only such, as Mens Humours may incline 'em to; and not Follies intirely abstracted from both Humour and Nature.

Sometimes, *Personal Defects are misrepresented for Humours.*

I mean, sometimes Characters are barbarously

exposed on the Stage, ridiculing Natural Deformities, Casual Defects in the Senses, and Infirmities of Age. Sure the Poet must both be very Ill-natur'd himself, and think his Audience so, when he proposes by shewing a Man Deform'd, or Deaf, or Blind, to give them an agreeable Entertainment; and hopes to raise their Mirth, by what is truly an object of Compassion. But much need not be said upon this Head to any body, especially to you, who in one /84/ of your Letters to me concerning Mr. *Johnson's Fox*,[3] have justly excepted against this Immoral part of *Ridicule* in *Corbaccio's* Character; and there I must agree with you to blame him, whom otherwise I cannot enough admire, for his great Mastery of true Humour in Comedy.

External Habit of Body is often mistaken for Humour.

By *External Habit*, I do not mean the Ridiculous Dress or Cloathing of a Character, thô that goes a good way in some received Characters. (But undoubtedly a Man's Humour may incline him to dress differently from other People.) But I mean a Singularity of Manners, Speech, and Behaviour, peculiar to all, or most of the same Country, Trade, Profession, or Education. I cannot think, that a *Humour*, which is only a Habit, or Disposition contracted by Use or Custom; for by a Disuse, or Complyance with other Customs, it may be worn off, or diversify'd.

Affectation is generally mistaken for Humour.

These are indeed so much alike, that at a Distance, they may be mistaken one for the other. For what is *Humour* in one, may be *Affectation* in another; and nothing is more common, than for some to affect particular /85/ ways of saying, and doing things, peculiar to others, whom they admire and would imitate. *Humour* is the Life, *Affectation* the Picture. He that draws a Character of *Affectation*, shews *Humour* at the Second Hand; he at best but publishes a Translation, and his Pictures are but Copies.

But as these two last distinctions are the Nicest, so it may be most proper to Explain them, by Particular Instances from some Author of Reputation. *Humour* I take, either to be born with us, and so of a Natural Growth; or else to be grafted into us, by some accidental change in the Constitution, or revolution of the Internal Habit of Body; by which it becomes, if I may so call it, Naturaliz'd.

Humour is from Nature, *Habit* from Custom; and *Affectation* from Industry.

Humour, shews us as we *are*.

Habit, shews us, as we appear, under a forcible Impression.

---

[2] A kind of false birth; hence, figuratively, an abortion, an abortive scheme.

[3] Ben Jonson, *Volpone, or The Fox* (1606).

Affectation, shews what we would be, under a Voluntary Disguise.

Thô here I would observe by the way, that a continued Affectation, may in time become a Habit.

The Character of *Morose* in the *Silent Woman*,[4] I take to be a Character of Humour. And I choose to Instance this Cha-/86/racter to you, from many others of the same Author, because I know it has been Condemn'd by many as Unnatural and Farce; And you have your self hinted some dislike of it, for the same Reason, in a Letter to me, concerning some of *Johnson's* Plays.

Let us suppose *Morose* to be a Man Naturally Splenetick and Melancholly; is there any thing more offensive to one of such a Disposition, than Noise and Clamour? Let any Man that has the Spleen (and there are enough in *England*) be Judge. We see common Examples of this Humour in little every day. 'Tis ten to one, but three parts in four of the Company that you dine with, are Discompos'd and Startled at the Cutting of a Cork, or Scratching a Plate with a Knife: It is a Proportion of the same Humour, that makes such or any other Noise offensive to the Person that hears it; for there are others who will not be disturb'd at all by it. Well; But *Morose* you will say, is so Extravagant, he cannot bear any Discourse or Conversation, above a Whisper. Why, It is his excess of this Humour, that makes him become Ridiculous, and qualifies his Character for Comedy. If the Poet had given him, but a Moderate proportion of that Humour, 'tis odds /87/ but half the Audience, would have sided with the Character, and have Condemn'd the Author, for Exposing a Humour which was neither remarkable nor Ridiculous. Besides, the distance of the Stage requires the Figure represented, to be something larger than the Life; and sure a Picture may have Features larger in Proportion, and yet be very like the Original. If this Exactness of Quantity, were to be observed in Wit, as some would have it in Humour; what would become of those Characters that are design'd for Men of Wit? I believe if a Poet should steal a Dialogue of any length, from the *Extempore* Discourse of the two Wittiest Men upon Earth, he would find the Scene but coldly receiv'd by the Town. But to the purpose.

The Character of Sir *John Daw* in the same Play, is a Character of Affectation. He every where discovers an Affectation of Learning; when he is not only Conscious to himself, but the Audience

4 Ben Jonson, *Epicoene, or The Silent Woman* (1609).

also plainly perceives that he is Ignorant. Of this kind are the Characters of *Thraso* in the Eunuch of *Terence*, and *Pyrgopolinices* in the *Miles Gloriosus* of *Plautus*. They affect to be thought Valiant, when both themselves and the Audience know they are not. Now such a boasting of Valour in Men who were /88/ really Valiant, would undoubtedly be a *Humour*; for a Fiery Disposition might naturally throw a Man into the same Extravagance, which is only affected in the Characters I have mentioned.

The Character of *Cob* in *Every Man in his Humour*, and most of the under Characters in *Bartholomew-Fair*, discover only a Singularity of Manners, appropriated to the several Educations and Professions of the Persons represented. They are not Humours, but Habits contracted by Custom. Under this Head may be ranged all Country-Clowns, Sailers, Tradesmen, Jockeys, Gamesters and such like, who make use of *Cants* or peculiar *Dialects* in their several Arts and Vocations. One may almost give a Receipt for the Composition of such a Character: For the Poet has nothing to do, but to collect a few proper Phrases and terms of Art, and to make the Person apply them by ridiculous Metaphors in his Conversation, with Characters of different Natures. Some late Characters of this kind have been very successful; but in my mind they may be Painted without much Art or Labour; since they require little more, than a good Memory and Superficial Observation. But true *Humour* cannot be shewn, without a Dissection of Nature, and a Narrow Search, /89/ to discover the first Seeds, from whence it has its Root and growth.

If I were to write to the World, I should be obliged to dwell longer, upon each of these Distinctions and Examples; for I know that they would not be plain enough to all Readers. But a bare hint is sufficient to inform you of the Notions which I have on this Subject: And I hope by this time you are of my Opinion, that Humour is neither Wit, nor Folly, nor Personal defect; nor Affectation, nor Habit; and yet, that each, and all of these, have been both written and received for Humour.

I should be unwilling to venture even on a bare Description of Humour, much more, to make a Definition of it, but now my hand is in, Ile tell you what serves me instead of either. I take it to be, *A singular and unavoidable manner of doing, or saying anything, Peculiar and Natural to one Man only; by which his Speech and Actions are distinguish'd from those of other Men.*

Our *Humour* has relation to us, and to what proceeds from us, as the Accidents have to a Substance; it is a Colour, Taste, and Smell, Diffused through all; thô our Actions are never so many, and different in Form, they are all Splinters of the same Wood, and have Naturally one Complexi-/90/on; which thô it may be disguised by Art, yet cannot be wholly changed: We may Paint it with other Colours, but we cannot change the Grain. So the Natural sound of an Instrument will be distinguish'd, thô the Notes expressed by it, are never so various, and the Divisions never so many. Dissimulation may, by Degrees, become more easy to our practice; but it can never absolutely Transubstantiate us into what we would seem: It will always be in some proportion a Violence upon Nature.

A Man may change his Opinion, but I believe he will find it a Difficulty, to part with his *Humour*, and there is nothing more provoking, than the being made sensible of that difficulty. Sometimes, one shall meet with those, who perhaps, Innocently enough, but at the same time impertinently, will ask the Question; *Why are you not Merry? Why are you not Gay, Pleasant, and Cheerful?* then instead of answering, could I ask such one; *Why are you not handsome? Why have you not Black Eyes, and a better Complexion?* Nature abhors to be forced.

The two Famous Philosophers of *Ephesus* and *Abdera*,[5] have their different Sects at this day. Some Weep, and others Laugh at one and the same thing. /91/

I dont doubt, but you have observed several Men Laugh when they are Angry; others who are Silent; some that are Loud: Yet I cannot suppose that it is the passion of *Anger* which is in it self different, or more or less in one than t'other; but that it is the Humour of the Man that is Predominant, and urges him to express it in that manner. Demonstrations of pleasure are as Various; one Man has a Humour of retiring from all Company, when any thing has happen'd to please him beyond expectation; he hugs himself alone, and thinks it an Addition to the pleasure to keep it Secret. Another is upon Thorns till he has made Proclamation of it; and must make other people sensible of his happiness, before he can be so himself. So it is in Grief, and other Passions. Demonstrations of Love and the Effects of that Passion upon several Humours, are infinitely different; but here the Ladies who abound in Servants are the best Judges. Talking of the Ladies, methinks some-

thing should be observed of the Humour of the Fair Sex; since they are sometimes so kind as to furnish out a Character for Comedy. But I must confess I have never made any observation of what I Apprehend to be true Humour in Women. Perhaps Passions are too powerful in that Sex, to let /92/ Humour have its Course; or may be by Reason of their Natural Coldness, Humour cannot Exert it self to that Extravagant Degree, which it often does in the Male Sex. For if ever any thing does appear Comical or Ridiculous in a Woman, I think it is little more than an acquir'd Folly, or an affectation. We may call them the weaker Sex, but I think the true Reason is, because our Follies are Stronger, and our Faults are more prevailing.

One might think that the Diversity of Humour, which must be allowed to be diffused throughout Mankind, might afford endless matter, for the support of Comedies. But when we come closely to consider that point, and nicely to distinguish the Difference of Humours, I believe we shall find the contrary. For thô we allow every Man something of his own, and a peculiar Humour; yet every Man has it not in quantity, to become Remarkable by it. Or, if many do become Remarkable by their Humours; yet all those Humours may not be Diverting. Nor is it only requisite to distinguish what Humour will be diverting, but also how much of it, what part of it to shew in Light, and what to cast in Shades; how to set it off by preparatory Scenes, and by opposing other humours to /93/ it in the same Scene. Thô a wrong Judgment, sometimes, Mens Humours may be opposed when there is really no specifick Difference between them; only a greater proportion of the same, in one than t'other; occasion'd by his having more Flegm, or Choller, or whatever the Constitution is, from whence their Humours derive their Source.

There is infinitely more to be said on this Subject; thô perhaps I have already said too much; but I have said it to a Friend, who I am sure will not expose it, if he does not approve of it. I believe the Subject is intirely new, and was never touch'd upon before; and if I would have any one to see this private Essay, it should be some one, who might be provoked by my Errors in it, to Publish a more Judicious Treatise on the Subject. Indeed I wish it were done, that the World being a little acquainted with the scarcity of true Humour, and the difficulty of finding and shewing it, might look a little more favourably on the Labours of them, who endeavor to search into Nature for it, and lay it open to the Publick View.

---

[5] St. Paul lived and preached in Ephesus, to the inhabitants of which city he directed one of his Epistles. Democritus (*c.* 460 B.C. – *c.* 370 B.C.) was born in Abdera; known as the "laughing philosopher," he was noted for his cheerfulness though blind.

I dont say but that very entertaining and useful Characters, and proper for Comedy, may be drawn from Affectations, and those other Qualities, which I have endeavoured to /94/ distinguish from Humour: but I would not have such imposed on the World, for Humour, nor esteem'd of Equal value with it. It were perhaps, the Work of a long Life to make one Comedy true in all its Parts, and to give every Character in it a True and Distinct Humour. Therefore, every Poet must be beholding to other helps, to make out his number of ridiculous Characters. But I think such a One deserves to be broke, who makes all false Musters; who does not shew one true Humour in a Comedy, but entertains his Audience to the end of the Play with every thing out of Nature.

I will make but one Observation to you more, and have done; and that is grounded upon an Observation of your own, and which I mention'd at the beginning of my Letter, *viz*, That there is more of Humour in our English Comick Writers than in any others. I do not at all wonder at it, for I look upon Humour to be almost of English Growth; at least, it does not seem to have found such Encrease on any other Soil. And what appears to me to be the reason of it, is the great Freedom, Privilege, and Liberty which the Common People of *England* enjoy. Any Man that has a Humour, is under no restraint, or fear of giving it Vent; they have a Proverb among them, /95/ which, may be, will shew the Bent and Genius of the People, as well as a longer Discourse: *He that will have a May-pole, shall have a May-pole*. This is a maxim with them, and their Practice is agreeable to it. I believe something Considerable too may be ascribed to their feeding so much on Flesh, and the Grossness of their Diet in general. But I have done, let the Physicians agree that. Thus you have my Thoughts of *Humour*, to my Power of Expressing them in so little Time and Compass. You will be kind to shew me wherein I have Err'd; and as you are very Capable of giving me Instruction, so, I think I have a very Just title to demand it from you; being without Reserve.

July 10. 1695

> *Your real Friend,*
> *and humble Servant,*
> W. CONGREVE   /96/

Bonamy Dobrée # Restoration Comedy: Drama and Values

Bonamy Dobrée, who was born in 1891, has had a distinguished career as critic, editor, and teacher, as well as having been on active service in both world wars. A Cambridge University graduate, he retired from his post as Professor of English Literature at Leeds University in 1955. His published works include studies of Pope and modern poetry, biographies of such diverse personalities as Sarah Churchill, Casanova, and John Wesley, and editions of the plays of Congreve and Vanbrugh as well as the letters of Lord Chesterfield. *Restoration Comedy, 1660-1720*, although published in 1924 (by the Oxford University Press), and its companion study, *Restoration Tragedy* (1929), still remain the standard works on the drama of the period. The footnotes are the editor's.

DRAMA AND VALUES

In the history of dramatic literature there are some periods that can be labelled as definitely "tragic," others as no less preponderatingly "comic," though of course both forms exist side by side throughout the ages. Taking the period of Aeschylus, Shakespeare, and Corneille as markedly "tragic," we find that these writers throve in a period of great national expansion and power, during which values were fixed and positive. At such times there is a general acceptation of what is good and what is evil. Out of this, as a kind of trial of strength, there arises tragedy, the positive drama; there is, as Nietzsche suggested, "an intellectual predilection for what is hard, awful, evil, problematical in existence owing to . . . fulness of life."

In the great "comic" periods, however, those of Menander, of the Restoration writers, and at the end of Louis XIV's reign and during the Regency, we find that values are changing with alarming speed. The times are those of rapid social readjustment and general instability, when policy is insecure, religion doubted and being revised, and morality in a state of chaos.

Yet the greatest names in comedy, Aristophanes, Jonson, Molière, do not belong here: these men flourished in intermediate periods, in which the finest comedy seems to be written. In form it still preserves some of the broad /9/ sweep of tragedy, and is sometimes hardly to be distinguished from the latter in its philosophy, its implications, and its emotional appeal. Think of *The Silent Woman* or *Le Festin de Pierre*. In this period we find that tragedy has lost its positive character, and begins to doubt if the old values are, after all, the best. It begins to have a sceptical or plaintive note, as in Euripides, Ford, and Racine. Values are beginning to change; they are not yet tottering.

Keeping this in mind, let us cast a cursory glance at the nature of comedy.

COMEDY

Everybody will agree that *Othello* is not a comedy, and that *The School for Scandal* is not a tragedy. But on the other hand *Volpone* is at least as different from Sheridan's play as the latter is from Shakespeare's. Similarly, in the period [1660–1720] under consideration, Etherege's *The Man of Mode* is not at all the same kind of thing as Wycherley's *Plain Dealer*, though both are called comedies. Again, if we are certain of the mood we get from *Lear* or *The Importance of Being Earnest*, what are we to say of *Measure for Measure*, *Le Tartuffe*, or *Le Cid*?

It is not surprising, then, that no theory of comedy yet developed, from Aristotle to Meredith or M. Bergson, seems to cover all the ground; and for the purposes of this book it will be useful to distinguish three kinds of comedy or at least three elements in comedy. This is not to elaborate a theory, but to provide a standpoint from which we may obtain a clearer view of the works we are about to consider.

1. *Critical Comedy*. The vast bulk of comedy is of the "critical" variety. What, for instance, was Aristophanes /10/ doing but "to laugh back into their senses 'revolting' sons and wives, to defend the orthodox faith against philosophers and men of science"? Menander, to judge from Terence, was doing the same kind of thing, as was Terence himself. This is the classical comedy from which much modern comedy is derived. It sets out definitely to correct manners by laughter; it strives to "cure excess."

This comedy, then, tends to repress eccentricity, exaggeration, any deviation from the normal: it wields the Meredithian "sword of common sense." It expresses the general feeling of the community, for which another name is morality; it is, to quote Meredith again, the "guardian of our civil fort," and it is significant that when comedy has been attacked, it has always been defended not on aesthetic but on moral grounds. But the defence has never been very successful, for the morality preached by comedy is not that of fierce ardour, of the passionate search for the utmost good, that in itself is excess, and subject for comedy (e.g., *Le Misanthrope*); but, as we continually find from Terence to the present day, it supports the happy mean, the comfortable life, the ideal of the *honnête homme*. Its lesson is to be righteous, but not to be righteous over much, which in the mouths of those who hold the doctrine becomes

J'aime mieux un vice commode
Qu'une fatigante vertu. [1]

Its object is to damp enthusiasm, to prick illusions. It is in a sense prig-drama; it flatters the vanity of the spectator, for whose amusement the weaknesses of his friends are held up.

One might imagine that confronted with comedy clothed in the garb of conscious virtue, the writers of comedy themselves would cry "Fudge." But these, in the seventeeth /11/ century at least always fell back upon the moral argument as though they lacked the defiance of their raillery. Jonson declared that comedy was "a thing throughout pleasant and ridiculous, and accommodated to the correction of manners," saying in the preface to *Epicene*:

The ends of all, who for the scene do write,
Are, or should be, to profit and delight!

a charming alternative, of which, fortunately, he sometimes took advantage. Molière, in his preface to *Le Tartuffe*, implicitly accepted the position when he wrote "If the use of comedy is to correct the vices of men . . .," as though merely restating an unquestionable axiom. "One can easily put up with a rebuke," he said, "but one cannot bear chaff. One may have no objection to being wicked, but one hates to be ridiculous." Corneille, however, declared that "Dramatic poesy has for object only the delight of the spectators," but he was forced to add that Horace was right, and that everybody would not be pleased if some useful precept were not at the same time slipped in, "et que les gens graves et sérieux, les vieillards, et les

[1] "I prefer a convenient vice to a tiresome virtue" (Molière, *Amphitryon*, I, iv).

amateurs de la vertu, s'y ennuieront s'ils n'y trouvent rien à profiter."[2]

In the period we are about to survey, the same ground was taken up. Shadwell, in attempting to continue the tradition of the Comedy of Humours, wrote of Jonson:

> He to correct, and to inform, did write,
> If poets aim at nought but to delight,
> Fiddlers have to the bays an equal right, [3]

a statement which reveals Shadwell's limitations as clearly as his point of view. Congreve and Vanbrugh—Wycherley's moral purpose is overwhelmingly evident in three of his plays—stimulated by Collier's declaration that "The business of plays is to recommend virtue and discountenance /12/ vice," were loud in their protestations. Congreve even forestalled the frenzied divine[4] in his preface to the *Double Dealer*, where he said "it is the business of the comic poet to paint the vices and follies of humankind." Vanbrugh in his heart thought that the object of plays was to divert, and to get full houses, but he accepted the moral standpoint in his *Short Vindication*, saying, "the business of comedy is to show people what they should do, by representing them on the stage doing what they should not." Who would refuse to be moralist on those terms? Farquhar, modifying the claims of comedy, declared in his preface to *The Twin Rivals*, "that the business of comedy is chiefly to ridicule folly; and that the punishment of vice falls rather into the province of tragedy," thus curiously forestalling Coleridge, who thought wickedness no subject for comedy.

Indeed the description of the morality as "a play enforcing a moral truth or lesson" might almost be taken as a definition of any comedy that deals with types, or "humours." For comedy, in so far as it is a generalization, can scarcely avoid type, and once this form has been accepted, the pontifical robes of the moralist descend almost inevitably upon it.

The foregoing may throw a light upon why it is that comedy appears when it does. Comedy of this type is not a phosphorescent gleam upon the surface of a decaying society, but a conservative reaction against change. It is, in short, a social corrective.

2. *"Free" Comedy*. There are, however, some comedies which seem to produce quite a different effect in us, comedies in which we feel no superiority, and which inculcate no moral, but in which we seem to gain a release, not only from what Lamb called the burden of our perpetual moral questioning, but from all things that appear to limit /13/ our powers. Of this kind of comedy, the plays of Etherege and Regnard are perhaps the best examples, though much of the laughter of Aristophanes is evoked in the same way. Here we feel that no values count, that there are no rules of conduct, hardly laws of nature. Certainly no appeal, however indirect, is made to our critical or moral faculties. We can disport ourselves freely in a realm where nothing is accountable; all we need to exact is that the touch shall be light enough. We take the same delight in the vagaries of Sir Fopling Flutter as we do at the sight of an absurd gambolling calf. Judgement, except the aesthetic, is out of place here. We are permitted to play with life, which becomes a charming harlequinade without being farce. It is all spontaneous and free, rapid and exhilarating; the least emotion, an appeal to common sense, and the joyous illusion is gone.

I have named this comedy "free" because it depends upon there being no valuations whatever; it is possible only in a world where nothing matters, either because one has everything, or because one has nothing. Since it can afford to be careless, it can be completely unmoral. Etherege wrote in the first exuberance of the return from exile of a court to which no moral argument could appeal. In the *Chanson Faite à Grillon* Regnard wrote:

> Il sera gravé sur la porte:
> Ici l'on fait ce que l'on veut, [5]

a motto that might be prefixed to each of his comedies. And if the above are examples of free comedy written by those who had everything, the Commedia dell'Arte may stand as an example of that performed by those who had nothing, and which flourished most when the spectators and actors had least; for when there is nothing more to be /14/ lost, there can be no further responsibility. Life and its appropriate comedy can be perfectly free.

---

[2] "And that serious-minded people, the aged, and those who are virtuous would be annoyed if they found nothing from which they might benefit."

[3] From the Prologue to *The Squire of Alsatia* (1688).

[4] Jeremy Collier (1650–1726), churchman, later bishop, is chiefly remembered for his "Short View of the Immorality and Profaneness of the English Stage" (1698). The work had an immediate effect; Congreve and other playwrights were prosecuted, actors were fined. But the futility of "The Short View" was shown by the continued success of the kind of play Collier condemned.

[5] "It will be written above the entrance: Here people do as they please." J. F. Regnard (1655–1709) was a French dramatist and satirist.

3. *Great Comedy.* There is, however, a third comedy, perilously near tragedy, in which the balance is so fine that it sometimes seems as though it would topple over into the other form, as in *Volpone* or *Le Misanthrope.* And here to leave the instances definitely recognized as comedy, are not *Troilus and Cressida* (Shakespeare's), *Measure for Measure,* and *All's Well That Ends Well* also of this kind? Is not Mr. Shaw right in regarding *Coriolanus* as the greatest of Shakespeare's comedies? Indeed the really great figures of comic literature can hardly be thought of apart from their tragedy: who can regard the melancholy knight of La Mancha without pity, or disentangle the elements of the tales that beguiled the road to Canterbury?

The greatest comedy seems inevitably to deal with the disillusion of mankind, the bitterness of a Troilus or an Alceste, the failure of men to realize their most passionate desires. And does this enable us to come to some conclusion as to what comedy really is? Cannot we see from the very periods in which it arises in its greatest forms with what aspect of humanity it needs must deal? It comes when the positive attitude has failed, when doubt is creeping in to undermine values, and men are turning for comfort to the very ruggedness of life, and laughing in the face of it all. "Je suis le rire en personne," says Maurice Sand's Polichinelle, "le rire triomphant, le rire du mal."[6] There he represents "great" comedy.

For comedy does not give us anything in exchange for our loss. Tragedy moves us in such a way that life becomes rich and glowing, in spite

[6] "I am laughter incarnate, laughter triumphant, the laughter of evil." The quote is from Chapter II, "Polichinelle," of Maurice Sand's *The History of the Harlequinade.*

of pain and all imaginable horror, perhaps because of them. In tragedy we are left in admiration of the grandiose spectacle of humanity stronger than /15/ its chains, and we are reconciled when a Cleopatra, hugging the asp, whispers:

> Peace, peace!
> Dost thou not see my baby at my breast
> That sucks the nurse asleep?

In tragedy we are made free by being taken outside the life of the senses into that of imaginative reality.

Comedy makes daily life livable in spite of folly and disillusion, but its vision, though as universal, is not that of tragedy, for it laughs at the spirit as much as at the flesh and will not take sides. Tragedy is all that is commonly said of it, in depth, revelation, and grandeur; but comedy is not its opposite. The latter is not necessarily more distant from life, nor is it life apprehended through the mind rather than through the emotions. Neither is it the triumph of the angel in man over our body of the beast, as one has said, nor, to quote another, the triumph of the beast in man over the divine. It is nothing so fleeting as a triumph. It is "a recordation in man's soul" of his dual nature.

Goethe sought in art courage to face the battle of life. But it is doubtful if life is a battle, or a game, or a chaos through which we walk with slippery feet. And comedy gives us courage to face life without any standpoint; we need not view it critically nor feel heroically. We need only to feel humanly, for comedy shows us life not at such a distance that we cannot but regard it coldly, but only so far as we may bring to it a ready sympathy freed from terror or too overwhelming a measure of pity. /16/

George Meredith # On Comedy and the Uses of the Comic Spirit

When he came to give his famous lecture, called "The Idea of Comedy and the Uses of the Comic Spirit," before the London Institution in 1877, George Meredith (1828-1909) was already an established novelist and poet. *The Ordeal of Richard Feverel* had appeared in 1859 and his series of poems, *Modern Love,* in 1862. He had been friendly with the Pre-Raphaelite group, had published widely in the journals, and was turning out a spate of novels to be climaxed by *The Egoist* (1879). His

statements on comedy reflected much of the thought of the Victorian age. The lecture was first printed in *The New Quarterly Magazine* for April, 1877; it was expanded and published as *An Essay on Comedy and the Uses of the Comic Spirit* by Archibald Constable & Co., London, in 1897 and by Charles Scribner's Sons, New York, in the same year. The text below follows The New York edition.

The footnotes are the editor's.

There are plain reasons why the Comic poet is not a frequent apparition, and why the great Comic poet remains without a /1/ fellow. A society of cultivated men and women is required, wherein ideas are current, and the perceptions quick, that he may be supplied with matter and an audience. The semi-barbarism of merely giddy communities, and feverish emotional periods, repel him; and also a state of marked social inequality of the sexes; nor can he whose business is to address the mind be understood where there is not a moderate degree of intellectual activity.

Moreover, to touch and kindle the mind through laughter demands, more than sprightliness, a most subtle delicacy. That must be a natal gift in the Comic poet. The substance he deals with will show him a startling exhibition of the dyer's hand, if he is without it. People are ready to surrender themselves to witty thumps on the back, breast, and sides; all except the head—and it is there that he aims. He must be subtle to penetrate. A corresponding acuteness must exist to welcome him. The necessity for the two conditions /2/ will explain how it is that we count him during centuries in the singular number.

"C'est une étrange entreprise que celle de faire rire les honnêtes gens," Molière says;[1] and the difficulty of the undertaking cannot be overestimated.

Then again, he is beset with foes to right and left, of a character unknown to the tragic and the lyric poet, or even to philosophers.

We have in this world men whom Rabelais would call "agelasts"; that is to say, non-laughers —men who are in that respect as dead bodies, which, if you prick them, do not bleed. The old gray boulder-stone, that has finished its peregrination from the rock to the valley, is as easily to be set rolling up again as these men laughing. No collision of circumstances in our mortal career strikes a light for them. . . .

We have another class of men who are /3/ pleased to consider themselves antagonists of the foregoing, and whom we may term "hypergelasts"; the excessive laughers, ever-laughing, who are as clappers of a bell, that may be rung by a breeze, a grimace; who are so loosely put together that a wink will shake them. "C'est n'estimer rien qu'estimer tout le monde";[2] and to laugh at everything is to have no appreciation of the Comic of Comedy.

Neither of these distinct divisions of non-laughers and over-laughers would be entertained by reading *The Rape of the Lock*, or seeing a performance of *Le Tartuffe*. In relation to the stage, they have taken in our land the form and title of Puritan and /4/ Bacchanalian; for though the stage is no longer a public offender, and Shakespeare has been revived on it, to give it nobility, we have not yet entirely raised it above the contention of these two parties. . . . .

Comedy, we have to admit, was never one of the most honored of the Muses. She was in her origin, short of slaughter, the loudest expression of the little civilization of men. The light of Athene over the head of Achilles illuminates the birth of Greek Tragedy.[3] But Comedy rolled in shouting under the divine protection of the Son of the Wine-jar, as Dionysus is made to proclaim himself by Aristophanes.[4] Our second Charles was the patron, of like benignity, of our Comedy of Manners, which began similarly as a combative performance, under a license to deride and outrage the Puritan, and was here and there Bacchanalian beyond the Aristophanic example—worse, inasmuch as a cynical licentiousness is more abominable than frank filth. . . . /5/

Our English idea of a Comedy of Manners might be imaged in the person of a blowsy country girl— say Hoyden, the daughter of Sir Tunbelly Clumsey, who, when at home, never disobeyed her father except in the "eating of green gooseberries"[5]—transforming to a varnished City Madam, with a loud laugh and a mincing step; the crazy ancestress /7/ of an accountably fallen descendant. She bustles prodigiously, and is punctually smart in her speech, always in a fluster to escape from Dulness, as they say the dogs on the Nile-banks drink at the river running to avoid the crocodile. If the monster catches her, as at times he does, she whips him to a froth, so that those who know Dulness only as a thing of ponderousness shall fail to recognize him in that light and airy shape.

When she has frolicked through her five acts, to surprise you with the information that Mr. Aimwell is converted by a sudden death in the

---

[1] "It is a strange undertaking, that, of making good people laugh," says Dorante in Scene vii of *La Critique de L'École des Femmes*.

[2] "To honor all men is to honor none" (*The Misanthrope*, I, i, 58).

[3] Meredith is here paraphrasing the *Iliad*, from which it may be assumed that with Aristotle he considers Greek tragedy to have begun with that work.

[4] In *The Frogs*.

[5] Miss Hoyden, a character in Vanbrugh's *The Relapse* (1696) speaks this line; the play was revised by Sheridan in 1777.

world outside the scenes into Lord Aimwell,[6] and can marry the lady in the light of day, it is to the credit of her vivacious nature that she does not anticipate your calling her Farce. Five is dignity with a trailing robe; whereas one, two, or three Acts would be short skirts, and degrading. . . . /8/ Her wit is at once, like steam in an engine, the motive force and the warning whistle of her headlong course; and it vanishes like the track of steam when she has reached her terminus, never troubling the brains afterward; a merit that it shares with good wine, to the joy of the Bacchanalians. As to this wit, it is warlike. In the neatest hands it is like the sword of the cavalier in the Mall, quick to flash out upon slight provocation, and for a similar office—to wound. Commonly its attitude is entirely pugilistic; two blunt fists rallying and countering. When harmless, as when the word "fool" occurs, or allusions to the state of husband, it has the sound of the smack of harlequin's wand upon clown, and is to the same extent exhilarating. Believe that idle, empty laughter is the most /9/ desirable of recreations, and significant Comedy will seem pale and shallow in comparison. . . .

The French have a school of stately comedy to which they can fly for renovation whenever they have fallen away from it; and their /13/ having such a school is mainly the reason why, as John Stuart Mill pointed out, they know men and women more accurately than we do. Molière followed the Horatian precept, to observe the manners of his age, and give his characters the color befitting them at the time. He did not paint in raw realism. He seized his characters firmly for the central purpose of the play, stamped them in the idea, and, by slightly raising and softening the object of study . . . generalized upon it so as to make it permanently human. Concede that it is natural for human creatures to live in society, and Alceste is an imperishable mark of one, though he is drawn in light outline, without any forcible human coloring. Our English school has not clearly imagined society; and of the /14/ mind hovering above congregated men and women it has imagined nothing. The critics who praise it for its downrightness, and for bringing the situations home to us, as they admiringly say, cannot but disapprove of Molière's comedy, which appeals to the individual mind to perceive and participate in the social. We have splendid tragedies, we have the most beautiful of poetic plays, and we have literary comedies passingly pleasant to read, and

occasionally to see acted. By literary comedies, I mean comedies of classic inspiration, drawn chiefly from Menander and the Greek New Comedy through Terence; or else comedies of the poet's personal conception, that have had no model in life, and are humorous exaggerations, happy or otherwise. These are the comedies of Ben Jonson, Massinger, and Fletcher. . . ./15/ The comic of Jonson is a scholar's excogitation of the comic; that of Massinger a moralist's.

Shakespeare is a well-spring of characters which are saturated with the Comic Spirit; with more of what we will call blood-life than is to be found anywhere out of Shakespeare; and they are of this world, but they are of the world enlarged to our embrace by imagination, and by great poetic imagination. They are, as it were—I put it to suit my present comparison—creatures of the woods and wilds, not in walled towns, not /16/ grouped and toned to pursue a comic exhibition of the narrower world of society. Jaques, Falstaff and his regiment, the varied troop of clowns, Malvolio, Sir Hugh Evans and Fluellen (marvelous Welshmen!) Benedick and Beatrice, Dogberry, and the rest, are subjects of a special study in the poetically comic. . . .

Politically, it is accounted a misfortune for France that her nobles thronged to the Court /17/ of Louis Quatorze. It was a boon to the Comic poet. He had that lively quicksilver world of the animalcule passions, the huge pretensions, the placid absurdities, under his eyes in full activity; vociferous quacks and snapping dupes, hypocrites, posturers, extravagants, pedants, rose-pink ladies and mad grammarians, sonnetteering marquises, highflying mistresses, plain-minded maids, interthreading as in a loom, noisy as at a fair. A simply bourgeois circle will not furnish it, for the middle class must have the brilliant, flippant, independent upper for a spur and a pattern; otherwise it is likely to be inwardly dull, as well as outwardly correct. Yet, though the King was benevolent toward Molière, it is not to the French Court that we are indebted for his unrivaled studies of mankind in society. For the amusement of the Court the ballets and farces were written, which are dearer to the rabble upper, as to the rabble lower, class than intellectual comedy. The French bourgeoisie /18/ of Paris were sufficiently quickwitted and enlightened by education to welcome great works like *Le Tartuffe*, *Les Femmes Savantes*, and *Le Misanthrope*, works that were perilous ventures on the popular intelligence, big vessels to launch on streams running to shallows. . . .

[6] A character in Farquhar's *The Beaux' Stratagem* (1707).

The *Misanthrope* was frigidly received.[7] Molière thought it dead. "I can not improve on it, and assuredly never shall," he said. It is one of the French titles to honor that this quintessential comedy of the opposition of Alceste and Célimène was ultimately understood and applauded. In all countries the middle class presents the public which, fighting the world, and with a good footing in the fight, knows the world best. It may be the most selfish, but that is a question leading us into sophistries. Cultivated men and women who do not skim the cream of life, and are attached to the duties, yet escape the harsher blows, make acute and balanced observers. Molière is their poet.

Of this class in England, a large body, neither Puritan nor Bacchanalian, have a sentimental objection to face the study of /20/ the actual world. They take up disdain of it, when its truths appear humiliating; when the facts are not immediately forced on them, they take up the pride of incredulity. They live in a hazy atmosphere that they suppose an ideal one. Humorous writing they will endure, perhaps approve, if it mingles with pathos to shake and elevate the feelings. They approve of satire, because, like the beak of the vulture, it smells of carrion, which they are not. But of Comedy they have a shivering dread, for Comedy enfolds them with the wretched host of the world, huddles them with us all in an ignoble assimilation, and cannot be used by any exalted variety as a scourge and a broom. Nay, to be an exalted variety is to come under the calm, curious eye of the Comic Spirit, and be probed for what you are. Men are seen among them, and very many cultivated women. You may distinguish them by a favorite phrase: "Surely we are not so bad!" and the remark: "If /21/ that is human nature, save us from it!"—as if it could be done; but in the peculiar paradise of the wilful people who will not see, the exclamation assumes the saving grace.

Yet, should you ask them whether they dislike sound sense, they vow they do not. And question cultivated women whether it pleases them to be shown moving on an intellectual level with men, they will answer that it does; numbers of them claim the situation. Now Comedy is the fountain of sound sense; not the less perfectly sound on account of the sparkle; and Comedy lifts women to a station offering them free play for their wit, as they usually show it, when they have it, on the side of sound sense. The higher the Comedy, the more prominent the part they enjoy in it. . . .

The heroines of Comedy are like women of the world, not necessarily heartless from being clear-sighted; they seem so to the sentimentally reared, only for the reason that they use their wits, and are not wandering vessels crying for a captain or a pilot. Comedy is an exhibition of their battle with men, and that of men with them; and as the two, however divergent, both look on one object, namely, Life, the gradual similarity of their impressions must bring them /23/ to some resemblance. The Comic poet dares to show us men and women coming to this mutual likeness; he is for saying that when they draw together in social life their minds grow liker. . . . Philosopher and Comic poet are of a cousinship in the eye they cast on life; and they are equally unpopular with our wilful English of the hazy region and the ideal that is not to be disturbed.

Thus, for want of instruction in the Comic Idea, we lose a large audience among our cultivated middle class that we should expect to support Comedy. The sentimentalist is as averse as the Puritan and as the Bacchanalian.

Our traditions are unfortunate. The public taste is with the idle laughers, and still inclines to follow them. It may be shown by an analysis of Wycherley's *Plain Dealer*, a coarse prose adaption of the *Misanthrope*, /24/ stuffed with lumps of realism in a vulgarized theme to hit the mark of English appetite, that we have in it the key-note of the comedy of our stage. It is Molière travestied, with the hoof to his foot, and hair on the pointed tip of his ear. . . .

These bad traditions of Comedy affect us, not only on the stage, but in our literature, and may be tracked into our social life. They are the ground of the heavy moralizings by which we are out-wearied, about life as a comedy, and comedy as a jade,[8] when popular /25/ writers, conscious of fatigue in creativeness, desire to be cogent in a modish cynicism; perversions of the idea of life, and of the proper esteem for the society we have wrested from brutishness, and would carry higher. Stock images of this description are accepted by the timid and the sensitive, as well as by the saturnine, quite seriously; for not many look abroad with their own eyes—fewer still have the habit of thinking for themselves. Life, we know too well, is not a Comedy, but something strangely mixed; nor is Comedy a vile mask. . . .

Comedy justly treated, as you find it in Molière, whom we so clownishly mishandled—the comedy

---

[7] A false notion; the play was a success.

[8] See *Tom Jones*, Book VIII, Chapter I, for Fielding's opinion of our Comedy. But he puts it simply; not as an exercise in the quasi-philosophical bathetiv. [Meredith's note]

of Molière throws no infamous reflection upon life. It is deeply conceived, in the first place, and therefore it cannot be impure. Meditate on that statement. Never did man wield so shrieking a scourge upon vice; but his consummate self-mastery is not shaken while administering it. . . . He strips Folly to the skin, displays the /27/ imposture of the creature, and is content to offer her better clothing. . . . He conceives purely, and he writes purely, in the simplest language, the simplest of French verse. The source of his wit is clear reason; it is a fountain of that soil, and it springs to vindicate reason, common sense, rightness, and justice—for no vain purpose ever. The wit is of such pervading spirit that it inspires a pun with meaning and interest. His moral does not hang like a tail, or preach from one character incessantly cocking an eye at the audience, as in recent realistic French plays, but is in the heart of his work, throbbing with every pulsation of an organic structure. If life is likened to the comedy of Molière, there is no scandal in the comparison. /28/

Congreve's *Way of the World* is an exception to our other comedies, his own among them, by virtue of the remarkable brilliancy of the writing, and the figure of Millamant. The comedy has no idea in it, beyond the stale one that so the world goes; and it concludes with the jaded discovery of a document at a convenient season for the descent of the curtain. A plot was an afterthought with Congreve. . . . Contrast the wit of Congreve with Molière's. That of the first is a Toledo blade, sharp, and wonderfully supple for steel; cast for dueling, restless in the scabbard, being so pretty when out of it. To shine, it must have an adversary. Molière's wit is like a running brook, with innumerable fresh lights on it at every turn of the wood through which its business is to find a way. It does not run in search of obstructions, to be noisy over them; but when dead leaves and viler sub-/30/ stances are heaped along the course, its natural song is heightened. Without effort, and with no dazzling flashes of achievement, it is full of healing, the wit of good breeding, the wit of wisdom.

"Genuine humor and true wit," says Landor,[9] require a sound and capacious mind, which is always a grave one. Rabelais and La Fontaine are recorded by their countrymen to have been *rêveurs*. Few men have been graver than Pascal; few have been wittier.

To apply the citation of so great a brain as Pascal's to our countryman would be unfair.

Congreve had a certain soundness of mind; of capacity, in the sense intended by Landor, he had little. Judging him by his wit, he performed some happy thrusts; and, taking it for genuine, it is a surface wit, neither rising from a depth nor flowing from a spring. . . .

Where Congreve excels all his English rivals is in his literary force, and a succinctness of style peculiar to him. He had correct judgment, a correct ear, readiness of illustra-/32/tion within a narrow range—in snap-shots of the obvious at the obvious—and copious language. He hits the mean of a fine style and a natural in dialogue. He is at once precise and voluble. If you have ever thought upon style, you will acknowledge it to be a signal accomplishment. In this he is a classic, and is worthy of treading a measure with Molière. *The Way of the World* may be read out currently at a first glance, so sure are the accents of the emphatic meaning to strike the eye, perforce of the crispness and cunning polish of the sentences. You have not to look over them before you confide yourself to him; he will carry you safe. Sheridan imitated, but was far from surpassing, him. . . . /33/

Rousseau, in his letter to D'Alembert on the subject of the *Misanthrope*,[10] discusses the character of Alceste as though Molière had put him forth for an absolute example of misanthropy; whereas Alceste is only a misanthrope of the circle he finds himself placed in—he has a touching faith in the virtue residing in the country, and a critical love of sweet simpleness. Nor is he the principal person of the comedy to which he gives a name. He is only passively comic. /36/ Célimène is the active spirit. While he is denouncing and railing, the trial is imposed upon her to make the best of him, and control herself, as much as a witty woman, eagerly courted, can do. By appreciating him she practically confesses her faultiness, and she is better disposed to meet him half-way than he is to bend an inch, only she is "*une âme de vingt ans*,"[11] the world is pleasant, and, if the gilded flies of the Court are silly, uncompromising fanatics have their ridiculous features as well. Can she abandon the life they make agreeable to her, for a man who will not be guided by the common sense of his class, and who insists on plunging into one extreme—equal to suicide in her eyes—to avoid another? That is the comic question of the *Misanthrope*. Why will he not continue to mix with the world

---

[9] *Imaginary Conversations, Alfieri and the Jew Salomon.* [Meredith's note]

[10] See pp. 263-67.
[11] "A creature of twenty years" (See *The Misanthrope*, V, vii, 42).

smoothly, appeased by the flattery of her secret and really sincere preference of him, and taking his revenge in satire of it, as she does from her own not very lofty /37/ standard, and will by and by do from his more exalted one?

Célimène is worldliness; Alceste is unworldliness. It does not quite imply unselfishness; and that is perceived by her shrewd head. Still, he is a very uncommon figure in her circle, and she esteems him, "*l'homme aux rubans verts*," who "sometimes diverts,"[12] but more often horribly vexes her—as she can say of him when her satirical tongue is on the run. Unhappily the soul of truth in him, which wins her esteem, refuses to be tamed, or silent, or unsuspicious, and is the perpetual obstacle to their good accord. He is that melancholy person, the critic of everybody save himself; intensely sensitive to the faults of others, wounded by them; in love with his own indubitable honesty, and with his ideal of the simpler form of life befitting it—qualities which constitute the satirist. He is a Jean Jacques of the Court. His proposal to Célimène, when he pardons her, that she should follow him in flying /38/ humankind, and his frenzy of detestation of her at her refusal, are thoroughly in the mood of Jean Jacques. He is an impracticable creature of a priceless virtue; but Célimène may feel that to fly with him to the desert (that is, from the Court to the country), "Où d'être homme d'honneur on ait la liberté,"[13] she is likely to find herself the companion of a starving satirist, like that poor princess who ran away with the waiting-man, and, when both were hungry in the forest, was ordered to give him flesh. She is a *fieffée*[14] coquette, rejoicing in her wit and her attractions, and distinguished by her inclination for Alceste in the midst of her many other lovers; only she finds it hard to cut them off— what woman with a train does not?—and when the exposure of her naughty wit has laid her under their rebuke, she will do the utmost she can: she will give her hand to honesty, but she cannot quite abandon worldliness. She would be unwise if she did. /39/

The fable is thin. Our pungent contrivers of plots would see no indication of life in the outlines. The life of the comedy is in the idea. As with the singing of the skylark out of sight, you must love the bird to be attentive to the song, so in this highest flight of the Comic Muse, you must love pure Comedy warmly to understand the *Misanthrope;* you must be receptive of the idea of Comedy. And to love Comedy you must know the real world, and know men and women well enough not to expect too much of them, though you may still hope for good. . . . /40/

[In the paragraphs omitted, Meredith discusses Roman, Italian, Spanish, German, and Arabian comedy; but except for Menander, he finds nothing to approach Molière.]

. . . There never will be civilization where Comedy is not possible; and that comes of some degree of social equality of the sexes. I am not quoting the Arab to exhort and disturb the somnolent East; rather for cultivated women to recognize that the Comic Muse is one of their best friends. They are blind to their interest in swelling the ranks of the sentimentalists. Let them look with their clearest vision abroad and at home. They will see that where they /54/ have no social freedom, Comedy is absent; where they are household drudges, the form of Comedy is primitive; where they are tolerably independent, but uncultivated, exciting melodrama takes its place, and a sentimental version of them. Yet the Comic will out, as they would know if they listened to some of the private conversations of men whose minds are undirected by the Comic Muse; as the sentimental man, to his astonishment, would know likewise, if he in similar fashion could receive a lesson. But where women are on the road to an equal footing with men, in attainments and in liberty—in what they have won for themselves, and what has been granted them by a fair civilization—there, and only waiting to be transplanted from life to the stage, or the novel, or the poem, pure Comedy flourishes, and is, as it would help them to be, the sweetest of diversions, the wisest of delightful companions.

Now, to look about us in the present time. . . . /55/ You see Folly perpetually sliding into new shapes in a society possessed of wealth and leisure, with many whims, many strange ailments and strange doctors. Plenty of common sense is in the world to thrust her back when she pretends to empire. But the first-born of common sense, the vigilant Comic, which is the genius of thoughtful laughter, which would readily extinguish her at the outset, is not serving as a public advocate.

You will have noticed the disposition of common sense, under pressure of some pertinacious piece of light-headedness, to grow impatient and angry. That is a sign of the absence, or at least of the

---

[12] A reference to Célimène's letter which Acaste reads to Alceste (see *The Misanthrope*, V, iv).

[13] "Where I'll be free to have an honest heart" (*The Misanthrope*, V, viii, 22).

[14] "By feudal right and necessity," hence "out and out" or "arrant."

dormancy, of the Comic Idea. For Folly is the natural prey of the Comic, known to it in all her transformations, in every disguise; and it is with the springing delight of hawk over heron, hound after fox, that it gives her chase, never fretting, never tiring, sure of having her, allowing her no rest. /56/

Contempt is a sentiment that cannot be entertained by Comic intelligence. What is it but an excuse to be idly-minded, or personally lofty, or comfortably narrow, not perfectly humane? If we do not feign when we say that we despise Folly, we shut the brain. There is a disdainful attitude in the presence of Folly, partaking of the foolishness to Comic perception; and anger is not much less foolish than disdain. The struggle we have to conduct is essence against essence. Let no one doubt of the sequel when this emanation of what is firmest in us is launched to strike down the daughter of Unreason and Sentimentalism—such being Folly's parentage, when it is respectable.

Our modern system of combating her is too long defensive, and carried on too ploddingly with concrete engines of war in the attack. She has time to get behind entrenchments. She is ready to stand a siege, before the heavily armed man of science and the writer of the leading article or elaborate essay have /57/ primed their big guns. It should be remembered that she has charms for the multitude; and an English multitude, seeing her make a gallant fight of it, will be half in love with her, certainly willing to lend her a cheer. Benevolent subscriptions assist her to hire her own man of science, her own organ in the Press. . . .

O for a breath of Aristophanes, Rabelais, Voltaire, Cervantes, Fielding, Molière! . . . /58/

No one would presume to say that we are deficient in jokers. They abound . . .

But the Comic differs from them in addressing the wits for laughter; and the sluggish wits want some training to respond to it, whether in public life or private, and particularly when the feelings are excited.

The sense of the Comic is much blunted by habits of punning and of using humoristic phrase: the trick of employing Johnsonian polysyllables to treat of the infinitely little . . .

But if the Comic Idea prevailed with us, and we had an Aristophanes to barb and wing it, we should be breathing air of Athens. Prosers now pouring forth on us like public fountains would be cut short in the street and left blinking, dumb as pillar-posts with letters thrust into their mouths. . . . There

would be a bright and positive, clear Hellenic perception of facts. The vapors of unreason and sentimentalism would be blown away before they were productive. . . . Yet possibly the change of despots, from good-natured old obtuseness to keen-edged intelligence, which /63/ is by nature merciless, would be more than we could bear. . . .

A political Aristophanes, taking advantage of his lyrical Bacchic license, was found too much for political Athens. I would not ask to have him revived, but that the sharp light of such a spirit as his might be with us to strike now and then on public affairs, public themes, to make them spin along more briskly.

He hated with the politician's fervor the Sophist who corrupted simplicity of thought, the poet who destroyed purity of style, the demagogue, "the saw-toothed monster,"[15] who, as he conceived, chicaned the mob; and he held his own against them by strength of /64/ laughter, until fines, the curtailing of his comic license in the chorus, and ultimately the ruin of Athens, which could no longer support the expense of the chorus, threw him altogether on dialogue, and brought him under the law. After the catastrophe, the poet, who had ever been gazing back at the men of Marathon and Salamis, must have felt that he had foreseen it; and that he was wise when he pleaded for peace, and derided military coxcombry and the captious old creature /65/ Demus, we can admit. . . .

He is not likely to be revived. He stands, like Shakespeare, an unapproachable. Swift says of him, with a loving chuckle:

> But as to comic Aristophanes,
> The rogue too vicious and too prófane is. [16]

. . . This laughing bald-pate, as he calls himself, was a Titanic pamphleteer, using laughter for his political weapon; a laughter without scruple, the laughter of Hercules. He was primed with wit, as with the garlic he speaks of giving to /67/ the gamecocks to make them fight the better. And he was a lyric poet of aerial delicacy, with the homely song of a jolly national poet, and a poet of such feeling that the comic mask is at times no broader than a cloth on a face to show the serious features of our common likeness. He is not to be revived; but, if his method were studied, some of the fire in him would come to us, and *we* might be revived.

---

[15] A reference to Cleon in *The Wasps*. Aristophanes ridiculed the Sophists in *The Clouds* and the poet (particularly Euripides) in *The Frogs*.
[16] In *Lines to Dr. Sheridan* (1718).

Taking them generally, the English public are most in sympathy with this primitive Aristophanic Comedy, wherein the Comic is capped by the grotesque, irony tips the wit, and satire is a naked sword. They have the basis of the Comic in them—an esteem for common sense. They cordially dislike the reverse of it. . . . /68/

It has been suggested that they have not yet spiritually comprehended the signification of living in society; for who are cheerfuller, brisker of wit, in the fields, and as explorers, colonizers, backwoodsmen? They are happy /69/ in rough exercise, and also in complete repose. The intermediate condition, when they are called upon to talk to one another, upon other than affairs of business or their hobbies, reveals them wearing a curious look of vacancy, as it were the socket of an eye wanting. The Comic is perpetually springing up in social life, and it oppresses them from not being perceived. . . .

In our prose literature we have had delightful Comic writers. Besides Fielding and Gold-/71/ smith, there is Miss Austen, whose Emma and Mr. Elton might walk straight into a Comedy, were the plot arranged for them. . . . In our poetic literature the Comic is delicate and graceful above the touch of Italian and French. Generally, however, the English elect excel in satire, and they are noble humorists. The national disposition is for hard-hitting, with a moral purpose to sanction it; or for a rosy, sometimes a larmoyant, geniality, not unmanly in its verging upon tenderness, and with a singular attraction for thickheadedness, to decorate it with asses' ears and the most beautiful sylvan haloes. But the Comic is a different spirit.

You may estimate your capacity for Comic perception by being able to detect the ridicule of them you love without loving them less; and more by being able to see yourself somewhat ridiculous in dear eyes, and accepting the correction their image of you proposes. /72/ . . .

If you detect the ridicule, and your kindliness is chilled by it, you are slipping into the grasp of Satire.

If, instead of falling foul of the ridiculous person with a satiric rod, to make him writhe and shriek aloud, you prefer to sting him under a semi-caress, by which he shall in his anguish be rendered dubious whether indeed anything has hurt him, you are an engine of Irony.

If you laugh all round him, tumble him, roll him about, deal him a smack, and drop a tear on him, own his likeness to you, and yours /73/ to your neighbor, spare him as little as you shun, pity him

as much as you expose, it is a spirit of Humor that is moving you.

The Comic, which is the perceptive, is the governing spirit, awakening and giving aim to these powers of laughter, but it is not to be confounded with them; it enfolds a thinner form of them, differing from Satire in not sharply driving into the quivering sensibilities, and from Humor in not comforting them and tucking them up, or indicating a broader than the range of this bustling world to them. . . . /74/

The Satirist is a moral agent, often a social scavenger, working on a storage of bile.

The Ironist is one thing or another, according to his caprice. Irony is the humor of satire; it may be savage, as in Swift, with a /76/ moral object, or sedate, as in Gibbon, with a malicious. . . .

The Humorist of mean order is a refreshing laugher, giving tone to the feelings, and sometimes allowing the feelings to be too much for him; but the Humorist of high has an embrace of contrasts beyond the scope of the Comic poet. . . .

The Comic poet is in the narrow field, or enclosed square, of the society he depicts; and he addresses the still narrower enclosure of /79/ men's intellects, with reference to the operation of the social world upon their characters. He is not concerned with beginnings or endings or surroundings, but with what you are now weaving. To understand his work and value it, you must have a sober liking of your kind, and a sober estimate of our civilized qualities. The aim and business of the Comic poet are misunderstood, his meaning is not seized nor his point of view taken, when he is accused of dishonoring our nature and being hostile to sentiment, tending to spitefulness and making an unfair use of laughter. Those who detect irony in Comedy do so because they choose to see it in life. "Poverty," says the satirist,[17] "has nothing harder in itself than that it makes men ridiculous." But poverty is never ridiculous to Comic perception until it attempts to make its rags conceal its bareness in a forlorn attempt at decency, or foolishly to rival ostentation. . . .

One excellent test of the civilization of a country, as I have said, I take to be the flourishing of the Comic Idea and Comedy; and the test of true comedy is that it shall awaken thoughtful laughter.

If you believe that our civilization is founded in common sense (and it is the first condition of sanity to believe it), you will, when contemplating men, discern a Spirit overhead; not more heavenly

[17] Juvenal.

than the light flashed upward from glassy surfaces, but luminous and watchful; never shooting beyond them, nor lagging in the rear; so closely attached to them that it may be taken for a slavish reflex, until its features are studied. It has the sage's brows, /82/ and the sunny malice of faun lurks at the corners of the half-closed lips drawn in an idle wariness of half-tension. That slim feasting smile, shaped like the long-bow, was once a big round satyr's laugh, that flung up the brows like a fortress lifted by gunpowder. The laugh will come again, but it will be of the order of the smile, finely-tempered, showing sunlight of the mind, mental richness rather than noisy enormity. Its common aspect is one of unsolicitous observation, as if surveying a full field and having leisure to dart on its chosen morsels, without any fluttering eagerness. Men's future upon earth does not attract it; their honesty and shapeliness in the present does; and whenever they wax out of proportion, overblown, affected, pretentious, bombastical, hypocritical, pedantic, fantastically delicate; whenever it sees them self-deceived or hoodwinked, given to run riot in idolatries, drifting into vanities, congregating in absurdities, planning short-sightedly, plotting dementedly; whenever they /83/ are at variance with their professions, and violate the unwritten but perceptible laws binding them in consideration one to another; whenever they offend sound reason, fair justice; are false in humility or mined with conceit, individually, or in the bulk; the Spirit overhead will look humanely malign, and cast an oblique light on·them, followed by volleys of silvery laughter. That is the Comic Spirit.

Not to distinguish it is to be bull-blind to the spiritual, and to deny the existence of a mind of man where minds of men are in working conjunction.

You must, as I have said, believe that our state of society is founded in common sense, otherwise you will not be struck by the contrasts the Comic Spirit perceives, or have it to look to for your consolation. You will, in fact, be standing in that peculiar oblique beam of light, yourself illuminated to the general eye as the very object of chase and doomed quarry of the thing obscure to you. But to feel its presence, and to see it, is your assurance that /84/ many sane and solid minds are with you in what you are experiencing; and this of itself spares you the pain of satirical heat, and the bitter craving to strike heavy blows. You share the sublime of wrath, that would not have hurt the foolish, but merely demonstrate their foolish-ness. . . . A perception of the Comic Spirit gives high fellowship. You become a citizen of the selecter world, the highest we know of in connection with our old world, which is not supermundane. Look there for your unchallengeable upper class! You feel that you are one of this our civilized community, that you cannot escape from it, and would not if you could. Good hope sustains you; weariness does not overwhelm you; in isolation you see no charms for vanity; personal pride is greatly moderated. Nor shall your title of citizenship exclude you from /85/ worlds of imagination or of devotion. The Comic Spirit is not hostile to the sweetest songfully poetic. Chaucer bubbles with it; Shakespeare overflows; there is a mild moon's ray of it (pale with superrefinement through distance from our flesh and blood planet) in *Comus*. Pope has it, and it is the daylight side of the night half-obscuring Cowper. . . . Laughter is open to perversion, like other /86/ good things; the scornful and the brutal sorts are not unknown to us; but the laughter directed by the Comic Spirit is a harmless wine, conducing to sobriety in the degree that it enlivens. It enters you like fresh air into a study, as when one of the sudden contrasts of the Comic Idea floods the brain like reassuring daylight. You are cognizant of the true kind by feeling that you take it in, savor it, and have what flowers live on, natural air for food. That which you give out—the joyful roar—is not the better part; let that go to good-fellowship and the benefit of the lungs. Aristophanes promises his auditors[18] that, if they will retain the ideas of the Comic poet carefully, as they keep dried fruits in boxes, their garments shall smell odoriferous of wisdom throughout the year. The boast will not be thought an empty one by those who have choice friends that have stocked themselves according to his directions. Such treasuries of sparkling laughter are wells in our desert. Sensitiveness to the comic laugh is a step in /87/ civilization. To shrink from being an object of it is a step in cultivation. We know the degree of refinement in men by the matter they will laugh at, and the ring of the laugh; but we know likewise that the larger natures are distinguished by the great breadth of their power of laughter, and no one really loving Molière is refined by that love to despise or be dense to Aristophanes, though it may be that the lover of Aristophanes will not have risen to the height of Molière. Embrace them both, and you have the whole scale of laughter in your breast. . . . Between these two stand Shakespeare

18 In *The Frogs*.

and Cervantes, with the richer laugh of heart and mind in one; with much of the Aristophanic robustness, something of Molière's delicacy.

The laughter heard in circles not pervaded /89/ by the Comic Idea will sound harsh and soulless, like versified prose, if you step into them with a sense of the distinction. You will fancy you have changed your habitation to a planet remoter from the sun. You may be among powerful brains, too. You will not find poets—or but a stray one, overworshiped. You will find learned men undoubtedly, professors, reputed philosophers, and illustrious dilettanti. They have in them, perhaps, every element composing light, except the Comic. They read verse, they discourse of art; but their eminent faculties are not under that vigilant sense of a collective supervision, spiritual and present, which we have taken note of. They build a temple of arrogance; they speak much in the voice of oracles; their hilarity, if it does not dip in grossness, is usually a form of pugnacity.

Insufficiency of sight in the eye looking outward has deprived them of the eye that should look inward. They have never weighed themselves in the delicate balance of the Comic /90/ Idea, so as to obtain a suspicion of the rights and dues of the world; and they have, in consequence, an irritable personality . . .

I do not know that the fly in amber is of any particular use, but the Comic Idea enclosed in a Comedy makes it more generally perceptible and portable, and that is an advantage. There is a benefit to men in taking the lessons of Comedy in congregations, for it enlivens the wits; and to writers it is beneficial, for they must have a clear scheme, and even if they have no idea to present, they must prove that they have made the public sit to them before the sitting, to see the picture. And writing for the stage would be a corrective of a too-incrusted scholarly style, into which some great ones fall at times. It keeps minor writers to a definite plan, and to English. Many of them now swelling a plethoric market in the composition of novels, in pun-manufactories, and in /98/ journalism—attached to the machinery forcing perishable matter on a public that swallows voraciously and groans—might, with encouragement, be attending to the study of art in literature. . . . /99/

Henri Bergson Laughter

Despite his ancestry (on his father's side he was descended from wealthy Polish Jewish merchants; his mother was English), Henri Bergson (1859-1941) was essentially French; ultimately he became, himself, a sort of cult. His three early epoch-making treatises dealt with, first, his famous "intuition of duration," a kind of declaration of independence of the mind; then, in *Matter and Memory*, he asserted the continuous flow of consciousness as opposed to the brain which is but an instrument of selection; finally (in *Creative Evolution*) he defined the mind itself as undiluted energy, an *élan vital*, ever "becoming," ever participating in universal creativeness. Many other works followed; he was an extremely popular professor at the Collège de France; he was elected to the French Academy (1914), and ultimately was awarded the Nobel Prize (in 1927). *Le Rire* (or *Laughter*) was first published in 1900. Coming from the eminent Bergson, it has been a significant document in the history of comic theory. Translated into English in 1911 by Cloudesley Brereton and Fred Rothwell, it was published by The Macmillan Company, New York.

CHAPTER I

The Comic in General—The Comic Element in Forms and Movements— Expansive Force of the Comic

I

The first point to which attention should be called is that the comic does not exist outside the pale of what is strictly *human*. A landscape may be beautiful, charming and sublime, or insignificant and ugly; it will never be laughable. You may laugh at an animal, but only because you have detected in it some human attitude or expression. You may laugh at a hat, but what you are making fun of, in this case, is not the piece of felt or straw, but the shape that men have given it—the human caprice whose mould it has assumed. It is strange that so important a fact, and such a simple one too, has not attracted to a greater degree the attention of philosophers. Several have defined man as "an animal which laughs." They might equally well have defined him as an animal /3/ which is laughed at; for if any other animal, or some lifeless object, produces the same effect, it is always because of some resemblance to man, of the stamp he gives it or the use he puts it to.

Here I would point out, as a symptom equally worthy of notice, the *absence of feeling* which usually accompanies laughter. It seems as though the comic could not produce its disturbing effect unless it fell, so to say, on the surface of a soul that is thoroughly calm and unruffled. Indifference is its natural environment, for laughter has no greater foe than emotion. I do not mean that we could not laugh at a person who inspires us with pity, for instance, or even with affection, but in such a case we must, for the moment, put our affection out of court and impose silence upon our pity. In a society composed of pure intelligences there would probably be no more tears, though perhaps there would still be laughter; whereas highly emotional souls, in tune and unison with life, in whom every event would be sentimentally prolonged and re-echoed, would neither know nor understand laughter. Try, for a moment, to become interested in everything that is being said and done; act, in imagina-/4/tion, with those who act, and feel with those who feel; in a word, give your sympathy its widest expansion: as though at the touch of a fairy wand you will see the flimsiest of objects assume importance, and a gloomy hue spread over everything. Now step aside, look upon life as a disinterested spectator: many a drama will turn into a comedy. . . . To produce the whole of its effect, then, the comic demands something like a momentary anesthesia of the heart. Its appeal is to intelligence, pure and simple.

This intelligence, however, must always remain in touch with other intelligences. And here is the third fact to which attention should be drawn. You would hardly appreciate the comic if you felt yourself isolated from others. Laughter appears to stand in need of an echo. Listen to it carefully: it is not an articulate, /5/ clear, well-defined sound; it is something which would fain be prolonged by reverberating from one to another, something beginning with a crash, to continue in successive rumblings, like thunder in a mountain. Still, this reverberation cannot go on for ever. It can travel within as wide a circle as you please: the circle remains, none the less, a closed one. Our laughter is always the laughter of a group. . . . /6/ To understand laughter, we must put it back into its natural environment, which is society, and above all must we determine /7/ the utility of its function, which is a social one. Such, let us say at once, will be the leading idea of all our investigations. Laughter must answer to certain requirements of life in common. It must have a *social* signification.

Let us clearly mark the point towards which our three preliminary observations are converging. The comic will come into being, it appears, whenever a group of men concentrate their attention on one of their number, imposing silence on their emotions and calling into play nothing but their intelligence.

II

A man, running along the street, stumbles and falls; the passers-by burst out laughing. They would not laugh at him, I imagine, could they suppose that the whim had suddenly seized him to sit down on the ground. They laugh because his sitting down is involuntary. /8/ Consequently, it is not his sudden change of attitude that raises a laugh, but rather the involuntary element in this change,—his clumsiness, in fact. Perhaps there was a stone on the road. He should have altered his pace or avoided the obstacle. Instead of that, through lack of elasticity, through absentmindedness and a kind of physical obstinacy, *as a result, in fact, of rigidity or of momentum*, the muscles continued to perform the same movement when the circumstances of the case called for something else. That is the reason of the man's fall, and also of the people's laughter.

Now, take the case of a person who attends to the petty occupations of his everyday life with mathematical precision. The objects around him, however, have all been tampered with by a mischievous wag, the result being that when he dips his pen into the inkstand he draws it out all covered with mud, when he fancies he is sitting down on a solid chair he finds himself sprawling on the floor, in a word his actions are all topsy-turvy or mere beating the air, while in every case the effect is invariably one of momentum. Habit has given the impulse: what was wanted was to check the /9/ movement or deflect it. He did nothing of the sort, but continued like a machine in the same straight line. The victim, then, of a practical joke is in a position similar to that of a runner who falls,—he is comic for the same reason. The laughable element in both cases consists of a certain *mechanical inelasticity*, just where one would expect to find the wideawake adaptability and the living pliableness of a human being. The only difference in the two cases is that the former happened of itself, whilst the latter was obtained artificially. In the first instance, the passer-by does nothing but look on, but in the second the mischievous wag intervenes.

All the same, in both cases the result has been brought about by an external circumstance. The comic is therefore accidental: it remains, so to speak, in superficial contact with the person. How is it to penetrate within? The necessary conditions will be fulfilled when mechanical rigidity no longer requires for its manifestation a stumbling-block which either the hazard of circumstance or human knavery has set in its way, but extracts by natural processes, from its own store, an inexhaustible series of oppor-/10/tunities for externally revealing its presence. Suppose, then, we imagine a mind always thinking of what it has just done and never of what it is doing, like a song which lags behind its accompaniment. Let us try to picture to ourselves a certain inborn lack of elasticity of both senses and intelligence, which brings it to pass that we continue to see what is no longer visible, to hear what is no longer audible, to say what is no longer to the point: in short, to adapt ourselves to a past and therefore imaginary situation, when we ought to be shaping our conduct in accordance with the reality which is present. This time the comic will take up its abode in the person himself; it is the person who will supply it with everything—matter and form, cause and opportunity. Is it then surprising that the absent-minded individual—for this is the character we have just been describing—has usually fired the imagination of comic authors? /11/ . . . Absentmindedness, indeed, is not perhaps the actual fountain-head of the comic, but surely it is contiguous to a certain stream of facts and fancies which flows straight from the fountain-head. It is situated, so to say, on one of the great natural watersheds of laughter.

Now, the effect of absentmindedness may gather strength in its turn. There is a general law, the first example of which we have just encountered, and which we will formulate in the following terms: when a certain comic effect has its origin in a certain cause, the more natural we regard the cause to be, the more comic shall we find the effect. Even now we laugh at absentmindedness when presented to us as a simple fact. Still more laughable will be the absentmindedness we have seen springing up and growing before our very eyes, with whose origin we are acquainted and whose life-history we can reconstruct. To choose a definite example: suppose a man has taken to reading nothing but romances of love and chivalry. Attracted and fascinated by his /12/ heroes, his thoughts and

intentions gradually turn more and more towards them, till one fine day we find him walking among us like a somnambulist. His actions are distractions. But then his distractions can be traced back to a definite, positive cause. They are no longer cases of *absence* of mind, pure and simple; they find their explanation in the *presence* of the individual in quite definite, though imaginary, surroundings. Doubtless a fall is always a fall, but it is one thing to tumble into a well because you were looking anywhere but in front of you, it is quite another thing to fall into it because you were intent upon a star. It was certainly a star at which Don Quixote was gazing. How profound is the comic element in the over-romantic, Utopian bent of mind! /13/ To realise this more fully, it need only be noted that a comic character is generally comic in proportion to his ignorance of himself. The comic person is unconscious. As though wearing the ring of Gyges[1] with reverse effect, he becomes invisible to himself while remain-/16/ing visible to all the world. A character in a tragedy will make no change in his conduct because he will know how it is judged by us; he may continue therein even though fully conscious of what he is and feeling keenly the horror he inspires in us. But a defect that is ridiculous, as soon as it feels itself to be so, endeavours to modify itself or at least to appear as though it did. . . . Indeed, it is in this sense only that laughter "corrects men's manners." It makes us at once endeavour to appear what we ought to be, what some day we shall perhaps end in being . . . /17/

What life and society require of each of us is a constantly alert attention that discerns the outlines of the present situation, together with a certain elasticity of mind and body to enable us to adapt ourselves in consequence. *Tension* and *elasticity* are two forces, mutually complementary, which life brings into play. If these two forces are lacking in the body to any considerable extent, we have sickness and infirmity and accidents of every kind. If they are lacking in the mind, we find every degree of mental deficiency, every variety of insanity. Finally, if they are lacking in the character, we have cases of the gravest inadaptibility to social life, which are the sources of misery and at times the causes of crime. Once these elements of inferiority that affect the serious side of existence are

---

[1] Gyges was the King of Lydia (seventh century B.C.) whose story is told in Plato's *Republic;* the legend is that he found a ring on a corpse by the turning of which he could make himself invisible; he is said to be the first ruler to be called tyrant.

removed—and they tend to eliminate themselves in what has been called /18/ the struggle for life—the person can live, and that in common with other persons. But society asks for something more; it is not satisfied with simply living, it insists on living well. What it now has to dread is that each one of us, content with paying attention to what affects the essentials of life, will, so far as the rest is concerned, give way to the easy automatism of acquired habits. Another thing it must fear is that the members of whom it is made up, instead of aiming after an increasingly delicate adjustment of wills which will fit more and more perfectly into one another, will confine themselves to respecting simply the fundamental conditions of this adjustment: a cut-and-dried agreement among the persons will not satisfy it, it insists on a constant striving after reciprocal adaptation. Society will therefore be suspicious of all *inelasticity* of character, of mind and even of body, because it is the possible sign of a slumbering activity as well as of an activity with separatist tendencies, that inclines to swerve from the common centre round which society gravitates: in short, because it is the sign of an eccentricity. And yet, society cannot intervene at this stage /19/ by material repression, since it is not affected in a material fashion. It is confronted with something that makes it uneasy, but only as a symptom —scarcely a threat, at the very most a gesture. A gesture, therefore, will be its reply. Laughter must be something of this kind, a sort of *social gesture*. By the fear which it inspires, it restrains eccentricity, keeps constantly awake and in mutual contact certain activities of a secondary order which might retire into their shell and go to sleep, and in short, softens down whatever the surface of the social body may retain of mechanical inelasticity. Laughter, then, does not belong to the province of esthetics alone, since unconsciously (and even immorally in many particular instances) it pursues a utilitarian aim of general improvement. And yet there is something esthetic about it, since the comic comes into being just when society and the individual, freed from the worry of self-preservation, begin to regard themselves as works of art. In a word, if a circle be drawn round those actions and dispositions—implied in individual or social life—to which their natural consequences bring their own penalties, there remains outside this sphere of /20/ emotion and struggle—and within a neutral zone in which man simply exposes himself to man's curiosity—a certain rigidity of body, mind and character that society would still like to get rid of in order to obtain from its members the greatest possible degree of elasticity and sociability. This rigidity is the comic, and laughter is its corrective . . . /21/

III

Let us begin at the simplest point. What is a comic physiognomy? Where does a ridiculous expression of the face come from? And what is, in this case, the distinction between the comic and the ugly? /22/

Now, certain deformities undoubtedly possess over others the sorry privilege of causing some persons to laugh; some hunchbacks, for instance, will excite laughter. Without at this point entering into useless details, we will simply ask the reader to think of a number of deformities, and then to divide them into two groups: on the one hand, those which nature has directed towards the ridiculous; and on the other, those which absolutely diverge from it. No doubt he will hit upon the following law: (*A deformity that may become comic is a deformity that a normally built person could successfully imitate.*)

Is it not, then, the case that the hunchback suggests the appearance of a person who holds himself badly? His back seems to have contracted an ugly stoop. By a kind of physical obstinacy, by *rigidity*, in a word, it persists in the habit it has contracted. Try to see with your eyes alone. Avoid reflection, and above all, do not reason. Abandon all your prepossessions; seek to recapture a fresh, direct and primitive impression. The vision /23/ you will reacquire will be one of this kind. You will have before you a man bent on cultivating a certain rigid attitude whose body, if one may use the expression, is one vast grin. . . . /24/

But a comic expression of the face is one that promises nothing more than it gives. It is a unique and permanent grimace. One would say that the person's whole moral life has crystallised into this particular cast of features. This is the reason why a face is all the more comic, the more nearly it suggests to us the idea of some simple mechanical action in which its personality would for ever be absorbed. Some faces seem to be always engaged in weeping, others in laughing or whistling, others, again, in eternally blowing an imaginary trumpet, and these are the most comic faces of all. Here again is exemplified the law according to which the more natural the explanation of the cause, the more comic is the effect. Automatism, *inelasticity*, habit that has been contracted and maintained, are clearly the causes why a face makes us laugh. But this effect gains in intensity when we are able to connect these characteristics with some deep-seated cause, a certain *fundamental absentmindedness*, as though the soul had allowed itself to be fascinated and hypnotised by the materiality of a simple action. /25/

We shall now understand the comic element in caricature. However regular we may imagine a face to be, however harmonious its lines and supple its movements, their adjustment is never altogether perfect: there will always be discoverable the signs of some impending bias, the vague suggestion of a possible grimace, in short, some favourite distortion towards which nature seems to be particularly inclined. The art of the caricaturist consists in detecting this, at times, imperceptible tendency, and in rendering it visible to all eyes by magnifying it. He makes his models grimace, as they would do themselves if they went to the end of their tether. Beneath the skin-deep harmony of form, he divines the deep-seated recalcitrance of matter. He realises disproportions and deformations which must have existed in nature as mere inclinations, but which have not succeeded in coming to a head, being held in check by a higher force. His art, which has a touch of the diabolical, raises up the demon who had been overthrown by the angel. Certainly, it is an art that exaggerates, and yet the definition would be very far from complete were exaggeration alone alleged to be its aim and object, for /26/ there exist caricatures that are more lifelike than portraits, caricatures in which the exaggeration is scarcely noticeable, whilst, inversely, it is quite possible to exaggerate to excess without obtaining a real caricature. For exaggeration to be comic, it must not appear as an aim, but rather as a means that the artist is using in order to make manifest to our eyes the distortions which he sees in embryo. It is this process of distortion that is of moment and interest. And that is precisely why we shall look for it even in those elements of the face that are incapable of movement, in the curve of a nose or the shape of an ear. For, in our eyes, form is always the outline of a movement. The caricaturist who alters the size of a nose, but respects its ground plan, lengthening it, for instance, in the very direction in which it was being lengthened by nature, is really making the nose indulge in a grin. Henceforth we shall always look upon the original as having determined to lengthen itself and start grinning. In this sense, one might say that Nature herself often meets with the successes of a caricaturist. In the movement through which she has slit that mouth, curtailed that chin and bulged out that /27/ cheek, she would appear to have succeeded in completing the intended grimace, thus outwitting the restraining supervision of a more reasonable force. In that case, the face we laugh at is, so to speak, its own caricature.

To sum up, whatever be the doctrine to which our reason assents, our imagination has a very clear-cut philosophy of its own: in every human form it sees the effort of a soul which is shaping matter, a soul which is infinitely supple and perpetually in motion, subject to no law of gravitation, for it is not the earth that attracts it. This soul imparts a portion of its winged lightness to the body it animates: the immateriality which thus passes into matter is what is called gracefulness. Matter, however, is obstinate and resists. It draws to itself the ever-alert activity of this higher principle, would fain convert it to its own inertia and cause it to revert to mere automatism. It would fain immobilise the intelligently varied movements of the body in stupidly contracted grooves, stereotype in permanent grimaces the fleeting expressions of the face, in short imprint on the whole person such an attitude as to make it appear immersed and absorbed in /28/ the materiality of some mechanical occupation instead of ceaselessly renewing its vitality by keeping in touch with a living ideal. Where matter thus succeeds in dulling the outward life of the soul, in petrifying its movements and thwarting its gracefulness, it achieves, at the expense of a body, an effect that is comic. If, then, at this point we wish to define the comic by comparing it with its contrary, we should have to contrast it with gracefulness even more than with beauty. It partakes rather of the unsprightly than of the unsightly, of *rigidness* rather than of *ugliness*.

IV

We will now pass from the comic element in *forms* to that in *gestures* and *movements*. Let us at once state the law which seems to govern all the phenomena of this kind. . . .

The attitudes, gestures and movements of the human body are laughable in exact proportion as that body reminds us of a mere machine. /29/

. . . To verify it directly, it would be sufficient to study closely the work of comic artists, eliminating entirely the element of caricature, and omitting that portion of the comic which is not inherent in the drawing itself. . . .

But if we devote our whole attention to the drawing with the firm resolve to think of nothing else, we shall probably find that it is generally comic in proportion to the clearness, as well as the subtleness, with which it enables us to see a man as a jointed puppet. The suggestion must be a clear one, for inside the person we must distinctly perceive, as though through a glass, a set-up mechanism. But the suggestion must also be a subtle one, for the general appearance of the person, whose every limb has been made rigid as a machine, must continue to give us the impression of a /30/ living being. The more exactly these two images, that of a person and that of a machine, fit into each other, the more striking is the comic effect, and the more consummate the art of the draughtsman. The originality of a comic artist is thus expressed in the special kind of life he imparts to a mere puppet.

In a public speaker, for instance, we find that gesture vies with speech. Jealous of the latter, gesture closely dogs the speaker's thought, demanding also to act as interpreter. Well and good; but then it must pledge itself to follow thought through all the phases of its development. An idea is something that grows, buds, blossoms and ripens from the beginning to the end of a speech. It never /31/ halts, never repeats itself. It must be changing every moment, for to cease to change would be to cease to live. Then let gesture display a like animation! Let it accept the fundamental law of life, which is the complete negation of repetition! But I find that a certain movement of head or arm, a movement always the same, seems to return at regular intervals. If I notice it and it succeeds in diverting my attention, if I wait for it to occur and it occurs when I expect it, then involuntarily I laugh. Why? Because I now have before me a machine that works automatically. This is no longer life, it is automatism established in life and imitating it. It belongs to the comic.

This is also the reason why gestures, at which we never dreamt of laughing, become laughable when imitated by another individual. /32/ . . . To imitate any one is to bring out the element of automatism he has allowed to creep into his person. And as this is the very essence of the ludicrous, it is no wonder that imitation gives rise to laughter. /33/

v

Before going further, let us halt a moment and glance around. /36/ . . . We might think of an immense avenue such as are to be seen in the forest of Fontainebleau, with *crosses* at intervals to indicate the crossways: at each of these we shall walk round the cross, explore for a while the paths that open out before us, and then return to our original course. Now, we have just reached one of these mental crossways. *Something mechanical encrusted on the living* will represent a cross at which we must halt, a central image from which the imagination branches off in different /37/ directions. What are these directions? There appear to be three main ones.

1. In the first place, this view of the mechanical and the living dovetailed into each other makes us incline towards the vaguer image of *some rigidity or other* applied to the mobility of life, in an awkward attempt to follow its lines and counterfeit its suppleness. Here we perceive how easy it is for a garment to become ridiculous. It might almost be said that every fashion is laughable in some respect. Only, when we are dealing with the fashion of the day, we are so accustomed to it that the garment seems, in our mind, to form one with the individual wearing it. We do not separate them in imagination. The idea no longer occurs to us to contrast the inert rigidity of the covering with the living suppleness of the object covered: consequently, the comic here remains in a latent condition. It will only succeed in emerging when the natural incompatibility is so deep-seated between the covering and the covered that even an immemorial association /38/ fails to cement this union: a case in point is our head and top hat. Suppose, however, some eccentric individual dresses himself in the fashion of former times our attention is immediately drawn to the clothes themselves; we absolutely distinguish them from the individual, we say that the latter *is disguising himself*,—as though every article of clothing were not a disguise!—and the laughable aspect of fashion comes out of the shadow into the light.

Here we are beginning to catch a faint glimpse of the highly intricate difficulties raised by this problem of the comic. One of the reasons that must have given rise to many erroneous or unsatisfactory theories of laughter is that many things are comic *de jure* without being comic *de facto*, the continuity of custom having deadened within them the comic quality. A sudden dissolution of continuity is needed, a break with fashion, for this quality to revive. Hence the impression that this dissolution of continuity is the parent of the comic, whereas all it does is to bring it to our notice. Hence, again, the explanation of laughter by *surprise*, *contrast*, etc., definitions which would equally apply to a host of cases in which we have no /39/ inclination whatever to laugh. The truth of the matter is far from being so simple. . . . /40/

Let us then follow this logic of the imagination in the special case in hand. A man in disguise is comic. A man we regard as disguised is also comic. So, by analogy, any disguise is seen to become comic, not only that of a man, but that of society also, and even the disguise of nature.

Let us start with nature. You laugh at a dog that is half-clipped, at a bed of artificially coloured flowers, at a wood in which the trees are plastered over with election addresses, etc. Look for the reason, and you will see that you are once more thinking of a masquerade. Here, however, the comic element is very faint; it is too far from its source. If you wish to strengthen it, you must go back to the source itself and /42/ contrast the derived image, that of a masquerade, with the original one, which, be it remembered, was that of a mechanical tampering with life. In "a nature that is mechanically tampered with" we possess a thoroughly comic theme, on which fancy will be able to play ever so many variations with the certainty of successfully provoking the heartiest hilarity. . . .

There are comic phrases /43/ in which this theme is audible, like a distant echo, coupled with an ingenuousness, whether sincere or affected, which acts as accompaniment. Take, as an instance, the exclamation of one of Gondinet's[2] characters on arriving in a town and learning that there is an extinct volcano in the neighbourhood, "They had a volcano, and they have let it go out!"

Let us go on to society. As we are both in and of it, we cannot help treating it as a living being. Any image, then, suggestive of the notion of a society disguising itself, or of a social masquerade, so to speak, will be laughable. Now, such a notion is formed when we perceive anything inert or stereotyped, or simply ready-made, on the surface of living society. There we have rigidity over again, clashing with the inner suppleness of life. The ceremonial side of social life must, therefore, always include a latent comic element, which is only waiting for an opportunity to burst into full view. It /44/ might be said that ceremonies are to the social body what clothing is to the individual body: they owe their seriousness to the fact that they are identified, in our minds, with the serious object with which custom associates them, and when we isolate them in imagination, they forthwith lose their seriousness. For any ceremony, then, to become comic, it is enough that our attention be fixed on the ceremonial element in it, and that we neglect its matter, as philosophers say, and think only of its form. Every one knows how easily the comic spirit exercises its ingenuity on social actions of a stereotyped nature, from an ordinary prize-distribution to the solemn sitting of a court of justice. Any form or formula is a ready-made frame into which the comic element may be fitted. . . . /45/

We might multiply examples, for all we need do would be to call up Molière's doctors, one after the other. However far, moreover, comic fancy may seem to go, reality at times under- /47/ takes to improve upon it. . . .

To sum up, then, we have one and the same effect, which assumes ever subtler forms as it passes from the idea of an artificial *mechanisation* of the human body, if such an expression is permissible, to that of any substitution whatsoever of the artificial for the natural. A less and less rigorous logic, that more and more resembles the logic of dreamland, transfers the same relationship into higher and higher spheres, between increasingly immaterial terms, till in the end we find a mere administrative /48/ enactment occupying the same relation to a natural or moral law that a ready-made garment, for instance, does to the living body. . . .

2. Our starting-point is again "something mechanical encrusted upon the living." Where did the comic come from in this case? It came from the fact that the living body became rigid, like a machine. Accordingly, it seemed to us that the living body ought to be the perfection of suppleness, the ever-alert activity of a principle always at work. But this activity would really belong to the soul rather than to the body. It would be the very flame of life, kindled within us by a higher principle and perceived through the body, as though through a glass. When we see only gracefulness and suppleness in the living body, it is because we disregard in it the elements of weight, of resistance, and, in a word, of matter; we forget its materiality and think only of its vitality, a vitality which we regard as derived from /49/ the very principle of intellectual and moral life. Let us suppose, however, that our attention is drawn to this material side of the body; that, so far from sharing in the lightness and subtlety of the principle with which it is animated, the body is no more in our eyes than a heavy and cumbersome vesture, a kind of irksome ballast which holds down to earth a soul eager to rise aloft. Then the body will become to the soul what, as we have just seen, the garment was to the body itself— inert matter dumped down upon living energy. The impression of the comic will be produced as soon as we have a clear apprehension of this putting the one on the other. And we shall experience it

2 Pierre Gondinet (1828-1888), author of popular, light comedies; his most famous work was the libretto of the opera, *Lakmé*.

most strongly when we are shown the soul *tantalised* by the needs of the body: on the one hand, the moral personality with its intelligently varied energy, and, on the other, the stupidly monotonous body, perpetually obstructing everything with its machine-like obstinacy. The more paltry and uniformly repeated these claims of the body, the more striking will be the result. But that is only a matter of degree, and the general law of these phenomena may be formulated as follows: *Any /50/ incident is comic that calls our attention to the physical in a person, when it is the moral side that is concerned.*

Why do we laugh at a public speaker who sneezes just at the most pathetic moment of his speech? Where lies the comic element in this sentence, taken from a funeral speech and quoted by a German philosopher: "He was virtuous and plump"? It lies in the fact that our attention is suddenly recalled from the soul to the body. Similar instances abound in daily life. . . . *A person embarrassed by his body* is the image suggested to us in all these examples. The reason that excessive stoutness is laughable is probably because it calls up an image of the same kind. I almost think that this too is what sometimes /51/ makes bashfulness somewhat ridiculous. The bashful man rather gives the impression of a person embarrassed by his body, looking round for some convenient cloak-room in which to deposit it.

This is just why the tragic poet is so careful to avoid anything calculated to attract attention to the material side of his heroes. No sooner does anxiety about the body manifest itself than the intrusion of a comic element is to be feared. On this account, the hero in a tragedy does not eat or drink or warm himself. He does not even sit down any more than can be helped. . . . /52/

Let us now give a wider scope to this image of *the body taking precedence of the soul.* We shall obtain something more general—*the manner seeking to outdo the matter, the letter aiming at ousting the spirit.* Is it not perchance this idea that comedy is trying to suggest to us when holding up a profession to ridicule? It makes the lawyer, the magistrate and the doctor speak as though health and justice were of little moment, the main point being that we should have lawyers, magistrates and doctors, and that all outward formalities pertaining to these professions should be scrupulously respected. And so we find the means substituted for the end, the manner for the matter; no longer is it the profession that is made for the public, but rather the public for the profession. Constant attention to form and the mechanical application of rules here bring about a kind of professional automatism analogous to that imposed upon the soul by the habits of the /53/ body, and equally laughable. Numerous are the examples of this on the stage. . . . /54/

3. Let us then return, for the last time, to our central image—something mechanical encrusted on something living. Here, the living being under discussion was a human being, a person. A mechanical arrangement, on the other hand, is a thing. What, therefore, incited laughter, was the momentary transformation of a person into a thing, if one considers the image from this standpoint. Let us then pass from the exact idea of a machine to the /57/ vaguer one of a thing in general. We shall have a fresh series of laughable images which will be obtained by taking a blurred impression, so to speak, of the outlines of the former and will bring us to this new law: *We laugh every time a person gives us the impression of being a thing.*

We laugh at Sancho Panza tumbled into a bed-quilt and tossed into the air like a football. We laugh at Baron Munchausen turned into a cannon-ball and travelling through space. But certain tricks of circus clowns might afford a still more precise exemplification of the same law. The clowns came and went, collided, fell and jumped up again in a uniformly accelerated rhythm, visibly intent upon effecting a *crescendo.* And it was more and more to the jumping up again, the *rebound,* /58/ that the attention of the public was attracted. Gradually, one lost sight of the fact that they were men of flesh and blood like ourselves; one began to think of bundles of all sorts, falling and knocking against each other. Then the vision assumed a more definite aspect. The forms grew rounder, the bodies rolled together and seemed to pick themselves up like balls. Then at last appeared the image towards which the whole of this scene had doubtless been unconsciously evolving,—large rubber balls hurled against one another in every direction. . . . /59/

A kind of dim, vague instinct may enable even an uncultured mind to get an inkling here of the subtler results of psychological science. We know that it is possible to call up hallucinatory visions in a hypnotised subject by simple suggestion. If he be told that a bird is perched on his hand, he will see the bird and watch it fly away. The idea suggested, however, is far from being always accepted with like docility. Not infrequently, the mesmeriser only succeeds in getting an idea into his subject's head by slow degrees through a carefully graduated series of hints. He will then start with objects really perceived by the subject, and will en- /60/ deavour to make the perception of these objects more and more indefinite; then, step by step, he will bring out of this state of mental chaos the precise form of the object of which he wishes to create an hallucination. Something of the kind happens to many people when dropping off to sleep; they see those coloured, fluid, shapeless masses, which occupy the field of vision, insensibly solidifying into distinct objects. Consequently, the gradual passing from the dim and vague to the clear and distinct is the method of suggestion *par excellence*. I fancy it might be found to be at the root of a good many comic suggestions, especially in the coarser forms of the comic, in which the transformation of a person into a thing seems to be taking place before our eyes. But there are other and more subtle methods in use, among poets, for instance, which perhaps unconsciously lead to the same end. By a certain arrangement of rhythm, rhyme and assonance, it is possible to lull the imagination, to rock it to and fro between like and like with a regular see-saw motion, and thus prepare it submissively to accept the vision suggested. . . . /61/

CHAPTER II
The Comic Element in Situations and the Comic Element in Words

I

Comedy is a game, a /68/ game that imitates life. And since, in the games of the child when working its dolls and puppets, many of the movements are produced by strings, ought we not to find those same strings, somewhat frayed by wear, reappearing as the threads that knot together the situations in a comedy? Let us, then, start with the games of a child, and follow the imperceptible process by which, as he grows himself, he makes his puppets grow, inspires them with life, and finally brings them to an ambiguous state in which, without ceasing to be puppets, they have yet become human beings. We thus obtain characters of a comedy type. And upon them we can test the truth of the law of which all our preceding analyses gave an inkling, a law in accordance with which we will define all broadly comic situations in general. *Any arrangement of acts and events is comic which gives us, in a single combination, the illusion of life and the distinct impression of a mechanical arrangement.*

1. *The Jack-in-the-box.*—As children we have all played with the little man who springs out of his box. You squeeze him flat, he /69/ jumps up again. Push him lower, and he shoots up still higher. Crush him down beneath the lid, and often he will send everything flying. It is hard to tell whether or not the toy itself is very ancient, but the kind of amusement it affords belongs to all time. It is a struggle between two stubborn elements, one of which, being simply mechanical, generally ends by giving in to the other, which treats it as a plaything. . . .

We will now pass on to the theatre, beginning with a Punch and Judy show. No sooner does the policeman put in an appearance on the stage than, naturally enough, he receives a blow which fells him. He springs to his feet, a second blow lays him flat. A repetition of the offence is followed by a repetition of the punishment. Up and down the constable flops and hops with the uniform rhythm of the bending and release of a spring, whilst the spectators laugh louder and louder.

Now, let us think of a spring that is rather of a moral type, an idea that is first expressed, /70/ then repressed, and then expressed again; a stream of words that bursts forth, is checked, and keeps on starting afresh. Once more we have the vision of one stubborn force, counteracted by another, equally pertinacious. This vision, however, will have discarded a portion of its materiality. No longer is it Punch and Judy that we are watching, but rather a real comedy. /71/

Let us scrutinise more closely the image of the spring which is bent, released, and bent again. Let us disentangle its central element, and we shall hit upon one of the usual processes of classic comedy, —*repetition*. . . . /72/

The repetition of a word is never laughable in itself. It makes us laugh only because it symbolises a special play of moral elements, this play itself being the symbol of an altogether material diversion. It is the diversion of the child pushing back the Jack-in-the-box, time after time, to the bottom of his box—but in a refined and spiritualised form, transferred to the realm of feelings and ideas. Let us then state the law which we think defines the main comic varieties of word-repetition on the stage: *In a comic repetition of words we generally find two terms: a repressed feeling which goes off like a spring, and an idea that delights in repressing the feeling anew.* /73/

2. *The Dancing-jack.*—There are innumerable comedies in which one of the characters /77/ thinks he is speaking and acting freely, and consequently, retains all the essentials of life, whereas, viewed from a certain standpoint, he appears as a mere toy in the hands of another, who is playing with him. . . . /78/

All that is serious in life comes from our freedom. The feelings we have matured, the passions we have brooded over, the actions we have weighed, decided upon and carried through, in short, all that comes from us and is our very own, these are the things that give life its ofttimes dramatic and generally grave aspect. What, then, is requisite to transform all this into a comedy? Merely to fancy that our seeming freedom conceals the strings of a dancing-jack, and that we are, as the poet says,

> . . . humble marionettes
> The wires of which are pulled by Fate.[3]

So there is not a real, a serious, or even a dramatic scene that fancy cannot render comic by simply calling forth this image. Nor is there a game for which a wider field lies open. /79/

3. *The Snow-ball.*—The farther we proceed in this investigation into the methods of comedy, the more clearly we see the part played by childhood's memories. These memories refer, perhaps, less to any special game than to the mechanical device of which that game is a particular instance. Take, for instance, the rolling snow-ball, which increases in size as it moves along. We might just as well think of toy soldiers standing behind one another. Push the first and it tumbles down on the second, this latter knocks down the third, and the state of things goes from bad to worse until they all lie prone on the floor. Or again, take a house of cards that has been built up with infinite care: the first you touch seems uncertain /80/ whether to move or not, its tottering neighbour comes to a quicker decision, and the work of destruction, gathering momentum as it goes on, rushes headlong to the final collapse. These instances are all different, but they suggest the same abstract vision, that of an effect which grows by arithmetical progression, so that the cause, insignificant at the outset, culminates by a necessary evolution in a result as important as it is unexpected. . . . /81/

It is the characteristic of a mechanical combination to be generally *reversible*. A child is delighted when he sees the ball in a game of ninepins knocking down everything in its way and spreading havoc in all directions; he laughs louder than ever when the ball returns to its starting-point after twists and turns and waverings of every kind. In other words, the mechanism just described is laughable even when rectilinear, it is much more so on becoming circular and when every effort the player makes, by a fatal interaction of cause and effect, merely results in bringing it back to the same spot. Now, a considerable number of light comedies revolve round this idea. An Italian

straw hat has been eaten up by a horse.[4] There is only one other hat like it in the whole of Paris; it *must* be secured regardless of cost. /83/ This hat, which always slips away at the moment its capture seems inevitable, keeps the principal character on the run, and through him all the others who hang, so to say, on to his coat tails, like a magnet which, by a successive series of attractions, draws along in its train the grains of iron filings that hang on to each other. And when at last, after all sorts of difficulties, the goal seems in sight, it is found that the hat so ardently sought is precisely the one that has been eaten. . . . /84/

When we think how intense and how common is this type of the comic, we understand why it has fascinated the imagination of certain philosophers. To cover a good deal of ground only to come back unwittingly to the starting-point, is to make a great effort for a result that is nil. So we might be tempted to define the comic in this latter fashion. And such, indeed, seems to be the idea of Herbert Spencer: according to him, laughter is the indication of an effort which suddenly encounters a void. Kant had already said something of the kind: "Laughter is the result of an expectation which, of a sudden, ends in nothing." /85/ The truth is, this second definition has scarcely more validity than the first. Lack of proportion between cause and effect, whether appearing in one or in the other, is never the direct source of laughter. What we do laugh at is something that this lack of proportion may in certain cases disclose, namely, a particular mechanical arrangement which it reveals to us, as through a glass, at the back of the series of effects and causes. Disregard this arrangement, and you let go the only clue capable of guiding you through the labyrinth of the comic. Any hypothesis you otherwise would select, while possibly applicable to a few carefully chosen cases, is liable at any moment to be met and overthrown by the first unsuitable instance that comes along.

But why is it we laugh at this mechanical arrangement? It is doubtless strange that the history of a person or of a group should sometimes appear like a game worked by strings, or gearings, or springs; but from what source does /86/ the special character of this strangeness arise? What is it that makes it laughable? To this question, which we have already propounded in various forms, our answer must always be the same. The rigid mechanism which we occasionally detect,

[3] . . . d'humbles marionnettes
Dont le fil est aux mains de la Nécessité.
                                        SULLY-PRUDHOMME.

[4] Labiche's play, *The Italian Straw Hat.*

as a foreign body, in the living continuity of human affairs is of peculiar interest to us as being a kind of *absentmindedness* on the part of life. Were events unceasingly mindful of their own course, there would be no coincidences, no conjunctures and no circular series; everything would evolve and progress continuously. And were all men always attentive to life, were we constantly keeping in touch with others as well as with ourselves, nothing within us would ever appear as due to the working of strings or springs. The comic is that side of a person which reveals his likeness to a thing, that aspect of human events which, through its peculiar inelasticity, conveys the impression of pure mechanism, of automatism, of movement without life. Consequently it expresses an individual or collective imperfection which calls for an immediate corrective. This corrective is laughter, a social gesture that singles /87/ out and represses a special kind of absentmindedness in men and in events. . . .

Life presents itself to us as evolution in time and complexity in space. Regarded in time, it is the continuous evolution of a being ever growing older; it never goes backwards and never repeats itself. Considered in space, it /88/ exhibits certain coexisting elements so closely interdependent, so exclusively made for one another, that not one of them could, at the same time, belong to two different organisms: each living being is a closed system of phenomena, incapable of interfering with other systems. A continual change of aspect, the irreversibility of the order of phenomena, the perfect individuality of a perfectly self-contained series: such, then, are the outward characteristics —whether real or apparent is of little moment— which distinguish the living from the merely mechanical. Let us take the counterpart of each of these: we shall obtain three processes which might be called *repetition, inversion,* and *reciprocal interference of series.* Now, it is easy to see that these are also the methods of light comedy, and that no others are possible. /89/

1. *Repetition.*—Our present problem no longer deals, like the preceding one, with a word or a sentence repeated by an individual, but rather with a situation, that is, a combination of circumstances, which recurs several times in its original form and thus contrasts with the changing stream of life. Everyday experience supplies us with this type of the comic, though only in a rudimentary state. Thus, you meet a friend in the street whom you have not seen for an age; there is nothing comic in the situation. If, however, you meet him again the same day, and then a third and a fourth time,

you may laugh at the "coincidence." Now, picture to yourself a series of imaginary events which affords a tolerably fair illusion of life, and within this ever-moving series imagine one and the same scene reproduced either by the same characters or by different ones: again you will have a coincidence, though a far more extraordinary one. /90/ Such are the repetitions produced on the stage. They are the more laughable in proportion as the scene repeated is more complex and more naturally introduced—two conditions which seem mutually exclusive, and which the playwriter must be clever enough to reconcile. . . . /91/

2. *Inversion.*—This second method has so much analogy with the first that we will merely define it without insisting on illustrations. Picture to yourself certain characters in a certain situation: if you reverse the situation and invert the *rôles,* you obtain a comic scene. The double rescue scene in *Le Voyage de M. Perrichon* belongs to this class.[5] There is no necessity, however, for both the identical scenes to be played before us. We may be shown only one, provided the other is really in our minds. Thus, we laugh at the prisoner at the bar lecturing the magistrate; at a child presuming to teach its parents; in a word, at everything that comes under the heading of "topsyturvydom."

Not infrequently comedy sets before us a character who lays a trap in which he is the first to be caught. The plot of the villain who is the victim of his own villainy, or the cheat cheated, forms the stock-in-trade of a good many plays. We find this even in primitive farce. . . . /94/

Here we apparently find the confirmation of a law, some illustrations of which we have already pointed out. When a comic scene has been reproduced a number of times, it reaches the stage of being a classical type or model. It becomes amusing in itself, quite apart from the causes which render it amusing. Henceforth, new scenes, which are not comic *de jure,* may become amusing *de facto,* on account of their partial resemblance to this model. /95/

3. We now come to the *reciprocal interference of series.* This is a comic effect, the precise formula of which is very difficult to disentangle, by reason of the extraordinary variety of forms in which it appears on the stage. Perhaps it might be defined as follows: *A situation is invariably comic when it belongs simultaneously to two altogether independent series of events and is capable of being interpreted in two entirely different meanings at the same time.* . . . /96/

---

[5] Labiche, *Le Voyage de M. Perrichon.*

We will not carry any further this analysis of the methods of light comedy. Whether we find reciprocal interference of series, inversion, or repetition, we see that the objective is always the same—to obtain what we called a *mechanisation* of life. You take a set of actions and relations and repeat it as it is, or turn it upside down, or transfer it bodily to another set with which it partially coincides—all these being processes that consist in /101/ looking upon life as a repeating mechanism, with reversible action and interchangeable parts. Actual life is comedy just so far as it produces, in a natural fashion, actions of the same kind; consequently, just so far as it forgets itself, for were it always on the alert, it would be ever-changing continuity, irreversible progress, undivided unity. And so the ludicrous in events may be defined as absentmindedness in things, just as the ludicrous in an individual character always results from some fundamental absentmindedness in the person, as we have already intimated and shall prove later on. This absentmindedness in events, however, is exceptional. Its results are slight. At any rate it is incurable, so that it is useless to laugh at it. Therefore the idea would never have occurred to any one of exaggerating absentmindedness, of converting it into a system, and creating an art for it, if laughter were not always a pleasure, and mankind did not pounce upon the slightest excuse for indulging in it. This is the real explanation of light comedy, which holds the same relation to actual life as does a jointed dancing-doll to a man walking, —being, as it is, an artificial /102/ exaggeration of a natural rigidity in things. The thread that binds it to actual life is a very fragile one. It is scarcely more than a game which, like all games, depends on a previously accepted convention. Comedy in character strikes far deeper roots into life. . . .

II

There may be something artificial in making a special category for the comic in words, since most of the varieties of the comic that we have examined so far were produced through the medium of language. We must make a distinction, however, between the comic *expressed* and the comic *created* by language. The former could, if necessary, be translated from one language into another, though at the cost of losing the greater portion of its significance when introduced into a fresh society different in manners, in literature, and above all in associa-/103/tion of ideas. But it is generally impossible to translate the latter. It owes its entire being to the structure of the sentence or to the choice of the words. It does not set forth, by means of language, special cases of absentmindedness in man or in events. It lays stress on lapses of attention in language itself. In this case, it is language itself that becomes comic.

Comic sayings, however, are not a matter of spontaneous generation; if we laugh at them, we are equally entitled to laugh at their author. This latter condition, however, is not indispensable, since the saying or expression has a comic virtue of its own. This is proved by the fact that we find it very difficult, in the majority of these cases, to say whom we are laughing at, although at times we have a dim, vague feeling that there is some one in the background.

Moreover, the person implicated is not always the speaker. Here it seems as though we should draw an important distinction between the *witty* (*spirituel*) and the *comic*. A word is said to be comic when it makes us laugh at the person who utters it, and witty when it makes us laugh either at a third party or at ourselves. But in most cases we can /104/ hardly make up our minds whether the word is comic or witty. All that we can say is that it is laughable. . . . /105/

Let us return to the comic in actions and in situations, consider the chief methods by which it is obtained, and apply them to the choice of words and the building up of sentences. We shall thus have every possible form of the comic in words as well as every variety of wit. /111/

1. Inadvertently to say or do what we have no intention of saying or doing, as a result of inelasticity or momentum, is, as we are aware, one of the main sources of the comic. Thus, absentmindedness is essentially laughable, and so we laugh at anything rigid, ready-made, mechanical in gesture, attitude and even facial expression. Do we find this kind of rigidity in language also? No doubt we do, since language contains ready-made formulas and stereotyped phrases. The man who always expressed himself in such terms would invariably be comic. But if an isolated phrase is to be comic in itself, when once separated from the person who utters it, it must be something more than ready-made, it must bear within itself some sign which tells us, beyond the possibility of doubt, that it was uttered automatically. This can only happen when the phrase embodies some evident absurdity, either a palpable error or a contradiction in terms. Hence the following general rule: *A comic meaning is invariably obtained when an absurd idea is fitted into a well-established phrase-form.* /112/

At times the commonplace phrase, under cover of which the absurdity slips in, is not so readily noticeable. "I don't like working between meals," said a lazy lout. There would be nothing amusing in the saying did there not exist that salutary precept in the realm /113/ of hygiene: "One should not eat between meals." . . .

2. "We laugh if our attention is diverted to the physical in a person when it is the moral /114/ that is in question," is a law we laid down in the first part of this work. Let us apply it to language. Most words might be said to have a *physical* and a *moral* meaning, according as they are interpreted literally or figuratively. Every word, indeed, begins by denoting a concrete object or a material action; but by degrees the meaning of the word is refined into an abstract relation or a pure idea. If then the above law holds good here, it should be stated as follows: "*A comic effect is obtained whenever we pretend to take literally an expression which was used figuratively*"; or, "*Once our attention is fixed on the material aspect of a metaphor the idea expressed becomes comic.*" . . . /115/

We said that wit often consists in extending the idea of one's interlocutor to the point of making him express the opposite of what he thinks and getting him, so to say, entrapt by his own words. We must now add that this trap is almost always some metaphor or comparison the concrete aspect of which is turned against him. You may remember the dialogue between a mother and her son in the *Faux Bonhommes:* "My dear boy, gambling on 'Change is very risky. You win one day and lose the next."—"Well, then, I will gamble only every other day.". . . /117/

We said that repetition is the favourite /121/ method of classic comedy. It consists in so arranging events that a scene is reproduced either between the same characters under fresh circumstances or between fresh characters under the same circumstances. Thus we have, repeated by lackeys in less dignified language, a scene already played by their masters. Now, imagine ideas expressed in suitable style and thus placed in the setting of their natural environment. If you think of some arrangement whereby they are transferred to fresh surroundings, while maintaining their mutual relations, or, in other words, if you can induce them to express themselves in an altogether different style and to transpose themselves into another key,—you will have language itself playing a comedy—language itself made comic. There will be no need, moreover, actually to set before us both expressions of the same ideas, the transposed expression and the

natural one. For we are acquainted with the natural one—the one which we should have chosen instinctively. So it will be enough if the effort of comic invention bears on the other, and on the other alone. No sooner is the second set before us than we spontaneously supply the /122/ first. Hence the following general rule: *A comic effect is always obtainable by transposing the natural expression of an idea into another key. . . .*

In the first place, we may distinguish two keys at the extreme ends of the scale, the solemn and the familiar. The most obvious effects are obtained by merely transposing the one into the other, which thus provides us with two opposite currents of comic fancy.

Transpose the solemn into the familiar and the result is parody. The effect of parody, thus defined, extends to instances in which the idea expressed in familiar terms is one that, if only in deference to custom, ought to be pitched in another key. . . . /123/

Summing up the foregoing, then, there are two extreme terms of comparison, the very large and the very small, the best and the worst, between which transposition may be effected in one direction or the other. Now, if the interval be gradually narrowed, the contrast between the terms obtained will be /126/ less and less violent, and the varieties of comic transposition more and more subtle.

The most common of these contrasts is perhaps that between the real and the ideal, between what is and what ought to be. Here again transposition may take place in either direction. Sometimes we state what ought to be done, and pretend to believe that this is just what is actually being done; then we have *irony.* Sometimes, on the contrary, we describe with scrupulous minuteness what is being done, and pretend to believe that this is just what ought to be done; such is often the method of *humour.* Humour, thus defined, is the counterpart of irony. Both are forms of satire, but irony is oratorical in its nature, whilst humour partakes of the scientific. Irony is emphasised the higher we allow ourselves to be uplifted by the idea of the good that ought to be: thus irony may grow so hot within us that it becomes a kind of high-pressure eloquence. On the other hand, humour is the more emphasised the deeper we go down into an evil that actually is, in order to set down its details in the most cold-blooded indifference. Several authors, Jean Paul amongst /127/ them, have noticed that humour delights in concrete terms, technical details, definite facts. If our analysis is correct, this is not an accidental trait of humour, it is its very essence. A humourist is a moralist disguised as a scientist, something like an anatomist who practises dissection with the sole object of filling us with disgust; so that humour, in the restricted sense in which we are here regarding the word, is really a transposition from the moral to the scientific. . . . /128/

CHAPTER III
The Comic in Character

Convinced that laughter has a social meaning and import, that the comic expresses, above all else, a special lack of adaptability to society, and that, in short, there is nothing comic apart from man, we have made man and character generally our main objective. Our chief difficulty, therefore, has lain in explaining how we come to laugh at anything else than character, and by what subtle processes of fertilisation, combination, or amalgamation the comic can worm its way into a mere movement, an impersonal situation, or an independent phrase. . . . /133/

Comedy can only begin at the point where our neighbour's personality ceases to affect us. It begins, in fact, with what might be called *a growing callousness to social life.* Any individual is comic who automatically goes his own way without troubling himself about getting into touch with the rest of his fellow-beings. It is the part of laughter to reprove his absentmindedness and wake him out of his dream. /134/

Therefore society holds suspended over each individual member, if not the threat of correction, at all events the prospect of a snubbing, which, although it is slight, is none the less dreaded. Such must be the function of laughter. Always rather humiliating for the one against whom it is directed, laughter is really and truly a kind of social "ragging." . . .

Hence the equivocal nature of the comic. It belongs neither altogether to art nor altogether to life. On the one hand, characters in real life would never make us laugh were we not capable of watching their vagaries in the same way as we look down at a play from our seat in a box; they are only comic in our eyes because they perform a kind of comedy before us. But, on the other hand, the pleasure caused by laughter, even on the stage, is not an unadulterated enjoyment; it is not a pleasure /135/ that is exclusively esthetic or altogether disinterested. It always implies a secret or unconscious intent, if not of each one of us, at all events of society as a whole. In laughter we always find an unavowed intention to humili-

ate, and consequently to correct our neighbour, if not in his will, at least in his deed. This is the reason a comedy is far more like real life than a drama is. The more sublime the drama, the more profound the analysis to which the poet has had to subject the raw materials of daily life in order to obtain the tragic element in its unadulterated form. On the contary, it is only in its lower aspects, in light comedy and farce, that comedy is in striking contrast to reality: the higher it rises, the more it approximates to life; in fact, there are scenes in real life so closely bordering on high-class comedy that the stage might adopt them without changing a single word. . . .

It has often been said that it is the *trifling* faults of our fellow-men that make us laugh. /136/ Evidently there is a considerable amount of truth in this opinion; still, it cannot be regarded as altogether correct. First, as regards faults, it is no easy matter to draw the line between the trifling and the serious; maybe it is not because a fault is trifling, that it makes us laugh, but rather because it makes us laugh that we regard it as trifling; for there is nothing disarms us like laughter. But we may go even farther, and maintain that there are faults at which we laugh, even though fully aware that they are serious,—Harpagon's avarice, for instance. And then, we may as well confess—though somewhat reluctantly— that we laugh not only at the faults of our fellow-men, but also, at times, at their good qualities. We laugh at Alceste. The objection may be urged that it is not the earnestness of Alceste that is ludicrous, but rather the special aspect which earnestness assumes in his case; and, in short, a certain eccentricity that mars it in our eyes. Agreed; but it is none the less true that this eccentricity in Alceste, at which we laugh, *makes his earnestness laughable,* and that is the main point. So we may conclude that the comic is not always an indication of a fault, in the moral meaning of the word, and if critics insist on seeing a fault, /137/ even though a trifling one, in the ludicrous, they must point out what it is here that exactly distinguishes the trifling from the serious.

The truth is, the comic character may, strictly speaking, be quite in accord with stern morality. All it has to do is to bring itself into accord with society. The character of Alceste is that of a thoroughly honest man. But then he is unsociable, and, on that very account, ludicrous. A flexible vice may not be so easy to ridicule as a rigid virtue. It is *rigidity* that society eyes with suspicion. Consequently, it is the rigidity of Alceste that makes us laugh, though here rigidity stands for honesty. The man who withdraws into himself is liable to ridicule, because the comic is largely made up of this very withdrawal. This accounts for the comic being so frequently dependent on the manners or ideas, or, to put it bluntly, on the prejudices, of a society.

It must be acknowledged, however, to the credit of mankind, that there is no essential difference between the social ideal and the moral. We may therefore admit, as a general /138/ rule, that it is the faults of others that make us laugh, provided we add that they make us laugh by reason of their *unsociability* rather than of their *immorality*. What, then, are the faults capable of becoming ludicrous, and in what circumstances do we regard them as being too serious to be laughed at?

We have already given an implicit answer to this question. The comic, we said, appeals to the intelligence pure and simple; laughter is incompatible with emotion. Depict some fault, however trifling, in such a way as to arouse sympathy, fear, or pity; the mischief is done, it is impossible for us to laugh. On the other hand, take a downright vice,—even one that is, generally speaking, of an odious nature,—you may make it ludicrous if, by some suitable contrivance, you arrange so that it leaves our emotions unaffected. Not that the vice *must* then be ludicrous, but it *may*, from that time forth, become so. *It must not arouse our feelings;* that is the sole condition really necessary, though assuredly it is not sufficient.

But, then, how will the comic poet set to work to prevent our feelings being moved? /139/ This art would appear to be governed by two methods, which are applied more or less unconsciously by the comic poet. The first consists in *isolating*, within the soul of the character, the feeling attributed to him, and making it a parasitic organism, so to speak, endowed with an independent existence. As a general rule, an intense feeling successively encroaches upon all other mental states, and colours them with its own peculiar hue; if, then, we are made to witness this gradual impregnation, we finally become impregnated ourselves with a corresponding emotion. To /140/ employ a different image, an emotion may be said to be dramatic and contagious when all the harmonics in it are heard along with the fundamental note. It is because the actor thus thrills throughout his whole being that the spectators themselves feel the thrill. On the contrary, in the case of emotion that leaves us indifferent, and that is about to become comic, there is always present a certain *rigidity* which pre-

vents it from establishing a connection with the rest of the soul in which it has taken up its abode. This rigidity may be manifested, when the time comes, by puppet-like movements, and then it will provoke laughter. . . . /141/

There is a second, which is far more obvious and arises out of the first. When a mental state is depicted to us with the object of making it dramatic, or even merely of inducing us to take it seriously, it gradually crystallises into *actions* which provide the real measures of its greatness. Thus, the miser orders his /142/ whole life with a view to acquiring wealth, and the pious hypocrite, though pretending to have his eyes fixed upon heaven, steers most skilfully his course here below. Most certainly, comedy does not shut out calculations of this kind; we need only take as an example the very machinations of Tartuffe. But that is what comedy has in common with drama; and in order to keep distinct from it, to prevent our taking a serious action seriously, in short, in order to prepare us for laughter, comedy utilises a method, the formula of which may be given as follows: *instead of concentrating our attention on actions, comedy directs it rather to gestures*. By *gestures* we here mean the attitudes, the movements and even the language by which a mental state expresses itself outwardly without any aim or profit, from no other cause than a kind of inner itching. Gesture, thus defined, is profoundly different from action. Action is intentional or, at any rate, conscious; gesture slips out unawares, it is automatic. In action, the entire person is engaged; in gesture, an isolated part of the person is expressed, unknown to, or at least apart from, the whole of the personality. Lastly—and /143/ here is the essential point— action is in exact proportion to the feeling that inspires it: the one gradually passes into the other, so that we may allow our sympathy or our aversion to glide along the line running from feeling to action and become increasingly interested. About gesture, however, there is something explosive, which awakes our sensibility when on the point of being lulled to sleep and, by thus rousing us up, prevents our taking matters seriously. Thus, as soon as our attention is fixed on gesture and not on action, we are in the realm of comedy. . . . /144/

To sum up, whether a character is good or bad is of little moment; granted he is unsociable, he is capable of becoming comic. We now see that the seriousness of the case is of no importance either: whether serious or trifling, it is still capable of making us laugh, provided that care be taken not to arouse our emotions. Unsociability in the performer and insensibility in the spectator—such, in a word, /145/ are the two essential conditions.

The third condition is automatism. We have pointed it out from the outset of this work, continually drawing attention to the following point: what is essentially laughable is what is done automatically. In a vice, even in a virtue, the comic is that element by which the person unwittingly betrays himself—the involuntary gesture or the unconscious remark. Absentmindedness is always comical. Indeed, the deeper the absentmindedness the higher the comedy. Take any comic character: however unconscious he may be of what he says or does, he cannot be comical unless there be some aspect of his person of which he is unaware, one side of his nature which he overlooks; on that account alone does he make us laugh.[6] Profoundly comic sayings are those /146/ artless ones in which some vice reveals itself in all its nakedness: how could it thus expose itself were it capable of seeing itself as it is? It is not uncommon for a comic character to condemn in general terms a certain line of conduct and immediately afterwards afford an example of it himself: for instance, M. Jourdain's teacher of philosophy flying into a passion after inveighing against anger. . . . What is the object of such contradictions except to help us to put our finger on the obliviousness of the characters to their own actions? Inattention to self, and consequently to others, is what we invariably find. And if we look at the matter closely, we see that inattention is here equivalent to what we have called unsociability. The chief cause of rigidity is the neglect to look around—and more especially within oneself: how can a man fashion his personality after that of another if he does not first study others as well as himself? Rigidity, automatism, absentmindedness and unsociability are all inextricably entwined; and all serve as ingredients to the making up of the comic in character. . . ./147/

In one sense it might be said that all *character* is comic, provided we mean by character the *ready-made* element in our personality, that mechanical element which resembles a piece of clockwork

wound up once for all and capable of working automatically. It is, if you will, that which causes us to imitate ourselves. And it is also, for that very reason, that which enables others to imitate us. Every comic character is a *type*. . . . /148/

Thus, to depict characters, that is to say, general types, is the object of high-class comedy. This has often been said. But it is as well to repeat it, since there could be no better definition of comedy. Not only are we entitled to say that comedy gives us general types, but we might add that it is the *only* one of all the arts that aims at the general; so that once this objective has been attributed to it, we have said all that it is and all that the rest cannot be. . . . /149/

And so we come back to the double conclusion we reached in the course of our investigations. On the one hand, a person is never ridiculous except through some mental attribute resembling absentmindedness, through something that lives upon him without forming part of his organism, /169/ after the fashion of a parasite; that is the reason this state of mind is observable from without and capable of being corrected. But, on the other hand, just because laughter aims at correcting, it is expedient that the correction should reach as great a number of persons as possible. This is the reason comic observation instinctively proceeds to what is general. It chooses such peculiarities as admit of being reproduced, and consequently are not indissolubly bound up with the individuality of a single person,—a possibly common sort of uncommonness, so to say,—peculiarities that are held in common. By transferring them to the stage, it creates works which doubtless belong to art in that their only visible aim is to please, but which will be found to contrast with other works of art by reason of their generality, and also of their scarcely confessed or scarcely conscious intention to correct and instruct. So we were probably right in saying that comedy lies midway between art and life. It is not disinterested as genuine art is. By organising laughter, comedy accepts social life as a natural environment; it even obeys an impulse of social life. And in this respect it turns its back upon /170/ art, which is a breaking away from society and a return to pure nature. /171/

---

[6] When the humourist laughs at himself, he is really acting a double part; the self who laughs is indeed conscious, but not the self who is laughed at. [Bergson's note]

Sigmund Freud — Wit and Its Relation to the Unconscious

Sigmund Freud's is one of the great names of modern times. The founder of psychoanalysis, he was born at Freiberg, in Moravia, in 1856, and early turned to medical studies, first in Vienna, then in Paris. His first published works were in the field of neurology; in the treatment of nervous disorders, Freud had already replaced hypnotism by his method of free association. His experimentations led him to make certain fundamental pronouncements about the human mind: the existence of the unconscious and its dynamic influence on consciousness; the splitting of the mind into layers, the result of intrapsychical conflicts between various sets of forces, one of which he named "repression"; the existence and importance of infantile sexuality. In 1906, Freud was joined by Adler, Brill, Jones, Jung, and others and under his leadership a "school" of psychoanalysis was formed. Eventually, he went to London where, in 1936, he was elected to the Royal Society. His last major publication, in 1939, was *Moses and Monotheism*. He died in 1939. *Wit and Its Relation to the Unconscious* was first published in Vienna in 1905. The English translation, by Dr. A. A. Brill, appeared in 1916; the present text is from The Modern Library edition, Random House, New York, 1938.

. . . Roughly speaking, one can distinguish three general stages in the formation of the dream: first, the transference of the conscious day remnants into the unconscious, a transference in which the conditions of the sleeping state /749/ must cooperate; secondly, the actual dream-work in the unconscious; and thirdly, the regression of the elaborated dream material to the region of perception, whereby the dream becomes conscious.

The forces participating in the dream-formation may be recognized as the following: the wish to sleep; the sum of cathexis which still clings to the day remnants after the depression brought about by the state of sleep; the psychic energy of the unconscious wish forming the dream; and the opposing force of the "*censorship*," which exercises its authority in our waking state, and is not entirely abolished during sleep. The task of dream-formation is, above all, to overcome the inhibition of the censorship, and it is just this task that is fulfilled by the displacement of the psychic energy within the material of the dream-thoughts.

Now we recall what caused us to think of the dream while investigating wit. We found that the character and activity of wit were bound up in certain forms of expression and technical means, among which the various forms of condensation, displacement, and indirect representation were the most conspicuous. But the processes which led to the same results—condensation, displacement, and indirect expression—we learned to know as peculiarities of dream-work. Does not this analogy almost force us to the conclusion that wit-work and dream-work must be identical at least in one essential point? I believe that the dream-work lies revealed before us in its most important characters, but in wit we find obscured just that portion of the psychic processes which we may compare with the dream-work, namely, the process of wit-formation in the first person. Shall we not yield to the temptation to construct this process according to the analogy of dream-formation? Some of the characteristics of dreams are so foreign to wit that the part of the dream-work corresponding to them cannot be carried over to the wit-formation. The regression of the stream of thought to perception is certainly lacking as far as wit is concerned. However, the other two stages of dream-formation, the sinking of a foreconscious thought into the unconscious, and the unconscious elaboration, would give us exactly the result which we might observe in wit if we assumed this process in wit-formation. Let us decide to assume that this is the proceeding of wit-formation in the case of the first person. *A foreconscious thought is left for a moment to unconscious elaboration and the results are forthwith grasped by the conscious perception.* . . . /750/

Wit possesses still another character which entirely corresponds to our conception of the wit-work as originally discovered in our study of dreams. It is true that it is common to hear one say "I *made* a joke," but one feels that one behaves differently during this process than when one pronounces a judgment or offers an objection. Wit shows in a most pronounced manner the character of an involuntary "inspiration" or a sudden flash of thought. A moment before one cannot tell what kind of joke one is going to make, though it lacks only the words to clothe it. One usually experiences something indefinable which I should like most to compare to an absence, or sudden drop of intellectual tension; then all of a sudden the witticism appears, usually simultaneously with its verbal investment. . . .

Let us now collect the properties of wit whose formation can be referred to the unconscious. Above all there is the peculiar brevity of wit which, though not indispensable, is a marked and distinctive characteristic feature. When we first encountered it we were inclined to see in it an expression of a tendency to economize, but owing to very evident objections we ourselves depreciated the value of this conception. At present we look upon it more as a sign of the unconscious elaboration which the thought of wit has undergone. The process of condensation which corresponds to it in dreams we can correlate with no other factor than with the local-/752/ization in the unconscious, and we must assume that the conditions for such condensations which are lacking in the foreconscious are present in the unconscious mental process. It is to be expected that in the process of condensation some of the elements subjected to it become lost, while others which take over their cathexis are strengthened by it, or are built up too energetically. The brevity of wit, like the brevity of dreams, would thus be a necessary concomitant manifestation of the condensation which occurs in both cases; both times it is a result of the condensation process. The brevity of wit is indebted also to this origin for its peculiar character, which though not further established produces a striking impression. . . . /753/

The most important difference lies in their [wit and dreams] social behavior. The dream is a perfectly asocial psychic product. It has nothing to tell to anyone else, having originated in an individual as a compromise between conflicting psychic forces it remains incomprehensible to the person himself and has therefore altogether no interest for anybody else. Not only does the dream /760/ find it unnecessary to place any value on intelligibleness, but it must even guard against being understood, as it would then be destroyed; it can only exist in disguised form. For this reason the dream may make use freely of the mechanism that controls unconscious thought processes to the extent of producing undecipherable distortions. Wit, on the other hand, is the most social of all those psychic functions whose aim is to gain pleasure. It often requires three persons, and the psychic process which it incites always requires the participation of at least one other person. It must therefore bind itself to the condition of intelligibleness; it may employ distortion made practicable in the unconscious through conden-

sation and displacement, to no greater extent than can be deciphered by the intelligence of the third person. As for the rest, wit and dreams have developed in altogether different spheres of the psychic life, and are to be classed under widely separated categories of the psychological system. No matter how concealed, the dream is still a wish, while wit is a developed play. Despite its apparent unreality, the dream retains its relation to the great interests of life; it seeks to supply what is lacking through a regressive detour of hallucinations; and it owes its existence solely to the strong need for sleep during the night. Wit, on the other hand, seeks to draw a small amount of pleasure from the free and unencumbered activities of our psychic apparatus, and later to seize this pleasure as an incidental gain. It thus *secondarily* reaches to important functions relative to the outer world. The dream serves preponderately to guard from pain, while wit serves to acquire pleasure; in these two aims all our psychic activities meet. /761/

. . . The comic differs from wit in its social behavior. The comic can be content with only two persons, one who finds the comical, and one in whom it is found. The third person to whom the comical may be imparted reinforces the comic process, but adds nothing new to it. In wit, however, this third person is indispensable for the completion of the pleasure-bearing process, while the second person may be omitted, especially when it is not a question of aggressive wit with a tendency Wit is made, while the comical is found; it is found first of all in persons, and only later by transference may be seen also in objects, situations, and the like. We know, too, in the case of wit that it is not a strange person's but one's own mental processes that contain the sources for the production of pleasure. . . . /762/

The comical appears primarily as an unintentional discovery in the social relations of human beings. It is found in persons—that is, in their movements, shapes, actions, and characteristic traits. In the beginning it is found probably only in their psychical peculiarities and later on in their mental qualities, especially in the expression of the latter. Even animals and inanimate objects become comical as the result of a widely used method of personification. However, the comical can be considered apart from the person in whom it is found, if the conditions under which a person becomes comical can be discerned. Thus arises the comical situation, and this knowledge enables us to make a person comical at will by putting him into situations in which the conditions necessary for the comic are bound up with his actions. The discovery that it is in our power to make another person comical opens the way to unsuspected gains in comic pleasure, and forms the foundation of a highly developed technique. It is also possible to make one's self just as comical as others. The means which serve to make a person comical are transference into comic situations, imitations, disguise, unmasking, caricature, parody, travesty, and the like. It is quite evident that these techniques may enter into the service of hostile or aggressive tendencies. A person may be made comical in order to render him contemptible or in order to deprive him of his claims to dignity and authority. But even if such a purpose were regularly at the bottom of all attempts to make a person comical this need not necessarily be the meaning of the spontaneous comic. . . . /768/

We will examine first the comic movement because we remember that the most primitive stage performance, the pantomime, uses this means to make us laugh. The answer to the question, "Why do we laugh at the actions of clowns?," would be that their actions appear to us immoderate and inappropriate; that is, we really laugh over the excessive expenditure of energy. Let us look for the same condition outside of the manufactured comic, that is, under circumstances where it may unintentionally be found. The child's motions do not appear to us comical, even if he jumps and fidgets, but it is comical to see a little boy or girl follow with the tongue the movement of his pen-holder when he is trying to master the art of writing; we see in these additional motions a superfluous expenditure of energy which under similar conditions we save. In the same way we find it comical to see unnecessary motions or even marked exaggeration of expressive motions in adults. Among the genuinely comic cases we might mention the motions made by the bowler after he has released the ball while he is following its course as though he were still able to control it. All grimaces which exaggerate the normal expression of the emotions are comical, even if they are involuntary, as in the case of persons suffering from St. Vitus' dance (chorea). The impassioned movements of a modern orchestra leader will appear comical to every unmusical person, who cannot understand why they are necessary. Indeed, the comic element found in bodily shapes and physiognomy is a branch of the comic of motion, in that they are conceived as though they were the result of motion that has been carried too far or motion that is purposeless. Wide exposed eyes, a crook-shaped nose bent towards the mouth,

handle-like ears, a hunch back, and all similar physical defects probably produce a comical impression only in so far as the movements that would be necessary to produce these features are imagined, whereby the nose and other parts of the body are pictured as more movable than they actually are. It is certainly comical if some one can "wiggle his ears," and it would undoubtedly be a great deal more comical if he could raise and lower his nose. A large part of the comical impression that animals make upon us is due to the fact that we perceive in them movements which we cannot imitate.

But how does it come about that we laugh as soon as we have recognized that the actions of some one else are immoderate and inappropriate? I believe that we laugh because we compare the motions observed in others with those which we ourselves should produce if we were in their place. The two persons must naturally be compared in accordance with the same standard. . . . /769/

The comic found in the mental and psychic attributes of another person is apparently again the result of a comparison between him and my own ego. But it is remarkable that it is a comparison which has more often /772/ furnished the opposite result than in the case of comic movement and action. In the latter case it was comical if the other person exerted a greater expenditure than I believed necessary for me; in the case of psychic activity it is just the reverse, it is comical if the other person economizes in expenditure, which I consider indispensable, for nonsense and foolishness are nothing but inferior functions. In the first case I laugh because he makes it too difficult for himself, and in the latter case because he makes it too easy for himself. As to the comic effect, it is obviously only a question of the difference between the two cathexes—the one of empathy, and the other of the ego—and not in whose favor this difference inclines. This peculiarity, which at first confuses our judgment, disappears, however, when we consider that it is in accord with our personal development towards a higher stage of culture to limit our muscular work and increase our mental work. By heightening our mental expenditure we produce a diminution of motion expenditure for the same activity. Our machines bear witness to this cultural success.

Thus, it coincides with a uniform understanding that that person appears comical to us who puts forth too much expenditure in his physical activities and too little in his mental activities; and it cannot be denied that in both cases our laughing is the expression of a pleasurably perceived superriority which we adjudge to ourselves in comparison with him. If the relation in both cases becomes reversed, that is, if the somatic expenditure of the other is less and the psychic expenditure greater, then we no longer laugh, but are struck with amazement and admiration. . . . /773/

Human beings are not satisfied to enjoy the comic as they encounter it in life, but they aim to produce it intentionally. Thus we discover more of the nature of the comic by studying the methods employed in producing the comic. Above all one can produce comical elements in one's personality for the amusement of others, by making one's self appear awkward or stupid. One then produces the comic exactly as if one were really so, by complying with the condition of comparison which leads to the difference of expenditure; but one does not make himself laughable or contemptible through this; indeed, under certain circumstances one can even secure admiration. The feeling of superiority does not come into existence in the other when he knows that the actor is only shamming, and this furnishes us a good new proof that the comic is independent in principle of the feeling of superiority.

To make another comical, the method most commonly employed is to transfer him into situations wherein he becomes comical regardless of his personal qualities, as a result of human dependence upon external circumstances, especially social factors; in other words, some one resorts to the comical situation. This transferring into a comic situation may be real as in practical jokes, such as placing the foot in front of one so that he falls like a clumsy person, or making one appear stupid by utilizing his credulity to make him believe some nonsense, etc., or it can be feigned by means of speech or play. It is a good aid in aggression, in the service of which, production of the comic is wont to place itself, in order that the comic pleasure may be independent of the reality of the comic situation; thus every person is really defenseless against being made comical.

But there are still other means of making one comical which deserve special attention and which in part also show new sources of comic pleasure. *Imitation*, for example, belongs here; it accords the hearer an extraordinary amount of pleasure and makes its subject comical, even if it still keeps away from the exaggeration of caricature. It is much easier to fathom the comic effect of caricature than that of simple imitation. Caricature, parody and travesty, like their practical counterpart unmasking, are directed against persons and objects who command authority and respect and who are exalted in some sense. These are procedures which /776/ tend to degrade. In the transferred psychic sense, the exalted is equivalent to something great and I want to make the statement, more accurately to repeat the statement, that psychic greatness like somatic greatness is exhibited by means of an increased expenditure. It needs little observation to ascertain that when I speak of the exalted I give a different innervation to my voice, I change my facial expression, an attempt to bring my entire bearing as it were into complete accord with the dignity of that which I present. I impose upon myself a dignified restriction, not much different than if I were coming into the presence of an illustrious personage, monarch, or prince of science. I can scarcely err when I assume that this added innervation of conceptual mimicry corresponds to an increased expenditure. The third case of such an added expenditure I readily find when I indulge in abstract trains of thought instead of in the concrete and plastic ideas. If I can now imagine that the mentioned processes for degrading the illustrious are quite ordinary, that during their activity I need not be on my guard and in whose ideal presence I may, to use a military formula, put myself "at ease," all that saves me the added expenditure of dignified restriction. Moreover, the comparison of this manner of presentation instigated by empathy with the manner of presentation to which I have been hitherto accustomed, which seeks to present itself at the same time, again produces a difference in expenditure which can be discharged through laughter.

As is known, caricature brings about the degradation by rendering prominent one feature, comic in itself, from the entire picture of the exalted object, a feature which would be overlooked if viewed with the entire picture. Only by isolating this feature can the comic effect be obtained which spreads in our memory over the whole picture. This has, however, this condition; the presence of the exalted itself must not force us into a disposition of reverence. Where such a comical feature is really lacking, caricature then unhesitatingly creates it by exaggerating one that is not comical in itself. It is again characteristic of the origin of comic pleasure that the effect of the caricature is not essentially impaired through such a falsifying of reality. . . . /777/

Two observations obtrude themselves upon the observer who reviews even only superficially the origin of comic pleasure from the difference of expenditure; first, that there are cases in which the comic appears regularly and as if necessarily; and, in contrast to these cases, others in which this depends on the conditions of the case and on the viewpoint of the observer. But secondly, that unusually large differences very often triumph over unfavorable conditions, so that the comic feeling originates in spite of it. In reference to the first point one may set up two classes, the inevitable comic and the accidental comic, although one will have to be prepared from the beginning to find exceptions in the first class to the inevitableness of the comic. It would be tempting to follow the conditions which are essential to each class.

What is important in the second class are the conditions, of which one may be designated as the "isolation" of the comic case. A closer analysis reveals something like the following relations:

(a) The favorable condition for the origin of comic pleasure is brought about by a general happy disposition in which "one is in the mood for laughing." In happy toxic states almost everything seems comic, which probably results from a comparison with the expenditure in normal conditions. For wit, the comic, and all similar methods of gaining pleasure from the psychic activities, are nothing but ways to regain this happy state—euphoria—from one single point, when it does not exist as a general disposition of the psyche.

(b) A similar favorable condition is produced by the expectation of the comic or by putting one's self in the right mood for comic pleasure. Hence when the intention to make things comical exists and when this feeling is shared by others, the differences required are so slight that they probably would have been overlooked had they been experienced in unpremeditated occurrences. He who decides to attend a comic lecture or a farce at the theater is indebted to this intention for laughing over things which in his everyday life would hardly produce in him a comic effect. He finally laughs at the recollection of having laughed, at the expectation of laughing, and at the appearance of the one who is to present the comic, even before the latter makes the attempt to make him laugh. It is for this reason that people admit that they are ashamed of that which made them laugh at the theater.

(c) Unfavorable conditions for the comic result from the kind of psychic activity which may occupy the individual at the moment. Imaginative or mental activity tending towards serious aims disturbs the dis-/790/charging capacity of the cathexis which the activity needs for its own displacements, so that only unexpected and great differences of expenditure can break through to form comic

pleasure. All manner of mental processes far enough removed from the obvious to cause a suspension of ideational mimicry are unfavorable to the comic; in abstract contemplation there is hardly any room left for the comic, except when this form of thinking is suddenly interrupted.

(d) The occasion for releasing comic pleasure vanishes when the attention is fixed on the comparison capable of giving rise to the comic. Under such circumstances the comic force is lost from that which is otherwise sure to produce a comic effect. A movement or a mental activity cannot become comical to him whose interest is fixed at the time of comparing this movement with a standard which distinctly presents itself to him. Thus the examiner does not see the comical in the nonsense produced by the student in his ignorance; he is simply annoyed by it, whereas the offender's classmates who are more interested in his chances of passing the examination than in what he knows, laugh heartily over the same nonsense. The teacher of dancing or gymnastics seldom has any eyes for the comic movements of his pupils, and the preacher entirely loses sight of humanity's defects of character, which the writer of comedy brings out with so much effect. The comic process cannot stand examination by the attention, it must be able to proceed absolutely unnoticed in a manner similar to wit. But for good reasons, it would contradict the nomenclature of "conscious processes" which I have used in *The Interpretation of Dreams*, if one wished to call it of necessity *unconscious*. It rather belongs to the *foreconscious*, and one may use the fitting name "automatic" for all these processes which are enacted in the foreconscious, and dispense with the attention cathexis which is connected with consciousness. The process of comparison of the expenditures must remain automatic if it is to produce comic pleasure.

(e) It is exceedingly disturbing to the comic if the case from which it originates gives rise at the same time to a marked release of affect. The discharge of the affective difference is then as a rule excluded. Affects, disposition, and the attitude of the individual in occasional cases make it clear that the comic comes or goes with the viewpoint of the individual person; that only in exceptional cases is there an absolute comic. The dependence or relativity of the comic is therefore much greater than that of wit, which never happens but is regularly made, and at its production one may already give attention to the conditions under which it finds acceptance. But affective development is the most intensive of the conditions which disturb the comic, the significance of which is well known. It is therefore said that the comic feeling comes most in tolerably indif-/791/ferent cases which evince no strong feelings or interests. Nevertheless it is just in cases with affective release that one may witness the production of a particularly strong expenditure-difference in the automatism of discharge. When Colonel Butler answers Octavio's admonitions with "bitter laughter," exclaiming: "Thanks from the house of Austria!" his bitterness has thus not prevented the laughter which results from the recollection of the disappointment which he believes he has experienced; and on the other hand, the magnitude of this disappointment could not have been more impressively depicted by the poet than by showing it capable of effecting laughter in the midst of the storm of unchained affects. It is my belief that this explanation may be applicable in all cases in which laughing occurs on other than pleasurable occasions, and in conjunction with exceedingly painful or tense affects.

(f) If we also mention that the development of the comic pleasure can be promoted by means of any other pleasurable addition to the case which acts like a sort of contact-effect (after the manner of the fore-pleasure principle in the tendency-wit), then we have discussed surely not all the conditions of comic pleasure, yet enough of them to serve our purpose. We then see that for these conditions, as well as for the inconstancy and dependence of the comic effect, no other assumption so easily lends itself as this one which traces the comic pleasure from the discharge of a difference, which under many conditions can be diverted to a different use than discharge.

It still remains to give a thorough consideration of the comic of the sexual and obscene, but we shall only skim over it with a few observations. Here, too, we shall take the act of exposing one's body as the starting-point. An accidental exposure produces a comical effect on us, because we compare the ease with which we attained the enjoyment of this view with the great expenditure otherwise necessary for the attainment of this object. The case thus comes nearer to the naive-comic, but it is simpler than the latter. In every case of exhibitionism in which we are made spectators—or, in the case of the smutty joke hearers—we play the part of the third person, and the person exposed is made comical. We have heard that it is the purpose of wit to replace obscenity and in this manner to reopen a source of comic pleasure that has been lost. On the contrary, spying out an exposure forms no example of the comic for the one spying, be-

cause the effort he exerts thereby abrogates the condition of comic pleasure; the only thing remaining is the sexual pleasure in what is seen. If the peeper relates to another what he has seen, the person looked at again becomes comical, because the viewpoint that predominates is that the expenditure was omitted which would have been necessary for /792/ the concealment of the private parts. At all events, the sphere of the sexual or obscene offers the richest opportunities for gaining comic pleasure beside the pleasurable sexual stimulation, as it exposes the person's dependence on his physical needs (degradation) or it can uncover behind the spiritual love the physical demands of the same (unmasking). . . . /793/

One reaches some solution of humoristic displacement if one considers it in the light of a defense process. The defense processes are the psychic correlates of the flight reflex and follow the task of guarding against the origin of pain from inner sources. In fulfilling this task they serve the psychic occurrence as an automatic adjustment, which, to be sure, finally proves harmful and, therefore, must be subjected to the control of the conscious thinking. A definite form of this defense, the failure of repression, I have demonstrated as the effective mechanism in the origin of the psychoneuroses. Humor can now be conceived as the loftiest variant of these de-/801/fense functions. It disdains to withdraw from conscious attention the ideas which are connected with the painful affect, as repression does, and it thus overcomes the defense automatism. It brings this about by finding the means to withdraw the energy from the ready held pain release, and through discharge changes the same into pleasure. It is even credible that it is again the connection with the infantile that puts at humor's disposal the means for this function. Only in childhood did we experience intensively painful affects over which today as grown-ups we would laugh, just as a humorist laughs over his present painful affects. The elevation of his ego, which is evidenced by the humoristic displacement—the translation of which would nevertheless read: I am too big to have these causes affect me painfully—he could find in the comparison of his present ego with his infantile ego. This conception is to some extent confirmed by the role which falls to the infantile in the neurotic processes of repression.

On the whole, humor is closer to the comic than wit. Like the former its psychic localization is in the foreconscious, whereas wit, as we had to assume, is formed as a compromise between the unconscious and the foreconscious. On the other hand, humor has no share in the peculiar nature in which wit and the comic meet, a peculiarity which perhaps we have not hitherto emphasized strongly enough. It is a condition for the origin of the comic that we be induced to apply—either *simultaneously or in rapid succession*—to the same thought function two different modes of ideas, between which the "comparison" then takes place and the comic difference results. Such differences originate between the expenditure of the stranger and one's own, between the usual expenditure and the emergency expenditure, between an anticipated expenditure and one which has already occurred.

The differences between two forms of conception resulting simultaneously, which work with different expenditures, comes into consideration in wit, in respect to the hearer. The one of these two conceptions, by taking the hints contained in wit, follows the train of thought through the unconscious, while the other conception remains on the surface and presents the witticism like any wording from the foreconscious which has become conscious. Perhaps it would not be considered an unjustified statement if we should refer the pleasure of the witticism heard to the difference between these two forms of presentation.

Concerning wit we here repeat our former statement concerning its /802/ Janus-like double-facedness, a simile we used when the relation between wit and the comic still appeared to us unsettled.

The character thus put into the foreground becomes indistinct when we deal with humor. To be sure, we feel the humoristic pleasure where an emotional feeling is evaded, which we might have expected as a pleasure usually belonging to the situation; and in so far humor really falls under the broadened conception of the comic of expectation. But in humor it is no longer a question of two different kinds of presentations having the same content; the fact that the situation comes under the domination of a painful emotional feeling which should have been avoided, puts an end to possible comparison with the nature of the comic and of wit. The humoristic displacement is really a case of that different kind of utilization of a freed expenditure, which proved to be so dangerous for the comic effect.

Now that we have reduced the mechanism of humoristic pleasure to a formula analogous to the formula of comic pleasure and of wit, we are at the end of our task. It has seemed to us that the pleasure of wit originates from an *economy of expenditure in inhibition*, of the comic from an *economy of expenditure in thought*, and of humor from an *economy of expenditure in feeling*. All three modes of activity of our psychic apparatus derive pleasure from economy. All three present methods which strive to bring back from the psychic activity a pleasure which has really been lost in the development of this activity. For the euphoria which we are thus striving to obtain is nothing but the state of a bygone time, in which we were wont to defray our psychic work with slight expenditure. It is the state of our childhood in which we did not know the comic, were incapable of wit, and did not need humor to make us happy. /803/

Northrop Frye The Argument of Comedy

Northrop Frye, a Canadian who holds degrees from Toronto and Oxford Universities, is currently Principal and Professor of English at Victoria College, Toronto. Mr. Frye is a leading critic, whose works have ranged widely from his study of William Blake (called *Fearful Symmetry*, published in 1947) to the recent all-embracing *Anatomy of Criticism* (Princeton University Press, 1957). Mr. Frye has steadily worked toward a larger, clearer, and more systematic vision of the art of literature; his criticism includes contemporary psychological and mythopoetic interpretations that throw fascinating new light on many old problems. The essay, "The Argument of Comedy," is reprinted from *English Institute Essays*, 1948, edited by D. A. Robertson, Jr., and published by Columbia University Press (New York, 1949).

The Greeks produced two kinds of comedy, Old Comedy, represented by the eleven extant plays of Aristophanes, and New Comedy, of which the best known exponent is Menander. About two dozen New Comedies survive in the work of Plautus and Terence. Old Comedy, however, was out of date before Aristophanes himself was dead; and today, when we speak of comedy, we normally think of something that derives from the Menandrine tradition.

New Comedy unfolds from what may be described as a comic Oedipus situation. Its main theme is the successful effort of a young man to outwit an opponent and possess the girl of his choice. The opponent is usually the father (*senex*), and the psychological descent of the heroine from the mother is also sometimes hinted at. The father frequently wants the same girl, and is cheated out of her by the son, the mother thus becoming the son's ally. The girl is usually a slave or courtesan, and the plot turns on a *cognitio* or discovery of birth which makes her marriageable. Thus it turns out that she is not under an insuperable taboo after all but is an accessible object of desire, so that the plot follows the regular wish-/58/fulfillment pattern. Often the central Oedipus situation is thinly concealed by surrogates or doubles of the main characters, as when the heroine is discovered to be the hero's sister, and has to be married off to his best friend. In Congreve's *Love for Love*, to take a modern instance well within the Menandrine tradition, there are two Oedipus themes in counterpoint: the hero cheats his father out of the heroine, and his best friend violates the wife of an impotent old man who is the heroine's guardian. Whether this analysis is sound or not, New Comedy is certainly concerned with the maneuvering of a young man toward a young woman, and marriage is the tonic chord on which it ends. The normal comic resolution is the surrender of the *senex* to the hero, never the reverse. Shakespeare tried to reverse the pattern in *All's Well That Ends Well*, where the king of France forces Bertram to marry Helena, and the critics have not yet stopped making faces over it.

New Comedy has the blessing of Aristotle, who greatly preferred it to its predecessor, and it exhibits the general pattern of Aristotelian causation. It has a material cause in the young man's sexual desire, and a formal cause in the social order represented by the *senex*, with which the hero comes to terms when he gratifies his desire. It has an efficient cause in the character who brings about the final situation. In classical times this character is a tricky slave; Renaissance dramatists often use some adaptation of the medieval "vice"; modern writers generally like to pretend that nature, or at least the natural course of /59/ events, is the efficient cause. The final cause is the audience, which is expected by its applause to take part in the comic resolution. All this takes place on a single

order of existence. The action of New Comedy tends to become probable rather than fantastic, and it moves toward realism and away from myth and romance. The one romantic (originally mythical) feature in it, the fact that the hero or heroine turns out to be freeborn or someone's heir, is precisely the feature that trained New Comedy audiences tire of most quickly.

The conventions of New Comedy are the conventions of Jonson and Molière, and a fortiori of the English Restoration and the French rococo. When Ibsen started giving ironic twists to the same formulas, his startled hearers took them for portents of a social revolution. Even the old chestnut about the heroine's being really the hero's sister turns up in *Ghosts* and *Little Eyolf*. The average movie of today is a rigidly conventionalized New Comedy proceeding toward an act which, like death in Greek tragedy, takes place offstage, and is symbolized by the final embrace.

In all good New Comedy there is a social as well as an individual theme which must be sought in the general atmosphere of reconciliation that makes the final marriage possible. As the hero gets closer to the heroine and opposition is overcome, all the right-thinking people come over to his side. Thus a new social unit is formed on the stage, and the moment that this social unit crystallizes is the moment of the comic resolution. In the last scene, when the drama-/60/tist usually tries to get all his characters on the stage at once, the audience witnesses the birth of a renewed sense of social integration. In comedy as in life the regular expression of this is a festival, whether a marriage, a dance, or a feast. Old Comedy has, besides a marriage, a *komos*, the processional dance from which comedy derives its name; and the masque, which is a by-form of comedy, also ends in a dance.

This new social integration may be called, first, a kind of moral norm and, second, the pattern of a free society. We can see this more clearly if we look at the sort of characters who impede the progress of the comedy toward the hero's victory. These are always people who are in some kind of mental bondage, who are helplessly driven by ruling passions, neurotic compulsions, social rituals, and selfishness. The miser, the hypochondriac, the hypocrite, the pedant, the snob: these are humors, people who do not fully know what they are doing, who are slaves to a predictable self-imposed pattern of behavior. What we call the moral norm is, then, not morality but deliverance from moral bondage. Comedy is designed not to condemn evil, but to ridicule a lack of self-knowledge. It finds the virtues of Malvolio and Angelo as comic as the vices of Shylock.

The essential comic resolution, therefore, is an individual release which is also a social reconciliation. The normal individual is freed from the bonds of a humorous society, and a normal society is freed from the bonds imposed on it by humorous individuals. The Oedipus pattern we noted in New Comedy /61/ belongs to the individual side of this, and the sense of the ridiculousness of the humor to the social side. But all real comedy is based on the principle that these two forms of release are ultimately the same: this principle may be seen at its most concentrated in *The Tempest*. The rule holds whether the resolution is expressed in social terms, as in *The Merchant of Venice*, or in individual terms, as in Ibsen's *An Enemy of the People*.

The freer the society, the greater the variety of individuals it can tolerate, and the natural tendency of comedy is to include as many as possible in its final festival. The motto of comedy is Terence's "Nothing human is alien to me." This may be one reason for the traditional comic importance of the parasite, who has no business to be at the festival but is nevertheless there. The spirit of reconciliation which pervades the comedies of Shakespeare is not to be ascribed to a personal attitude of his own, about which we know nothing whatever, but to his impersonal concentration on the laws of comic form.

Hence the moral quality of the society presented is not the point of the comic resolution. In Jonson's *Volpone* the final assertion of the moral norm takes the form of a social revenge on Volpone, and the play ends with a great bustle of sentences to penal servitude and the galleys. One feels perhaps that the audience's sense of the moral norm does not need so much hard labor. In *The Alchemist*, when Lovewit returns to his house, the virtuous characters have proved so weak and the rascals so ingenious that the /62/ action dissolves in laughter. Whichever is morally the better ending, that of *The Alchemist* is more concentrated comedy. *Volpone* is starting to move toward tragedy, toward the vision of a greatness which develops *hybris* and catastrophe.

The same principle is even clearer in Aristophanes. Aristophanes is the most personal of writers: his opinions on every subject are written all over his plays, and we have no doubt of his moral attitude. We know that he wanted peace with Sparta and that he hated Cleon, and when his comedy depicts the attaining of peace and the defeat of Cleon we know that he approved and wanted his audience to approve. But in *Ecclesiazusae* a band of women in disguise railroad a communistic scheme through the Assembly, which is a horrid parody of Plato's *Republic*, and proceed to inaugurate Plato's sexual communism with some astonishing improvements. Presumably Aristophanes did not applaud this, yet the comedy follows the same pattern and the same resolution. In *The Birds* the Peisthetairos who defies Zeus and blocks out Olympus with his Cloud-Cuckoo-Land is accorded the same triumph that is given to the Trygaeus of the *Peace* who flies to heaven and brings a golden age back to Athens.

Comedy, then, may show virtue her own feature and scorn her own image—for Hamlet's famous definition of drama was originally a definition of comedy. It may emphasize the birth of an ideal society as you like it, or the tawdriness of the sham society which is the way of the world. There is an important parallel /63/ here with tragedy. Tragedy, we are told, is expected to raise but not ultimately to accept the emotions of pity and terror. These I take to be the sense of moral good and evil, respectively, which we attach to the tragic hero. He may be as good as Caesar, and so appeal to our pity, or as bad as Macbeth, and so appeal to terror, but the particular thing called tragedy that happens to him does not depend on his moral status. The tragic catharsis passes beyond moral judgment, and while it is quite possible to construct a moral tragedy, what tragedy gains in morality it loses in cathartic power. The same is true of the comic catharsis, which raises sympathy and ridicule on a moral basis, but passes beyond both.

Many things are involved in the tragic catharsis, but one of them is a mental or imaginative form of the sacrificial ritual out of which tragedy arose. This is the ritual of the struggle, death, and rebirth of a God-Man, which is linked to the yearly triumph of spring over winter. The tragic hero is not really killed, and the audience no longer eats his body and drinks his blood, but the corresponding thing in art still takes place. The audience enters into communion with the body of the hero, becoming thereby a single body itself. Comedy grows out of the same ritual, for in the ritual the tragic story has a comic sequel. Divine men do not die: they die and rise again. The ritual pattern behind the catharsis of comedy is the resurrection that follows the death, the epiphany or manifestation of the risen hero. This is clear /64/ enough in Aristophanes, where the hero is treated as a risen God-Man, led in triumph with the divine honors of the Olympic victor, rejuvenated, or hailed as a new Zeus. In New Comedy the new human body is, as we have seen, both a hero and a social group. Aristophanes is not only closer to the ritual pattern, but contemporary with Plato; and his comedy, unlike Menander's, is Platonic and dialectic: it seeks not the entelechy of the soul but the Form of the Good, and finds it in the resurrection of the soul from the world of the cave to the sunlight. The audience gains a vision of that resurrection whether the conclusion is joyful or ironic, just as in tragedy it gains a vision of a heroic death whether the hero is morally innocent or guilty.

Two things follow from this: first, that tragedy is really implicit or uncompleted comedy; second, that comedy contains a potential tragedy within itself. With regard to the latter, Aristophanes is full of traces of the original death of the hero which preceded his resurrection in the ritual. Even in New Comedy the dramatist usually tries to bring his action as close to a tragic overthrow of the hero as he can get it, and reverses this movement as suddenly as possible. In Plautus the tricky slave is often forgiven or even freed after having been threatened with all the brutalities that a very brutal dramatist can think of, including crucifixion. Thus the resolution of New Comedy seems to be a realistic foreshortening of a death-and-resurrection pattern, in which the struggle /65/ and rebirth of a divine hero has shrunk into a marriage, the freeing of a slave, and the triumph of a young man over an older one.

As for the conception of tragedy as implicit comedy, we may notice how often tragedy closes on the major chord of comedy: the Aeschylean trilogy, for instance, proceeds to what is really a comic resolution, and so do many tragedies of Euripides. From the point of view of Christianity, too, tragedy is an episode in that larger scheme of redemption and resurrection to which Dante gave the name of *commedia*. This conception of *commedia* enters drama with the miracle-play cycles, where such tragedies as the Fall and the Crucifixion are episodes of a dramatic scheme in which the divine comedy has the last word. The sense of tragedy as a prelude to comedy is hardly separable from anything explicitly Christian. The serenity of the final double chorus in the St. Matthew Passion would hardly be attainable if composer and audience did not know that there was more to the story. Nor would the death of Samson lead to "calm of mind all passion spent" if Samson were not a prototype of the rising Christ.

New Comedy is thus contained, so to speak, within the symbolic structure of Old Comedy, which in its turn is contained within the Christian conception of *commedia*. This sounds like a logically exhaustive classification, but we have still not caught Shakespeare in it.

It is only in Jonson and the Restoration writers that English comedy can be called a form of New Comedy. /66/ The earlier tradition established by Peele and developed by Lyly, Greene, and the masque writers, which uses themes from romance and folklore and avoids the comedy of manners, is the one followed by Shakespeare. These themes are largely medieval in origin, and derive, not from the mysteries or the moralities or the interludes, but from a fourth dramatic tradition. This is the drama of folk ritual, of the St. George play and the mummers' play, of the feast of the ass and the Boy Bishop, and of all the dramatic activity that punctuated the Christian calendar with the rituals of an immemorial paganism. We may call this the drama of the green world, and its theme is once again the triumph of life over the waste land, the death and revival of the year impersonated by figures still human, and once divine as well.

When Shakespeare began to study Plautus and Terence, his dramatic instinct, stimulated by his predecessors, divined that there was a profounder pattern in the argument of comedy than appears in either of them. At once—for the process is beginning in *The Comedy of Errors*—he started groping toward that profounder pattern, the ritual of death and revival that also underlies Aristophanes, of which an exact equivalent lay ready to hand in the drama of the green world. This parallelism largely accounts for the resemblances to Greek ritual which Colin Still has pointed out in *The Tempest*.

The Two Gentlemen of Verona is an orthodox New Comedy except for one thing. The hero Valentine becomes captain of a band of outlaws in a forest, and all /67/ the other characters are gathered into this forest and become converted. Thus the action of the comedy begins in a world represented as a normal world, moves into the green world, goes into a metamorphosis there in which the comic resolution is achieved, and returns to the normal world. The forest in this play is the embryonic form of the fairy world of *A Midsummer Night's Dream*, the Forest of Arden in *As You Like It*, Windsor Forest in *The Merry Wives of Windsor*, and the pastoral world of the mythical sea-coasted Bohemia in *The Winter's Tale*. In all these comedies there is the same rhythmic movement from normal world to green world and back again. Nor is this second world confined to the forest comedies. In

The Merchant of Venice the two worlds are a little harder to see, yet Venice is clearly not the same world as that of Portia's mysterious house in Belmont, where there are caskets teaching that gold and silver are corruptible goods, and from whence proceed the wonderful cosmological harmonies of the fifth act. In *The Tempest* the entire action takes place in the second world, and the same may be said of *Twelfth Night*, which, as its title implies, presents a carnival society, not so much a green world as an evergreen one. The second world is absent from the so-called problem comedies, which is one of the things that makes them problem comedies.

The green world charges the comedies with a symbolism in which the comic resolution contains a suggestion of the old ritual pattern of the victory of summer over winter. This is explicit in *Love's Labour's |68| Lost*. In this very masque-like play, the comic contest takes the form of the medieval debate of winter and spring. In *The Merry Wives of Windsor* there is an elaborate ritual of the defeat of winter, known to folklorists as "carrying out Death," of which Falstaff is the victim; and Falstaff must have felt that, after being thrown into the water, dressed up as a witch and beaten out of a house with curses, and finally supplied with a beast's head and singed with candles while he said, "Divide me like a brib'd buck, each a haunch," he had done about all that could reasonably be asked of any fertility spirit.

The association of this symbolism with the death and revival of human beings is more elusive, but still perceptible. The fact that the heroine often brings about the comic resolution by disguising herself as a boy is familiar enough. In the Hero of *Much Ado About Nothing* and the Helena of *All's Well That Ends Well*, this theme of the withdrawal and return of the heroine comes as close to a death and revival as Elizabethan conventions will allow. The Thaisa of *Pericles* and the Fidele of *Cymbeline* are beginning to crack the conventions, and with the disappearance and revival of Hermione in *The Winter's Tale*, who actually returns once as a ghost in a dream, the original nature-myth of Demeter and Proserpine is openly established. The fact that the dying and reviving character is usually female strengthens the feeling that there is something maternal about the green world, in which the new order of the comic resolution is nourished and brought to birth. How-/69/ever, a similar theme which is very like the rejuvenation of the *senex* so frequent in Aristophanes occurs in the folklore motif of the healing of the impotent king

on which *All's Well That Ends Well* is based, and this theme is probably involved in the symbolism of Prospero.

The conception of a second world bursts the boundaries of Menandrine comedy, yet it is clear that the world of Puck is no world of eternal forms or divine revelation. Shakespeare's comedy is not Aristotelian and realistic like Menander's, nor Platonic and dialectic like Aristophanes', nor Thomist and sacramental like Dante's, but a fourth kind. It is an Elizabethan kind, and is not confined either to Shakespeare or to the drama. Spenser's epic is a wonderful contrapuntal intermingling of two orders of existence, one the red and white world of English history, the other the green world of the Faerie Queene. The latter is a world of crusading virtues proceeding from the Faerie Queene's court and designed to return to that court when the destiny of the other world is fulfilled. The fact that the Faerie Queene's knights are sent out during the twelve days of the Christmas festival suggests our next point.

Shakespeare too has his green world of comedy and his red and white world of history. The story of the latter is at one point interrupted by an invasion from the comic world, when Falstaff *senex et parasitus* throws his gigantic shadow over Prince Henry, assuming on one occasion the role of his father. Clearly, if the Prince is ever to conquer France he must re-/70/assert the moral norm. The moral norm is duly reasserted, but the rejection of Falstaff is not a comic resolution. In comedy the moral norm is not morality but deliverance, and we certainly do not feel delivered from Falstaff as we feel delivered from Shylock with his absurd and vicious bond. The moral norm does not carry with it the vision of a free society: Falstaff will always keep a bit of that in his tavern.

Falstaff is a mock king, a lord of misrule, and his tavern is a Saturnalia. Yet we are reminded of the original meaning of the Saturnalia, as a rite intended to recall the golden age of Saturn. Falstaff's world is not a golden world, but as long as we remember it we cannot forget that the world of *Henry V* is an iron one. We are reminded too of another traditional denizen of the green world, Robin Hood, the outlaw who manages to suggest a better kind of society than those who make him an outlaw can produce. The outlaws in *The Two Gentlemen of Verona* compare themselves, in spite of the Italian setting, to Robin Hood, and in *As You Like It* Charles the wrestler says of Duke Senior's followers: "There they live like the old Robin Hood of England: they say many young gentlemen flock to him every day, and fleet the time carelessly, as they did in the golden world."

In the histories, therefore, the comic Saturnalia is a temporary reversal of normal standards, comic "relief" as it is called, which subsides and allows the history to continue. In the comedies, the green world suggests an original golden age which the normal world has usurped and which makes us wonder if it /71/ is not the normal world that is the real Saturnalia. In *Cymbeline* the green world finally triumphs over a historical theme, the reason being perhaps that in that play the incarnation of Christ, which is contemporary with Cymbeline, takes place offstage, and accounts for the halcyon peace with which the play concludes. From then on in Shakespeare's plays, the green world has it all its own way, and both in *Cymbeline* and in *Henry VIII* there may be suggestions that Shakespeare, like Spenser, is moving toward a synthesis of the two worlds, a wedding of Prince Arthur and the Faerie Queene.

This world of fairies, dreams, disembodied souls, and pastoral lovers may not be a "real" world, but, if not, there is something equally illusory in the stumbling and blinded follies of the "normal" world, of Theseus' Athens with its idiotic marriage law, of Duke Frederick and his melancholy tyranny, of Leontes and his mad jealousy, of the Court Party with their plots and intrigues. The famous speech of Prospero about the dream nature of reality applies equally to Milan and the enchanted island. We spend our lives partly in a waking world we call normal and partly in a dream world which we create out of our own desires. Shakespeare endows both worlds with equal imaginative power, brings them opposite one another, and makes each world seem unreal when seen by the light of the other. He uses freely both the heroic triumph of New Comedy and the ritual resurrection of its predecessor, but his distinctive comic resolution is different from either: it is a de-/72/tachment of the spirit born of this reciprocal reflecton of two illusory realities. We need not ask whether this brings us into a higher order of existence or not, for the question of existence is not relevant to poetry.

We have spoken of New Comedy as Aristotelian, Old Comedy as Platonic and Dante's *commedia* as Thomist, but it is difficult to suggest a philosophical spokesman for the form of Shakespeare's comedy. For Shakespeare, the subject matter of poetry is not life, or nature, or reality, or revelation, or anything else that the philosopher builds on, but poetry itself, a verbal universe. That is one reason why he is both the most elusive and the most substantial of poets. /73/

Susanne K. Langer The Great Dramatic Forms: The Comic Rhythm

Susanne K. Langer is a distinguished American philosopher. Her background includes study at Radcliffe College and in Vienna; she has taught at her alma mater and at Delaware, New York University, Northwestern, Ohio State, and Michigan. Since 1954, she has been a professor at Connecticut College. She has held numerous fellowships and grants. Mrs. Langer's fame, however, rests securely on her books, all widely influential, all published by Charles Scribner's Sons, New York; they include: *Introduction to Symbolic Logic* (1937), *Philosophy in a New Key* (1942), *Feeling and Form* (1953), *The Problems of Art* (1957). She is an aesthetician of note, whose discourse has extended and given greater meaning to comedy; her words are provocative and she writes with skill. What follows is chapter eighteen of *Feeling and Form*. Mrs. Langer's footnotes have been retained.

Of all the arts, the most exposed to non-artistic interpretation and criticism are prose fiction and the drama. As the novel has suffered from being treated as a psycho-biographical document, drama has suffered from moralism. In the theater, most people—and especially the most competent spectators—feel that the vision of destiny is the essence of the work, the thing that unfolds before their eyes. In critical retrospect they forget that this visibly growing future, this destiny to which the persons in the play are committed, is the artistic form the poet set out to make, and that the value of the play lies in this creation. As critics, they treat the form as a device for conveying a social and moral content; almost all drama analysis and comment is concerned with the moral struggle involved in the action, the justice of the outcome, the "case" of society against the tragic hero or the comic villain, and the moral significance of the various characters.

It is true that tragedy usually—perhaps even always—presents a moral struggle, and that comedy very commonly castigates foibles and vices. But neither a great moral issue, nor folly inviting embarrassment and laughter, in itself furnishes an artistic principle; neither ethics nor common sense produces any image of organic form. Drama, however, always exhibits such form; it does so by creating the semblance of a history, and composing its elements into a rhythmic single structure. The moral content is thematic material, which, like everything that enters into a work of art, has to serve to make the primary illusion and articulate the pattern of "felt life" the artist intends.

"The tragic theme" and "the comic theme"—guilt and expiation, vanity and exposure—are not the essence of drama, not even the deter-/326/minants of its major forms, tragedy and comedy; they are means of dramatic construction, and as such they are, of course, not indispensable, however widespread their use. But they are to European drama what the representation of objects is to painting: sources of the Great Tradition. Morality, the concept of deed and desert, or "what is coming to the doer," is as obvious a subject for the art of creating a virtual future as the depiction of objects is for the art of creating virtual space. The reason for the existence of these two major themes, and for their particular respective contents, will be apparent as soon as we consider the nature of the two great forms, comic drama and tragic.

It is commonly assumed that comedy and tragedy have the same fundamental form, but differ in point of view—in the attitude the poet and his interpreters take, and the spectators are invited to take, toward the action.[1] But the difference really goes deeper than surface treatment (i.e. relative levity or pathos). It is structural and radical. Drama abstracts from reality the fundamental forms of consciousness: the first reflection of natural activity in sensation, awareness, and expectation, which belongs to all higher creatures and might be

called, therefore, the pure sense of life; and beyond that, the reflection of an activity which is at once more elaborate, and more integrated, having a beginning, efflorescence, and end—the personal sense of life, or self-realization. The latter probably belongs only to human beings, and to them in varying measure.

The pure sense of life is the underlying feeling of comedy, developed in countless different ways. To give a general phenomenon one name is not to make all its manifestations one thing, but only to bring them conceptually under one head. Art does not generalize and classify; art sets forth the individuality of forms which discourse, being essentially general, has to suppress. The sense of life is always new, infinitely complex, therefore infinitely variable in its possible expressions. This sense, or "enjoyment" as Alexander would call it,[2] is the realization in direct /327/ feeling of what sets organic nature apart from inorganic: self-preservation, self-restoration, functional tendency, purpose. Life is teleological, the rest of nature is, apparently, mechanical; to maintain the pattern of vitality in a non-living universe is the most elementary instinctual purpose. An organism tends to keep its equilibrium amid the bombardment of aimless forces that beset it, to regain equilibrium when it has been disturbed, and to pursue a sequence of actions dictated by the need of keeping all its interdependent parts constantly renewed, their structure intact. Only organisms have needs; lifeless objects whirl or slide or tumble about, are shattered and scattered, stuck together, piled up, without showing any impulse to return to some pre-eminent condition and function. But living things strive to persist in a particular chemical balance, to maintain a particular temperature, to repeat particular functions, and to develop along particular lines, achieving a growth that seems to be preformed in their earliest, rudimentary, protoplasmic structure.

That is the basic biological pattern which all living things share: the round of conditioned and conditioning organic processes that produces the life rhythm. When this rhythm is disturbed, all activities in the total complex are modified by the break; the organism as a whole is out of balance. But, within a wide range of conditions, it struggles to retrieve its original dynamic form by overcoming and removing the obstacle, or if this proves impossible, it develops a slight variation of its typical form and activity and carries on life with a new balance of functions—in other words, it

---

[1] Cf., for instance, the letters of Athene Seyler and Stephen Haggard, published under the title: *The Craft of Comedy.* Miss Seyler writes: ". . . comedy is simply a point of view. It is a comment on life from outside, an observation on human nature. . . . Comedy seems to be the standing outside a character or situation and pointing out one's delight in certain aspects of it. For this reason it demands the cooperation of . . . the audience and is in essence the same as recounting a good story over the dining-table." (P. 9.)

[2] S. Alexander, *Space, Time and Deity.* See Vol. I, p. 12.

adapts itself to the situation. A tree, for instance, that is bereft of the sunshine it needs by the encroachment of other trees, tends to grow tall and thin until it can spread its own branches in the light. A fish that has most of its tail bitten off partly overcomes the disturbance of its locomotion patterns by growing new tissue, replacing some of the tail, and partly adapts to its new condition by modifying the normal uses of its fins, swimming effectively without trying to correct the list of its whole body in the water, as it did at first.

But the impulse to survive is not spent only in defense and accommodation; it appears also in the varying power of organisms to seize on opportunities. Consider how chimney swifts, which used to nest in crevasses among rocks, have exploited the products of human architecture, and how unfailingly mice find the warmth and other delights of /328/ our kitchens. All creatures live by opportunities, in a world fraught with disasters. That is the biological pattern in most general terms.

This pattern, moreover, does not develop sporadically in midst of mechanical systems; when or where it began on the earth we do not know, but in the present phase of this planet's constitution there appears to be no "spontaneous generation." It takes life to produce further life. Every organism, therefore, is historically linked with other organisms. A single cell may die, or it may divide and lose its identity in the reorganization of what was formerly its protoplasm round two nuclei instead of one. Its existence as one maturing cell is a phase in a continuum of biological process that varies its rhythm at definite points of growth, starting over with multiplied instances of the immature form. Every individual in this progression that dies (i.e. meets with disaster) instead of dividing is an offshoot from the continuous process, an end, but not a break in the communal biography.

There are species of such elementary life that are diffused in air and water, and some that cohere in visible colonies; above all, there are genetically related organic structures that tend to interact, modify each other, vary in special ways, and together—often by hundreds, thousands, millions together—produce a single higher organism. In such higher organisms, propagation no longer occurs by binary fission, and consequently the individual is not a passing phase in an endless metabolic process; death, which is an accident in amoeboid existence, becomes the lot of every individual—no accident, but a phase of the life

pattern itself. The only "immortal" portion of such a complex organism is a class of cells which, during its lifetime, forms new individuals.

In relatively low forms of individualized life, for instance the cryptogams, new specimens may spring entirely from one parent, so that the entire ancestry of an organism forms a single line. But the main evolutionary trend has been toward a more complex form of heredity: two cells of complementary structure, and from different individuals, fuse and grow into a common offspring. This elaborate process entails the division of the race into two sexes, and radically affects the needs and instincts of its members. For the jellyfish, the desire for continuity is enough; it seeks food and avoids destructive influence. Its rhythm is the endless metabolic cycle of cellular growth, punctuated by fissions and /329/ rearrangements, but ageless except for the stages of each passing individuation, and in principle deathless. The higher organisms, however, that do not give themselves up by division into new units of life, are all doomed to die; death is inherent in a form of life that achieves complete individuation. The only vestige in them of the endless protoplasmic life passing through organism after organism is their production of the "immortal" cells, ova or spermatozoa; this small fraction of them still enjoys the longer life of the stock.

The sex impulse, which presumably belongs only to bisexual creatures (whatever equivalents it may have in other procreative processes), is closely intertwined with the life impulse; in a mature organism it is part and parcel of the whole vital impetus. But it is a specialized part, because the activities that maintain the individual's life are varied and adaptable to many circumstances, but procreation requires specific actions. This specialization is reflected in the emotional life of all the higher animals; sexual excitement is the most intense and at the same time the most elaborately patterned experience, having its own rhythm that engages the whole creature, its rise and crisis and cadence, in a much higher degree than any other emotive response. Consequently the whole development of feeling, sensibility, and temperament is wont to radiate from that source of vital consciousness, sexual action and passion.

Mankind has its rhythm of animal existence, too—the strain of maintaining a vital balance amid the alien and impartial chances of the world, complicated and heightened by passional desires. The pure sense of life springs from that basic rhythm, and varies from the composed well-being of sleep to the intensity of spasm, rage, or ecstasy. But the process of living is incomparably more complex for human beings than for even the highest animals; man's world is, above all, intricate and puzzling. The powers of language and imagination have set it utterly apart from that of other creatures. In human society an individual is not, like a member of a herd or a hive, exposed only to others that visibly or tangibly surround him, but is consciously bound to people who are absent, perhaps far away, at the moment. Even the dead may still play into his life. His awareness of events is far greater than the scope of his physical perceptions. Symbolic construction has made this vastly involved and extended world: and mental adroitness is his chief asset for exploiting it. The pat-/330/tern of his vital feeling, therefore, reflects his deep emotional relation to those symbolic structures that are his realities, and his instinctual life modified in almost every way by thought—a brainy opportunism in face of an essentially dreadful universe.

This human life-feeling is the essence of comedy. It is at once religious and ribald, knowing and defiant, social and freakishly individual. The illusion of life which the comic poet creates is the oncoming future fraught with dangers and opportunities, that is, with physical or social events occurring by chance and building up the coincidences with which individuals cope according to their lights. This ineluctable future—ineluctable because its countless factors are beyond human knowledge and control—is Fortune. Destiny in the guise of Fortune is the fabric of comedy; it is developed by comic action, which is the upset and recovery of the protagonist's equilibrium, his contest with the world and his triumph by wit, luck, personal power, or even humorous, or ironical, or philosophical acceptance of mischance. Whatever the theme—serious and lyrical as in *The Tempest*, coarse slapstick as in the *Schwänke* of Hans Sachs, or clever and polite social satire—the immediate sense of life is the underlying feeling of comedy, and dictates its rhythmically structured unity, that is to say its organic form.

Comedy is an art form that arises naturally wherever people are gathered to celebrate life, in spring festivals, triumphs, birthdays, weddings, or initiations. For it expresses the elementary strains and resolutions of animate nature, the animal drives that persist even in human nature, the delight man takes in his special mental gifts that make him the lord of creation; it is an image of human vitality holding its own in the world amid the surprises of unplanned coincidence. The most

obvious occasions for the performance of comedies are thanks or challenges to fortune. What justifies the term "Comedy" is not that the ancient ritual procession, the Comus, honoring the god of that name, was the source of this great art form—for comedy has arisen in many parts of the world, where the Greek god with his particular worship was unknown—but that the Comus was a fertility rite, and the god it celebrated a fertility god, a symbol of perpetual rebirth, eternal life.

Tragedy has a different basic feeling, and therefore a different form; that is why it has also quite different thematic material, and why char- /331/ acter development, great moral conflicts, and sacrifice are its usual actions. *It is also what makes tragedy sad*, as the rhythm of sheer vitality makes comedy happy. To understand this fundamental difference, we must turn once more to the biological reflections above, and carry them a little further.

In the higher forms of life, an organism is not split up into other organisms so as to let its career as an individual properly end without death and decay; each separate body, on the higher levels, having completed its growth, and normally having reproduced, becomes decadent and finally dies. Its life has a definite beginning, ascent, turning point, descent, and close (barring accidental destruction of life, such as simple cells may also suffer); and the close is inevitably death. Animals—even highly developed ones—instinctively seek to avoid death when they are suddenly confronted with it, and presumably do not realize its coming if and when they die naturally. But human beings, because of their semantically enlarged horizon, are aware of individual history as a passage from birth to death. Human life, therefore, has a different subjective pattern from animal existence; as "felt life" (to borrow Henry James' phrase once more) it has a different dimension. Youth, maturity, and age are not merely states in which a creature may happen to be, but are stages through which persons must pass. Life is a voyage, and at the end of it is death.

The power to conceive of life as a single span enables one also to think of its conduct as a single undertaking, and of a person as a unified and developed being, a personality. Youth, then, is all potentiality, not only for physical growth and procreation, but also for mental and moral growth. Bodily development is largely unconscious and involuntary, and the instincts that aid it are bent simply upon maintaining the vital rhythms from moment to moment, evading destruction, letting the organism grow in its highly specialized fashion.

Its maturation, procreative drive, then a fairly long period of "holding its own" without further increase, and finally the gradual loss of impetus and elasticity—these processes form one organic evolution and dissolution. The extraordinary activity of man's brain, however, does not automatically parallel his biological career. It outruns the order of animal interests, sometimes confusing his instincts, sometimes exaggerating them (as simple sexual /332/ passion, for instance, is heightened by imagination into romantic passion and eternal devotion), and gives his life a new pattern dominated by his foreknowledge of death. Instead of simply passing through the natural succession of his individualized existence, he ponders its uniqueness, its brevity and limitations, the life impulses that make it, and the fact that in the end the organic unity will be broken, the self will disintegrate and be no more.

There are many ways of accepting death; the commonest one is to deny its finality, to imagine a continued existence "beyond" it—by resurrection, reincarnation, or departure of the soul from the body, and usually from the familiar world, to a deathless existence in hades, nirvana, heaven or hell. But no matter how people contrive to become reconciled to their mortality, it puts its stamp on their conception of life: since the instinctive struggle to go on living is bound to meet defeat in the end, they look for *as much life as possible* between birth and death—for adventure, variety and intensity of experience, and the sense of growth that increase of personality and social status can give long after physical growth has stopped. The known limitation of life gives form to it and makes it appear not merely as a process, but as a career. This career of the individual is variously conceived as a "calling," the attainment of an ideal, the soul's pilgrimage, "life's ordeal," or self-realization. The last of these designations is, perhaps, the most illuminating in the present context, because it contains the notion of a limited potential personality given at birth and "realized," or systematically developed, in the course of the subject's total activity. His career, then, appears to be preformed in him; his successive adventures in the world are so many challenges to fulfill his individual destiny.

Destiny viewed in this way, as a future shaped essentially in advance and only incidentally by chance happenings, is Fate; and Fate is the "virtual future" created in tragedy. The "tragic rhythm of action," as Professor Fergusson calls it, is the rhythm of man's life at its highest powers in the limits of his unique, death-bound career. Tragedy is the image of Fate, as comedy is of Fortune. Their basic structures are different; comedy is essentially contingent, episodic, and ethnic; it expresses the continuous balance of sheer vitality that belongs to society and is exemplified briefly in each individual; tragedy is a fullfillment, and its /333/ form therefore is closed, final and passional. Tragedy is a mature art form, that has not arisen in all parts of the world, not even in all great civilizations. Its conception requires a sense of individuality which some religions and some cultures—even high cultures—do not generate.

But that is a matter for later discussion, in connection with the tragic theater as such. At present I wish only to point out the radical nature of the difference between the two types of drama, comedy and tragedy; a difference which is, however, not one of opposites—the two forms are perfectly capable of various combinations, incorporating elements of one in the other. The matrix of the work is always either tragic or comic; but within its frame the two often interplay.

Where tragedy is generally known and accepted, comedy usually does not reach its highest development. The serious mood is reserved for the tragic stage. Yet comedy may be serious; there is heroic drama, romantic drama, political drama, all in the comic pattern, yet entirely serious; the "history" is usually exalted comedy. It presents an incident in the undying life of a society that meets good and evil fortunes on countless occasions but never concludes its quest. After the story comes more life, more destiny prepared by the world and the race. So far as the story goes, the protagonists "live happily ever after"—on earth or in heaven. That fairy-tale formula is tacitly understood at the close of a comedy. It is implicit in the episodic structure.

Dante called his great poem a comedy, though it is entirely serious—visionary, religious, and sometimes terrible. The name *Divina Commedia*, which later generations attached to it, fits it, even if not too literally since it is not actually a drama as the title suggests.[3] Something analogous to the comedy pattern, together with the tones of high seriousness that European poets have generally

[3] Professor Fergusson and Mr. T. S. Eliot both treat *The Divine Comedy* as an example of genuine drama. The former even speaks of "the drama of Sophocles and Shakespeare, the *Divina Commedia* of Dante—in which the idea of a theater has been briefly realized." (*The Idea of a Theater*, p. 227.) But between drama and dramatic narrative there is a world of difference. If everything these two eminent critics say of great drama holds also for Dante's poem, this does not mean that the poem is a drama, but that the critics have reached a generalization applying to more than drama.

struck only in tragedy, yields a work that invites the paradoxical name. /334/

Paradoxical, however, only to our ears, because our religious feeling is essentially tragic, inspired by the contemplation of death. In Asia the designation "Divine Comedy" would fit numberless plays; especially in India triumphant gods, divine lovers united after various trials (as in the perennially popular romance of Rama and Sita), are the favorite themes of a theater that knows no "tragic rhythm." The classical Sanskrit drama was heroic comedy—high poetry, noble action, themes almost always taken from the myths—a serious, religiously conceived drama, yet in the "comic" pattern, which is not a complete organic development reaching a foregone, inevitable conclusion, but is episodic, restoring a lost balance, and implying a new future.[4] The reason for this consistently "comic" image of life in India is obvious enough: both Hindu and Buddhist regard life as an episode in the much longer career of the soul which has to accomplish many incarnations before it reaches its goal, nirvana. Its struggles in the world do not exhaust it; in fact they are scarcely worth recording except in entertainment theater, "comedy" in our sense—satire, farce, and dialogue. The characters whose fortunes are seriously interesting are the eternal gods; and for them there is no death, no limit of potentialities, hence no fate to be fulfilled. There is only the balanced rhythm of sentience and emotion, upholding itself amid the changes of material nature.

The personages in the nataka (the Sanskrit heroic drama) do not undergo any character development; they are good or evil, as the case may be, in the last act as they were in the first. This is essentially a comedy trait. Because the comic rhythm is that of vital continuity, the protagonists do not change in the course of the play, as they normally do in tragedy. In the latter there is development, in the former developments. The comic hero plays against obstacles presented either by nature (which includes mythical monsters such as dragons, and also "forces," personified like the "Night Queen," or impersonal like floods, fires, and pests), or by society; that is, his fight is with obstacles and enemies, which his strength, wisdom, virtue, or other assets let him overcome.[5] It /335/ is a fight with the uncongenial world, which he

shapes to his own fortunes. Where the basic feeling of dramatic art always has the comic rhythm, comedy enjoys a much fuller development than it does where tragedy usurps its highest honors. In the great cultures of Asia it has run through all moods, from the lightest to the most solemn, and through all forms—the one-act skit, the farce, the comedy of manners, even to dramas of Wagnerian proportions.

In the European tradition the heroic comedy has had a sporadic existence; the Spanish *Comedia* was perhaps its only popular and extended development.[6] Where it reaches something like the exalted character of the nataka, our comedy has generally been taken for tragedy, simply because of its dignity, or "sublimity," which we associate only with tragedy. Corneille and Racine considered their dramas tragedies, yet the rhythm of tragedy—the growth and full realization of a personality—is not in them; the Fate their personages meet is really misfortune, and they meet it heroically. This sad yet non-tragic character of the French classical drama has been noted by several critics. C. V. Deane, for instance, in his book, *Dramatic Theory and the Rhymed Heroic Play*, says of Corneille: "In his tragedies the incidents are so disposed as to bring out to the full the conflict between an overmastering will and the forces of Fate, but the interest centres in the dauntless endurance of the individual, and there is little attempt to envisage or suggest the universal moral problem inherent in the nature of Tragedy, nor do his chief characters submit to ordinary morality; each is a law unto himself by virtue of his particular kind of heroism."[7] Earlier in the book he had already remarked on the fact that the creation of human personalities was not the aim of these playwrights;[8] and in a comment on Otway's translation of Racine's *Bérénice* he really exposed—perhaps without realizing it himself—the true nature of their tragedies, for he said that Otway /336/ was able "to reproduce the spirit of the original," though he was not scrupulously true to the French text. "Even Otway, however, adapts rather than translates," he observed, "and the tilt toward the happy ending in his version betrays an acquiescence in

[4] Cf. Sylvain Lévi, *Le Théâtre indien*, p. 32: "The heroic comedy (nataka) is the consummate type of Indian drama; all dramatic elements can find their place in it."

[5] In Chinese drama, even exalted heroes often conquer their enemies by ruse rather than by valor; see Zucker, *The Chinese Theater*, especially p. 82.

[6] Brander Matthews describes the *Comedia* as "often not a comedy at all in our English understanding of the term, but rather a play of intrigue, peopled with hot-blooded heroes. . ." (Introduction to Lope De Vega Carpio's *The New Art of Writing Plays*.)

[7] *Dramatic Theory and the Rhymed Heroic Play*, p. 33.

[8] *Ibid.*, p. 14: "It is true that during the course of its history the heroic play seldom succeeded in creating characters which were credible as human beings; this, however, was really foreign to its purpose."

the stereotyped poetic justice which the English playwrights (appreciably influenced by Corneille's practice) deemed inseparable from the interplay of heroism and honor." (P. 19.)

How could a translator-editor bring a tragic play to a happy ending and still "reproduce the spirit of the original"? Only by virtue of the non-tragic structure, the fundamentally comic move-ment of the piece. These stately Gallic classics are

Romantic drama such as Schiller's *Wilhelm Tell* illustrates the same principle. It is another species of serious heroic comedy. Tell appears as an ex-emplary personage in the beginning of the play, as citizen, husband, father, friend and patriot; when an extreme political and social crisis devel-ops, he rises to the occasion, overcomes the enemy, frees his country, and returns to the peace, dignity and harmonious joy of his home. The balance of
ed. As a personage he is impressive; as
y he is very simple. He has the standard
righteous indignation, paternal love,
vor, pride, anxiety, etc.—under their
ditions. Nothing in the action requires
nore than a man of high courage, in-
spirit, and such other virtues as the
rs of Switzerland boasted, to oppose
ce and vanity of foreign oppressors.
al male he was from the start, and the
ode merely gives him opportunity to
domitable skill and daring.
the serious products of comic art; they
rarer examples. The natural vein of
humorous—so much so that "comic"
synonymous with "funny." Because
comic" is here used in a somewhat
nse (contrasting "the comic rhythm"
ragic rhythm"), it may be well to say
where the popular sense is intended.
ll degrees of humor in comedy, from
partee that elicits a smile by its clever-
t being intrinsically funny at all, to the
nat sets young and old, simple or so-
houting with merriment. Humor has
all the arts, but in comic drama it has
Comedy may be frivolous, farcical,
crous to any degree, and still be true
er springs from its very structure. /338/
close relation between humor and the
fe," and several people have tried to
n order to find the basis of that char-
y human function, laughter; the chief
their attempts has been, I think, that
ll started with the question: What sort
akes us laugh? Certainly laughter is
d by ideas, cognitions, fancies; it ac-
specific emotions such as disdain, and
he feeling of pleasure; but we also laugh
when we are tickled (which may not be pleasur-able at all), and in hysterics. Those predominantly physiological causes bear no direct relation to humor; neither, for that matter, do some kinds of pleasure. Humor is one of the causes of laughter.

Marcel Pagnol, who published his theory of

Bibliography

Bergson, Henri. Laughter.

conflict between Oedipus and Tiresias, wherein the moral beings of the antagonists are at stake. . . . [In *Bérénice*] the moral being is unmistakable and impossible to lose while the stage life continues at all . . . the very possibility of the interchange depends upon the authority of reason, which secures the moral being in any contingency. . . . But if the moral being is *ex hypothesi* secure, . . . there cannot be a pathos in the Sophoclean sense at all." (*Op. cit.*, p. 52.)

laughter in a little book entitled *Notes sur le rire*, remarks that his predecessors—he names particularly Bergson, Fabre, and Mélinand—all sought the source of laughter in funny things or situations, i.e. in nature, whereas it really lies in the subject who laughs. Laughter always—without exception—betokens a sudden sense of superiority. "Laughter is a song of triumph," he says. "It expresses the laugher's sudden discovery of his own momentary superiority over the person he laughs at." This, he maintains, "explains all bursts of laughter in all times and all countries," and lets us dispense with all classifications of laughter by different kinds or causes: "One cannot classify or arrange in categories the radii of a circle."[12]

Yet he proceeds directly to divide laughter into "positive" and "negative" kinds, according to its social or antisocial inspiration. This indicates that we are still dealing with *ludicrous situations*, though these situations always involve the person to whom they are ludicrous, so it may be said that "the source of the comical is in the laugher."[13] The situation, moreover, is something the subject must discover, that is, laughter requires a conceptual element; on that M. Pagnol agrees with Bergson, Mélinand, and Fabre. Whether, according to Bergson's much-debated view, we see living beings following the law of mechanism, or see absurdity in midst of plausibility as Mélinand says, or, as Fabre has it, create a /339/ confusion only to dispel it suddenly, we feel our own superiority in detecting the irrational element; more particularly, we feel superior to those who perform mechanical actions, introduce absurdities, or make confusions. Therefore M. Pagnol claims that his definition of the laughable applies to all these supposedly typical situations.

It probably does; but it is still too narrow. *What is laughable* does not explain the nature of laughter, any more than what is rational explains the nature of reason. The ultimate source of laughter is physiological, and the various situations in which it arises are simply its normal or abnormal stimuli.

Laughter, or the tendency to laugh (the reaction may stop short of the actual respiratory spasm, and affect only the facial muscles, or even meet with complete inhibition) seems to arise from a surge of vital feeling. This surge may be quite small, just so it be sudden enough to be felt distinctly; but it may also be great, and not particularly swift, and

reach a marked climax, at which point we laugh or smile with joy. Laughter is not a simple overt act, as the single word suggests; it is the spectacular end of a complex process. As speech is the culmination of a mental activity, laughter is a culmination of feeling—the crest of a wave of felt vitality.

A sudden sense of superiority entails such a "lift" of vital feeling. But the "lift" may occur without self-flattery, too; we need not be making fun of anyone. A baby will laugh uproariously at a toy that is made to appear suddenly, again and again, over the edge of the crib or the back of a chair. It would take artful interpretation to demonstrate that this fulfillment of his tense expectation makes him feel superior. Superior to whom? The doll? A baby of eight or nine months is not socialized enough yet to think: "There, I knew you were coming!" and believe that the doll couldn't fool him. Such self-applause requires language, and enough experience to estimate probabilities. The baby laughs because his wish is gratified; not because he believes the doll obeyed his wishing, but simply because the suspense is broken, and his energies are released. The sudden pleasure raises his general feeling tone, so he laughs.

In so-called "gallows humor"—the harsh laugh in distress—the "lift" of vital feeling is simply a flash of self-assertion. Something similar probably causes the mirthless laughter of hysterics: in the disorganized re-/340/sponse of a hysterical person, the sense of vitality breaks through fear and depression spasmodically, so that it causes explosive laughter, sometimes alternating with sobs and tears.

Laughter is, indeed, a more elementary thing than humor. We often laugh without finding any person, object, or situation funny. People laugh for joy in active sport, in dancing, in greeting friends; in returning a smile, one acknowledges another person's worth instead of flaunting one's own superiority and finding him funny.

But all these causes of laughter or its reduced form, smiling, which operate directly on us, belong to actual life. In comedy the spectator's laugh has only one legitimate source: his appreciation of humor in the piece. He does not laugh with the characters, not even at them, but at their acts—at their situations, their doings, their expressions, often at their dismay. M. Pagnol holds that we laugh at the characters directly, and regards that as a corroboration of his theory: our pleasure in the comic theater lies in watching people to whom we feel superior.[14]

---

[12] *Notes sur le rire*, p. 41. His argumentation is, unfortunately, not as good as his ideas, and finally leads him to include the song of the nightingale and the rooster's crow as forms of laughter.

[13] *Ibid.*, p. 17.

[14] *Ibid.*, p. 92. There is further discussion of this problem at the end of the present chapter.

There is, however, one serious defect in that view, namely that it supposes the spectator to be aware of himself as a being in the same "world" as the characters. To compare them, even subconsciously, to himself he must give up his psychical Distance and feel himself co-present with them, as one reads an anecdotal news item as something apart from one's own life but still in the actual world, and is moved to say: "How could she do such a thing! Imagine being so foolish!" If he experiences such a reaction in the theater, it is something quite aside from his perception of the play as a poetic fabrication; he has lost, for the moment, his Distance, and feels himself inside the picture.

Humor, then, would be a by-product of comedy, not a structural element in it. And if laughter were elicited thus by the way, it should not make any difference to the value of the work where it occurred; a stage accident, a bad actor who made every amateur actor in the audience feel superior, should serve as well as any clever line or funny situation in the play to amuse the audience. We do, in fact, laugh at such failures; but we do not praise the comedy for that entertainment. In a good play the "laughs" are poetic elements. Its humor as well as its pathos belongs /341/ to the virtual life, and the delight we take in it is delight in something created for our perception, not a direct stimulus to our own feelings. It is true that the comical figures are often buffoons, simpletons, clowns; but such characters are almost always sympathetic, and although they are knocked around and abused, they are indestructible, and eternally self-confident and good-humored.

The buffoon is, in fact, an important comic personage, especially in folk theater. He is essentially a folk character, that has persisted through the more sophisticated and literary stages of comedy as Harlequin, Pierrot, the Persian Karaguez, the Elizabethan jester or fool, the *Vidusaka* of Sanskrit drama; but in the humbler theatrical forms that entertained the poor and especially the peasantry everywhere before the movies came, the buffoon had a more vigorous existence as Hans Wurst, as Punch of the puppet show, the clown of pantomime, the Turkish Karagöz (borrowed from Persian tradition) who belongs only to the shadow play.[15] These anciently popular personages show what the buffoon really is: the indomitable living creature fending for itself, tumbling and stumbling (as the clown physically illustrates) from one situation into another, getting into scrape after scrape and getting out again, with or without a thrashing. He is the personified *élan vital;* his chance adventures and misadventures, without much plot, though often with bizarre complications, his absurd expectations and disappointments, in fact his whole improvised existence has the rhythm of primitive, savage, if not animalian life, coping with a world that is forever taking new uncalculated turns, frustrating, but exciting. He is neither a good man nor a bad one, but is genuinely amoral,—now triumphant, now worsted and rueful, but in his ruefulness and dismay he is funny, because his energy is really unimpaired and each failure prepares the situation for a new fantastic move.[16] The most forthright of these infantilists is the English Punch, who carries out every impulse by force and speed of action— chastises his wife, throws his child out of the window, beats the policeman, and finally spears the devil and carries him out triumphantly on a pitchfork. Punch is not a real buffoon, he is too successful; his appeal is probably a sub-/342/ jective one, to people's repressed desires for general vengeance, revolt, and destruction. He is psychologically interesting, but really a degenerated and stereotyped figure, and as such he has little artistic value because he has no further poetic progeny. What has caused his persistence in a single, mainly vulgar, and not particularly witty role, I do not know, nor is this the place to investigate it; but when he first appeared in England as Punchinello, borrowed from the Italian marionettes, he was still the pure comic protagonist. According to a statement of R. M. Wheeler in the *Encyclopaedia Britannica*, which we may, presumably, take as authority, "The older Punchinello was far less restricted in his actions and circumstances than his modern successor. He fought with allegorical figures representing want and weariness as well as with his wife and with the police, was on intimate terms with the patriarchs and the seven champions of Christendom, sat on the lap of the queen of Sheba, had kings and dukes for his companions, and cheated the Inquisition as well as the common hangman."

The high company this original Punch keeps is quite in accordance with the dignified settings in which he makes his appearance. From the same article we learn that the earliest recorded appearances of Punch in England were in a puppet play

---

[15] See N. N. Martinovitch, *The Turkish Theater, passim.*

[16] Falstaff is a perfect example of the buffoon raised to a human "character" in comedy.

of the Creation of the World, and in another representing the Deluge. To the modern, solemn religious mind, scriptural stories may seem a strange context for such a secular character, and perhaps this apparent incongruity has led to the widespread belief that the clown in modern comedy derives from the devil of mediaeval miracle plays.[17] The devil is, of course, quite at home in sacred realms. It is not impossible that this relation between devil and fool (in his various forms as clown, jester, freak) really holds; yet if it does, that is a historical accident, due to the peculiar Christian conception that indentifies the devil with the flesh, and sin with lust. Such a conception brings the spirit of life and the father of all evil, which are usually poles apart, very close together. For there is no denying that the Fool is a red-blooded fellow; he is, in fact, close to the animal world; in French tradition he wears a cockscomb on his cap, and Punchinello's nose is probably the residue of a beak. He is all motion, whim, and impulse—the "libido" itself. /343/

But he is probably older than the Christian devil, and does not need any connection with that worthy to let him into religious precincts. He has always been close to the gods. If we view him as the representative of mankind in its struggle with the world, it is clear at once why his antics and impertinences are often an integral part of religious rites—why, for instance, the clowning orders in Pueblo society were held in high honor:[18] the clown is Life, he is the Will, he is the Brain, and by the same token he is nature's fool. From the primitive exuberant religions that celebrate fertility and growth he tends ever to come into the ascetic cults, and tumble and juggle in all innocence before the Virgin.

In comedy the stock figure of the buffoon is an obvious device for building up the comic rhythm, i.e. the image of Fortune. But in the development of the art he does not remain the central figure that he was in the folk theater; the lilt and balance of life which he introduced, once it has been grasped, is rendered in more subtle poetic inventions involving plausible characters, and an *intrigue* (as the French call it) that makes for a coherent, over-all, dramatic action. Sometimes he remains as a jester, servant, or other subsidiary character whose comments, silly or witty or shrewd, serve

to point the essentially comic pattern of the action, where the verisimilitude and complexity of the stage-life threaten to obscure its basic form. Those points are normally "laughs"; and that brings us to the aesthetic problem of the joke in comedy.

Because comedy abstracts, and reincarnates for our perception, the motion and rhythm of living, it enhances our vital feeling, much as the presentation of space in painting enhances our awareness of visual space. The virtual life on the stage is not diffuse and only half felt, as actual life usually is: virtual life, always moving visibly into the future, is intensified, speeded up, exaggerated; the exhibition of vitality rises to a breaking point, to mirth and laughter. We laugh in the theater at small incidents and drolleries which would hardly rate a chuckle off-stage. It is not for such psychological reasons as that we go there to be amused, nor that we are bound by rules of politeness to hide our hilarity, but these trifles at which we laugh are really funnier *where they occur* than they would /344/ be elsewhere; they are *employed* in the play, not merely brought in casually. They occur where the tension of dialogue or other action reaches a high point. As thought breaks into speech—as the wave breaks into foam—vitality breaks into humor.

Humor is the brilliance of drama, a sudden heightening of the vital rhythm. A good comedy, therefore, builds up to every laugh; a performance that has been filled up with jokes at the indiscretion of the comedian or of his writer may draw a long series of laughs, yet leave the spectator without any clear impression of a very funny play. The laughs, moreover, are likely to be of a peculiar sameness, almost perfunctory, the formal recognition of a timely "gag."

The amoral character of the comic protagonist goes through the whole range of what may be called the comedy of laughter. Even the most civilized products of this art—plays that George Meredith would honor with the name of "comedy," because they provoke "thoughtful laughter" —do not present moral distinctions and issues, but only the ways of wisdom and of folly. Aristophanes, Menander, Molière—practically the only authors this most exacting of critics admitted as truly comic poets—are not moralists, yet they do not flaunt or deprecate morality; they have, literally, "no use" for moral principles— that is, they do not use them. Meredith, like practically all his contemporaries, labored under the belief that poetry must teach society lessons, and that comedy was valuable for what it revealed

[17] See the article "Clown" (unsigned) in the *Encyclopaedia Britannica*.
[18] On the secret societies of clowns, see F. H. Cushing, *Zuni Creation Myths* (Report of the Bureau of American Ethnology, 1892), concerning the order of "Koyemshi" ("Mudheads").

concerning the social order.[19] He tried hard to hold its exposé of foibles and vindication of common sense to an ethical standard, yet in his very efforts to justify its amoral personages he only admitted their amoral nature, and their simple relish for life, as when he /345/ said: "The heroines of comedy are like women of the world, not necessarily heartless from being clear-sighted. . . . Comedy is an exhibition of their battle with men, and that of men with them. . . ."

There it is, in a nutshell: the contest of men and women—the most universal contest, humanized, in fact civilized, yet still the primitive joyful challenge, the self-preservation and self-assertion whose progress is the comic rhythm.

This rhythm is capable of the most diverse presentations. That is why the art of comedy grows, in every culture, from casual beginnings —miming, clowning, sometimes erotic dancing— to some special and distinctive dramatic art, and sometimes to many forms of it within one culture, yet never seems to repeat its works. It may produce a tradition of dignified drama, springing from solemn ritual, even funereal, its emotional movement too slow to culminate in humor at any point; then other means have to be found to lend it glamor and intensity. The purest heroic comedy is likely to have no humorous passages at all, but to employ the jester only in an ornamental way reminiscent of tragedy, and in fact to use many techniques of tragedy. It may even seem to transcend the amoral comic pattern by presenting virtuous heroes and heroines. But their virtue is a formal affair, a social asset; as Deane remarked of the French classic heroes, they do not submit to ordinary morality; their morality is "heroism," which is essentially strength, will, and endurance in face of the world. Neither have the divinities of oriental drama any "ordinary morality"; they are perfect in virtue when they slay and when they spare, their goodness is glory, and their

will is law. They are Superman, the Hero, and the basic pattern of their conquest over enemies whose only wickedness is resistance, is the amoral life of fencing with the devil—man against death.

Humor, then, is not the essence of comedy, but only one of its most useful and natural elements. It is also its most problematical element, because it elicits from the spectators what appears to be a direct emotional response to persons on the stage, in no wise different from their response to actual people: amusement, laughter.

The phenomenon of laughter in the theater brings into sharp focus the whole question of the distinction between emotion symbolically presented, /346/ and emotion directly stimulated; it is, indeed, a *pons asinorum* of the theory that this distinction is radical, because it presents us with what is probably the most difficult example. The audience's laugh at a good play is, of course, self-expressive, and betokens a "lift" of vital feeling in each laughing person. Yet it has a different character from laughter in conversation, or in the street when the wind carries off a hat with the "hair-do" attached, or in the "laugh house" at an amusement park where the willing victims meet distorting mirrors and things that say "boo." All these laughs of daily life are direct responses to separate stimuli; they may be as sporadic as the jokes bandied in a lively company, or may be strung along purposely like the expected and yet unforeseen events in the "laugh house," yet they remain so many personal encounters that seem funny only if one is in the mood for them. Sometimes we reject witticisms and are bored with tricks and clowning.

It is different in the theater: the play possesses us and breaks our mood. It does not change it, but simply abrogates it. Even if we come in a jovial mood, this does not notably increase our appreciation of humor in the play; for the humor in a good comedy does not strike us directly. What strikes us directly is the dramatic illusion, the stage action as it evolves; and the joke, instead of being as funny as our personal response would make it, seems as funny as its occurrence in the total action makes it. A very mild joke in just the right place may score a big laugh. The action culminates in a witticism, an absurdity, a surprise; the spectators laugh. But after their outburst there is not the letdown that follows an ordinary laugh, because the play moves on without the breathing spell we usually give our own thought and feeling after a joke. The action carries over from one laugh to another, sometimes fairly far spaced; peo-

---

[19] His well-known little work is called *An Essay on Comedy, and the Uses of the Comic Spirit*. These uses are entirely non-artistic. Praising the virtues of "good sense" (which is whatever has survival value in the eyes of society), he says: "The French have a school of stately comedy to which they can fly for renovation whenever they have fallen away from it; and their having such a school is the main reason why, as John Stuart Mill pointed out, they know men and women more accurately than we do." (Pp. 13-14.) And a few pages later: "The *Femmes Savantes* is a capital instance of the uses of comedy in teaching the world to understand what ails it. The French had felt the burden of this new nonsense [the fad of academic learning, new after the fad of excessive nicety and precision in speech, that had marked the *Précieuses*]; but they had to see the comedy several times before they were consoled in their suffering by seeing the cause of it exposed." (Pp. 19-20.)

ple are laughing *at the play*, not at a string of jokes.

Humor in comedy (as, indeed, in all humorous art) belongs to the work, not to our actual surroundings; and if it is borrowed from the actual world, its appearance in the work is what really makes it funny. Political or topical allusions in a play amuse us because they are *used*, not because they refer to something intrinsically very comical. This device of playing with things from actual life is so sure to bring laughs that the average comic writer and improvising comedian overdoes it to the point of artistic ruin; hence the constant flood of "shows" that have /347/ immense popularity but no dramatic core, so they do not outlive the hour of their passing allusions.

Real comedy sets up in the audience a sense of general exhilaration, because it presents the very image of "livingness" and the perception of it is exciting. Whatever the story may be, it takes the form of a temporary triumph over the surrounding world, complicated, and thus stretched out, by an involved succession of coincidences. This illusion of life, the stage-life, has a rhythm of feeling which is not transmitted to us by separate successive stimulations, but rather by our perception of its entire *Gestalt*—a whole world moving into its own future. The "livingness" of the human world is abstracted, composed, and presented to us; with it the high points of the composition that are illuminated by humor. They belong to the life we see, and our laugh belongs to the theatrical exhilaration, which is universally human and impersonal. It is not what the joke happens to mean to us that measures our laughter, but what the joke does in the play.

For this reason we tend to laugh at things in the theater that we might not find funny in actuality. The technique of comedy often has to clear the way for its humor by forestalling any backsliding into "the world of anxious interest and selfish solicitude." It does this by various devices—absurd coincidences, stereotyped expressions of feeling (like the clown's wails of dismay), a quickened pace of action, and other unrealistic effects which serve to emphasize the comic structure. As Professor Fergusson said, "when we understand a comic convention we see the play with godlike omniscience. . . . When Scaramouche gets a beating, we do not feel the blows, but the idea of a beating, at that moment, strikes us as funny. If the beating is too realistic, if it breaks the light rhythm of thought, the fun is gone, and the comedy destroyed."[20]

[20] *Op. cit.*, pp. 178-179.

That "light rhythm of thought" is the rhythm of life; and the reason it is "light" is that all creatures love life, and the symbolization of its impetus and flow makes us really aware of it. The conflict with the world whereby a living being maintains its own complex organic unity is a delightful encounter; the world is as promising and alluring as it is dangerous and opposed. The feeling of comedy is a feeling of heightened /348/ vitality, challenged wit and will, engaged in the great game with Chance. The real antagonist is the World. Since the personal antagonist in the play is really that great challenger, he is rarely a complete villain; he is interesting, entertaining, his defeat is a hilarious success but not his destruction. There is no permanent human triumph except in tragedy; for nature must go on if life goes on, and the world that presents all obstacles also supplies the zest of life. In comedy, therefore, there is a general trivialization of the human battle. Its dangers are not real disasters, but embarrassment and loss of face. That is why comedy is "light" compared to tragedy, which exhibits an exactly opposite tendency to general exaggeration of issues and personalities.

The same impulse that drove people, even in prehistoric times, to enact fertility rites and celebrate all phases of their biological existence, sustains their eternal interest in comedy. It is in the nature of comedy to be erotic, risqué, and sensuous if not sensual, impious, and even wicked. This assures it a spontaneous emotional interest, yet a dangerous one: for it is easy and tempting to command an audience by direct stimulation of feeling and fantasy, not by artistic power. But where the formulation of feeling is really achieved, it probably reflects the whole development of mankind and man's world, for feeling is the intaglio image of reality. The sense of precariousness that is the typical tension of light comedy was undoubtedly developed in the eternal struggle with chance that every farmer knows only too well— with weather, blights, beasts, birds and beetles. The embarrassments, perplexities and mounting panic which characterize that favorite genre, comedy of manners, may still reflect the toils of ritual and taboo that complicated the caveman's existence. Even the element of aggressiveness in comic action serves to develop a fundamental trait of the comic rhythm—the deep cruelty of it, as all life feeds on life. There is no biological truth that feeling does not reflect, and that good comedy, therefore, will not be prone to reveal.

But the fact that the rhythm of comedy is the

basic rhythm of life does not mean that biological existence is the "deeper meaning" of all its themes, and that to understand the play is to interpret all the characters as symbols and the story as a parable, a disguised rite of spring or fertility magic, performed four hundred and fifty times on Broadway. The stock characters are probably symbolic both in origin and in appeal. /349/ There are such independently symbolic factors, or residues of them, in all the arts,[21] but their value for art lies in the degree to which their significance can be "swallowed" by the single symbol, the art work. Not the derivation of personages and situations, but of the rhythm of "felt life" that the poet puts upon them, seems to me to be of artistic importance: the essential comic feeling, which is the sentient aspect of organic unity, growth, and self-preservation. /350/

[21] E.g., the symbolization of the zodiac in some sacred architecture, of our bodily orientation in the picture plane, or of walking measure, a primitive measure of actual time, in music. But a study of such non-artistic symbolic functions would require a monograph.

IV
Criticism

THE BIRDS

The two critical discussions on *The Birds* reprinted below are the work of two European scholars, Francis M. Cornford and Victor Ehrenberg; they represent the remarkable growth in recent times of interest in and knowledge about the history and literature of the ancient world.

Before the student plunges into these scholarly discussions, he might profitably scan the following few lines from a Chorus of the *Peace* (a play which Aristophanes wrote in 421 B.C.) in which the dramatist has described himself:

> He has scorned from the first to descend and to dip
> Peddling and meddling in private affairs:
> To detect and collect every petty defect
> Of husband and wife and domestical life;
> But intrepid and bold, like Alcides of old,
> When the rest stood aloof, put himself to the proof
> In his country's behoof . . . .

Francis M. Cornford from *The Origin of Attic Comedy*

Francis M. Cornford's *The Origin of Attic Comedy* (London, Edward Arnold, 1914) has been a controversial book for almost fifty years. During his lifetime Professor Cornford, who died in 1943, was continuously identified with Cambridge University, where he was both student and teacher. His many publications dating from 1907 made him outstanding in the field of Ancient Philosophy.

Footnotes in this selection are the editor's.

THE STRUCTURE OF AN ARISTOPHANIC PLAY

Of all the strange characteristics of a play by Aristophanes, the one which most forcibly strikes the modern reader is the *Parabasis* of the Chorus—a long passage which cuts the play in two about half way through its course and completely suspends the action. This passage is almost wholly undramatic. It is delivered by the Chorus and its Leaders, and it normally opens with a farewell to the actors, who leave the stage clear till it is over, and then return to carry on the business of the piece to the end. The Chorus, meanwhile, turn their backs on the scene of action and advance across the orchestra to address the audience directly—the movement from which the *Parabasis* takes its name. The action of the play is thus divided into two parts.

Of these two parts, the first normally consists of the *Prologue*, or exposition scenes; the Entrance of the Chorus (*Parados*); and what is now generally called the *Agon*, a fierce "contest" between the representatives of two parties or principles, which are in effect the hero and villain of the whole piece. In the *Acharnians*, for instance, the conflict is between Peace and War; in the *Lysistrata*, between Man and Woman; in the *Wasps*, between the political ideals of the elder and the younger generation. The victorious principle is usually incarnated in the protagonist or hero of the play. In this contest the interest of the first part centres and culminates.

The second part, after the *Parabasis*, contains the rest of the action. . . . When we compare the plays with one another, it is /2/ soon evident, in the first place, that nearly all of them end with an incident no less canonical than the *Agon*—a festal procession (*Kômos*) and a union which I shall call a "Marriage." . . . But that is not all. We shall also find in almost every play two other standing incidents which fall between the *Agon* and the final *Kômos*—a scene of Sacrifice and a Feast. In several of the earlier plays these form nearly the whole of the action, and fill nearly the whole time of presentation, in the second part. In the later plays, from the *Birds* onwards, plots of a more complicated type are developed, chiefly in this latter half of the play; but still the old sequence of fixed incidents in the old order remains as the substructure of the action: *Agon*, Sacrifice, Feast, Marriage, *Kômos*. Another regularly recurring type of incident is the interruption of the Sacrifice or the Feast, or both, by a series of unwelcome intruders, who are successively put to derision by the protagonist and driven away with blows.

Meanwhile, for the sake of clearness, it will be well to state here the hypothesis we shall offer in explanation of these facts. It is that *this canonical plot-formula preserves the stereotyped action of a ritual or folk-drama, older than literary Comedy, and of a pattern well known to us from other sources.* /3/

THE NEW ZEUS IN THE *Birds*

When Pisthetairos propounds to the Birds his design of founding a new City in the air, he begins with the startling declaration that the Birds were once kings over all, even over Zeus himself; nay, their sovereignty is older than Kronos and the Titans. If they had duly thumbed their Aesop, they would remember that the Lark was the first bird, and, being older than the Earth itself, had nowhere to bury her father, save in her own head. How much more are they older than the gods. ("Zeus," interposes Euelpides, "will soon give back his sceptre to the woodpecker.") After other proofs of the royal powers once enjoyed by the Cock over the Persians, the Hawk over the Greeks, and the Cuckoo over the orientals, Pisthetairos, in the second part of his discourse, tells the Birds how to recover their kingdom. They must fortify the air all around, like Babylon, with baked bricks, and then, if Zeus refuses to abdicate, declare a holy war upon Heaven, debar the Gods from visiting mortal women, and send a herald to mankind to bid them sacrifice first to the Birds, before they offer anything to the Gods. ("Now let Zeus thunder!" interjects Euelpides.) If man will not

respect them, all the seed of his crops will be eaten up by the fieldfares and the eyes of his cattle pecked out. Then let Demeter give them corn, if she can! If mankind is submissive, the Birds will spare their fruits, give them omens, find hidden treasure to enrich them, and bestow on them health and lives as long as the crow's. They will make much better kings than Zeus. The Birds are beside themselves with enthusiasm, and in the *Parabasis* they confirm /21/ these promises. The City is built, and the Gods are starved into making terms.

The final scene shows us Pisthetairos, dressed in his bridal robe, and hailed not only as King of the new city, with the Queen of Heaven for his bride, but also as a new Zeus—a new master of the thunder and fertilising rain. The details here are significant, because the whole passage institutes an elaborate comparison between Pisthetairos and the Olympic victor. This analogy is peculiarly instructive.

We have seen how the appearance of Pisthetairos and his bride, Basileia, is compared by the messenger in words of almost Aeschylean grandeur, to the Sun and Moon shining in all the splendour of their golden rays, and how, in the hymenaeal song that follows, their wedding is likened to the marriage of Zeus and Hera, driven by Eros in a chariot with gold reins. The same conjunction of ideas seems to have been attached to the pair of Olympic victors—the winner of the chariot race and the winner of the Virgins' race at the Heraea. As I have argued elsewhere, this couple, whose prototypes are Pelops and Hippodameia in Pindar's First Olympian Ode, were regarded as periodic representatives of Zeus and Hera, and also as impersonating the Sun and Moon, united in one form of that sacred marriage which was often celebrated at midsummer feasts. Like Pelops and Hippodameia, the Sun and Moon are represented both in art and in literature, though in despite of natural /22/ facts, as driving together in one chariot across the sky. The story of Pelops also preserves the *Agon* between the young king and the old weather and fertility king, Oenomaus, who is slain with his own spear. The Olympic victor, as a new incarnation of Zeus, wields his royal and divine powers of control over the weather. His attributes are worn by Salmoneus, who defied Zeus and essayed to mimic the sky-god's thunder. So, in the *Birds*, Pisthetairos comes "brandishing the thunderbolt, the winged shaft of Zeus" while all the circle of the sky is filled with the smoke of incense.

For we have already been told that Basileia, like Athena in Aeschylus, has the keys of her father's thunder, with which go all the attributes of the Heaven-father. When the Chorus are bidden, after their hymenaeal song, to celebrate "the thunders underground and the fiery lightnings of Zeus and the dread flashing thunderbolt," they break out into a song which declares that Pisthetairos is now "master of everything that belongs to Zeus": it is he who now will shake the earth with rumbling thunders that bring the rain. He is not merely *like* Zeus, but, transfigured in the beauty of his renewed youth, he is a new Zeus, a new lord of the thunders and dispenser of the fertilising rain. He demands to be escorted to "the floor of Zeus and his bridal bed."

The whole point is summed up in the last words of the *Exodos*: "Hurrah for the victor! O Highest of the Gods"—Pisthetairos, leading the procession of the Chorus, as the Olympic /23/ victor led the *Kômos* of his friends in the evening celebration, is hailed in the words of the Song of Archilochos, consecrated to that occasion. We have noted already that the same song seems to have served for the *Exodos* of the *Acharnians*, and perhaps also of the *Knights*. When we remember that the protagonist who is fêted in the torchlit *Kômos* of Comedy, is normally also the victor in the *Agon* at the beginning of the play, we may suspect something more than a superficial analogy between the programme of ritual action which we suppose to underlie the comic plot, and the programme of the great panhellenic festival.

THE SACRED MARRIAGE OF DIONYSUS AND THE QUEEN AT ATHENS

The identity of Pisthetairos' bride, Basileia, has been much debated. Whoever she may be, she is certainly the partner in a sacred marriage and her husband is a God. She is a "Queen" and her husband is a new King. Mr. J. T. Sheppard has pointed out that the last scene of the *Birds* could not fail to recall to the Athenian spectator the sacred marriage of Dionysus to the Queen, the wife of the King Archon, which was annually celebrated, perhaps at the Anthesteria. "Whatever the date of the wedding," says Dr. Frazer,[1] "its object can hardly have been any other than that of ensuring the fertility of the vines and other /24/ fruit-trees, of which Dionysus was the god. Thus both in form and in meaning the ceremony would answer to the nuptials of the King and Queen of May." It is not, of course, necessary to suppose an exclusive reference to this ceremony; the secular rite of marriage between Zeus and Hera is also clearly referred to, and, as we have argued above, probably the marriage of the pair of Olympic victors. What is important to our argument is the indisputable fact that the yearly ritual of Dionysus at Athens included precisely that rite which we have supposed to be the basis of the canonical *Exodos* of Aristophanes' plays. /25/

[1] Sir James George Frazer (1854-1941), anthropologist, historian, and critic. His best known study was the multivolumed work, *The Golden Bough*, first published in 1890 and subsequently much expanded, subtitled "A Study in Comparative Religion," and later "A Study in Magic and Religion." The influence of this great and impressive piece of research on modern literature is incalculable.

Victor Ehrenberg # from *The People of Aristophanes*

Victor Ehrenberg's discussion of *The Birds* relates the play to contemporary events and is taken from the same work from which "The Poet and His Audience" in Part II was drawn (see headnote, p. 175).

Footnotes in this selection are by the editor.

. . . the *Birds* of Aristophanes, however it may be interpreted in relation to contemporary events, is an escape from reality into the least material of all regions, the air, the realm of the birds, and at the same time the realm of pure poetry. Hence, to discover what is relevant to the inner meaning of this comedy two questions must be discussed: why

the two Athenian citizens who are the principal figures in the plot have left their home, and what sort of superiority the new Birds' City has over the earthly Polis.

Of the two Athenians the one, Euelpides, "the man of good hope," is a typical good-natured citizen. His only part in the play is to act as interlocutor to the ingenious creator of Cloudcuckooland, whose name and character we may assume to have been "the persuasive friend" (Peithetairos) rather than "the reliable friend" (Pisthetairos). Though both are "citizens among citizens" and respectable men of mature age, they have left Athens not because of any hatred of it, but because they are completely disgusted with the prevailing mania for litigation. It appears, however, to be a case of putting *pars pro toto*.[1] The two men are in search of a *polis apragmon*, a city where one can stretch one's limbs on soft cushions and live one's own quiet and private life. The emigrants wish to be free of their debts; but their chief concern is to find a place free of politics where food and love are of paramount importance. They have had enough of the endless difficulties, of the troubles and violence of life at Athens, dominated by politics. Their desire, then, is not to escape from democracy, and their adherence to tribe and clan does not involve any oligarchic or even conservative /57/ tendency. Euelpides denies explicitly that he is looking for an aristocratic State. They are not anxious to avoid war and danger, they do not even mention them. Nor are they fleeing from the irreligion of the new age: there is no allusion to the Hermocopids[2] or the profanation of the mysteries. Yet, all these troubles derive from the same world from which they try to escape, the restless and joyless, even malignant, atmosphere of the Athenian law-courts and Athenian politics. Aristophanes' old ideal of peace has not changed, but there seems now no chance left of realizing it on earth. The result, born of a general sense of estrangement from the State, is the flight of the two old men, and therefore of the poet. This poetical and fanciful escape is the victory of the unpolitical man.

Of course, like will stick to like, and the Athenian to politics. The escape from the State is succeeded by the foundation of a new State. The goal, the achievement of non-political life, is to be approached only by the path of true politics. When the new Polis is built in imagination, Euelpides thinks of nothing beyond the money he will be able to make out of it; Peithetairos, however, stands above this level which we can easily believe to be the general and natural level of the Athenian middle-class. Peithetairos is a born leader. He continues a tradition which, in Aristophanes' plays, has hardly any connection with the real statesmen of the past, and which has certainly no representative in the poet's time, a tradition which

perhaps goes only back to Agorakritos[3] in the last scenes of the *Knights*. It is a type of leadership which could hardly be found outside comedy, and which the poet could not have created without himself being guided by the spirit of sophistic individualism, and without doing a certain injustice at least to the politicians of the "good old times." Peithetairos is rewarded by receiving as his prize Basileia, the daughter of Zeus and embodiment of all political virtue. She does not make an ordinary monarch out of the cunning bourgeois. In a fairytale myth the marriage /58/ crowns the picture of an ascent that is tied to no reality, and gives to the ruler the full dignity and grace, the *charisma*, that is the right of his position.

Yet in spite of its fabulous character the "ideal Polis," this fantasy-city Cloudcuckooland, shows some connection with reality—at least negatively, in the nature of the people driven away from it by Peithetairos. First come persons who usually appeared when a new Athenian colony was to be founded, a priest and a poet, that is to say, a beggarpriest and an opportunist poet, followed by an oracle-monger and the mathematician Meton, here a town-planning architect, likewise a quack and an impostor. After Meton comes an "inspector" (one of the officials elected by lot) and a "decree-seller." The priest and poet, Peithetairos dismisses with words, to the poet he even gives some clothes: the others, however, he drives from the stage with whips, convinced that all those who try to make money as sophists or by profiting from, and corrupting, politics are impostors. This impression is confirmed by a second scene which shows the would-be members of the new city. The first to appear is one of those unpleasant youths who beat their fathers and drain their resources. Peithetairos makes a soldier of him, that is to say, turns him into a useful citizen. On the other hand, the well-known poet Kinesias is treated like the sycophant and whipped. The principle underlying this representation of the founder of a State as one who is always ready to use the lash is moral, not political. It is exemplified again in the fact that democracy is not renounced in Cloudcuckooland, nor are democratic institutions; only those who make a selfish profit out of them are repudiated. The inclusion of Meton amongst the impostors is, of course, to be attributed to the same attitude of mind in the poet which made him

---

[1] A part for the whole.

[2] The mysterious and sacrilegious mutilation of the Hermae (pillars, originally small piles of stones, set up at street corners and at doors of houses, used initially to mark boundaries but later having religious significance) on the eve of the Sicilian expedition (415 B. C.) created alarm and indignation in Athens.

[3] Literally "The Choice of the Agora" (the assembly of citizens). In Aristophanes' play, *The Knights* (424 B. C.), he is the character who overcomes Cleon to become the reformer and savior of the State.

depict Socrates as a mere sophist and an observer of the stars. Although Aristophanes' chief aim was to make fun of anyone who in one way or another was different from the average, it is hardly rash to conclude from his emphasis on the money point that to him intellectual pursuits were as wicked a source of economic gain as politics. The greater his contempt for sophists and sycophants, the more fervently must he have believed in the worth of those who earned their living as farmers, crafts-men, or merchants. He does not name them here, but together with the defenders of the State (who of /59/ course come first) they are its true pillars. Significantly enough, Peithetairos sends his *alter ego*, his comrade Euelpides, to take part in the building of the wall, and to supervise workmen and guards. Disinterested service to the community and a life spent in real work, those are the forces that maintain the State. /60/

TWELFTH NIGHT

Joseph H. Summers The Masks of *Twelfth Night*

Joseph H. Summers, a native of Kentucky who received his doctorate at Harvard, now teaches English literature at Washington University, St. Louis. He has taught previously at the University of Connecticut and was, in 1952–53, in Italy on a fellowship from The Fund for the Advancement of Learning. He has published both in the field of the Renaissance and in that of modern literature. His essay on *Twelfth Night* is reprinted from *The University of Kansas City Review* (Vol. 22, Autumn, 1955).

Love and its fulfillment are primary in Shakespeare's comedies. Its conflicts are often presented in terms of the battle of the generations. At the beginning of the plays the bliss of the young lovers is usually barred by an older generation of parents and rulers, a group which has supposedly experienced its own fulfillment in the past and which is now concerned with preserving old forms or fulfilling new ambitions. The comedies usually end with the triumph of young love, a triumph in which the lovers make peace with their elders and themselves assume adulthood and often power. The revolutionary force of love becomes an added element of vitality in a re-established society.

Twelfth Night does not follow the customary pattern. In this play the responsible older generation has been abolished, and there are no parents at all. In the first act we are rapidly introduced into a world in which the ruler is a love-sick Duke—in which young ladies, fatherless and motherless, embark on disguised actions, or rule, after a fashion, their own households, and in which the only individuals possibly over thirty are drunkards, jokesters, and gulls, totally without authority. All the external barriers to fulfillment have been eliminated in what becomes almost a parody of the state desired by the ordinary young lovers, the Hermias and Lysanders—or even the Rosalinds and Orlandos. According to the strictly romantic formula, the happy ending should be already achieved at the beginning of the play: we should abandon the theater for the rites of love. But the slightly stunned inhabitants of Illyria discover that they are anything but free. Their own actions provide the barriers, for most of them know neither themselves, nor others, nor their social world.

For his festival entertainment, Shakespeare freshly organized all the usual material of the romances—the twins, the exile, the impersonations—to provide significant movement for a dance of maskers. Every character has his mask, for the assumption of the play is that no one is without a mask in the serio-comic business of the pursuit of happiness. The character without disguises who is not ridiculous is outside the realm of comedy. Within comedy, the character who thinks it is possible to live without assuming a mask is merely too naive to recognize the mask he has already assumed. He is the chief object of laughter. As a general rule, we laugh with the characters who know the role they are playing and we laugh at those who do not; we can crudely divide the cast of *Twelfth Night* into those two categories.

But matters are more complicated than this, and roles have a way of /25/ shifting. All the butts except perhaps Sir Andrew Aguecheek have moments in which they are the masters of our laughter; yet all the masters have moments in which they appear as fools. In our proper confusion, we must remember the alternative title of the play, "What You Will." It may indicate that everyone is free to invent his own title for the proceedings. It also tells the author's intention to fulfill our desires: we wish to share in the triumphs of love and we wish to laugh; we wish our fools occasionally to be wise, and we are insistent that our wisest dramatic figures experience our common fallibility. Most significantly, the title may hint that what "we" collectively "will" creates all the comic masks—that society determines the forms of comedy more directly than it determines those of any other literary genre.

At the opening of the play Orsino and Olivia accept the aristocratic (and literary) ideas of the romantic lover and the grief-stricken lady as realities rather than as ideas. They are comic characters exactly because of that confusion. Orsino glories in the proper moodiness and fickleness of the literary lover; only our own romanticism can blind us to the absurdities in his opening speech. Orsino first wishes the music to continue so that the appetite of love may "surfeit"; immediately, however, he demands that the musicians stop the music they are playing to repeat an isolated phrase—an awkward procedure and a comic bit of stage business which is rarely utilized in productions. Four lines later the music must stop entirely because the repeated "strain" no longer *is* sweet, and the appetite is truly about to "surfeit." He then exclaims that the spirit of love is so "quick and fresh" that like the sea (hardly a model of freshness)

> naught enters there,
> Of what validity and pitch soe'er,
> But falls into abatement and low price,
> Even in a minute!

Orsino is a victim of a type of madness to which the most admirable characters are sometimes subject Its usual causes are boredom, lack of physical love, and excessive imagination, and the victim is unaware that he is in love with love rather than with a person.

In the same scene, before we ever see the lady, Olivia's state is as nicely defined. Valentine, Orsino's messenger, has acquired something of his master's extraordinary language, and his report on his love mission manages both to please the Duke and to convey his own incredulity at the excess of Olivia's vow for her brother. In his speech the fresh and the salt are again confused. It is impossible to keep fresh something so ephemeral as grief; Olivia can make it last and "season" it, however, by the process of pickling—the natural effect of "eye-offending brine." Orsino feels unbounded admiration for the depth of soul indicated by Olivia's vow and at the same time he assumes that the vow can easily be broken by a lover. He departs for "sweet *beds* of flow'rs" which are somehow to provide a *canopy* for "love-thoughts."

Both Orsino and Olivia have adopted currently fashionable literary postures; yet neither of them is a fool. We are glad to be reassured by the Captain that Orsino is "A noble duke, in nature as in name," and that his present infatuation is /26/ only a month old. Sir Toby's later remark "What a plague means my niece, to take the death of her brother thus?" indicates that Olivia too had seemed an unlikely candidate for affectation. She is also an unconvincing practitioner. Although at our first glimpse of her she is properly the grief-stricken lady ("Take the fool away"), her propriety collapses under Feste's famous catechism. We discover that Olivia is already bored and that she really desires to love. Outraged nature has its full and comic revenge when Olivia falls passionately in love with a male exterior and acts with an aggressiveness which makes Orsino seem almost feminine. Still properly an actor in comedy, Olivia quickly changes from the character who has confused herself with a socially attractive mask to one who fails to perceive the mask which society has imposed on another.

Viola's situation allows time for neither love nor grief-in-idleness. A virgin, shipwrecked in a strange land, possessing only wit and intelligence and the Captain's friendship, she must act immediately if she is to preserve herself. She, like Olivia, has "lost" a brother, but the luxury of conventional mourning is quickly exchanged for a *willed* hope that, as she was saved, "so perchance may he be." With Viola's wish for time to know what her "estate is," before she is "delivered to the world," we are reminded that society often requires a mask, neither for the relief of boredom nor the enjoyment of acting, but merely for self-preservation. While Antonio, "friend to Sebastian," almost loses his life because of his failure to assume a disguise, Viola suffers from no failure of discretion or imagination. She must assume a disguise as a boy and she must have help in preparing it.

Although she knows the ways of the world, Viola takes the necessary chance and wills to trust the Captain:

> There is a fair behavior in thee, Captain.
> And though that Nature with a beauteous wall
> Doth oft close in pollution, yet of thee
> I will believe thou hast a mind that suits
> With this thy fair and outward character.

We have in this second scene not only the beginning of one strand of the complicated intrigue, but also the creation of the one character active in the intrigue who provides a measure for the comic excesses of all the others. (Feste's role as observer is analogous to Viola's role as "actor.") Although Viola chooses to impersonate Cesario from necessity, she later plays her part with undisguised enjoyment. She misses none of the opportunities for parody, for confession, and for *double entendre* which the mask affords, and she never forgets or lets us forget the biological distance between Viola and Cesario. Except in the fencing match with Sir Andrew Aguecheek, she anticipates and directs our perception of the ludicrous in her own role as well as in the roles of Orsino and Olivia.

Sebastian is the reality of which Cesario is the artful imitation. Viola's twin assumes no disguise; Viola and the inhabitants of Illyria have assumed it for him. He is, to the eye, identical with Viola, and his early scenes with Antonio serve to remind us firmly of his existence as well as to introduce an initial exhil-/27/arating confusion at the entrance of either of the twins. When he truly enters the action of the play in Act IV he is certainly the object of our laughter, not because he has confused himself with an ideal or improper mask, but because he so righteously and ineffectually insists on his own identity in the face of unanimous public opposition. Our attitude quickly changes, however, to a mixture of amused patronization and identification: we do, after all, *know* so much more than does Sebastian; yet, within the context of the play, we can hardly keep from identifying with the gentleman who, practically if not idealistically, decides not to reject the reality of a passionate Olivia just because he has never seen her before:

> Or I am mad, or else this is a dream.
> Let fancy still my sense in Lethe steep.
> If it be thus to dream, still let me sleep!

The other characters in the play do not truly belong to an aristocracy of taste and leisure. For some of them, that is the chief problem. Malvolio and Sir Andrew Aguecheek are ruled by their mistaken notions of the proper role of an upper-class gentleman, and they fail to perceive the comic gaps between themselves and their ideal roles, and

between those ideals and the social reality. Sick with self-love as he is, Malvolio is also sick with his desire to rise in society: "an affectioned ass, that cons state without book and utters it by great swaths: the best persuaded of himself, so crammed, as he thinks, with excellencies, that it is his grounds of faith that all that look on him love him." Although he knows it without, he has learned his "state" by book—but such a pupil inevitably distorts the text. He dreams of ruling a thrifty and solemn household while he plays with "some rich jewel," a dream characteristically attractive to the *arriviste* and absolutely impossible to the *arrivé*. We, like Maria, "can hardly forbear hurling things at him." His is as absurd as the reverse image which possesses Sir Andrew, a carpet-knight rightly described by Sir Toby as "an ass-head and a coxcomb and a knave, a thin-faced knave, a gull!" In the gallery of false images Sir Andrew's roaring boy hangs opposite Malvolio's burgher. Although in a low moment Sir Andrew may think that he has "no more wit than a Christian or an ordinary man has," he never has such grave self-doubt for long. Like a true gull, he tries to assume the particular role which, of all others, he is most poorly equipped to play: drinker, fighter, wencher.

Sir Andrew, however, would hardly exist without Sir Toby Belch: the gull must have his guller. Sir Toby may fulfill Sir Andrew's idea of what a gentleman should be, but Sir Toby himself has no such odd idea of gentility. (Sir Andrew may be "a dear manikin to you, Sir Toby," but Sir Toby has a superlatively good reason for allowing him to be: "I have been dear to him, lad, some two thousand strong, or so.") Even at his most drunken, we are delightfully unsure whether we laugh at or with Sir Toby, whether he is or is not fully conscious of the effects as well as the causes of his "mistakes," his verbal confusions, and even his belches. Like another drunken knight, and like Viola, Toby possesses a range of dramatic talents and he enjoys using /28/ them. He is equally effective as the fearless man of action, as the practitioner of noble "gentleness" with the "mad" Malvolio, and as the experienced alcoholic guide to Sir Andrew. His joy is in the jest as well as in the bottle, and he can bring himself to abandon the latter long enough to marry Maria simply in admiration for her ability as an intriguer. But like other knowing players, Sir Toby is vulnerable to deception. He is object rather than master of our laughter from the time when he mistakes Sebastian for Cesario and attempts to assert his masculine ability as a swordsman.

In the business of masking, Feste is the one professional among a crowd of amateurs; he does it for a living. He never makes the amateur's mistake of confusing his personality with his mask—he wears not motley in his brain. Viola recognizes his wisdom and some kinship in the fact that each "must observe their mood on whom he jests." But though Feste may have deliberately chosen his role, society determines its conditions. Now that he is growing old, the conditions become difficult: "Go to, you're a dry fool, I'll no more of you. Besides, you grow dishonest." While all the other characters are concerned with gaining something they do not have, Feste's struggle is to retain his mask and to make it again ingratiating. He is able to penetrate all the masks of the others, and he succeeds in retaining his own.

However fanciful its dreams of desire, the play moves within a context of an almost real world, from one disguise and half-understood intrigue to another, until all its elements are whirled into a complexly related and moving figure. With the constant contrasts and parallels and reversals in character, situation, and intrigue, we find ourselves at last, along with Malvolio and Olivia and Viola and the rest, in a state of real delirium. Until the concluding scene, however, we can largely agree with Sebastian: if we dream, we do not wish to wake; if this is madness, it is still comic madness, and we do not envy the sane. The attempts at false and inflexible authority are being defeated, the pretentious are being deflated, and the very sentimentality of the likable sentimentalists has led them close to biological reality. We are particularly delighted with Viola. Young, intelligent, zestful, she is a realist. She cuts through the subterfuges and disguises of the others with absolute clarity, and she provides us with a center for the movement, a standard of normality which is never dull. In her rejection of the artificial myths of love, moreover, Viola never becomes the advocate of a far more terrifying myth, the myth of absolute rationality. In a completely rational world, Shakespeare never tires of pointing out, what we know as love could not exist. We have never desired such a world.

From the time of her first aside to the audience after she has seen Orsino ("Yet a barful strife!/ Whoe'er I woo, myself would be his wife"), Viola directly admits her irrational love. She differs, then, from Orsino and Olivia not in any invulnerability to blindness and passion, but in the clarity and simplicity with which she recognizes and accepts her state. Reason is not abandoned: she rationally admits her irrationality and her /29/ inability to cope with the situation:

> O Time, thou must untangle this, not I!
> It is too hard a knot for me to untie!

Viola needs a miracle. Although she may imagine herself as "Patience on a monument, smiling at grief," she remains as close as possible to her loved one and waits for the miracle to happen. Since we have seen Sebastian, we know that the miracle will occur; yet through our identification with Viola we come to know the comic burden, the masker's increasing weariness of the mask which implies that love is still pursued rather than possessed.

The burden becomes comically unbearable only in the final scene, when it is cast off. Here Shakespeare underscores all those possibilities of violence and death which are usually submerged in comedy. Antonio is arrested and in danger of his life. Orsino, finally recognizing the hopelessness of his suit to Olivia, shows the vicious side of sentimentality. After considering the possibility of killing Olivia "like to the Egyptian thief," he determines to do violence to "Cesario":

> Come, boy, with me. My thoughts are ripe in mischief.
> I'll sacrifice the lamb that I do love,
> To spite a raven's heart within a dove.

Olivia is hysterical at what seems to be the baseness of Cesario. Sir Toby has a broken pate to show for his one major failure to penetrate a mask. The dance must stop. The miracle must occur.

The entrance of Sebastian is "what we will." It is the most dramatic moment of the play. The confrontation of Sebastian and Cesario-Viola, those identical images, concludes the formal plot and provides the means for the discarding of all the lovers' masks. The moment must be savored and fully realized. As Viola and Sebastian chant their traditional formulas of proof, both the audience and the other characters on the stage undistractedly view the physical image of the duality which has made the confusion and the play. The masks and the play are to be abandoned for a vision of delight beyond delight, in which lovers have neither to wear nor to penetrate disguises since they are at last invulnerable to error and laughter.

Yet the play does not resolve into a magic blessing of the world's fertility as does A Midsummer Night's Dream. We have been promised a happy ending, and we receive it. We are grateful that the proper Jacks and Jills have found each other, but the miracle is a limited miracle, available only to the young and the lucky. Not every Jack has his Jill even in Illyria, and after the general unmasking, those without love may seem even lonelier. Malvolio, of course, is justly punished. He has earned his mad scene, and with the aid of Feste he has made it comic. As a result of his humiliation he has also earned some sort of redress. Yet he is ridiculous in his arrogance to the end, and his threatened revenge, now that he is powerless to effect it, sustains the comedy and the characterization and prevents the obtrusion of destructive pathos.

It is Feste rather than Malvolio who finally reminds us of the limitations and the costs of the romantic vision of happiness with which we have been seduced. However bur-/30/densome, masking is his career, and romantic love provides no end for it. Alone on the stage at the end of the play, he sings a song of unfulfilled love which shows the other side of the coin. For Feste, as for his audience, the mask can never be finally discarded: the rain it raineth every day. His song has those overtones, I believe, but they are only overtones. The music, here and elsewhere in the play, provides an element in which oppositions may be resolved. And the song itself, like the movement which must accompany it, is crude and witty as well as graceful and nostalgic. However far it may have missed the conventionally happy ending, Feste's saga of misfortunes in love is comic, even from his own point of view. The exaggeration so often operative in the refrains of Elizabethan lyrics emphasizes that the watery as well as the sunny vision can become funny: it doesn't rain every day by a long shot.

The song, which begins as the wittiest observer's comment on the denouement of the play, ends as a dissolution of the dramatic fiction:

> A great while ago the world begun,
>   With hey, ho, the wind and the rain,
> But that's all one, our play is done,
>   And we'll strive to please you every day.

The audience has been a participant in the festivity. As the fictional lovers have unmasked to reveal or realize their "true" identities, it is only proper that the clown, the only character who might move freely in the environs of Bankside, as well as in the realm of Illyria, should unmask the whole proceeding for the imitation of a desired world which it has been. The audience must be returned from "What You Will" to its own less patterned world where the sea rarely disgorges siblings given up for lost, where mistaken marriages rarely turn out well, where Violas rarely catch Dukes, and where Malvolios too often rule households with disturbing propriety. The lovers have met, and Feste announces that present laughter has come to an end. But the actors, those true and untiring maskers, will continue to "strive to please" us. They will find few occasions in the future in which their efforts will be more sure of success.

Twelfth Night is the climax of Shakespeare's early achievement in comedy. The effects and values of the earlier comedies are here subtly embodied in the most complex structure which Shakespeare had yet created. But the play also looks forward: the pressure to dissolve the comedy, to realize and finally abandon the burden of laughter, is an intrinsic part of its "perfection." Viola's clear-eyed and affirmative vision of her own and the world's irrationality is a triumph and we desire it; yet we realize its vulnerability, and we come to realize that virtue in disguise is only totally triumphant when evil is not in disguise— is not truly present at all. Having solved magnificently the problems of this particular form of comedy, Shakespeare was evidently not tempted to repeat his triumph. After *Twelfth Night* the so-called comedies require for their happy resolutions more radical characters and devices—omniscient and omnipresent Dukes, magic, and resurrection. /31/ More obvious miracles are needed for comedy to exist in a world in which evil also exists, not merely incipiently but with power. /32/

Jean-Jacques Rousseau

M. Rousseau to M. D'Alembert

The two essays on *The Misanthrope* present widely divergent attitudes toward the play. Rousseau's attack is famous, both for its rhetorical brilliance and its revelation of the great man's attitude toward the stage. His strictures on *The Misanthrope* are part of a long essay, *A Letter to M. D'Alembert on the Theatre;* the letter was inspired by D'Alembert's article on "Geneva" (Rousseau's "home-town") in *L'Encyclopédie* (seventh edition, 1757), where D'Alembert, with Voltaire's connivance, suggested that the city needed a theatre. Rousseau, replying to the distinguished member of seven academies merely as J.-J. Rousseau, citizen, wrote immediately and vigorously. His reply was first printed in 1758, and was revised many times. The text reprinted here is from the first English translation (London: Printed for J. Nourse at the Lamb opposite Katherine-Street in the Strand. 1759). Some minor changes and a few modernizations, particularly of the punctuation, have been made by the editor, but in general the eighteenth-century tone has been allowed to stand.

In both this essay and the next one by Turnell, whenever there are direct quotes from Molière's French text, the editor has inserted lines from Richard Wilbur's translation of *The Misanthrope*.

. . . It is agreed on all hands, and daily experience convinces us, that among the various writers of comedy, whose works have come down to us, Molière is the most perfect; and yet who can deny that the plays of this very writer, whose abilities no man admires more than myself, are a school of vice and corruption, more dangerous than the very books where vice is professedly taught? His chief concern is to turn goodness and simplicity into ridicule; and to represent characters, whose interest we are to espouse, as men of craft and deceit: his honest people are honest only in words; his knaves are such in their actions and are often crowned with the most signal success; in short, applause is an honor seldom bestowed on persons of the greatest worth, but almost always on those of the most craftiness.

Examine this author's talent of ridicule and you will find that vice is its instrument, and natural defects are its subject; that the malice of the one punishes the simplicity of the other, and that fools are the victims of knaves; which, for being /38/ but

too true in common life, ought not to be acted on the stage with an air of approbation, as if he encouraged knaves to punish the simplicity of honest men in the name of folly.

Dat veniam corvis, vexat censura columbas.[1]

Such is the general tendency of Molière and all his imitators. The most that can be said of them is that they sometimes ridicule vice, but without ever making us fall in love with virtue; they resemble those people, says an ancient writer, who know how to snuff a lamp, but never fill it with oil.

Do but see in what manner this man, to indulge his vein of pleasantry, inverts the whole order of society; how scandalously he strikes at even the most sacred ties on which it is founded; how he derides the valuable rights of fathers over their children, of husbands over the wives, and of masters over their servants! He makes us laugh, it is true; but he only incurs a greater guilt, in compelling even philosophers themselves, by an invincible charm, to countenance such raillery as merits their indignation. I know it is said that he combats vice, but I should like you to compare the vices he combats with those he encourages. Which is the worst character of the two, a vain stupid citizen who acts the fine gentleman, or the knavish gentleman who defrauds him? And yet in the play we have been speaking of,[2] is not the latter the chief character? Does not he interest the audience in his favor? And does not the public applaud the several tricks he plays up-/39/on the other? Who is the most criminal, a peasant so foolish as to marry a lady, or a wife who seeks to dishonor her marriage bed? What are we to think of a play where the audience applauds the infidelity, the deceit, and the impudence of the latter and laughs at the stupidity of the clown? I own it is a great vice to be avaricious and to lend money out at usury, but is it not a much greater for a son to rob his father, to behave disrespectfully to him, to reproach and insult him a thousand times; and when the father is so provoked as to

[1] "Censure is indulgent to crows, hard on pigeons" (Juvenal, *Satires*, II, 63).

[2] *Le Bourgeois Gentilhomme.*

give him curse, to answer then with a sneer that he will have nothing to do with his father's presents? If the jokes are pleasing, are they the less evil? And if the play makes you fond of the son, who cracks those jokes, does this make it less a school of immorality?

I shall not spend time in examining his valets: they are condemned by all the world,[3] and it would be unfair to charge Molière with the errors of the times he lived in, or of those he imitates, since he corrected them himself. Let us not take advantage of the irregularities, which we may find /40/ in his youthful pieces, nor of those passages which are less perfect in his other plays; but let us skip at once to that, which by all voices is allowed to be his masterpiece, the *Misanthrope*.

I find that of all Molière's comedies, this gives us the best insight into the aims with which he wrote for the stage; and best enables us to judge of the real effects of his writings. As he had the public to please, he consulted the general taste of those who compose it: on this taste he formed a plan, and according to this he drew a sketch of contrary failings, from which he developed his comic characters, and interspersed the different ones among his plays. His intent, therefore, was not to draw an honest man but a man of the world; consequently, he did not want to correct vice, but folly and, as I observed already, he found vice a proper instrument for effecting his design. Therefore being determined to expose to public derision the several defects opposite to the qualifications of an agreeable or sociable person, after having exposed so many other subjects of ridicule, there remained only to try his talent on that form of the ridiculous which the world least of all forgives, that of virtue; this is what he has done in the *Misanthrope*.

Two things there are which you cannot deny: one, that the character of Alceste in this play is that of a fair, open and in short truly honest man; the other, that the poet makes him a subject of ridicule. This, in my opinion, is sufficient to condemn Molière. O, say you, the object of his /41/ raillery is not Alceste's virtue, but a real failing, misanthropy, or aversion to mankind. But it is not true that Alceste has any such aversion. Let

not the name of misanthrope impose on the world, as if the person who bore it were an enemy to the human race. Such an aversion would not be a foible or defect, but natural depravity and the greatest of vices. Since all social virtues relate back to benevolence, nothing can be so diametrically contrary to them as inhumanity. The real misanthrope is a monster: could he exist, he would not excite our laughter, but strike us with horror.

What sort of a misanthrope then is Molière's? An honest man who detests the corrupt manners [morals] of his age, and the iniquity of his contemporaries; who, merely because he loves his fellow creatures, hates the mischief which they do to one another and the vices from which this mischief arises. Were he less affected with the failings of humanity, less incensed at the iniquities he daily sees, would he be more humane himself? As well might you pretend that a fond father loves another man's children better than his own because he is vexed at the faults of the latter and is silent in regard to those of the former.

These notions of the misanthrope are perfectly explained in the course of the play. He says, I acknowledge, that he has conceived an immortal ha-/42/tred against mankind, but on what accasion does he say it?[4] Just at the time when provoked to see his friend basely betraying his conscience, deceiving the man who asks him his opinion, he finds this friend making fun of him in the midst of his anger. It is natural that this anger should rise to the very height of passion and make him say more than he would in cold blood. Besides, the reason he gives for this universal hatred is very just:

Some men I hate for being rogues; the others
I hate because they treat the rogues like brothers.

It is not then that he is an enemy to mankind, but to the viciousness of some and to the encouragement which this viciousness receives from others. Were there to be neither knaves nor sycophants, he would love all the world. Every honest man is a misanthrope in this sense, or rather the real misanthropes are those who do not think thus; for upon the whole I do not know a greater enemy to society than the man who is everybody's friend,

[3] I will not take upon me to say whether we ought really to condemn them. Perhaps the valets are no more than the tools of their wicked masters, since the latter have deprived them of the honor of inventiveness. Yet I question whether too natural a picture of society be proper for the stage. Suppose there was a necessity for some knavish tricks in a play, I wonder whether it would not be better that the valets only were charged with performing them and that honest people should still be honest, at least upon the stage. [Rousseau's note]

[4] I must acquaint the reader that having no books or papers by me, and all my materials consisting of a confused remembrance of the remarks which I formerly made at the playhouse, I may be mistaken in my quotations and invert the order of the plays. But even if my examples are not exact, this would not hinder my reasons from being just, since they are not drawn from this or that particular play, but from the general spirit of the stage, which I have thoroughly studied. [Rousseau's note]

who is pleased with everything, so as /43/ to give constant encouragement to knaves and to flatter those vices from which every ill arises in society.

A strong proof that Alceste is not a misanthrope in the literal sense is this: with all his bluntness and grumbling, still he engages and pleases the audience. The spectators, indeed, would not choose to resemble him because so much uprightness is very troublesome. But there is not one of them all that would be sorry to have dealings with a man of his character which could never be the case were he a declared enemy of mankind. In the rest of Molière's plays, the ridiculous person is generally odious or contemptible; here, although Alceste has real foibles which we may innocently laugh at, yet in the bottom of our hearts we feel such respect for him as is not in our power to stifle. On this occasion the force of virtue prevails over the poet's art and does honor to his character. Though Molière wrote some plays deserving of censure, yet he himself was an honest man, but never did the pencil of an honest man disguise the features of justice and sincerity in such odious colors. Further, Molière has put such a number of his own maxims into the mouth of Alceste, that a great many people are of the opinion that he intended to draw his own picture. This appeared from the concern the audience was in the first night, for not being of the misanthrope's opinion in regard to the sonnet; it was very plain the poet thought as did Alceste.

And yet this good, this virtuous character is represented as a subject of ridicule and such he is /44/ indeed in some respects, but what shows that the poet's aim is to render him ridiculous is the character of his friend, Philinte, which he contrasts with that of Alceste. This Philinte is the sage of the play, one of those honest men in high life, whose maxims greatly resemble those of knaves, one of those mild, those moderate persons who are sure to tell you that things go well because their interest is they should not go better, who are content with everybody because they care for nobody, who, around a plentiful table, maintain it is false that poor people are starving, who, with their pockets well lined, find fault with preaching in favor of the poor, who, when their own house is secure, would not make the least stir, if the whole world besides were ransacked, murdered and destroyed, because God has blessed them with an eminent degree of patience to bear the misfortunes of other people.

It is obvious that so calm a reasoner as Philinte is a very fit person to work up the other into a ridiculous excess of passion and Molière's fault is not for having made the misanthrope a choleric man but for making him break out into childish fits on points that ought not to move him. The character of the misanthrope is not at the poet's disposal; his predominant passion determines it. This is a violent hatred of vice, owing to an ardent love of virtue and irritated by the continual sight of human iniquity. None, therefore, but a great and noble soul is capable of it. The horror and contempt which this same passion encourages against those very vices by which it was aroused /45/ serves to exclude these vices from that person's breast. Besides, this constant contemplation of the vices of society detaches him from himself, to fix his whole attention upon mankind. This habit raises and ennobles his ideas while it destroys all those base inclinations which strengthen self-love, while the soul disdains to amuse itself with sentiments unbecoming its dignity.

Not but that man is always man, but that his passion oftentimes renders him weak, unjust and unreasonable; but that he spies out the hidden motives of other people's actions with a secret pleasure at seeing the corruption of their hearts; but that a trifling evil will frequently throw him into a great passion and an artful knave will be able by frequent provocation to make him pass for one as bad as himself. However it is still true that all means are not proper to produce these effects and that they ought to be suited to his character before he can be brought into action; otherwise, it would be substituting another person instead of the misanthrope and representing him with features not his own.

Here we see the tendency of those foibles for which the misanthrope's character is distinguished and what an excellent use Molière makes of this in the several scenes between Alceste and his friend where the quaint sentences and the raillery of the latter disconcert the former every instant and make him say a thousand fooleries which are extremely well placed. But this same morose character which fills him with so much acrimony /46/ and gall should prevent him at the same time from falling into a childish, groundless passion or from having any strong personal prejudice to which he ought by no means to be subject. Let him rail against the several vices which he sees prevail, this will only add a few new features to the portrait; but let him be cool in regard to that which is levelled at himself. For, having declared war against all villains, he must expect that they will declare it against him in their turn. Had he not foreseen the mischief which his freedom will do him, it would be stupidity and not a virtue. Let a wanton wife dishonor his bed, let traitors betray him, his false friends forsake him, he ought to bear it without repining. He knows mankind.

Should these distinctions be just, Molière has not hit off the misanthrope. Do you imagine it was through mistake? Not in the least. But you see how the desire of exciting laughter at the expense of this character has obliged him to degrade an honest man, contrary to dramatic truth.

After the adventure of the sonnet, how comes it that Alceste does not expect the bad usage of Orontes? Can he be surprised when he is informed of it as if it was the first time in his life that he had been sincere or the first time that his sincerity had procured him an enemy? Ought not he to prepare himself quietly for the loss of his suit instead of previously expressing a childish spite? /47/

It may cost twenty thousand francs; but I
Shall pay their twenty thousand, and gain thereby
The right to storm and rage at human evil.

A misanthrope has no occasion to purchase the privilege of storming at so dear a rate, he need only to open his eyes. And he does not set a sufficient value upon money to imagine he has acquired a new privilege of this kind by losing his cause. But the audience must be made to laugh.

In the scene with Dubois, the more Alceste has reason to be angry the more he ought to command his temper because the valet's stupidity is not a vice. A misanthrope and a hasty, passionate man are two very different characters and here was an occasion to distinguish them. Molière knew this very well, but the audience must be made to laugh.

Though I run the risk of making the reader laugh at my expense, I dare charge this author with having missed an opportunity of showing a greater regard to decency, to truth and perhaps to beauty of character. This would have been in changing his plot in such a manner that Philinte would enter as a necessary actor in the intricate part of the play and the actions of Philinte and Alceste might be set in apparent opposition with their principles and in perfect conformity to their characters. What I mean is that the misanthrope should have been always raving mad upon the subject of public vice, and /48/ perfectly calm in regard to the personal injuries done to himself. On the contrary, the philosopher Philinte ought to behold the vices of society with a Stoic phlegm and to run mad upon the least hurt done directly to himself. And indeed I observe that those people who are so easy in regard to public injustice always make the most noise upon the least injury done to their own persons and preserve their philosophy only so long as they have no occasion for it for themselves. They are like the Irishman who would not get out of bed though the house was on fire. "What's that to me?" said he. "I am but a lodger." At length the flames having reached his room, he jumps up, runs about, cries out, bestirs himself and begins to be convinced that we ought sometimes to be concerned for the house we dwell in though it be not our property. If those characters were handled in this manner each would have been more just, more regular and that of Alceste in particular would have produced a better effect. But then the audience could have laughed only at the expense of the man of the world and the author's intention was that they should laugh at the misanthrope.[5] /49/

With the same purpose Molière puts Alceste into a scene of humor but gives him a taste quite different from that of a man of his character. An example of the tastelessness is the following pun from the scene of the sonnet:

. . . blast the close; you'd better close your face
Before you send your lying soul to hell.

A pun is so much the more out of place in the misanthrope's mouth as he himself has found fault with some much better phrasing in the sonnet of Orontes; and it is very extraordinary that the person who makes it proposes a moment afterwards the *Song of King Henry* for a model of taste. It means nothing to say that this word drops from him at a time when he is in a passion, for passion seldom dictates puns. And Alceste having been all his life a grumbler ought even when he grumbles to assume a tone suitable to his character.

You know the thing is trash. How dare you praise it? In this manner ought the misanthrope to have expressed himself in a passion. A pun will never do. But the audience must be made to laugh. And by such means is virtue debased. . . .

One thing very remarkable in this play is that the features which the poet has given to the /50/ misanthrope have obliged him to dilute the essential part of the character so that whereas in all his other plays the parts are over-done in order to

---

[5] I do not doubt but that upon the plan above mentioned a man of genius might make a new *Misanthrope*, of equal merit with that of Molière and incomparably more instructive. I see but one inconveniency in this new play; it would be impossible for it to succeed. For, say what you will, nobody chooses to laugh at his own dishonor. And thus we come back to first principles. [Rousseau's note]

produce a better effect in this alone the features are deadened with a view to render the character more ridiculous. This is demonstrated by the very scenes of which I have been speaking. There we see Alceste using evasions and shifts to tell Orontes his opinion. This is not the misanthrope, but the man of the world who feels some reluctance to deceive the person that consults him. To act up to his character, Alceste should have said to him, bluntly, your sonnet is good for nothing, throw it into the fire. But this would have prevented the laughter arising from the misanthrope's perplexity and from his frequent repetition of *I don't say that* which, however, is in the main a lie. If Philinte, after his example, had said to him on this occasion, *What else d'you call it, you hypocrite?* what answer could he have made? Really it is not worth while to be only a misanthrope by halves; for if once he is allowed the least evasion or the least deviation from the truth, what reason can he have to stop till he becomes as false as any gentleman of them all?

Alceste's friend ought to know him. How durst he propose to pay a visit to the judges, that is, in plain terms, to endeavor to corrupt them? How can he suppose that a man who neglects all forms of civility through love of virtue should be capable of not doing his duty through a motive of interest? To solicit a judge! One need /51/ not be a misanthrope, it is sufficient to be an honest man to make no such attempt. For which way soever the thing turns, either the person who solicits a judge exhorts him to do his duty and then he affronts him, or he proposes an exception for personal reasons and then he wants to seduce him. For every exception for personal reasons is criminal in a judge who should take cognizance of the principles and not of the parties and see that the law is executed. Now I say that to induce a judge to commit a criminal action is committing it yourself and that it is much better to lose a just cause than to be guilty of a criminal action. This is plain, clear doctrine and there is no gainsaying it. I am not ignorant that the world is directed by other maxims of morality, but it is sufficient to me to show that wherever the misanthrope was exposed to ridicule he did but act the part of an honest man and that it was out of character if his friend supposed he could act otherwise.

If the ingenious author sometimes gives full scope to this character, this is only when it enlivens the scene and produces a more sensible contrast or comic opposition. Such is, for instance, the sullen taciturnity of Alceste and the animated censure of the conversation at the coquette's apartment.

> How bravely, Sirs, you cut and thrust at all
> These absent fools, till one by one they fall.

Here the author has plainly distinguished the detractor from the misanthrope. The latter, with /52/ all his gall and sourness, detests calumny and satire. His attack is against public vice and knaves in general; private detraction is mean and unworthy of him; he despises, he hates it in others; and when he says anything ill of a person, he begins by telling it to him to his face. Thus in the whole play he acts his part nowhere so well as in this scene because here he is what he ought to be and, if he makes the audience laugh, honest people are not ashamed of having joined with the crowd.

In general, however, we cannot deny that if Alceste was more of the misanthrope he would be less amusing: because his frankness and resolution would then admit of no evasions nor shifts and of course he would never be at a loss. It is, therefore, you will say, out of respect for him that the poet sometimes waters down his character; on the contrary it is to render him more ridiculous. Besides, another reason obliges him to it; this is, the misanthrope must talk of what he sees, he must live in society and of course must temper his sincerity and manners with some of those regards to falsehood and deception which constitute politeness and which are required of every one that wants to be tolerated in the world. Were he to behave otherwise, what he says would be of no effect. The author's business is to render him ridiculous, but not a fool and such he would appear in the eye of the public if he were to be altogether a sage.

I am loathe to leave this admirable play, when once I have begun. The more I examine it, the /53/ more beauties disclose themselves to my view. But, since it is of all Molière's plays that which contains the best and soundest morality, you may judge from thence of the rest and I doubt not but you will agree that the author's intention being to please a corrupt people either his moral has a tendency to vice or the apparent good which it recommends is more dangerous than vice itself: because it seduces by a semblance of reason; because it teaches us to prefer the uses and maxims of the world to exact probity; because it makes wisdom consist in a certain medium between vice and virtue; because to the great conveniency of the spectators it persuades them that to be an honest man it is sufficient not to be a downright villain. /54/

Martin Turnell Le Misanthrope

This essay is the work of the British scholar, Martin Turnell, and has been taken from *The Classical Moment*, a brilliant critical study of Corneille, Molière, and Racine, published in the United States by New Directions Press (New York, 1948). An earlier book, *The Novel in France*, and later works on Baudelaire and on more novelists, *The Art of French Fiction* (1959), have established Turnell's reputation as a penetrating and meticulous scholar-critic.

1

Le Misanthrope is by common consent the greatest of Molière's plays, but attempts to discover the nature of its peculiar excellence have sometimes led critics into unprofitable paths. The Romantic critics found in it the main support for their theory of "the tragic Molière"; Ramon Fernandez, the stern champion of "philosophical criticism," has spoken of "this comedy in which the very essence of the comic has been jeopardized"; and a German writer has used it to /90/ propound a theory of "the diabolical element in great comedy." These theories have one factor in common. They suggest that the *Misanthrope* is in some way "deeper," more "profound," more "serious" than Molière's other works, overlooking perhaps the fact that comedy is essentially a serious activity. Compare it with *Tartuffe* and the dangers of such a criterion are at once apparent. It is not difficult to see in what sense the *Misanthrope* and *Tartuffe* are more "serious" than *les Femmes savantes* or *l'Avare*, but we should be on very uncertain ground in claiming that the *Misanthrope* is more serious than *Tartuffe*. Indeed, it would be less difficult to prove the contrary. *Tartuffe* has obvious affinities with primitive comedy. The most striking of them is the sacrificial element. Tartuffe is the scapegoat whose chastisement provides a release for the audience's primitive desires and emotions, and Molière knew very well what he was about when he underlines the sexual propensities of his victim. The play appeals to some of the deepest, though not the most admirable, of human instincts, and it has a ferocity which is unparalleled in Molière's work. "My opinion of *Tartuffe*," wrote Baudelaire in his diary, "is that it is not a comedy, but a pamphlet." This is an over-statement, but it helps us to understand the limitations of that masterpiece and the superiority of the *Misanthrope*.

The *Misanthrope* in the seventeenth century was the connoisseur's play and a contemporary described it with felicity as "a play which creates laughter in the soul." Its pre-eminence lies not in greater depth or profundity, but in a greater variety of tone, a wider social reference, more complex and more delicate shades of feeling. It is one of the most personal of Molière's plays. *Tartuffe* was a magnificent onslaught on a narrow, vindictive puritanism which had all but succeeded in driving comedy from the stage. The *Misanthrope* was written during a personal crisis and is certainly coloured by /91/ Molière's own domestic difficulties. We must be careful not to read too much into the play, but those critics who have found its laughter "sad" are on the right track; there is no doubt that personal suffering helped to give Molière the astonishing insight into the human heart which he displays in the *Misanthrope* and which contributes to its richness and maturity.

2

"He did not set out to write a comedy full of incidents," said Visé in a commentary which is believed to have been published with Molière's approval, "but simply a play in which he could speak against the manners of the age."

There is one striking difference between the *Misanthrope* and Molière's other plays. He does not confine himself to the study of the psychology of an individual seen against the background of a stable society. His irony is turned on society as well as on Alceste, and the play ends, as we shall see, not with the restoration of order, but with something that is very like a mark of interrogation.

The theme is presented by means of a triple conflict—the conflict between Alceste and social convention, Alceste and justice, Alceste and Célimène. It is the constant shifting of the focus from one to the other and the way in which Molière plays on our divided sympathies that give the *Misanthrope* its variety, so that it calls for a greater effort of attention from the reader than any of the other comedies.

Mr. L. C. Knights has suggested that a close examination of the tone and intention of each line in the first scene is the best way of discovering how the play as a whole should be read. The opening scene is so carefully constructed and the theme stated with such clarity and force that almost

268

everything which follows is a development of hints and suggestions contained in it.

> *Philinte:* Now, what's got into you?
> *Alceste [seated]:*   Kindly leave
>   me alone./92/
> *Philinte:* Come, come, what is it? This lugubrious
>   tone . . .
> *Alceste:* Leave me, I said; you spoil my solitude.
> *Philinte:* Oh, listen to me, now, and don't be rude.
> *Alceste:* I choose to be rude, Sir, and to be hard
>   of hearing.
> *Philinte:* These ugly moods of yours are not
>   endearing;
> Friends though we are, I really must insist . . .
> *Alceste [abruptly rising]:* Friends? Friends, you say?
>   Well, cross me off your list.
> I've been your friend till now, as you well know;
> But after what I saw a moment ago
> I tell you flatly that our ways must part.
> I wish no place in a dishonest heart.

The play opens as usual on a note which sounds uncommonly like farce, but the intention is serious. There is something wrong with Alceste and most of the play is devoted to discovering what it is. It makes his behaviour so unreasonable that he becomes incomprehensible to the tolerant and reasonable Philinte. The violent tone is characteristic of Alceste and an understanding of it leads to an understanding of the *motifs* behind it. The *spoil* and the *ugly moods* are important clues—the unobtrusive stage direction, *abruptly rising*, illustrates the close connection between word and gesture in Molière—and their recurrence in the play emphasizes the closeness of its texture.

The dialogue that follows explains the origin of Alceste's *mood*, but before examining it in detail, I wish to jump eighty lines and look at the next use of the word:

> *Alceste:* I fall into deep gloom and melancholy
> When I survey the scene of human folly,
> Finding on every hand base flattery,
> Injustice, fraud, self-interest, treachery. . . .
> *Philinte:* This philosophic rage is a bit extreme;
> You've no idea how comical you seem. . . . /93/

It is clear that for Alceste the *deep gloom* and *melancholy* are a matter of deadly seriousness, but it is also clear from the change of tone and the ironical *philosophic rage* that they have a different value for Philinte, for the ordinary, reasonable man. It is characteristic of the peculiar ambiguity of the play, and of Philinte's place in it, that we feel doubtful at this point whether the *rage* is or is not a laughing matter. There is still room for doubt when he goes on four lines later:

> Then let's have no more tirades, if you please.
> The world won't change, whatever you say or do;
> And since plain speaking means so much to you,
> I'll tell you plainly that by being frank
> You've earned the reputation of a crank,
> And that you're thought ridiculous when you rage.

Philinte drops the tone of easy banter and proceeds to give a serious warning. The *mood* (or *philosophic rage*) is now described as *being frank* and we are meant to take the phrase at its face value, but it is still a *reputation* which in the eyes of the world *earns* [him] *the reputation of a crank* (of being *ridiculous* in his *rage*). There is a conflict of values. *Mood* (or *rage*) has a different significance for different individuals. The doubt lies in deciding what importance should be attached to the respective valuations of Alceste, Philinte and *the world*. Are they all right or all wrong, or partly right and partly wrong?

This doubt is really the crux of the whole play, and it is interesting to glance at the use of this and similar words—the *desert* and the *spot . . . apart*—in other contexts:

1. My God! It chills my heart to see the ways
   Men come to terms with evil nowadays;
   Sometimes, I swear, I'm moved to flee and find
   Some *desert* land unfouled by humankind. (I, i)

2. Men, Sir, are always wrong, and that's the reason
   That *righteous anger's* never out of season. . . . (II, v)

3. She lets the world believe that she's a prude
   To justify her *loveless solitude*. (Célimène of Arsinoé,
   III, iii)/94/

4. Go to her, do; and leave me with my *gloom*
   Here in the *darkened corner* of this room. (V, i)

5. My one condition is that you agree
   To share my chosen fate, and fly with me
   To that wild, trackless, *solitary place*
   In which I shall forget the human race. (V, vii)

6. Meanwhile, betrayed and wronged in everything,
   I'll flee this bitter world where vice is king,
   And seek some *spot unpeopled and apart*
   Where I'll be free to have an honest heart. (V, viii)

It is tempting but dangerous to compare Alceste's *mood* (or *rage*) with Pascal's vision of *the abyss* or even with Baudelaire's *spleen*, because in doing so we run the risk of serious misinterpretation. Alceste is painfully conscious of his perplexity and frustration, but it is evident from these examples that his attitude is a *personal* one. It does not spring from a vision which transcends the deceptive appearances of everyday life. It is largely negative, is directed *against* [mankind]; and in the fourth example, where he caricatures himself, he

seems for a moment to be aware that there is
something a little absurd about his *gloom*. There is
a burlesque note, too, in the fifth and sixth
examples. Alceste strikes a pose. He renounces the
world and goes off to play at being "an honest
heart" in a "solitary place." Now, this "solitary
place" (this "spot unpeopled and apart") is both
objective and subjective, and it has certain affinities with Arsinoé's *loveless solitude* which are suggested by a passage in M. Mauriac's interesting
essay on the play:

> "In a world where a decent man and a Christian
> has so many reasons if not for protest, at least for
> examining his own conscience, Alceste not only attacks
> the most harmless practices, those 'lies' which do not
> take anyone in but which are necessary if social life
> is to go on at all. He is indignant over slanders which
> only affect people indirectly, which do not penetrate
> the hidden vices and merely provoke laughter. In a
> world where injustice is rife, where crime is every-
> where, he is up in arms against trivialities. He feels
> no horror for what is really horrible—beginning with
> himself. All his attacks are directed to things outside
> himself; he /95/ only compares himself with other
> people in order to demonstrate his own superiority."

M. Mauriac's criticism of Alceste seems to me
to be unduly severe and there is, perhaps, a
tendency to simplify the issues; but it does illu-
minate one side of his character. A good deal of his
rage against mankind springs from a psychological
need to distract his attention from his own sense of
frustration, from "what is horrible" in his own
nature, and in this he is representative of the
society that he is attacking. For all the characters
on whom Molière turns his irony are in a greater
or lesser degree aware of their own interior
emptiness, of a *loveless solitude* from which they are
trying to escape. This explains their restless
activity, their desperate preoccupation with gossip
and *manners*. While the struggle to escape from
themselves by losing themselves in the world of
minor social events is one of the principal themes
of the play, it must be emphasized that Molière's
study of their vacancy and fatuity is not a tragic
one. The *Misanthrope* is pre-eminently a comedy;
it is not a bourgeois tragedy in the manner of
l'Éducation sentimentale.

3

It is time to turn to consideration of the individual characters and their place in the pattern of
the play, and to the sources of Alceste's *rage*. His
first long speech is a denunciation of social convention:

I see you almost hug a man to death,
Exclaim for joy until you're out of breath,
And supplement these loving demonstrations
With endless offers, vows, and protestations;
Then when I ask you "Who was that?", I find
That you can barely bring his name to mind!/96/
Once the man's back is turned, you cease to love him,
And speak with absolute indifference of him!
By God, I say it's base and scandalous
To falsify the heart's affections thus;
If I caught myself behaving in such a way,
I'd hang myself for shame, without delay.

The tone of nervous exasperation, the taste for
extremes, signified by *hug . . . to death*, *loving demonstrations, endless offers, vows, and protestations*, and
the piled up words rising to a crescendo—*base and
scandalous to falsify*—is peculiar to Alceste, and
there is an obvious disproportion between the
language used and the "most harmless practices"
which he is attacking. He uses precisely the same
tone in speaking of his lawsuit and his love affair:

Did not truth, honor, decency, and the laws
Oppose my enemy and approve my cause?
My claims were justified in all men's sight;
I put my trust in equity and right;
Yet, to my horror and the world's disgrace,
Justice is mocked, and I have lost my case!
A scoundrel whose dishonesty is notorious
Emerges from another lie victorious!
Honor and right condone his brazen fraud,
While rectitude and decency applaud!
Before his smirking face, the truth stands charmed,
And virtue conquered, and the law disarmed!

Madam, I've had a mortal, mortal blow.
If Chaos repossessed the universe,
I swear I'd not be shaken any worse.
I'm ruined. . . . I can say no more. . . . My soul . . .

The uniformity of tone shows that he reacts in
precisely the same way to three different situations,
that he places the same valuation on his campaign
against convention, his lawsuit and his love affair.
There is certainly a connection between the three,
but they are very far from being of the same importance. His cult of sincerity is a fetish. If his
principles were adopted, social intercourse would
come to an end, and it is perhaps because he is a
threat to a brittle society that his attitude is unpopular. There is more to be /97/ said for his other
preoccupations. Philinte admits that he has a
grievance over the unfortunate lawsuit, and
Célimène confesses that she has treated him
badly. But though they sympathize with him,
they are at one in protesting against the violence
of his denunciation and the extravagance of his

remedies. "I agree with all you say," remarks Philinte.

> . . . all you say I'll readily concede:
> This is a low, conniving age indeed;
> Nothing but trickery prospers nowadays,
> And people ought to mend their shabby ways.
> Yes, man's a beastly creature; but must we then
> Abandon the society of men?

In short, Alceste's attitude betrays a confusion of values, an extraordinary lack of discrimination, which alone would make him ludicrous. Minor mishaps are the pretext for wild generalizations about human nature; the perfidy of a shallow, frivolous society woman assumes the proportions of a universal catastrophe in his disordered imagination, and his denunciation peters out in a strangled cry:

> I'm ruined. . . . I can say no more. . . . My soul. . .

The more we study his pronouncements, the more evident it becomes that his attitude is the reverse of disinterested. When he declares:

> I'd have them be sincere, and never part
> With any word that isn't from the heart.

we may feel that though this is a counsel of perfection, it is not altogether unreasonable. A few lines later, however, his real objections to the insincere enthusiasm with which people greet one another emerge very clearly:

> I spurn the easy tribute of a heart
> Which will not see the worthy man apart:
> I choose, Sir, to be chosen; and in fine,
> The friend of mankind is no friend of mine.

There is a strong element of vanity in his protests. He is determined that people shall be made to distinguish *him* from his fellows, /98/ and the lines betray a sense of insecurity, a need of psychological affirmation. When Philinte suggests in the first scene that he should visit some of the judges who will try his suit, he refuses angrily:

> No, I refuse to lift a hand. That's flat.
> I'm either right, or wrong.

The second line is a curious illustration of the rigidity of Alceste's mind which prevents any compromise with society; but it is interesting for another reason. It has not always been understood by contemporary readers who have felt that his attitude is commendable and have compared it favourably with Célimène's assiduous "touting" in *her* lawsuit. Now it must be remembered that in the seventeenth century the practice of visiting one's judges was universal and was not regarded as being in any way improper. The explanation of Alceste's refusal is to be found in his reaction to Philinte's suggestion that he should appeal against the decision when he loses his case:

> No, no, let the verdict rest.
> Whatever cruel penalty it may bring,
> I wouldn't have it changed for anything.
> It shows the times' injustice with such clarity
> That I shall pass it down to our posterity
> As a great proof and signal demonstration
> Of the black wickedness of this generation.
> It may cost twenty thousand francs; but I
> Shall pay their twenty thousand, and gain thereby
> The right to storm and rage at human evil,
> And send the race of mankind to the devil.

These are not the words of a fighter or a reformer. Alceste is convinced that there has been a miscarriage of justice; but instead of trying to set it right, he is delighted at the loss of his suit because he feels that it gives him a *right* to fulminate against human nature, and this right seems cheap at twenty thousand francs. This is characteristic of his general behaviour. He is always on the lookout for some abuse that he can attack or someone with whom he can pick a quarrel, and the slightest excuse is sufficient to set the machinery of excited denunciation in motion. "What!" cries the horrified Philinte, /99/

> Then you'd tell old Emilie it's pathetic
> The way she daubs her features with cosmetic
> And plays the gay coquette at sixty-four?
>   *Alceste:* I would.
>   *Philinte:*   And you'd call Dorilas a bore,
> And tell him every ear at court is lame
> From hearing him brag about his noble name?
>   *Alceste:* Precisely.

This suggests that his attitude is to a certain extent *desired*. While it is true that denunciation is a form of self-indulgence, a substitute for *action*, this does not exhaust the question. It is noticeable that in most of the plays the *perfect gentleman* treats this heated denunciation as the danger point. It is the point at which the normative influence of society ceases to be effective and the comic character's hysterical mood may well lead to some desperate act. It is for this reason that Philinte's warnings are nearly always directed against Alceste's *tone* and not against what he says. Now Alceste's violence deserves a closer examination than it has perhaps received. In some of the lines lifted from *Dom Garcie de Navarre* Alceste denounces Célimène's perfidy:

I mean that sins which cause the blood to freeze
Look innocent beside your treacheries;
That nothing Hell's or Heaven's wrath could do
Ever produced so bad a thing as you.

Again:

My temper's out of hand; I've lost my head;
Shocked by the knowledge of your double-dealings,
My reason can't restrain my savage feelings;
A righteous wrath deprives me of my senses. . . .

At such moments we have the illusion that we are listening to a Cornelian *tirade*, but it is an illusion. Alceste is not, even at these moments, a tragic figure. His denunciation, though undeniably serious, belongs peculiarly to comedy, and there is an interesting passage at the beginning of the play which helps us to appreciate why this is so: /100/

No, no, this formula you'd have me follow,
However fashionable, is false and hollow,
And I despise the frenzied operations
Of all these barterers of protestations,
These lavishers of meaningless embraces,
These utterers of obliging commonplaces,
Who court and flatter everyone on earth
And praise the fool no less than the man of worth.

What is striking about these lines is a curious air of unreality, the sense that we are watching a Punch-and-Judy show. This is no accident. The violence and the jerkiness have a different function here. The focal phrase is *frenzied operations* and it colours the rest of the passage. The element of caricature is deliberate. This is not abstract denunciation of real people; it is society as it appears to Alceste. We feel ourselves looking at it through his eyes and seeing a world of grinning, gesticulating marionnettes, going through their grotesque performance as some unseen showman pulls the strings. For Alceste's violence leads to a state of hysteria—Molière's word for it is *emportement* (literally, carried away)—in which the actual world is transformed into a comic nightmare, reminding us a little oddly of a Disney cartoon. The nightmare is in Alceste's mind, and the contrast between his distorted outlook and unreasonable behaviour and the humdrum world in which he lives makes him at once a comic and a moving figure. Our response to this passage, and indeed to the whole play, is a balance between two impulses which superficially appear to exclude one another—the impulse to laugh at Alceste's absurdity and the impulse to pity the obvious waste of his gifts. The art of the comic writer depends on preserving this nice balance between two apparently contradictory emotions, on the continual switch

from one set of feelings to another and back again without ever allowing the balance to tip over to the extremes of tragedy or farce. There are moments when he takes us to the brink of tragedy. George Dandin will go to the edge of the water and will stand there gazing at his own reflection, wondering whether to throw himself in or not; but in the end he will turn his back on it and return slowly homewards, will return to the cultivation of his farm and to the problem of finding a *modus vivendi* with his impossible wife—as Molière himself did. In the same way, Alceste reaches the point at which reason totters, but he too will retreat into the world /101/ of words and harmless denunciation. It is not the least of the dramatist's achievements that he establishes this feeling of confidence in his audience and convinces us that it will be so.

It is the failure to understand this that has led to many of the attempts to turn the *Misanthrope* into a tragedy. Fernandez, for example, has suggested that in the course of the play Alceste's character undergoes a radical change and that the man who departs for the "desert" as the curtain falls is no longer the same man as the fiery reformer of Act I. The change is supposed to lie in the collapse of the will. It is an entertaining theory, but I can find no evidence for it in the text of the play. It is true that Alceste is always using expressions of great determination but, as I have already suggested, there is no real volition behind the words which are a sort of smoke screen used to hide a complete absence of determination. The Alceste of Act V is identical with the Alceste of Act I. His *physical* exile is the logical outcome of the *psychological* exile—the retreat into a private world—which is studied with such profound insight in the course of the play.

I stress this point because Fernandez' theory seems to me to rest on a misunderstanding of Molière's method of presentation in this play. Alceste is constructed partly by direct statement and partly by his action on other characters. Certain essential traits are presented in the opening scene and driven home by deliberate repetition all through the play. Once he has sketched the outlines, Molière proceeds to fill in the details. A series of impressions of Alceste as he appears to other characters is superimposed one on another. These impressions add to our knowledge both of Alceste and of the other characters. They are not always in agreement and sometimes, as we shall see, they qualify or contradict one another. This is a point of considerable importance and it is one

of the things that force the reader to follow the dialogue with such minute care, to decide what weight must be attributed to the constant shift and change of tone.

This brings us to a consideration of Philinte's role in the play. In one of the central passages he declares:

> This world requires a pliant rectitude;
> Too stern a virtue makes one stiff and rude;/102/
> Good sense views all extremes with detestation,
> And bids us to be noble in moderation.
> The rigid virtues of the ancient days
> Are not for us; they jar with all our ways
> And ask of us too lofty a perfection.
> Wise men accept their times without objection,
> And there's no greater folly, if you ask me,
> Than trying to reform society.
> Like you, I see each day a hundred and one
> Unhandsome deeds that might be better done,
> But still, for all the faults that meet my view,
> I'm never known to storm and rave like you.
> I take men as they are, or let them be,
> And teach my soul to bear their frailty;
> And whether in court or town, whatever the scene,
> My phlegm's as philosophic as your spleen.

We recognize this passage, which recalls Cléante's plea for a devotion which is *humane* and *tractable*, as the familiar statement of Molière's positives. It is also a good example of the patterned movement of his verse. It is not a mere catalogue of "the great abstractions." There are life and warmth in his *wisdom*, *perfect reason* and *sobriety*. They have behind them centuries of European civilization which is vividly felt. The *inflexibility of the ages* underlines the peculiar and disabling rigidity of Alceste's outlook and, at the same time, reflects a delicate appreciation of the graciousness of contemporary civilization which exists in spite of human imperfection. The passage closes on a personal note; precept merges into practice and one becomes aware of the urbanity and good sense of the civilized man. Philinte's tone is intended to act as a foil to Alceste's, to moderate his transports. When Alceste cries

> Sometimes, I swear, I'm moved to flee and find
> Some desert land unfouled by humankind.

Philinte replies:

> Come, let's forget the follies of the times
> And pardon mankind for its petty crimes.

The sharp *find-kind* creates a sense of physical constriction and the relief provided by *times-crimes* is palpable. The *pardon* and *leniency* (two lines below) prolong the process on the logical plane. It is not without /103/ significance, however, that

Philinte's attempts to moderate Alceste's transports are seldom successful. The very gentleness of tone seems to heighten his exasperation, and he reserves some of his bitterest shafts for his friend. In these exchanges his tactics vary and he is decidedly *crafty*. When he retorts:

> This phlegm which you so eloquently commend,
> Does nothing ever rile it up, my friend?

commend is balanced against *rile up*. He feels instinctively that *phlegm* puts the brake on his *anger* and he tries to discredit it by suggesting that it is an excuse for tolerating injustice. There is a curious eagerness to brush aside obstacles. The verse stumbles and almost comes to a halt over the repeated *phlegm*, then moves breathlessly forward to the word *rile up* which is sufficient to set the machinery of denunciation in motion.

"Sir, you're a matchless reasoner," he begins with icy politeness in another place,

> Sir, you're a matchless reasoner, to be sure;
> Your words are fine and full of cogency;
> But don't waste time and eloquence on me.
> *My* reason bids me go, for my own good.
> My tongue won't lie and flatter as it should;
> God knows what frankness it might next commit,
> And what I'd suffer on account of it.

In order to keep up the appearance of rational behaviour, he pretends that his proposal to retire to the desert is a reasoned one, but there is a world of difference between the *cogency* attributed to Philinte and Alceste's *reason*. "Reason" ceases to be universal and becomes a private and very misleading label that he attaches to the demon which is driving him into the desert. The last three lines are double-edged. It is because he is unreasonable and not because society is unreasonable that he is likely to find himself in trouble if he remains where he is.

I have already spoken of the peculiar ambiguity of the play and of Philinte's place in it. In the *Misanthrope* there is a skilful modification of the pattern of Molière's comedies which becomes more subtle and more varied. Although Philinte is certainly Molière's spokesman in many places and certainly helps to provide the background of reason and sanity which contributes largely to /104/ the poise of the play, his role is a shifting one. We do not feel, as we do with Cléante, that the whole of the play is behind his words, and the explanation is be to found in Éliante's observations on Alceste in Act IV, scene i:

> His conduct has been very singular lately;
> Still, I confess that I respect him greatly,

> The honesty in which he takes such pride
> Has—to my mind—its noble, heroic side.
> In this false age, such candor seems outrageous;
> But I could wish that it were more contagious.

Éliante is the only wholly sympathetic character in the play. It would not be accurate to say that she represents Molière's own point of view more completely than Philinte, but her role is of the first importance. In the *Misanthrope*, as in *Tartuffe*, Molière felt the need of two spokesmen; but the function of Éliante and Philinte goes beyond that of Dorine and Cléante. Dorine and Cléante complete one another, but Éliante qualifies the role of Philinte and it is this that gives the play a mellowness which is unique in Molière's work. For Éliante's words display a fresh attitude towards the comic hero. Arnolphe, Harpagon and Orgon (in spite of his conversion to a *docile devotion*) are and remain completely unsympathetic; but Alceste awakens the sympathies of the audience to a degree which is exceptional in seventeenth-century and indeed in all comedy.

Éliante minimizes Alceste's peculiarities and by placing the emphasis on his "candor" she corrects Philinte. Alceste is not a buffoon in the same sense as Molière's other comic characters. There is always a foundation of good sense behind his criticisms and, in spite of their exaggeration, this is true of his attacks on convention. In the scene where Oronte's sonnet is criticized, which is significantly placed immediately after the exposition of the principal theme of the play in scene i, his good taste and sound judgment obviously compare favourably with Philinte's flattery. There is a less obvious but more impressive example towards /105/ the end of the play, when, after commiserating with Alceste on the loss of his lawsuit, Philinte proceeds to expound the virtues of his own philosophy:

> Here in the world, each human frailty
> Provides occasion for philosophy,
> And that is virtue's noblest exercise;
> If honesty shone forth from all men's eyes,
> If every heart were frank and kind and just,
> What could our virtues do but gather dust . . .

Philinte's logic may be unexceptionable, but is not the attitude that he is defending in danger of becoming abstract and unreal? Is there not a gap between life and thought, a gap which can only be closed by the more human and more generous approach of Éliante? Does not his attitude overlook the fact that the ordinary man is not a mere logician and that the "occasion for philosophy" cannot impose order on the tangled feelings and desires which Molière perceived as clearly as Racine? The neat maxims which appealed so much to the reasonable seventeenth century are useless in solving the central problem of the play—the conflict between what Gutkind calls with true Teutonic violence "the pert, frivolous, fickly, coquettish young widow and Alceste, the heavy-blooded man who is eaten up by his passion and who is fighting for his love."

The conclusion seems to me to be unmistakable. In this play Molière criticizes his own standards. The urbanity and moderation of the *perfect gentleman* are felt to be insufficient. When Éliante speaks of the "noble, heroic side," she is referring to the potentialities of Alceste's character; but these potentialities are prevented from realizing themselves by his lack of balance and his impatience of all restraint. His virtues are converted into negation, into the *virile hatreds* of one passage and the *undying hatred* of another; his violence leads him away from the world of common experience into a world of private mania where, deprived of the normative influence of society, he thunders against wildly exaggerated abuses in the void. This makes him a comic figure, but it is the consciousness of his potential virtues and of his profound humanity which gives the play its peculiar resonance. /106/

4

The triple conflict represents the three points of contact between Alceste and society. The continual switching from one to the other and back again enables Molière to present both Alceste and society in a perpetually changing light until, as the play moves towards its climax, the three blend and give it its cumulative force. The direct conflict with convention underlines Alceste's absurdity and prevents comedy from turning into tragedy; the lawsuit redresses the balance and seems at times to justify his violence; the affair with Célimène is the richest and most serious of all and in a way contains them both. Alceste's rage over convention and his lawsuit is the point at which he separates himself from his fellow men and his love affair is the point at which he rejoins them. It stands for normality; it is the side of his character by which (in Mauriac's words) "he becomes our brother." "It much surprises me," remarks Philinte:

> It much surprises me that you, who seem
> To view mankind with furious disesteem,
> Have yet found something to enchant your eyes
> Amidst a species which you so despise.
> And what is more amazing, I'm afraid,
> Is the most curious choice your heart has made.
> The honest Éliante is fond of you,

Arsinoé, the prude, admires you too;
And yet your spirit's been perversely led
To choose the flighty Célimène instead,
Whose brittle malice and coquettish ways
So typify the manners of our days.
How is it that the traits you most abhor
Are bearable in this lady you adore?
Are you so blind with love that you can't find them?
Or do you contrive, in her case, not to mind them?

Alceste replies at once, with his curious mixture of arrogance and perspicacity, that he has no illusions about the shortcomings of Célimène:

My love for that young widow's not the kind
That can't perceive defects; no, I'm not blind.
I see her faults, despite my ardent love,
And all I see I fervently reprove.
And yet I'm weak; for all her falsity,
That woman knows the art of pleasing me, /107/
And though I never cease complaining of her,
I swear I cannot manage not to love her.
Her charm outweighs her faults; I can but aim
To cleanse her spirit in my love's pure flame.

Célimène's importance is twofold. She is the complete representative of the society that Alceste and through him Molière is attacking. When some of her retainers tell Alceste that he should blame her and not them for the spiteful remarks that she is making about acquaintances and friends, he retorts acutely:

No, no, by God, the fault is yours, because
You lead her on with laughter and applause.

Part of his problem is to "convert" Célimène, to carry her away from the vicious circle in which she lives; but the problem remains unsolved because of Alceste's eccentricity, because he can only convert her by transporting her into his own world, by carrying her off with him into the "desert" to which he eventually retires. What distinguishes him from Molière's other characters is an extraordinary insight into his own feelings. There are moments when he suddenly forgets his grievances against society, drops the tone of violent denunciation and sees himself as he really is—not a reformer, but a man sadly perplexed by his passion for a woman who is unworthy of him. It is at such moments that we become aware of his immense superiority over the brittle society that is trying to laugh him out of criticisms which are felt to be a threat to it:

Philinte: If I were you, and had your choice to make,
Éliante, her cousin, would be the one I'd take;
That honest heart, which cares for you alone,
Would harmonize far better with your own.
Alceste: True, true: each day my reason tells me so;
But reason doesn't rule in love, you know.

In the last two lines *reason* is used in its normal sense, which is not the sense of

My reason bids me go, for my own good.

Célimène stands for the tangled feelings and desires which, as I have already suggested, the seventeenth century tried in vain to /108/ enclose in its neat formulas. It is at this point that the "systems" of both Alceste and Philinte break down. The obstinate fanaticism of the one and the philosophical maxims of the other are alike impotent to solve the problems of life. For in this play Molière explores regions in which conventional formulas have no validity, and the insight with which he does so gives the *Misanthrope* its exceptional place in French comedy. Nor must we overlook the irony of *honest heart* which is echoed later in the play by Alceste's

I see, dear lady, that you could make a case
For putting up with the whole human race.

Alceste, Célimène and Éliante form a triangle. Alceste places himself at a point outside society, Célimène is entirely absorbed in it; Éliante occupies an intermediate position. She is of society, but is wholly uncontaminated by it. *Alceste's contact with the world of common experience is seen to be intermittent.* He is continually rebounding from its polished surface into the world of his private mania. The victory of either Alceste or Célimène in the tug-of-war would fail to solve the problem. For Alceste the only solution, the only way back to the norm of sanity and common sense, lies in marriage with Éliante and he refuses it. This is true of nearly all the characters in their different ways. They are all looking for something solid and sincere, for some philosophy on which to base their lives, but they meet with disappointment at every turn. Custom, justice and love prove equally hollow and unreal and they suddenly find themselves face to face with the void.

A large part of the play is thus taken up with the tug-of-war between Alceste and Célimène as each tries to draw the other into his or her own sphere. Célimène is shallow and frivolous but she too is dimly conscious of her shortcomings, and it is only because she is not beyond redemption that she provides Alceste with an adequate foil. From time to time the glitter and polish of the exchanges between them are disturbed by a deeper note:

Alceste: Well, if I mustn't be jealous, tell me, then,
Just how I'm better treated than other men.
Célimène: You know you have my love. Will that
not do? /109/

This note only occurs at rare intervals. Célimène's normal tone bears a marked similarity to
Philinte's. She answers Alceste's over-wrought dec-
larations either in a mood of light banter or with
mild surprise which lowers the tension:

Alceste: Why, why am I doomed to love you?
I swear that I shall bless the blissful hour
When this poor heart's no longer in your power!
I make no secret of it: I've done my best
To exorcise this passion from my breast;
But thus far all in vain; it will not go;
It's for my sins that I must love you so.
    Célimène: Your love for me is matchless, Sir; that's
    clear.
Alceste: Indeed, in all the world it has no peer;
Words can't describe the nature of my passion,
And no man ever loved in such a fashion.
    Célimène: Yes, it's a brand-new fashion, I agree;
You show your love by castigating me,
And all your speeches are enraged and rude.
I've never been so furiously wooed.
    Alceste: Yet you could calm that fury, if you chose.
Come, shall we bring our quarrels to a close?
Let's speak with open hearts, then, and begin. . .

This illustrates very well the constant change of
tone. Alceste begins in a mood of deadly seriousness. The turns and twists of the dialogue reflect the
turns and twists of the trapped animal—"the
heavy-blooded man who is eaten up by his passion
and who is fighting for his love"—to escape this
passion, and recalls ironically Philinte's

And yet your spirit's been perversely led
To choose the flighty Célimène instead.

For Alceste's struggle is no laughing matter, and
the gravity of Célimène's

Your love for me is matchless, Sir; that's clear /110/

shows that she is impressed in spite of herself, is
faced with something which is outside her experience. But when Alceste continues in the same tone,
her mood changes and she comments light-heart-
edly on the "brand-new fashion" of making love.
The reference to his notorious ill-humour not only
lowers the tension of the scene, it brings Alceste
back to his usual level—the comic figure who is at
odds with society. The relief, however, is only
momentary, and the scene closes with something
that sounds like a cry for mercy. "Shall we bring
our quarrels to a close?"—Alceste's arrogance vanishes and he knows that he has been defeated in the
encounter.

5

With Act II, scene ii the work of exposition is
complete. The stage is cleared and Molière brings

his batteries to bear on the procession of vain,
empty, frivolous courtiers who have nothing better
to do than engage Célimène in malicious chatter
or attend some small function at court.

Acaste: I'm free to linger, unless I should perceive
Madame is tired, and wishes me to leave.
    Clitandre: And as for me, I needn't go today
Until the hour of the King's *coucher*.

It is noticeable that almost every word uttered
by these people about their friends or in the bitter
exchanges between themselves is double-edged. It
returns like a boomerang to the speaker. Acaste
remarks complacently:

By Jove, when I survey myself, I find
No cause whatever for distress of mind.

The implication is that the game of self-decep-
tion is so successful, that he is so shallow and empty,
that he is incapable of perceiving his shortcomings
or experiencing the torment which infects Alceste.
This becomes clearer in the brilliant portrait of the
fop which emerges innocently as the speech continues: /111/

Then as to courage, that most precious trait,
I seem to have it, as was proved of late
Upon the field of honor, where my bearing,
They say, was very cool and rather daring.
I've wit, of course; and taste in such perfection
That I can judge without the least reflection,
And at the theater, which is my delight,
Can make or break a play on opening night,
And lead the crowd in hisses or bravos,
And generally be known as one who knows.
I'm clever, handsome, gracefully polite;
My waist is small, my teeth are strong and white;
As for my dress, the world's astonished eyes
Assure me that I bear away the prize.
I find myself in favor everywhere,
Honored by men, and worshiped by the fair;
And since these things are so, it seems to me
I'm justified in my complacency.

The small, flat words contrast with the solemnity
of the performance. When he uses a word like *cool*
the thin, mincing lilt of the line robs it of its power
and gives it a grotesque air. When we come to *judge
without the least reflection*, there is a note of fatuity
which is heightened by the eulogy of his teeth and
waist which are given the same importance as his
skill as a critic. And with a final pirouette he turns
to survey the admiring world of his peers. The
brittle, artificial style reflects the poverty of experience of all these people.

One of the best demonstrations of the vigour
and subtlety of Molière's style occurs in the great

scene between Célimène and Arsinoé which is one of the high-lights of the play. Thus Célimène:

> It's all an act.
> At heart she's worldly, and her poor success
> In snaring men explains her prudishness.
> It breaks her heart to see the beaux and gallants
> Engrossed by other women's charms and talents,
> And so she's always in a jealous rage
> Against the faulty standards of the age.
> She lets the world believe that she's a prude
> To justify her loveless solitude,
> And strives to put a brand of moral shame
> On all the graces that she cannot claim.
> But still she'd love a lover; and Alceste /112/
> Appears to be the one she'd love the best.
> His visits here are poison to her pride;
> She seems to think I've lured him from her side;
> And everywhere, at court or in the town,
> The spiteful, envious woman runs me down.

The more one studies Molière's style, the more impressed one is by its concrete particularity. It is possible to argue, as some critics have done, that his prose is superior to his verse and that the alexandrine was on occasion too rigid an instrument for his purpose. This may be true, but it can be seen in this play that the verse registers the changing expressions of his characters with remarkable vividness and that, without seeming to do so, the words do an immense amount of work. Words almost invariably issue in action and the actions of the characters mirror conflicting feelings. There was nothing absurd or discreditable about the *prude* in the seventeenth century. A prude was simply an austere and rather puritanical woman; it was only later that the word acquired its present-day suggestion of affectation and insincerity. Molière's prudes, however, are all "false prudes" and they are used as negative symbols—as symbols of a hypocritical rejection of the life of the senses in which Molière himself believed so firmly. So it is here. *Act* sets the tone of the passage and it is sufficient to give us a picture of the stiff, puritanical old maid, trying to hide her lack of success behind a mask; but "It's all an act," a mask which hides nothing and simply draws attention to her hypocrisy. For in spirit she belongs to the world of Célimène and Acaste, accepts its values and does her best to "hook" or "angle" for a husband. We see the prude stretching out her hand furtively, but she misses the mark. She is left looking enviously at the procession of gallants who pass her by, without so much as a glance, in the train of some other beauty. She is the withered old maid—this is the cruel sense of *jealous rage*—completely abandoned

in a world, in an age, in which favours are only too lightly distributed. *She lets the world believe that she's a prude*, reinforces the *act*, makes it more explicit, more pictorial. It is a veil which she puts between herself and the world, a veil which she uses vainly to cover the *loveless solitude*, the terrible, consuming sexual frustration of the ageing spinster. But her deception extends further than that. It is used to conceal her intrigues /113/ and it is also a weapon which she uses to attack other women who are more successful than herself. The hand which is stretched out, pathetically, to "hook" a gallant is now stretched out to stab Célimène as a relief to her bitterness. The image of the pose of prudery is caught up and developed in the encounter between Célimène and Arsinoé which follows. Célimène is pretending to quote some unfavourable comments on Arsinoé's deportment which she has overheard in someone's drawing-room:

> "What good," they said, "are all these outward shows,
> When everything belies her pious pose?
> She prays incessantly; but then, they say,
> She beats her maids and cheats them of their pay;
> She shows her zeal in every holy place,
> But still she's vain enough to paint her face;
> She holds that naked statues are immoral,
> But with a naked *man* she'd have no quarrel."

The procedure is the same as in the earlier passage. We see life going on simultaneously on different sides of a "show," the contrast between the public and private life of a false prude. *These outward shows* are the masks which hide, or are intended to hide, an interior disorder. She is exact in carrying out her religious duties; we see her sink to her knees and rise to her feet in church; but behind the locked doors of her house, the pious gestures merge into the savage rise and fall of the whip as she thrashes her servants. She gives alms, but has no money to pay her servants their just wages. She is the centre of attention at the cenacle where the pious meet, ostentatiously crossing herself; but in the fastness of her boudoir the pious gestures are replaced by the hand painting the face in a vain effort to repair its *jealous rage*. The last two lines are one of the glories of the play. The prude solemnly hangs a veil over some statues of nude figures to hide them from a shocked world, but it is another subterfuge, another attempt to hide her own frustration. The final truth conveys an extraordinary sense of hot, guilty intimacy, a morbid brooding over the intimate details of sexual relations, and the spiteful Célimène is only too conscious of the bitterness of the shaft.

I have dwelt on these passages not only because of their intrinsic merits, but also because the image of "shows" and the /114/ "mask" explains the intention behind the play. It is to an even greater extent than *Tartuffe* a comedy of unmasking, but the unmasking is a game in which author and characters all take part. Alceste tries to abolish conventional politeness because he feels that it encourages insincerity and prevents him from seeing into the human heart. He attacks his opponent in the lawsuit because he is accepted at his face value and is able to secure an unjust decision:

> His social polish can't conceal his nature;
> One sees at once that he's a treacherous creature;
> No one could possibly be taken in
> By those soft speeches and that sugary grin.

In another place:

> . . . we should condemn with all our force
> Such false and artificial intercourse.

Célimène is busy stripping the mask from Arsinoé and from other members of her circle in order to reveal their hypocrisy and absurdity, but at the end of the encounter with Arsinoé she makes a far more damaging admission than she realizes:

> Madame, I think we either blame or praise
> According to our taste and length of days.
> There is a time of life for coquetry,
> And there's a season, too, for prudery.
> When all one's charms are gone, it is, I'm sure,
> Good strategy to be devout and pure:
> It makes one seem a little less forsaken.
> Some day, perhaps, I'll take the road you've taken:
> Time brings all things. But I have time aplenty,
> And see no cause to be a prude at twenty.

For here Molière himself takes a hand. The fragile prettiness of the verse reflects the fragile values by which Célimène lives. She accept them absolutely and uncritically, and the future holds out little for her beyond Arsinoé's own fate.

The characters enter wholeheartedly into the game of unmasking which reaches its climax with the reading of Célimène's letter in the last Act; but as with Arsinoé they only do it as a distraction, as a means of veiling their own interior emptiness from themselves.

Now the game is of the utmost seriousness when played by /115/ Alceste and Célimène. They are doubtful about their feelings for one another. Alceste *thinks* that he is madly in love with Célimène, but the very violence of his protestations betrays an element of doubt. He is not at all sure that she loves him, and he sets to work to find out because it distracts him from his doubts about his own feelings. The play enters on its last phase when

Arsinoé undertakes to prove to Alceste that Célimène is not in love with him:

> Yes, though she *is* my friend, I say again
> You're very much too good for Célimène.
> She's wantonly misled you from the start.

Alceste bridles at this:

> You may be right; who knows another's heart?
> But ask yourself if it's the part of charity
> To shake my soul with doubts of her sincerity.

"Who knows another's heart?" is a defence mechanism: it describes exactly what Alceste wants to know and directs his attention uncomfortably back to his own doubts. The damage is done in spite of his protests:

> Madam, you know that doubt and vague suspicion
> Are painful to a man in my position;
> It's most unkind to worry me this way
> Unless you've some real proof of what you say.

Arsinoé gleefully undertakes the job—on condition that he goes home with her:

> I've ocular evidence which will persuade you
> Beyond a doubt, that Célimène's betrayed you.
> Then, if you're saddened by that revelation,
> Perhaps I can provide some consolation.

She is extremely successful in giving Célimène away, but not in replacing her. In the last two acts Molière rings the changes so rapidly, the feelings are so complex, that one is doubtful whether "comic," "moving" or "horrible" is the proper description of some of the scenes.

"The whole misfortune of Alceste," writes M. Mauriac, "of that Alceste who is in all of us, lies in a psychological need of the absolute that we bring to love which is the most relative of human feelings. /116/ Alceste angrily brushes aside all false appearances; he is determined to advance on firm ground into this *pays du Tendre* which is essentially the home of fickleness and change; and it is precisely because it is the home of fickleness and change that it is the domain of Célimène."

Alceste's

> No, I refuse to lift a hand. That's flat.
> I'm either right, or wrong.

of which I have already spoken, has its parallel in the story of his love affair. When he remarks

> The more one loves, the more one should object
> To every blemish, every least defect,

his pure love is the absolute love described by Mauriac, the absolute necessity of fixing his love in a formula and compelling the loved one to conform to it. It is here that he fails with Célimène. He feels that he is in the realm of change, that the ground is shifting under his feet, threatening to plunge him into chaos at any moment. When he discovers the letter to Oronte, he loses all control over himself; the whole universe rocks:

If Chaos repossessed the universe,
I swear I'd not be shaken any worse.

Éliante comes to the rescue with her moderate and reasonable

Are you quite certain? Can you prove these things?

recalling the *honest heart* and the desperate hunt for a sound foundation of earlier scenes. This produces an extraordinary reaction in Alceste who suddenly sees in her a refuge against the devouring doubt. "Avenge a crime your pure soul must detest," he cries. "But how?"

Madam, this heart within my breast
Is yours; pray take it; redeem my heart from her,
And so avenge me on my torturer.

When we recall that Éliante is Alceste's one chance of salvation, we can appreciate the grimness of Molière's irony here.

It becomes clearer as the play draws towards its conclusion that /117/ Célimène is a means to an end, that Alceste's chief preoccupation is deliverance from his own obsession, is a need to achieve a startling success to rehabilitate himself in the eyes of the world and to make himself feel that he is rooted in society:

I love you more than can be said or thought;
Indeed, I wish you were in such distress
That I might show my deep devotedness.
Yes, I could wish that you were wretchedly poor,
Unloved, uncherished, utterly obscure;
That fate had set you down upon the earth
Without possessions, rank, or gentle birth;
Then, by the offer of my heart, I might
Repair the great injustice of your plight;
I'd raise you from the dust, and proudly prove
The purity and vastness of my love.

This shows to what extent Alceste lives in a private world, how impossible it is to prevent the "noble, heroic side" from being swamped and destroyed by his eccentricities. For he is obliged to invent a situation, in which he can repair imaginary injustices by imaginary sacrifices, to convince himself not merely of the reality of his own feelings, but of his very existence.

While Alceste is hunting desperately to discover some sure foundation in the realm of change, Célimène is clinging no less tenaciously to her shifting, changing world. For her whole existence depends upon maintaining a state of doubt—doubt about her own feelings, doubt in the minds of her retainers about her feelings for them. When Alceste and Oronte deliver their ultimatum—"Choose between us two"—it is she who assumes the role of a trapped animal, or perhaps of the trapped butterfly, struggling desperately to avoid a commitment:

Enough: this inquisition's gone too far:
How utterly unreasonable you are!
Not that I couldn't make the choice with ease;
My heart has no conflicting sympathies;
I know full well which one of you I favor,
And you'd not see me hesitate or waver.
But how can you expect me to reveal
So cruelly and bluntly what I feel?
I think it altogether too unpleasant /118/
To choose between two men when both are present;
One's heart has means more subtle and more kind
Of letting its affections be divined,
Nor need one be uncharitably plain
To let a lover know he loves in vain.

Finally, when she can no longer avoid making a choice, she discovers that she does not love Alceste enough to follow him into his desert, and his vanity is too great to allow of any compromise:

Alas, at twenty one is terrified
Of solitude. I fear I lack the force
And depth of soul to take so stern a course.

6

I have already spoken of the differences between the *Misanthrope* and Molière's other plays. When the curtain comes down on the *École des femmes*, *Tartuffe*, *l'Avare* and les *Femmes savantes*, the audience is left in no doubt about the author's intentions. It is able to "determine... exactly what attitude is broken down and what takes its place." In *Tartuffe* religious mania is satirized, a criminal is brought to book and the play closes with the triumph of society.

The same cannot be said of the *Misanthrope*. Molière has richly fulfilled his intention of speaking against the morals of the times; but the doubt, which is an integral part of our experience, persists. We are, perhaps, able to determine what attitude is broken down, but it is less easy to decide what takes its place. It is idle to pretend that order is re-established and that a chastened buffoon is brought back to the norm of sanity. At the close of the play society, in the persons of Célimène and her retainers, leaves by one exit and Alceste abandons society by another, leaving an empty stage. The line that echoes in the mind is not profession of belief, but a profession of complete disbelief, is not Philinte's

Good sense views all extremes with detestation,

but Alceste's

But reason doesn't rule in love, you know. /119/

Indeed, so far from ending in another triumph for perfect reason, it is perfect reason which dissolves into Alceste's

My reason can't restrain my savage feelings.

Ramon Fernandez seems to put his finger on the point when, in the course of his stimulating but highly erratic study of Molière, he remarks that Molière lived in an age of intellectual scepticism. For when one considers the play as a whole, it is difficult not to feel that Molière had come to share Alceste's own scepticism. The *perfect gentleman* no doubt contributes to the poise of each of the plays in which he appears, but his urbane, polished discourses never succeed in converting anyone; and even in *Tartuffe* conversion is brought about by a sudden change of situation—the intervention of the "great Prince"—and not by Cléante. In the *Misanthrope*, more than in any of the other plays, the *perfect gentleman* is a symbolical figure and Molière is particularly careful to avoid the appearance of imposing a solution. The most that he does is to suggest that a blending of the virtues of Philinte and Éliante may have some bearing on the complicated situation which he has created. In no other play does he reveal such variety and complexity of feelings, but in no other does he show such reluctance to judge the individual or so marked a tendency to call in question all accepted standards and formulas. It is a masterly exploration of the motives behind social behaviour; feelings are tracked down, as surely as in Racine, to the moment of their formation; but judgment on them is suspended. There is in truth no formal ending to the play. The catharsis lies in the clarifying of our feelings, in the perception that social adjustment is a personal matter where in the last resort no facile slogan or philosophical system can help us; and the "message," if we must have one, is that we must have the courage to create our own "order," whatever the cost, instead of yielding to the temptation of an easy escape. /120/

Otto Reinert # Satiric Strategy in *The Importance of Being Earnest*

Otto Reinert specializes in the drama, both that written in his native tongue, Norwegian, and the drama in English. Professor Reinert (Ph. D., Yale, 1952) teaches at the University of Washington. Currently he is lecturing at the University of Oslo. His essay on *The Importance of Being Earnest* is reprinted from *College English* (Vol. 18, No. 1, October, 1956).

Almost everyone agrees that *The Importance of Being Earnest* is good fun, but few have tried to show that it is also a good play. To say that Wilde has written a brilliant farce is not to say why it seems both funnier and more significant than other superior farces, and to say that the farce satirizes Victorianism is not, at this late date, to tell us why it amuses at all. From some of the incidental comments one gets the impression that the play is untouchable, so exquisite that criticism would be fatal—stupid abuse of something bright and fragile. A few critics, who take their business more seriously, refuse even to be charmed. The play "never transcends . . . the incomplete or the trivial," Edouard Roditi writes in his generally perceptive book on Wilde (1947). "Its tone is that of satire, but of a satire which, for lack of a moral point of view, has lost its sting and degenerated into the almost approving banter of a P. G. Wodehouse."

But only a curious form of critical blindness can dismiss *Earnest* as a trifle of dialogues. It merits attention both as satire and as drama. The farce is meaningful. Tone and plot have been successfully integrated, and the whole is more truly comic—because normative—than a well-made play to end all well-made plays, a vehicle for the utterance of witty nonsense. Awareness of its satirical strategy precludes the criticism that it is elusive of reasoned analysis for lack of any kind of rationale.

Wilde first employed a pattern of ironic inversion in *An Ideal Husband*, the play immediately preceding *Earnest*. Its hero, Lord Goring, is not the irresponsible dandy he seems to be, the surface frivolity is not the real man, and his flippant paradoxes emphasize the irony of his moral position relative to that of Lord Chiltern, the pretended pillar of society. For the first time in his plays Wilde puts the fine art of epigram to serious purposes: it participates in the total meaning of the play.

Lord Goring's wit expresses that ironic attitude to life that guarantees moral salvation in Wilde's world. But though the brand of wit is similar in *Earnest*, such an attitude cannot be attributed to any one or several of the characters in the later play, simply because it has no hero (or heroine) in the sense in which Lord Goring is the hero of *An Ideal Husband*. The characters in *Earnest* never stop being flippant; their flippancy is their whole nature and not, like Lord Goring's, the mocking mask of enlightened irony in a pompous society. The only ironist in *Earnest* is Wilde himself, who not only has abandoned the simple ethics of thesis melodrama but also /14/ has deliberately sacrificed the illusionistic conventions of naturalism in order to gain what Francis Fergusson calls (in *The Idea of a Theater*, 1949) a "limited perspective, shared with the audience, as the basis of the fun," showing "human life *as* comic . . . because . . . consistent according to some narrowly defined, and hence unreal, basis."

That is why there is no reason to be embarrassed by the farce label. The play's merit is that it is *all* farce, capable of serving as a lucid image of the non-farcical reality that is kept strictly outside the play. Wilde has respected his paradoxes. He is no longer putting them to menial service as bright spots in sentimental thesis plays or as devices of crude melodramatic irony. *The Importance of Being Earnest* is one sustained metaphor, and esthetic detachment is the only mood in which it can be intelligently enjoyed. It insists on being acted straight, for if we should feel, even for a moment, that the characters are aware of what absurdities they are saying, the whole thing vanishes. Once object and image are confused there is a blurring of vision. No one in his right mind gets emotionally involved with the destinies of Algernon and Cecily, Gwendolen and Jack. But it is precisely their

emotive neutrality as figures of farce that allows Wilde's characters to establish his "limited perspective": Wilde's basic formula for satire is their assumption of a code of behavior that represents the reality that Victorian convention pretends to ignore.

Algernon is explaining his reluctance to attend Lady Bracknell's dinner party: "She will place me next Mary Farquhar, who always flirts with her own husband across the dinner table. That is not very pleasant. Indeed, it is not even decent . . . and that sort of thing is enormously on the increase. The amount of women in London who flirt with their own husbands is perfectly scandalous. It looks so bad. It is simply washing one's clean linen in public." To say that Algernon's tone here is consciously flippant is to miss the joke altogether. The quip is not a quip; it means what is says. Algernon is indignant with a woman who spoils the fun of extramarital flirtation and who parades her virtue. He is shocked at convention. And his tone implies that he is elevating break of convention into a moral norm. He is not the first figure in English satire to do so; among his ancestors are Martin Scriblerus, other assumed identities in Pope and Swift (including Gulliver), and the apologist for Jonathan Wild. What they all have in common is that they derive their ideals for conduct from the actual practice of their societies, their standards are the standards of common corruption, they are literal-minded victims of their environments, realists with a vengeance.

Here is Algernon on conventional love institutions: "I really don't see anything romantic in proposing. It is very romantic to be in love. But there is nothing romantic about a definite proposal. Why, one may be accepted. One usually is, I believe. Then the excitement is all over." And here is his vision of the post honeymoon tea table:

> *Algernon:* Have some bread and butter. The bread and butter is for Gwendolen. Gwendolen is devoted to bread and butter.
> *Jack:* And very good bread and butter it is too.
> *Algernon:* Well, my dear fellow, you need not eat as if you were going to eat it all. You behave as if you were married to her already. . . .

The girls, too, implicitly accept this inverted code. In the proposal scene between Jack and Gwendolen the latter acts out reality: girls about to be proposed to quite realize the situation and are annoyed by their suitors' conventionally bungling approach. In the second act Gwendolen explains to Cecily that she always travels with her diary in order to "have something sensational to read in the train." One of Cecily's first speeches expresses her concern for "dear Uncle Jack" who is so "very serious" that "I think he cannot be quite well." When Algernon, at their /15/ first meeting, begs her not to think him wicked, she sternly replies: "If you are not, then you have certainly been deceiving us all in a very inexcusable manner. I hope you have not been leading a double life, pretending to be wicked and being really good all the time. That would be hypocrisy." Paradoxical morality cannot be argued much further than this, and the speech upsets even Algernon. In context it cuts down to the very core of the problem of manners with which Wilde is concerned. It epitomizes the central irony of the play, for the Bunburying Algernon, in escaping the hypocrisy of convention, becomes a hypocrite himself by pretending to be somebody he is not. (Even Miss Prism participates. She is telling Cecily about her youthful novel: "The good ended happily, and the bad unhappily. That is what Fiction means.")

Only Jack and Lady Bracknell seem at first glance to be outside the pattern of inversion, expressing shock when confronted with the code of cynical realism. But their conventionality is not genuine. Jack is a confirmed Bunburyist long before Algernon explains the term to him, and Bunburyism is most simply defined as a means of escape from convention. He occasionally acts the role of naive elicitor of Algernon's discourses on Bunburyism and is not such a consistent theorist of the realist code, but his behavior is certainly not conventional.

One of Lady Bracknell's main plot functions is to be an obstacle to Jack's romance with Gwendolen, but a systematic analysis of her speeches will show, I think, that she has no illusions about the reality her professed convention is supposed to conceal: ". . . I do not approve of mercenary marriages. When I married Lord Bracknell I had no fortune of any kind." To her the speech is neither cynical nor funny. It represents that compromise between practical hardheadedness and conventional morality that she has worked out to her own satisfaction and behind which she has retired in dignified immunity. In other speeches she advocates Algernon's code with as much sanctimoniousness as he: "Well, I must say, Algernon, that I think it is high time that Mr. Bunbury made up his mind whether he was going to live or to die. This shilly-shallying with the question is absurd. Nor do I in any way approve of the modern sympathy with invalids. I consider it morbid." She moralizes on behalf of people who take it for granted that illness in others is always faked and that consequently sympathy with invalids is faked also, a concession to an artificial and—literally—morbid code. The frivolous banter accomplishes something serious. It exposes the polite cynicism that negates all values save personal convenience and salon decorum. Life and death have become matters of *savoir-vivre*.

The following speech presents a somewhat more complex case, because Lady Bracknell is here simultaneously deferring to convention and exposing its sham: "French songs I cannot possibly allow. People always seem to think that they are improper, and either look shocked, which is vulgar, or laugh, which is worse. But German sounds a thoroughly respectable language, and indeed, I believe is so." To laugh at presumably improper songs is to fly in the face of convention and break the delicate fabric of social decorum. But the opposite reaction is hardly less reprehensible. To register shock at indecency is indecently to call attention to something people realize the existence of but refuse to recognize. In her last sentence she quietly gives away the polite fiction that people in society know foreign languages.

When the pattern of inversion operates the characters either express or assume a morality that is deduced from the actual behavior of high society, though the existence of conventional morality is sometimes recognized as a fact to come to terms with. What the accumulation of paradox adds up to is an exposure both of hypocrisy and of the unnatural convention that necessitates hypocrisy. In elegant accents of pompous bigotry Wilde's puppets turn /16/ moral values upside down. "Good heavens," Algernon exclaims when Lane tells him that married households rarely serve first-rate champagne. "Is marriage so demoralizing as that?" We are made to share Wilde's view of the ludicrous and sinister realities behind the fashionable façade of an over-civilized society where nothing serious is considered serious and nothing trivial trivial.

But *Earnest* is, before anything else, a play, an imitation of *action*, and no discussion of tone apart from its dramatic setting can account for the extraordinary impact of the play as play. It is rather odd, therefore, to notice that even critics who have been aware of serious satiric implications in the dialogue have been prone to dismiss the plot as negligible, as, at best, "inspired nonsense." "The plot," writes Eric Bentley, in *The Playwright as Thinker* (1946), "is one of those Gilbertian absurdities of lost infants and recovered brothers which can only be thought of to be laughed at," and he defines the function of "the ridiculous action" as constantly preventing the play from "breaking into bitter criticism." There is truth in that, but the action has another and far more important function as well: it informs the satiric dialogue with coherent meaning.

The action of *The Importance of Being Earnest* is about just that—the importance of being earnest. The title is as straightforward a statement of theme as any literalist could ask for. Specifically, the play deals with the consequences of that way of not being earnest that Algernon calls Bunburying, and it is Bunburying that gives the plot moral significance. The key speech in the play is Algernon's little lecture to Jack: "Well, one must be serious about something, if one wants to have any amusement in life. I happen to be serious about Bunburying. What on earth you are serious about I haven't got the remotest idea. About everything, I should fancy. You have an absolutely trivial nature." Bunburying means to invent a fictitious character, who can serve as a pretext for escaping a frustrating social routine, regulated by a repressive convention. The pretended reason for getting away is perfectly respectable, even commendable, according to convention: to comfort a dying friend, to rescue a fallen brother. Thus defined, Bunburying is simply the mechanism that sets in motion the preposterously elaborate plot of mistaken identities. But the word has also a wider meaning. Significantly, Algernon *happens* to be serious about Bunburying—that is, it is not the subterfuge itself that is important, but the commitment to a course of action that will provide fun. The Bunburyist in the wider sense is serious about not being serious, and Bunburyism is the alternative to a convention that fails to reckon with the facts of human nature. It stands for behavior that will give experience the shading and perspective that convention denies it. To be serious about everything is to be serious about nothing; that is, to trifle. Algernon charges Jack (unfairly, as it happens) with a failure to discriminate among life values, to see that monotone of attitude blunts the spirit and deadens joy. And this is precisely Wilde's charge against Victorianism.

The Bunburyist lives in a world of irresponsibility, freed from the enslavement of a hypocritical convention. He enjoys himself. But life beyond hypocrisy is life in a dangerous climate of moral anarchy, and, like most states of revolt, Bunburyism is not ideal. The escape from convention is itself a flagrant instance of hypocrisy: pretense is the price the Bunburyist pays for freedom from the pretense of convention. In his title pun Wilde catches the moral failure of dandyism. Just as the conformist pretends to be, but is not, earnest, so Algernon and Jack pretend to be, but are not, Ernest.

What Wilde is saying, then, is that all normal Victorians who want to retain the respect of their conventional society are, perforce, Bunburyists, leading double /17/ lives, one respectable, one frivolous, neither earnest. Bunburyism, as Algernon confesses in the opening of the play, is the application of science to life, to the exclusion of sentiment. Sentiment properly belongs to art. The science is the science of having a good time. These are obviously false distinctions, and all that can be said for Bunburyism as a way of life is that it offers relief from a social round where, in Lady Bracknell's words, good behavior and well being "rarely go together," and where, according to Jack, "a high moral tone can hardly be said to conduce very much to either one's health or one's happiness." Bunburyism marks one of the extreme points in the swing of the pendulum, Victorianism the other.

Neither of the two Bunburyists is either earnest or Ernest—before the very end.[1] It is only then that they become, and in more than a single sense, themselves. When the action begins they have already escaped the mortifying seriousness of convention, but it takes them three acts and the movement from town to country—the movement has symbolic relevance as a return to "naturalness"— to regain their balance and become earnest, that is, neither conventionally nor frivolously hypocritical. At the end of the play the respectable (though amorous) Miss Prism (her name suggests "prim prison") has been unmasked, the four young people are romantically engaged, Jack has discovered his Bunburying identity to be his true self, and Lady Bracknell must recognize the contemptible orphan of Act 1, "born, or at any rate, bred in a handbag," as her own sister's son. The plot, as it were, makes a fool of respectability and proves the two Bunburyists "right" in their escapade. But it also repudiates Bunburyism. Algernon, who as a

---

[1] It is the one flaw in a superbly constructed play that Algernon remains Algernon at the end and thus ineligible as a husband for Cecily. To say that she does not seem to mind at that point or that Dr. Chasuble is quite ready for the christening cannot conceal the flaw. It staggers the imagination to try to think of any way in which Wilde could have turned Algernon into a second Ernest, but, given the plot, he ought to have done so.

Bunburyist spoke cynically about proposals and matrimony in Act I, is happily proposing marriage to Cecily in Act II, and at the end his initial false dichotomies between life and art, science and sentiment, have been resolved in romance. The radical remedy of Bunburying has effected a cure, the pendulum rests in the perpendicular, and we share Jack's final conviction of "the vital Importance of Being Earnest." The two adjectives have not been chosen lightly. /18/

Suggestions for Writing

I. SHORT PAPERS

1. Write a synopsis of the events in *The Birds* (or *Twelfth Night*, or *The Misanthrope*) from the beginning to the close of the play which makes clear the causal relations among the events.

2. Describe the ideal state in *The Birds*.

3. Is the chastisement of Malvolio warranted?

4. What are the dramatic functions of Feste?

5. Célimène's refusal to marry Alceste can be regarded as a wise decision.

6. Rousseau charges that in *The Misanthrope* Molière has attempted to make virtue (Alceste) ridiculous. Do you agree?

7. Are the characters in *The Critic* more than puppets?

8. The relation between Wilde's aphorisms and the morality of his play.

9. The purpose of the farcical elements in *A Wedding*.

10. By analyzing the speeches of the young Bonaparte, can you isolate Shaw's attitude toward history?

11. Fry has been most praised for his jeweled verse. Pick out an image and trace it through *A Phoenix Too Frequent*. What does your study reveal about poetic drama?

12. What aspects of your own comic experience remain unaccounted for in Bergson's theory of the comic? If there is a discrepancy between your experience and Bergson's theory, how seriously is the latter impaired?

13. Define what Mrs. Langer means by the "rhythm" of comedy.

14. Demonstrate the validity of Freud's theory of wit by citing examples from your own experience.

15. Dobrée is describing the same comedies as Congreve: compare and contrast their views.

16. Take one of the sources Kenneth Muir describes and show what Shakespeare does with it in *Twelfth Night*.

17. What light does Victor Ehrenberg's "The People of Aristophanes" throw upon *The Birds*?

18. Define the four kinds of source studies which the four essays in Part II illustrate.

19. Is "strategy" as Otto Reinert uses it a helpful term for describing comedy? Why?

20. What connections do Bergson and Freud make between childhood and wit? Are they valid, do you think?

II. LONGER PAPERS

1. Is Aristotle a helpful guide to the comedy of Aristophanes? In what ways do the theories of Mrs. Langer and Northrop Frye help us to understand *The Birds*?

2. Trace the theme of music through *Twelfth Night*. What is Shakespeare's attitude toward music?

3. Contrast and compare the three feminine characters in *Twelfth Night*.

4. Compare the women in *Twelfth Night* with those in *The Misanthrope*. What do your comparisons reveal about the two societies?

5. Molière makes a game of "serious" life. Sober, moralistic Rousseau cannot tolerate this "corruption." A modern critic, like Turnell, finds meaning in the game. Contrast the two points of view. Which do you find more congenial?

6. Sheridan's criticism extends beyond his parody of the theatre. What has he to say that is pertinent for comedy today?

7. Meredith seems to have written his essay with Wilde as his model. Demonstrate how the two go together. What picture do we get from them of Victorian society?

8. Shaw is considered to have been greatly influenced by the philosophy of Bergson and to have incorporated many of Bergson's ideas into his plays. Can you demonstrate this opinion on the basis of your reading of Bergson's "Laughter" and Shaw's *The Man of Destiny*?

9. Is Chekhov a realist? Is Wilde? Is Shaw? All three of the plays in the text were written within a five-year span, from 1890 to 1895. Can you detect any unifying artistic concepts? Or must we speak of the three as totally distinct from one another?

10. G. B. Shaw and Christopher Fry both go to the past for characters and situations to dramatize. What are the significant differences in their uses of "history"?

11. How does the position of Northrop Frye in "The Argument of Comedy" illustrate the practices of Christopher Fry?

12. Kronenberger's book, *The Thread of Laughter*, is an account of English stage comedy. Is the essay reprinted here a good introduction to the comedies of Shakespeare, Sheridan, Wilde, Shaw, and Fry? What comments on dramatic techniques would you add?

13. Contrast and compare the comic worlds of any pair: Aristophanes and Shakespeare, Aristophanes and Molière, Shakespeare and Molière, Molière and Wilde.

14. Does the one-act form give us an adequate comic point of view? Does it sufficiently incorporate the comic "rhythm" described by Mrs. Langer?

15. English stage wit has been called "the talk that never was nor could be." The same position continues in this form: "The glittering chatter from Sheridan's comedies to the clever sparkle of Christopher Fry, while persuasive enough in the darkened theatre, falls to pieces in the daylight. Not so the authentic masters of continental comedy. Aristophanes and Molière, to note but two immensities, manage to do two things these English theatre-men cannot: (1) they rise above mere nationality and (2) by doing so make a perma-

nently valuable gloss on the persistent folly—not of ancient Greeks and seventeenth-century Frenchmen—but of humankind at all times." This combative position carefully chooses its ground and then dismisses the whole line of English comedy from Sheridan to Fry. Notice that Shakespeare is left out. Using only the plays in Part I, and whatever supporting evidence you care to draw from Parts II, III, and IV of this volume, write a well-documented paper refuting or supporting the contentions given in the critical position above.

16. First, write out a scenario of *The Misanthrope*. Then, compare it with the plot outline of the *commedia* described by Allardyce Nicoll. What developments beyond the essential *commedia* situation can you discern in Molière? In what respects does he show dependence upon the older comic form?

17. In *A Phoenix Too Frequent* what changes does Christopher Fry make in retelling the story of the famous Widow of Ephesus? Which version of the episode seems to you the more modern?

18. First, read Kenneth Muir's essay on Shakespeare's sources. Then, discuss the parts of *Twelfth Night* that are strictly Shakespeare's original creation. What value do these sections have?

19. In his essay on Restoration Comedy Bonamy Dobrée states that Aristophanes' purpose was "to laugh back into their senses 'revolting sons and wives,' to defend the orthodox faith against philosophers and men of science." What evidence is there in *The Birds* to support such an interpretation?

20. Can Joseph Summers' notion of "masks" be extended to apply to comedy in general? Could his method throw light on *The Importance of Being Earnest?* *The Misanthrope?*

III. RESEARCH TOPICS

1. Comic utopias from Aristophanes to Huxley.
2. Comic characters or comic caricatures.
3. Romantic versus realistic comedy.

4. The reputation of Aristophanes.

5. *The Importance of Being Earnest* as a document in the "Art for Art's Sake" movement.

6. The role of women in the comic world.

7. Modern attitudes toward comedy.

8. The necessarily neo-classic impulse in the modern attempt to revive poetic drama.

9. Pre-Shakespearean comedy in England.

10. The influence of Molière on English comic dramatists.

11. Traces of Roman comedy in *commedia dell'arte*.

12. Show how the conditions of the French (or Elizabethan) stage account for differences between *The Misanthrope* (or *Twelfth Night*) and *The Importance of Being Earnest*.

13. Read two famous modern comedies—Shaw's *Man and Superman* and Chekhov's *The Cherry Orchard*—and then in a comparative paper using several plays written since 1925 evaluate the following statement: "Without Chekhov and Shaw, what is distinctly modern in twentieth century stage comedy would be impossible to define."

14. The stage history of *Twelfth Night* (or *The Critic*).

15. Cristopher Fry's role in the revival of poetic drama in the contemporary theatre.

16. The relationship between the "happy ending" and comedy. Is the former necessary to the latter?

17. Define comedy: (a) Does it have its origin in external, objective situations or in the individual's subjective, psychological state? (b) Does it reside in language, situation, or character? (c) Must it always see man in a social context?

18. The significance of exaggeration or understatement—in language, character, situation—in the creation of comedy.

19. The relation between wit and comedy.

20. "The business of comedy is to paint the follies of the age," wrote Voltaire. Do you agree? Must comedy have a moral purpose? Is there such a thing as pure amusement?

Suggestions for Further Reading

I

For the student interested in comedy, one can recommend, first of all, that he read more comedies. Aristophanes wrote a great many, eleven of which are extant. Of these, Dudley Fitts has translated *The Frogs*, *Ladies' Day*, and *Lysistrata*. New translations are appearing all the time, so it is not difficult to find modern versions of the other comedies. The student might also enjoy a modern treatment of a classic comic myth such as Jean Giraudoux's *Amphitryon 38*, which has been translated by S. N. Behrman.

In the process of moving on to Shakespeare and Molière, the conscientious reader should read the Roman comedies of Plautus (such pieces as the *Menaechmi* or the *Rudens*) and Terence. Or, again, there is the rich field of the *commedia dell'arte*, translations of which are now becoming more accessible, e.g., Eric Bentley's *The Classic Theatre*, Vol. I, where one can find works by Goldoni, Gozzi, and others; also Bentley has reprinted *La Mandragola* (*c.* 1518), Machiavelli's bitter and bawdy comedy.

No pursuit of comedy can succeed without a careful transit of Shakespeare's comic vision, especially as it is incorporated in that great wit, Falstaff, who appears in *Henry IV* (1597–98), Parts I and II. Other major comedies need only be mentioned to remind us of the richness there: *A Midsummer Night's Dream* (1594), *The Merchant of Venice* (1595), *Much Ado About Nothing* (1599), *As You Like It* (1600), *The Tempest* (1611). To mention Shakespeare is to bring the wealth of Elizabethan and Jacobean drama into view. A conscientious investigator will want to look at some of the comedies of Ben Jonson (especially *Every Man Out of His Humour*, 1599, *Volpone*, 1606, *The Alchemist*, 1610, and *Bartholomew Fair*, 1614), of Thomas Dekker (*The Shoemaker's Holiday*, 1599), of Francis Beaumont and John Fletcher (*The Knight of the Burning Pestle*, 1608) and of Philip Massinger (*A New Way to Pay Old Debts*, 1625).

The plays of Molière range as widely in the field of comedy as those of Shakespeare. The student has only to look into any volume of translations to find examples of his amazing skill from *Les Précieuses Ridicules* (1658) and *L'École des Femmes* (1662) through *Tartuffe* (1664) to *Le Bourgeois Gentilhomme* (1671) and *Le Malade Imaginaire* (1672). Ben Jonson and Molière were, in turn, the two most significant influences upon the English Restoration dramatists. The outstanding comic writers of the period were Wycherley (*The Plain Dealer*, 1676, is a reworking of *The Misanthrope*, 1666, whereas *The Country Wife*, 1674, stands midway between *L'École des Femmes*, 1662, and Sheridan's *The School for Scandal*, 1777) and Congreve (*Love for Love*, 1695, and *The Way of the World*, 1700, are his masterpieces). One must not neglect Dryden, whose best comedy is undoubtedly *Marriage à la Mode* (1672). Dryden's tragedies, it is worth

mentioning, evoked the Duke of Buckingham's satirical play, *The Rehearsal* (1671), which was then used by Sheridan as the model for *The Critic* (1779). Other notable eighteenth-century burlesques are John Gay's vivid musical, *The Beggar's Opera* (1728), and Henry Fielding's farce, *Tom Thumb* (1730). Sheridan's two magnificent comedies of manners, *The School for Scandal* and *The Rivals* (1775), are necessary additions to this list, as is *She Stoops to Conquer* (1773) by his contemporary, Oliver Goldsmith.

When one turns to Wilde and Shaw, one is again overwhelmed by the quantity of distinguished plays. To begin with there are Wilde's *A Woman of No Importance* (1893), *Lady Windermere's Fan* (1892) and *An Ideal Husband* (1895). In the Shavian canon are *Arms and the Man* (1894), *Major Barbara* (1907), *Androcles and the Lion*, (1912), plus more than twenty others, most of them standard theatrical fare. Irish contemporaries include O'Casey, Synge, Lady Gregory, and the poet, W. B. Yeats. On the English scene are the playwrights W. Somerset Maugham, James Barrie, and Noel Coward. To these can be added the Americans Philip Barry, Thornton Wilder, James Thurber, and Eugene O'Neill, who wrote one comedy, *Ah, Wilderness!* (1933). The revival of poetic comedy is another notable aspect of the modern theatre. In addition to the major works of Christopher Fry (*The Lady's Not for Burning*, 1949, *Venus Observed*, 1950), there are the plays of T. S. Eliot, especially *The Cocktail Party* (1949) and *The Confidential Clerk* (1954).

Modern Continental comic drama begins, in a sense, with Chekhov, who labeled *The Cherry Orchard* (1904) a comedy; perhaps his *Uncle Vanya* (1899), however, would be a more clear-cut example. For Chekhov's short farces, the reader should consult Eric Bentley's edition of these pieces. In addition to the plays of Chekhov, one other Russian comedy needs to be mentioned, *The Inspector-General* (1836), by Gogol. Other Continental comedies of note are, generally speaking, French. Here one thinks of the plays of Giraudoux and Anouilh and, more recently, of Ionesco and Beckett.

II

For the student who wishes to read more widely in the general area of the theory of comedy, a few procedures can be recommended. In actual fact, there are not many documents, so that he may start where he pleases.

Two general collections of materials should be mentioned first, however. Barrett H. Clark's *European Theories of the Drama* (rev. ed. 1947) reprints significant texts from Aristotle to William Archer. There, the student will find of particular value famous critical statements by Goldoni, Ben Jonson, and Molière together with well-known essays by Addison (from *The Spectator*), Lamb, and Hazlitt. An equally useful book is A. M. Nagler's *Source Book in Theatrical History* (1959), which ranges even more widely through supporting documents; Professor Nagler has included some three hundred selections here, all interesting and some very revealing indeed. To round out this particular area, there are *The Oxford Companion to the Theatre* (1957), edited by Phyllis Hartnoll, an indispensable reference guide; Blanch M. Baker's bibliography, *Theatre and Allied Arts, A Guide to Books Dealing with the History, Criticism and Technic of the Drama and Theatre* (1952); and Rosamond Gilder's selective, annotated list, *A Theatre Library* (1932).

At this point, there should also be mentioned three recent anthologies of interest. Edited by Sylvan Barnet, Morton Berman, and William Burto, *Eight Great Comedies* (1958) ranges from Aristophanes to Shaw and includes four brief excerpts on comedy. *The Comic in Theory and Practice* (1960), edited by John J. Enck, Elizabeth T. Forter, and Alvin Whitley, reprints a wide variety of materials including definitions and theoretical essays as well as examples of the comic from other literary genres; the stories and poems are particularly valuable. Finally, Wylie Sypher has edited the complete texts of Bergson's and Meredith's essays in a volume called *Comedy* (1956); to the more familiar selections, he has appended a stimulating essay of his own.

Other useful modern works on comedy include:

Cook, Albert S. *The Dark Voyage and the Golden Mean* (1949).
Cooper, Lane. *An Aristotelian Theory of Comedy* (1923).
Eastman, Max. *The Enjoyment of Laughter* (1936).
Feibleman, James. *In Praise of Comedy* (1939).
Frye, Northrop. *Anatomy of Criticism* (1957).
Grotjahn, Martin. *Beyond Laughter* (1957).
Huizinga, Johan. *Homo Ludens* (1955).
Koestler, Arthur. *Insight and Outlook* (1949).
Lynn, Kenneth S., ed. *The Comic Tradition in America* (1958).
Potts, L. J. *Comedy* (1950).
Rourke, Constance. *American Humor* (1955).
Smith, Willard M. *The Nature of Comedy* (1930).
Swabey, Marie Collins. *Comic Laughter* (1961).
Thompson, Alan R. *The Anatomy of Drama* (1949).
Wimsatt, W. K., ed. *English Stage Comedy* (1955).

The student is also reminded that the various head-notes supplied by the editor contain many references to works which have a vital bearing on the subject.